PROPERTY AND CONVEYANCING LIBRARY

THE LAW AND PRACTICE OF INTESTATE SUCCESSION

by

C. H. SHERRIN, LL.M., PH.D.
Barrister; Senior Lecturer in Law, University of Bristol

R. C. BONEHILL, LL.M.
Solicitor

LONDON
SWEET & MAXWELL
1987

Published in 1987 by
Sweet & Maxwell Limited of
11 New Fetter Lane, London
Computerset by Burgess & Son (Abingdon) Ltd.
Printed in Great Britain by
The Garden City Press Ltd., Letchworth, Herts.

British Library Cataloguing in Publication Data

Sherrin, C.H.
The law and practice of intestate succession.
—(Property and conveyancing library)
1. Inheritance and succession—England
I. Title II. Bonehill, Roger III. Series
344.2065'2 KD1522

ISBN 0–421–32630–1

Property and Conveyancing Library

THE LAW AND PRACTICE OF INTESTATE SUCCESSION

AUSTRALIA AND NEW ZEALAND
The Law Book Company Ltd.
Sydney : Melbourne : Perth

CANADA AND U.S.A.
The Carswell Company Ltd.
Agincourt, Ontario

INDIA
N.M. Tripathi Private Ltd.
Bombay
and
Eastern Law House Private Ltd.
Calcutta and Delhi
M.P.P. House
Bangalore

ISRAEL
Steimatzky's Agency Ltd.
Jerusalem : Tel-Aviv : Haifa

MALAYSIA : SINGAPORE : BRUNEI
Malayan Law Journal (Pte.) Ltd.
Singapore and Kuala Lumpar

PAKISTAN
Pakistan Law House
Karachi

PREFACE

It can be said with some statistical justification that intestate rather than testate succession is currently normal practice in England and Wales. Certainly the law of intestacy is central to the modern law of family property and must serve as one of the cornerstones of any understanding of that law. It is surprising, therefore, that, although the law of succession in general is well served with texts, there has hitherto been no specialist book devoted primarily to the modern law and practice of intestate succession. Hence the conception of this book, the aim of which is to provide a full exposition of the modern law and practice which might be regarded as an authoritative work for practitioners and a useful source of reference for students.

To this end we have sought to highlight matters of practical importance, such as small estates, taxation, the position of the matrimonial home and variation of the beneficial entitlement, and to provide a more detailed discussion of distribution on intestacy than has previously been available in a single text in addition to dealing with the processes of obtaining a grant and of the administration of the estate. The emphasis has been placed on those areas of the law or practice which are central or particular to intestate succession and thus some of the more general aspects of administration which are fully discussed in other texts receive shorter treatment.

The important supplementary family provision jurisdiction embodied in The Inheritance (Provision for Family and Dependants) Act 1975 is discussed with particular reference to its application to intestate succession. We have also felt that it would be useful to include an Appendix of relevant legislation, rules and orders.

The present law of intestacy in England and Wales is still essentially that which was promulgated in the Administration of Estates Act 1925, although it was reconsidered in mid-century and modified in some respects by the Intestates' Estates Act 1952. The changes which have taken place since that revision in familial, social, economic, fiscal and legal circumstances have been dramatic and have largely bypassed the law of intestacy. We consider that a further revision of the law is necessary to reflect these changes and we have taken the opportunity to include some critical comment and suggestions for reform. Many Commonwealth codes which originally shared our provisions have been modernised and we have referred to them where appropriate.

We have attempted to state the law and practice applicable in England and Wales as at October 1 1986 and have taken the opportunity to make reference to the relevant provisions of the Insolvency Act 1986 even though they had not been brought into force at that date. We have also been able to include references to inheritance tax where appropriate and have referred to the 1984 Act as the "Inheritance Tax Act 1984."

We would wish to express our gratitude to our respective wives for their forebearance during the long period of gestation of this work, to Mrs. Pat Jones, Mrs. Susan Clee and Miss Lesley Willey for the typing of the manuscript and to our publishers for their support and encouragement as well as for producing the tables of cases and statutes. Our thanks also to Robert Spicer who prepared the index. The responsibility for any errors is, of course, our own.

C. H. SHERRIN
R. C. BONEHILL

October 1, 1986

CONTENTS

TABLE OF CASES

TABLE OF STATUTES

BIBLIOGRAPHY

British Tax Encyclopaedia.
Bromley, *Family Law* (6th ed., 1981).
Cheshire and North, *Private International Law* (11th ed., 1986).
Cretney, *Principles of Family Law* (4th ed., 1984).
Cross on Evidence (6th ed., 1984).
Dymond's Capital Taxes (1986).
Dicey and Norris, *Conflict of Laws* (10th ed., 1980).
Emmet on Title (19th ed., 1986).
Foster, *Capital Taxes Encyclopaedia.*
Halsbury's Laws of England (4th ed., 1980).
Hardingham, Neave and Ford, *Wills and Intestacy* (1983).
Hill and Redman's *Law of Landlord and Tenant* (17th ed., 1982).
Holdsworth, *A History of English Law* (7th ed., 1956).
Ing, *Bona Vacantia* (1971).
Keeton, *An Introduction to Equity* (5th ed., 1961).
Lee, *Manual of Queensland Succession Law* (1975).
Megarry and Wade, *The Law of Real Property* (5th ed., 1984).
Mellows, *The Law of Succession* (4th ed., 1983).
Morris, *The Conflict of Laws* (3rd ed., 1984).
Parry and Clark, *The Law of Succession* (8th ed., 1983).
Pettit, *Equity and the Law of Trusts* (5th ed., 1984).
—— *Private Sector Tenancies* (2nd ed., 1981).
Pollock and Maitland, *History of the English Law* (2nd ed., 1898).
Scammell and Densham, *Law of Agricultural Holdings* (6th ed., 1978) and *Supplement* (1980).
Simon's Taxes (revised 3rd ed.).
Smith, *Law of Theft* (5th ed., 1984).
Snell's Principles of Equity (28th ed., 1982).
Tyler and Oughton, *Family Provision* (2nd ed., 1984).
Williams, Mortimer and Sunnucks, *Executors, Administrators and Probate* (16th ed., 1982).
Williams on Title (4th ed., 1975).
Williams on Wills (5th ed., 1980).
Woodfall, *Landlord and Tenant* (28th ed., 1978).

Part One

INTRODUCTION AND HISTORY

CHAPTER 1

GENERAL PRINCIPLES AND TERMINOLOGY

INTRODUCTION

It is a fundamental incident of the ownership of property long recognised by the Common Law that property can pass by inheritance on the death of the owner to another person. The manner of this transmission is regulated by the law of succession and the twin pillars of the law are the complementary rules of testamentary and intestate succession. The former provides the more effective way of regulating the inheritance, and lawyers would always urge that the power of testamentary disposition should be exercised.[1] However, a great many people do not make effective testamentary dispositions of their property and thus die intestate. Although the majority of intestate estates are small, it sometimes happens, through accident or design, that a substantial estate becomes subject to the intestacy code. Thus Lord Ashton died intestate in 1934 leaving an estate of £10 million.[2] It is no doubt true that a number of people die intestate intentionally, *i.e.* that after due consideration of the law of intestate succession they make a conscious decision not to make a will. Goff L.J. recognised this possibility in *Re Coventry (decd.)*,[3]

> "... a deceased person may have deliberately chosen to be intestate, and the provisions provided by the legislature to cover the case where there is no will, or an incomplete will, may be as much the wishes of the deceased as those which he has expressed in a will."

However, it would be naive to assume that more than a small number of intestacies can be so explained. The Russell Committee[4] were undoubtedly correct in their assessment that the majority of people die intestate through accident, idleness, ignorance or through an aversion from taking a formal step that recognises that death is the lot

[1] Not only does a will enable the inheritance to be tailored to the testator's own wishes, but enables executors and guardians to be chosen, and facilitates the administration of the estate. It can hardly be claimed that people are deterred from making a will on the grounds of expense, since wills can be made very cheaply on published will forms and legal aid is available for professionally drawn wills (see s.2(1)(*b*) of the Legal Advice and Assistance Act 1972, now s.2(1)(*b*) of the Legal Aid Act 1974).

[2] See *Re Ashton (decd.)* (1934) 78 S.J. 803.

[3] [1979] 3 All E.R. 815, 822; see also *Re Edwards* [1906] 1 Ch. 570; *Re Abbott* [1944] 2 All E.R. 457, 459. Further this wish can be expressed in a will, see *Williams on Wills* (5th ed.), p. 1209, see *post*.

[4] 1966 Cmnd. 3051; para. 31.

of all. Mr Michael Wheeler Q.C. (sitting as a Deputy High Court Judge) recently summarised the position as follows[5]:

> "For my part, whilst I accept that a person may deliberately choose to die intestate, in the absence of proof I would be slow to accept this as a calculated decision. I suspect that in the majority of cases intestacy is a combination of procrastination and the not uncommon belief that 'there's no hurry: I'm not going to die tomorrow', coupled, all too often, with an ignorance of the law regarding intestacy."

MEANING OF TERMS

Total intestacy

Intestacy

An intestacy can be either total or partial. Neither concept is expressly defined by the Administration of Estates Act 1925[6] but a total intestacy can be described as the situation where a person dies leaving undisposed of by testamentary disposition the whole of his estate.[7] Such a situation will arise where on death there is no effective or operative will. This can be because:

—the deceased never made a will[8] or
—all previous wills have been revoked, without replacement, by destruction[9] or by marriage[10] or
—all previous wills are invalid by reason of defective formalities[11] or lack of capacity.[12]

A total intestacy will also arise where the testator leaves a will, which is wholly ineffective because the gift (or gifts) to the sole

[5] In *Re Leach (decd.) Leach* v. *Lindeman*, [1984] Fam.L.R. 590, 602; affirmed on appeal, [1985] 2 All E.R. 754.
[6] The 1925 Act does however define "intestate." See s.55(1)(vi); and *post* p. 6. The only statutory definition of intestacy in English law would appear to be that contained in s.7 of the Intestates' Estates Act 1884: "Where any beneficial interest in the real estate of any deceased person, whether the estate or interest of such deceased person therein was legal or equitable, is, owing to the failure of the objects of the devise, or other circumstances happening before or after the death of such person, in whole or in part not effectually disposed of, such person shall be deemed, for the purposes of this Act, to have died intestate in respect of such part of the said beneficial interest as is ineffectively disposed of."
[7] See Succession (Scotland) Act 1964, s.36(1).
[8] See the comments of the Russell Committee, 1966, Cmnd.3051, para. 31, on the reasons why persons fail to make a will.
[9] See *Williams on Wills* (5th ed.), p. 133, and s.20 of the Wills Act 1837.
[10] *Ibid.* p. 123 and s.18 of the Wills Act 1837, as substituted by s.18(1) of the Administration of Justice Act 1982. See *e.g. Re Coleman* [1976] Ch. 1.
[11] *Ibid* pp. 72–93 and s.9 of the Wills Act 1837, as substituted by s.17(1) of the Administration of Justice Act 1982. See *e.g. Re Groffman* [1969] 1 W.L.R. 733; *Re Colling* [1972] 1 W.L.R. 1440.
[12] *Ibid.* pp. 23–37; see *e.g. Re Park* [1954] P. 112.

beneficiary (or all the beneficiaries) wholly fails because of lapse,[13] or witnessing the will,[14] or uncertainty[15] or contravention of some rule of law such as the rule against perpetuities.[16]

Although an intestacy is said to arise when a person dies without leaving a valid will it is submitted that the existence of a will is not the correct test. This is because wills have functions other than the disposition of property. Thus a will that merely appoints executors will be admitted to probate but, if it fails to make any effective disposition of property, there will be a total intestacy.[17] Similarly the will might merely revoke a previous will, appoint testamentary guardians, or exercise a testamentary special power of appointment. It is suggested that the test of a total intestacy is not whether there is a valid will, which is determined by reference to Probate, but whether there is a will which makes any effective testamentary disposition of property.[18]

In all cases of total intestacy section 33 of the 1925 Act applies imposing a trust for sale and leading to the identification of "the residuary estate of an intestate."[19] This property is distributed in accordance with the statutory code of entitlement contained in Part IV of the Act, and principally set out in section 46(1) of the Act.

Intestate

The word "intestate" is used in two senses in the 1925 Act. First, it is used to describe the state of affairs that exists when a person dies without leaving a valid will. Thus section 33(1) refers to "the death of a person intestate as to any real or personal estate. . . . "[20] When used in this sense the word also covers cases of partial intestacy; thus

[13] See *e.g.* *Re Ford* [1902] 2 Ch. 605, where the deceased made a will by which he appointed his wife his sole executrix and gave her all his property. She died in his lifetime and the result was that there was no-one in whose favour the will could operate. Vaughan Williams L.J. stated at p. 605: "It is not true to say that the deceased did not die intestate. He did die intestate, and therefore the Statute [*i.e.* Distributions] applies." See also *Re Cuffe* [1908] 2 Ch. 550, where there was a complete failure by lapse of all the beneficial interests under the will and the person named as executor had predeceased the testator; held, an intestacy and the widow entitled under Intestates' Estates Act 1890 to the statutory legacy of £500.

[14] See *Williams on Wills* (5th ed.), p. 56.

[15] *Ibid* p. 450.

[16] *Ibid* p. 689.

[17] *Re Skeats, Thain* v. *Gibbs* [1936] Ch. 683, where the only will was on a printed form containing an appointment of the testator's wife as executrix and a direction to pay debts and funeral and testamentary expenses, but no gift or disposition of property to any person. Held, widow must distribute property in the manner indicated in s.46 of the 1925 Act; s.55(1)(vi) definition of "intestate" considered. Contrast the historical position, see *Re Roby* [1908] 1 Ch. 71 at p. 81.

[18] See the American cases of *Re Shestack's Estate*, 267 Pa.115; *Re Cameron's Estate*, 47 App.Div. 120; *Messmann* v. *Egenberger*, 46 App.Div. 46.

[19] See *post* p. 82.

[20] s.33 uses the word "intestate" in the state of affairs sense in subs. (1), and in the identification sense in subs. (4): See also s.51(2) ". . . who thereafter dies intestate . . . ," and s.9, "Where a person dies intestate. . . . "

section 33(7) provides that "where the deceased leaves a will, this section has effect subject to the provisions contained in the will." The Act also refers to "an intestacy"[21] in the same state of affairs sense. However the Act uses the word "intestate" more usually in the second sense of identifying the deceased. Thus virtually all the references in Part IV of the Act are to "an intestate"[22] or "the intestate"[23] and it is in this sense that the word is defined in section 55(1)(vi) of the Act.[24]

> "Intestate includes a person who leaves a will but dies intestate as to some beneficial interest in his real or personal estate."[25]

It is apparent from this definition that when used in this sense it includes a person who dies partially intestate. It is suggested that it would have been preferable for the legislation to have avoided using the word in these dual senses, and that "intestate" would have been better used simply to describe the person whilst "intestacy" could have been used to describe the state of affairs.[26] It is however convenient to use the word in both senses and in this work it is so used.

"As on intestacy"

If a testator wholly revokes without replacement his last will and testament, then, in the absence of dispositive provisions he will die intestate. It is thought that the same result would follow if a testator makes a will in the following form:

> "I . . . of . . . hereby revoke a will dated . . . and all other testamentary dispositions made by me and hereby declare that it is my intention to die intestate."[27]

Such a will is merely declaratory and contains no dispositive intent. However, if the will revokes all previous wills and the testator declares that he wishes his property to be distributed "as if I had died intestate" or simply "as on intestacy,"[28] then it is likely to be regarded as a case of testate succession, "where the intestacy provisions operate only by a species of incorporation by reference."[29] A useful illustrative

[21] s.7(3)(*a*).
[22] s.46(1); s.47(1), (3), etc.
[23] s.46(1)(3); s.47(1), (2), (3), (4), etc.
[24] See *Re Skeats* [1936] Ch. 683 ". . . the word intestate means a person who has not made an effective disposition of the beneficial interest in the whole of his property," per Clauson J. at p. 689.
[25] See also the similar definitions in Australian and New Zealand legislations, Hardingham, Neave and Ford, *Wills and Intestacy*; and Succession (Scotland) Act 1964, s.36(1); Republic of Eire's Succession Act 1965, s.3(1).
[26] More modern codes, for example, those applicable in some Australian states, define both "intestate" and "intestate estate" using the former term to identify the person and the latter phrase to identify the property; see Hardingham, *op. cit.*
[27] See *Williams on Wills*, (5th ed.), p. 1209.
[28] See the precedent in *Williams on Wills, op. cit.* p. 1084.
[29] Prichard (1981) 45 Conv.(N.S.) 343 at p. 345; see *Re Morgan* [1920] 1 Ch. 196.

case is *Brenchley* v. *Lynn*[30] where the testatrix's will contained the following wording:

> "... whereas I am desirous to revoke and make void my said will and disposition aforesaid and to die intestate, in order that all my property both real and personal, may go to and devolve upon my heirs or next of kin ... the same as if I had made no will and had died utterly intestate ... now therefore I, the said Elizabeth Lynn, do, by this instrument in writing, revoke, annul, and make void my said will in toto ... so that I may die intestate both as to my real and personal estate."

The judge thought[31] that this wording rendered the instrument not merely revocatory but dispositive as well, in that it contained a bequest of the property to the next of kin.

> "Intestacy can only arise when a person dies without legally bequeathing his property, that is, without a will. If a man by will declares he dies intestate, and that his property shall go as in case of intestacy, such paper does not constitute an intestacy but a bequest of the property to *personae designatae*—designated by the statute, as it might be by any other description. The property in the present instance goes not in virtue of the statute, but in virtue of the will, exactly as if the ultimate limitation in Mrs. Minnitt's will had been to AB and not to the next of kin. That the property would go by the statute in the same direction as by the will cannot divest it of the character of property bequeathed by will.[32]

More modern wills may expressly incorporate the statutory provisions as a clear formula to identify the person or persons who are to take, as if the relevant provisions of section 46 of the Administration of Estates Act 1925 had been written out in full in the will.[33] This was the case in *Re Mitchell (decd.)*[34] where in default of appointment the testator provided that the residuary estate should be held "... in trust for such person or persons who would have been entitled thereto under Part IV of the Administration of Estates Act 1925 at the death of my said wife had she died possessed thereof intestate without having been married such persons to take (and if more than one) in

[30] (1852) 2 Rob.Ecc. 441.
[31] *Per* Dr. Lushington at p. 468.
[32] Thus the beneficiary took as a legatee and had to pay duty as a legatee and could not take the oath as in case of intestacy.
[33] *Per* Wynn-Parry J. in *Re Mitchell (decd.)* [1954] 1 Ch. 525, at p. 528; see also *Re Jackson, Holliday* v. *Jackson* [1943] 113 L.J. Ch. 78.
[34] *Supra.*

the shares and manner in which they would have taken under the said part of the said Act."[35]

The Administration of Estates Act 1925 contains express provisions in section 50 regarding the construction of such clauses with reference to either the Statutes of Distribution or to Part IV of the 1925 Act.[36] Whether such wills are regarded as cases of testate or intestate succession, is not without practical importance with regard to, for example, the entitlement of illegitimate relatives[37] or the application of the rules of hotchpot.[38]

Gift to "relations"

The courts had adopted before 1925, a rule of convenience that a gift to "relations" was to be construed as meaning the persons who would have taken under the Statutes of Distribution[39]; otherwise the gift would be void as requiring an inquiry into everyone between whom and the testator or testatrix there was a nexus of blood.[40] This rule has been adopted and applied with reference to the new scheme of distribution introduced by the Administration of Estates Act 1925.[41] Thus a testamentary disposition of "all my possessions to be held in trust after my death and divided equally amongst all my relations" was construed as meaning those persons who on an intestacy would actually have taken under Part IV of the 1925 Act in the circumstances of each case, and not as including the whole class defined by Part IV as potential beneficiaries on intestacy.[42] Such a gift

[35] The wife was illegitimate and thus as the law stood at the date of her death in 1949, there was no person other than the Crown entitled. It will be apparent from this result that such "as on intestacy" clauses should not be used unless the factual circumstances are explored very carefully and the facts and the law kept continually under review. Thus if the facts of *Re Mitchell supra*, were to recur now, it is arguable that the mother of the illegitimate wife would be entitled under s.14 of the Family Law Act 1969, see *post* and Prichard (1981) 45 Conv.(N.S.). This case is further discussed, with reference to the nature of the Crown's entitlement, *post*, p. 276.

[36] As to which see *e.g. Re Sutton*, [1934] 1 Ch. 217; *Re Sutcliffe* [1929] 1 Ch. 123; and *post* p. 188.

[37] This is because the entitlement of illegitimate persons on intestacy is governed by s.14 of the Family Law Reform Act 1969, essentially limited to inheritance by children and parents, see *post* p. 173, whereas the entitlement of illegitimate persons under a will is governed by s.15 of the 1969 Act, which is expressed more widely.

[38] Thus a widow or issue taking by virtue of a partial intestacy will have a duty to account for testamentary benefits, under s.49(1)(*aa*), (*a*), of the 1925 Act, see *post* pp. 288, 292. There will be no such requirement if the beneficiaries take wholly under the will. Likewise with the application of s.47(1)(iii), see *post* p. 249.

[39] *Widmore* v. *Woodroffe* (1766) Amb. 636; *Green* v. *Howard* (1779) 1 Bro. C.C.30.

[40] See Lord Campden L.C. in *Widmore* v. *Woodroffe, supra* at p. 640; Clauson J. in *Re Bridgen, Chaytor* v. *Edwin* [1938] 1 Ch. 205 at p. 209.

[41] See Clauson J. in *Re Bridgen, supra*, rejecting an argument that a different construction should now be adopted.

[42] *Re Bridgen, supra.* In this case no difficulty arose by reason of any claimant entitled to benefit being a minor and thus the judge expressed no view on whether a minor would take absolutely (as he would have done under the Statute of Distribution) or contingently (as he would now do under the 1925 Act).

constitutes an effective universal testamentary disposition of the testatrix's property and is not a case of intestacy.[43]

Partial intestacy

Definitions

It is expressly provided by the Administration of Estates Act 1925 that "intestate" includes a person who leaves a will but dies intestate as to some beneficial interest in his real or personal estate.[44]

Section 49 of the 1925 Act, which is concerned with the application to cases of partial intestacy, refers to situations "where any person dies leaving a will effectively disposing of part of his property" but where there is "... part of his property not so disposed of...."[45] Thus a partial intestacy arises when there is a will which effectively disposes of some of the testator's assets but which fails to provide for the totality of the property included in the net estate or fails to dispose of every interest in such property.[46] The reasons for this failure can be diverse; the testator may have overlooked specific property or have drafted a defective residuary clause or some of the provisions of his will may contravene a technical rule, such as section 15 of the Wills Act 1837.[47] These situations are considered more fully in Chapter 15 on partial intestacies. Suffice it to note at this stage that, whatever the reason for the failure,[48] when a partial intestacy occurs the undisposed of property is basically subject to the same scheme of distribution as applies to a total intestacy.[49]

SOURCES

Introduction

The modern code of intestate succession stems from the comprehensive revision of English property law that took place at the beginning of this century and which found expression in the series of Acts which are often referred to as "The 1925 legislation." Indeed, the complete and fundamental reform of the law of intestacy that was effected by the Administration of Estates Act 1925 is one of the most

[43] *Ibid. per* Clauson J, at p. 208.
[44] s.55(1)(vi).
[45] See more fully discussed *post* in Chap. 15 on Partial Intestacy.
[46] See *e.g.* Romer L.J. in *Re Thornber* [1937] 1 Ch. 29 at p. 35.
[47] Which disentitles a beneficiary who has witnessed the will.
[48] See *Re McKee* [1931] 2 Ch. 145 and *Re Bowen-Buscarlet's Will Trusts* [1972] 1 Ch. 463 which illustrate the necessity to distinguish between immediate partial intestacies and contingent partial intestacies, at least so far as the application of the 1925 Act s.33 and the statutory trust for sale, is concerned, see *post* p. 86.
[49] See the 1925 Act s.49(1) applying "this Part of this Act" to cases of partial intestacy, subject to the provisions contained in the will, and subject to statutory modifications which are mainly concerned with the duty to account for testamentary benefits; see *post* p. 288.

striking features of that legislation. The historical dichotomy between the rules of inheritance to realty, based largely on tenurial concepts, and the succession to personalty, embodied in the Statutes of Distribution 1670 and 1685, was swept aside.[50] A new code of distribution and entitlement common to both forms of property was enacted in Part IV of the Administration of Estates Act 1925, and it is in that legislation, as amended, that the modern code of intestate succession is to be found.[51] However, the code as originally enacted was found to be inadequate within a generation of its coming into being, necessitating the radical revision of the law effected by the Intestates' Estates Act 1952. The changes introduced by that legislation to the basic scheme of distribution on intestacy were effected by amendments to section 46(1) of the original code and by the re-enactment of Part IV of the 1925 Act as so amended. Accordingly, the source of the modern law of intestate succession is still to be found in the 1925 Act. There has been no major restructuring of the law since 1952, although various family and property law statutes have affected the law in incidental ways, and the basic entitlement has been greatly affected by the dramatic increases in the statutory legacy payable to a surviving spouse.

The statutory sources

As already indicated, the primary source of the modern law of intestate succession is to be found in Part IV of the 1925 Administration of Estates Act as re-cast by the 1952 Intestates' Estates Act. In the case of deaths before January 1, 1926[52] the real estate of persons who died intestate was governed by the old rules of inheritance,[53] with the distribution of the personalty being subject to the provisions of the Statutes of Distribution 1670 and 1685.[54] The uniform code as originally enacted by the 1925 Act governed intestate succession in the case of deaths on or after January 1, 1926 and before January 1, 1953.[55] The revision of the original code by the Intestates' Estates Act 1952[56] and the amendments effected by the Family Provision Act

[50] The rules of inheritance previously applicable to realty were retained for exceptional and insignificant purposes after 1925, and are briefly considered in Chap. 2. The pre-1925 rules governing the distribution of personalty are now only of historical interest and are briefly considered on that basis in Chap. 2.

[51] The assimilation of the law relating to realty and personalty was, of course, one of the aims of the 1925 legislation. Other objects of those reforms, such as the simplification of conveyancing and the removal of anachronisms, are also apparent in the revision of the law of intestate succession.

[52] The date when the A.E.A. 1925 came into force.

[53] See discussed *post* in the next Chapter.

[54] *Ibid.*

[55] The amount of the statutory legacy under the 1925 Act as originally enacted was a constant £1,000; see *post.* p. 204.

[56] See *post* p. 42.

1966[57] and the subsequent increases in the statutory legacy payable to a spouse[58] necessitate noting the following dates:

—deaths intestate on or after January 1, 1953 and before January 1, 1967[59] when the fixed net sums were £5,000 (where there were also issue surviving) and £20,000 (where there were no issue but specified relatives)[60];
—deaths on or after January 1, 1967 and before July 1, 1972 when the fixed net sums were £8,750 and £30,000 respectively[61];
—deaths on or after July 1, 1972 and before March 15, 1977 when the fixed net sums were £15,000 and £40,000 respectively[62];
—deaths on or after March 15, 1977 and before March 1, 1981 when the fixed net sums were £25,000 and £55,000 respectively[63];
—deaths on or after March 1, 1981 when the fixed net sums are £40,000 and £85,000.[64]

Variations in the rate of interest payable on the statutory legacy necessitate noting the following dates:

—with effect from January 1, 1926 the rate was 5 per cent.[65];
—with effect from January 1, 1953 the rate was 4 per cent.[66];
—with effect from September 15, 1977 the rate was 7 per cent.[67];
—with effect from October 1, 1983, the rate is 6 per cent.[68];

Amendments to the age of majority and the entitlement of illegitimate children effected by the Family Law Reform Act 1969, necessitate a distinction between deaths before and after January 1, 1970. The original code has also been affected in minor ways by the Administration of Estates (Small Payments) Act 1965, the Matrimonial Causes Act 1973, the Inheritance (Provision for Family and Dependants) Act 1975[69], the Children Act 1975, the Legitimacy Act

[57] See *post* p. 205.
[58] See *post* p. 205.
[59] The dates when the Intestates' Estates Act 1952, and the Family Provision Act 1966 came into force; see commencement order, S.I. 1966 No. 1453.
[60] The amounts fixed by the Intestates' Estates Act 1952.
[61] The amounts originally fixed by the Family Provision Act 1966 which also provided that the amounts could be subsequently increased by statutory instrument, s.1(3)(4). See *post* p. 205.
[62] Family Provision (Intestate Succession) Order 1972 (S.I. 1972 No. 916).
[63] Family Provision (Intestate Succession) Order 1977 (S.I. 1977 No. 415).
[64] Family Provision (Intestate Succession) Order 1981 (S.I. 1981 No. 255).
[65] Governed by the 1925 Act as originally enacted.
[66] Governed by the 1952 Act.
[67] Governed by the Intestate Succession (Interest and Capitalisation) Order 1977 (S.I. 1977 No. 1491): see enabling legislation Administration of Justice Act 1977, s.28(1).
[68] Governed by the Intestate Succession (Interest and Capitalisation) Order 1983 (S.I. 1983 No. 1374).
[69] Also affected by earlier, now repealed, legislation.

1976[70], the Adoption Act 1976[71], and the Mental Health Act 1983,[72] amongst others.

Case law

The decisions relevant to the law of intestacy tend in the main to be interpretive of the statutory code although there are areas, such as the meaning of "personal chattels," where the case law provides useful sources of principle. In other areas the decisions highlight difficulties or anomalies, such as with reference to section 49(1)(*a*) of the 1925 Act or with reference to the application of the statutory code to "contingent partial intestacies." Other cases provide clarification of statutory terms, such as the meaning of "advancement." Some Commonwealth jurisdictions have enacted statutory codes modelled on the English scheme and cases on those provisions can sometimes provide guidance with reference to the English law.

The statutory code concentrates on the basic distribution on intestacy and contains few provisions on the ancillary matters that can affect entitlement, where judicial decisions can be relevant. For example, the rule of public policy disinheriting a murderer from his victim's estate is wholly a case law creation; likewise the principles governing, and the effect of, disclaimers. Similarly, there is no statutory code of private international law governing the entitlement on intestacy and such cases are subject to established judicial precedents.

CHARACTERISTICS

Uniform code

The 1925 Administration of Estates Act provides a uniform code of devolution[73] and distribution applicable to both realty and personalty.[74] The outstanding characteristic of the modern law is the pre-eminent position of the surviving spouse with the issue next entitled.[75] The classes of relatives entitled on intestacy are closely defined and take in defined order of priority with the Crown as the ultimate taker.[76] The Act operates by way of provision not disposition: it was established by the Court of Appeal in *Re Buttle's Will Trusts*[77] that the

[70] *Ibid.*
[71] *Ibid.*
[72] *Ibid.*
[73] With reference of course to property which devolves on the personal representatives; some categories of property are excluded—see *post* p. 79.
[74] See especially 1925 Act s.33 and s.46. The only true exception relates to personal chattels which are specifically dealt with by the legislation.
[75] See *post* pp. 157–160.
[76] See *post* Chap. 10.
[77] [1977] 1 W.L.R. 1200 at p. 1211.

Administration of Estates Act 1925 "... was not a disposition of the testator's property[78] and played no part in disposing of it. It simply provided how so much of it as was undisposed of should be dealt with."[79]

Mandatory

In cases to which it applies the code is mandatory in the sense that it dictates, without scope for discretion, the manner of distribution,[80] and is applicable to the whole of the intestate part of "the residuary estate of the deceased."[81] This appears from the mandatory wording of section 46 of the 1925 Act "... the residuary estate of an intestate shall be distributed in the manner...." Indeed it was at one time argued, even assumed,[82] that an interest on intestacy could not be disclaimed since the interest was conferred by statute. This proposition no longer seems tenable in view of the decision in *Re Scott*[83] where it was accepted[84] that such an interest could be disclaimed,[85] but this does not fundamentally negate the imperative effect of the statutory provisions.

Voluntary

Although mandatory if it is applicable, the statutory code can also be regarded as a voluntary scheme of inheritance since it can be wholly or partly supplanted by an effective testamentary provision.[86] Further, even in cases to which the statute applies, if the intestate beneficiaries are all of full age and *sui juris* and collectively entitled to the whole estate (usually as the spouse and children of the deceased) then they can join together and agree upon the manner of distribution of the estate.[87] In such cases they can in effect rewrite the intestate entitlement in accordance with their own wishes. Where this takes the form of a variation within section 142(1) Inheritance Tax Act 1984 and section 49(6) of the Capital Gains Tax Act 1979, it can be done

[78] *i.e.* of that part of the property in respect of which the testator died partially intestate.

[79] Because a "disposition" (for the purposes of s.36(5)(*a*)(i)(*aa*) of the Finance Act 1969; estate duty charge) connotes a disposer and the legislation there being considered drew a distinction between a disposition and a devolution.

[80] Subject, of course, to the jurisdiction under the Inheritance (Provision for Family and Dependants) Act 1975; this is a supplementary jurisdiction which strictly forms no part of the intestate code. The *commorientes* provision in s.46(3) could perhaps be regarded as an exception, see *post* p. 164.

[81] English law has no overriding "fixed rights of inheritance" or "*reserve*" familiar in Scottish or French law, or "elective share" as in many states of America.

[82] See Goodhart, (1976) 40 Conv. 292.

[83] *Widdows* v. *Friends of the Clergy Corporation* [1975] 2 All E.R. 1033.

[84] Although the point was not fully argued.

[85] See full discussion *post* in Chap. 17.

[86] See *ante* p. 9.

[87] *Saunders* v. *Vautier* (1841) Cr. & Ph. 240.

without capital taxes disadvantages.[88] Additionally in cases of partial intestacy it is possible for the next of kin to elect to take under the will and abandon their rights on intestacy.[89]

Basis of the Law

Presumed intention

It would appear that the reformers of the law in 1925 had little difficulty in deciding that the law of intestate succession should be fixed and certain. There is no indication that any method of discretionary entitlement based on an application to some judicial or quasi-judicial authority to determine the distribution was seriously considered, but the questions remained how that entitlement should be structured, who was to be entitled, in what order of preference, and to what? The first step in the resolution of those questions was to determine the criteria on which the new law should be based. There were various alternatives. Regard could have been had to historical precedent and the entitlement based on the method of identifying next-of-kin according to degrees of relationship in the Statute of Distribution 1670. Alternatively, a distribution consistent with objective notions of fairness or propriety could have been imposed. Neither of these approaches was adopted. It was decided that the code of entitlement on the death of a person intestate should be based on the presumed intention or wishes of that deceased person. In other words, the law of intestate succession should effect a distribution of the estate analogous to the distribution that the deceased would have wished, if he had been consulted at his death, or consistent with a will that the deceased might have, but did not, leave. This essentially subjective approach owes something to the notion expressed by Lord Cairns in an often-quoted remark that the provisions as to intestate succession should be regarded as no more than a will made by the legislature for the intestate.[90]

In order to arrive at this result a requisite preliminary is to ascertain the usual or common form of testamentary provision in particular family situations. This can be obtained by a thorough and systematic

[88] See full discussion, *post* p. 119. A benefit on intestacy can also be disclaimed, see *post* p. 339 thus affecting the prima facie entitlement. A claim under the family provision legislation can also be settled by compromise, see *post* Chap. 18.

[89] See *Re Sullivan* [1930] 1 Ch. 84.

[90] *Cooper* v. *Cooper* (1874) L.R. 7 H.L. 53 at p. 66 on the Statutes of Distribution. Thus in cases of partial intestacy the provisions should be read into the testator's will; see *Re McKee* [1931] 2 Ch. 145 at pp. 155, 157–158; *Re Bowen-Buscarlet's Will Trusts* [1972] 1 Ch. 463 at pp. 468, 469. But see Maitland, Collected Papers, Vol. I, p. 122, writing in 1879, "... the law makes a will for intestates which no sane testator would make for himself" referring to the dichotomy between the succession to real property and to personalty; see Morris, 85 L.Q.R. 339 at p. 346.

survey of many wills which have been proved within a recent period.[91] Such a survey was carried out prior to the drafting of the 1925 Act and a similar process was gone through by the Morton Committee on Intestate Succession[92] which was set up in 1950 to consider what changes, if any, were needed in the law of intestate succession. The recommendations of that Committee were strongly influenced by the evidence provided by the survey.[93] The other major investigation into the law of intestacy carried out in recent years was that of the Russell Committee[94] in relation to the entitlement of illegitimate persons.[95] Although that Committee expressed reservations whether "... the suggested theory of assumed intention is of great weight,"[96] the Report recognised that the "... provisions for intestacy are basically designed to carry out the presumed wishes of the deceased who has not expressed his or her wishes by will."[97]

A final illustration of the same approach is provided by the Law Commission[98] who, in recommending a change in the law relating to the entitlement on intestacy of a judicially separated spouse,[99] commented:

> "The law of intestacy is intended to give effect to the likely dispositions of the deceased had he made a will and it seems clear that a rule that disinherits the separated spouse is more likely to achieve that result than one which preserves his or her rights."

A code based on "presumed intentions"

The desire to bring the statutory provisions into line with the

[91] This approach was explained in the New Zealand Parliament by the Minister of Justice (introducing the Administration Amendment Bill 1965, see 3 N.Z.L.R. 169) as follows: "In providing for the distribution of an intestate estate there must be some kind of averaging out of what a deceased person might have been expected to do if he had made a will. To achieve this, the most satisfactory approach is to try to relate the rules governing intestacy to the most common dispositions made by those who do leave wills." The modern law of intestate succession in New Zealand has been tested against such a survey by a research student in 1964–65 who published his findings in 3 N.Z.L.R. 169. The results indicated general agreement with that country's statutory code with one or two inconsistencies.

[92] (1951) Cmnd. 8310, set up as a result of prompting by the Law Society. The recommendations of this Committee are considered in Chap. 2 *post*.

[93] The Principal Probate Registry analysed all wills proved in England and Wales on two successive days in each of five successive weeks. See (1951) 48 L.S.Gaz. 383; see also para. 8 of the Morton Committee's report where the survey is referred to. The recommendations relating to the size of the statutory legacy in particular were based on the figures revealed by the survey.

[94] 1966 Cmnd. 3051.

[95] See *post* p. 173.

[96] *Supra*, para. 31.

[97] *Supra*, para. 30. This principle was reflected in the Committee's recommendation that succession in cases of illegitimacy should be confined to the parents and the child thus excluding an illegitimate grandchild or nephew from any share in his grandfather's or uncle's estate; see Chap. 10, *post*.

[98] Working Paper No. 9, para. 212.

[99] The legislation is discussed in Chap. 10 *post*.

deceased's presumed intention is apparent in both the 1925 Administration of Estates Act and in the 1952 Intestates' Estates Act. Thus the paramount entitlement of the spouse, particularly in cases where there are no issue, reflects the presumed wishes of the intestate. Further, the order of entitlement and the limitation within defined boundaries of the classes of relatives possibly entitled is also thought to be in accordance with modern ideas regarding the proper division of family assets.

If one looks from the general to the specific, it is clearly possible to identify specific provisions of both Acts whose principal *raison d'être* is to effectuate the deceased's presumed wishes. An illustration from the 1925 Act is section 51(2), which preserves the old rules of succession as applicable, in exceptional circumstances, to govern the inheritance of real property of a "lunatic or defective."[1] The required conditions for the application of the old rules are that the lunatic or defective was living and of full age at the commencement of the Act; that he was at that time unable by reason of his incapacity to make a will; and that he died intestate after that time without having recovered his testamentary capacity. The (somewhat fictional) idea in such cases seems to be that the defective would have known and understood the pre-1925 rules and not made a will in reliance thereon. Since he is in such a case unable to vary by will the post-1925 scheme of distribution, it cannot be assumed that the modern scheme accords with his intention. Thus his presumed intention relates to the old and not the new rules.

An illustration of a specific provision based on presumed intention in the 1952 Act is section 46(3).[2] This section provides that where a husband and wife die intestate in a *commorientes* situation (*i.e.* it is uncertain which survived the other) each will be regarded as having predeceased the other. Thus the husband will be deemed to have died intestate without a surviving spouse and his property will pass (in the absence of children) to his parents or brothers and sisters and the wife's property to her family. In the absence of such a provision, section 184 of the Law of Property Act 1925 would apply. This assumes that the younger (say the wife) would have survived the older and thus the husband's estate would pass to the wife, and both his and the wife's estate would pass (in the absence of children) to her relations. This result is not regarded as consistent with the parties' intentions and so the law was modified in 1952.

Further illustrations of the same point are not difficult to find, *e.g.* the spouse's entitlement to the "personal chattels"[3] and the liability of children to account.[4] Although in cases of total intestacy the statutory

[1] See full discussion, *post* p. 29.
[2] Added to the 1925 Act by the 1952 Act. See full discussion, *post* p. 164.
[3] See full discussion, *post*, in Chap. 11.
[4] See full discussion, *post*, in Chap. 13.

code is imperative, in cases of partial intestacy the provisions in the Act can be modified by an expression of a contrary intention. Thus section 33(7) provides "where the deceased leaves a will, this section has effect subject to the provisions contained in the will"[5]; section 49(1) is likewise expressed to be "subject to the provisions contained in the will."[6] The requirement in section 47(1)(iii) to bring a child's advance into account is "subject to any contrary intention expressed or appearing from the circumstances of the case."[7] Section 50(1) states that references to any Statutes of Distribution shall be construed as references to the new code, "unless the context otherwise requires."[8] A similar qualification appears in section 55(1).

Inconsistent provisions

However, inevitably perhaps, it is possible to find statutory provisions in the code which do not seem to accord with the deceased's presumed intention. The entitlement of grandchildren is one such case. The distribution under the statutory trusts in favour of issue is *per stirpes*; grandchildren are not entitled *per se* but merely take, by representation, their deceased parent's share, and take, ". . . through all degrees, according to their stocks, in equal shares if more than one, the share which their parent would have taken if living at the death of the intestate."[9] Thus the size of the share which a grandchild will take will depend upon the number of brothers or sisters that he might have. Consider an example where the deceased intestate had three children A, B, and C, and A survives the deceased and has a child D; B predeceased the intestate leaving four children E, F, G and H; and C predeceased the intestate leaving one child J. The *per stirpes* distribution dictated by the statute will mean that A will take a one-third share (D will get nothing); E, F, G and H, will share a further third share, *i.e.* will take one-twelfth each, and J will take the other one-third share.[10] Thus the grandchildren are benefited entirely unequally whereas the deceased, if asked hypothetically during his lifetime, might well have presumed or preferred the grandchildren to share equally. Further, if J had also predeceased the intestate leaving a child K, then that child would take the one-third share, a case of a

[5] See *post*, Chap. 15.

[6] See full discussion, *post* p. 280. The requirement in s.49(1)(*a*) that issue should account for testamentary benefits can be regarded as consistent with the deceased's presumed intentions. As Megarry commented, 72 L.Q.R. 484, "As the Act stands, it does not interfere with planned inequality, but in the case of issue it rejects accidental inequality in favour of the equality produced by hotchpot; surely few testators would think this a great mistake."

[7] *Ibid.*

[8] *Ibid.* However, s.46(1) is imperative and cannot be ousted or modified by expressions of a contrary intention in, say, an invalid will.

[9] s.47(1)(i).

[10] See full discussion, *post* p. 244.

more remote relative taking a larger share than closer relatives.[11] It can be questioned whether that accords with the deceased's presumed wishes.

Another situation where it is at least doubtful whether the modern code fully accords with most intestates' intentions concerns the entitlement of brothers and sisters of the half-blood, *i.e.* step-brothers and step-sisters. Where there are also brothers and sisters of the whole blood, they will take to the exclusion of the step-brothers and sisters.[12] Where all of these children have been brought up in a family without differentiation, an intestate might well be surprised to realise that (in the absence of a spouse, issue or parent) only his full brothers and sisters would share his estate and no part would go to his half-brothers and sisters.[13]

In addition to these points of inconsistency embodied in the statutory provisions a striking anomaly arises from the rules of private international law regarding the entitlement on intestacy. These rules are contained in long-standing case law and have regrettably not been the subject of statutory modernisation. The point is simply that the law of intestate succession to movables is governed by the domicile of the intestate, but the law relating to immovables is that of the *lex situs*.[14] This can lead to all sorts of anomalies of double entitlement and foreign succession. Would a Scot domiciled in Scotland realise or intend that his land in England should devolve according to English law?

Comment

Although it is submitted that the idea of presumed intention is the correct basis for the law of intestate succession, the concept is open to criticism. The first point relates to the idea of knowledge which is implicit in any scheme theoretically based on subjective not objective considerations, *i.e.* the basis of the statutory code of distributions on what the deceased would have wished, not on what is thought to be just and proper in the circumstances. It is tempting to say that as such the theory of presumed intention is based on two fallacies: one, that the average intestate knows and approves the statutory scheme of distribution and, two, that he deliberately decides not to make a will being content that his estate should be distributed in that way. It is in fact easily provable that few non-lawyers fully know and understand

[11] This result could be easily avoided by statutory provision, see *e.g.* South Australia's Administration and Probate Act 1919–1975, s.72(i).

[12] s.46(1)(v).

[13] See *e.g. Re Groffman* [1969] 1 W.L.R. 733 where the testator wished to leave the interest in remainder in his residuary estate, equally between his daughter and his step-daughter.

[14] See *Re Collens (decd.)* [1986] 1 All E.R. 611 and *post* Chap. 16.

the statutory rules relating to the distribution of intestate estates.[15] Secondly, it can be pointed out that it is obvious that in many cases the statutory distribution does not accord with the manifest wishes of the deceased, *e.g.* in those cases where there is a will which fails for technical reasons and the estate falls to be distributed on intestacy in an entirely different manner.[16] Perhaps, however, this must be regarded as an inevitable circumstance which does not necessarily destroy the fundamental validity of the theory. The same may be said of those cases in which the statutory distribution does not accord with the relatives' consensus as to what is right and proper and they, regularly or irregularly, agree to an inconsistent distribution.[17]

Thirdly, it is apparent that any code of inheritance based on a survey of wills is likely to arrive at a model of distribution based on the wishes of the "average testator." Like all averages it will be strictly correct only in some cases and will fail to reflect the range of possible circumstances or the diversity of wishes and opinions of the population as a whole. This is incontestable but is a factor not of the theory of presumed intention but of a code of succession providing fixed entitlement and is inevitable with all such codes.[18] English law has decided that the law of intestate succession should be fixed and

[15] If proof be needed reference can be made to the survey conducted by the Office of Population, Censuses and Surveys, in 1972, in Todd and Jones, *Matrimonial Property*. That survey indicated that 76 per cent. of the husbands and 90 per cent. of the wives in their sample, had not made a will. These people were asked if they thought that they understood the law of intestacy, and a third of the husbands, and one half of the wives admitted that they knew nothing about the law of intestate succession (para. 5.3). Of those who claimed some understanding of the law the researchers found predictable confusion and misconceptions and were forced to conclude (para. 5.3) "Thus, detailed knowledge of the intestacy law is confined to a very few people indeed. About half of our sample had some idea of the laws of intestacy, though the degree of knowledge varied considerably. Only three people, that is about one spouse per thousand, knew in detail the parts of the intestacy laws which affect the family, and they all had close connection with legal work."

[16] As in *Re Groffman* [1969] 1 W.L.R. 733 the deceased's will provided for his widow, daughter and step-daughter; the will failed and on intestacy the property passed to the first two, to the exclusion of the step-daughter. In *Ross* v. *Caunters* [1980] Ch. 297 the testamentary gift to a sister-in-law failed and on intestacy the property went elsewhere.

[17] See the small survey carried out in 1972 by Abel-Smith, Zander and Brooke, *Legal Problems and the Citizen* (1973), pp. 130–135, who discovered that in some 12 per cent. of the sample (where the property exceeded £50), the property of a deceased who died intestate had not been distributed in accordance with the intestacy rules. Two typical situations were where the property was given in response to an *inter vivos* verbal promise and where an unmarried daughter who had lived with and cared for her parents took the whole property to the exclusion of the other brothers and sisters. In such cases the property is distributed by agreement in accordance with the sense of fairness.

[18] Thus the present code works best where the deceased is married, or a widow or widower, leaving children surviving, and owning few assets other than the matrimonial home. It works less well if a business is involved or other more substantial assets. The intestacy laws also make no provision for a *de facto* spouse and can operate unsatisfactorily when a marriage is contracted shortly before death: see *Re Davey (decd.)* [1981] 1 W.L.R. 164; and *Re Park* [1954] P. 89.

certain and that the essential flexibility necessary to deal with exceptional circumstances should be provided by an overriding system of discretionary family provision.[19] So long as this saving and redeeming jurisdiction is present, it can be argued that the law of intestacy cannot be unduly criticised for failing to provide for all circumstances but should rather be judged on how effectively it provides for the average situation.[20]

A fourth point that can easily be made is that it is possible for different interpretations to be made of the majority opinion by different bodies in different jurisdictions. Thus in 1951 England,[21] Scotland[22] and Northern Ireland[23] all had committees reporting on proposed changes to the respective succession laws in each jurisdiction.[24] All were based on the theory of presumed intention and yet the resultant legislation, although perhaps fundamentally similar, varied significantly in detail. Thus the Mackintosh Committee on the Law of Succession in Scotland stated that their proposals were designed to effectuate the principle, "that when a man dies without a will the law should try to provide so far as possible for the distribution of his estate in the manner he would most likely have given effect to himself if he had made a will."[25] Despite this the law in Scotland is markedly different in some respects from the modern English law. For example, the class of next of kin entitled to inherit is very much wider than is the case under the English 1925 Act, and includes, *e.g.* great aunts and uncles (brothers and sisters of a grandparent) and second cousins (children of parents' first cousins).[26] A lawyer might well accept and explain such differences as inevitably flowing from the different sources that influence Scottish law, but the theory of presumed intention is based on factual and practical considerations rather than jurisprudential ones. It can be said with some justification that, as a

[19] Under the Inheritance (Provision for Family and Dependants) Act 1975. See *post* in Chap. 18.

[20] The extent to which the modern code does reflect the wishes of the average person has been tested only once in recent years by an official scientific survey. In 1971 the Office of Population, Censuses and Surveys commissioned a survey on Matrimonial Property (see Todd and Jones, *Matrimonial Property*), which included questions relating to the law of intestate succession. The investigators asked their sample to indicate how they thought an estate should be distributed on intestacy in three situations, and tested the responses against the actual position; see para. 9. There was some considerable divergence of views as to how the estates ought most properly to be distributed.

[21] Morton Committee, Cmd. 6310 (1951).

[22] Mackintosh Committee, Cmd. 8144 (1951).

[23] Johnson Committee, Cmd. 308 (N.I.) (1951).

[24] See Morris (1969) 85 L.Q.R. 363. See also the variations in Commonwealth codes that are purportedly also based on presumed intentions. See Hardingham, Neave and Ford; *op. cit.*

[25] Cmd. 8144 (1951) para. 6. See Morris (1969) 85 L.Q.R. 363, and the critical comments of Browne-Wilkinson V.C. in *Re Collens (decd.), Royal Bank of Scotland (London) Ltd.* v. *Krogh*, [1986] 1 All E.R. 611 at p. 616.

[26] Succession Act 1964, s.2; See Walker, *Principles of Scottish Private Law*, 2nd ed. pp. 1920 *et seq.*

matter of fact, it is unlikely that a resident of Edinburgh would markedly differ in his presumed intentions to a resident of Bristol. The same point can also be made on the Northern Irish Law[27] which likewise includes a much wider class of next of kin ascertained according to the old degrees of relationship theory.[28]

It is submitted, however, that despite these defects the English law of intestate succession is correctly based on theoretically subjective considerations. If the alternative objective basis is considered for a moment, the statutory distribution would owe little to what the deceased might have intended, but would be based simply on an objective view of what was fair and reasonable in the particular circumstances of each factual situation. Such a code might well in the end be very similar to the present distribution but would give rise to two difficulties. The first is that a code of intestate succession based on objective criteria would seem to give little scope for the effective operation of the law of family provision which is, and must be, based on objective considerations. Although a code based on objective general considerations would not necessarily preclude a system based on objective specific considerations, it is submitted that it would make the task of the applicant challenging the intestate distribution very much more difficult. This would be a grave defect since it is regarded as essential that any fixed code of intestate succession should be supplemented by a flexible system of discretionary variation. The second difficulty relating to an intestacy code based on objective criteria arises in cases of partial intestacy. It would seem to be essential that, as at present, the intestate entitlement should be subject to the wishes of the deceased as expressed in his will. In other words that the will should be capable of modifying the statutory code. In so far as both are based on subjective considerations this is obviously possible but subjective wishes of the testator would seem to be less apt to modify an objective system of intestacy.

Further it is submitted that a system of fixed entitlement based on subjective considerations is preferable to any system of discretionary entitlement based on objective considerations. It is suggested that the Morton Committee[29] were correct in thinking that the first essential of any system of intestate succession is that it should be fixed, clear and easy to understand. A discretionary system, or any system with built-in flexibility, is none of these things. It would result in persons being

[27] See the Report of the Johnson Committee on the Law of Intestate Succession in Northern Ireland, Cmd. 308 (N.I.) 1951, para. 13; discussed, 10 N.I.L.Q. 3 which formed the basis of the Administration of Estates Act (N.I.) 1955 (hereafter also referred to as the "A.E.A. (N.I.) 1955").

[28] See A.E.A. (N.I.) 1955, ss.11 and 12. The Johnson Committee, *op. cit.* para. 13, had recommended that the guiding principle should be that the law "... should as nearly as possible provide for the distribution of the estate in the same manner as the deceased would probably have done had he made a will" although no survey of wills was carried out, see 10 N.I.L.Q. 3 at p.11.

[29] 1951 Cmd. 8310.

unsure how their estate would be distributed on their death, it would require resolution by a judicial figure or process and thus would create dispute, expense and delay in the distribution of estates.

Although, no doubt, the system of fixed entitlement can be shown to operate arbitrarily and unfairly in some cases, this is more than outweighed by the advantages in the majority of cases of certainty, simplicity and ease of operation. Thus it is suggested that the code of entitlement on intestacy should be fixed and certain and that the English approach of supplementing the statutory scheme with a system of application for modification by discretionary awards under the Inheritance (Provision for Family and Dependants) Act 1975 is the best solution.

Reform of the Law

It is submitted that the fundamental structure of the prevalent law of intestate succession, a fixed code based on presumed intention, is generally satisfactory. However, within that structure it is the opinion of many that the law relating to the entitlement on intestate succession is in need of another thorough review and amendment. By the middle of the century the status of wives and the attitudes of married couples to property owned by each or both of them had rendered the original provision in favour of a widow patently inadequate, but the changes in legal, social and familial conditions and attitudes have been even more marked in the second half of the century than in the first. Consider the growth in the incidence of the ownership of the matrimonial home by married couples and the move towards the joint ownership of that house,[30] the development of the notion of "family assets," the introduction of capital taxes and the increasing recognition of the rights of co-habitants and mistresses. The law of intestate succession is indisputably part of the general structure of family property law and must operate in conjunction with, and therefore reflect and relate to, such law.

Further it is obvious that the law cannot operate independently of its social and economic context and therefore must be affected by changes in social circumstances and attitudes. A few relevant developments that readily come to mind are the decline in the "extended family;" the high incidence of divorce and remarriage, the number of single parent families and the changed attitudes to unmarried cohabitation and illegitimacy. Most of these developments have occurred since the last major review of the law in 1952 and the

[30] In 1971 Todd and Jones *op. cit.* discovered that only 20 per cent. of houses purchased in the 1930s were jointly owned whereas the figure for houses purchased more recently was as high as 74 per cent.

conclusion that the law is overdue for another thorough review and reassessment is inescapable.[31]

[31] The only significant development in the law of succession in recent years which in fact reflects some of these social changes has been the extension of the family provision jurisdiction by the Inheritance (Provision for Family and Dependants) Act 1975. This is to be welcomed but, of course, leaves the basic structure of the law of intestate succession unchanged.

Chapter 2

THE HISTORICAL CONTEXT

Introduction

At the beginning of the twentieth century the law of intestate succession was basically that which had endured for centuries; the succession to real property remained rooted in tenurial concepts,[1] whilst the rules applicable to personalty were to be found in the Statutes of Distribution of 1670 and 1685. The 1925 legislation swept away the old rules for most purposes and replaced them with the modern statutory code applicable to both realty and personalty. Indeed the aims of that legislation—to simplify titles, to assimilate the law of realty and personalty and to remove anachronisms—is nowhere more apparent than in the modernisation of the law of intestate succession. Although the pre-1926 rules are now largely of historical interest rather than substantive effect, it is thought essential to consider them for the following reasons. First, the rules relating to the ascertainment of the heir were expressly preserved by the 1925 legislation for certain exceptional situations and the old rules may be relevant to the proof of titles extending beyond 1926. Secondly, the modern code, although intended as a new uniform system, inevitably owes something to the rules applicable before 1926 to the succession to personal property.

Succession to Realty—Pre-1926

The rules of inheritance

Ascertainment of the heir

It is necessary to consider initially the rules governing the identification of the heir and to follow with some discussion of the rights of a widow and widower. The rules were conveniently codified with some amendments in the Inheritance Act 1833 which governed

[1] The rules of inheritance identifying the heir evolved at an early date and were based partly on custom and partly on the decisions of the King's Courts which enforced them as the common law of the land; see Pollock and Maitland, *History of English Law*, 2nd ed, Vol. 2, pp. 260–313; Holdsworth, *A History of English Law*, Vol. III, pp. 171–185. These rules were among the most enduring principles of the English legal system constituting part of the common law from the 13th to the 19th century (until they were codified in the Inheritance Act 1833) and remaining in force until 1925 in England, and until 1956 in Northern Ireland, and in fact retaining some relevance in the modern law, see *post*.

intestate succession to realty[2] from January 1, 1834[3] until January 1, 1926.[4] Some general characteristics of these rules can be noted at the outset.

First, the heir was ascertained at the moment of death and a living person had no heir. Secondly, the process was essentially concerned with identifying a single person as heir, rather than with ascertaining a class of next of kin. Thirdly, the real estate passed on death directly to the heir (subject to the rights of the surviving spouse) and the personal representatives, as their name implied, were concerned only with personal estate. This remained the position until the Land Transfer Act 1897 provided that realty should also vest in the representatives, who thus became, for the first time, both real and personal.[5]

The heir was ascertained by the application of a number of rules,[6] the first of which was that descent must be traced from the last purchaser,[7] who was defined as the last person who acquired the land otherwise than by descent, or by escheat, or inclosure.[8] In order to facilitate this rule it was provided that the last owner should be considered to be a purchaser, unless the contrary be proved.[9] The heir under a will took as a devisee and a limitation to the grantor or his heirs created an estate by purchase.[10] Further, when heirs took by purchase under limitations to the heirs of their ancestor, the land descended as if the ancestor had been the purchaser.[11] The Act failed to provide for the case where there had been a total failure of heirs of the purchaser and so the Law of Property Amendment Act 1859, ss.19 and 20, provided that in such a case the descent should be traced from the person last entitled to the land as if he had been a purchaser.

The second major rule was that issue were preferred to other relatives and male issue were preferred to female. Thirdly, by virtue of the principle of primogeniture the eldest male heir took in priority to

[2] Further 19th-century amendments need to be noted, principally the Dower Act 1833, the Law of Property Amendment Act 1859, the Intestates' Estates Act 1884, the Intestates' Estates Act 1890, and the Land Transfer Act 1897. Of these amendments the 1890 Act was the most significant, so far as the modern law is concerned since it imposed a charge of £500 in favour of the widow, rateably on both the real and the personal estate. This was the initial intrusion into the rights of the heir and the first statutory entitlement affecting both realty and personalty alike.

[3] The date when the 1833 Act came into operation.

[4] The date when the Administration of Estates Act 1925 came into operation.

[5] Although the former terminology of "personal representative" has been retained. See generally Morris (1969) 85 L.Q.R. pp. 345–347.

[6] Only a brief summary of the rules is possible here. A detailed exposition of the common law rules can be found in the texts noted in note 1 to page 24 *ante*. A useful summary of the post-1833 position can be found in *Halsbury's Laws of England* 3rd ed., Vol. 17, paras. 1421–1447; and in Megarry and Wade, *The Law of Real Property*, 5th ed., pp. 540 *et seq.*

[7] Inheritance Act 1833, s.2.

[8] *Ibid.* s.1 *i.e.* otherwise than by operation of law.

[9] *Ibid.* s.2.

[10] *Ibid.* s.3.

[11] *Ibid.* s.4.

younger males but females took as coparceners, *i.e.* equally together. Fourthly, the lineal descendants of a deceased person *ad infinitum* represented and took the share of their ancestor. Thus the issue of the deceased eldest son took before younger sons and their issue.

The lineal ancestors inherited only on failure of lineal descendants and the Act provided that the lineal ancestor was to be heir in preference to collateral persons claiming through him.[12] This fifth rule meant that a father was preferred to a brother. The sixth rule provided that the male line was to be preferred, so that none of the maternal ancestors would inherit until all the paternal ancestors and their descendants had failed[13] and the male paternal ancestors were preferred to the female paternal ancestors.[14] The seventh rule was that the mother of more remote male paternal ancestors was to be preferred to the mother of the less remote male paternal ancestors[15] and, where there was a failure of male maternal ancestors, the mother of the more remote male maternal ancestor was preferred to the mother of a less remote male maternal ancestor.[16] Eighthly, a relative of the half blood could be the heir and inherit next after a relative of the same degree of the whole blood, if the common ancestor was a male, or next after the common ancestor if that person was a female.[17]

Finally, if there was no ascertainable heir, the land escheated to the feudal lord, or to the Crown.[18]

Entailed interests were capable of inheritance only by descendants[19] and the above general rules could be varied by local customs such as gavelkind[20] or borough english.[21]

Curtesy and dower

It will be observed that the old rules of inheritance had no place for the widow. The scant entitlement of a surviving spouse to real property on intestacy was embodied in the doctrines of curtesy[22] and dower.[23] By virtue of the former a widower was entitled to a life interest in the whole of the real property in which the wife had been entitled in possession to an estate of inheritance, provided that issue capable of inheriting had been born alive, whether or not they were

[12] s.6, this represented a change in the law, before 1833 an ancestor could not succeed, see Morris (1969) 85 L.Q.R. p. 345.

[13] 1833 Act, s.7.

[14] Including issue of such persons.

[15] *Ibid.* s.8, including her descendants.

[16] *Ibid.* s.8.

[17] *Ibid.* s.9. Before 1834, relatives of the half blood were not entitled, the 1833 Act effecting a change in this respect.

[18] See Halsbury's Laws, Vol. 17, paras. 1435–1441, and Intestate Estates Act 1884.

[19] *Ibid.*, paras. 1442–1443.

[20] *Ibid.*, para. 1446.

[21] *Ibid.*, para. 1447.

[22] See Megarry and Wade, *The Law of Real Property*, 5th ed., pp. 543 *et seq.*; Morris (1969) 85 L.Q.R. p. 346.

[23] *Ibid.* p. 544.

living at the death. After the Married Women's Property Act 1882 the wife could defeat curtesy by disposition of the property either *inter vivos* or by will.

The widow was less generously treated and was entitled only to a life interest in one third of her husband's freehold land, provided that the land had been held for an inheritable estate. The right to dower could be defeated easily either by alienation of the land *inter vivos* or by will or by declaration by deed or will of a denial of the right.[24] The widow had to wait until the end of the nineteenth century for a more secure inheritance on her husband's death. The Intestates' Estates Act 1890 provided that, where the intestate's estate did not exceed £500 and there were no issue, the whole estate should belong to the widow absolutely and exclusively[25] and, where it did exceed that sum, that the widow should be entitled to a sum of £500 which was charged rateably on the whole real and personal estate.[26]

Abolition of the old rules subject to preservation for limited purposes

The rules of inheritance noted above were expressly abolished for most purposes by section 45 of the 1925 Act and replaced by a statutory code common to both realty and personalty.[27] However, this abolition relates only to the estates of persons dying after the commencement of the Act, January 1, 1926, and the Inheritance Act 1833[28] is not repealed. Accordingly the old rules remain of significance, although of rapidly diminishing relevance, in the case of deaths before January 1, 1926. Thus, if the root of title of real property extends beyond 1925, the rules of inheritance will apply to any earlier intestacy relevant to that property. Further, the conveyancer might still be concerned with the construction of pre-1925 trusts or wills which provide for the distribution of the property to the persons entitled under the Statutes of Distribution.[29] It is also possible that a partial intestacy might arise subsequent to 1925 out of a pre-1925 will and such property will fall to be distributed in accordance with the old rule.

In addition to such cases section 45(2) of the Act of 1925 expressly preserves the old rules as applicable to the descent of an entailed interest and section 51 also preserves the application of these rules in two other situations. First, the construction of the word "heir," when

[24] Dower Act 1833, ss.4, 6, 7, 8, 9. The reason for this somewhat odd provision was that dower tended to clog titles to land and ways were sought to avoid this. The Act however conferred a general right of dower in equitable interests to which the husband was beneficially entitled at his death, s.2, a change dictated by the fact that previously there was no recognition of rights of dower in equitable interests.

[25] 1890 Act, s.1.

[26] *Ibid.* ss.2, 3.

[27] See Appendix A.

[28] And the amending legislation, *e.g.* Law of Property Amendment Act 1859, s.19.

[29] Any reference in modern wills or trusts to the Statutes of Distribution will be construed as references to Pt. IV of the 1925 Act, s.50(1) see discussed *post* p. 188.

used as a word of purchase, is still governed by the old rules.[30] Secondly, the new code does not apply in certain strictly defined circumstances to the devolution of a beneficial interest in real estate of a "person of unsound mind or a defective" living and of full age at the commencement of the Act.[31] None of these exceptions is of great practical significance in the modern law but they will have to be noted shortly in the following sections.

Entailed interests

An entailed interest after 1925 is deemed to be an interest ceasing on death and thus strictly forms no part of the deceased's estate.[32] This of course applies only where the entail has not been barred either *inter vivos* or by will.[33] The old rules of inheritance are preserved by section 45(2) to govern the descent or devolution of entailed interests. In such cases section 130(4) of the Law of Property Act 1925 will apply so that the estate will devolve as an equitable interest, from time to time, upon the persons who would have been successively entitled thereto as the heirs of the body (either generally or of a particular class) of the tenant in tail or other person, or as a tenant by the curtesy, if the entailed interest had before January 1, 1926 been limited in respect of freehold land governed by the general law in force immediately before that date and such law had remained unaffected.[34] This provision will apply whether the entail is in realty or personalty[35] but in the case of realty only to the devolution of the equitable beneficial interest in the estate. After 1925 the legal estate will be vested by the Settled Land Act 1925 in the tenant for life and will devolve according to the usual rules applicable to such an estate.[36]

Heir

Section 51(1) of the Administration of Estates Act 1925 excludes the application of the new code to the right of any person to take beneficially, by purchase,[37] as heir either general or special. The Law of Property Act 1925 provides in section 132 that in such a case the limitation shall operate to confer a corresponding equitable interest in

[30] s.51(1).

[31] s.51(2), s.51(3) refers to the distribution of property of a minor who dies after 1925 unmarried who is equitably entitled under a settlement to a vested interest in freehold land. In such cases it is provided that the infant shall be deemed to have had an entailed interest. The succession in such cases will be considered in Chap. 17.

[32] Administration of Estates Act 1925, s.3(3) (hereinafter also referred to as the "A.E.A. 1925").

[33] Law of Property Act 1925, s.176 (hereinafter also referred to as the "L.P.A. 1925"). The general power for a tenant in tail in possession to dispose of property by specific devise or bequest and so defeat the heirs, will, of course, be frequently exercised and so limit the number of cases to which s.45(2) can apply.

[34] *i.e.* by the Inheritance Act 1833; and the Law of Property Amendment Act 1859.

[35] s.130(1).

[36] See Settled Land Act 1925, ss.1–37.

[37] As to the distinction between words of purchase and words of limitation, see Megarry and Wade, *The Law of Real Property*, 5th ed., pp. 48–58.

the property on the person who would, under the old rules, have answered the description of the heir either at the death of the deceased or at the time named in the limitation, as the case may be. It will be noticed that the preceding section[38] abolishes the so-called rule in *Shelley's* case[39] so that in appropriate cases the word "heir" is now to be regarded as a word of purchase and not a word of limitation. The old rules apply by virtue of section 132(1) whether the deceased person died before or after 1925 but only to limitations or trusts created by an instrument coming into force after 1925.[40] A recent illustration of the application of these rules is provided by *Re Bourke's Will Trusts*,[41] where there was a gift to "heirs and surviving issue." It was held that "heirs" had to be construed in the strict pre-1926 sense since it would, if it had been limited in respect of freehold land immediately before January 1, 1926, have conferred on the heir an estate in land by purchase.[42] Accordingly the persons entitled were ascertained in accordance with section 132 of the Law of Property Act 1925.

Persons of unsound mind

The old rules of inheritance remain applicable in certain strictly defined circumstances to govern the devolution of any beneficial interest in real estate to which a person of unsound mind was entitled at his death intestate. It will be seen that it will be rarely, if at all, that the conditions precedent to the operation of this exception will be satisfied in the modern law but the point remains theoretically applicable. The exception also provides a graphic illustration of the principle that the modern law of intestate succession is based on the presumed intentions of the intestate. The exception is contained in section 51(2) which requires the following conditions to be satisfied: first, that the "person of unsound mind[43] or defective" should have been living and of full age on January 1, 1926[44]; secondly, that at that time he should have been incapable by reason of his incapacity to make a valid will and, thirdly, that he should die after January 1, 1926 intestate without having recovered his testamentary capacity.[45] It is provided that such a person shall not be deemed to have recovered his

[38] s.131.
[39] (1581) 1 Co. Rep. 88b, see Megarry and Wade, *op.cit.* pp. 1161–1163.
[40] s.132(2).
[41] *Re Bourke's Will Trusts, Barclays Bank Trust Co. Ltd.* v. *Canada Permanent Trust Co.* [1980] 1 W.L.R. 539.
[42] This is the hypothesis which s.132 poses. Thus on the death of a half-brother without issue, the half-sisters became his heirs in the strict sense.
[43] Originally enacted as "lunatic," the alternative phrase was substituted by the Mental Treatment Act 1930, s.20(5); the section was also amended in a minor way by the Mental Health Act 1959. See now Mental Health Act 1983.
[44] The date when the Administration of Estates Act 1925 came into effect.
[45] s.51(2); see (1936–37) 1 Conv. 62; (1951) 15 Conv. 38.

testamentary capacity unless his receiver has been discharged.[46] These conditions are unlikely to be met in the modern law but, where they are, then "any beneficial interest in real estate[47] shall . . . without prejudice to any will of the deceased, devolve in accordance with the general law in force before the commencement of the 1925 Act applicable to freehold land and that law shall, notwithstanding any repeal, apply to the case."[48] However, the exclusion of the new code of intestacy law in such cases is restricted to the devolution of the beneficial interest[49] and so the real estate must bear its rateable share of the funeral, testamentary and administration expenses, debts and liabilities under sections 32, 33, 34 and Schedule I of the Administration of Estates Act 1925.[50]

An illustration of the effect of the section is provided by the case of *Re Berrey*,[51] where it was held that a legitimated person could not take any part of the estate of a person of unsound mind within section 51(2), because, although such a person would have rights to succeed under the Legitimacy Acts in the modern law, he or she would have had no claim at all under the old law. A modern illustration of the application of the section is *Re Sirett*[52] where the court decided that an interest in copyholds was within the section. Having been satisfied on a balance of probabilities that the deceased had been continuously of unsound mind since 1952, the property was held to devolve on the heir at law of the deceased's father, he being the last person to take by purchase. The exception only applies to real estate[53] and thus personal estate, including leaseholds (which are excepted as "chattels real"), will devolve according to the provisions of the 1925 Act. The extent to which the section applies to interests in real estate held on trust for sale has been the subject of some judicial disagreement. The governing authority must now be regarded to be the majority decision in *Re Bradshaw*[54] where Lord Evershed M.R. thought that the phrase "any beneficial interest in real estate" was one of wide import and

[46] *Ibid.* But it is not necessary that a receiver should have been appointed. *Re Gates* [1930] 1 Ch. 199.

[47] Not including chattels real, *cf.* s.55(1)(xix), the intestate's interest in the land had to be, at the moment when A.E.A. 1925 came into operation, a beneficial interest in real estate and then to have devolved as real estate, see Buckley J. in *Re Sirett* [1969] 1 W.L.R. 60 at p. 63.

[48] s.51(2), *i.e.* the heir as ascertained in accordance with the rules of inheritance and thus not according to a local custom such as gavelkind, *Re Higham, Higham* v. *Higham*, [1937] 2 All E.R. 17.

[49] *i.e.* "The foregoing provisions of this part of this Act", s.51(2).

[50] *Re Gates, supra.*

[51] *Re Berrey, Lewis* v. *Berrey* [1936] Ch. 274.

[52] *Pratt* v. *Burton* [1969] 1 W.L.R. 60.

[53] Defined in s.55(1)(xix). The section has been held to apply to the proceeds of sale of freehold land sold in 1923 which by virtue of an earlier enactment devolved on the heir, *Re Harding* (1934) Ch. 271, and also an interest in copyholds, *Re Sirett, supra*; and also to money when treated as real estate, *Re Silva, Silva* v. *Silva* [1929] 2 Ch. 198.

[54] [1950] 1 Ch. 582, Jenkins L.J. dissenting, reversing Danckwerts J. [1950] 1 Ch. 78.

would, according to the ordinary usage of language, cover an interest in the proceeds of sale of real estate held on trust for sale.[55] Such interests will fall within section 51(2) if they possess three characteristics. First, they must exist or have existed and belonged to the person of unsound mind or the defective on January 1, 1926; secondly, they must also exist or belong to the defective at the time of the defective's death and thirdly, the beneficial interests must be such that, at the date of the coming into operation of the 1925 Act, or immediately before the coming into operation of the 1925 Act, they would have devolved as real property and gone to the heir.[56] These requirements were held to be satisfied in *Re Bradshaw*[57] where a defective was entitled before 1925 to a beneficial interest in an undivided share of real estate. It was held, notwithstanding the imposition of the statutory trust for sale by the Law of Property Act 1925, that the defective had a beneficial interest in real estate within section 51(2) which accordingly devolved upon the heir at law as determined by the law of inheritance in force immediately before January 1, 1926. The alternative view that the nature of the property should be determined at the intestate's death was not accepted by the majority.[58]

The making of wills for mentally disordered persons

It has been noted above that the personal estate (including leaseholds) of mentally disordered persons who die intestate after 1925 will be distributed in accordance with the statutory code. The same will apply to the realty save where the conditions in section 51(2) of the 1925 Act are satisfied so as to render the old rules of inheritance applicable. Mental defectives are incapable of making a will and it is obviously undesirable that such persons should inevitably have to die intestate so that power has been conferred on the court to make wills and settlements of property for such persons. The original jurisdiction was contained in section 171 of the Law of Property Act 1925 which was repealed and replaced by section 103 of the Mental Health Act 1959 and consolidated in section 96 of the

[55] *Ibid.* at p. 591.

[56] *Ibid.*

[57] *Supra.* Subject to the judicial disagreement noted above. The difficulty arose because clearly the section did not contemplate the statutory trust for sale introduced by the Law of Property Act 1925. Jenkins L.J., dissenting, thought that for the purposes of devolution, the nature of the property of a "lunatic" dying intestate should be determined at the date of that person's death and at no other time. On this view, since the interest had been converted into personalty by the Law of Property Act 1925 it did not devolve as real estate would have devolved before 1926. This view is perhaps strictly correct on a literal view of the statutes but the majority opinion is to be preferred as avoiding any unfairness caused by the somewhat arbitrary operation of the doctrine of conversion.

[58] *Re Donkin, Public Trustee* v. *Cairns* [1948] Ch. 74 distinguished in *Re Bradshaw, supra.*

Mental Health Act 1983. However, that legislation as originally enacted, although empowering a settlement of the patient's property, did not confer a specific power to make a will for the patient.[59] This power was conferred by the Administration of Justice Act 1969 which added a new paragraph, (*dd*), to section 103(1) of the 1959 Act, since consolidated as paragraph (*e*) of section 96(1) of the Mental Health Act 1983.[60] This provision confers specific power "... for the execution for the patient of a will making any provision (whether by way of disposing of property or exercising a power or otherwise) which could be made by a will executed by the patient if he were not mentally disordered."[61]

Section 96(4) provides that the power to order the execution of a will for a patient relates only to adult patients and "shall not be exercised unless the judge has reason to believe that the patient is incapable of making a valid will." It is beyond the scope of this work to discuss the jurisdiction in detail, for which reference can be made to texts on wills,[62] but its importance in avoiding undesirable intestacies can be emphasised. The recent case of *Re Davey (deceased)*[63] graphically illustrates the point. A very elderly patient of declining mental capacity went through a ceremony of marriage with a much younger employee of the nursing home in which she was resident. Even if this marriage was voidable owing to want of capacity, the decision in *Re Roberts (deceased)*[64] clearly established that it would be effective to revoke an earlier will made by the patient in favour of relatives. Since it seemed apparent that the lady did not have capacity to make a new will after the marriage, the inevitable result would have been an intestacy to the advantage of the husband and disadvantage of the relatives who were the testamentary beneficiaries. The Court of Protection made a new will for the patient pursuant to the powers conferred by the Mental Health Act 1959 in identical terms to the earlier will. Such a solution is obviously preferable to the alternative course of an application under the Inheritance (Provision for Family and Dependants) Act 1975.[65] The jurisdiction has been fully reviewed by Vice-Chancellor Megarry in

[59] See Cross J. in *Re W.J.G.L.* [1966] Ch. 135, who reviews the jurisdiction. Under the 1925 legislation an inter vivos settlement could be made which would operate as a will substitute, as in *Re W.J.G.L. supra*, but this was not entirely satisfactory, see also *Re H.M.F.* [1976] Ch. 33.

[60] With effect from September 30, 1983, see *Practice Direction* [1983] 3 All E.R. 255.

[61] The power is exercisable by the Lord Chancellor, a nominated judge or a Master of the Court of Protection, see s.94 of the 1983 Act. Apart from the inclusion of Officers of the Court of Protection the wording of the legislation in the 1983 Act is the same as that in the 1959 Act.

[62] See *Williams on Wills*, 5th ed., p. 26.

[63] [1981] 1 W.L.R. 164.

[64] [1978] 1 W.L.R. 653.

[65] It is doubtful whether the relatives, in a *Re Davey* type of case, could prove the necessary dependency anyway. The 1975 Act is more fully discussed *post* p. 353.

the case of *Re D. (J.)*[66] where legal and procedural guidelines are laid down. Although expressed with reference to the 1959 Act,[67] the judgment seems equally applicable to the consolidating 1983 Act.[68]

Succession to Personal Estate—Pre-1926

Introduction

It has been seen above that the historical succession to real estate was based on tenurial concepts administered by the King's Courts and reflected the pre-eminent position of land in a feudal society. Personal property was viewed differently and the process of intestate succession applicable to personalty developed quite separately. Thus English law was accustomed until the reforms of 1925 to a dichotomy between succession to realty and to personalty. The latter was very largely neglected by the common law and for many centuries depended on local custom which led to uncertainty and irregularity, although the ecclesiastical courts took an interest and tried to curb abuse of the system.[69] However, the position was far from satisfactory and, because of continuous confusion between the common law courts and the ecclesiastical courts over jurisdiction to intestate estates, it has been said that by the beginning of the seventeenth century "... the law practically ceased to have any clear rules as to the persons entitled to succeed to movables upon the death of one who had died intestate."[70] The confusion so caused was graphically illustrated by the case of *Hughes* v. *Hughes*[71] in 1666 which led to the enactment of the Statute of Distribution in 1670.[72] This Act had two main objects: first, to strengthen the jurisdiction of the ecclesiastical courts over the administration of the estates of intestates and, secondly, to define the rights of persons entitled to take on intestacy.[73] Although the Act failed to achieve the first object, it clarified and established the rules as to entitlement and remained the primary source of the rules governing the intestate succession to personal property until 1925.[74] Two fundamental characteristics of the system can be identified which provide a striking contrast to the contemporaneous position of realty. First, personal estate vested on death in the personal representative

[66] [1982] 2 W.L.R. 373; see Sherrin, 13 Fam.Law 135.
[67] ss.103(1)(*dd*); 103A.
[68] ss.96(1); 97.
[69] It is not necessary for this discussion to consider the pre-1670 position in any detail, since it is fully documented in Holdsworth, *A History of English Law*, Vol. III, pp. 550–563; and in Pollock and Maitland, *History of English Law*, 2nd ed. Vol. II, pp. 356–361.
[70] Holdsworth, *op.cit.* p. 558.
[71] Carter's Rep.125; see the facts, but not the result, set out in Holdsworth, *op.cit.* p. 559.
[72] See Holdsworth, *op.cit.*
[73] *Op.cit.* p. 560.
[74] Although added to subsequently by the Statute of Distribution 1685 (and hence "the Statutes of Distribution") and amended in important respects by the Intestates' Estates Act 1890; see *Re Hughes* [1916] 1 Ch. 493 at p. 500.

and did not pass directly to the heir or the next of kin. Secondly, the statutory process was aimed at identifying a class of persons to take as next of kin rather than a single person to take as heir.

The Statutes of Distribution were repealed in 1925 and replaced by the modern scheme and, with one single exception,[75] have no substantive relevance at the present day. Nonetheless the 1670 Act remains of crucial importance, since in the words of Holdsworth: "The clauses of the Act which define the rights of the persons entitled to take on intestacy have made our modern law."[76] Although the influence of the old statutes on what was intended to be a new code must not be exaggerated, it can be said that the modern statutory code of intestate succession applicable to both realty and personalty evolved out of these statutory provisions which were previously applicable to personalty. This can be illustrated by the basic structure of that code, namely a primary provision for the spouse and children, with the next of kin[77] taking thereafter in a strictly defined order of priority and with the Crown ultimately entitled to *bona vacantia.* Other characteristics of the modern scheme can be identified in the 1670 statute: the duty of children to account for advancements, the equal entitlement of male and female children and of the younger with the elder. For these reasons as well as considerations of historical interest the pre-1926 rules of intestacy, as set out in the Statutes of Distribution 1670 and 1685, need briefly to be considered. First, however, the exceptional case where these rules might still have substantive effect must be noted.

Preservation of the old rules

The single exception where the 1670 and 1685 Statutes remain relevant in the modern law is provided by section 50(2) of the Administration of Estates Act 1925. Trusts declared in an instrument *inter vivos* made, or in a will coming into operation, before January 1, 1926 (the commencement of the 1925 Act) by reference to the Statutes of Distribution must, unless the contrary thereby appears,[78] be construed as referring to the enactments (other than the Intestates' Estates Act 1890)[79] relating to the distribution of effects of intestates which were in force immediately before the commencement of the 1925 legislation. A similar reference in a post-1925 trust or will is

[75] See *post* p. 188.
[76] *Op.cit.* p. 561.
[77] Defined according to a different formula to the modern approach.
[78] *Re Sutcliffe, Sutcliffe* v. *Robertshaw* [1929] 1 Ch. 123; *Re Sutton, Evans* v. *Oliver* [1934] Ch. 209; *Re Hooper's Settlement, Phillips* v. *Lake* [1943] Ch. 116; see further discussed *post* p. 188.
[79] Consistently with the decision in *Re Morgan* [1920] 1 Ch. 196. See further discussed, *post* p. 188.

construed (unless the context otherwise requires) as referring to Part IV of the 1925 Act.[80]

Total intestacy

Statute of Distribution 1670. The Statute of 1670 (subject to two minor provisions noted below) contained all the law on the entitlement to personal estate on intestacy for two centuries until further amended in 1890. The Statute of Frauds 1677 made it clear that the husband's right to take administration to his wife's estate was still a beneficial interest[81] and in 1685 it was provided that the brothers and sisters of an intestate shared equally with the intestate's mother.[82] The entitlement under the Statute of 1670 as so amended can now be shortly noted.

Widow and widower. A widower was entitled to the whole of his wife's personalty to the exclusion of other relatives.[83] A widow was entitled to one-third of the personal estate where there were surviving issue,[84] and to one-half if there were no issue.[85] After 1890 the widow was additionally entitled to a "statutory legacy of £500."[86]

Issue. Subject to the rights of a surviving spouse the issue[87] were primarily entitled with children of deceased children taking their parents' share *per stirpes.*[88] Males were entitled equally with females and there was no preference for the eldest child.[89] Advancements by way of portion made by a father to his children had to be brought into account.[90]

Next of kin. Where the intestate left a widow but no issue, then the next of kin were entitled to a half share in the estate.[91] In the absence of a surviving spouse or issue the relatives were then entitled in order, according, in theory at least, to their degrees of relationship to the deceased.[92] The degree of relationship was ascertained by counting the

[80] s.50(1); see *Re Krawitz's Will Trusts, Krawitz* v. *Crawford* [1959] 1 W.L.R. 1192.

[81] s.25. See Holdsworth, *A History of English Law,* 5th ed., Vol. III, p. 561.

[82] Statute of Distribution, 1685, s.7. The 1670 Act and the 1685 Act are known collectively as the Statutes of Distribution; but not including the Intestates' Estates Act 1890; *Re Morgan* [1920] 1 Ch. 196. See generally on the Statutes of Distribution, *Re Cullen* (1976) 14 S.A.S.R. 456.

[83] Statute of Frauds 1677, s.25. The 1670 Act did not affect the widower's entitlement to the personal estate of his intestate wife.

[84] Statute of Distribution 1670, s.5.

[85] *Ibid.,* s.6.

[86] Intestates' Estates Act 1890, s.1, see *post.*

[87] Including issue *en ventre sa mère.*

[88] 1670 Statute, s.5, so that if there was no widow the children took the whole estate, s.2.

[89] 1670 Statute, s.3.

[90] *Ibid.* s.5. This only applied in cases of total, and not partial intestacy, *Re Roby* [1908] 1 Ch. 71. S.5 is set out and further discussed *post* in Chap. 13.

[91] 1670 Statute, s.6.

[92] *Ibid.* ss.6, 7.

number of steps that the relative was removed from the deceased, counting the generations down in the case of descendants and computing up to the common ancestor and then down in the case of other relatives.[93] Relatives more closely connected were entitled as a class in priority to relatives more remotely connected.[94] However, this formula was not always followed strictly since policy considerations tended to overrule strict logic. Thus a father was the person primarily entitled to the whole estate in the absence of a spouse and issue[95] and excluded, rather than took equally with, the mother. In the absence of a father then the mother shared equally with brothers and sisters and children of deceased brothers and sisters were equally entitled to their parents' share.[96]

It could be that relatives of the first degree (mother), second degree (brothers and sisters) and third degree (nephews and nieces) were all equally entitled. In the absence of a spouse, issue or parents the persons entitled were the brothers and sisters, including children of deceased brothers and sisters,[97] but if *all* the brothers and sisters had predeceased the intestate, then their children took in their own right as relatives of the third degree *per capita*.[98] Grandparents[99] came after brothers and sisters followed by uncles and aunts. Relatives of the fourth degree, *e.g.* first cousins etc., then took and so on, subject to the two overriding rules that a relative more closely connected to the deceased excluded a relative more remotely connected and that within equal degrees of relationship the relatives took equally.[1] In the absence of ascertainable relatives the Crown was entitled to personalty as *bona vacantia*.[2]

The modern scheme of intestate succession embodied in the 1925 Act rejects the degrees of relationship approach in favour of the identification of persons by descriptive name but, apart from the entitlement of a surviving spouse, the modern order of entitlement is not dramatically different to that provided by the 1670 Act.[3]

[93] The surviving spouse and the issue of the deceased (children and their representatives) were expressly provided for by the Statute of Distribution 1670, and strictly speaking were not regarded as next of kin for the purpose of distribution under that statute. See the Table of relatives indicating degrees of relationship, *post* p. 183 note 45. For a modern statute which contains a similar formula for ascertaining the next of kin see the Republic of Eire's, Succession Act 1965, s.71.

[94] Holdsworth, *op.cit.* p. 561.

[95] *Ibid.* p. 562, *Blackborough* v. *Davies* (1701), 1.P.Wms pp. 48, 49.

[96] 1685 Statute, s.7; but not more remote issue.

[97] 1670 Statute, s.7.

[98] 1670 Statute, s.7.

[99] Relatives of the second degree, who would thus exclude nephews and nieces when they took as relatives of the third degree.

[1] Relatives of the half blood took equally with relatives of the whole blood, see Holdsworth, *op.cit.* p. 562 and cases there cited.

[2] At common law, and not under the Statute.

[3] See *post*, pp. 157–160. The modern scheme embraces a more restrictive class of relatives.

Intestates' Estates Act 1890. The law of intestate succession was significantly amended by the 1890 Act which reflected a desire to make better provision for a widow on the intestacy of her husband. Although the Act was, as Morris described it, "a timid half measure of reform,"[4] it did contain two ideas seminal to the 1925 reforms. First, the rights conferred by the Act were applicable equally to both real and personal property. Secondly, the effect of the Act was to provide the widow with a "statutory legacy" in priority to all other relatives. The limitations of the Act are, however, equally apparent since it perpetuated the distinction between widows and widowers and had no application where there were also surviving issue.

The Act applied in the case of deaths intestate after September 1, 1890[5] and provided that, where the real and personal estate of a man did not exceed £500, then, if he left a widow but no issue, the whole estate should belong to the widow absolutely.[6] Where the estate exceeded £500 in value the widow was entitled "... to five hundred pounds part thereof absolutely and exclusively and shall have a charge upon the whole of such real and personal estates for such five hundred pounds, with interest thereon from the date of the death of the intestate at four per cent per annum until payment."[7] This charge was to be borne and paid in proportion to the values of the real and personal estates respectively[8] and was to be in addition to the widow's entitlement to a share of residue.[9] It will be noticed that the Act only applied to intestacies where there was a widow but no issue.[10]

It was decided in *Re Twigg's Estate*[11] that the Act was only intended to apply to the case of a man dying totally intestate and that it had no application to cases of partial intestacy.[12] However, the Act was applied in a case where there had been a complete failure by lapse of all the beneficial interests under a will and the person named as executor had predeceased the testator, who had died leaving a widow but no issue.[13]

The 1890 Act was repealed in respect of deaths after 1926 by the Administration of Estates Act 1925.[14]

[4] (1969) 85 L.Q.R. 339 at p. 348.
[5] s.1.
[6] s.1.
[7] s.2.
[8] s.3.
[9] s.4.
[10] s.1 and *Re Morgan* [1920] 1 Ch. 196.
[11] [1892] 1 Ch. 579.
[12] *Ibid. per* Chitty J. at p. 582.
[13] *In Re Cuffe, Fooks* v. *Cuffe* [1908] 2 Ch. 500.
[14] s.56 and Sched. 2, Pt. I.

Partial intestacy

Rules applicable. The distribution of estates in cases of partial intestacy before 1925 is now only of historical interest and can be noted shortly. The Statute of Distribution 1670 did not apply originally to the intestate part of an estate where an executor had been appointed. In such a case the executor took the undisposed of property beneficially.[15] ". . . The executor having been appointed he, by virtue of his office, took the property, but he took the property, not by reason of any disposition by the testator of the beneficial interest, but by reason of his appointment as executor."[16]

The position under the Statutes of Distribution before the passing of the Executors Act 1830 was stated by Farwell L.J. in *Re Roby*[17] as follows:

> "The Statute of Distribution applied only to intestacy. When the testator appointed an executor he was not intestate, and at common law the executor took the whole of his estate. Equity, however, thought that to be hard, and in cases in which there was any ground on the terms of the will for turning the executor by construction into a trustee, the Court seized upon very small indicia of intention so to turn him. Then the question arose, Trustee for whom? Now the Statute of Distribution, as I have already said, does not apply; it is therefore only by analogy that it has been brought in at all. . . . The Statute is to be read to ascertain the persons to take the shares and the proportion in which they take."

This position was regularised by the Executors Act 1830 which prevented the executor from taking the undisposed of residue beneficially and constituted him a trustee for the persons entitled under the Statute. The Act provided that where any person died after September 1, 1830, ". . . having by his or her will, or any codicil or codicils thereto, appointed any person or persons to be his or her executor or executors, such executor or executors shall be deemed by Courts of Equity to be a trustee or trustees for the person or persons (if any) who would be entitled to the estate under the Statute of Distributions, in respect of any residue not expressly disposed of, unless it shall appear by the will, or any codicil thereto, the person or

[15] *Re Skeats* [1936] 1 Ch. 683; *Re Roby* [1908] 1 Ch. 71.
[16] *Ibid. per* Clauson J. at p. 689. Although in certain cases a court of equity would have treated the executor as a trustee for the next of kin, *ibid.* at p. 686. See also *Re Twigg's Estate, Twigg* v. *Black* [1892] 1 Ch. 57.
[17] [1908] 1 Ch. 71 at pp. 81, 82, which decided that in cases of partial intestacy where the Statute of Distribution is applied by analogy to the undisposed of residue, there is no rule that advances made by the testator in his lifetime have to be brought into hotchpot, following *Vachell* v. *Jeffereys*, (1701) Prec. Ch. 170; *Wheeler* v. *Sheer* (1730) Mos. 301 and *Cowper* v. *Scott*, (1731) 3 P.Wms. 119.

persons so appointed executor or executors was or were intended to take such residue beneficially."[18]

The 1830 Act was repealed by the Administration of Estates Act 1925[19] and in *Re Skeats*[20] it was argued that the effect of the repeal was to restore the position after 1925 to the law as it stood before the enactment of the 1830 Act, so that the executor took beneficially in cases of partial intestacy. This conclusion would have put the law back by a century and certainly could not have been intended by the draftsmen of the Administration of Estates Act 1925. Clauson J. in *Re Skeats*[21] was able to reject this argument in view of the clear definition of "intestate" in section 55(1) of the 1925 Act to include a person who dies partially intestate. In the words of the judge:

> "When a man has made only a partial disposition of the beneficial interest in his property, or has made no disposition at all of that beneficial interest, although he has made a will, his property must be dealt with in the manner indicated by section 46, with the modification, where there has been a partial disposition, indicated in section 49 of the Act. The result of that is that the law applicable to such a case as the present remains exactly the same as it was before this Act, [*i.e.* the *Administration of Estates Act 1925*] was enacted with the modification that the class of next of kin to take has been altered."

As indicated above it was held in pre-1926 cases[22] that the Intestates' Estates Act 1890 did not apply to cases of partial intestacy which were accordingly governed by the Statutes of Distribution unaffected by that Act.

Deaths Intestate After January 1, 1926 And Before January 1, 1953

The 1925 Act

The distribution of the estate of an intestate who died after January 1, 1926[23] and before January 1, 1953 was, and is, governed by Part IV of the Administration of Estates Act 1925 as originally enacted. The latter date refers to the date when the Intestates' Estates Act 1952

[18] The Act only applied as between an executor and the next of kin and had no application where the Crown claimed the estate for want of heirs. Such cases therefore depended on whether there was any testamentary indication that the executors were not to take beneficially. See *Re Jones* [1925] 1 Ch. 340, indication that executor to take as trustee and thus on failure of the trusts, Crown entitled as *bona vacantia*; and *Att.Gen* v. *Jeffreys*, [1908] A.C. 411, no such indication, executors entitled.

[19] s.56.

[20] *Supra*.

[21] *Supra* at p. 689.

[22] *Re Twigg's Estate* [1892] 1 Ch. 579; *Re Cuffe* [1908] 2 Ch. 500, discussed in the previous section, p. 37.

[23] 1925 Act, s.58(2).

came into force[24] and deaths subsequent to that date will be subject to the amended entitlement provided for by that statute. The pre-1953 law will remain significant in some cases, for example where the death occurred before 1953 and a partial intestacy arises subsequently by reason of the failure of an interest in remainder after an effective life interest.[25] Likewise where the deceased died before that date and by will provided that any interest which might fail should be distributed among the next of kin entitled on intestacy. For this reason it is necessary to consider briefly the pre-1953 position. The discussion will also indicate important contrasts between the old and the new rules illustrating the policy considerations which underlie the modern law. The Report of the Morton Committee, The Committee on The Law of Intestate Succession,[26] will also be discussed because the provisions of the 1952 Act, and thus the modern law of intestate succession, largely flowed from those recommendations.

Entitlement of spouse pre-1953

Spouse and no issue and no close relations. The intestate's spouse was[27] entitled to the whole estate absolutely if there were no surviving issue, or parents, or brothers or sisters of the whole, or half blood, or issue thereof, or grandparents, or uncles and aunts of the whole, or half blood, or issue thereof.[28]

Spouse and issue. If the intestate was survived by a spouse and issue, then the spouse was entitled to the personal chattels absolutely,[29] a net sum of £1,000 with interest thereon at 5 per cent[30] and a life interest in one-half of the estate, which was held subject thereto on the statutory trusts for the issue.[31] The other half of the estate was held on the statutory trusts for the issue.[32] If these trusts failed, by reason of all the issue failing to attain a vested interest,[33] in the lifetime of the spouse, then the spouse took a life interest in that part also,[34] if there were other surviving relatives.

[24] 1952 Act, s.9(2).
[25] As in *Re Grover's Will Trust, National Provincial Bank Ltd.* v. *Clarke* [1971] Ch. 168, where the testator died in 1949 and the distribution of the estate on partial intestacy had to be determined in 1969.
[26] 1951 Cmd. 8310.
[27] For convenience the position will be expressed in the past tense.
[28] s.46(1)(v). The references to the 1925 Act in this and the succeeding sections, are to the Act as originally enacted.
[29] s.46(1)(i), s.55(1)(x). See discussion *post.* The meaning of personal chattels has not changed.
[30] s.46(1)(i). Although this sum was expressed to be charged on the residuary estate, it was in effect an absolute gift.
[31] s.46(1)(i)(*b*).
[32] *Ibid.*
[33] *i.e.* attaining the age of 21, or marrying under that age, s.47(1)(i) and s.47(2)(*b*).
[34] s.46(1)(i)(*b*) and s.47(2)(*a*) and also, by that section, the income accumulated under those trusts.

Spouse and no issue but specified relatives. Where the intestate left no surviving issue, but was survived by any of the relatives noted below, then the surviving spouse took the personal chattels absolutely[35] and a statutory legacy of £1,000.[36] The remaining estate was held on trust for the surviving spouse for life[37] with remainder to the following relatives in the following order: to the parents, in equal shares absolutely if more than one[38]; on the statutory trusts for brothers and sisters of the whole blood (including issue of deceased ones); on the statutory trusts for the brothers and sisters of the half blood (including issue of deceased ones); for the grandparents if more than one in equal shares absolutely; failing any of these, on the statutory trusts for the uncles and aunts of the whole blood, (including issue of deceased ones) or if none, of the half blood[39] (including issue of deceased ones).

It will be noticed that, irrespective of the class of the other relatives also surviving, the spouse was entitled only to a net sum of £1,000. This sum could, if desired, be raised by a charge on the estate[40] or satisfied by appropriation.[41]

The life interest of the surviving spouse could, with his or her consent, be redeemed by the personal representatives.[42] The capital value of the interest was calculated according to specified tables,[43] and could be raised if necessary by a charge on the residuary estate.[44]

Other relatives

Specified relatives. In the absence of a spouse or issue, the other relatives were entitled in the following order: parents[45]; brothers and/or sisters of the whole blood or issue thereof[46]; brothers and/or sisters of the half blood or issue thereof[47]; grandparents[48]; uncles and/or aunts of the whole blood or issue thereof[49]; uncles and/or aunts of the half blood or issue thereof.[50] Parents and grandparents took

[35] See s.55(1)(*x*).
[36] With interest at 5 per cent., s.46(1)(i).
[37] s.46(1)(i)(*a*).
[38] s.46(1)(iii), (iv).
[39] s.46(1)(v). If none of those relatives survived, or the trusts failed, then the surviving spouse took absolutely.
[40] s.48(2)(*a*).
[41] s.41.
[42] s.48(1).
[43] Life insurance society tables, or the tables in the Schedule to the Succession Duty Act 1853.
[44] s.48(2)(*b*).
[45] s.46(1)(iii), (iv).
[46] s.46(1)(v).
[47] s.46(1)(v).
[48] s.46(1)(v).
[49] s.46(1)(v).
[50] s.46(1)(v).

absolutely, in equal shares if more than one[51]; the other relatives took on the statutory trusts.[52] These were the only relatives entitled to the exclusion of more distant relatives, *e.g.* second cousins or great aunts, thus the class was confined within degrees of grandparents or descendants of grandparents.[53] In the absence of any of the specified relatives, the Crown took the whole estate as *bona vacantia*.[54] It can be observed that the 1952 Act did not extend the class of relatives entitled as next of kin or affect the order of entitlement.

Other rules. Other aspects of the intestacy scheme as originally enacted, such as the entitlement of the Crown to *bona vacantia*,[55] the meaning of the statutory trusts[56] and the definition of "personal chattels"[57] have remained largely unaffected by the 1952 Act. The analogous application of the rules in cases of partial intestacy[58] has also remained unchanged, except for the requirement that the spouse should account for testamentary benefits.[59]

REFORM IN 1952

The Morton Committee and the Intestates' Estates Act 1952

By the middle of the century it had become apparent that the 1925 Act as originally drafted was no longer adequate, particularly with reference to the entitlement of the surviving spouse. Accordingly, as a result of prompting by the Law Society, the Committee on The Law of Intestate Succession (usually referred to shortly as the Morton Committee) was established.[60] The corner stone of the Morton Committee's recommendations[61] was that the statutory legacy in

[51] s.46(1)(iii), (iv).
[52] As to which see s.47(1), made applicable to other relatives by s.47(3).
[53] See Clausen J., *Re Bridgen* [1938] 1 Ch. 205 at p. 209, in contrast to the pre-1926 rules.
[54] s.46(1)(vi).
[55] s.46(1)(vi), see *post*, Chap. 14.
[56] s.47(1), see *post*, Chap. 13.
[57] s.55(1)(x), see *post*, Chap. 11.
[58] s.49.
[59] Introduced by the 1952 Act, see *post*, Chap. 11.
[60] 1951 Cmd. 8310. Despite the wide ranging title, the terms of reference were in fact limited to considering the rights under s.46 of the 1925 Act of a surviving spouse in the residuary estate of an intestate, and to considering whether the Inheritance (Family Provision) Act 1938 should be made applicable to intestacies. The major concern of the committee was the provision for the surviving spouse and their recommendations were based on four main considerations. First, that the surviving spouse's entitlement on intestacy should be increased. Secondly, that the spouse should have a right to acquire the matrimonial home. Thirdly, that life estates should be avoided in small estates. Fourthly, that the family provision legislation should apply to cases of total intestacy.
[61] See para. 20.

favour of the spouse[62] should be increased to £5,000 where there were surviving issue, and £20,000 where there were specified relations but no issue.[63] The Committee were aware that this would have the effect in the majority of estates of the spouse being entitled to the whole estate.[64] The 1952 Act also effected two changes with reference to the payment of interest on this sum, consequential to recommendations from the Committee. First, the rate of interest on the statutory legacy was reduced to 4 per cent.[65] and, secondly, it was provided that the interest should be charged against and be payable primarily out of income.[66]

Elimination of life interests

The Morton Committee[67] were concerned to reduce the number of occasions on which a life interest arose on intestacy in order both to enlarge the beneficial interest of the spouse and to simplify the administration of estates.[68] Accordingly, under the restructured section 46(1)(i) of the 1925 Act a life interest, in one-half of the estate, can only arise in cases where there is a spouse and issue and the estate exceeds in value the amount of the statutory legacy.[69] Further, it was thought that the life interest might be attended by difficulties in administration and might be regarded as being less beneficial to the spouse than a capital sum.[70] Accordingly, the Committee recommended that the power of the spouse to capitalise the life interest should be widened and changed so as to confer a right on the spouse

[62] The committee considered the problem of the unmarried "wife", *i.e.* the long term, perhaps lifetime, co-habitation as husband and wife without the formality of marriage. Although they had some sympathy with such persons they did not think it desirable that the legislation should make any specific provision for co-habitees or for the illegitimate children of such a union.

[63] Subsequently, enacted by the Intestates' Estates Act 1952.

[64] At the time of the Report evidence derived from an analysis of wills conducted by the Principal Probate Registry showed that 87 per cent. of estates were valued at under £5,000. Further where the estate was less than £2,000, 73 per cent. of male testators left the whole estate to their widows; where the estate was between £2,000 and £5,000, 65 per cent.; and where the estate was over £5,000, 45 per cent.

[65] Subsequently increased to 7 per cent. and then reduced to 6 per cent., see *post* p. 206. The terminology "fixed net sum" was introduced by the Family Provision Act 1966.

[66] Para. 22, rather than out of capital, s.46(4). This can have consequences relating to the valuation of the estate to determine whether the spouse is solely entitled, because the interest is no longer a permitted deduction since January 1, 1953, when determining the capital value of the estate. The original reason for the change, however, was fiscal.

[67] Cmd. 8310, para. 32.

[68] The ascertainment of the correct balance between the spouse and the issue caused the Committee much thought. They considered, but rejected, a proposal that the spouse should have a life interest in the whole estate, since it was not thought appropriate that the children should be deprived of any immediate interest in substantial (*i.e.* exceeding the amount of statutory legacy) estates, see para. 29.

[69] The terminology "fixed net sum" was introduced by the Family Provision Act 1966.

[70] Para. 32.

rather than a power on the personal representatives.[71] These recommendations were ultimately embodied in the new section 47A of the Administration of Estates Act 1925[72] by the 1952 Act.

Increase in the spouse's absolute entitlement

Several organisations, notably the Council of the Law Society, suggested to the Morton Committee that, where there was a spouse and no issue, the surviving spouse should take the whole estate to the exclusion of all other classes of kin.[73] Although rejected in terms, this result is, to a large extent, achieved in effect in the majority of cases by virtue of two major changes proposed by the Committee and enacted by the 1952 Act. First, after 1953 only parents, and brothers and sisters of the whole blood and their issue, are entitled to share in an estate with a spouse.[74] Where there are such relatives, the spouse takes one-half of the estate absolutely and the parents or brothers and sisters are entitled to the other half. It will be noticed that this change has the effect of excluding brothers and sisters of the half-blood and their issue, grandparents, and uncles and aunts of both the whole and the half blood, and their issue from any entitlement where there is a surviving spouse. This change was justified on the principle that "we think that the average individual would not wish next-of-kin who are remoter than brothers and sisters of the whole blood or the issue of such deceased brothers and sisters to benefit from the estate at the expense of the surviving spouse."[75] It will also be observed that the comment indicates that the Morton Committee accepted that the presumed intention of the intestate should be the basis of modern intestacy law.[76]

The second change recommended by the Committee and enacted in 1952 was that, even where parents and brothers or sisters survived, the statutory legacy to which the spouse was entitled as a first charge on the estate should be increased to £20,000.[77] Thus, in all cases where the residuary estate is less in value than this (subsequently greatly

[71] s.48(1) already provided that the personal representatives could purchase or redeem the life interest of the spouse by paying to the spouse a capital sum out of the estate, para. 32; s.48(1) was repealed as respects death after January 1, 1953 and replaced by the new s.47A.

[72] It was not thought desirable that issue should have a similar power, nor was it thought appropriate that the surviving spouse's interest in the estate should be reduced on remarriage; para. 32.

[73] see para. 34.

[74] paras. 34–36.

[75] para. 36. This results in the curious distinction in the modern law between brothers and sisters of the whole blood and brothers and sisters of the half blood. The Report contains no specific justification for the exclusion of half brothers and sisters in such circumstances.

[76] There is no discussion in the Report on the fundamental policy question that should underlie the rules of intestate succession. The Committee assumed that presumed intention was, and should continue to be, the basis. See also para. 10.

[77] Para. 34.

increased) "fixed net sum,"[78] the spouse takes the whole estate to the exclusion of other kin. In cases where the estate exceeds that amount, the spouse takes the legacy and an absolute interest in one-half of the residue.[79]

Matrimonial home

The Committee were concerned to ensure that in most cases the spouse should be protected in occupation of the matrimonial home. The Committee considered but rejected a proposal that the spouse should be given some direct right of inheritance to the matrimonial home in lieu of, or in diminution of, the statutory legacy.[80] They thought that a better solution would be to give the spouse an option to purchase from the estate the intestate's interest in the matrimonial home.[81] This recommendation was subsequently modified to a right of appropriation in satisfaction of the statutory legacy as embodied in the rules set out in the Second Schedule to the 1952 Act. Clearly, the Committee were influenced by a desire to see a correlation between the statutory legacy and the value of the matrimonial home and this is reflected in subsequent increases in the amount of the statutory legacy. The committee did not think it desirable that the spouse should be given any right of occupation in the house since this would give rise to difficulties regarding liability, for example, to effect repairs and to pay rates and taxes.[82]

Partial intestacies

The Morton Committee were not inclined to formulate separate rules to govern the distribution of partially intestate estates and thought that the existing approach of the 1925 Act should continue. The 1952 Act did, however, introduce as section 49(1)(*aa*) the requirement that a spouse should account against his or her entitlement to the statutory legacy for any testamentary benefits received in a partial intestacy.[83]

[78] Terminology introduced by the Family Provision Act 1966—see *post* p. 205.
[79] In the case of estates exceeding this sum then it will be noticed that the change has the effect of increasing the parent's and the brother's and sister's share since they become immediate interests rather than interests in reversion. The previous entitlement of a parent in reversion after the spouse's life interest was very largely illusory for obvious reasons.
[80] Para. 23.
[81] *Ibid.*
[82] para. 27. The personal representatives have a power to permit a person entitled to take possession of land, before assenting or making a conveyance, A.E.A. 1925, s.43, see *post* p. 124.
[83] A change consequential to the increased amount of the statutory legacy. See also s.49(2), (3), (4) added by the 1952 Act.

The Intestates' Estates Act 1952

This Act, consequential to the report of the Morton Committee,[84] effected a significant alteration in the law of intestate succession where there is a surviving spouse.[85] The legislation retained the structure of the 1925 scheme but substantially recast and amended section 46(1)(i) and other provisions of Part IV of the Administration of Estates Act 1925. The amended rules apply to deaths intestate, wholly or partially, after January 1, 1953[86] and are set out in detail in the following chapters. It can be stated with some justification that the 1952 Act is poorly drafted and that some of the new provisions in, for example, section 46(3) and section 49(4) are defective and in need of amendment.[87] These points will be explored more fully in due course. In addition to the changes noted above the 1952 Act added the following subsections to the 1925 Act: section 46(3) which negates the application of section 184 to cases of the simultaneous deaths of husband and wife where one or both died intestate; section 47(4) to the effect that references to the intestate leaving or not leaving a member of the class of brothers or sisters of the whole blood should be construed as reference to the intestate leaving or not leaving a member of that class who attained a vested interest; and section 47(5), since repealed.[88]

[84] See *supra*, 1951 Cmd. 8310.

[85] But left untouched the position where there is no surviving spouse; thus s.46(1)(i) is entirely recast, but there are only minor amendments to s.46(1)(ii), (iii), (iv), (v), (vi).

[86] s.9(2).

[87] Indeed s.47(5), which was added by the 1952 Act was shown in *Re Lockwood, Atherton* v. *Brooke* [1958] Ch. 231, to have such absurd consequences, that it was repealed by the Family Provision Act 1966, ss.9, 10, Sched. 2. See discussed *post*.

[88] By Family Provision Act 1966, ss.9 and 10, Sched. 2, see *supra*, n. 87.

1. Table of Distribution of Intestate Estate
Death on or After January 1, 1926 and Before January 1, 1953

Spouse Surviving

Relative Surviving		*Entitlement*
Spouse and estate not exceeding £1,000 in value		All to surviving spouse absolutely
Spouse and none of relatives specified below		All to surviving spouse absolutely
	Statutory Legacy and Personal Chattels	*Residue*
Spouse and issue	Surviving spouse takes the personal chattels absolutely and £1,000 absolutely. Residue is distributed as in next column	One-half to surviving spouse for life, then to issue on statutory trusts; other half to issue on statutory trusts
Spouse and parent(s)	Ditto	All to surviving spouse for life, then to parent, or parents in equal shares, absolutely
Spouse and brother(s) and /or sister(s) of the whole blood, and/or issue thereof	Ditto	All to surviving spouse for life, then to brother(s) and/or sister(s) on the statutory trusts
Spouse and brother(s) and /or sister(s) of the half blood, and/or issue thereof	Ditto	Ditto
Spouse and grandparent(s)	Ditto	All to surviving spouse for life, then to grandparent, or grandparents in equal shares, absolutely
Spouse and uncle(s) and /or aunt(s) of the whole blood, and/or issue thereof	Ditto	All to surviving spouse for life, then to uncle(s) and /or aunt(s) on the statutory trusts
Spouse and uncle(s) and /or aunt(s) of the half-blood, and/or issue thereof	Ditto	Ditto

No Spouse Surviving

Relative Surviving	*Entitlement*
Issue	All to issue on statutory trusts
Parents	All to parent, or parents in equal shares, absolutely
Brother(s) and/or sister(s) of the whole blood, and/or issue thereof	All to brother(s) and/or sister(s) on the statutory trusts; issue of deceased brother or sister taking their parents share on the statutory trusts
Brother(s) and/or sister(s) of the half blood, and/or issue thereof	Ditto
Grandparent(s)	All to grandparent, or grandparents in equal shares, absolutely
Uncle(s) and/or aunt(s) of the whole blood, and/or issue thereof	All to uncle(s) and/or aunt(s) on the statutory trusts; issue of deceased uncle or aunt taking their parents share on the statutory trusts
Uncle(s) and/or aunt(s) of the half blood and/or issue thereof	Ditto
None of these rélatives	All to Crown, Duchy of Lancaster or Duke of Cornwall, as *bona vacantia*

Part Two

PERSONAL REPRESENTATIVES AND THE ADMINISTRATION

CHAPTER 3

NECESSITY FOR A GRANT

INTRODUCTION

A grant of probate where there are proving executors, or a grant of letters of administration where there are no proving executors, is required with respect to all estates which include realty and is usually required in all cases in order to enable the estate to be properly administered. A grant of probate effectively proves the will and establishes the formal title of the proving executors to deal with the estate. Letters of administration with the will annexed likewise prove the will and also confer title to the assets upon the administrator. Where there is no will, letters of administration in effect establish the intestacy and confer title on the administrators. The grant will be essential to prove title to realty and to enable an effective transfer of it to be made to the beneficiaries, and the production of a grant is generally necessary to establish the right to receive and to deal with any part of the deceased's assets. Exceptionally, however, statute has authorised the payment of specified small sums and the disposition of some personal property of small value to the person entitled without the necessity for the production of a grant. In addition some forms of property and kinds of disposition can operate effectively on death without being subject to a grant.

Powers before grant

It is axiomatic that an executor derives his authority from the will and an administrator from the grant.[1] In a testate estate, the real and personal property vests at death in the executor; in an intestate estate the property vests at death in the President of Family Division of the High Court[2] until administration is granted.[3]

The powers of an administrator to act before grant are exceptional and limited in effect to essential actions to preserve and protect the deceased's estate. The general powers of administration which are

[1] Always the case with personalty; by statute now Administration of Estates Act 1925 (hereinafter also referred to as the "A.E.A. 1925"), ss.1(1) and (3) in the case of realty.

[2] A.E.A. 1925, s.9, as amended, so that, for example, a notice to quit may be served on him by sending it by post addressed to him c/o The Treasury Solicitor, Queen Anne's Chambers, 28 Broadway, London SW1H 9JS, Practice Direction of 13 February 1985 [1985] 1 All E.R. 832.

[3] See *post* p. 60. In so far as this text is concerned with intestacies and thus usually with the position of administrators it is not necessary to discuss the powers of an executor to act before probate in any detail.

available immediately to an executor are vested in an administrator only by the grant of letters of administration.[4] There is, however, a limited doctrine of relation back in that the grant has been held to relate back to the death of an intestate so as to give validity to the acts before the letters were obtained.[5] However, it is clear that relation back is an exception to the general rule that an administrator derives title from the grant and it has been recently confirmed that the doctrine will only be applied where to do so would clearly be regarded as beneficial to the estate.[6] The test of benefit is to be applied by viewing the matter objectively from the date of the grant and not subjectively from the position of the actor or at the date of the action.[7] Thus, where a father had negotiated the settlement of a fatal accident claim on behalf of his son's estate and subsequently had obtained letters of administration, it was held that the estate was not bound and that the damages could be renegotiated. This was necessary because the decision in *Gammell* v. *Wilson*[8] indicated that a higher level of damages would be obtainable.[9]

Personal Property of Small Value

Small payments

In order to avoid the trouble and expense of obtaining a formal grant in small estates, it has been established that payment of particular sums within specified limits can be made without the necessity to obtain a grant. The Administration of Estates (Small Payments) Act 1965 specified a limit of £500[10]; this was increased to £1,500 by The Administration of Estates (Small Payments) (Increase of Limit) Order 1975[11]; and has now been increased with effect from April 11, 1984, by a 1984 order of the same name[12] to £5,000. The 1965 Act lists in Schedule 1 the enactments authorising the disposal of property on death without the necessity for a grant.[13] The two main categories of such property are sums invested in various forms of saving schemes and the personal effects, pay and pensions of specified

[4] *Wankford* v. *Wankford* (1784) 1 Salk 299; *Ingall* v. *Moran* [1944] K.B. 160, commencement of action by administrator pre-grant ineffective, see *Austin* v. *Hart* [1983] 2 A.C. 640.

[5] Benet Hytner Q.C. (sitting as a deputy judge of the High Court) in *Mills* v. *Anderson* [1984] Q.B. 704 at p. 542 citing Williams, Mortimer and Sunnucks on *Executors, Administrators and Probate*, 16th ed. 1982, p. 91.

[6] *Mills* v. *Anderson* [1984] Q.B. 704.

[7] *Ibid.*

[8] [1982] A.C. 27; reported after the initial settlement had been agreed.

[9] *Mills* v. *Anderson, supra.* Nor was the father estopped from denying the validity of his acts pre-grant or of an agreement entered into by him in relation to the estate before he was granted letters of administration since any representation made pre-grant could not have been made by him in his capacity as administrator, *ibid.*

[10] This figure was inserted into the list of specified provisions in Sched. 1 to the Act.

[11] S.I. 1975 No. 1137.

[12] S.I. 1984 No. 539.

[13] For a full list see *Halsbury's Laws*, 4th ed., Vol. 17 paras. 967–976.

public employees. The former include payments due to the deceased in respect of deposits in friendly societies,[14] trustee savings banks,[15] national savings bank,[16] building societies,[17] industrial and provident societies[18] and loan societies,[19] trade unions[20] and in respect of social security payments.[21] Similar provisions apply to government stock and war loans[22] and savings certificates.[23] The rules governing each type of payment must be sought in the statutory provisions applicable in each case, but the following section from the Friendly Societies Act 1974 is typical, bearing in mind that the sum of £500 has been replaced as above.

> "s.68(1) If any member of a registered society or branch entitled from the funds thereof to a sum not exceeding £500 dies without having made any nomination thereof then subsisting, the society or branch may, without letters of administration or probate of any will or, in Scotland without any grant of confirmation, distribute the sum among such persons as appear to the committee, upon such evidence as they may deem satisfactory, to be entitled by law to receive that sum.
> (2) If any such member is illegitimate, the society or branch may pay the sum of money which that member might have nominated to or among the persons who, in the opinion of the committee, would have been entitled thereto if that member had been legitimate, or if there are no such persons, the society or branch shall deal with the money as the Treasury may direct."

It will be noticed that the section is permissive or enabling and not mandatory. Protection is afforded to the officers who so act[24] but the next of kin or personal representative of the deceased member is given a remedy for recovery of the money paid under section 68 against the person who has received it.[25]

Pay and personal effects of public employees

Arrears of pay, allowances and pensions due to the following deceased public employees are payable without production of a grant: members of the armed forces, civilian employees in naval dockyards, police pensioners, firemen, civil servants, employees of various public

[14] Friendly Societies Act 1974, ss.66–68.
[15] Trustee Savings Bank Act 1981, s.27(4).
[16] National Savings Bank Act 1971, s.9.
[17] Building Societies Act 1962, s.46.
[18] Industrial and Provident Societies Act 1965, ss.23–27.
[19] Loan Societies Act 1840, s.11.
[20] Trade Union and Labour Relations Act 1974, s.1(1), (2)(*d*).
[21] Social Security Act 1975, s.8(4)(*e*).
[22] National Debt Act 1972, s.6.
[23] Savings Certificates Regulations 1972, S.I. No. 641.
[24] s.69.
[25] *Ibid.*

services, school teachers and local authority employees.[26] The Merchant Shipping Act 1970 also enables the personal effects of merchant seamen dying at sea to be handed over without production of a grant.[27]

Other cases

Other property which can be dealt with without a grant includes funds in court,[28] certain property in the hands of consular officers[29] and moneys due under a policy of life insurance effected by a person not domiciled in the United Kingdom.[30]

In addition it may be possible in practice to avoid having to obtain a grant in respect of a small estate even if the property does not fall within any of the categories previously mentioned. In the case, for example, of money in a current or a deposit account with a clearing bank, payment can often be obtained against an indemnity given by the recipient, particularly if such recipient is the spouse or child of the deceased.

Statutory Nominations

Money in savings accounts with friendly societies,[31] industrial provident societies[32] and trade unions[33] can effectively be disposed of on death by written nomination. The same facility was also previously applicable to money in the Trustee Savings Bank (withdrawn May 1, 1979),[34] the National Savings Bank (withdrawn May 1, 1981)[35] and in respect of National Savings Certificates (withdrawn May 1, 1981).[36] There was no limit to the amount that could be nominated with respect to the last two named, but in the case of the others the limit was £1,500.[37] Where an effective nomination is made, the money will pass accordingly and not under the will or the intestacy provisions.

[26] For the enabling legislation and regulations see *Halsbury's Laws*, 4th ed., Vol. 17 para. 969. Since these provisions are particularly liable to change it is suggested that the most up to date supplement to that text be consulted.

[27] s.66(2).

[28] Subject to the usual limit.

[29] Consular Conventions Act 1949.

[30] See Halsbury, *op. cit.*, para. 972.

[31] Friendly Societies Act 1974, ss.66, 67.

[32] Industrial and Provident Societies Act 1965, ss.23, 24.

[33] Trade Union and Labour Relations Act 1974, Sched. 1, para. 31; Trade Union (Nominations) Regulations 1977, S.I. 1977 No. 789.

[34] Trustee Savings Banks Regulations 1972, S.I. 1972 No. 583; as amended by S.I. 1979 No. 259.

[35] National Savings Banks Regulations 1972, S.I. 1972 No. 764; as amended by S.I. 1981 No. 484.

[36] Savings Certificates Regulations 1972, S.I. 1972 No. 641; as amended by S.I. 1981 No. 486.

[37] Administration of Estates (Small Payments) (Increase of Limit) Order 1975, S.I. No. 1137; the limit previously was £500; see now the 1984 Order of the same name, S.I. 1984 No. 539, raising the amount to £5,000.

The full details of this form of disposition must be sought elsewhere but some points can shortly be noted.

All such nominations are required to be in due form and the rules relating to each are similar, the provisions in section 66 of the Friendly Societies Act 1974 being typical:

> "... a member of a registered society or of a branch thereof who is not under the age of sixteen years may, by writing under his hand delivered at or sent to the registered office of the society or branch, or made in a book kept at that office, nominate a person or persons to whom any sum of money payable by the Society or Branch on the death of that member or any specified amount of money so payable shall be paid at his decease."

Such a nomination is revoked by marriage,[38] or by a similar document conforming with the rules above,[39] but is not revoked by a will.[40] However, it should be noted that property nominated is treated as part of the net estate of the deceased for the purposes of the Inheritance (Provision for Family and Dependants) Act 1975.[41]

Property Not Subject to Probate

Joint property

The interest of a deceased person under a joint tenancy where another joint tenant survives the deceased is an interest ceasing on his death.[42] As such it does not devolve on the personal representative and is not regarded as assets of the estate.[43] No grant is required in respect of such property, which provides an effective method of bypassing administration and the code of intestate succession. The automatic inheritance ensures immediate entitlement of the survivor on death and avoids the delay and expense of probate and administration.[44] Although property can be jointly owned by any persons whether related or not, it is most commonly encountered with reference to husbands and wives, the two most significant circumstances being the joint ownership of the matrimonial home and joint bank accounts.

Where the matrimonial home is subject to registered title, the husband and wife may be registered as joint proprietors and on the death of one joint tenant his or her name will be removed from the register on proof of death. Production of the probate or letters of

[38] s.66(7).
[39] s.66(6).
[40] *Lavin* v. *Howley* (1897) 102 L.T.J. 560; *Bennett* v. *Slater* [1899] 1 Q.B. 45.
[41] s.25(1) and s.8 of the 1975 Act; see *post.*
[42] A.E.A. 1925, s.3(4).
[43] *Ibid.* s.1(1).
[44] Joint tenancies are widely used for this purpose in the United States where there is a keen desire to avoid the expense of probate.

administration is not generally required.[45] This is subject of course to the important proviso that no *inter vivos* severance has taken place.[46] In unregistered land the absolute entitlement of the survivor of two joint tenants can similarly be established by proof of death. Where the parties are not legally entitled as joint tenants, but the sole legal owner is shown to hold on trust for himself and another as joint tenants then the *jus accrescendi* can apply to the beneficial interest. However, in the absence of an express declaration of trust, it is more likely that the beneficial interest will be held in common and a grant of administration will then be necessary in the usual way.

The advantage of a joint bank or savings account is that the survivor has immediate access to the money without the necessity for a grant. It is desirable for all married couples to have some money held in this way to ensure that in the interval between death and grant the survivor has ready access to money as of right. The terms on which such joint accounts are held will be subject to the contractual basis on which the account was opened and this will usually be governed by the standard conditions of the financial institution.

It can be noted that the deceased's severable share of joint property can be treated, if the court so orders, as part of the net estate of the deceased for the purposes of the Inheritance (Provision for Family and Dependants) Act 1975.[47]

Donationes mortis causa

Property which is subject to a *donatio mortis causa* does not devolve on the personal representative and is not subject to a grant. This exceptional form of gift was described as follows by Buckley J. in *Re Beaumont*[48]:

> "A *donatio mortis causa* is a singular form of gift. It may be said to be of an amphibious nature, being a gift which is neither entirely inter vivos nor testamentary. It is an act *inter vivos* by which the donee is to have an absolute title to the subject at the gift not at once but if the donor dies. If the donor dies the title becomes absolute not under but as against his executor. In order to make the gift valid it must be made so as to take complete effect on the donor's death. The court must find that the donor intended it to be absolute if he died, but he need not actually say so."

To constitute an effective *donatio mortis causa* three conditions must be satisfied. First, the gift must have been intended by the donor to be conditional on death, *i.e.* it must have been made on the terms

[45] Land Registration Rules 1925, r. 172. Further evidence may however be required.
[46] As to which see Megarry and Wade, *The Law of Real Property,* 5th ed. pp. 429 *et seq.*
[47] s.25 and s.9 of the 1975 Act; see *post.*
[48] *Beaumont* v. *Ewbank* [1902] 1 Ch. 889 at p. 892.

that, if the donor should not die, he should be entitled to resume complete dominion of the property.[49] Secondly, it must have been made in contemplation of death within the near future, *i.e.* death which is for some reason believed to be impending.[50]

Thirdly, the donor must have parted with dominion over the subject-matter of the gift. This involves three elements.[51] First, there must be a sufficient delivery of the subject-matter of the alleged gift to the donee. Secondly, there must be the requisite *animus donandi* having regard especially to acts done after the delivery. Thirdly, where the subject-matter of the gift is a chose in action, such as money in a bank account, there must be a transfer of essential documents amounting to the *indicia* of title.

Where an effective donation is established then the donee's title becomes absolute on the donor's death and no assent or other act is required by the deceased's personal representative to perfect the title.[52] It will be apparent that property subject to such a gift devolves in accordance with the gift and does not form part of the residuary estate of the deceased for the purposes of intestate succession. Exceptionally, however, such property is treated as part of the net estate of the deceased for the purposes of the Inheritance (Provision for Family and Dependants) Act 1975.[53]

Social Security Payments

Some reference must be made to the entitlement on death of a widow to social security payments by way of allowance or pension, which are payable directly on the death. The most important of these are the widow's allowance, the widowed mother's allowance and the various categories of widow's pension. The widow's allowance is payable during the period of 26 weeks following the husband's death to a widow who was under pensionable age at the date of the death or whose husband was not then entitled to a full retirement pension provided that the requisite contributions had been made by the husband and that she is not cohabiting with a man as his wife.[54] The widowed mother's allowance is payable subject to specified conditions to a widowed mother who does not qualify for a widow's allowance[55]

[49] *Per* Wynn-Parry J. in *Re Lillingston (decd.), Pembery* v. *Pembery* [1952] 2 All E.R. 184 at p. 187; *Gardner* v. *Parker* [1818] 3 Madd. 184. See more fully discussed, Parry and Clarke, *Law of Succession*, 8th ed., pp. 17–24.

[50] *Per* Farwell J. in *Re Craven's Estate* [1937] Ch. 423 at p. 426.

[51] *Per* Lord Evershed M.R. in *Birch* v. *Treasury Solicitor* [1951] 1 Ch. 298 at pp. 300, 301.

[52] *Ward* v. *Turner* (1752) 2 Ves.Sen. 431; *Tate* v. *Hilbert* (1793) 2 Ves.Jun. 111.

[53] s.25, and s.8(2) of the 1975 Act; see *post.*

[54] Social Security Act 1975, s.24 as amended; as to effect of conviction for manslaughter see R. v. *Chief National Commissioner, ex p. Connor* [1981] 1 Q.B. 758; *R.* v. *Secretary of State for the Home Department, ex p. Puttick* [1981] 2 W.L.R. 440; *Re K.* [1985] Ch. 85 affirmed by C.A. [1986] Ch. 180.

[55] *Ibid.* s.25, as amended.

and the widow's pension is payable, provided that the requisite contributions had been made by the deceased husband, to a widow who was over the age of 40 but under the age of 65 at the date of the husband's death, until she attains the age of 65 except for any period during which she is entitled to a widow's or widowed mother's allowance.[56] Additionally, there could be an entitlement in some cases to industrial benefits[57] or to war pensions.[58] A death grant, currently of a maximum of £30, may also be claimed by the next-of-kin independently of a personal representative.[59]

Pension and life assurance schemes

Many pension schemes enable the employee to nominate a third party to receive the contributions in the event of the employee's death before becoming entitled to the pension. Such a power was considered in *Re Danish Staff Pension Fund, Christensen* v. *Arnett*.[60] The scheme provided that, if a member should die while in the company's service, an amount equal to his contributions with compound interest up to the date of his death should be paid out to his personal representative. However, it was provided further that a member might appoint, in approved manner, a nominee to receive the money which under the rules might on his death fall to be paid to his personal representative. Such a nomination could be changed by the member during his life if he so wished. A member of the fund originally nominated his wife and then by letter instructed the secretary of the pension fund to change the nominee to another person, which was done. It was held that the alteration was effective and the changed nomination was valid.[61]

Megarry J. commented[62]:

> "Non-statutory nominations are odd creatures, and the cases provide little help on their nature. I do not, however, think that a nomination under the trust deed and rules in the present case requires execution as a will. It seems to me that such a nomination operates by force of the provisions of those rules, and not as a testamentary disposition by the deceased. Further, although the nomination has certain testamentary characteristics, I do not think that these suffice to make the paper on which it is written a testamentary paper. Accordingly, in my judgment the requirements of the Wills Act 1837 have no application."

[56] *Ibid.* s.26, as amended.
[57] Social Security Act 1975, ss.67–75.
[58] See Williams, Mortimer and Sunnucks, *Executors, Administrators and Probate* (16th ed.) p. 505.
[59] Social Security Act 1975, s.32.
[60] [1971] 1 W.L.R. 248.
[61] In so far as the alteration to the nomination was "a disposition of an equitable interest" within s.53(1)(*e*) of the Law of Property Act 1925, there was held to be sufficient writing for the purposes of the section.
[62] [1971] 1 W.L.R. 248 at p. 256.

Thus such dispositions, although operating at death, are not subject to a grant or to inheritance tax.

In the case of life assurance schemes it is common for the death benefit to be payable to such person or persons as the trustees of the scheme shall at their sole discretion determine. In practice the trustees will invariably exercise that discretion in favour of the deceased employee's next-of-kin but the effect of the arrangement is again to avoid both the need for a grant and liability to inheritance tax.

Insurance policies

Money payable under an insurance policy on the death of the deceased will without more form part of the deceased's estate and be subject to a grant in the usual way. However, it is possible for the insured to have declared a trust of the proceeds of the policy and in such cases the money will be payable directly to the named beneficiaries without the necessity for a grant. The most common form of such trusts are those declared under section 11 of the Married Woman's Property Act 1882 in favour of the spouse and or the children. However, an express trust can be declared in favour of anyone. The use of such policies can be an effective substitute for a will avoiding the need for a grant.

Policies effected for the benefit of a spouse and/or children can be a useful means of providing a fund for payment of inheritance tax on the death since the policy money will itself be exempt from tax if the payment of the premiums by the deceased, as will usually be the case, constitutes normal expenditure out of income.[63]

Inter Vivos Trusts

Property which the deceased has effectively conveyed to trustees on a fully constituted *inter vivos* trust will form no part of the deceased's estate. Even where the deceased retained a life interest under the trust, it will be an interest ceasing on death and will not vest in the personal representative.[64] Such a trust with declared remainders over can operate as an effective will substitute.[65] Similar cases are where the remainder interests are made subject to a power of appointment and where the whole property is made subject to a discretionary trust.

Contracts to devise or bequeath property on death, mutual wills and secret trusts can also operate as will substitutes but will not normally obviate the necessity for a grant.[66]

[63] Inheritance Tax Act 1984, s.21.
[64] A.E.A. 1925, s.1(1).
[65] Such settlements were used by judges in the Court of Protection with reference to the property of mentally defective patients as will substitutes in the days before they had jurisdiction to make wills for such persons; see Cross J. in *Re W.J.G.L.* [1965] 3 All E.R. 865, at p. 871.
[66] See discussion in Chap. 17, *post*.

Chapter 4

OBTAINING A GRANT

Entitlement

Number of administrators

A grant of administration cannot be made to more than four persons in respect of the same property[1] and, if a minority or life interest arises on the intestacy or, in the case of a grant of administration with the will annexed, under the will, administration must be granted to not less than two individuals or a trust corporation unless it appears to the court to be expedient in all the circumstances to appoint an individual as sole administrator.[2] However, if a grant of administration is made to two individuals in accordance with the rule and one of them dies, there is no requirement that another administrator must be appointed to act with the survivor.[3]

Capacity of administrators

A grant of administration cannot be made to a minor or to a person who, by reason of mental or physical incapacity, is incapable of managing his or her own affairs or to a corporation aggregate other than a trust corporation.[4]

Where a minor would otherwise be entitled to a grant, administration for his or her use and benefit until he or she attains the age of eighteen years is to be granted[5]:

(a) to both parents[6] of the minor jointly or to the surviving parent as the statutory guardian[7] of the minor or to the person appointed by a deceased parent either by deed or will as the testamentary guardian[8] of the minor or to any guardian appointed by a court of competent jurisdiction,[9] or

(b) if there is no such guardian able and willing to act and the minor has attained the age of sixteen years, to any next-of-kin

[1] Supreme Court Act 1981 (hereinafter also referred to as the "S.C.A. 1981"), s.114(1).
[2] *Ibid.* s.114(2). This rule does not apply to a grant of administration *pendente lite* under s.117 or to a grant of administration limited to settled land.
[3] The court has power to appoint one or more additional administrators on the application of any person interested or of the guardian, committee or receiver of any such person, *ibid.* s.114(4).
[4] *Ibid.* s.115(1), Non-Contentious Probate Rules 1954 (hereinafter also referred to as the "N.-C.P.R. 1954") as amended, r. 34(3).
[5] *Ibid.* r. 31(1).
[6] Including parents of an adopted or legitimated child, Children Act 1975 and Legitimacy Act 1976 respectively.
[7] Guardianship of Minors Act 1971, ss.3 and 14(3).
[8] *Ibid.* ss.4 and 14(3).
[9] *Ibid.* ss.5 and 14(3).

nominated by the minor or, where the minor is a married woman, any next-of-kin or her husband,[10] or

(c) in default of, or jointly with, or to the exclusion of, any person mentioned above, to any person assigned as guardian of the minor by order of a registrar, which may be made on application by the intended guardian.[11]

Where a person who, by reason of mental or physical incapacity is incapable of managing his or her own affairs, would otherwise be entitled to a grant, administration for his or her use and benefit, limited during the incapacity or otherwise as may be directed by the registrar, may be granted:

(a) in the case of mental incapacity, to the person authorised by the Court of Protection to apply,[12] or

(b) where there is no such person or in the case of physical incapacity, to the person who would be entitled to a grant in respect of the estate of the incapacitated person if he or she had died intestate or to such other person as a registrar may by order direct.[13]

Order of priority

Section 127 of the Supreme Court Act 1981 provides for the making of rules of court to regulate the practice and procedure of the High Court with respect to non-contentions or common form probate business and for such rules to regulate in particular the classes of persons entitled to grants of probate or administration in particular circumstances and the relative priorities of their claims. The current rules[14] are the Non-Contentious Probate Rules 1954[15] as amended which specify the following order of priority:

(i) the surviving spouse,
(ii) the children[16] of the deceased or the issue of any such child who has died during the lifetime of the deceased,
(iii) the father or mother of the deceased,[17]
(iv) brothers and sisters of the whole blood, or the issue of any deceased brother or sister of the whole blood (who has died).

If the deceased has not been survived by any person in one of the degrees mentioned above, the following order of priority applies:

[10] N.-C.P.R. 1954 as amended, r. 31(1).
[11] *Ibid.* r. 31(3).
[12] *Ibid.* r. 33(1).
[13] *Ibid.*
[14] Made under Judicature Act 1925, s.100 (since repealed).
[15] r. 21.
[16] Including illegitimate children, r. 21(6) as amended.
[17] Including an illegitimate deceased, *ibid.*

(i) brothers and sisters of the half blood, or the issue of any deceased brother or sister of the half blood (who has died),
(ii) grandparents,
(iii) uncles and aunts of the whole blood, or the issue of any deceased uncle or aunt of the whole blood (who has died),
(iv) uncles and aunts of the half blood, or the issue of any deceased uncle or aunt of the half blood (who has died).

It should be noted, however, that an applicant in any of the specified degrees must have a beneficial interest in the estate of the deceased intestate so that it is necessary to apply the rules of succession on intestacy[18] in order to determine entitlement to a grant. All persons with a prior right to a grant must be cleared off[19] and, where there is more than one person who is entitled to a grant in the same degree, the grant may be made to any of them without notice to the others[20] unless a caveat has been entered.[21] The personal representative of any deceased person has the same right to a grant as that person would have had if alive, but living persons who are entitled in the same degree are to be preferred.[22] Persons who are not under a disability are similarly to be preferred to minors who are entitled in the same degree.[23]

If there is no person who has a beneficial interest in the estate, the Treasury Solicitor is entitled to a grant if he claims *bona vacantia* on behalf of the Crown[24] and a grant may be made to a creditor[25] of the deceased or to any person who may have a beneficial interest in the estate in the event of an accretion to it, provided in either case that all persons with a prior right have been cleared off.[26]

If all the persons who are entitled to the estate have assigned their whole interest, the assignee or assignees take the place of the assignor or, if there are two or more assignors, the one with the highest priority, in the order of priority for a grant.[27] If there are two or more assignees, administration may be granted to any one or more (not exceeding four) of them with the consent of the others.[28]

If the beneficial interest in the whole estate is vested absolutely in a person[29] who has renounced his right to a grant and has consented to

[18] Administration of Estates Act 1925 (hereinafter also referred to as the "A.E.A. 1925"), s.46 and see Chap. 10 *post*.
[19] N.-C.P.R 1954 as amended, r. 6(2).
[20] *Ibid.* r. 25(1).
[21] See *post*, p. 69.
[22] *Ibid.* r. 25(3).
[23] *Ibid.*
[24] *Ibid.* r. 21(3).
[25] As to grants to creditors, see *post*, p. 73.
[26] *Ibid.* r. 21(4).
[27] *Ibid.* r. 22(1).
[28] *Ibid.* r. 22(2).
[29] A surviving spouse is not regarded as such a person unless there is no issue or parent or brother or sister of the whole blood or issue of a brother or sister of the whole blood.

administration being granted to the person or persons who would be entitled to his estate if he himself had died intestate administration may be granted to such person or one or more (not exceeding four) of such persons.[30]

PROCEDURE

Jurisdiction

The High Court of Justice has exclusive jurisdiction to issue grants of administration in England and Wales.[31] Where there is no contention as to the right to a grant,[32] the business of obtaining administration is assigned to the Family Division[33] but, if there is a dispute as to a person's entitlement to a grant, the proceedings must be brought in the Chancery Division[34] or, if the net estate does not exceed £30,000, the county court for the area in which the deceased resided.[35] Nevertheless, once the contest has been terminated, any grant of administration is made by the Family Division of the High Court. No grant may be made, however, within 14 days of the death of the deceased except with the leave of two registrars.[36]

Inheritance tax[37]

Except in the circumstances mentioned below, the personal representatives[37a] are required to deliver to the Commissioners of Inland Revenue within twelve months from the end of the month in which the deceased died[38] an account specifying to the best of their knowledge and belief all the property which formed part of the deceased's estate immediately before his death and its value.[39] On delivery of the account they must pay all the tax for which they are liable[40] and interest is charged at the rate of 9 per cent. per annum on all unpaid tax after six months from the end of the month in which the death occurred.[41] No grant of administration can be made until the

[30] *Ibid.* r. 27.
[31] S.C.A. 1981 ss.25, 61(1), 128 and Sched. 1, para. 3.
[32] *i.e.* where no proceedings have been instituted.
[33] S.C.A. 1981, s.61(1) and Sched. 1, para. 1.
[34] *Ibid.*
[35] County Courts Act 1984, s.62; A.J.A. 1977, s.15(3) and Administration of Justice Act 1982 (hereinafter also referred to as the "A.J.A. 1982"), s.37 and Sched. 3, Pt. II; County Courts Jurisdiction Order 1981 (S.I. 1981 No. 1123).
[36] N.-C.P.R. 1954 as amended, r. 5(3).
[37] Being the erstwhile Capital Transfer Tax as renamed and remodeled by the Finance Act 1986 and applying to deaths occurring on or after March 18, 1986.
[37a] *i.e.* the person(s) by whom or on whose behalf an application for a grant of administration is made.
[38] or (if later) within 3 months from the date on which they first acted; Inheritance Tax Act 1984, s.216(6).
[39] *Ibid.* s.216(1), (3).
[40] *Ibid.* s.226(2). Tax attributable to certain kinds of property may be paid by instalments, *ibid.* ss.227–229 and *post*, p. 65.
[41] *Ibid.* s.233(2) as amended by Finance Act 1986, Sched. 18, Pt. I.

account has been delivered and the tax for which the personal representatives are liable has been paid.[42]

If, however, the value of the estate is attributable wholly to property passing under the intestacy, or under a nomination taking effect on death, or by survivorship in beneficial joint tenancy and the total gross value of the property does not exceed £40,000 an account is not normally required to be delivered in the case of deaths on or after April 1, 1983.[43]

Inheritance tax is charged on the value of the estate[44] immediately before the death of the deceased[45] and so any property which passes on the death by survivorship in beneficial joint tenancy will form part of the estate for inheritance tax purposes. The estate will also include any property which passes under a nomination taking effect on the death or is the subject of a valid *donatio mortis causa*[46] and any property which was the subject of a gift made by the deceased on or after March 18, 1986, and either the donee did not assume *bona fide* possession and enjoyment of it at or before the beginning of the period of seven years ending on the date of the death of the deceased or it was not enjoyed by the donee to the entire exclusion, or virtually to the entire exclusion, of the deceased and of any benefit to him by contract or otherwise during the whole of the period of seven years ending on the date of the deceased's death.[46a] Certain property, which otherwise would form part of the estate, is however excluded by statute.[47] The principal categories of such excluded property comprise property situated outside the United Kingdom, provided that the deceased was himself domiciled outside the United Kingdom,[48] and, subject to exceptions, reversionary interests.[49]

The property comprised in the estate is to be valued for inheritance tax purposes at the price which it might reasonably be expected to fetch if sold in the open market but without regard to the fact that the whole property is to be placed on the market at the same time.[50] The

[42] S.C.A. 1981, s.109.

[43] Inheritance Tax (Delivery of Accounts) (No. 3) Regulations 1983 (S.I. 1983 No. 1039). By regulation 7 of the Principal Regulations (S.I. 1981 No. 880), as amended, the Commissioners of Inland Revenue may require an account to be delivered even if the gross value of the estate does not exceed £40,000 by a notice in writing issued not later than 35 days after the making of the first grant of representation. This is done in a number of cases taken at random in order to monitor the working of the Regulations.

[44] The aggregate of all the property to which the deceased was beneficially entitled: Inheritance Tax Act 1984, s.5(1).

[45] *Ibid.* s.4(1). Reasonable funeral expenses may, however, be deducted: *ibid.* s.172. So also may the value of all liabilities incurred for a consideration in money or money's worth: *ibid.* s.5(5).

[46] See *ante*, p. 56.

[46a] Finance Act 1986, s.81.

[47] Inheritance Tax Act 1984, ss.6(1) and 48(1).

[48] *Ibid.* s.6(1).

[49] *Ibid.* s.48(1).

[50] *Ibid.* s.160.

rate at which the tax is to be paid in respect of the estate is then determined by deducting from the value of the estate as a whole the entire value of any property, the transfer of which is exempted from tax,[51] and the appropriate proportion of the value of any property, in respect of which relief is available.[52] To the resultant figure is then added, because the tax is a cumulative one, the total value of all chargeable transfers made by the deceased during the seven years immediately preceding his death.[53] Tax is charged at a reduced rate, however, on the value transferred by a chargeable transfer made more than three but not more than seven years before the death[53a] and relief may be available by way of a reduction in the amount of the tax payable in respect of property which was the subject of a chargeable transfer to the deceased not more than five years before the date of his death.[54]

The Inland Revenue account

A simplified form of account (Cap Form 202) is provided for use where the deceased died domiciled in the United Kingdom and the gross value of the estate situated in the United Kingdom including any nominated property and the entirety of any jointly held property passing by survivorship does not exceed the inheritance tax thresh-hold.[54a] Where Form 202 is not appropriate, Cap Form 200 or, if the deceased died domiciled outside the United Kingdom, Cap Form 201 should be used. Prints of the forms can be obtained either from the Capital Taxes Office or, except in the case of Form 201 from head post offices.

Cap Form 200 contains four sections.[55] In Section 1A should be set out the property of the deceased situated in the United Kingdom in respect of which the grant is to be made but for which the instalment option[56] is not available and in section 1B all such property which is subject to the instalment option. Section 2 is for property of the deceased situated outside the United Kingdom together with nominated property and joint property accruing by survivorship. Section 3 comprises all other property in which the deceased had a beneficial interest in possession immediately before his death or over which the deceased had, and exercised by will, a general power of appointment. The personal representatives are liable to pay the tax on the assets in

[51] *e.g.* property passing to a surviving spouse: *ibid.* s.18.
[52] *e.g.* business property: *ibid.* ss.103–114; or agricultural property: *ibid.* ss.115–124.
[53] *Ibid.* s.7(1), as amended by Finance Act 1986, Sched. 18, Pt. I.
[53a] Inheritance Act 1984, s.7(4).
[54] Inheritance Act 1984, s.141.
[54a] Currently £71,000, Inheritance Tax (Indexation) Order 1986 (S.I. 1986 No. 528).
[55] Form 201 is similar.
[56] Tax may be paid by instalments in respect of land, controlling shareholdings, unquoted shares (subject to conditions) interests in businesses and woodlands: Inheritance Tax Act 1984, ss.227–229.

Sections 1A and 1B and on the foreign assets in Section 2.[57] The tax on the other property in Section 2 and the property in Section 3 is the liability of the persons in whom the property is vested after the death of the relevant trustees.[58]

Where additional assets are discovered later, or for some other reason[59] the account requires to be amended, a corrective account in Form D.3 should be completed and submitted to the Capital Taxes Office.

The oath

Every application for a grant of administration must be supported by an oath contained in an affidavit sworn or affirmed by each applicant.[60] The oath must state

(a) the true full name, address[61] and description[62] of each applicant;
(b) the true full name,[63] address, age and description of the deceased;
(c) the date of the deceased's death;
(d) the domicile of the deceased;
(e) whether or not any minority or life interest arises under the intestacy;
(f) whether or not there was land vested in the deceased which was settled previously to his death and remained settled land notwithstanding his death;
(g) how the persons, if any, who have a prior right to a grant have been cleared off;
(h) the relationship of the applicant(s) to the deceased;
(i) the gross and the net value of the estate as shown in the Inland Revenue Account or, if an Inland Revenue Account is not required, that the gross value of the estate does not exceed £40,000 and the net value of the estate does not exceed £40,000 or £25,000 or £10,000, as the case may be.[64]

[57] *Ibid.* s.200(1)(*a*).
[58] *Ibid.* s.200(1)(*c*).
[59] *e.g.* quoted shares and securities or units in authorised unit trusts are sold for a lower value within 12 months after the death, *ibid.* s.179; or an interest in land is sold for a lower value within 3 years after the death, *ibid.* s.191.
[60] N.-C.P.R. 1954 as amended, r. 6.
[61] *i.e.* place of residence or (in the case of a professional executor) professional address.
[62] *i.e.* occupation or (in the case of a female) status.
[63] Any alias which it is desired to include in the grant (*e.g.* because part of the estate was held in a different name) should also be given with the reason for its inclusion: N.-C.P.R. 1954 as amended, r. 7.
[64] *Practice Direction* [1981] 1 W.L.R. 1185. If the net value of the estate does not exceed £10,000, no fee is payable on an application for a grant and if it exceeds £10,000 but does not exceed £25,000 the fee is fixed at £40: N.-C.P. Fees Order 1981 (S.I. 1981 No. 861). If the net value of the estate exceeds £25,000 but does not exceed £40,000, the fee is fixed at £80: N.-C.P. Fees (Amendment) Order 1983 (S.I. 1983 No. 1180).

Guarantees

The High Court may require[65] as a condition of a grant of administration that one or more persons guarantee to make good within such limit as may be imposed by the court any loss suffered by any person interested in the administration of the estate as a result of a breach of the administrator's duties.[66] It is provided, however, that a guarantee shall not be required save in certain specified cases or where the registrar considers that there are special circumstances which make a guarantee desirable.[67]

The specified cases are where administration is proposed to be granted:

(a) to a creditor, or the personal representative of a creditor, or to a person who has no immediate beneficial interest in the estate of the deceased but may have such an interest in the event of an accretion to the estate;
(b) to a person, or some of the persons, who would, if the person beneficially entitled to the whole of the estate died intestate, be entitled to his estate;
(c) to the attorney of a person entitled to a grant;
(d) for the use and benefit of a minor;
(e) for the use and benefit of a person who is by reason of mental or physical incapacity incapable of managing his affairs;
(f) to an applicant who appears to the registrar to be resident elsewhere than in the United Kingdom.

If the applicant, or one of the applicants, is a trust corporation, or a solicitor holding a current practising certificate under the Solicitors Act 1974, or a servant of the Crown acting in his official capacity, or a nominee of a public department or of a local authority within the meaning of the Local Government Act 1972, no guarantee is required except in special circumstances, even in one of the specified cases.[68] Furthermore, the power of the court to require a guarantee does not apply where administration is to be granted to the Treasury Solicitor, the Public Trustee, the Solicitor to the Duchy of Lancaster or the Duchy of Cornwall, the Chief Crown Solicitor for Northern Ireland or the Consular officer of a foreign state to which section 1 of the Consular Convention Act 1949 applies.[69]

Where a guarantee is required, there must be two sureties unless the gross value of the estate does not exceed £500 or the guarantee is given by a corporation, and only a person resident in the United Kingdom

[65] The applicant or the solicitor through whom the application is made is entitled to be heard with respect to the requirement, *ibid.* r. 5(4).
[66] S.C.A. 1981, s.120.
[67] N.-C.P.R. 1954 as amended, r. 38(1).
[68] *Ibid.* r. 38(2).
[69] S.C.A. 1981, s.120(5). Other cases may be prescribed but there is none to date.

will be accepted as a surety.[70] Liability under a guarantee is limited to the gross amount of the estate and every surety, other than a corporation, must justify,[71] which means swear an affidavit showing that he is worth the amount of the limit of his liability.

If a corporation is to be a surety, there must be filed an affidavit by its proper officer to the effect that it has power to act as such and has executed the guarantee in the manner prescribed by its constitution. The affidavit must also contain sufficient information as to the financial position of the corporation to satisfy the registrar that its assets are sufficient to satisfy all claims which may be made against it under any guarantee which it has given, or is likely to give for a similar purpose.[72] Alternatively, a corporation may be permitted by the Senior Registrar to make such an affidavit not less often than once in every year instead of in every case with an undertaking to notify forthwith any alteration in its constitution affecting its power to become a surety for the purpose.[73]

Guarantees must be in the prescribed form[74] and, except where the surety is a corporation, the signature of the surety must be attested by an authorised officer, commissioner for oaths or other person authorised by law to administer an oath.[75] The seal of a corporate surety will be affixed in the manner prescribed by its constitution.

Manner of application

Application for a first grant may be made personally,[76] or through a solicitor,[77] either at the Principal Registry of the Family Division[78] or at one of the district registries or sub-registries which have been established at various places in England and Wales.[79] The papers[80] may be lodged by post if the application is made through a solicitor,

[70] N.-C.P.R. 1954 as amended, r. 38(5).
[71] *Ibid.*
[72] N.-C.P.R. 1954 as amended, r. 38(6).
[73] *Ibid.*
[74] *Ibid.* r. 38(3) and Sched. 1, Form 1.
[75] *Ibid.* r. 38(4).
[76] *Ibid.* r. 4.
[77] *Ibid.* r. 3.
[78] Personal applications are made to the Personal Applications Department, 4th Floor, Adelphi Building, John Adam Street, London WC2N 6BB and applications through solicitors are made to the Receiver's Department, Somerset House, Strand, London WC2R 1LP.
[79] Namely Birmingham, Brighton (sub-registry Maidstone), Bristol (sub-registries Bodmin and Exeter), Ipswich (sub-registries Norwich and Peterborough), Leeds (sub-registries Hull and York), Liverpool (sub-registry Lancaster), Llandaff (sub-registries Bangor and Carmarthen), Manchester, Newcastle (sub-registries Carlisle and Middlesborough), Nottingham (sub-registries Leicester and Lincoln), Oxford (sub-registry Gloucester), Sheffield (sub-registries Chester and Stoke-on-Trent) and Winchester.
[80] The Oath, the guarantee (if any), the Inland Revenue Account and any other documents which the circumstances of the case may require.

but not if made personally.[81] The requisite fee[82] is paid together with any inheritance tax.

A draft of the oath and of any other necessary document, other than an affidavit of fact, may be submitted to the Probate Department of the Principal Registry, or to a district registry or sub-registry, for settling before the application is made. An additional fee of £5.00 is payable for each document settled[83] and the settled draft should be lodged with the other papers.

After the application has been made, a search is made in the registry to find out whether a grant has been made previously in respect of the estate or whether a *caveat*[84] has been entered. No grant may be made if there is a conflicting application[85] or if the registrar has knowledge of an effective *caveat*.[86] The Inland Revenue account and any inheritance tax are forwarded to the Capital Taxes Office of the Inland Revenue.

In the absence of any prior grant or application, or of any *caveat*, the grant is prepared, signed by an authorised Probate Officer or by the District Probate Registrar and sealed.

If the grant is issued by the Principal Registry, a photographic copy is filed and, if the grant issued by a district registry, a photographic copy is sent to the Principal Registry for filing with a weekly list of the grants made by that registry.[87] The grant is issued by post and sealed copies, which are accepted throughout the United Kingdom as evidence of the grant,[88] may be obtained on payment of an additional fee.[89]

Caveats, Citation, Renunciation and Passing Over

Caveats

Purpose

The entry of a *caveat* operates to prevent a grant from being issued so long as it remains in force. It ensures that the person by whom or on whose behalf, it is entered, and who is called "the caveator" will be notified of the making of any application for a grant.[90] Since it is designed to prevent the issue of a grant, it is essentially a hostile act and may well lead to further proceedings.[91]

[81] *Ibid.* r. 3(1) and 4(1).
[82] Calculated in accordance with N.-C.P. Fees Order 1981 as amended.
[83] N.-C.P. Fees Order 1981.
[84] See *post*, p. 71.
[85] S.C.A. 1981, s.107.
[86] *Ibid.* s.108; N.-C.P.R. 1954 as amended, r. 44(6).
[87] N.-C.P.R. 1954 as amended, r. 57(2).
[88] S.C.A. 1981, s.132.
[89] Currently 25 pence per copy, Non-Contentious Probate Fees Order 1981.
[90] N.-C.P.R. 1954 as amended, r. 44(1).
[91] *e.g.* an application that a guarantee be given.

If it is desired merely to have notice of the issue of a grant[92] and not to prevent it, the entry of a *caveat* is inappropriate and instead an application should be made for a standing search.[93] This will ensure that the applicant will receive an office copy of any grant which is issued within the following six months.[94]

Duration

Once entered a *caveat* remains in force for six months initially,[95] but may be withdrawn earlier,[96] and will cease to have effect when application for a grant is made by the person shown to be entitled thereto by the decision of the court in a probate action of which the caveator has had notice, unless a registrar of the Principal Registry directs otherwise.[97] It may be extended for one or more further periods of six months on written application being lodged at the registry in which the *caveat* was entered within the last month of the first, or any successive period of six months[98] and any *caveat* in respect of which an appearance to a warning[99] has been entered remains in force until the commencement of a probate action, unless a registrar of the Principal Registry directs otherwise.[1] In addition, unless again a registrar of the Principal Registry directs otherwise, any *caveat* which is in force at the commencement of proceedings by way of citation or motion remains in force until an application for a grant is made by the person shown to be entitled thereto by the decision of the court in such proceedings unless previously withdrawn.[2] When such an application is made, any *caveat* entered by a party who had notice of the proceedings ceases to have effect, unless a registrar of the Principal Registry directs otherwise.[3] Whilst a *caveat* remains in force, or after it has ceased to have effect, no further *caveat* may be entered by or on behalf of the same caveator without the leave of a registrar of the Principal Registry.[4]

Procedure

A *caveat* may be entered in any registry[5] by completing a prescribed

[92] *e.g.* with a view to the making of an application for provision under the Inheritance (Provision for Family and Dependants) Act 1975.
[93] The application is made to the Record Keeper at the Principal Registry with the prescribed fee.
[94] The application may be renewed for one or more similar periods on payment of further fees.
[95] N.-C.P.R. 1954 as amended, r. 44(4).
[96] *Ibid.* r. 44(8).
[97] *Ibid.* r. 44(12).
[98] *Ibid.* r. 44(4A).
[99] See *post* p. 71.
[1] *Ibid.* r. 44(12).
[2] *Ibid.*
[3] *Ibid.*
[4] *Ibid.* r. 44(13).
[5] N.-C.P.R. 1954 as amended, r. 44(1).

form[6] at the registry, or by sending a notice in the prescribed form through the post,[7] and may be entered either personally or by a solicitor on the caveator's behalf.[8] An index of *caveats* is maintained at the Principal Registry by the Senior Registrar and notice of a *caveat* entered in a district registry is given to the Principal Registry immediately.[9]

If a *caveat* has been entered, and is still in force at the time when an application for a grant is made, the applicant is notified and the papers are retained in the registry until the *caveat* has been withdrawn or has ceased to have effect. The applicant may then issue a warning to the caveator in a prescribed form[10] that the court may proceed to issue a grant notwithstanding the *caveat* unless the caveator, within six days after service of the warning upon him, either enters an appearance in person or by solicitor at the Principal Registry setting out what interest he has in the estate of the deceased person contrary to that of the applicant or, if he has no contrary interest, but wishes to show cause against the sealing of a grant to the applicant, issues and serves a summons for directions by a registrar.[11]

If the caveator fails to enter an appearance within the specified time, and the applicant files an affidavit showing that the warning was duly served and that he has not received a summons for directions, the *caveat* will cease to have effect and the application for a grant may proceed.[12] If on the other hand the caveator or his solicitor does enter an appearance in the prescribed form[13] within the specified time, or later if no affidavit has been filed as mentioned above, and serves a sealed copy of the appearance on the applicant,[14] no grant can be issued to any person other than the caveator without an order of the court unless the proceedings are discontinued at that stage or a registrar of the Principal Registry directs otherwise.[15] Following the entry of an appearance the caveator will usually commence a probate action by the issue of a writ in the Chancery Division and a copy of the writ will be sent to the Principal Registrar of the Family Division. The court will then determine whether or not the pending application for a grant should be permitted to proceed.

If, however, the caveator does not have an interest which is contrary to that of the applicant, so that the entry of an appearance is not appropriate, but he wishes nevertheless to show cause against the

[6] *Ibid.* 1st Sched., Form 4.
[7] *Ibid.* r. 44(2).
[8] *Ibid.* r. 44(3). If a *caveat* is entered by a solicitor, the name of the caveator must be stated.
[9] S.C.A. 1981, s.108.
[10] N.-C.P.R. 1954 as amended, 1st Sched., Form 5.
[11] *Ibid.* r. 44(7).
[12] *Ibid.* r. 44(11).
[13] *Ibid.* 1st Sched., Form 6.
[14] *Ibid.* r. 44(9).
[15] *Ibid.* r. 44(12).

issue of a grant to the applicant, he must issue and serve within the specified time, or later if no affidavit has been filed by the applicant as mentioned above, a summons for directions returnable before a registrar of the Principal Registry.[16] The caveator will then apply on the hearing of the summons for such relief as he may require.

Renunciation

A person who is entitled to take a grant of administration cannot be compelled to do so even if he has intermeddled with the estate.[17] He is free to renounce his right to a grant by filing at a probate registry a formal renunciation in writing signed by him. The renunciation does not take effect until it has been filed and may be retracted at any time before then.[18] After filing retraction is possible only on the order of a registrar[19] but will be permitted if it is necessary or expedient.[20]

Unless a registrar directs otherwise, a person who has renounced administration in one capacity may not obtain a grant in another capacity[21] but the renunciation will not bind his own personal representative who may still take a grant if one has not been made and subject to the provisions of rule 25(3) of the Non-Contentious Probate Rules 1954 as amended.[22]

Citation

If a person who is entitled to take a grant of administration fails to do so and does not renounce his right, an application may be made to the court by a person with an inferior right to the grant for the issue of a citation to accept or refuse a grant.[23] In default of an appearance by the person cited the citor may apply to a registrar for an order for a grant to himself.[24]

Passing over

The court has a discretion to pass over the person who would otherwise have been entitled to a grant if it appears to the court to be necessary or expedient by reason of the insolvency of the deceased's estate or any other special circumstances and to appoint another person as administrator.[25] An application for the discretion to be exercised may be made to a registrar and must be supported by an affidavit setting out the grounds of the application.[26] Successful

[16] *Ibid.* r. 44(10).
[17] *In the Goods of Davis* (1860) 4 Sw. & Tr. 213.
[18] *In the Goods of Morant* (1874) L.R. 3 P. & D. 151.
[19] N.-C.P.R. 1954 as amended, r. 35(3).
[20] *In the Goods of Thacker* [1900] P. 15.
[21] N.-C.P.R. 1954 as amended, r. 35(2).
[22] *Ante*, p. 62.
[23] *Ibid.* r. 46(1).
[24] *Ibid.* r. 46(5).
[25] S.C.A. 1981, s.116(1).
[26] N.-C.P.R. 1954 as amended, r. 51.

applications have been made in a wide variety of circumstances, examples of which are where the person primarily entitled was abroad[27] or was missing[28] or was of bad character.[29]

An interesting recent example of the use of the court's discretion is to be found in the case of *Re Clore (decd.)*[30] where the Court of Appeal dismissed an appeal by the executors named in the will of the late Sir Charles Clore against the issue to the Official Solicitor of a grant *ad colligenda bona* under section 161(1)(*b*). The executors were directors of Stype Investments (Jersey) Ltd. which had procured the transfer to Jersey after Sir Charles' death of some £20 million worth of his property in the United Kingdom and they shared responsibility for opposing the efforts of the Inland Revenue to obtain payment by Stype Investments of any capital transfer tax found to be payable in respect of Sir Charles' English estate. In the circumstances the Court of Appeal considered that "the appointment of the executors as personal representatives duly constituted in this country would be bizarre."[31]

SPECIAL AND LIMITED GRANTS

Grants to creditors

It has been seen[32] that a grant may be made to a creditor of the deceased if all persons with a prior right to a grant have been cleared off by renunciation or by citation.[33] This is so whether or not the debt has become statute-barred.[34] In some cases[35] a grant has been made to a creditor under the provisions of section 116 of the Supreme Court Act 1981,[36] passing over those with a prior right. A guarantee is invariably required[37] and the creditor-administrator is under a duty to pay the debts of the deceased in accordance with the priority prescribed by law and not to prefer his own or any other debt.[38]

If the estate is solvent, it is unlikely that the person or persons who are entitled to it will fail to apply for a grant unless the estate can be administered without one.[39] If, however, there is a failure to apply for a grant, so that there is no personal representative who can be sued by an unpaid creditor of the deceased, the creditor, instead of seeking to

[27] *Re Hagger* (1863) 3 Sw. & Tr. 65; *Re Hughes* (1873) L.R. 3 P. & D. 140; *Re Webb* (1888) 13 P.D. 71; *Re Nares* (1888) 13 P.D. 35; *Re Wallas* [1905] P. 326.
[28] *Re Peck* (1860) 2 Sw. & Tr. 506; *Re Harling* [1900] P. 59.
[29] *Re Arden* [1898] P. 147; *Re Paine* [1916] 115 L.T. 935.
[30] [1982] Ch. 456.
[31] *Ibid.* at p. 476.
[32] *Ante*, p. 62.
[33] N.-C.P.R. 1954 as amended, r. 21(4).
[34] *Coombs* v. *Coombs* (1866) L.R. 1 P. & D. 288.
[35] *e.g. Re Heerman* [1910] P. 357.
[36] Re-enacting Judicature Act 1925, s.162.
[37] S.C.A. 1981, s.120(1).
[38] A.E.A. 1925, s.10(1).
[39] See *ante*, Chap. 3.

apply for a grant himself, can bring an action against the estate of the deceased.[40] He must then apply to the Court within the time for service of the proceedings for an order appointing a person to represent the deceased's estate in the action.[41]

If, however, the estate is known to be insolvent, the person or persons who otherwise would be entitled to it may well refrain from applying for a grant. In such circumstances a substantial creditor, particularly a substantial secured creditor, may consider that it would be to his advantage to take on the onerous responsibilities of an administrator and to apply for a grant himself after citing all persons with a prior right.[42]

Alternatively, the creditor may commence an administration action[43] and apply to the court for the appointment of a receiver[44] or of an administrator pending suit.[45] The other available course of action[46] is for the creditor to petition the bankruptcy court for an order for the administration of the deceased's estate in bankruptcy.[47]

Settled land grants

If the deceased was a tenant for life under the Settled Land Act 1925 and the legal estate in the land was vested in him at the date of his death and the land remains settled land after his death, a grant of administration limited to settled land will be made to the trustees of the settlement at the time of the application for the grant or, if the trustees are cleared off or passed over, the personal representative of the deceased.[48]

Grants de bonis non

If the sole or last surviving administrator of the deceased has died, or has disappeared,[49] without having completed the administration of the estate,[50] it will be necessary to obtain a grant of administration *de bonis non administratis* for the purpose of dealing with the unadministered estate.[51] The same rules of priority apply to applications for

[40] Proceedings Against Estates Act 1970, s.2 as amended by A.J.A. 1977, s.27; R.S.C. Ord. 15, r. 6A.
[41] *Ibid.*
[42] *Ante*, p. 72.
[43] *Re Hargreaves* (1890) 44 Ch.D. 236; see *post* p. 112.
[44] *Re Sutcliffe* [1942] Ch. 453. In this case the creditor may be required by the court to give an undertaking that he will take a grant himself.
[45] S.C.A. 1981, s.117.
[46] If the debt would have been sufficient to support a bankruptcy petition against the deceased had he lived.
[47] Insolvency Act 1985, s.228.
[48] N.-C.P.R. 1954 as amended, r. 28(3).
[49] *Re Saker* [1909] P. 233; *Re French* [1910] P. 169.
[50] *e.g.* without having made any assent or conveyance of the deceased's freehold or leasehold land.
[51] 2 Bl.Comm. (14th ed.) 506.

grants *de bonis non* as are applicable to original grants[52] and all persons with a prior right to a grant must be cleared off unless the court exercises its discretion to pass them over.[53]

An applicant for administration *de bonis non* must take an appropriate form of oath[54] and complete the appropriate form of Inland Revenue account.[55] The estate is sworn at the present value of the unadministered assets but no further tax will be payable if tax was paid originally on the full value of the estate.[56]

The Inland Revenue account must be submitted to the Capital Taxes Office for the endorsement of a certificate stating either the amount of tax paid already or that no tax is payable, as the case may be, before the application is filed at the probate registry.

Grants for the use and benefit of minors

If the person to whom a grant would otherwise be made is a minor, administration for his use and benefit until he attains the age of 18 years must be granted to both parents of the minor jointly or to the statutory[57] or testamentary guardian of the minor or to a guardian appointed by a court of competent jurisdiction.[58] If there is no such guardian able and willing to act and the minor has attained the age of 16 years, the grant is made to any next-of-kin[59] nominated by the minor.[60] A registrar may, however, pass over all such persons in favour of a guardian assigned by him.[61]

Two administrators will be required because of the minority interest unless the court considers it expedient to appoint an individual as sole administrator[62] and, if there is only one person competent and willing to take a grant, that person may nominate a fit and proper person to act as co-administrator and the grant will be made to them jointly unless a registrar otherwise directs.[63] The grant will determine when the minor comes of age and he may then apply for a cessate grant of administration himself.

Grants during incapacity

If the person entitled to a grant is by reason of mental or physical incapacity incapable of managing his affairs, administration may be granted for his use and benefit, limited during his incapacity or in

[52] N.-C.P.R. 1954 as amended, r. 21; see *ante* p. 61.
[53] S.C.A. 1981, s.116(1).
[54] *e.g.* 8 Encyclopaedia of Forms & Precedents (4th ed.) 729, Form 1:7.
[55] Form A-5C.
[56] Or if the full value of the estate was within the nil rate band.
[57] *i.e.* the surviving parent, Guardianship of Minors Act 1971, s.3(1), (2).
[58] N.-C.P.R. 1954 as amended, r. 31(1)(*a*).
[59] Or, if the minor is a married woman, her husband.
[60] *Ibid.* r. 31(1)(*b*).
[61] *Ibid.* r. 31(3).
[62] S.C.A. 1981, s.114(2).
[63] N.-C.P.R. 1954 as amended, r. 31(4).

such other way as the registrar may direct.[64] Such a grant will not be made, however, unless all persons with an equal right to a grant have been cleared off or unless the registrar otherwise directs.[65]

In the case of mental incapacity the grant will be made to the person who is authorised by the Court of Protection to apply for it.[66] If there is no such person, the grant will be made to the person who would be entitled to a grant in respect of the estate of the incapable person if he had died intestate.[67] Notice of intention to apply for a grant must be given to the Court of Protection in either case.[68]

In the case of physical incapacity the grant will be made to the person who would be entitled to a grant in respect of the estate of the incapable person if he had died intestate[69] and notice of intention to apply for the grant must be given to the person who is alleged to be incapable unless a registrar otherwise directs.[70]

Grants ad colligenda bona

If there is likely to be a delay in obtaining a full grant and the delay may prove detrimental to the estate, a grant *ad colligenda bona* may be made to any suitable person for the purpose of collecting and preserving the estate until a full grant is made.[71] Application for the grant is made *ex parte* to a registrar and must be supported by an affidavit setting out the grounds.[72] Such applications are, however, uncommon as it is generally preferable to apply for a grant of administration under section 116 of the Supreme Court Act 1981,[73] limited as appropriate, which confers wider powers. The procedure is the same.[74]

Revocation of Grants

Jurisdiction

The High Court of Justice and the county courts have jurisdiction over the revocation of grants of probate or administration equivalent to their respective jurisdictions over the making of such grants.[75] Accordingly the jurisdiction is exercised in respect of contentious cases, which will be the subject of a revocation action, by the Chancery Division of the High Court or, if the value of the net estate

64 *Ibid.* r. 33(1).
65 *Ibid.* r. 33(2).
66 *Ibid.* r. 33(1)(*a*).
67 *Ibid.* r. 33(1)(*b*).
68 *Ibid.* r. 33(3).
69 *Ibid.* r. 33(1)(*b*).
70 *Ibid.* r. 33(4).
71 *Re Clarkington* (1861) 2 Sw. & Tr. 380; *Re Wyckoff* (1862) 3 Sw. & Tr. 20; *In the Goods of Bolton* (1899) P. 186. See also *Re Clore* [1982] Ch. 456.
72 N.-C.P.R. 1954 as amended, r. 51.
73 *Ante*, p. 72.
74 *Ibid.*
75 See *ante*, p. 63.

does not exceed £30,000,[76] by the county court for the district in which the deceased died and in non-contentious cases by the Family Division of the High Court.

If the person to whom the grant was made applies for or consents to its revocation, or if there are special circumstances,[77] an order revoking the grant may be made by a registrar of the Family Division[78] and, if the grant was made wrongly or contains an error, the court may revoke it of its own accord.[79] A revocation action will usually be required, however, if the person to whom the grant was made opposes its revocation and there are no special circumstances.

Grounds for revocation

The principal grounds for revocation of a grant are that it was made wrongly in the first place, as mentioned above, or that it ought to be revoked because of the happening of a later event such as the incapacity[80] or disappearance[81] of the grantee.

Effect of revocation

Payments or dispositions made in good faith by the grantee prior to the revocation of the grant are protected[82] and the grantee is entitled to reimburse himself in respect of any such payments or dispositions before handing over the remaining assets of the estate to the new personal representative.[83] Similar protection is provided for payments or dispositions made in good faith to the grantee prior to the revocation of the grant.[84] There is no protection, however, for a beneficiary entitled under the revoked but not under the new grant to whom a distribution was made before the original grant was revoked. Finally, a purchaser in good faith and for valuable consideration from the grantee is protected if the grant is revoked subsequently.[85]

[76] *Ante*, p. 63.
[77] *e.g.* the grant was made in error at a time when a *caveat* was in force.
[78] N.-C.P.R. 1954 (as amended), r. 42.
[79] S.C.A. 1981, s.121.
[80] *In the Goods of Newton* (1843) 3 Curt. 428; *In the Estate of Shaw* [1905] P. 92; *In the Goods of Galbraith* [1951] P. 422. It should be noted, however, that this applies only on the supervening incapacity of one of two more personal representatives. If a sole or sole surviving administrator becomes incapable, the original grant is impounded and a grant of administration *de bonis non* is made for the incapable grantee's use and benefit during his incapacity: *In the Goods of Cooke* [1895] P. 68.
[81] *In the Goods of Bradshaw* (1888) 13 P.D. 18; *In the Goods of Covell* (1890) 15 P.D. 8; *In the Goods of Loveday* [1900] P. 154.
[82] A.E.A. 1925, s.27(1).
[83] *Ibid.* s.27(2).
[84] *Ibid.*
[85] *Ibid.* s.37; L.P.A. 1925, s.204(1); *Hewson* v. *Shelley* [1914] 2 Ch. 13.

CHAPTER 5

DEVOLUTION OF ASSETS AND TRUST FOR SALE

DEVOLUTION OF THE ESTATE ON THE PERSONAL REPRESENTATIVES

Introduction

Part IV of the Administration of Estates Act 1925 provides in the case of the death of a person intestate after January 1, 1926 that,[1] "... the residuary estate of an intestate shall be distributed in the manner or be held on the trusts mentioned in this section[2]..." The crucial phrase is "the residuary estate of an intestate" and it is necessary initially to identify what this is. The devolution and vesting of the estate in the personal representatives will be discussed and will be followed by a discussion of the nature of a beneficiary's interest after death and before assent. The scope and effect of the statutory trust for sale imposed in cases of intestacy by Part III of the 1925 Act will then be considered.

Property subject to intestate succession

Devolution before 1925

The whole of a deceased person's personal property[3] has always vested in his representatives, who were thus "personal" representatives, and in the administration of the estate it was this property which was liable primarily for expenses, debts and legacies. Where the deceased had died intestate, the distribution of the estate would have been decided historically by those customary rules, codified by the Statute of Distribution 1670, which have been considered in Chapter 3 *ante*. However, as noted above, a deceased person's interest in freeholds historically did not pass to his representatives but vested in the heir and so was free to some extent from the demands of administration.[4] This position was changed by the Land Transfer Act 1897 which provided in the case of deaths after January 1, 1898 that real estate which was vested in the deceased[5] was to vest in his

[1] The date of the commencement of the Act, ss.54, 58.

[2] *i.e.* s.46.

[3] Including "chattels real" and real property subject to the equitable doctrine of conversion but not joint property subject to the *jus accrescendi* or property subject to the testamentary exercise of a general power of appointment. After 1925 by virtue of s.55(3) the estate of a deceased person includes property over which the deceased exercised a general power of appointment. Joint property would be regarded now as an "interest ceasing on death" and would not be included.

[4] See discussion *ante*, in Chap. 3.

[5] Otherwise than as a joint tenant, s.1(1), but including real estate over which a person exercised by will a general power of appointment, s.1(2).

representatives.[6] The representatives thus became for the first time both "real" and "personal" representatives but the latter terminology was retained.

If an executor had been appointed, the realty vested directly in him but in the case of intestacy the legal estate still vested initially in the heir pending the appointment of an administrator.[7] The personal representatives held the real property as trustees[8] and the rules and powers of administration previously applicable to personal estate were made applicable to real estate.[9]

Devolution after 1925

Personal property. Little change was necessary in 1925 in the case of personal property since such property always had effectively devolved at common law on the personal representatives. Personal property is not defined in the 1925 Act and thus comprehends all property not included in the definition of real property.[10] The devolution of particular forms of personal property, such as leaseholds,[11] partnership assets, stocks and shares and causes of action, is subject to special rules which it is beyond the scope of this work to consider because they apply generally and are not limited to cases of intestacy. Reference should be made to specialist texts where the topic is considered fully.[12]

Real property. By virtue of section 1 of the 1925 Act real estate to which a deceased person was entitled for an interest not ceasing on his death devolves on the personal representative(s) whether the deceased died testate or intestate.[13] For this purpose "real estate" includes chattels real[14] and land[15] in possession, remainder, or reversion and every interest in or over land to which a deceased person was entitled at the time of his death and real estate held on trust (including settled land) or by way of mortgage or security, but not money to arise under a trust for sale of land nor money secured or charged on land.[16] Also included is real property over which the deceased had a testamentary

[6] s.1(1). Probate and letters of administration could be granted in respect of real estate only although there was no personal estate, s.1(3).
[7] *Re Griggs* [1914] 2 Ch. 547.
[8] Land Transfer Act 1897, s.2(1).
[9] *Ibid.* s.2(2).
[10] Including choses in action, 2.55(1)(xvii). See *Halsbury's Laws*, Vol. 17, para. 1071.
[11] Historically regarded as contractual rather than real interests and thus personalty, now included as "real estate," 1925 Act, s.3(1)(i).
[12] Williams Mortimer and Sunnucks *Executors, Administrators and Probate*, (16th ed.) 1982, Pt. Six; *Halsbury's Laws of England*, Vol. 17, paras. 1071–1099.
[13] s.3(1)(i).
[14] "Chattels real" historically included those interests in real property which were not recoverable in a real action as lacking the characteristics of an indeterminate estate, *i.e.* leaseholds.
[15] s.55(1)(xxiv), 1925 Act, incorporating s.117(1)(ix), Settled Land Act 1925 (hereinafter also referred to as the "S.L.A. 1925").
[16] s.3(1)(i), (ii).

power of appointment[17] and entailed property disposed of by will under section 176 of the Law of Property Act 1925.[18]

An important exclusion is that the residuary estate of the deceased does not include real estate to which the deceased was entitled for an interest "ceasing on his death."[19] There are three main categories of such property, namely entailed interests, joint tenancies and life interests, and they can be discussed briefly. First, it is provided by section 3(3) that "an entailed interest of a deceased person shall (unless disposed of under the testamentary power conferred by statute)[20] be deemed an interest ceasing on his death. . . . " The devolution of an entailed interest as an equitable interest remains subject to the old rules of inheritance,[21] and has been considered earlier.[22] However, any further or other interest in the same property in remainder or reversion after the entail, which is capable of being disposed of by will, is not to be regarded as an interest ceasing on death.[23]

The second category is property owned by the deceased as a joint tenant which ". . . where another tenant survives the deceased is an interest ceasing on his death.[24] The importance of this category will be apparent particularly as regards the matrimonial home[25] and, to a smaller extent, joint bank accounts and it will be appreciated that the whole law of intestate succession can be bypassed by putting property into joint names.[26] In addition the holding of the matrimonial home in joint names can lead to a double entitlement of the surviving spouse, who will take the house by virtue of the *jus accrescendi* and the statutory legacy as well.[27]

The third category of property which the deceased will own for an interest ceasing on death is property in respect of which the deceased only has a life interest. This will be met less frequently now[28] and the exclusion of such property is self-explanatory and requires no further discussion here, save only to remark that, if the property includes realty, the interest will give rise, in the absence of a trust for sale, to settled land, necessitating a settled land grant.[29]

It can be noted finally that, by virtue of section 3(5), the interest of a

[17] s.3(2).
[18] s.3(2). For a full discussion see Williams Mortimer and Sunnucks, *Executors, Administrators and Probate* (16th ed.) 1982 p. 523.
[19] s.1 of the 1925 Act.
[20] s.176 of the Law of Property Act 1925 (hereinafter also referred to as "the L.P.A. 1925").
[21] See s.51(4).
[22] See Chap. 3 *ante*.
[23] s.3(3).
[24] s.3(4).
[25] See fuller discussion in Chap. 16.
[26] But not of course the tax legislation or the Inheritance (Provision for Family and Dependants) Act 1975, see *post*.
[27] See *post*, Chap. 11.
[28] The dangers of the realty becoming settled land in such cases will be apparent.
[29] See *ante*, Chap. 4.

corporation sole in the corporation's real and personal estate is deemed to be an interest ceasing on his death and devolves on his successor.

Vesting of estate

Vesting of estate between death and grant of representation

Where there is an intestacy it is unlikely that there will have been an express appointment of any executors and so the estate will fall to be administered by the person[30] who is appointed administrator by the grant of letters of administration. In such cases there will be a *lacuna* between the death and the grant and so it is provided,[31] "where a person dies intestate, his real and personal estate, until administration is granted in respect thereof, shall vest in the Probate Judge[32] in the same manner and to the same extent as formerly in the case of personal estate it vested in the ordinary."

Where a person dies wholly intestate without a will this section will clearly apply. However, it is expressed to apply where a person dies "intestate," which is defined in section 55(1)(vi) as including a person who leaves a will but dies intestate as to some beneficial interest in his real or personal estate. Prima facie, therefore, the section will also apply in cases of partial intestacy where an executor has been appointed. This cannot have been intended, however, and so the section is usually construed as meaning "leaving no executor in whom his estate vests."[33]

The effect of section 9 has been considered in several cases[34] including *Long and Sons Ltd.* v. *Burgess*,[35] where Bucknill L.J. commented as follows:

> "I think that, on principle and historically, the vesting of the estate in the President is a positive act with some legal substance. Normally the court, formerly composed of the Probate Judge, appoints a person or persons to deal with the property of the intestate through a grant of letters of administration, but I see no reason why in a case of necessity the President should not have legal power to give directions about the property. If he cannot do so, no one can. That is why the property is vested in him."

[30] Or persons.

[31] Administration of Estates Act 1925 (hereinafter also referred to as "the A.E.A. 1925"), s.9.

[32] *i.e.* the President of the Family Division of the High Court of Justice. See *Practice Direction* [1985] 1 All E.R. 832.

[33] See Parry and Clark, *The Law of Succession*, 8th ed., p. 162. This construction also covers the situation where a person dies wholly testate but where there is no executor.

[34] See *e.g. Smith* v. *Mather* [1948] 2 K.B. 212; *Thynne* v. *Salmon* [1948] 1 K.B. 482; *Re Deans* [1954] 1 W.L.R. 332.

[35] [1950] 1 K.B. 115 at p. 119. In that case the President was held to have the legal capacity to receive a valid notice to quit a tenancy.

Vesting of estate on change of administrator

The estate will "devolve from time to time on the personal representative of the deceased"[36] so that, if there should be a change in the administrator(s), the estate will devolve on the successor.

THE TRUST FOR SALE

Total intestacies

Section 33

In all cases of total intestacy section 33(1) of the Administration of Estates Act 1925 imposes a trust for sale on the real and personal estate of the intestate. The real estate is put upon trust to sell[37] and the personal estate upon trust to call in, sell and convert into money such property as does not already consist of money.[38] The trust to sell is subject to a power to postpone and to the protection of certain property.[39] This trust for sale will produce a mixed fund of money and unconverted assets. The fund is then subject to the administration trusts provided in section 33(2) which require the personal representatives to discharge the funeral, testamentary and administration expenses, debts and other liabilities out of the fund of converted and unconverted assets.[40] In addition there is a direction to set aside out of the residue a fund sufficient to provide for any pecuniary legacies bequeathed by the will (if any) of the deceased.[41]

The residue of the money, any investments for the time being representing the same,[42] and any part of the estate of the deceased which has been retained unsold and is not required for administration purposes, forms, and is referred to in the Act as "the residuary estate of the intestate."[43]

Protection of certain property

It is provided expressly in section 33(1) that personal chattels[44] are not to be sold except for special reason unless required for purposes of

[36] 1925 Act, s.1(1).
[37] s.33(1)(*a*).
[38] s.33(1)(*b*).
[39] s.33(1); both points are discussed *post*.
[40] s.33(2).
[41] *Ibid.*
[42] By s.33(3) the personal representatives are given power to invest the converted residue in authorised trustee investments pending the distribution of the estate of the deceased in cases where an immediate distribution is not possible because of the minority of any beneficiary or during the subsistence of any life interest.
[43] s.33(4). If the deceased leaves a will, these provisions are subject to the terms of the will, s.33(7), so that property subject to an express trust for sale is not within the statutory trust for sale, see *Re McKee* [1931] 2 Ch. 145, *post* p. 90, but without regard to provisions which have become inoperative by disclaimer or lapse, *Re Sullivan, Dunkley* v. *Sullivan* [1930] 1 Ch. 84, see *post* p. 85.
[44] As defined in s.55(1)(x), see *post*.

administration. This has the effect of preserving such chattels *in specie* for the benefit of the surviving spouse. The matrimonial home is protected similarly by the provision in the Second Schedule to the 1952 Act[45] that during the period of twelve months from the first taking out of representation with respect to the intestate's estate, "... the personal representatives shall not without the written consent of the surviving husband or wife sell or otherwise dispose of the said interest in the dwelling house except in the course of administration owing to want of other assets." This is to enable the surviving spouse to invoke the power of appropriation of the house contained in the Schedule if he or she so desires.[46] The protection of the chattels and the house would seem to apply only where there is a surviving spouse but this is not stated specifically at least with reference to the chattels.[47]

Also protected is a reversionary interest which is not to be sold until it falls into possession unless the personal representatives see special reason for sale.[48] A reversionary interest within the section means

> "... a future interest vested in the intestate at the moment of his death in some specific property which at that moment is in the possession or enjoyment of some other person. They do not mean or include a mere promise made to a man to pay his legal personal representatives a sum or sums of money at a specified time or times after his death. The language of this section points, ... quite clearly, to specific property which at the intestate's death is in the possession of another, which property will, on the happening of an event after the intestate's death, come into the possession of his legal personal representatives. A debt payable in the future is not ... such property."[49]

Power to postpone

Section 33(1) confers expressly upon the personal representatives a power to postpone sale and conversion under the trust for sale for such period as the personal representatives, without being liable to account, may think proper. This essential power will implicitly be invoked in the majority of intestate estates, at least in respect of part

[45] Para. 4(1).
[46] See *post*, Chap. 12.
[47] See the general wording of s.33(1).
[48] s.33(1). The reversionary interests referred to are those which form part of the deceased's estate and do not include undisposed of reversionary interests created by the will, see *Re McKee* [1931] 2 Ch. 145, see *post*. p. 90.
[49] *In Re Fisher, Harris* v. *Fisher* [1943] 1 Ch. 377 at p. 383, *per* Bennett J. Applying these principles it was held that money secured by a policy of life insurance and payable by instalments or by a lump sum in the future was not a reversionary interest excluded from the trust for conversion in s.33(1). See further discussion *post*. See also Maugham J. in *Re McKee* [1931] 2 Ch. 145 at p. 150, contrasting the situation where the deceased creates an undisposed of reversionary interest, *e.g.* to A for life, with no provision in remainder.

of the assets, and ensures that the personal representatives will not be liable for losses arising from the failure to convert. It would seem that, where the power has effectively been exercised, the rules of conversion and apportionment in *Howe* v. *Lord Dartmouth*[50] and the *Earl of Chesterfield's Estate*[51] will be excluded. This was stated clearly in *Re Fisher*[52] by Bennett J. who thought that it was obvious that, if the power to postpone had been exercised, the whole of the income of a wasting security was receivable by a tenant for life. He thought that the rules generally had no application to a case where, as in *post*-1925 intestacies, the trust is one to convert with a power to postpone. In such cases the terms of the trusts have to be observed. The judge thought, however, that the rules were applicable "... when the terms of the trust have not been complied with and there has not been an adjustment of the rights of the tenant for life and remainderman."[53] Applying these principles in *Re Fisher*,[54] it was held that monthly instalments paid under a policy of insurance in respect of which the deceased had died intestate had to be regarded as capital and not income and thus fell to be converted as a wasting security under the rule in *Howe* v. *Lord Dartmouth*.[55] Bennett J. distinguished the case of *Re Sullivan*,[56] commenting[57]

> "I feel equally sure that the learned judge could not have decided that all the income of a wasting security such as a copyright was receivable by the tenant for life unless there had been an exercise of the power to postpone conversion. Of course, if that power has been exercised, the whole of the income of a wasting security is receivable by the tenant for life."

It is difficult, however, to see how this conclusion can be supported for two reasons. First, the personal representatives are unlikely to invoke the power to postpone in a formal way, so that a distinction between cases where the power has been exercised and cases where it has not will be difficult to make. Secondly, it is difficult to see how the decision in *Re Fisher*[58] can be reconciled with section 33(5) of the 1925 Act. This subsection provides:

[50] (1802) 7. Ves. 137; see generally Pettit, *Equity and the Law of Trusts*, 4th ed., pp. 355–360. In many cases of intestacy the residuary personal estate will be held for successive interests thus prima facie giving rise to the applicability of the rule.

[51] (1883) 24 Ch.D. 643, *ibid.*

[52] [1943] 1 Ch. 377 at p. 385; see also *Re Hay's Settlement Trusts* [1945] 1 Ch. 294, at p. 315.

[53] *Re Fisher, supra,* at p. 387.

[54] *Supra.*

[55] *Supra.*

[56] [1930] 1 Ch. 84, a case concerning the disclaimer of an interest giving rise to a partial intestacy of *inter alia* royalties received by the trustees in respect of copyright, discussed *post.*

[57] *Supra* at p. 385.

[58] *Supra.*

> "The income . . . of so much of the real and personal estate of the deceased as may not be disposed of by his will, if any, or may not be required for the administration purposes aforesaid, may, however such estate is invested, as from the death of the deceased be treated and applied as income, and for that purpose any necessary apportionment may be made between tenant for life and remainderman."

In view of this provision it would seem that the better view is, as submitted by Williams, Mortimer and Sunnucks,[59] that the true effect of subsections (1), (4) and (5) of the A.E.A. 1925, section 33, is to exclude the rules of apportionment on an intestacy whether the power to postpone is exercised or not.[60]

The applicability of all the provisions of section 33, including subsection (5), will be subject to the provisions of the will, if any, and can be modified or excluded thereby.[61] However, it was held in *Re Sullivan*[62] that only effective provisions will have this effect so that provisions which are inoperative by reason of lapse or disclaimer are to be disregarded. In that case the will disposed of the whole of the residuary personalty to the widow for life, with ultimate trust in favour of issue. The will contained a direction that certain royalties[63] should be treated as capital monies. The wife disclaimed her life interest and the question arose, in the resultant partial intestacy, whether the royalties were to be regarded as income in accordance with section 33(5) or as capital in accordance with the will.[64] It was held that the provision in the will was inserted in order to diminish the widow's life interest in favour of children, who did not in fact exist, and was not intended to determine the nature of the interests to be taken in property in respect of which the testator had died intestate. Accordingly, the widow took a life interest in the residue and took the royalties as income in accordance with section 33(5).

A further point arising from the power to postpone concerns the carrying on by the personal representatives of a business of the deceased after his death. It is clear that this can be done with a view to the proper realisation of the estate or where there is authority in the will so to do.[65] However, it is thought, in cases of intestacy to which

[59] See Williams, Mortimer and Sunnucks, *Executors, Administrators and Probate* (16th ed.) 1982 p. 965. See also *Re Trollope's Will Trusts* [1927] 1 Ch. 596 at p. 604; and *Re Sullivan, supra*, at p.87.

[60] An alternative view is that "necessary apportionment" applies only to the rule in *Allhusen* v. *Whittell* (1867) L.R. 4 Eq. 295, and does not affect the rule in *Howe* v. *Lord Dartmouth, supra.*

[61] s.33(7).

[62] *Supra.*

[63] The will in question was that of the nephew of the famous composer Sir Arthur Sullivan and the royalties in question were in respect of the latter's musical copyright.

[64] s.33(7); s.49(1).

[65] See Parry and Clark, *Law of Succession*, 8th ed., pp. 215 *et seq.*

section 33 applies, that the statutory power to postpone sale will also enable the personal representatives to carry on the business.[66]

Power to invest

The personal representatives are given power to invest the residue of the money not required for the payment of taxes, expenses, debts or legacies, in authorised investments with power to change these investments into other authorised investments as necessary.[67] This power can be used where the immediate distribution of the estate is not possible by reason of the minority of any beneficiary or the subsistence of any life interest.[68]

Trust for sale in cases of partial intestacy

Partial intestacy

Section 33(1) refers to "the death of a person intestate[69] as to any real or personal estate . . . " and declares that "such estate" shall be held by the personal representatives on trust to sell. Section 33(2) clearly envisages cases where there are testamentary pecuniary legacies and section 33(7) states that "where the deceased leaves a will, this section has effect subject to the provisions contained in the will." This provision must mean that the section applies only so far as the estate is not disposed of by a will,[70] although there can be no doubt that the statutory trust for sale can apply to the undisposed part of the estate where the deceased dies partially intestate.[71] The trust for sale can, however, be excluded by the terms of the will either wholly, by an express trust for sale of residue where the undisposed property is a share of residue, or partly, by express provisions of the will which modify the administration trusts set out in section 33(2).

[66] *Ibid.* at p. 28, applying the reasoning in *Re Crowther* [1895] 2 Ch. 56; see also Pritchard (1974) 118 S.J. 355.

[67] s.33(3).

[68] *Ibid.*

[69] It is interesting to note that this is one of the few sections of the Act where the word "intestate" is used in its state of affairs sense, rather than as referring to the deceased. The word is defined in s.55(1) only in its latter sense but then clearly includes a person who dies partially intestate.

[70] *Per* Tomlin J. in *Re Trollope's Will Trusts, Public Trustee* v. *Trollope* [1927] 1 Ch. 596 at p. 604. See also Maugham J. and Lawrence L.J. in *Re McKee, supra*, at pp. 151, 160. The application of s.49 and the controversy between *Re McKee, supra*, and *Re Bowen-Buscarlet's Will Trusts* [1972] Ch. 463 is discussed *post* p. 208.

[71] See Romer L.J. in *Re Thornber, Crabtree* v. *Thornber* [1937] 1 Ch. 29 at p. 35 referring to *Re McKee, supra.* It was argued in *Re Berreys Will Trusts* [1959] 1 W.L.R. 30 at p. 40 that the provisions of s.33 could not apply where the only intestacy was not as regards particular assets of the whole estate but as regards a share in the residuary estate. This was firmly rejected by Danckwerts J., at p. 40, who thought that *Re Worthington* [1933] 1 Ch. 777 disposed of that argument conclusively.

Express trust for sale

The statutory trust for sale imposed by section 33 in cases of intestacy can clearly be excluded by an express inconsistent provision in the will.[72] Such a situation will only arise in cases of partial intestacy,[73] where, for example, the residue is put upon express trust for sale and divided into shares, one of which fails. The position in such cases has been stated clearly in *Re McKee*[74] by Maugham J. as follows[75]

> "... I have come to the conclusion that a trust for sale in the usual form for sale and conversion of the residue of the real and personal estate of a testator contained in his will altogether precludes the operation of the statutory trust for sale under section 33(1).... There is in the present case an effective trust for conversion and an effective life interest created by the will, and for the reasons given it follows that the statutory trust for sale mentioned in subsection 1 of section 33 is not applicable, and that subsection 2 is not applicable because the testator has stated how the funeral and testamentary expenses and debts and the legacies bequeathed by his will are to be paid."[76]

Similarly, where the will contains administrative directions or trusts inconsistent with section 33(2), then the latter can have no place. There cannot be two subsisting trusts for conversion of the testator's estate and for application of the proceeds with different incidents.[77] For example, the will may include a requirement of the consent of the tenant for life to a sale, or a special provision as to the legacies which are to be discharged out of the proceeds, or directions

[72] In *Re McKee* [1931] 2 Ch. 145 at p. 148, Maugham J. pointed out that the wording in subsection (7) is wider than the more usual statutory qualification "unless a contrary intention is expressed in the will." In *Re Gillett's Will Trusts* [1950] 1 Ch. 102 at p. 112, Roxburgh J. seemed to preclude the possibility that there could be an implied inconsistency, "If anything is clear, I think it is that the testator was not consciously leaving property undisposed of. In those circumstances I think it difficult to imply from anything he has said what he would have said if he had been aware that some property was undisposed of."

[73] Although it is possible to envisage a situation where the will includes an express trust for sale and detailed administrative trusts and all the distributive provisions fail, when it could be argued that the estate is wholly undisposed of but that the statutory trust for sale should be regarded as excluded by the will.

[74] *Supra.*

[75] At pp. 150, 151; followed in *Re Taylor's Estate* [1969] 2 Ch. 265 at p. 251 where the contrary was thought to be unarguable, "both of them [counsel] agree that section 33 does not touch the issue, having regard to clause 5 of the will and the overriding express trust for sale of the total mixed residue therein contained."

[76] See also Lord Hanworth in the Court of Appeal in *Re McKee, supra,* at p. 165.

[77] *Supra,* Maugham J. at p. 149; followed in *Re Taylor's Estate* [1969] 2 Ch. 245 at p. 250.

as to the application of the rules of apportionment.[78] In such cases the will prevails. The effect of an express trust for sale can be illustrated by reference to the cases concerning the incidence of debts and legacies. In *Re Martin*[79] there was an express trust for sale which cast the just debts, funeral and testamentary expenses on the personal estate. Accordingly the provisions of the Act were held to have been varied, so that the personal estate and not the undisposed of realty was the primary fund to meet these obligations.

The same also applies with reference to the vexed question of the incidence of legacies.[80] Section 33(2) provides that

> "... The personal representatives shall pay all such funeral, testamentary and administration expenses, debts and other liabilities as are properly payable thereout, having regard to the rules of administration contained in this part of this Act, and out of the residue of the said money the personal representatives shall set aside a fund sufficient to provide for any pecuniary legacies bequeathed by the will (if any) of the deceased."

If section 33(2) applies, the legacies will be discharged primarily out of the undisposed of property, usually the lapsed share of residue.[81] It has been said that, in view of the direction to set aside the fund, it is a modest implication to draw that it is mandatory that the legacies should be so paid.[82] Thus in *Re Berrey's Will Trusts*[83] no trust for sale was contained in the will and section 33 was applied so that the legacies were payable out of the undisposed of share of residue.

If, however, there is an express trust for sale in the will, it will exclude section 33(2)[84] and it may be that the proper construction of the will is that legacies have to be paid first, before the residue is ascertained. In that case they will be borne by the whole estate before the residue is divided into shares and will not fall wholly on the

[78] *Ibid.* If a will is so drawn as to give property *in specie* to any beneficiary for life or for some other period, the subsections *pro tanto* must obviously be superseded, *ibid.* But subject, of course, only to effective testamentary provisions, *Re Sullivan* [1930] 1 Ch. 84 and *Re Thornber* [1937] 1 Ch. 29, discussed *ante* p. 285.

[79] [1955] 1 Ch. 698; see also *Re Petty* [1929] 1 Ch. 726; *Re Kempthorne* [1930] 1 Ch. 268; *Re Harland Peck* [1941] 1 Ch. 182 and *Re Berry's Will Trusts* [1959] 1 W.L.R. 30.

[80] As to which see Ryder, [1956] C.L.J. 80. It will be appreciated that this discussion is concerned only with the effect of an express trust for sale on the application of s.33(2), and not with the general question as to the incidence of pecuniary legacies.

[81] As in *Re Martin* [1955] Ch. 698, where the express trust for sale applied only to the personalty and the undisposed of realty was subject to s.33(1), (2); and in *Re Worthington* [1933] Ch. 771, there being no provision in the will to the contrary, the debts, funeral and testamentary expenses and the legacies were payable primarily out of the lapsed share of the residue.

[82] *Per* Salt Q.C. in *Re Taylor's Estate* [1969] 2 Ch. 245 at p. 251; see also Danckwerts J. in *Re Berrey's Will Trusts* [1959] 1 W.L.R. 30 at p. 40.

[83] [1959] 1 W.L.R. 30, where the previous, not necessarily consistent, cases were reviewed.

[84] See *Re McKee, supra.*

undisposed of share.[85] In these cases there has been a failure only of one object of the trust for sale. If there has been a complete failure of the objects of the trust, for example, all the beneficiaries entitled to residue have predeceased the deceased, it would seem that the express testamentary trust would fail and that section 33(1) and (2) would apply.[86]

A final point can be noted. It was stated at the outset of this Chapter that the statutory administration trusts provided in section 33(2) are crucial in that they lead to the identification of the property which is defined as "the residuary estate of an intestate"[87] to which the scheme of distribution in Part IV applies. Accordingly, where the statutory trusts are excluded by express provision in the will, this crucial concept will not become identifiable in the manner specified in section 33. It could be argued, therefore, that section 46 of the Act, which is expressed to relate to "the residuary estate of an intestate," cannot strictly apply. This must be regarded, however, as a technicality on which no point is taken and in cases of express provision section 46 is applied to the net undisposed of residue ascertained according to the trusts of the will.[88]

Immediate and contingent partial intestacies

Most intestacies will be both "immediate," *i.e.* the property or the interest is undisposed of at the death and immediately available for distribution on intestacy, and "immediately apparent," *i.e.* that these facts are apparent at the death.[89] So far as these cases are concerned, section 33 will clearly be applicable to impose the statutory trust for sale.[90] More difficult questions arise in cases where the intestacy is either not immediate, such as a gift of a life interest with no provision

[85] As in *Re Beaumont's Will Trusts* [1950] Ch. 462, and *Re Taylor's Estate* [1969] 2 Ch. 245. In both cases there was an express trust for sale which was held to exclude s.33(2) and *Re Martin, supra,* was distinguished on the grounds that there was no express trust for sale applicable to the undisposed of share in that case. However, in *Re Gillett's Will Trusts* [1950] Ch. 102 it was held that the undisposed of income bore the legacies and this was followed in *Re Midgley* [1955] 1 Ch. 576, where there was an express trust for sale and the legacies were held to be payable out of the undisposed of estate by virtue of the schedule to the 1925 Act.

[86] See Harman J. in *Re Midgley* [1955] 1 Ch. 576 at p. 583 and Parry and Clarke, *op. cit.*, p. 307.

[87] s.33(4).

[88] There is a further theoretical difficulty in applying s.33 to cases of partial intestacy, namely that s.49(1) of the A.E.A. 1925 strictly only applies Pt. IV of the Act applies to partial intestacies, and s.33 is in Pt. III; see Lord Hanworth M.R. in *Re McKee, supra,* at p. 159. However, this argument can easily be met by the terms of the express provisions of s.33, which clearly contemplate application to cases of partial intestacy, and by the fact that s.46, in Pt. IV, relates only to "the residuary estate of an intestate" which is defined in s.33(4) and is meaningless without reference to s.33.

[89] See *ante,* Chap. 1 and *post,* Chap. 15.

[90] See *Re Berrey's Will Trusts* [1959] 1 W.L.R. 30, following *Re Worthington* [1933] Ch. 771, and specifically rejecting an argument that s.33 did not apply. See also *Re Sullivan* [1930] 1 Ch. 84, where s.33(5) was held to apply to an immediate partial intestacy.

on the remainder, or not immediately apparent, such as a gift of a life interest with a contingent gift in remainder which wholly fails subsequent to the death. In such cases there is authority to the effect that the statutory trust for sale imposed by section 33 does not apply.[91] First, however, the statutory provisions must be considered.

Section 33(1) opens with the words "on the death of a person intestate. . . . " and this seems clearly to be envisaging the situation where an intestacy arises on, or is apparent at, the death. Where the will creates successive interests in property which are capable of taking full effect, although subject to the possibility that the remainder will not vest in interest, the deceased is not intestate at death and section 33 seems inappropriate to create an immediate trust for sale.[92] If it becomes apparent subsequently that the remainder interests have failed, resulting in the property becoming undisposed of after the prior interest, it might be argued that section 33 should then apply. However, such a conclusion seems inconsistent with the opening words of the section, which relate to the death, and with the provisions in subsection (2). They govern the administration of the estate and clearly relate to, and are appropriate for, the usual administration period immediately after the death. For example, there is a reference to the payment of funeral, testamentary and administration expenses[93] which is entirely inappropriate for the operation of the statutory trust for sale when the remainder fails, perhaps many years from the death. In addition section 33 is expressed to apply, where the deceased leaves a will, subject to the provisions contained in the will.[94] It could be said, therefore, that in the sort of contingent partial intestacy situations under discussion, the creation of an effective prior interest is consistent with the application of the statutory trust, which must be regarded as having been excluded by the will.[95]

Accordingly it is submitted that an analysis of section 33 precludes its application to cases where the partial intestacy is not immediately apparent at the death. The authorities support this conclusion and must now be considered.

The leading decision is *Re McKee*.[96] In that case the testator, who died in 1928, devised and bequeathed his residuary estate to trustees on trust for sale to pay the income to his wife for life and after her death to divide the same between his surviving brothers and sisters. The last of the brothers and sisters died in 1930 while the widow was still living. It was held as a matter of construction that "surviving

[91] *Re McKee, supra,* see Romer L.J. at p. 165, *Re Thornber* [1937] 1 Ch. 29 at pp. 35, 36.

[92] It could happen that the whole estate becomes undisposed of, *e.g.* "All to X for life remainder to Y if he survives X," and Y dies during X's lifetime.

[93] s.33(2).

[94] s.33(7). See *ante.*

[95] See Maugham J. in *Re McKee, supra,* at p. 149.

[96] [1931] 2 Ch. 145.

brothers and sisters" meant brothers and sisters surviving the widow and therefore that there was an intestacy as to the reversionary interest in the testator's residuary estate expectant on the widow's death. The question then arose of the applicability of section 33. Maugham J. identified the situation as a "contingent partial intestacy" not immediately apparent at the death and continued[97]:

> "The subsections may no doubt be construed as applicable to any item of property as to which there is an immediate intestacy, in the sense above explained; for there would be no serious difficulty in applying an immediate trust for sale to that item of property. . . . It is suggested that in the case of a contingent partial intestacy, such as I have to deal with in the present case, the statutory trust for sale may apply to the property undisposed of. As I have already indicated there is plainly great difficulty in the contention that in such a case the statutory for sale arises at the date when the intestacy became certain or probable; for section 33 subsections (1) and (2) are framed as if they applied only as from the death of the testator. Moreover, to take one out of many instances of the result of the suggestion I am testing, the funeral expenses of the deceased have, under subsection 2, to be paid out of the proceeds of the statutory trust for sale. It does not seem to be possible to suppose that the legislature can be contemplating that the various sums paid for funeral and testamentary expenses and debts out of the general estate pursuant to the provisions of the will must be recouped out of the item of property in question at some future date; nor is this, in my opinion, giving full effect to the provisions contained in the will."

The Court of Appeal confirmed the decision, Romer L.J. commenting[98]:

> "Now in connection with this matter, our attention was called to the provisions of section 33 of the Act dealing with the case of a person dying intestate as to any real or personal estate. If that section applied to the present case, it would no doubt create much difficulty. In my opinion, however, the section is confined to the case of a person dying intestate as to some one or more specific items of his real or personal estate, and does not extend to a case like the present, where there is a will which deals with every item of the testator's estate, but omits to dispose of every interest in that estate."[99]

[97] At pp. 148, 149, 150.
[98] At p. 165.
[99] In *Re Plowman* [1943] 1 Ch. 269 at p. 274, Cohen J. thought that it was clear from these passages that s.33 applied only to cases of intestacy affecting the whole interest in the estate or some part thereof and not to an intestacy as to a partial interest in the residuary estate such as the life interest in that case.

Trust for sale or trust?

Comment

A trust for sale on intestacy is imposed for two apparent reasons. The first is to avoid any suggestion that the real estate would become settled land on intestacy. In the absence of a trust for sale section 1 of the Settled Land Act 1925 might well apply, either because of the charge of the fixed net sum in favour of the spouse,[1] or because of the succession of interests where there is a spouse and issue.[2] A trust for sale will avoid any such result.[3] The second reason is simply to provide some machinery for the liquidation of the assets for the purpose of paying tax, debts, expenses and legacies (if any). Both of these objectives could be achieved by other means. The application of the Settled Land Act could be avoided by specific statutory exclusion in cases of intestacy and the necessary liquidation of assets could be achieved by a simple trust with a power of sale vested in the personal representatives.

It is submitted that this is the better solution and that the statutory trust for sale on intestacy should be abandoned for the following reasons.[4] First, a simple trust is more consistent with the actual position on intestacy and the trust for sale is in many respects an artificial device suggesting, as it does, that the assets will be sold when in reality many of the assets will remain unsold. This leads to the inclusion of the equally artificial power to postpone and the power of appropriation. A trust of the assets with a power to sell would avoid this artificiality. Secondly, such a simple trust would be more consistent with the presumed intention of the intestate and would be understood more readily by the layman. It can be said, of course, that the intestate's presumed intention underlies only the distribution of the assets and not the machinery of administration but, in view of the fact that many letters of administration are taken by laymen, it is desirable that the position should be easily understandable. Thirdly, the trust for sale requires the protection by special exclusion of certain categories of property, for example, the chattels and the matrimonial home, and this complication would be avoided by a simple trust. Fourthly, although section 33 imposes a trust for sale for administration purposes, the statutory trusts governing the entitlement are simple trusts (albeit in the converted residue). It would seem simpler to avoid this dichotomy. Finally, it is suggested that a simple trust would avoid the problem highlighted by *Re McKee* as to the

[1] A.E.A. 1925, s.46(1); S.L.A. 1925, s.1(1)(v). S.L.A. 1925 includes situations where the land satisfies the definition of settled land by virtue of an Act of Parliament, s.1(1).

[2] A.E.A., s.46(1); S.L.A. 1925, s.1(1)(*i*).

[3] S.L.A. 1925 s.1(7) added by Law of Property Amendment Act 1926, (hereinafter also referred to as the "L.P.A.A. 1926"), s.7, schedule.

[4] It is interesting to note that New Zealand and the most of Australian states have abandoned the trust for sale in favour of a trust with power of sale; see Hardingham, Neave and Ford *Wills and Intestacies*, pp. 345 *et seq.*

inapplicability of an immediate trust for sale to a contingent partial intestacy. A mere power of sale would not be inconsistent with a prior life interest and the trust could apply at the outset in such cases, with the estate being realised by exercise of the power at the death of the life tenant or whenever the property ceased to be effectively disposed of.

Nature of Beneficiary's Interest

It has been seen that on the death of a person intestate the estate vests automatically in the Probate judge.[5] It will then pass to the administrator on the grant of letters of administration and ultimately to the beneficiary entitled by assent. Questions accordingly arise as to the nature of the beneficiary's interest under an intestacy during the course of administration. Has he, for instance, an interest which is capable of being bequeathed by his will or of being disclaimed?

The leading decisions

There is considerable authority on this point and the answers to the questions posed are to be found in the House of Lords decisions in *Lord Sudeley* v. *Attorney General*,[6] and *Dr. Barnado's Homes National Incorporated Association* v. *Commissioners for Special Purposes of the Income Tax Acts*[7] and in the Privy Council decision in *Commissioner of Stamp Duties (Queensland)* v. *Livingston*.[8] Although these cases were all concerned with testate succession, the principles stated are usually regarded as being applicable equally to the nature of a beneficiary's right on intestacy.[9] The basic principle appears from the *Barnado's* case, where it was clearly stated[10]:

> "When the personal estate of a testator has been fully administered by his executors and the net residue ascertained, the residuary legatee is entitled to have the residue as so ascertained, with any accrued income, transferred and paid to him; but until that time he has no property in any specific investment forming part of the estate or in the income from any such investment, and both *corpus* and income are the property of the executors and are

[5] A.E.A. 1925, s.9.
[6] [1897] A.C. 11.
[7] [1921] 2 A.C. 1.
[8] [1965] A.C. 694.
[9] So far as the cases concern residuary legatees and not specific legatees, see Williams, Mortimer and Sunnucks, *Executors, Administrators and Probate*, (16th ed.), 1982, p. 944 Pinkerton, (1978) 42 Conv. 213, 215. See *post* p. 95.
[10] *Supra* at p. 10, *per* Viscount Cave. Accordingly the payment by deduction of income tax made by the executors in respect of the income was not made on behalf of the charitable institutions entitled to residue, and therefore the institution was not entitled to repayment of the income tax so paid. This decision has since been affected by statutory provisions in the Income Tax Acts.

> applicable by them as a mixed fund for the purposes of administration."

Similarly, Viscount Finlay said[11]

> "... the legatee of a share in the residue has no interest in any of the property of the testator until the residue has been ascertained. His right is to have the estate properly administered and applied for his benefit when the administration is complete."

This was explained by the House of Lords in the *Lord Sudeley* case[12] on the basis that until the claims against the testator's estate for debts, legacies, testamentary expenses have been satisfied, the residue does not come into actual existence.[13] It is a non-existent thing until that event has occurred and the probability that there will be a residue is not enough: the residue must be actually ascertained.[14] The right of the residuary legatees is simply a right to have the administration completed and the residuary estate ascertained and realised, either wholly or so far as may be necessary for the purpose, and to have the appropriate shares paid in due course.[15] These two cases were regarded as conclusive of the issue by the Privy Council in the *Livingston*[16] case. Viscount Radcliffe stated the position as follows[17]:

> "What equity did not do was to recognise or create residuary legatees a beneficial interest in the assets in the executor's hands during the course of administration. Conceivably, this could have been done, in the sense that the assets, whatever they might be from time to time, could have been treated as a present, though fluctuating, trust fund held for the benefit of all those interested in the estate according to the measure of their respective interests. But it never was done. It would have been a clumsy and unsatisfactory device from a practical point of view; and, indeed, it would have been in plain conflict with the basic conception of equity that to impose the fetters of a trust upon property, with the

[11] *Ibid.* at p. 8, both judges relying on the *Lord Sudeley* case, *supra.*

[12] *Ibid.*

[13] *Supra,* at p. 15, *per* Lord Halsbury. See, so far as intestacy is concerned, A.E.A. 1925, s.33.

[14] *Per* Lord Atkinson in *Barnardo's* case, *supra,* at p. 11.

[15] *Sudeley's* case, *supra,* at p. 21, *per* Lord Davey. In that case a wife was entitled under her husband's will to a share of the residue which included mortgages on foreign property. She died before the administration of her husband's estate had been completed. It was held that she had a chose in action in her husband's estate which was an English asset and on which probate duty had to be paid but that she did not have a right in respect of the overseas property on which probate duty would have been payable: "I do not think that they (*i.e.* the wife's executors) have any estate, right or interest, legal or equitable, in these New Zealand mortgages so as to make them an asset of her estate," *supra,* at p. 18 *per* Lord Herschell. The position in England with reference to inheritance tax would now be different.

[16] [1965] A.C. 694.

[17] *Supra* at p. 707.

resulting creation of equitable interests in that property, there had to be specific subjects identifiable as the trust fund. An unadministered estate was incapable of satisfying this requirement. The assets as a whole were in the hands of the executor, his property; and until administration was complete no one was in a position to say what items of property would need to be realised for the purposes of that administration or of what the residue, when ascertained, would consist or what its value would be. Even in modern economies, when the ready marketability of many forms of property can almost be assumed, valuation and realisation are very far from being interchangeable terms."[18]

The recent Court of Appeal decision in *Re K.*[19] is consistent with this approach. It was held that a beneficiary in an unadministered estate had not "acquired . . . any interest in property" within section 2(7) of the Forfeiture Act 1982.[20]

Intestate estate

The principles set out in the cases above are usually regarded as being applicable equally to determine the nature of the rights of the next of kin on intestacy, on the basis that the rights of the next of kin are analogous to those of a residuary legatee.[21] Thus in the *Livingston* case[22] the Privy Council doubted expressly the observations in *Cooper* v. *Cooper*,[23] that the next of kin on intestacy analogously to the residuary legatees under a will,[24] had "a clear and tangible interest *in specie*" in the assets of the estate. Viscount Radclife commented in *Livingston*[25]:

"It is said that Lord Cairns' description of the next of kin as having a substantial proprietorship in every item of an intestate's personal estate and of residuary legatees of what, presumably, he was regarding as an unadministered estate as possessing a clear and tangible interest *in specie* in a particular item of the estate

[18] In the case a widow was entitled to the residuary estate of her husband but died before the administration of his estate was completed. It was held that the husband's property was vested in his executors in full ownership and that the widow had no beneficial interest in it so that her estate was not liable to succession duty on that property. The Privy Council doubted observations in *Cooper* v. *Cooper* [1874] L.R. 7 H.L. 53, see *post; McCaughey* v. *Commissioner of Stamp Duties* [1945] 46 S.R. N.S.W. 192; *Smith* v. *Lagh* [1953] 90 C.L.R. 102. The decision in *Skinner* v. *Att.Gen.* [1940] A.C. 350 was not regarded as having qualified the *Sudeley* case.

[19] [1986] Ch. 180 at pp. 188–190, C.A.

[20] See *post,* Chap. 17.

[21] For the ascertainment of the residuary estate on intestacy see A.E.A. 1925, s.33.

[22] [1965] A.C. 694 at p. 709.

[23] (1874) L.R. 7 H.L. 53 at pp. 64 and 65, and therefore decided before the imposition of the statutory trust for sale on intestacy by the 1925 Act.

[24] The Statute of Distribution was regarded in substance as nothing more than a will made by the legislature for the intestate, *supra,* at p. 66, *per* Lord Cairns.

[25] *Supra,* at pp. 710 and 698.

contradicts the clear statement of the position which was made by Lord Herschell and others in the *Sudeley* case.[26] So indeed it does, in the sense that Lord Cairns' words cannot be treated as an accurate statement of the law in the light of the later decision. . . ."

His Lordship concluded that the language of Lord Cairns' speech in *Cooper* v. *Cooper* was picturesque, but inexact, and could not be regarded as an authoritative statement of the rights of next of kin or residuary legatees in opposition to the *Sudeley* and *Barnado* cases.[27]

Subsequent decisions on intestate succession have followed this approach. Thus in *Eastbourne Mutual Building Society* v. *Hastings Corporation*[28] the occupier of a house died intestate and her husband was the sole person entitled to her residuary estate. He died before any grant of administration to his wife's estate had been taken out. A claim was made to money payable under a compulsory purchase order on the basis that the husband, as a member of the family of his deceased wife, was entitled to an interest in the house[29] under the intestacy.[30] The court held[31] that the word "interest" in the relevant Housing Act was confined to an interest of a proprietary nature and therefore that the husband, as the sole next-of-kin of his wife, could not be said to have had any interest in the house which formed part of the unadministered estate of his wife or in the proceeds of sale of that house.[32] In *Lall* v. *Lall*[33] the widow of an intestate sought to defend an action for possession of the matrimonial home on the ground that the provision of Schedule 2 to the Intestates' Estates Act 1952 conferred on her sufficient interest in the matrimonial home to give her *locus standi*. She failed[34] because

"... if a residuary legatee who has some sort of interest in the totality of the assets cannot be said to have a particular interest in a particular asset, I think it must be equally true that a surviving spouse who has a particular sort of interest in the matrimonial

[26] [1897] A.C. 11 at p. 18.
[27] *Ibid.* at pp. 711, 712.
[28] [1965] 1 W.L.R. 861.
[29] Under the Housing Act 1959 (see now 1985 Act).
[30] An alternative claim was as the surety under certain legal charges.
[31] [1965] 1 W.L.R. 861 at p. 870.
[32] Following *Commissioner of Stamp Duties (Queensland)* v. *Livingston* [1965] A.C. 694. The principle thus worked against the beneficiary in the case. See, however, *Re Servers of the Blind League* [1960] 1 W.L.R. 564 at p. 565 "Equally the order [under s.352(19) the Companies Act 1948] would now divest the interest which the next of kin took on the date of death, and with which they were in a position to deal from that date," *per* Pennycuick J.
[33] [1965] 1 W.L.R. 1249. No grant of representation to the estate had been made.
[34] Applying the *Eastbourne Building Society* case, *supra,* and the *Livingston* case, *supra*; see also *Barclay* v. *Barclay* [1970] 2 Q.B. 677, and *Williams and Glyn's Bank Ltd.* v. *Boland* [1981] A.C. 487, *Irani Finance Ltd.* v. *Singh* [1971] Ch. 59, on the nature of the beneficial interest under a trust for sale.

home, conferred by the Intestates' Estates Act 1952, by parity of reasoning has not got any equitable interest in that asset of the deceased's estate recognisable by the law."[35]

Accordingly it would seem that a beneficiary on intestacy has no more than a right to apply for a grant of administration or a right to compel the personal representative to duly administer the estate. However, once the residuary estate of the intestate has been ascertained,[36] it is arguable that the persons entitled on intestacy then have a beneficial interest in the estate.[37]

Transmissibility by will

In *Re Leigh's Will Trusts*,[38] Buckley J. thought that the *Livingston*[39] case had established the following propositions. First, the entire ownership of the property comprised in the estate of a deceased person which remains unadministered is in the deceased's legal personal representatives for the purposes of administration without any differentiation between legal and equitable interests. Secondly, no residuary legatee or person entitled upon the intestacy of the deceased has any proprietary interest in any particular asset comprised in the unadministered estate of the deceased. Thirdly, each such legatee or person so entitled is entitled to a chose in action, namely a right to require the deceased's estate to be duly administered, whereby he can protect those rights to which he hopes to become entitled in possession in the due course of the administration of the deceased's estate. Fourthly, each such legatee or person so entitled has a transmissible interest in the estate notwithstanding that it remains unadministered.[40] This transmissible or disposable interest can consist only of the chose in action in question which carries with it the right to receive the fruits of the chose in action when they mature.

In *Leigh's* case[41] the widow was entitled on the intestacy of her husband to his entire estate which included some shares in a company. She was also sole administratrix of the estate. She died soon after her husband without having made any formal assent of the shares in her own favour and by her will she specifically devised her interest in the shares to the defendant. Buckley J. held that as sole beneficiary she could not be said to have held any shares in the company when she died but that she had an interest in the company in respect of the shares sufficient to answer the description in the specific

[35] *Per* Buckley J. at p. 1251.
[36] Which must be a matter of fact.
[37] The statements of the principle in *Barnardo's* case, *supra*, and *Livingston's* case, *supra*, noted above, are qualified by the phrase "until the residue has been ascertained."
[38] [1970] 1 Ch. 277.
[39] [1965] A.C. 694.
[40] Clearly recognised by the *Livingston* case (*supra*) at p. 710.
[41] [1970] 1 Ch. 277.

bequest to the defendant.[42] In addition as sole administratrix and sole beneficiary, she had, while she lived, complete dominion over the conduct of the administration of the estate. Although she could not tie the hands of her successor as administrator[43]:

> "... what she could transmit was her own right to require the administrator of her husband's estate, whoever he might be, to administer his estate in any manner she or her personal representative might require consistent with the rights of any other persons having rights against the estate. This right she could transmit to her executor, coupled with a duty to exercise it in a particular manner."[44]

Disclaimer

A further question to be considered is whether a beneficiary in an intestacy can disclaim his entitlement to the advantage of the other beneficiaries entitled on intestacy. It was assumed in *Re Scott (decd.)*[45] that he could, and this decision and its implications are more fully considered *post*, in Chapter 17. This decision has been justified[46] on the basis that, on the authority of the cases discussed above, there is no automatic vesting of the interest in the beneficiary on death so as to preclude a disclaimer by the application of the rule that an interest once accepted or vested cannot be disclaimed. The only automatic vesting on death is in the Probate judge[47] and it is certain that a disclaimer can validly be made at any time up to, and probably after, the issue of the grant of letters of administration.[48]

Possession

Section 43(i) of the 1925 Act confers a power on personal representatives to permit "any person entitled" to take possession of any land in the estate before an assent or conveyance has been made.[49] The section applies both to testate and intestate succession.[50] It is thought that the reference to a person being "entitled" is not meant to indicate a statutory recognition of any interest in the land before assent but merely to identify persons prima facie entitled to succeed to the land in due course.

[42] *Ibid.* at p. 283.
[43] *Ibid.* at p. 284.
[44] Would the decision have been the same if the widow had been sole beneficiary but not also sole administratrix? See also *Re Edward's Will Trusts* [1982] Ch. 30, discussed *post* p. 134.
[45] *Widdows* v. *Friends of the Clergy Corporation* [1975] 1 W.L.R. 1260.
[46] Pinkerton (1978) 42 Conv. 213. Not following the view of Goodhart, (1976) 40 Conv. 260; see also Oughton (1977) 41 Conv. 260.
[47] 1925 Act s.9, see *supra.*
[48] Pinkerton, *supra,* at pp. 215, 216.
[49] Without prejudice, however, to the right of the personal representative to take or resume possession, *ibid.*
[50] s.43(3).

CHAPTER 6

ADMINISTRATION OF THE ESTATE

Personal representatives are under a duty to collect and get in the real and personal estate of the deceased and administer it according to law.[1] The real and personal estate of the deceased are assets for payment of the deceased's debts and liabilities[2] and an administrator will be concerned both to get in the assets as quickly as possible and to establish what debts and liabilities are due for payment out of them. The powers which are available to him for the purpose of collecting and managing the assets will be described[3] and there will then follow a discussion of the ascertainment and payment of the debts[4] and an explanation of the action to be taken by an administrator to settle the deceased's tax liability.[5] Finally, some consideration will be given to the question of administration proceedings.[6] First, however, it is necessary to consider further what property may properly be regarded as assets for payment of the deceased's debts and liabilities.

PROPERTY CONSTITUTING ASSETS

The deceased's estate

The real estate of the deceased, including chattels real, which devolves upon the personal representative[7] and the personal estate of the deceased, whether legal or equitable in either case, are assets to the extent of the deceased's beneficial interest.[8] It follows that property which devolves upon the personal representative by virtue of the fact that it was held by the deceased as a sole trustee does not constitute an asset if the deceased had no beneficial interest in it.[9]

Property appointed under a general power

If the deceased has exercised by deed prior to his death a general power of appointment which did not take effect until his death and was in favour of a volunteer, the appointed property constitutes assets

[1] Administration of Estates Act 1925 (hereinafter also referred to as "the A.E.A. 1925"), s.25(*a*); A.E.A. 1971, s.9. See *Harvell* v. *Foster* [1954] 2 Q.B. 367.
[2] *Ibid.* s.32(1).
[3] See *post.*
[4] See *post.*
[5] See *post*; the taxation of the estate is dealt with in the next Chapter.
[6] See *post.*
[7] A.E.A. 1925, s.55(1)(xix).
[8] *Ibid.* s.32(1).
[9] *Re Webb* [1941] Ch. 225.

to which a creditor may resort if the assets of the deceased's estate are insufficient.[10]

Property in respect of which the deceased has exercised a general power of appointment by his will, as may be the case in a partial intestacy, constitutes assets for payment of the deceased's debts in like manner as the deceased's own real and personal estate.[11] Property over which the deceased has exercised a special power of appointment, whether by deed or by will, does not constitute assets, however, unless the power has been exercised in the deceased's own favour.[12]

Entailed interests

If in a case of partial intestacy the deceased has disposed by his will of the fee simple of land, in which he held an entailed interest at the time of his death, in exercise of the statutory power in that behalf,[13] the fee simple devolves upon the deceased's personal representative and constitutes assets.[14]

Donationes mortis causa

Property which is the subject of a *donatio mortis causa* also constitutes assets but only if the assets of the deceased's estate are insufficient.[15]

Property subject to the rule in Strong v. Bird

It seems, although there is no direct authority on the point, that such property also constitutes assets of last resort.

Income arising after death

Income produced after the death of the deceased by his real and personal estate constitutes assets.[16]

Property accruing after death

Property which accrues to the estate of the deceased after his death, whether by natural increase[17] or by acquisition, similarly constitutes assets.[18]

POWERS RELATING TO ASSETS

The source of the powers

The powers vested in a personal representative derive either from

[10] *O'Grady* v. *Wilmot* [1916] 2 A.C. 231; *Re Phillips* [1931] 1 Ch. 347.
[11] A.E.A. 1925, s.32(1).
[12] *Re Penrose* [1933] Ch. 793.
[13] Law of Property Act 1925 (hereinafter also referred to as the "L.P.A. 1925"), s.176.
[14] A.E.A. 1925, s.32(1).
[15] *Re Korvine's Trust* [1921] 1 Ch. 343.
[16] *Re Tong* [1931] 1 Ch. 202.
[17] *e.g.* young produced by the deceased's animals after his death.
[18] *Re Tong* [1930] 2 Ch. 400.

common law[19] or from statute and an executor can often point to additional powers conferred by the will. In a partial intestacy such additional powers might also be available but in total intestacies the administrators have only the common law and statutory powers and it is on these that this discussion will concentrate. The statutory powers are to be found in sections 12–25 of the Trustee Act 1925 and in sections 39–44 of the Administration of Estates Act 1925. The former are rendered applicable by section 68(1) of the Trustee Act 1925 which states expressly that a "trustee" includes a personal representative where the context admits so that powers conferred on the former are also available to the latter.[20] This is not of course to equate the two offices since the functions and duties of each are distinct. The questions whether, and at what time, a personal representative becomes a trustee of estate assets is discussed later,[21] as is the linked, and somewhat vexed, question of the power of a personal representative to appoint a trustee.[22]

Power to bring actions

The general rule, which is embodied in the Law Reform (Miscellaneous Provisions) Act 1934, is that causes of action survive for the benefit of the estate so that the personal representatives can bring actions in respect of contracts or torts. The duty to ensure that they obtain possession of the assets of the estate means that they can where necessary also bring actions to recover property in the hands of third parties. There is express statutory power[23] to distrain upon land for arrears of rent as the deceased could have done if living.[24]

Power of sale

An administrator has absolute power both at common law and in equity to dispose of the personal estate and chattels real of the deceased on the basis that realisation of assets may be required to enable debts to be paid and the estate to be distributed. This power has been given statutory effect[25] and extended to the deceased's real estate.[26]

[19] In the sense of being developed by case law; in fact developed in ecclesiastical chancery or probate courts in the main.
[20] Note the power in s.57 of the Trustee Act 1925 for the court to authorise any dealings with trust property which can also be invoked by personal representatives.
[21] See *post.*
[22] See *post.*
[23] A.E.A. 1925, s.26(4).
[24] Including the right to distrain for arrears after the termination of the lease if the distress is made (a) within six months after termination of the lease and (b) during the continuance of the possession of the lessee from whom the arrears are due; *ibid.*, s.26(4).
[25] A.E.A. 1925, s.39(1)(i). The section restricts the exercise of these powers . . . "for the purposes of administration, or during a minority of any beneficiary or the subsistence of any life interest, or until the period of distribution arrived . . . ".
[26] *Ibid.* s.2(1).

In addition an administrator has all the powers conferred by statute on trustees for sale,[27] which includes the powers of a tenant for life and of the trustees of a settlement under the Settled Land Act 1925.[28] Furthermore, any real or personal estate as to which the deceased died intestate is to be held on trust for sale with power to postpone such sale[29], although it is provided that reversionary interests shall not be sold before they fall into possession and that personal chattels shall not be sold if other assets are available, unless in either case there is a special reason.[30]

A sale may be effected by public auction or by private contract and subject to such conditions as the administrator thinks fit[31] and no sale may be impeached by a beneficiary on the ground that any of the conditions may have been unnecessarily depreciating unless the consideration for the sale was thereby rendered inadequate.[32]

Power to mortgage

An administrator has power at common law to mortgage or pledge assets vested in him as such in order to raise money for the purpose of the administration of the estate and this power has also been given statutory effect.[33]

Power to grant leases

The power of an administrator to grant leases is limited at common law to the grant of an underlease out of a term of years which has devolved upon him[34] and even then only if that is the best way to administer the asset.[35] Since 1925, however, administrators have enjoyed a wide statutory power of leasing, namely a power to grant a lease of the deceased's land or any part of it for a term not exceeding 999 years for building or forestry, 100 years for mining and 50 years in any other case.[36]

The power extends to the grant of leases in accordance with covenants for renewal and to confirm void or voidable leases[37] as well as to the grant of an option for a lease,[38] the acceptance of a surrender

[27] *Ibid.* s.39(1)(ii) and (iii).
[28] L.P.A. 1925, s.28(1) as amended.
[29] A.E.A. 1925, s.33(1), see *ante* p. 82.
[30] *Ibid.*
[31] Trustee Act 1925, s.12(1).
[32] *Ibid.* s.13(1).
[33] Settled Land Act 1925 (hereinafter also referred to as the "the S.L.A. 1925"), s.39(1)(ii).
[34] *Re Owen* [1912] 1 Ch. 519.
[35] *Oceanic Steam Co.* v. *Sutherberry* (1880) 16 Ch.D. 236; *Johnson* v. *Clarke* [1928] Ch. 847.
[36] A.E.A. 1925, s.39(1)(iii); L.P.A. 1925, s.28(1) as amended; Settled Land Act 1925 (hereinafter also referred to as the "S.L.A. 1925"), s.41.
[37] S.L.A. 1925, s.43.
[38] *Ibid.* s.51.

of a lease[39] and the making of a contract for a lease.[40] In addition there is power to vary leases and give licences[41] and to apportion rents.[42]

Power to carry on business

In the absence of express authority personal representatives generally have no power to carry on the deceased's business. However, they may do so for a limited period for the purpose of selling it as a going concern.[43] Section 33 of the Administration of Estates Act 1925, which confers the statutory trust for sale on intestacy, expressly includes a power to postpone and thus authorises the continuation of a business during the period of administration.[44] Care is needed to limit the extent of the personal liability of the personal representative in such cases, particularly in cases of intestacy because of the absence of express testamentary authority. If the business is carried on only for the minimum period required for the purposes of realisation, the personal representatives will be protected.[45] Where the power in section 33 is implicitly invoked and the business is carried on for longer than required for realisation, but within the period of distribution, it would seem that the personal representatives are entitled to an indemnity in priority to the general creditors and the beneficiaries.[46]

Power to employ agents

The power of personal representatives to employ agents, such as solicitors, stockbrokers and valuers, is co-extensive with the power of trustees laid down in the Trustee Act 1925.[47] Section 23 confers a general power on personal representatives to employ agents "... to transact any business or do any act required to be transacted or done in the administration of the testator's or intestate's estate...." There is no liability for the default of such an agent if he was employed in good faith[48] and there is also the well-known protection afforded by section 30 of the Trustee Act 1925 which states that the trustee or personal representative is not liable for loss occasioned by the act of the agent "unless the same happens through his own wilful default."[49]

[39] *Ibid.* s.52.
[40] *Ibid.* s.90.
[41] *Ibid.* s.59.
[42] *Ibid.* s.60.
[43] *Dowse* v. *Gorton* [1891] A.C. 190, see *post*, Chap. 9.
[44] *Re Crowther* [1895] 2 Ch. 56; *i.e.* during the executor's year even presumably, if this is longer than is strictly necessary for the purpose of realisation.
[45] The debts will rank as administration expenses.
[46] *Dowse* v. *Gorton, supra.*
[47] For the pre-1925 position see *Speight* v. *Gaunt* (1883) 9 App.Cas. 1, see *post*, Chap. 9.
[48] s.23(1); see *Re Vickery* [1931] 1 Ch. 572; *Re Lucking's Will Trusts* [1968] 1 W.L.R. 866.
[49] See cases above and *Bartlett* v. *Barclays Bank Trust Co. (No. 1)* [1980] Ch. 515.

A fuller discussion of these questions of liability is contained in Chapter 9.

It is usually stated that only ministerial acts or duties can be delegated under section 23 and not discretions. A full delegation can only be achieved under section 23(2) in respect of property abroad or by power of attorney in accordance with section 25 of the Trustee Act.[50] The latter authority permits delegation for a period not exceeding twelve months but the donor of a power of attorney given under the section is liable for the acts or defaults of the donee in the same manner as if they were the acts or defaults of the donor.[51]

Other powers

Other powers of personal representatives which can be noted include power to postpone,[52] power to give receipts,[53] power to deposit documents,[54] power to insure[55] and power to compromise.[56]

Payment of Debts

Duty of personal representatives

It is the duty of personal representatives to pay the debts of the deceased, including unpaid taxes, with due diligence having regard both to the assets in their hands which are properly applicable for the purpose and to all the circumstances of the case.[57] The duty is owed to the beneficiaries as well as to the creditors of the estate and personal representatives will be liable to the beneficiaries for any loss[58]

[50] As substituted by Powers of Attorney Act 1971. See now Enduring Powers of Attorney Act 1985, s.2(8) and Oerton (1986) 130 S.J. on the effect of s.3(3).

[51] s.25(5).

[52] A.E.A. 1925, s.44 in the sense that they are not bound to distribute the estate before the expiration of one year from the death.

[53] Trustee Act 1925, s.14 in respect of any money, securities or other personal property which is payable, transferable, or deliverable to him.

[54] Trustee Act 1925, s.21 in any banking or other safe deposit company for safekeeping.

[55] Trustee Act 1925, s.19(1). It is a rather curious feature of this provision that the power to insure against loss or damage by fire is limited to an amount not exceeding three quarters of the full value of the property. Further this is expressed as a power not a duty. The Law Reform Committee, 23rd Report on the Powers and Duties of Trustees, para. 4.33, have recommended that trustees should be under a duty to insure against any risk in all the circumstances in which an ordinary prudent man of business would insure. Further it has been recommended that the power should extend to the full replacement value of the property.

[56] Trustee Act 1925, s.15 confers on personal representatives acting in good faith power *inter alia* to allow time to a debtor for payment of a debt or to compromise, compound, abandon, submit to arbitration or otherwise settle any debt, account, claim, relating to the deceased's testate or intestate estate. It will be noticed that the protection conferred by the section on personal representatives, "without being responsible for any loss occasioned by any act or thing done by him or them" is confined to actions done in good faith.

[57] *Re Tankard* [1942] Ch. 69.

[58] *e.g.* the costs of proceedings brought by a creditor, *ibid.*

resulting from their failure to pay debts with due diligence when there are properly applicable assets in hand.[59]

The duty extends, however, only to debts which are recoverable by the creditors at law. If a legitimate defence is available,[60] a personal representative should rely upon it[61] although, exceptionally, he has a discretion to pay a debt which has become statute-barred[62] unless the court has declared it to be such[63] or the estate is insolvent.[64]

Protection of personal representatives

A personal representative can, and should, protect himself by advertising for claims against the estate in accordance with the provisions of section 27 of the Trustee Act 1925.[65] The advertisement should require any person having a claim to send particulars of it to the personal representative within a specified time[66] and should be inserted[67] in the *London Gazette*, in a newspaper circulating in the district in which any land of the deceased is situated[68] and, if the deceased resided outside London, in a newspaper circulating in the neighbourhood of the deceased's residence.[69]

If the necessary advertisements are placed and if in addition the personal representative makes such searches as would be made by a prudent purchaser,[70] the personal representative will be at liberty after the expiration of the time specified in the advertisements to distribute the assets, having regard only to the claims of which he has notice.[71] He will not be under any liability in respect of the distributed assets to any person of whose claim he has no notice at all.[72]

Solvent estates

If the estate is solvent[73], the expenses, debts and liabilities will be paid in full and the creditors will not be concerned with the incidence

[59] *Ibid.*
[60] *e.g.* under L.P.A. 1925, s.40.
[61] *Re Rownson* (1885) 29 Ch.D. 358.
[62] *Norton* v. *Frecker* (1737) 1 Atk. 524.
[63] *Midgley* v. *Midgley* (1893) 3 Ch. 282.
[64] A.E.A. 1925, Sched. 1, Pt. 1, para. 2.
[65] Law of Property Amendment Act 1926 (hereinafter also referred to as the "L.P.A.A. 1926"), ss.7, 8(2), Sched. extends the principle to real property.
[66] Being not less than two months from the date of the advertisement; Trustee Act 1925, s.27(1).
[67] Once only unless there are special circumstances; *Re Bracken* (1889) 43 Ch.D. 1.
[68] Trustee Act 1925, ss.27(1), 68(1), (4); L.P.A.A. 1926, ss.7, 8(2), Sched.; A.J.A. 1965, s.17(1), Sched.
[69] *Wood* v. *Weightman* (1872) L.R. 13 Eq. 434.
[70] Trustee Act 1925, s.27(2)(6).
[71] Whether or not by way of a claim made in response to the advertisements; *Re Land Credit Co. of Ireland* (1872) 21 W.R. 135; *Guardian Trust and Executors Co. of New Zealand Ltd.* v. *Public Trustee of New Zealand* [1942] A.C. 115.
[72] Trustee Act 1925, s.27(2); *Re Burke* [1919] 54 L.J. 430.
[73] *i.e.* if the assets are sufficient to pay all the funeral, testamentary and administration expenses, debts and liabilities; *Re Leng* [1895] 1 Ch. 642.

of the debts upon the various parts of the estate. The order in which the assets are applied for payment of the expenses, debts and liabilities is, however, of concern to the beneficiaries and is determined, subject to any contrary directions contained in a will of the deceased,[74] by statutory rules which are based upon the presumed intentions of the deceased.[75] The incidence of unsecured debts is governed by section 34(3) of the Administration of Estates Act 1925 and that of secured debts by section 35 of the same Act.

In the case of unsecured debts section 34(3) provides that, subject to rules of court[76] and to the provisions (if any) contained in the deceased's will, the real and personal estate of the deceased shall be applicable towards the discharge of the funeral, testamentary and administration expenses, debts and liabilities payable thereout in the order mentioned in Part II of the First Schedule to the Act. That order is (1) property undisposed of[77] by will, subject to the retention out of it of a fund sufficient to meet any pecuniary legacies; (2) property included in a residuary gift, subject to the retention out of it of a fund sufficient to meet any pecuniary legacies so far as the fund retained out of the undisposed of property is insufficient to meet them, (3) property the subject of specific gifts for the payment of debts; (4) property charged with the payment of debts; (5) the fund for pecuniary legacies; (6) property specifically devised or bequeathed; and (7) property appointed under a general power. It follows that, if the deceased died wholly intestate, resort may be had to any part or parts of the estate since the deceased will not have disposed of any part of it by will. In the case of a partial intestacy, however, the statutory order will be applicable unless the will of the deceased provides otherwise.

With regard to secured debts section 35 provides that, where a person dies possessed of or entitled to an interest in property[78] which, at the time of his death, is charged with the payment of money, whether by way of legal mortgage, equitable charge[79] or otherwise,[80] including a lien for unpaid purchase money,[81] and the deceased has not by will, deed or other document signified a contrary or other

[74] *e.g.* a gift of residue "subject to" or "after" payment of the expenses and debts; *Re Kempthorne* [1930] 1 Ch. 268, C.A. A direction to pay the expenses and debts followed by a gift of residue will not, however, suffice; *Re Lamb* [1929] 1 Ch. 722; *Re Tong* [1931] 1 Ch. 202, C.A.

[75] A.E.A. 1925, s.34(3), Sched. 1, Pt. II; *ibid.* s.35.

[76] *e.g.* Non-Contentious Probate Rules 1954 (hereinafter also referred to as the "N.-C.P.R. 1954").

[77] Including a lapsed share of residue: *Re Lamb* [1929] 1 Ch. 726; *Re Worthington* [1933] Ch. 771, C.A.; *Re Sanger* [1939] 1 Ch. 238; or of income: *Re Tong* [1931] 1 Ch. 202, C.A.; and a lapsed devise of real estate: *Re Atkinson* [1930] 1 Ch. 47.

[78] "Property" includes a thing in action and any interest in real or personal property: A.E.A. 1925 s.55(1)(xvii).

[79] *Re Turner* [1938] Ch. 593.

[80] *e.g.* see *Re Riddell* [1936] Ch. 747.

[81] *Re Cockcroft* (1833) 24 Ch.D. 94.

intention,[82] the interest so charged is primarily liable for the payment of the charge, and every part of the interest bears, according to its value, a proportionate part of the charge on the whole.

Insolvent estates

If the estate is insolvent, or becomes insolvent when the costs of administration are added to the debts and liabilities of the deceased,[83] or is shown to be insolvent when the capitalised value of an annuity is taken into account,[84] or there is sufficient reason to believe that the estate will turn out to be insolvent,[85] the real and personal estate is to be administered in accordance with the rules set out in Part I of the First Schedule to the Administration of Estates Act 1925.[86] Those rules provide that the funeral, testamentary and administration expenses shall have priority and, subject thereto, that the same rules are to prevail and be observed as may be in force for the time being under the law of bankruptcy with respect to the assets of persons adjudged bankrupt.

The effect of the Insolvency Act 1986 replacing the Bankruptcy Act 1914 is to create four categories of debts which, in order of priority, are preferential debts,[87] ordinary debts,[88] payments of interest on preferential and ordinary debts[89] and deferred debts.[90] All of the debts which fall within the same category are to be paid *pari passu* and preferential debts rank equally with ordinary debts for interest purposes.[91]

Preferential debts comprise,[92]

> (a) debts due to the Inland Revenue in respect of deductions of income tax from emoluments paid during the 12 months preceding the date of death; (b) debts due to the Customs and Excise in respect of value added tax referable to the six months preceding the date of death; (c) sums due in respect of class 1 or class 2 social security contributions during the 12 months preceding the date of death and sums due in respect of Class 4 contributions up to April 5 next before the date of death subject

[82] By words referring expressly or by necessary implication to all or some part of the charge: A.E.A. 1925, s.35(2).
[83] *Re Leng* [1895] 1 Ch. 652, C.A.
[84] *Re Pink* [1927] 1 Ch. 237.
[85] *Re Hopkins* (1881) 18 Ch.D. 370. The court may direct an enquiry whether the estate is insolvent: *Re Smith* (1883) 22 Ch.D 586.
[86] A.E.A. 1925, s.34(1).
[87] Insolvency Act 1986, s.328(1).
[88] *Ibid.* s.328(3).
[89] *Ibid.* s.328(4).
[90] *Ibid.* s.329.
[91] *Ibid.* s.328(4).
[92] *Ibid.* s.386(1) and Sched. 6.

to a maximum of one year's assessment; (d) sums owed in respect of contributions to occupational pension schemes and state scheme premiums; (e) amounts (up to a prescribed maximum) owed by way of remuneration to an employee in respect of the four months preceding the date of death and amounts owed by way of accrued holiday remuneration to a former employee and sums owed in respect of money advanced for and applied towards payments of remuneration or accrued holiday remuneration as aforesaid and amounts (up to a prescribed maximum) ordered to be paid under the Reserve Forces (Safeguard of Employment) Act 1985.

Ordinary debts comprise all debts which do not fall within any of the other categories[93] and interest on both preferential and ordinary debts is payable, if a surplus remains after payment of those debts, at the greater of the rate specified in section 17 of the Judgments Act 1838 at the date of death or the rate applicable to each debt apart from the bankruptcy.[94]

Deferred debts comprises debts owed in respect of credit provided by a person who (whether or not the bankrupt's spouse at the time the credit was provided) was the bankrupt's spouse at the commencement of the bankruptcy and are payable with interest at the rate specified above calculated from the commencement of the bankruptcy.[95]

If, however, a creditor has security for his debt, he is entitled to realise the security and to retain sufficient of the proceeds to discharge the debt regardless of the category in which the debt may lie. In the event of the debt exceeding the value of the security the creditor may realise the security and prove for the balance of his claim[96] or value the security and prove for the balance[97] or surrender the security and prove for the full amount of his claim.[98] The first course will usually be the appropriate one.

It should be noted also that the priorities specified above do not prejudice the effect of any provision of the Insolvency Act itself or of any other Act[99] under which the payment of any debt or the making of any other payment is to have a particular priority or is to be postponed.[1]

Contingent liabilities

In the case of an insolvent estate provision is made for the valuation

[93] *Ibid.* s.328(3).
[94] *Ibid.* s.328.
[95] *Ibid.* s.329.
[96] Bankruptcy Act 1914, Sched.II which is to be replaced by (as yet unpublished) rules under Insolvency Act 1986, s.322(1).
[97] *Ibid.*
[98] *Ibid.*
[99] *e.g.* Friendly Societies Act 1974.
[1] Insolvency Act 1986, s.328(6).

of contingent liabilities by the bankruptcy rules.[2-3] Where the estate is solvent, contingent liabilities do not become debts until the contingency has occurred and creditors of all degrees are entitled to be paid in full without regard to any contingent liabilities.[4-5] Such liabilities cannot be disregarded, however, in the distribution of the net assets among the beneficiaries. Personal representatives will become liable to satisfy any contingent liability which does in fact ripen into a debt[6] and it would be highly imprudent to distribute the net assets of the estate without protecting themselves against such liability.

Statutory protection[7] is afforded to personal representatives in respect of (1) any rent, covenant or agreement reserved by or contained in any lease[8]; (2) any rent, covenant or agreement payable under or contained in any grant made in consideration of a rentcharge[9]; or (3) any indemnity given in respect of any such rent, covenant or agreement.[10] Provided that the personal representative has not entered into possession of the property,[11] has satisfied all liabilities which have accrued, and been claimed up to date and, where necessary, has set aside a fund sufficient to meet any future claim in respect of any fixed sum which the lessee or grantee agreed to expend upon the property, he may convey the property to a purchaser or to a beneficiary who is entitled to it and thereafter will not be liable in respect of any subsequent claim under the lease or grant.[12]

In other cases personal representatives may seek an order of the court to authorise distribution and such an order will provide a complete indemnity provided that full disclosure has been made to the court.[13] Alternatively, an indemnity may be required from a beneficiary as a condition of making an assent in his favour,[14] although any such indemnity may prove worthless if it is not secured by, for example, a mortgage or a bond. The only other means of protection is for a fund to be retained to cover possible future liabilities.

Funeral testamentary and administration expenses

Reasonable funeral expenses are payable out of the estate in priority

[2-3] Insolvency Act 1986, s.322(3),(4).
[4-5] *Eeles* v. *Lambert* [1648] 2 Vern. 101n; *Read* v. *Blunt* (1832) 5 Sim. 567.
[6] *Nector and Sharp* v. *Gennet* (1590) Cro.Eliz. 466; *Hawkins* v. *Day* (1753) Amb. 160; *Pearson* v. *Archdeaken* (1831) 1 Alcock & Nap. 23; *Taylor* v. *Taylor* (1870) L.R. 10 Eq. 477.
[7] Trustee Act 1925 (hereinafter also referred to as the "T.A. 1925"), s.26.
[8] *Ibid.* s.26(1)(*a*).
[9] *Ibid.* s.26(1)(*b*).
[10] *Ibid.* s.26(1)(*c*).
[11] *Re Owers* [1941] Ch. 389.
[12] T. A. 1925, s.26(1)(ii).
[13] *Dean* v. *Allen* (1855) 20 Bear 1; *Waller* v. *Barrett* (1857) 24 Beav. 413; *Smith* v. *Smith* (1861) 1 Drow & Son 384; *Re King* [1907] 1 Ch. 72.
[14] A.E.A. 1925, s.26(10).

to any other debt.[15] This applies to insolvent as well as to solvent estates[16] but, if the estate is insolvent, a stricter test of reasonableness will be applied. In the case of a solvent estate the relevant factors are the deceased's position in life,[17] his religious belief[18] and his expressed wishes. Where the estate is insolvent, the insolvency itself is also a relevant factor, at least if it is known or anticipated,[19] and the expenses will be restricted to those which are necessary.[20] Such expenses will be payable to a personal representative who has incurred liability in contract[21] or in quasi-contract[22] to the undertaker and to any other person who has ordered and paid for the funeral unless he did so gratuitously.[23]

The general costs of administering the estate, so far as they are incidental to the proper performance by the personal representative of his duties,[24] are testamentary expenses[25] and as such are properly payable out of the estate. They include the costs of obtaining the grant,[26] any inheritance tax payable in respect of the deceased's free personal and real estate in the United Kingdom,[27] the expense of collecting and preserving the assets of the estate,[28] the costs of obtaining legal advice as to the administration of the estate or of necessary proceedings,[29] the expense incurred in discharging the debts[30] and the cost of distribution.[31] They do not include the expenses of the execution or administration of trusts arising after the estate has been administered or an assent has been made.[32]

[15] *R.* v. *Wade* (1818) 5 Price 621.
[16] *Re Walter* [1929] 1 Ch. 647.
[17] *Stag* v. *Punter* (1744) 3 Atk. 119; *Re Walter, supra.*
[18] *Gammell* v. *Wilson* [1982] A.C. 27.
[19] *Stag* v. *Punter, supra*; *Edwards* v. *Edwards* (1834) 2 Cro. & M. 612.
[20] *Shelley's Case* (1693) 1 Salk. 296; *Re Wester Wemyss* [1940] Ch. 1.
[21] Because he has ordered the funeral and is liable to pay for it, *Corner* v. *Shaw* (1838) 3 M. & W. 350.
[22] Because no other person is contractually liable to pay the undertaker, *Rogers* v. *Price* (1829) 3 Y. & J. 28; *Corner* v. *Shaw, supra.*
[23] *Colely* v. *Colely* (1866) 12 Jur. (N.S.) 496.
[24] *Sharp* v. *Lush* (1879) 10 Ch.D. 468; *Re Clemow* [1900] 2 Ch. 182.
[25] The expression applies to an intestacy as well as to a testate estate, *Sharp* v. *Lush, supra*; it is prima facie synonymous with "administration expenses," *Re Taylor's Estate* [1969] 2 Ch. 245.
[26] *Re Clemow, supra.*
[27] *Ibid.* (payment of estate duty was "a necessary incident to the obtaining of the grant"); Inheritance Tax Act 1984, s.211. The same principle applies to inheritance tax.
[28] *Peter* v. *Stirling* (1878) 10 Ch.D. 279; *Re Goetze* [1953] Ch. 96; *Re Sebba* [1959] Ch. 166.
[29] *Sharp* v. *Lush, supra*; *Re Buckton* [1907] 2 Ch. 406; *Morrell* v. *Fisher* (1851) 4 De G. & Sm. 422; *Harloe* v. *Harloe* (1875) L.R. 20 Eq. 471; *Re Clarke* [1907] 97 L.T. 707; *Miles* v. *Harrison* (1874) 9 Ch.App. 316; *Re Young* (1881) 44 L.T. 499 C.A.; *Penny* v. *Penny* (1879) 11 Ch.D. 440; *Re Groom* [1897] 2 Ch. 407; *Re Vincent* [1909] 1 Ch. 810; *Re Hall-Dare* [1916] 1 Ch. 272.
[30] Including, for example, the cost of advertising for claimants.
[31] *Sharp* v. *Lush, supra.*
[32] *Re Fitzpatrick* [1952] Ch. 86.

Settlement of the Deceased's Tax Liability

Before the administration of the estate is completed it will be necessary for the personal representatives to make returns to the appropriate inspector of taxes[33] of the income and capital gains of the deceased for the period or periods up to the date of his death and to pay any tax which is outstanding or to reclaim any tax which has been overpaid. He will be personally liable to the Revenue if he distributes all the assets of the estate without having paid, or made provision for, any tax due up to the date of the deceased's death and he will be similarly liable to the beneficiaries if he fails to obtain any repayment of tax to which the estate is entitled. The personal representative should bear in mind also that the amount of any income or capital gains tax which is payable or repayable must be taken into account in any assessment of the estate to inheritance tax.

Income tax

The return to be made by the personal representative will cover the period commencing on April 6 immediately preceding the deceased's death and ending on the date of the death. Additional returns may be required in respect of earlier tax years, if the deceased did not submit returns for those years himself, but an assessment cannot be raised against the personal representative for any tax year which ended more than six years prior to the date of death[34] and any assessment must in any event be made within three years from the end of the tax year in which the death occurred.[35]

It may be noted that full personal reliefs may be set against the deceased's income[36] for the period ending on the date of his death even though the period in question is less than a full tax year. It is also worthy of mention that, if the deceased was a widow whose husband died earlier in the same tax year or in the preceding tax year, a widow's bereavement allowance equivalent to the difference between the single person's allowance and the married man's allowance will be available in addition to the single person's allowance for the tax year in which the deceased widow died and, if her husband died during the preceding tax year and she had not remarried before the end of that year, the preceding year also.[37]

[33] *i.e.* the inspector to whom the deceased made his returns: usually the inspector for the district in which the deceased worked or, if he had retired or was unemployed, had his principal residence.

[34] Taxes Management Act 1970, s.40(2). In the absence of wilful default, neglect (which includes failure to make returns) or fraud on the part of the deceased, an assessment cannot be raised in respect of a tax year which ended more than six years prior to the date of the assessment; *ibid.* s.34(1).

[35] *Ibid.* s.40(1).

[36] Which, if the deceased was a married man, will include the income of his wife unless an application has been made for separate assessments.

[37] Income and Corporation Taxes Act 1970, s.15A; Finance Act 1983, s.15. A similar allowance is of course available to the widow if the deceased was a married man.

Capital gains tax

The return made by the personal representative for the period which ended on the date of the deceased's death and for any earlier period in respect of which the deceased did not submit a return[38] must include particulars of any chargeable gains which accrued to the deceased[39] in the period in question taking into account any allowable losses which were sustained during the same period and any unrelieved losses carried forward from a previous period.

It should be noted, however, that no charge to capital gains tax will arise if the taxable amount for a tax year does not exceed the exempt amount for the year,[40] that allowable and/or unrelieved losses are not to be deducted if and to the extent that their deduction would reduce the taxable amount below the exempt amount for the year[41] and that the full exempt amount is available for the period up to the date of the deceased's death even though that period may be less than a full tax year.

Any losses which remain unrelieved at the date of death cannot be carried forward to be set off against gains realised by the personal representative in the administration of the estate but, contrary to the usual rule, an allowable loss, which was sustained by the deceased during the tax year in which he died and which otherwise would remain unrelieved, may be deducted from any chargeable gains which accrued to the deceased in the three preceding tax years, gains which accrued in a later year being taken before those which accrued in an earlier year.[42]

ADMINISTRATION PROCEEDINGS

If a matter of doubt or difficulty, for example the composition of the class of beneficiary entitled to the estate of the deceased under the intestacy rules, arises in the course of the administration, the personal representative[43] may seek the guidance of the Chancery Division of the High Court of Justice[44] by the issue of an originating summons.[45]

[38] The rules governing the time within which and the tax years in respect of which capital gains tax assessments can be made are the same as those which apply to income tax assessments, Taxes Management Act 1970, s.40(3); *ante* p. 111.

[39] And, if the deceased was a married man, to his wife unless an application has been made for separate assessment, Capital Gains Tax Act 1979, s.45.

[40] *Ibid.* s.5. Currently (1986) £6,300.

[41] *Ibid.* s.5(1B), (1C).

[42] *Ibid.* s.49(2).

[43] Or a beneficiary or creditor: *Peacock* v. *Colling* (1885) 54 L.J.Ch. 743; *Re Hargreaves* (1890) 44 Ch.D. 236; *Re Shorey* [1898] 79 L.T. 349.

[44] Or the county court if the value of the estate does not exceed £30,000, or if the parties agree to extend the jurisdiction of that court: County Courts Act 1984 ss.23(*a*) and 145; County Courts Jurisdiction Ord. 1981 (S.I. 1981 No. 1123); County Courts Act 1984, s.24.

[45] R.S.C., Ord. 85, r. 4.

The personal representative's costs of the proceedings will be payable out of the estate unless he has acted unreasonably or substantially for his own benefit rather than that of the estate.[46] The costs of other parties will usually also be allowed out of the estate.[47]

In other cases, for example where a beneficiary or creditor is dissatisfied with the personal representative's conduct of the administration, an action may be commenced[48] for the estate to be administered by the court. The personal representative, or each personal representative if there is more than one, must be made a party to the action[49] and, if an order for administration is made, the personal representative or representatives will be unable to exercise any of their powers without having first obtained the approval of the court.[50] The costs thus incurred are likely to be substantial. However, such an order will not usually be made unless the court considers that the issue between the parties cannot be resolved in any other way.[51] In many instances a limited order may be sufficient.[52]

A less drastic course in a case where a beneficiary is not satisfied with the conduct of the administration is that of an application to the Chancery Division for the appointment of a judicial trustee[53] to act jointly with or even in place of the personal representatives.[54] A judicial trustee, unlike a personal representative when a full administration order has been made, can exercise his powers without the court's prior approval.[55] The expense to the estate will be less than if the entire administration of the estate were to be carried out under the direction of the court, although the court may assign remuneration to a judicial trustee.[56] Alternatively, an application may be made by a beneficiary or by a personal representative for the exercise of the court's discretion to appoint a substituted personal representative in place of the existing representative or representatives or, if there are two or more existing representatives, to terminate the appointment of one or more, but not all of them.[57] The appointment, if made, will be

[46] *Ibid.* Ord. 62, r. 6(2).
[47] *Re Buckton* [1907] 2 Ch. 406.
[48] By writ or originating summons: R.S.C., Ord. 5, r. 1; *ibid.*, Ord. 85, r. 4.
[49] *Ibid.* r. 3(1).
[50] *Re Viscount Furness* [1943] Ch. 415; *Minors* v. *Battison* (1876) 1 App.Cas. 428.
[51] R.S.C., Ord. 85, r. 5(1).
[52] *e.g.* in a case where a beneficiary alleges that no or insufficient accounts have been provided by the personal representative, an order that the action be stayed for a fixed period and that proper accounts be provided by the personal representative within that time: *ibid.* r. 5(2).
[53] Judicial Trustees Act 1896, ss.1, 2 (as amended by A.J.A. 1982, s.57); Judicial Trustee Rules 1972 (S.I. 1972 No. 1096).
[54] *Ibid.*; *Re Ratcliff* [1898] 2 Ch. 352.
[55] Judicial Trustees Act 1896, ss.1(3), (4).
[56] *Ibid.* s.1(5); Judicial Trustee Rules 1972, *supra*, r. 16; *Re Ratcliff*, *supra*.
[57] A.J.A. 1985, s.50(1).

effective from its date and the person appointed may be authorised by the court to charge remuneration for his services on such terms as the court may think fit.[58]

[58] *Ibid.* s.50(2), (3).

CHAPTER 7

TAXATION OF THE ESTATE

This chapter is concerned with the taxation of income and of capital gains arising during the administration of the estate and with the effect on the inheritance tax liability in respect of the estate of certain events which may occur during the administration. It is not concerned with the personal liability of the deceased to income or any other tax or with the assessment of the amount of inheritance tax payable by reason of the death. The action to be taken by an administrator to deal with the deceased's personal tax liability has been considered in the previous chapter[1] and the procedure for the assessment of the inheritance tax liability in respect of the estate was mentioned in Chapter 4.[2]

It is not intended to discuss the detailed rules and principles of the law relating to income tax, capital gains tax and capital transfer tax, which are beyond the scope of this work. In this connection reference should be made to the relevant standard texts.[3]

INCOME TAX

General principles

The charging provisions of the Income Tax Acts apply during the administration of an estate as at other times so that, if a receipt would be subject to income tax in the hands of an individual, it will be taxable in the hands of an administrator. There are, however, a number of provisions which apply only during the "administration period." This is the period from the date of the death of the deceased until the date of completion of the administration of the estate,[4] which is when the residue of the estate has been ascertained and is available for distribution.[5]

Although an administrator is, or two or more joint administrators are, considered to be a separate taxpayer, there is no entitlement to personal reliefs even if the deceased's personal reliefs have not been fully used up in the period prior to his death. Such reliefs are available only to "individuals" and an administrator is not an individual for income tax purposes. Conversely, and for the same reason, adminis-

[1] *Ante*, p. 111.
[2] *Ante*, p. 63.
[3] *e.g. British Tax Encyclopedia, Simon's Taxes* (3rd ed.) and *Dymond's Capital Transfer Tax* (3rd ed.).
[4] Income and Corporation Taxes Act 1970, s.426.
[5] *Lilley* v. *Public Trustee of the Dominion of New Zealand* [1981] A.C. 839.

trators are not liable to income tax at the higher rates.[6] It follows that administrators are liable to tax at the basic rate on the whole of the income which they receive subject only to the availability of non-personal reliefs.

Interest

The interest paid on money borrowed for the purpose of paying inheritance tax prior to the issue of a grant of administration is deductible from the income of the estate in computing the income tax liability.[7]

Trading

The profits of a business which was owned by the deceased and which is carried on by an administrator of the deceased's estate with a view to its disposal as a going concern are taxable in the ordinary way. If, however, the administrator merely disposes of the assets of the business and does so quickly without trading, no income tax will be payable.[8]

Statutory legacies

A surviving spouse of the deceased is entitled to a statutory legacy[9] and such a legacy carries interest[10] from the date of the death of the deceased until the date of payment. The amount of the interest is paid without deduction of tax by the administrator and is subject to income tax in the hands of the spouse to the extent (if at all) that it exceeds the income of the estate.

Position of residuary beneficiaries

If the deceased is survived by a spouse and by a child or children and if the estate is sufficiently large, the spouse will be entitled, as will be seen,[11] to a life interest in one-half of the residue in addition to the appropriate statutory legacy and the personal chattels. In such a case the income of the share of the residue in which the life interest subsists is allocated to the spouse as if it had accrued due from day to day during the administration period.[12] The income of the remaining half of the residue (or of the whole of the residue if there is no life interest) is allocated to the beneficiaries according to the year of assessment in

[6] *I.R.C.* v. *Countess of Longford* [1928] A.C. 252.
[7] Finance Act 1974, Sched. 1.
[8] *I.R.C.* v. *Nelson* [1939] 22 T.C. 716, but see *J. and R. O'Kane & Co.* v. *I.R.C.* [1920] 12 T.C. 303.
[9] *Post*, Chap. 11.
[10] At 6 per cent., Intestate Succession (Interest and Capitalisation) Order 1977 (Amendment) Order 1983.
[11] *Post*, Chap. 11.
[12] Income and Corporation Taxes Act 1970, s.426.

which it arises.[13] All income of the estate will, of course, have suffered income tax at the basic rate in the hands of the administrator and each beneficiary will be liable to higher rates of tax, or will be entitled to a repayment of tax, if his or her total income[14] is at an appropriate level.

Capital Gains Tax

Acquisition of assets by administrators

All assets of which the deceased was competent to dispose at the date of his death are deemed to have been acquired by the administrator at their market value at that time.[15] This includes any share of the deceased in jointly-owned property[16] but not property over which the deceased had a power of appointment. As a rule the market value of an asset which forms part of the deceased's estate will be the value which is determined for purposes of inheritance tax[17] but disregarding any inheritance tax relief.[18] Thus, if shares or securities which are quoted on a stock exchange at the date of the death of the deceased or holdings in authorised unit trusts are sold in the course of the administration of the estate within twelve months from the death at a price which is less than their market value at the date of the deceased's death, the sale price can be subsisted for the value at the date of death for inheritance tax purposes[19] and likewise for the purposes of capital gains tax.[20] It should be noted, however, that, although the proceeds of an interest in land which is sold within three years of the date of the deceased's death can be substituted for the market value of the interest at the date of death for inheritance tax purposes,[21] no alteration can be made for capital gains tax purposes.[22]

Disposal of assets by administrators

If an asset is transferred to a beneficiary or a beneficiary becomes absolutely entitled to it, it is deemed to be acquired by the beneficiary at its market value at the date of the death of the deceased[23] so that no liability to capital gains tax can arise in respect of any actual increase in the value of the asset during the intervening period. If, however, an asset is sold in the course of the administration of the estate at a price which is more or less than its market value at the date of the

[13] *Ibid.* s.427.
[14] Including the grossed-up amount of the income derived from the estate.
[15] Capital Gains Tax Act 1979, s.49(1)(*a*).
[16] *Ibid.* s.49(10).
[17] *Ibid.* s.153.
[18] *e.g.* business or agricultural property relief; Inheritance Tax Act 1984, ss.104 and 115–124.
[19] *Post*, p. 118.
[20] *Ibid.* s.187.
[21] *Post*, p. 119.
[22] *Ibid.* ss.190–198.
[23] Finance Act 1982, ss.86–89 and Sched. 13.

deceased's death, a taxable gain or loss will arise subject to the availability and extent of an indexation allowance. Allowable losses can only be relieved by deduction from chargeable gains accruing from the sale of other assets by the administrator in the same or a subsequent year of assessment. Administrators are, however, entitled for the year of assessment in which the deceased died and for the two subsequent years of assessment to the same annual exemption as individuals.[24] In each of those three years, therefore, a capital gains tax liability will arise only if and to the extent that the chargeable gains less the allowable losses exceed the amount of the annual exemption.[25]

Treatment of expenses

If an asset is transferred to a beneficiary, the administrator may deduct the cost of the transfer from the amount of any chargeable gains accruing to him on the sale of other assets and, if this deduction is not claimed, the beneficiary may add the cost of the transfer to the value at which he is deemed to have acquired the asset with the result that there will be an equivalent reduction in the amount of any gain accruing to the beneficiary on a subsequent disposal.[26]

In the case of the sale of an asset, the administrator can deduct from the amount of any chargeable gain arising from the sale the expenses of the sale itself,[27] the amount of any expenditure wholly and exclusively incurred for the purposes of enhancing its value[28] and a proportion of the cost of administering the estate.[29] If the value of the gross estate does not exceed £400,000 a scale is applied to ascertain the amount of the allowable costs[30] except in the case of quoted shares or securities, to which a flat rate deduction not exceeding £5 per transaction is applied unless the circumstances are exceptional.[31] If the gross estate exceeds £400,000 in value, the amount of the allowable costs is determined by negotiation with the Inland Revenue.

Inheritance Tax

If certain assets are sold by the administrator within a specified period after the date of the deceased's death at a price which is less than their market value at the date of death, the sale price can be substituted for the market value at death subject to specified

[24] Capital Gains Tax Act 1979, s.5(6).

[25] Currently £6,300, Capital Gains Tax (Annual Exempt Amount) Order 1986 (S.I. 1986 No. 528).

[26] Capital Gains Tax Act 1979, s.47(1).

[27] *Ibid.* s.32(2).

[28] *Ibid.* s.32(1)(*b*).

[29] *e.g.* the legal costs of obtaining the grant of administration and of the valuation of the estate for inheritance tax purposes; *I.R.C.* v. *Executors of Dr. Richards* [1971] 1 All E.R. 785, H.L.

[30] SP 7/81, [1981] L. S. Gaz. 1112.

[31] [1975] L.S.Gaz. 876.

conditions.[32] The assets in question are "qualifying investments" and interests in land.

Qualifying investments

If quoted shares or securities or holdings in an authorised unit trust which were held by the deceased immediately before his death are sold within the period of twelve months immediately following his death, the administrator can substitute the sale price[33] for the market value at the date of death if he does not purchase other qualifying investments during the period from the date of the deceased's death until the expiry of two months after the date of the last sale.[34]

Interests in land

The position is similar if an interest in land is sold within the period of three years immediately following the date of the deceased's death[35] provided that the sale price does not differ from the market value at the date of death by more than £1,000 or 5 per cent. of the value of the death, whichever is the lower figure[36] and that the sale is not to a beneficiary or to a person connected with a beneficiary.[37]

Post–Mortem Variations

The effect of the rules of intestate succession may be varied after the death of the deceased by the agreement of all the beneficiaries concerned, by the disclaimer by a particular beneficiary of his entitlement, by an order of the court in accordance with the provisions of the Inheritance (Provision for Family and Dependants) Act 1975 or by the election of a surviving spouse to commute the life interest to which he or she may be entitled under the rules.[38] Any such variation will or may affect the taxation of the estate.

Income tax

Both a variation of the beneficial interests by agreement and a disclaimer of a beneficial interest take effect for income tax purposes on the date of execution[39] so that the liability to tax on the income arising prior to the date of the variation or disclaimer is not affected. It should be borne in mind also that, if there is an element of bounty, a

[32] Inheritance Tax Act, ss.178–189 and 190–198.
[33] Or, if the sale was made at an undervalue, the market value at the time of the sale, *ibid.* s.179(1). The expenses of the sale are not taken into account; *ibid.* s.178(5).
[34] *Ibid.* s.180(1).
[35] The date of the contract for sale or, in the case of sale resulting from the exercise of an option granted not more than six months previously, the date of the grant of the option being the operative date, *ibid.* s.198.
[36] *Ibid.* s.191(2).
[37] *Ibid.* s.191(3).
[38] *Post*, Chaps. 17 and 18.
[39] *Waddington* v. *O'Callaghan* [1931] 16 T.C. 187.

variation, but not a disclaimer, will be a "settlement" for the purposes of the Income and Corporation Taxes Act 1970 with the result that, if, for example, a variation is made for the benefit of a minor unmarried child of one of the parties, the income which is transferred from the parent to the child will be deemed to remain the income of the parent for tax purposes.

Orders made under the provisions of the Inheritance (Provision for Family and Dependants) Act 1975 also take effect for income tax purposes from the date on which they are made, as do elections by surviving spouses to commute their residuary life interests under the intestacy rules. In neither case, however, will there be a "settlement" for income tax purposes as no element of bounty will be present.[40]

Capital gains tax

The parties to a variation of the beneficial interests can elect in writing that the variation shall be regarded as having been effected by the intestacy rules so that it will not constitute a disposal for capital gains tax purposes provided that the variation is made within the two years immediately following the date of the deceased's death and that notice of the election is given to the Inland Revenue within six months from the date of the variation.[41] There are, however, no similar provisions in relation to an order under the Inheritance (Provision for Family and Dependants) Act 1975 or an election by a surviving spouse to commute a life interest. In the case of a disclaimer no election is required as it is regarded as taking effect from the date of death.

The relief is not in any case of much practical value because it will apply only to gains which have accrued since the date of death. Nevertheless, it will usually be advisable to make the election if only to avoid the need for valuation.

Inheritance tax

As with capital gains tax the persons affected, or who may be affected, by a variation can elect in writing that the variation shall be regarded as having been effected by the intestacy rules so that it will not constitute a transfer of value for inheritance tax purposes provided that the variation is made within the two years immediately following the date of the deceased's death, that the election is made by all the affected persons[42] and that notice of it is given to the Inland Revenue within six months from the date of the variation.[43]

[40] *Sed quaere* if a claim under the Inheritance (Provision for Family and Dependants) Act 1975 is compromised in favour of the minor unmarried child of a statutory beneficiary.

[41] Capital Gains Tax Act 1979, s.49(6).

[42] Including, if the variation results in additional tax becoming payable, the personal representatives.

[43] Inheritance Tax Act 1984, s.142.

The relief is a valuable one because it can be used, for example, to redirect the estate of the deceased, or a larger part of it, to a surviving spouse or to grandchildren with a consequent saving of inheritance tax either immediately or in the future. It should be noted, however, that the Capital Taxes Office adopted the position[44] that a deed which does not state expressly[44a] that it is varying the dispositions of the property of the deceased comprised in his estate immediately prior to his death, or is operating as a disclaimer of the benefit of those dispositions, does not operate as a variation or disclaimer for the purpose of relief under section 142.[45] The matter has since been reviewed[45a] but prudence must dictate compliance with the Revenue's earlier interpretation of the requirements for the grant of relief.

There is no requirement for an election to be made in respect of an order under the Inheritance (Provision for Family and Dependants) Act 1975 but it is in any event regarded for inheritance tax purposes as if it had been effected by the intestacy rules so that it does not constitute a transfer of value.[46] Similar provisions apply to an election by a surviving spouse to commute a life interest[47] and in the case of a disclaimer the position is the same as that which obtains in respect of capital gains tax.

Stamp duty

All qualifying deeds are liable only to a fixed duty of 50 pence although an adjudication stamp is also required.[48]

[44] [1984] L.S. Gaz. 3058.
[44a] In the body of the deed and not merely in the recitals!
[45] So that, for example, the precedent contained in the additional forms section of the service volume of the *Encyclopaedia of Forms & Precedents* on p. 5(47) was not accepted as valid.
[45a] [1985] L.S. Gaz. 1454.
[46] Inheritance Tax Act 1984, s.146.
[47] *Ibid.* s.145.
[48] Finance Act 1985, s.84.

CHAPTER 8

THE DUTIES AND POWERS OF A PERSONAL REPRESENTATIVE

INTRODUCTION

The duties of an administrator to collect and get in the estate, to pay the due debts and expenses and to pay any tax due on the estate have been considered in an earlier Chapter. It is now necessary to consider the position and powers of a personal representative *vis-à-vis* the beneficial interests in the residuary estate. Lord Evershed M.R. stated in *Harvell* v. *Foster*[1] that the duties of an administrator were to pay the funeral and testamentary expenses and debts and legacies (if any) and, where immediate distribution of the estate was not possible owing to the infancy of the person beneficially entitled, to retain the net residue in trust for the infant. The question of the capacity in which the personal representative holds and deals with the residuary estate will also need to be considered.

POWERS OF A PERSONAL REPRESENTATIVE

Powers relating to assets

The powers of a personal representative relating to the collection and realisation of assets have been considered above in Chapter 6.

Powers relating to the beneficial interest

Power to act severally

Trustees must act jointly in the exercise of their powers[2] but personal representatives can act severally with reference to personal assets although they must act jointly to effect a sale of realty.[3] The power of one administrator to act alone and to bind his fellow administrator is not entirely settled but in the most recent case of *Fountain Forestry* v. *Edwards*[4] it was held that one of two administra-

[1] [1954] 2 Q.B. 367 at p. 383.

[2] See, for example, Pettit, *Equity and the Law of Trusts*, 5th ed. p. 316, 317.

[3] Administration of Estates Act 1925 (hereinafter also referred to as the "A.E.A. 1925"), s.2(2).

[4] [1975] Ch. l. Earlier authorities are *Hudson* v. *Hudson* (1737) 1 Atk. 460 (which denied that one administrator acting alone could bind the other); *Jacomb* v. *Harwood* (1751) 2 Ves.Sen. 265 (where the earlier case was not followed and the position of administrators was regarded as analogous to that of executors); *Warwick* v. *Greville* (1809) 1 Phill. 123; *Stanley* v *Bernes* (1828) 1 Hag.Ecc. 221 and *Smith* v. *Everett* (1859) 29 L.J.Ch. 236 where Romilly M.R. seemed to accept that administrators had the same power as executors to act alone.

tors could enter into a binding contract to sell real estate. Brightman J. commented[5]:

> "It appears to me that there is no decisive authority which answers the question whether one administrator, acting without his co-administrator, has the same power of disposition as an executor acting without the concurrence of his co-executor. But having regard to the statement of Romilly M.R.[6] that the question was settled by 1859 in favour of the administrator who acts alone, I am content to assume for present purposes that the view which he expressed was a correct interpretation of the law with the result that an administrator has power, at the present day, to bind the intestate's estate by his own act without the concurrence of his co-administrator."

Remuneration

The general principle is that an administrator "... cannot charge for work done as administrator but must give his services gratuitously."[7] In this respect personal representatives are analogous to trustees and as in the case of trustees the general rule is subject to exceptions. A testator may authorise an executor to charge by means of a properly drawn charging clause. Administrators, however, will normally have the benefit of no such clause and will have to rely either on the inherent jurisdiction of the court to authorise remuneration or on the consent of the beneficiaries. The former power has been extensively reviewed recently by the Court of Appeal in *Re Duke of Norfolk's Settlement Trusts*[8] to which reference should be made. The beneficiaries can only consent according to the usual rule that they are all *sui juris* and collectively absolutely entitled to the estate.[9] Additionally a solicitor personal representative can charge for work done in connection with litigation under the rule in *Cradock* v. *Piper*.[10] A personal representative is, of course, entitled to an indemnity in respect of expenses properly incurred in administering the estate.[11]

The duration of the office

Appointment to the office of administrator can be made only by the

[5] At p. 285.
[6] In *Smith* v. *Everett*, *supra*, at p. 239, 240.
[7] *per* Upjohn J. in *Re Worthington* [1954] 1 W.L.R. 526 at p. 527; *Re Barbour's Settlement Trusts* [1974] 1 W.L.R. 1198; *Re Codd (decd.)* [1975] 1 W.L.R. 1139; *Re Duke of Norfolk's Settlement Trusts* [1981] 3 W.L.R. 455 where these and many earlier authorities are reviewed.
[8] *Supra*; where the court ordered the payment of increased remuneration. Additionally there is power in the Trustee Act 1925 s.42 to authorise remuneration for a corporation where the court appoints the corporation to be a personal representative.
[9] Analogous to the principle in *Saunders* v. *Vautier* (1841) Cr. & Ph. 240.
[10] (1850) 1 Mac. & G. 664, as to which see, *e.g.* Pettit, *Equity and the Law of Trusts*, 5th ed., p. 372.
[11] See A.E.A. 1925 s.27(1).

court and once appointed an administrator retains the office for the remainder of his life,[12] irrespective of whether he continues to hold any property in that capacity, unless the grant is expressly limited in duration or is revoked.[13] Accordingly he retains the capacity after the estate has been administered to act on behalf of the estate in legal proceedings and to be sued as administrator.[14] He may also deal with any assets which subsequently accrue to the estate. However, there is no transmission of the office on the death of a sole or surviving administrator. If any part of the estate remains unadministered at that time, it will be necessary for a new appointment to be made by a grant of letters of administration *de bonis non administratis.*[15]

Powers of maintenance and advancement

The statutory power of advancement and the statutory provisions which relate to maintenance and accumulation of surplus income apply to the statutory trusts which arise on intestacy.[16] These powers, contained in section 30 and section 31 of the Trustee Act 1925, are well documented elsewhere and need not be considered here.[17]

Power to appoint trustees of infant's property

There is a limited power to appoint trustees in the rare circumstance of a minor being absolutely entitled on intestacy.[18] The effect of the appointment is to discharge the personal representatives from any further liability in respect of such property.[19]

Power to permit possession

A personal representative can permit a person entitled to property to go into possession of it before assent without prejudice either to the right of the personal representative to take and resume possession or to his power to convey the land as if he were in possession of it.[20]

Powers in respect of interests of the surviving spouse on intestacy

Section 48 of the Administration of Estates Act 1925 confers two powers. First, a power is given to raise the fixed net sum or any part of it, and the interest on it, on the security of the whole or any part of the

[12] *Attenborough* v. *Soloman* [1913] A.C. 76; *Harvell* v. *Foster* [1954] 2 Q.B. 367.

[13] See *ante* pp. 75 *et seq.*

[14] *Harvell* v. *Foster, supra.*

[15] See *ante* pp. 74 *et seq.* The chain of representation provided by A.E.A. 1925 s.7 is broken by an intestacy.

[16] A.E.A. 1925 s.47(1)(ii).

[17] See, for example, Pettit, *Equity and the Law of Trusts*, 5th ed., pp. 392 *et seq.*

[18] A.E.A. 1925 s.42(1). This situation will only arise on intestacy if the surviving spouse is an infant or under the statutory trusts where the infant is married; see *post.*

[19] This does not confer a general power on personal representatives to appoint trustees; for the circumstances in which this can be done see *ante.*

[20] Administration of Estates Act 1925 s.43, see *post* with reference to the matrimonial home.

residuary estate of the intestate.[21] Secondly, power is conferred to raise the capital sum, if any, required for the purchase or redemption of the life interest of the spouse or any part thereof.[22]

Power of appropriation

The right of the surviving spouse to require appropriation of the matrimonial home in satisfaction of absolute interests under the intestacy, will be discussed in detail later.[23] The general power to appropriate contained in section 41 of the Administration of Estates Act 1925 can be considered here.[24] The section provides as follows:

> "The personal representative may appropriate any part of the real or personal estate, including things in action, of the deceased in the actual condition or state of investment thereof at the time of appropriation in or towards satisfaction of any legacy bequeathed by the deceased, or of any other interest or share in his property, whether settled or not, as to the personal representative may seem just and reasonable, according to the respective rights of the persons interested in the property of the deceased."[25]

In general an appropriation can only take effect with the consent of the person to be benefited. If the appropriation is made for the benefit of a person absolutely and beneficially entitled in possession, then he consents on his own behalf.[26] If it is made in respect of any settled legacy, share or interest, then the appropriation must be with the consent of the trustee (not being also the personal representative).[27]

If the person entitled to the income in such a case is of full age, then he can consent.[28] It is provided that, if there is no trustee of a settled share other than the personal representative and no person of full age and capacity entitled to the income, no consent is required.[29] The personal representatives are empowered to ascertain and fix the value of the respective parts of the estate and may employ a valuer for this

[21] Other than the personal chattels; so far as the estate may be sufficient for the purpose or the fixed net sum and interest may not have been satisfied by an appropriation under s.41; *ibid.*

[22] s.48(1)(*b*); not satisfied by the application for that purpose of any part of the residuary estate of the intestate; *ibid.* The costs of either transaction can also be raised in like manner; *ibid.*

[23] *See post*, Chap. 12 and see Intestates' Estates Act 1952, 2nd Sched.

[24] s.41 is expressed to apply to intestacy, see sub-section (9).

[25] A *power* not a *right*, see Pennycuick V.-C. in *Robinson* v. *Collins* [1975] 1 W.L.R. 309.

[26] s.41(1)(ii)(*a*).

[27] s.41(1)(ii)(*b*).

[28] s.41(1)(ii)(*b*). Where an infant or a person suffering from mental disorder within the meaning of the Mental Health Act 1983 is involved then basically, the parent or receiver consents on his behalf; *ibid.*

[29] s.41(1)(v). In this case the appropriation can only be of authorised investments; *ibid.*

purpose.[30] As one might expect, the personal representatives in exercising this power are directed to have regard to the rights of any other person who is, or may be, a beneficiary,[31] but subject thereto the appropriation binds all persons interested in the estate whose consent is not required.[32] In intestate estates the power of appropriation will be particularly relevant to satisfy the spouse's entitlement to the fixed net sum.[33]

An appropriation with consent will attract *ad valorem* stamp duty[34] and the express provision in many wills dispensing with consent for this reason, will not assist in cases of total intestacy. However, there is no stamp duty to pay where the surviving spouse exercises the right to require appropriation of the matrimonial home under the Second Schedule to the Intestates' Estates Act 1952.[35]

Power to invest

The Trustee Investments Act 1961 confers specific powers of investment on trustees and, in the absence of any enlargement by will, personal representatives have similar powers. The Act is fully discussed in books on trusts[36] and need not be given further consideration here. It may be noted, however, that the Trustee Act confers power to open and operate a bank account and to pay money into a bank to a deposit or other account.[37] Additionally with specific reference to intestacy, section 33(3) of the Administration of Estates Act 1925 confers power to invest the residue of the money subject to the statutory trust for sale, "during the minority of any beneficiary or the subsistence of any life interest and pending the distribution of the whole or any part of the estate of the deceased. . . . " Such money may be invested in any investment for the time being authorised by statute for the investment of trust money, with power at the discretion of the personal representatives to change such investments for others of a like nature.[38] The income of the intestate estate which is not required for the purposes of administration is treated and applied as income however such estate is invested.[39] It is submitted that the rule in *Howe*

[30] s.41(3). The value of the appropriated property is ascertained at the date of the appropriation; *Robinson* v. *Collins* [1975] 1 W.L.R. 309 a case on the right of appropriation of the matrimonial home under the Second Schedule to the Intestates' Estates Act 1952, discussed *post*. p. 228.

[31] s.41(5).

[32] s.41(4).

[33] See *post*; Chap. 11.

[34] See *Jopling* v. *I.R.C.* [1940] 2 K.B. 282.

[35] See *post*.

[36] See for example, Pettit, *Equity and the Law of Trusts*, 5th ed., pp. 333 *et seq.*

[37] 1925 Act, s.11(1).

[38] A.E.A. 1925, s.33(3).

[39] s.33(5), *ibid.*

v. *Earl of Dartmouth*[40] is excluded and any necessary apportionment may be made between tenant for life and remainderman.[41]

Assents

Statutory power

An assent in relation to personal property is regarded merely as an indication that the personal representatives do not require that property for the purposes of administration. Accordingly there is no general requirement for a formal assent at all, although it will be appreciated that particular forms of personalty, such as shares, require a particular formality to pass title. Such special property aside, an assent may be made by informal words or inferred from conduct; indeed the completion of the administration itself might be sufficient to raise that inference.[42] However, assents are essential[43] with respect to real property and the term is often employed to indicate the document which passes legal title to land. It is quite clear that an administrator administering a totally intestate estate has such power. Section 36(1) of the Administration of Estates Act 1925 provides:

> "A personal representative may assent to the vesting, in any person who (whether by devise, bequest, devolution, appropriation or otherwise) may be entitled thereto, either beneficially or as a trustee or personal representative, of any estate or interest in real estate to which the testator or intestate was entitled or over which he exercised a general power of appointment by his will, including the statutory power to dispose of entailed interests, and which devolved upon the personal representative."[44]

The reference to "devolution" would seem to refer to the succession on intestacy and section 36(1) expressly states that the provision applies to both testators and intestates.[45]

Such a document operates to vest in the beneficiary the estate to which the assent relates and, unless the contrary intention appears,

[40] (1802) 7 Ves. 137; see *Re Sullivan* [1930] 1 Ch. 84; *Re Fisher* [1943] Ch. 377.

[41] s.33(5), *ibid.*; see discussion *ante*, p. 84.

[42] *Attenborough* v. *Soloman* [1913] A.C. 76. Indeed it is often stated that an administrator dealing with a totally intestate estate has no power to assent to the passing of pure personalty. William, *Law Relating to Assents* (1947) p. 96, is invariably cited as authority for this proposition for which there does not seem to be specific case law authority.

[43] A deed is normally required to transfer a legal estate, Law of Property Act 1925 (hereinafter also referred to as the "L.P.A. 1925"), s.52(1) but an assent can pass title by written document not under seal.

[44] It could be argued that the statutory trust for sale on intestacy effects a conversion of the realty into personalty and that thus a formal assent is not necessary on intestacy. This is negated by the legislation which clearly renders an assent necessary in cases of intestacy, see s.36(12) and s.36(2).

[45] Although of course the latter could be referring to partial intestacies; see definition of "intestate" s.55(vi).

relates back to the death of deceased.[46] In order to pass a legal estate in land the following formalities are required: the document must be in writing, it must be signed by the personal representative and it must name the person in whose favour it is given.[47] An equitable interest may be passed orally or in writing without formality.[48]

A purchaser dealing with a personal representative will require a written statement to the effect that there has been no previous assent or conveyance of a legal estate in the property in question.[49] If he obtains such an assurance and if no notice of a previous assent or conveyance is indorsed on, or annexed to, the probate or the letters of administration, the purchaser will take a good title.[50] In the same way a purchaser from a person in whose favour an assent was made can assume that such person was entitled to have the legal estate conveyed to him unless notice of a previous assent or conveyance affecting that title has been indorsed on, or annexed to, the probate or letters of administration.[51] However, an assent or conveyance does not prejudice the right of the personal representative or any other person to trace and recover the asset except against a purchaser of the legal estate.[52]

A personal representative who is not entirely convinced that all obligations of the estate have been discharged may require security for the discharge of any duties, debts or liabilities as a condition of giving the assent.[53] Further protection is offered in section 36(9) which enables the personal representative to be indemnified out of the property conveyed in respect of duties debts or liabilities of the estate. This right of indemnity does not apply against a purchaser of a legal estate in the property.[54]

CAPACITY OF THE PERSONAL REPRESENTATIVES

Personal representative or trustee?

The problems which will be explored briefly in this section are familiar ones, namely: at what time, if at all, does a personal representative hold the deceased's estate as a trustee and is a formal assent in his own favour necessary to mark this transaction? These

[46] s.36(2).

[47] s.36(4). Any person in whose favour an assent or conveyance of a legal estate has been made can require that notice of the assent or conveyance be written or indorsed on or permanently annexed to the probate or the letters of administration, s.36(5).

[48] See *ibid.*

[49] s.36(6) which only protects purchasers not beneficiaries.

[50] *See ibid.* A conveyance of a legal estate by a personal representative to a purchaser is not invalidated by reason only that the purchaser may have notice that all the debts, expenses etc. have been discharged or provided for; s.36(8).

[51] s.36(7).

[52] s.36(9).

[53] s.36(10). Note also the power under s.43, discussed above to allow a beneficiary into possession before making a formal assent.

[54] s.36(9).

questions have been considered fully by the textbook writers[55] and commentators[56] and, so far as the discussion concerns wills, need not be repeated here. The position on intestacy must however be noted.

Some initial propositions can be regarded as axiomatic and can be stated without the necessity for further comment. First, a personal representative once appointed holds office for life.[57] Secondly, a person can hold simultaneously the two offices of personal representative and trustee but he cannot hold the same property in both capacities at the same time.[58] Thirdly, the offices of personal representative and trustee are different and must be distinguished.[59] Fourthly, in some cases of intestacy it becomes necessary at some stage for the residuary estate to be held on trust for the beneficiaries.[60] Fifthly, although a trustee can appoint a new trustee under section 36 of the Trustee Act 1925, the statutory power does not extend to personal representatives.[61] The power vested in personal representatives to appoint new trustees is contained in section 42 of the Administration of Estates Act 1925 and is limited to cases where "an infant is absolutely entitled . . . on the intestacy. . . . " As such it is of little assistance in cases of intestacy because under the statutory trusts minor issue are only entitled contingently on attaining the age of eighteen or on marriage under that age.[62] Thus the power to appoint trustees under section 42 will only apply in cases of intestacy where the minor is absolutely entitled as the surviving spouse or where there is no preceding life interest and the child has married under the age of eighteen.[63]

In the usual case where infant children are beneficially entitled on intestacy, the statutory trusts will come into effect and the necessity for trustees to hold the property on such trusts will arise. The question is, therefore, whether the personal representatives automatically become trustees for this purpose at some stage, so that they can hold the property themselves in that capacity or so that they can appoint new trustees in their place by virtue of the power of section 36 of the Trustee Act. It is in this context, *i.e.* the power of the persons appointed initially as personal representatives to appoint new trustees, that the issues of whether, and at what time, personal representatives become trustees, have arisen. The question of the necessity for an assent in their own favour to mark a change of

[55] See *e.g.* Parry and Clark, *The Law of Succession*, 8th ed., pp. 369–373.

[56] See Ryder 29 C.L.P. pp. 60–73.

[57] See Parry and Clark, *op. cit.* 367; *Harvell* v. *Foster* [1954] 2 Q.B. 367, at p. 383.

[58] See Mellows, *op. cit.* p. 277. But see *Harvell* v. *Foster, supra*, at pp. 379–380 and 382–383.

[59] See Parry and Clark, *op. cit.* pp. 367, 368; Mellows, *op. cit.* pp. 277, 278.

[60] See ss.46, 47 A.E.A. 1925, *i.e.* where the statutory trusts are applicable.

[61] Mellows, *op. cit.* p. 278.

[62] s.47(1).

[63] See Parry and Clark, *op. cit.* p. 350.

capacity is closely related. If personal representatives become trustees for the purpose of appointing new trustees automatically, it would seem to follow that the estate must effectively have been vested in them in that capacity. However, the decision in *Re King's Will Trusts*[64] casts doubt on this proposition.

Personal representatives on intestacy

The questions whether, and at what time, a personal representative becomes also a trustee of the estate have been canvassed in cases concerning both testate and intestate succession. It is submitted that the two situations should be kept distinct and that cases on wills are not necessarily relevant to intestacies. This is because the statutory provisions of the 1925 Administration of Estates Act apply on an intestacy and not only impose a trust for sale upon personal representatives but also put the residuary estate of the intestate on trust, in some cases, for the persons entitled. Clearly the problem relating to the transition from personal representative to trustee is more difficult where there is a will which imposes no trusts at all. If the will includes an express trust for sale of the residue, there will be some analogy with the position on intestacy but a distinction could be drawn between the statutory trust for sale imposed on the assets immediately by section 33 and a testamentary trust for sale of residue. It is submitted that in order to ascertain the position on intestacy regard must first be had to the relevant statutory provisions and then to the relevant cases on intestacy. Reference must be made initially to section 33 of the Administration of Estates Act 1925 which imposes an immediate statutory trust for sale, sets out the administration trusts and identifies "the residuary estate of the intestate."[65] Section 46 of the same Act provides that this estate is to be distributed or "held on the trusts mentioned in this section," *i.e.* "the statutory trusts" which are set out in section 47. Further, section 49(1)(*b*) relating to partial intestacy states expressly:

> "the personal representative shall, subject to his rights and powers for the purposes of administration, be a trustee for the persons entitled under this Part of this Act. . . . "

Two distinct trusts are created, therefore, by the statutory provisions on intestacy. First, there is a trust for sale which is imposed on the personal representatives immediately on appointment for the purposes of the administration and, secondly, there are trusts of the residuary estate which apply in some cases to govern the beneficial entitlement.[66] The two trusts can be distinguished because the trust for

[64] [1964] 1 Ch. 542, see discussion *post* p. 133.
[65] s.33(1), (2), (3), (4), discussed *ante*.
[66] See Lord Evershed M.R. in *Harvell* v. *Foster* [1954] 2 Q.B. 367 at p. 380. See also *Re Trollope's Will Trusts* [1927] 1 Ch. 596 at p. 604.

sale is an administration trust which is clearly co-extensive and not inconsistent with the office and function of a personal representative. However, the trusts of the residuary estate only come into being when the net residue has been ascertained and are continuing trusts under which the property is clearly held in the capacity of trustee rather than personal representative. The legislation suggests an automatic transition from personal representative to trustee where the net residuary estate of an intestate is held on the statutory trusts and the authorities support this conclusion.

The first case to consider is *Re Ponder*,[67] where the deceased died intestate leaving a widow and two minor children. The widow was the administratrix and after realising all the intestate's personalty she paid the expenses and debts and invested the residue which included the proceeds of sale of a freehold house. She applied for the appointment of the Public Trustee as trustee of the proceeds of sale of the realty, and of the shares of the children in the residuary personalty, jointly with her. The court made the appointment, Sargant J. commenting[68]:

> "That the Court may appoint a new trustee to act with an executor where all the debts and the expenses of the estate have been paid, and the estate has been cleared, and the executor is left merely a trustee for the residuary legatees, seems quite clear. That is so because, when the estate has been wound up and the residue ascertained, the executor has ceased to be an executor and has become a trustee for the persons entitled to the residue. And I cannot see why the same reasoning should not apply to the case of the administratrix before me. The widow has divided the personalty into three portions for herself and her two infant sons, and from the time she did this she became a trustee of each of two of the shares for each son."

This case was decided in 1921 before the 1925 legislation imposed the modern trusts on intestacy and so after 1925 it would seem *a fortiori* that the administrator would in such a case become a trustee.

Re Ponder[69] was applied in *Re Pitt*[70] where an administratrix with the will annexed had executed a deed appointing two trustees of the will in her place and the Court held the appointment to be good. In

[67] [1921] 2 Ch. 59; following *Eaton* v. *Daines* (1894) W.N. 32 which "... shows clearly that when an estate has been wound up, and the trust property is in the hands of an executor freed from the administration of the estate, the office is changed from that of executor to that of a trustee, and therefore a power exists to appoint a trustee; and I see no reason why the same result should not follow in the case of an administratrix" *per* Sargant J. at p. 62.

[68] At p. 61.

[69] *Supra.*

[70] [1928] 44 T.L.R. 371.

another post-1925 case, *Re Yerburgh*,[71] it was again accepted that administrators on an intestacy "...ceased to be legal personal representatives and became trustees at a particular date."[72]

Finally, there is a clear support for this view in the modern case of *Re Cockburn's Will Trusts*[73] which, although concerned with testate succession, contains the following statement by Danckwerts J.[74]:

> "...I feel no doubt about the matter at all whether persons are executors or administrators, once they have completed the administration in due course, they become trustees holding for the beneficiaries either on an intestacy or under the terms of the will, and are bound to carry out the duties of trustees, though in the case of personal representatives they cannot be compelled to go on indefinitely acting as trustees and are entitled to appoint new trustees in their place and thus clear themselves from those duties which were not expressly conferred on them under the terms of the testator's will and which, for that purpose, they are not bound to accept."

Danckwerts J. accepted the authority of *Re Ponder*[75] and distinguished the Court of Appeal decision in *Harvell* v. *Foster*,[76] where the Court had cast some doubts upon the decision in *Re Ponder*,[77] comments which as Danckwerts J. pointed out were *obiter* and which he thought were not justified.

At first instance in *Harvell* v. *Foster*[78] Lord Goddard C.J. had applied *Re Ponder*[79] and had decided that sureties to an administration bond were not liable for acts done after the residue had been ascertained since at that time the character of the person appointed as administrator had changed to that of trustee. The Court of Appeal reversed that decision and held that the sureties were liable on the bond until the administrator had "well and truly administered the estate according to law." The decision can be distinguished since the liability on the bond could be regarded as having nothing to do with the question whether a personal representative, who has completed his duties in a proper way, is or is not in a position to appoint new trustees.[80] However, the case does raise difficulties because, if the offices of an administrator and a trustee are mutually exclusive,

71 [1928] W.N. 208.

72 *Supra, per* Homer J., at p. 208.

73 [1957] 1 Ch. 438; see also *Attenborough* v. *Soloman* [1913] A.C. 76.

74 See *supra*, at p. 439. It is to be noticed that there was unsold realty in the estate in question and no distinction was drawn between realty and personalty, see *post*.

75 *Supra.*

76 [1954] 2 Q.B. 367.

77 *Supra.*

78 [1954] 2 Q.B. 591.

79 *Supra.*

80 *Per* Danckwerts J. in *Re Cockburn's Will Trusts, supra*, at p. 440; Ryder, 29 C.L.P. 60, at pp. 67, 68.

liability as an administrator would seem to preclude trusteeship. Further, Lord Evershed M.R. commented[81]:

> "We would add that, in our view, the duty of an administrator, as such, must at least extend to paying the funeral and testamentary expenses and debts and legacies (if any) and where, as here, immediate distribution is impossible owing to the infancy of the person beneficially entitled, retaining the net residue in trust for the infant. At least until the administrator can show that he has done this, it cannot in our judgment, be said of him that he has duly administered the estate according to law."

In so far as this suggests that the administrator does not become a trustee when he has ascertained the residuary estate and therefore cannot appoint a new trustee in his place, it is submitted that the comment is incorrect and that *Re Ponder*[82] is to be preferred.[83]

Personal representatives assenting in favour of themselves

The question arises whether it is necessary for the personal representatives to assent in their own favour when they cease to hold the real estate in that capacity and come to hold it as trustees. A further question is whether this transition in capacity can take place without any such assent. It could be argued that an assent is not necessary in such cases since there is no "passing" of the legal estate[84] but merely a change in capacity or character, and for many years this was the assumption made by text books and practitioners.[85] The assumption was shown to be unjustified in 1964 by the decision in *Re King's Will Trusts*,[86] a case, as the name indicates, on testate succession. Pennycuick J. held that under section 36 a personal representative could make an assent vesting an estate or interest in himself in another capacity and that, until and unless he did so, he could not hold the estate or interest in that other capacity. He further held that, where the estate was vested in a person as personal representative, a deed of appointment of a new trustee jointly with

[81] See *supra*, at p. 383.
[82] See *supra*. Such a decision would be exceedingly inconvenient!
[83] See also *Commissioner of Stamp Duties* v. *Livingston* [1965] A.C. 604 discussed above. Viscount Radcliffe's comments, at p. 707, deny any trust creating a beneficial interest in the persons entitled to residue before the residue is ascertained, but are consistent with such a trust arising once the residuary estate has been ascertained.
[84] See Ryder, 29 L.C.P. 60, at p. 61.
[85] See Farrand, 108 S.J. 698, 719, and the authorities there cited. See also 80 L.Q.R. 328; 28 Conv. 298. It was apparently in reliance on this assumption that the administrator in *Re Edwards' Will Trusts* [1982] Ch. 30 (see discussed *post*) did not execute as administrator a formal assent of land in his own favour as beneficiary. Although the case gave rise to litigation in 1977 the facts relevant to the assent point, took place in 1930, and 1950. See Buckley L.J. at p. 40.
[86] [1964] 1 Ch. 542. In *Re Yerburgh* [1928] W.N. 208 there is a statement relating to the desirability of personal representatives making an assent in favour of themselves but no statement that this was essential.

himself did not operate by virtue of section 40 of the Trustee Act 1925 to vest the legal estate in the new trustee. The estate was accordingly held to be vested in the executor by representation of the testatrix.

Pennycuick J. specifically rejected the suggestion that, where the personal representative is also entitled to the estate or interest in some other capacity, for example, as trustee of the will, as beneficiary or otherwise, he may come to hold the estate or interest in that capacity without any written assent. This decision was both out of line with established probate practice and inconsistent with such authority as there was at the time on the point.[87] However, the decision is now established and acted on and it is interesting to note that the Court of Appeal has recently declined to take an opportunity to overrule the *Re King* rule. This was in the case of *Re Edwards' Will Trusts*,[88] which was concerned with the death intestate in 1930 of a woman whose husband was solely entitled to her estate and who took out letters of administration. He never executed any assents in respect of two plots of land which formed part of the estate but occupied and used them as his own for many years.

Buckley L.J. commented[89] that the failure to execute any assent in writing in his own favour,

> "... may very probably be explained by the fact that until the decision in *Re King's Will Trusts*[90] it was fairly generally thought by conveyancers that, where the legal estate in land had become vested in a person beneficially entitled to that land but had become so vested in some capacity (*e.g.* as the executor of the previous owner) other than the capacity of beneficial owner, no assent in writing was necessary to clothe that person with the legal estate in his capacity as beneficial owner."

Subsequently the husband died and his executors executed what purported to be a written assent in respect of the two plots, vesting the fee simple in themselves as trustees for sale. A question arose as to the validity of their title. Buckley L.J. stated that[91]:

[87] See also *Re Yerburgh* [1928] W.N. 208, which was considered and *Re Ponder* [1921] 2 Ch. 59 which was not. In the latter case a widow had completed the first stage of administration of the estate as administratrix and the court decided to appoint the Public Trustee as joint trustee with her of the children's beneficial shares. This implies that the widow had automatically become a trustee and although the case concerned a pre-1925 intestacy the reasoning could be argued to apply after 1925. See Ryder, 20 C.L.P. 60 at p. 70 who concludes that personal representatives entitled to have the estate vested in them as trustees may change the capacity in which they hold that legal estate by either (a) assenting in writing in their own favour or (b) discharging all the debts and liabilities of the estate, in which case they will automatically become trustees without any assent, *op. cit.* at p. 73.

[88] [1982] Ch. 30.

[89] See *supra* at p. 33.

[90] See *supra*.

[91] See *supra*, at p. 33.

> "If, however, *Re King's Will Trusts*[92] was rightly decided, and the contrary has not been suggested, the purported assent cannot have had that effect, for the legal estate was never vested in [the husband] in any capacity other than that of administrator of [his wife's] estate."

However, the facts were that the husband had been in beneficial occupation of the two plots for some twenty years after her death and that he was beneficially entitled to them under the intestacy. On this basis the Court of Appeal in *Re Edwards*[93] thought that there could have been an implied passing of the beneficial equitable interest.[94] This seems to be an acceptable proposition since section 36(4) requires formalities for the passing of a legal estate in real property but all the texts assume that an assent to the vesting of an equitable interest in real estate may be expressed or implied and need not be in writing.[95] It has been said[96] that only executors, and not administrators, can make an implied assent by conduct and *Re Edwards* has been criticised on that basis. This seems, however, to be unduly technical. *Re Hedge*[97] was the authority mainly relied on in *Re Edwards* and, although the case was concerned with executors, the judgment did not expressly qualify the principle to the exclusion of administrators. Farwell J. commented[98]:

> "His equitable interest as devised depends upon equities and upon whether or not he has done acts which must be treated as amounting to sufficient evidence of assent so as to make it impossible for him now to say that he has never accepted the gift."

Although *Re Edwards* provides a solution[99] to a conveyancing dilemma in some cases, there seems no doubt that it is desirable to follow the established practice of assenting formally to the passing of the legal estate where there is a change in capacity from that of personal representative to that of trustee or beneficiary. Not only does this put the matter beyond doubt but it provides documentary proof of the title.

92 See *supra*.
93 See *supra*.
94 *Per* Buckley L.J. at p. 39.
95 *Halsbury's Laws of England*, 4th ed., Vol. 17, para. 1347.
96 P. W. Smith (1982) Conv. 4–6, in view of the historical dichotomy relating to the vesting and passing of the estate, between executors and administrators.
97 [1940] 1 Ch. 260, at pp. 264, 265.
98 At pp. 264, 265.
99 Another possible solution in cases of intestacy is to argue the effect of the statutory provisions. The A.E.A. 1925 s.33 vests the estate in the personal representatives upon trust to sale and thus automatically they hold as trustees. Note also that ss.46 and 47 put certain beneficial interests upon "the statutory trusts." There is also the reference in s.49(1)(*b*) to a personal representative being a trustee for the persons entitled under Part IV of the Act.

Personal representative as beneficiary

Where the personal representative is also a beneficiary of the estate, as will frequently be the case on intestacy, a formal assent will be necessary in respect of real property to transfer the legal estate.[1] *Re Edwards' Will Trusts*[2] is directly in point here since the case was concerned with the validity of the title to two plots of land of a husband who was both sole administrator and sole beneficiary of his wife's intestate estate. It has been seen above that in the light of the decision in *Re King's Will Trusts*[3] the legal title to these two plots had never been effectively transferred since the husband had never executed any formal assent in respect of the land. However, it was held by virtue of the continued use and occupation of the land by the husband for over twenty years that it was to be inferred that the testator had assented to the vesting of the equitable estate in himself.[4] Accordingly on the husband's death the equitable interest in the land had passed to his executors and had become subject to the husband's will trusts. Thus it is clear that the beneficial interest in property can pass by implication without the need for a formal assent in some cases, although the nature and extent of the beneficial use and enjoyment of the property necessary to give rise to this implication is not clear. The fact remains, however, that in such a case a formal assent should be made by the personal representative in his own favour in order to complete the legal title and clarify the beneficial ownership.

[1] A.E.A. 1925, s.36.
[2] [1981] 3 W.L.R. 15.
[3] [1964] 1 Ch. 542.
[4] Writing within the L.P.A. 1925, s.53(1)(*c*), is apparently not necessary in these cases. This is presumably on the basis that the equitable interest is already vested in the person who is the personal representative/beneficiary and there is no passing of this interest to a third party, merely a change of capacity in which the interest is held by the same person.

CHAPTER 9

LIABILITY OF PERSONAL REPRESENTATIVES

LIABILITY IN CONTRACT

Nature of liability

The liability on contracts entered into by the deceased survives against the estate so that the personal representatives are liable to the extent of the assets for debts and other contractual claims for which the deceased was liable.[1] The extent of the liability of the personal representatives for contracts entered into by them after death needs to be considered in more detail.

A personal representative who enters into unauthorised contracts runs the risk of rendering himself personally liable on such contracts. Thus "... upon a contract of borrowing made by an executor after the death of the testator, the executor is only liable personally, and cannot be sued as executor so as to get execution against the assets of the testator."[2] However, by confining himself to authorised contracts a personal representative will usually avoid such liability. Where the personal representative contracts expressly in exercise of the powers conferred by section 39 of the Administration of Estates Act 1925, he will be liable only as administrator, *i.e.* to the extent of the deceased's assets in his hands, and not personally. The position would seem to be similar with any contract entered into expressly in a representative capacity, *i.e.* as administrator.[3]

Three contractual situations call for special mention, namely funeral expenses, leases and business debts.

Funeral expenses

It is the duty of an administrator to "... bury the deceased in a manner suitable to the estate which he leaves behind."[4] The necessary funeral expenses are a first charge on the estate having priority to other debts[5] and an executor has absolute priority of reimbursement

[1] Law Reform (Miscellaneous Provisions) Act 1934 s.1 but with the exception of contracts which are purely personal to the deceased.

[2] *Farhall* v. *Farhall* (1871) L.R. 7 Ch. 123, per Sir G. Mellish L.J. at p. 126; distinguishing cases such as *Dowse* v. *Coxe* (1825) 3 Bing. 20, where the consideration for the promise of the executor was a contract or transaction with the testator.

[3] See *Dowse* v. *Coxe* (1825) 3 Bing. 20; *Powell* v. *Graham* (1817) 7 Taunt. 580.

[4] Bl. Comm. Bk. 2, Ch. 32 at p. 508, cited by Tucker L.J. in *Rees* v. *Hughes* [1946] 1 K.B. 517 at p. 528; *Sharp* v. *Lush* (1879) 10 Ch.D. 468; *Green* v. *Salmon* (1838) 8 Ad. & E. 348; *Brice* v. *Wilson (ibid.)*; *Williams* v. *Williams* (1882) 20 Ch.D. 659.

[5] *Ibid.*

out of the estate.[6] Personal liability for such expenses may arise where the estate is insolvent,[7] or insufficient to meet the full cost, or where the costs incurred in relation to the funeral or burial exceed what is regarded as reasonable in the circumstances.[8] Such liability may arise not only where the personal representative himself ordered the funeral but also, it is said,[9] where the personal representative ratifies or adopts the acts of another party who gave orders for the funeral.[10]

Where no other person is contractually liable to pay the funeral expenses, then the personal representatives will be liable to meet reasonable claims but it is thought that this liability is limited to the extent of the assets in his hands and thus would not give rise to personal liability.[11]

Leasehold covenants

In accordance with the usual rules the estate will be liable for any breaches of covenant by the deceased during his lifetime. For breaches occuring after the death a personal representative can be liable either in his representative capacity or, if he takes possession, as an assignee, in which case he can incur personal liability.

Liability in his representative capacity

On the death of a lessee the lease will devolve on his personal representatives and thus the representative will become liable for the payment of rent and the observance of the covenants in the lease.[12] However, if the personal representative does not take possession, his liability is limited to the extent of the deceased's assets.[13] In *Youngmin*

[6] *Edwards* v. *Edwards* (1834) 2 Cr. & M. 612; even a stranger can recover from the estate his voluntary expenditure on funeral expenses.

[7] See *Edwards* v. *Edwards, supra*, Parke B. at p. 616 "... I take the rule to be, that the executor is entitled to be allowed reasonable expenses, and if he exceeds those he is to take the chance of the estate turning out insolvent."

[8] As to which, see most recently, *Hart* v. *Griffiths-Jones* [1948] 2 All E.R. 729: *Stanton* v. *Ewart F. Youldon Ltd.* [1960] 1 W.L.R. 543; and see *Gammell* v. *Wilson* [1980] 3 W.L.R. 391 affirmed [1982] A.C. 27.

[9] See Williams, Mortimer and Sunnucks, *Executors, Administrators and Probate*, 16th ed., p. 701, citing *inter alia, Brice* v. *Wilson* (1834) 8 Ad. & E. note to p. 350. "... the defendant has made himself individually the party ordering the funeral, by adopting the acts of another."

[10] Thus in *Lucy* v. *Walrond* (1837) 3 Bing (N.C.) 841 the defendant before taking out letters of administration sanctioned an expensive funeral which a relation had ordered for the deceased. It was held that after taking out administration the defendant was liable in the capacity of administrator for this expense, the court leaving open the question whether he could have been sued in his personal capacity.

[11] *Tingwell* v. *Heyman* (1812) 3 Camp. 298; *Rogers* v. *Price* (1829) 3 Y. & J. 28, see Tucker L.J. in *Rees* v. *Hughes* [1946] 1 K.B. 517 at p. 528.

[12] See Megarry and Wade, *The Law of Real Property*, 5th ed., p. 748. See Stamp L.J. in *Youngmin* v. *Heath* [1974] 1 W.L.R. 135 at p. 463: "The personal representative of a deceased is, however, bound to perform all the contracts of the deceased if he has assets, and is accordingly bound to discharge any contractual liability of the deceased under a tenancy."

[13] *Ibid.*

v. *Heath*[14] a tenant who had been paying £3 a week for rent for furnished accommodation died intestate. Letters of administration were taken out by the defendant as attorney administrator, and he did not enter or take possession of the accommodation. It was held that the landlord was entitled to claim rent from the administrator for the period commencing with the tenant's death and ending when the administrator gave formal notice to terminate the tenancy. This liability was limited, however, to the extent of the deceased's assets.

This representative liability can be limited by a plea of *plene administravit*, *i.e.* that the estate has been wholly administered. In addition section 26 of the Trustee Act provides statutory protection against liability as a personal representative or trustee, but not as an assignee if possession has been taken,[15] in respect of rents and covenants under a lease. Provided that the personal representative has satisfied all existing liabilities under the lease, made provision by way of a fund to meet any future claims in respect of agreed fixed sums to be laid out on the property, if any, and assigned the lease to a purchaser or to a person entitled to it, the residue can safely be distributed without fear of personal liability under the lease.[16]

Liability of assignee

If, as will usually be the case, a personal representative enters into possession of the demised premises, he becomes liable on the covenants in the same way as an ordinary assignee.[17] The usual rule that an assignee is liable only for breaches of covenant that occur during his period of assignment applies.[18] The personal representative can protect himself against this liability either by taking an indemnity from the beneficiaries or, more usually, by setting aside out of the estate a fund to provide by way of indemnity against possible liability.[19] There is no need, however, to retain such a fund after the expiration of the period beyond which any possible action by the lessors against the personal representatives would be statute-barred.[20] It should be noted also that the personal representatives are not

[14] [1974] 1 W.L.R. 135.
[15] See *Re Owers* [1941] 1 Ch. 389.
[16] Provided that possession was not taken of the property giving rise to liability under privity of estate.
[17] See Megarry and Wade, *op. cit.*, citing *inter alia, Stratford upon Avon Corpn.* v. *Parker* [1914] 2 K.B. 562. By proper pleading he may limit his liability for rent to the annual value of the land, *ibid.*
[18] See *ibid.*
[19] *Re Owers, Public Trustee* v. *Death* [1941] 1 Ch. 389, no such fund will be authorised where there is no personal liability but representative liability which can be protected by the application of the Trustee Act 1925, s.26.
[20] In *Re Lewis, Jennings* v. *Hemsley* [1939] 1 Ch. 232.

entitled to any indemnity out of the estate in respect of properties as to which they have assented.[21]

Business debts

Continuation of a business

Where the deceased was engaged in a trade or business, the devolution of the assets of the business will depend upon the manner in which the assets were held, which could be as sole proprietor, as a partnership or as a limited company.[22] In many such cases it will be desirable to continue the enterprise after the death to the advantage of the beneficiaries but the basic rule is that personal representatives have no such power.[23] This rule is subject, however, to important exceptions.

First, authority to carry on the business might be conferred expressly by the will.[24] Secondly, a personal representative is always entitled to carry on the business with a view to its effective realisation.[25] Thirdly, in cases of intestacy the statutory trust for sale and power to postpone sale contained in section 33 of the 1925 Act will apply and this will enable the personal representatives to continue the business during the period of postponement.[26] Fourthly, where all the beneficiaries are *sui juris*, they can consent and provide an indemnity by way of protection for the personal representatives. Finally, in the absence of other authority the personal representatives may apply to the court for an order authorising them to carry on the business.[27]

Liability for business debts

A personal representative who carries on the business of the deceased renders himself liable personally for debts incurred under all contracts entered into after the death.[28] However, this liability is

[21] *Re Bennett, Midland Bank Executor and Trustee Co. Ltd.* v. *Fletcher* [1943] 1 All E.R. 467.

[22] See *ante*.

[23] See, for example, Williams, Mortimer and Sunnucks, *Executors, Administrators and Probate* (16th ed.) at p. 702; citing *Barker* v. *Parker* (1786) 1 T.R. 295.

[24] See *Re Crowther* (1895) 2 Ch. 56; *Re Chancellor* (1884) 26 Ch.D. 42. This will obviously be inapplicable in cases of total intestacy.

[25] *Ibid.*; this authorisation is usually regarded as being commensurate with the duration of the executor's year, *ibid.* See also *Re East* [1914] 111 L.T. 101 at p. 105.

[26] *Re Chancellor*, *supra*; *Re Crowther*, *supra*—Contrast *Re Rooke* [1953] 1 Ch. 716 where the power to postpone conferred by the L.P.A. 1925 s.25 was excluded by a contrary intention. It is probable that the power will terminate once the estate becomes divisible, see *Re Ball* [1930] W.N. 111.

[27] Under the Trustee Act 1925, s.57. An alternative would be to seek the consent and indemnity of the beneficiaries where they are all of full age and absolutely entitled.

[28] *Labouchere* v. *Tupper* (1857) 11 Moo.P.C. 198; whether or not he contracts as personal representative, *ibid.* and even at the risk of personal bankruptcy, *ex p. Garland* (1803) 10 Ves. 110.

modified by the right to an indemnity out of the estate in certain cases. The law on this point has been settled for 100 years since the House of Lords' case of *Dowse* v. *Gorton*[29] where Lord Herschell laid down the following propositions.[30] First, where the business has been carried on under authority in the will, the personal representatives will be entitled to a general indemnity out of the estate as against all persons claiming under the will, but this right cannot be maintained against the creditors.[31] Secondly, where the personal representatives have carried on the business for such reasonable time as was necessary to enable them to sell the business property as a going concern, they will be entitled even as against the creditors to an indemnity in respect of the liabilities properly incurred in so doing.[32]

Thirdly, where the personal representatives carry on the business with the assent of the pre-death creditors, they are entitled to an indemnity out of the estate in priority to those creditors.[33] The court will require strict proof of assent or consent in such cases and mere acquiescence will not suffice.[34]

Where the personal representative is entitled to an indemnity out of the estate in respect of a debt incurred in properly carrying on the business, the creditor may be entitled to claim by subrogation the right of indemnity.[35]

DEVASTAVIT

Liability for devastavit

The literal meaning of *devastavit* is wasting of the assets and a personal representative will be liable personally to both the beneficiaries and the creditors for losses arising out of such actions.[36] In practice a *devastavit* is any breach of the duty of administration. In *Re Stevens*[37] Vaughan Williams L.J. approved the statement in *Williams on Executors* that an executor[38] is liable as on a *devastavit* not only for loss arising from a direct abuse of the assets by spending or consuming

[29] [1891] A.C. 190; applied in *Re East, supra.*

[30] At p. 199.

[31] For the simple reason that the beneficiaries are bound by the terms of the will but the creditors are not. See *Re East, supra*, where a business was carried on for over three years were considerable debts incurred, and no indemnity was granted in priority to the creditors. This is obviously inapplicable to a total intestacy.

[32] *Ibid.* In *Dowse* v. *Gorton, supra*, the business was carried on for three years and not merely for the purpose of effecting a sale; see *Re East, supra*, likewise.

[33] *Ibid.*, such an indemnity was obtained on the facts of *Dowse* v. *Gorton, supra.*

[34] See *Re Oxley* [1914] 1 Ch. 604, where it was held that merely standing by with knowledge that the business was being carried on and abstaining from interference with it were not of themselves sufficient to constitute the original creditors of the testator persons entitled to the subsequent assets and therefore bound to give effect to the indemnity.

[35] See Williams, Mortimer and Sunnucks, *op. cit.* p. 706.

[36] See Williams, Mortimer and Sunnucks, *op. cit.* Chap. 60.

[37] [1898] 1 Ch. 162 at pp. 176, 177.

[38] Or, of course, an administrator.

them but also for waste by such acts of negligence and wrong administration as will disappoint the claimants to the assets. It would seem[39] that this liability may include a loss to the estate arising by reason of the estate having to bear charges which it would not have had to bear but for the culpable negligence of the personal representative. In *Re Tankard*[40] it was stated that it is the duty of personal representatives as a matter of the due administration of the estate to pay the debts of the testator with due diligence and that this duty is owed not only to the creditors but also to the beneficiaries.

Instances of devastavit

Any breach by a personal representative of the duties of his office, or any loss to the estate caused by wilful or negligent acts, is capable of amounting to a *devastavit*. Some examples can be given from the decided cases. The payment of a declared statute-barred debt has been held to be a *devastavit* since it is the duty of a personal representative to protect the assets of the estate.[41]

The position with regard to payment of an unenforceable debt is similar since, although it is a duty of a personal representative to pay just debts and to satisfy just claims against a testator's estate, "... it is clearly his duty not to waste an estate not his own, which he is administering for the benefit of others, in satisfying demands that are equally untenable in law and in equity."[42] The personal representatives were similarly held to be liable where by mistake they divided the residuary estate between five legatees when six were entitled.[43] More recently in *Marsden* v. *Regan*[44] a personal representative was thought clearly to be guilty of a *devastavit* in giving away furniture and bedding belonging to the estate without getting anything for them.[45] A personal representative has a duty to safeguard the assets of the estate but will not now be liable for their loss unless that is caused by his own wilful default.[46]

39 From the case of *Hall* v. *Hallet* (1784) 1 Cox. 134. In *Re Stevens, supra* it was thought that no action would lie for a failure to take out probate; the remedy being a citation.
40 [1942] 1 Ch. 69, per Uthwatt J.
41 *Midgley* v. *Midgley* [1893] 3 Ch. 282; "If an executor pays what he ought not to pay he is guilty of a *devastavit* ...," *per* A. L. Smith L.J. *supra*, at p. 304. Williams, Mortimer and Sunnucks, *op.cit.* suggest that a personal representative is entitled to pay a debt which is barred by the Limitation Act unless the payment is against the declared wish of his co-representatives or it has been judicially declared to be statute-barred.
42 *Re Rownson* (1885) 29 Ch.D. 358, per Bowen L.J. at p. 363.
43 *Hilliard* v. *Fulford* (1876) 4 Ch.D. 389.
44 [1954] 1 W.L.R. 423.
45 She had also incurred costs in commencing and then abandoning an appeal to the Court of Appeal relating to possession of leasehold premises. This was also alleged to be a *devastavit* but the Court of Appeal were doubtful since she was conducting that litigation for the benefit of the estate generally. In any event the Court thought that she was entitled to relief under the Trustee Act 1925, s.61, see *post*.
46 *Job* v. *Job* (1877) 6 Ch.D. 562; see Trustee Act 1925, s.30 and *Re Vickery* [1931] 1 Ch. 572.

If a beneficiary, with full knowledge of what was being done, has acquiesced in the *devastavit*, he is precluded from claiming against the personal representative in respect thereof.[47] The onus of proving such concurrence is on the personal representative who must show actual, not constructive, knowledge on the part of the beneficiary.[48]

Where a personal representative commits a *devastavit*, or "converts to his own use any part of the real or personal estate of the deceased," and then dies, his personal representative is liable and chargeable for such waste or conversion in the same manner as the defaulter would have been if living.[49]

Liability for breach of trust

The circumstances in which a personal representative will be deemed to become a trustee have been considered above.[50] When this transition has taken place, liability as a trustee for breach of trust can arise, and such liability is similar to but can be wider than liability as a personal representative for *devastavit*. Reference must be made in this connection, to books on the law of trusts.[51]

Competing with the estate

A rule of universal application is that a personal representative having duties to discharge under the will or intestacy shall not be allowed to enter into any engagement in which he has or can have a personal interest which conflicts, or which possibly may conflict, with the interests of those whom he is bound to protect.[52]

LIABILITY FOR ACTS OF OTHERS

Liability for acts of agents

A personal representative has general power to employ an agent under section 23(1) of the Trustee Act 1925.[53] This provision has, in the well-known words of Maugham J. in *Re Vickery*[54]

> "revolutionise[d] the position of a trustee or an executor[55] so far as regards the employment of agents. He is no longer required to do any actual work himself, but he may employ a solicitor or

[47] *Re Marsden* (1884) 26 Ch.D. 783; analogous to breach of trust cases see, *Fletcher* v. *Collis* [1905] 2 Ch. 24; *Holder* v. *Holder* [1968] Ch. 353.
[48] *Ibid.*; the claim was not made out on the facts of the case.
[49] A.E.A. 1925, s.29.
[50] See *ante*, p. 130.
[51] Such as Pettit, *Equity and the Law of Trusts*, 5th ed., pp. 425–445.
[52] *per* Clauson J. in *Re Thomson, Thomson* v. *Allen* [1930] 1 Ch. 203 at p. 215, in that case the duty of a fiduciary nature was to carry on the business of the testator to the best advantage of the beneficiaries. See also *Keech* v *Sandford* (1726) Sel.Cas. Ch. 61; *Re Biss* [1903] 2 Ch. 40.
[53] As to which generally, see Parry and Clark, *The Law of Succession*, 8th ed., p. 229.
[54] [1931] 1 Ch. 572, at p. 581.
[55] Or, of course, an administrator.

other agent to do it, whether there is any real necessity for the employment or not."[56]

Specific power to appoint an agent in respect of any property forming part of the testator's or intestate's estate in any place outside the United Kingdom is conferred by section 23(2), whereas section 23(3) contains provisions relating to the receipt by agents of money.[57]

The Powers of Attorney Act 1971[58] substitutes a wider provision for section 25 of the Trustee Act 1925 enabling complete delegation, by power of attorney, by a personal representative for a period not exceeding 12 months.[59]

The liability of the personal representative for the acts of an agent employed under these sections is governed by statutory provisions which, as judicially interpreted, are unfortunately not as clear as might be desired. Section 23(1) states that the principal "... shall not be responsible for the default of any such agent if employed in good faith." At first sight this would seem to restrict liability to cases of subjective fault and to exclude liability where the agent has been negligently (although honestly) employed or supervised.[60] However, this seems unduly lenient and other judges have stated that the principal should be judged by the standard applied in *Speight* v. *Gaunt*,[61] namely a trustee[62] is bound to conduct the business of the trust in such a way as an ordinary prudent man would conduct a business of his own.[63] It is submitted that this states correctly the standard of conduct required, at least so far as a professional representative is concerned.[64]

The Trustee Act 1925, s.23(2) states, so far as delegations under that provision are concerned, that the principals shall not "... by reason only of their having made such appointment, be responsible for any loss arising thereby." However, section 23(3) states that a trustee can

[56] It is usually stated that only administrative acts and not discretions may be delegated under this provision; for example, the decision whether to sell particular property or not cannot be delegated but the mechanical acts incidental to effecting such a sale can be.

[57] See Parry and Clark, *ibid.* It is expressly stated that this subsection enables any discretion or trust or power vested in the personal representatives in relation to such property to be delegated.

[58] s.2.

[59] For a period not exceeding 12 months. The section enables the personal representatives to delegate all or any of the trusts, powers and discretions vested in them.

[60] See Maugham J. in *Re Vickery, supra*, referring to *Re City Equitable Fire Insurance Co.* [1925] C.R. 407.

[61] (1883) 22 Ch.D. 727.

[62] There seems no reason to differentiate between the liability of a trustee and a personal representative in this respect.

[63] See Cross J. in *Lucking's Will Trusts* [1968] 1 W.L.R. 866, at pp. 873–875; and Brightman J. in *Bartlett* v. *Barclays Bank Trust Co. (No. 1)* [1980] Ch. 515; at p. 533. It could be argued that the good faith referred to in s.23(1) governs only the act of appointment and does not qualify the continuing duty to supervise the activities of the agent once appointed.

[64] See *Bartlett* v. *Barclays Bank Trust Co., supra.*

be liable if he permits the money "... to remain in the hands or under the control of the banker or solicitor for a period longer than is reasonably necessary to enable the banker or solicitor, as the case may be, to pay or transfer the same to the trustee." The liability under the Trustee Act 1925 section 25 is clear: "The donor of a power of attorney given under this section shall be liable for the acts or defaults of the donee in the same manner as if they were the acts or defaults of the donor."

The final provision to consider is section 30(1) of the Trustee Act[65] which provides:

> "A trustee shall be chargeable only for money and securities actually received by him notwithstanding his signing any receipt for the sake of conformity, and shall be answerable and accountable only for his own acts, receipts, neglects, or defaults, and not for those of any other trustee, nor for any banker, broker, or other person with whom any trust money or securities may be deposited, nor for the insufficiency or deficiency of any securities, nor for any loss, unless the same happens through his own wilful default."

In *Re Vickery*,[66] Maugham J. decided that the effect of this provision was that:

> "... where an executor[67] employs a solicitor or other agent to receive money belonging to the estate in reliance on section 23(1) of the Trustee Act 1925, he will not be liable for a loss of the money occasioned by the misconduct of the agent unless the loss happens through the wilful default of the executor, using those words as implying, as the Court of Appeal have decided[68] either a consciousness of negligence or a breach of duty, or a recklessness in the performance of a duty."[69]

Although these comments demand respect as being directly in point, Maugham J.'s views have been criticised severely[70] as being unduly favourable to the trustee or representative and as being inconsistent with decisions[71] on the earlier sections to which section 30 is the successor.[72] The decision has not found favour with other

[65] The section applies to a personal representative as well as trustees, Trustee Act 1925, s.68(17).
[66] [1931] 1 Ch. 572 at pp. 583, 584.
[67] Or, of course, an administrator.
[68] Referring to *Re City* and *Equitable Fire Insurance Co.* [1925] C.R. 407 a decision concerning liability in company law not trust law.
[69] Applying this test in *Re Vickery*, the court decided that the executor was guilty only of an error of judgment and thus not liable for losses to the estate occasioned by the dishonest solicitor.
[70] See Parry and Clark, *op.cit.* pp. 232–234.
[71] Namely *Speight* v. *Gaunt* (1883) 23 Ch.D. 727 and *Re Chapman* [1896] 2 Ch. 763.
[72] Lord Cranworth's Act 1859, s.31; repealed and replaced by Trustee Act 1893, s.24.

judges and the more recent cases of *Lucking's Wills Trusts*[73] and *Bartlett* v. *Barclays Bank Trust Co. Ltd.*,[74] although not directly in point on section 30, indicate a judicial preference for liability for conduct which falls short of that to be expected of a reasonably prudent man of business, *i.e.* an objective standard.

Liability for acts of co-representatives

The liability of a personal representative for the acts of his co-representative is governed by section 30 which has been set out and considered above.[75] There seems little doubt that a representative would be liable under the section only for his own acts and not for any losses occasioned to the estate by his co-representatives "... unless the same happens through his own wilful default." This statutory provision is consistent with the principles of equity expounded in earlier cases.[76] Accordingly "... a *devastavit* by one of two executors or administrators will not charge his companion provided he has not intentionally or otherwise contributed to it."[77] There is little modern authority to which reference can be made by way of illustration of these principles but the old case of *Styles* v. *Guy*[78] is instructive. Two of three executors who knew that there were unsettled accounts subsisting at the death between the testator and their co-executor took no steps to compel him to account and pay or secure the amounts owing. The debtor executor went bankrupt and it was held that the other executors were liable since they had a duty to keep a check on each other and should not have allowed the money to remain outstanding simply on personal security.

In cases where a representative can satisfy the court that the default was solely that of his colleague and that he himself was in no way at fault, he is entitled to claim an indemnity from the defaulting party.[79]

CRIMINAL LIABILITY

Personal representatives are, of course, not immune from the ordinary criminal law and dishonest conduct can result in prosecution. Indeed, the Theft Act 1968 singles out trustees and personal representatives for particularly unfavourable treatment. The general rule under that Act is that a person is not dishonest if he appropriates property in the belief that the person to whom the property belongs

[73] [1968] 1 W.L.R. 866.
[74] [1980] Ch. 515.
[75] See *ante*.
[76] Such as *Re Brier* (1884) 26 Ch.D. 238; *Re Munton* [1927] 1 Ch. 262.
[77] *Williams* v. *Nixon* (1840) 2 Beav. 472.
[78] (1849) 1 M. & G. 422.
[79] See *Bahin* v. *Hughes* (1886) 31 Ch.D. 390, at pp. 395, 396. Most of the cases relate to the joint and several liability of trustees as to which reference should be made to books on trusts such as Pettit, *Equity and the Law of Trusts*, 5th ed. p. 429.

cannot be discovered by taking reasonable steps. Trustees and personal representatives, however, are expressly *excluded* from this rule so that they may be deemed to be dishonest in these circumstances.[80] The explanation[81] for this provision lies in the fiduciary nature of the offices so that in no circumstances can the trustee or personal representative regard the property as his own; failing beneficiaries it will go to the Crown as *bona vacantia*.[82] Care is needed in such cases therefore, and, if the beneficiary cannot be traced, the property should be paid into court or directions should be taken for the protection of the personal representative.

Defence to Liability

If a personal representative is sued by a creditor in respect of a debt, he may plead *plene administravit, i.e.* that he has fully administered all the assets of the estate which may have come into his hands.[83-84] It is essential that this plea (or the analogous *plene administravit praeter*)[85] be raised by the personal representative before judgment otherwise it will be lost and the failure to plead will be taken as conclusive evidence that the representative had assets.[86]

Protection from Claims

Under the well-known procedure embodied in section 27 of the Trustee Act 1925 a personal representative can protect himself against liability for claims from beneficiaries and creditors by advertising for such claims.[87] Once the specified time limit (not less than two months) has expired, a personal representative can safely distribute the assets to those creditors and beneficiaries of whom he has notice without liability to claimants who come forward later.[88] The section does not, of course, provide any protection against unpaid claims of which the personal representative had notice at the time of distribution.

If the personal representatives are aware of the existence of a beneficiary but cannot find him, they can secure protection by means

[80] s.2(1)(*c*); by virtue of s.4(2) a trustee or personal representative may, exceptionally, be capable of stealing land where "... he appropriates the land or anything forming part of it by dealing with it in breach of the confidence reposed in him." See also s.5(2) relating to property subject to a trust.

[81] See Smith, *The Law of Theft*, 4th ed., p. 60.

[82] See *post*, chap. 14.

[83-84] See Williams, Mortimer and Sunnucks, *op. cit.* pp. 802–804.

[85] *i.e.* fully administered with the exception of specified assets.

[86] *Re Marvin* [1905] 2 Ch. 490; *Midland Bank Trust Co. Ltd.* v. *Green (No. 2)* [1979] 1 W.L.R. 460.

[87] It is not thought necessary to discuss this provision in detail here. See *ante*, p. 105 and Williams, Mortimer and Sunnucks, *Executors, Administrators and Probate*, 16th ed., pp. 559 *et seq.*

[88] Without prejudice to the rights of the disappointed creditor or beneficiary to seek to recover the asset from the person wrongly paid.

of a *Benjamin* order.[89] This enables the estate to be distributed on the basis of a particular assumption, *e.g.* that a beneficiary is dead or that all the creditors have been ascertained.

Possible future or contingent liabilities, *e.g.* possible legal proceedings against the estate, can be met in a number of ways. If the amount of the liability is small, or the chances of it arising are remote, a satisfactory solution is to obtain from the beneficiaries an indemnity against the liability if it should arise. The estate can then be distributed safely. Alternative courses of action are to set aside and retain a sum sufficient to meet the liability should it arise, to insure against the claim or to seek the direction of the court. Any of these actions should ensure the protection of the personal representatives.

RELIEF FROM LIABILITY

Relief by the court

The court has power under section 61 of the Trustee Act 1928 to relieve, wholly or partially, a personal representative from personal liability in respect of his actions in the administration.[90] Such relief may be granted where the person acted "... honestly and reasonably ..." and "... ought fairly to be excused for the breach. ..."[91] Most of the cases illustrating the exercise of this jurisdiction are concerned with the liability of trustees for breach of trust and reference to such cases can be found in the appropriate texts.[92] The section was invoked successfully by an executrix in the Court of Appeal case of *Marsden* v. *Regan*[93] where the estate consisted of a

[89] [1902] 1 Ch. 723. See *Re Green's Will Trust, Fitzgerald-Hart* v. *Att.-Gen.* [1985] 3 All E.R. 455.

[90] The section is expressly for the relief of a trustee from liability for breach of trust but also applies to a personal representative see Trustee Act 1925, s.68(17) and *Marsden* v. *Regan* [1954] 1 W.L.R. 423 where relief was granted to an executor. See also *Re Kay* [1897] 2 Ch. 518, *post*, where it was held expressly that s.3 of the Judicial Trustees Act 1896 (forerunner to s.61 of the 1925 Act) applied to an executor who had committed a *devastavit.*

[91] See *National Trustee Company of Australasia* v. *General Finance Company of Australasia* [1905] A.C. 373; *Re Windsor Steam Coal Company* [1929] 1 Ch. 151; *Re Houghton, Hawley & Blake* [1904] 1 Ch. 622 where an executor who compromised a claim by his co-executor against the estate was held to have acted "honestly and reasonably"; *Re Allsop, Whittaker & Bamford* [1914] 1 Ch. 1, it was held that the earlier Judicial Trustee Act 1896 provision was not confined to cases where the breach of trust arose from some executive or administrative blunder, but may extend to cases where money is paid to a person not entitled according to the true construction of the instrument. Relief was not granted however, in this case nor in *Khoo Tek Keong* v. *Ch'ng Joo Tuan Neoh* [1934] A.C. 529 where, although a trustee acted honestly, he did not act prudently.

[92] See Pettit, *Equity and the Law of Trusts*, 5th ed., pp. 442–444. Recent cases concerning trustees include *Bartlett* v. *Barclays Bank Trust Co. Ltd.* [1980] Ch. 515; *Re Rosenthal (decd.)* [1972] 1 W.L.R. 1273; *Re Pauling's Settlement Trusts* [1964] Ch. 303.

[93] [1954] 1 W.L.R. 423.

second-hand clothes business carried on in premises held on a weekly tenancy. The owner of the freehold reversion obtained judgment against the executrix for possession of the premises and for sums totalling £50 in respect of the mesne profits and costs. The executrix applied under the Landlord and Tenant Act 1927 for a new lease but this was refused. Action was then taken by the owner against the executrix to recover the £50, and a further £55 in respect of mesne profits, alleging a *devastavit* in that she had improperly wasted the assets of the estate on the unsuccessful application for a new lease. The court were by no means clear that this action was a *devastavit* since she had acted on the advice of solicitors and the litigation was conducted for the benefit of the estate. The court was quite clear, however, that the executrix had acted honestly and reasonably in the circumstances and thus was entitled to relief under section 61.[94]

Other cases where a personal representative has been granted relief under analogous provisions in previous legislation[95] can be noted shortly. In *Re Lord De Clifford's Estate*[96] the executors had paid large sums to their solicitors in reliance on their statements that these sums were required for the payment of debts, disbursements and other administration purposes. Some of the money was lost in the subsequent bankruptcy of the solicitors. It was held that the executors should be relieved from personal liability since they had acted honestly and reasonably on the advice of the solicitors whom they had no reason to suspect were not financially sound. A similar result occurred in *Re Grindley*,[97] where money was lost to the estate by reason of the bankruptcy of the debtor whom the executors believed to be a man of good credit.

A striking illustration of the limitations to such relief is afforded in *Re Kay*,[98] where an executor, who had no reason to believe that an estate was insolvent, allowed the widow to enjoy the income for nearly two years until judgment was pronounced against the estate for a sum exceeding its total value. The deceased had died in June and the action (to which the executor believed there was a complete answer) was commenced in December. The executor defended the action and continued to make disbursements out of the estate until judgment was given against the estate some sixteen months later. It was held that the executor was entitled to relief from liability for his actions up to the

[94] The executrix had also given away furniture and bedding to the value of £22 which was clearly a *devastavit* and in respect of which she could have no relief.
[95] The Judicial Trustees Act 1896, s.3(1).
[96] [1900] 2 Ch. 707.
[97] [1898] 2 Ch. 593, where the executors were also entitled to rely on a clause in the will to justify their conduct and relief was granted upon the combined effects of the will and the Act.
[98] [1897] 2 Ch. 518.

date when the writ was issued but not thereafter.[99] In *Re Mackay*[1] an executor and trustee was held not liable for losses to the estate by reason of misappropriations by a solicitor since he was justified in believing that, having regard to the terms of the will, he might safely pay the money to the solicitor, and that he had acted honestly and reasonably and ought fairly to be excused in the circumstances. Finally, in *Re Roberts*,[2] relief was granted to an executor who had failed to recover certain costs which were due to the estate because he honestly believed, on the basis of what the testator (his father) and the residuary legatee (his brother) had told him, that the costs were irrecoverable.

Acquiescence or concurrence by the beneficiary

A beneficiary will be barred from claiming against a personal representative for a *devastavit* where he can be shown to have acquiesced in the breach.[3] The onus of proving acquiescence is on the party alleging it and it is necessary to show "a standing by with full knowledge of what was being done and an acquiescence in the *devastavit*."[4] Further the beneficiary must be *sui juris* at the time of the alleged concurrence. This principle is analogous to the rule in the law of trusts where the *cestui que trust* joins with the trustees in that which is a breach of trust. Either concurrence in the act or acquiescence without original concurrence will release the trustees.[5] This rule was considered fully by Wilberforce J. in *Re Pauling's Settlement Trusts*[6] and he concluded that the court should consider all the circumstances in which the concurrence of the *cestui que trust* was given with a view to seeing whether it is fair and equitable that, having given his concurrence, he should afterwards turn round and sue the trustees. It is not necessary however, that he should know that what he is concurring in is a breach of trust, provided that he fully understands what he is concurring in, nor that he should himself have benefited directly by the breach of trust.[7]

[99] "I believe the defendant acted honestly; but it would lead to grave results if I were to hold that an executor having notice of a serious and substantial claim against his testator's estate could disregard it with impunity, merely because he believed, or was advised, that the claim could be defeated. . . . " per Romer J., *supra*, at p. 524.

[1] [1911] 1 Ch. 300. See also *Palmer* v. *Emerson* [1911] 1 Ch. 758.

[2] (1897) 96 L.T. 479, applying *Clark* v. *Holland* (1854) 19 Beav. 262.

[3] *Re Marsden* (1884) 26 Ch.D. 783, see *ante*.

[4] *Ibid. per* Kay J. at p. 790.

[5] See Lord Eldon L.C. in *Walker* v. *Symonds* (1818) 3 Swan 1 at p. 64; see also *Fletcher* v. *Collis* [1905] 2 Ch. 24.

[6] [1962] 1 W.L.R. 86, at pp. 106–108; referring to *Walker* v. *Symonds*, *supra*; *Evans* v. *Benyon* (1887) 37 Ch.D. 329; *Re Garnett* (1885) 31 Ch.D. 1; *Re Somerset* [1894] 1 Ch. 231; and *Chillingworth* v. *Chambers* [1896] 1 Ch. 685.

[7] *Per* Wilberforce J. in *Re Pauling's Settlement Trusts*, *supra*, at p. 107; followed in *Holder* v. *Holder* [1968] 1 Ch. 353 at p. 369.

Impounding a beneficiary's interest

Where trustee or personal representative[8] commits a breach of trust at the instigation or request or with the consent in writing of a beneficiary, section 62 of the Trustee Act 1925 enables the court to order that all or part of the interest of such beneficiary shall be impounded and applied by way of indemnity to the party liable. Most of the cases on this discretionary jurisdiction are concerned with trustees and breaches of trust and reference can be made to specialist works.[9]

Further litigation concerning *Re Pauling's Settlement Trusts*[10] is the only modern case where the jurisdiction is considered. Cases on earlier statutory formulations[11] indicate that the words "in writing" apply only to "consent" and not to "instigation" or "request."[12] It has been held that it must be shown that the beneficiary not only instigated, requested or consented in writing to the breach not also that he knew the facts which would make it a breach of trust.[13]

LIMITATION OF ACTIONS

Actions against personal representatives are subject to periods of limitation analogous to other actions and the relevant law is now to be found in the Limitation Act 1980.[14] This area of the law is fully documented elsewhere and so will be only shortly noted here. It is necessary to distinguish between actions by creditors and actions by beneficiaries.

Actions by creditors

The usual limitation period of six years applies to actions by creditors against the estate in respect of contract debts.[15] The same applies to actions founded on tort,[16] while actions to recover land are subject to the usual twelve year period.[17] An executor can plead the Limitation Act in respect of a *devastavit* so that such an action will be

[8] See Trustee Act 1925, s.68(17).
[9] See Pettit, *Equity and the Law of Trusts* 5th ed., pp. 436–438.
[10] [1963] Ch. 576.
[11] Trustee Act 1888, s.6.
[12] *Griffith* v. *Hughes* [1892] 3 Ch. 105.
[13] *Re Somerset* [1894] 1 Ch. 231.
[14] Consolidating previous legislation, with effect from May 1, 1981. See Williams, Mortimer and Sunnucks *Executors, Administrators and Probate* (16th ed.) *op. cit.*, Chap. 67; and Parry and Clark, *op. cit.*, pp. 379–382.
[15] 1980 Act, s.5. Time runs continually with no suspension for the period between death and grant, *Rhodes* v. *Smethurst* (1840) 6 M. & W. 351, and notwithstanding that the creditor becomes the executor of the debtor, *Bowring-Hanbury's Trustees* v. *Bowring-Hanbury* [1943] Ch. 104.
[16] 1980 Act, s.2.
[17] 1980 Act, ss.15, 18.

barred after six years from the date of the wrongful distribution.[18] Thus in *Lacons* v. *Warmoll*[19] the executors had wrongfully handed over the assets of the testator to a beneficiary without making any provision for future liability under a guarantee. This was adjudged to be a *devastavit* but, since more than six years had elapsed following the distribution, the executor was held to be entitled to plead the Statute of Limitations as a defence. Buckley L.J. commented[20]:

> "It seems to be perfectly plain both upon principle and authority[21] . . . that if an act of *devastavit* has been committed and six years have run, the Statute of Limitations applies and a creditor is thereby precluded from setting up that act."

Actions by beneficiaries

It is necessary to distinguish between cases in which there is an allegation of fraud against the representative and other cases. In the former case section 21(1)provides[22]:

> "No period of limitation prescribed by this Act shall apply to an action by a beneficiary under a trust, being an action—

(a) in respect of any fraud or fraudulent breach of trust to which the trustee was a party or privy; or

(b) to recover from the trustee trust property or the proceeds of trust property in the possession of the trustee, or previously received by the trustee and converted to his use."[23]

Subject to this provision the basic limitation period applicable to actions to recover trust property or in respect of any breach of trust is six years.[24]

However, where the action relates to any claim to the personal estate of a deceased person, or to any share or interest in any such estate, whether under a will or an intestacy, then the period of limitation is twelve years from the date on which the right to receive the share or interest accrued.[25] The same period applies as a general rule to the recovery of land.[26] Where the personal representative has ceased to hold the assets as such and has become a trustee of the

[18] *Re Blow, Governors of St. Bartholomew's Hospital* v. *Cambden* [1914] 1 Ch. 233. Likewise with an action for account, 1980 Act, s.23.

[19] [1907] 2 K.B. 350; following *Thorne* v. *Kerr* (1855) 2 K. & J. 54 and in *Re Gale* (1883) 22 Ch.D. 820.

[20] At p. 366.

[21] See the cases referred to in note 19.

[22] 1980 Act.

[23] This provision applies to personal representatives, see 1980 Act, s.38(1) and the Trustee Act 1925, s.68(17).

[24] 1980 Act, s.21(3), which is also the period applicable to the recovery of arrears of interest in respect of any legacy.

[25] 1980 Act, s.22.

[26] As to the transition from personal representative to trustee, see the discussion *ante*, p. 130.

estate, then it would seem that the six-year period referred to above will apply.[27]

It is provided expressly by the 1980 Act that the equitable jurisdiction to refuse relief on the grounds of acquiescence or otherwise is unaffected.[28] Thus the personal representative may be able to plead the equitable doctrine of laches.[29]

Extension of period

A creditor may be able to obtain an extension of the period if he can point to an acknowledgment by the personal representative of his debt.[30] Such an acknowledgment must be in writing and signed by the person making it.[31] An acknowledgment by one personal representative will bind the others.[32] The effect of such an acknowledgment is to make time run afresh (repeatedly if applicable) but a cause of action once barred cannot be revived.[33]

The period of limitation will also be extended if the plaintiff was under a disability at the time when the cause of action accrued[34] and the period will be postponed in cases of fraud, concealment or mistake.[35]

[27] 1980 Act, s.15(1), which includes any interest in the proceeds of the sale of land held upon trust for sale, see 1980 Act, s.38(1).
[28] s.36(2).
[29] See *Snell's Principles of Equity*, 28th ed., pp. 34–37.
[30] See 1980 Act, s.29; *Re Bowring-Hanbury's Trustees* v. *Bowring-Hanbury* [1943] Ch. 104. A payment in respect of the debt will amount to an acknowledgment, 1980 Act, s.29(5); s.29(7); s.30(2).
[31] 1980 Act, s.30.
[32] 1980 Act, s.31(7).
[33] 1980 Act, s.29(7).
[34] 1980 Act, s.28.
[35] 1980 Act, s.32.

Part Three

THE ENTITLEMENT AND DISTRIBUTION

TABLE OF DISTRIBUTION OF INTESTATE ESTATES DEATHS ON OR AFTER JANUARY 1, 1953

Spouse Surviving

Relative Surviving	*Size of Estate*	*Entitlement*
A. *Spouse*	Estate not exceeding: (i) £40,000 in value death on or after March 1, 1981; (ii) £25,000 in value, death on or after March 15, 1977; (iii) £15,000 in value, death on or after July 1, 1972; (iv) £8,750 in value, death on or after January 1, 1967; (v) £5,000 in value, death on or after January 1, 1953	All to spouse
B. *Spouse and no issue*	Estate not exceeding: (i) £85,000 in value, death on or after March 1, 1981; (ii) £55,000 in value, death on or after March 15, 1977; (iii) £40,000 in value, death on or after July 1, 1972; (iv) £30,000 in value, death on or after January 1, 1967; (v) £20,000 in value, death on or after January 1, 1953	All to spouse
C. *Spouse and no issue or parent or brother or sister of the whole blood or their issue*	Of whatever value	All to spouse
D. *Spouse and issue*	Estate exceeding in value: £40,000; or £25,000; or £15,000; or £8,750; or £5,000 as the case may be with reference to the dates noted in A above	*Spouse entitled to:* —personal chattels absolutely; —£40,000; or £25,000; or £15,000; or £8,750; or £5,000 as the case might be with reference to the dates noted in A above, with interest —a life interest in half of the remaining estate.

Spouse Surviving

Relative Surviving	*Size of Estate*	*Entitlement*
D. *(continued).*		*Issue entitled subject to the spouse's entitlement above:* —one-half of the remaining estate on the statutory trusts —a reversionary interest on the statutory trusts in the other half of the remaining estate after the spouse's life interest
E. *Spouse. No issue but parent(s)*	Estate exceeding in value: £85,000; or £55,000; or £40,000; or £30,000; or £20,000, as the case might be with reference to the dates noted in B above	*Spouse entitled to:* —personal chattels absolutely; —£85,000; or £55,000; or £40,000; or £30,000; or £20,000, as the case might be with reference to the dates noted in B above —an absolute interest in one half of the remaining estate. *Parent(s) entitled to:* —an interest in the other half of the remaining estate, either absolutely if only one parent, or in equal shares absolutely if two parents.
F. *Spouse. No issue but brother(s) and or sister(s) of the whole blood, or issue of a brother or sister of the whole blood*	Estate exceeding in value: £85,000; or £55,000; or £40,000; or £30,000; or £20,000 as the case might be with reference to the dates noted in B above	*Spouse entitled to:* —personal chattels absolutely; —£85,000; or £55,000; or £40,000; or £30,000; or £20,000; as the case might be with reference to the dates in B above —an absolute interest in one-half of the remaining estate *Brother(s) and/or sister(s) entitled to:* —the other half of the remaining estate on the statutory trusts; issue of deceased brother or sister taking their parents share on the statutory trusts.

No Spouse Surviving

No Spouse: Other Relative Surviving	*Size of Estate*	*Entitlement*
G. *Issue*	Of whatever value	*Issue entitled to:* the whole estate on the statutory trusts
H. *Parent(s)*	Of whatever value	*Parent(s) entitled to:* the whole estate absolutely or in equal shares absolutely
I. *Brother(s) and/or sister(s) of the whole blood or issue of a brother or sister of the whole blood*	Of whatever value	*Brother(s) and/or sister(s) entitled to:* the whole estate on the statutory trusts; issue of deceased brother or sister taking their parents share on the statutory trusts
J. *Brother(s) and/or sister(s) of the half blood or issue of a brother or sister of the half blood*	Of whatever value	*Half-brother(s) and/or sister(s) entitled to:* the whole estate on the statutory trusts: issue of deceased brother or sister taking their parents share on the statutory trusts
K. *Grandparent(s)*	Of whatever value	*Grandparent(s) entitled to:* the whole estate absolutely or in equal shares absolutely
L. *Uncle(s) and/or aunt(s) of the whole blood or issue of an uncle or aunt of the whole blood*	Of whatever value	*Uncle(s) and/or aunt(s) entitled to:* the whole estate on the statutory trusts; issue of a deceased uncle or aunt taking their parents share on the statutory trusts
M. *Uncle(s) and/or aunt(s) of the half blood or issue of an uncle or aunt of the half blood*	Of whatever value	*Half uncle(s) and/or aunt(s) entitled to:* the whole estate on the statutory trusts; issue of a deceased uncle or aunt taking their parents share on the statutory trusts
N. *None of the above relatives*	Of whatever value	*The Crown; or the Duchy of Lancaster; or the Duchy of Cornwall entitled to:* the whole estate absolutely

CHAPTER 10

PERSONS ENTITLED ON INTESTACY

PERSONS ENTITLED AS A SPOUSE

Husband or wife

Introduction

Section 46 of the 1925 Act, which governs the entitlement on intestacy after 1925, refers to the intestate leaving "a husband or wife"[1] and the entitlement is expressed to be in favour of "the surviving husband or wife."[2] In order to inherit on intestacy as a spouse it is necessary for a person to have the status of a legally married husband or wife at the date of the death. Strictly speaking a marriage is dissolved by death,[3] and so perhaps it is literally incorrect to refer to the deceased's husband or wife, but this can be regarded as a technicality on which no point is taken. However, so long as a person has this status then it is noticeable that all spouses are equally entitled under the law of intestate succession and it matters not that the surviving spouse, for example, was living apart from the deceased in adultery, provided that no decree absolute of divorce or judicial separation has been obtained. Nor does it matter how long the marriage has lasted. Thus in *Re Park*[4] a wife inherited a substantial estate as the surviving spouse on intestacy, although the marriage had only lasted seventeen days. However, a person without that status has no claim, even if that person has been deceived into thinking that he or she is the lawful spouse of the other by a fraudulent bigamous marriage. Thus in *Shaw* v. *Shaw*[5] a woman had gone through a ceremony of marriage with a man and had lived with him, as she thought, as his lawful wife for many years until his death intestate. In fact at the time of the ceremony the man was already lawfully married and it was held that the woman had no entitlement to his estate as his

[1] s.46(1)(i), s.49(1), or conversely "leaves no husband or wife," s.46(1)(ii), (iii), (iv), (v).

[2] s.46(1)(i); s.47A(1); s.49(1)(*aa*). The Intestates' Estates Act 1952, Sched. 2 is headed "Rights of Surviving Spouse as respects the Matrimonial Home," but the reference throughout is then to the "surviving husband or wife." There is no reference in the legislation to a "widow" or "widower."

[3] See Bromley, *Family Law*, 6th ed., p. 185, and *Re Seaford* (*decd.*) [1968] P. 53 at p. 70; Willmer L.J. citing Fry L.J. in *Stanhope* v. *Stanhope* (1886) 11 P.D. 103, at p. 111, "... no power can dissolve a marriage which has been already dissolved by the act of God."

[4] [1954] P. 89.

[5] [1954] 2 Q.B. 429.

spouse.[6] The denial of intestate succession rights to unmarried cohabitants (or so called "common law husbands or wives"), however long-standing or permanent the relationship, is a striking illustration of the policy of the law to uphold marriage. In recent years such persons have received some legal recognition in other contexts,[7] and in more modern Commonwealth codes of intestate succession,[8] but the English law still insists on the strict legal definition of a husband or wife.[9]

Judicial separation

A decree of judicial separation does not dissolve the marriage or alter the status of husband and wife and therefore such a decree should not affect the intestate entitlement of the survivor on the death intestate of the other party to the marriage.[10] This position has, however, been affected by statute.

In the case of deaths before 1970 the relevant legislation was section

[6] In fact she was able to recover damages equal to what she would have been entitled to as a widow on intestacy against the administrators of the intestate's estate, for breach of promise of marriage. This remedy would no longer be available to her: Law Reform Miscellaneous Provisions Act 1970, s.1. An application under the Inheritance (Provision for Family and Dependants) Act 1975 would now be the solution, under which an innocent party to a void marriage can apply as a spouse, see s.25(4), and more fully discussed, *post* p. 357.

[7] See *e.g.* Domestic Violence and Matrimonial Proceedings Act, 1976, s.1(2); *Davis* v. *Johnson* [1979] A.C. 264. See also *Pascoe* v. *Turner* [1979] 1 W.L.R. 431.

[8] See *e.g.* the definition of "common law spouse" in British Columbia Administration Act, s.91, as amended by a 1972 Act, where a discretionary allowance is provided, for the common law spouse on intestacy. See also South Australian legislation where there is statutory recognition of a "putative spouse" on intestacy. Such a spouse is defined as a person who has co-habited with the other partner as husband and wife *de facto* for five years. Where an intestate is survived by a lawful spouse and by a putative spouse so defined, the two are entitled to the "spouse's share" in equal parts; Family Relationships Act 1975, s.11; Administration and Probate Act 1919–1980, s.4, s.72G. See Hardingham Neave and Ford, *Wills and Intestacy*, pp. 388, 389.

[9] However that is not to say that the unmarried cohabitant never, in fact, succeeds on intestacy since the established presumption of marriage which arises when a man and a woman co-habit and hold themselves out to be husband and wife, might apply. In such cases the burden of disproving the marriage will fall on those who allege that the parties are not married. This must be proved beyond reasonable doubt and can present a formidable obstacle. See Bromley, *Family Law*, 6th ed., p. 65, and the cases there cited, *viz. Mahadervan* v. *Mahadervan*, [1964] P. 233; *Hill* v. *Hill* [1959] 1 W.L.R. 1279; *Piers* v. *Piers* (1849) H.L. Cas. 331. *Re Taylor* [1961] 1 W.L.R. 9. Further the entitlement of the long term cohabitant is recognised and provided for in the law of succession by the Inheritance (Provision for Family and Dependants) Act 1975, which permits an application for discretionary provision out of an intestate's estate by "... any person ... who immediately before the death of the deceased was being maintained, either wholly or partly, by the deceased," s.1(1)(e); s.1(3). See generally, *Re Wilkinson (decd.)*, [1977] 3 W.L.R. 514; *Re Beaumont (decd.)* [1980] Ch. 444, where a claim by a "common law" husband failed; and *Jelley* v. *Iliffe* [1981] 2 W.L.R. 801. Both cases are more fully discussed *post* in Chap. 18.

[10] See Bromley, *Family Law*, 6th ed., pp. 180–184.

20(3) of the Matrimonial Causes Act 1965,[11] a most unsatisfactory provision which was described by the Law Commission as an "extraordinary relic."[12] The section only applied to the wife[13] and as regards reversionary property only if she was the party who obtained the decree. It drew an arbitrary and inconvenient distinction between property acquired before and after the decree. In 1970[14] it was replaced by section 40 of the Matrimonial Proceedings and Property Act 1970, which has been reproduced as section 18(2) of the Matrimonial Causes Act 1973, as follows:

> "If while a decree of judicial separation is in force and the separation is continuing either of the parties to the marriage dies intestate, as respects all or any of his or her real or personal property, the property as respects which he or she dies intestate shall devolve as if the other party to the marriage had then been dead."[15]

This provision makes no distinction between husbands or wives or when the property was acquired. In so far as a decree of judicial separation represents in many cases the termination of the marriage, the current provision more accurately reflects the presumed intention of the parties. However, it will be noticed that the section only governs intestate property and thus will not affect the entitlement to property subject to testamentary provision in a partial intestacy. If, therefore, in a partial intestacy, property is specifically bequeathed to the wife, husband or spouse described as such, then a judicially-separated spouse will take that property.

It is provided that a non-cohabitation order obtained in a magistrates' court[16] is not to have the effect of a decree of judicial separation for the purposes of section 18(2) and thus does not prejudice the rights of intestate succession on the death of a spouse.[17]

[11] The section was the successor to previous legislation in similar terms and provided as follows: "In a case of judicial separation—(*a*) any property which is acquired by or devolves upon the wife on or after the date of the decree whilst the separation continues; and (*b*) where the decree is obtained by the wife, any property to which she is entitled for an estate in remainder or reversion on the date of the decree, shall, if she dies intestate, devolve as if her husband had then been dead." For a critical discussion see Law Commission Working Paper No. 9.

[12] *Op.cit.*, para. 211.

[13] On the death intestate of the husband, the wife was entitled in the usual way notwithstanding any decree of judicial separation.

[14] The relevant provision came into force on August 1, 1970.

[15] The 1973 Act came into force on January 1, 1974. See Law Commission Report No. 25, para. 79. It is based on Australian legislation, see Law Commission Working Paper No. 9, para. 212. New Zealand has similar legislation, Matrimonial Proceedings Act 1963, s.12(2).

[16] s.2(1)(*a*) of the Matrimonial Proceedings (Magistrates Courts) Act 1960, which provided that generally such an order was to have the effect of a decree of judicial separation, but this is expressly excluded by the 1973 Act s.18(3).

[17] s.18(3), previously s.40(2) of the 1970 Act, see Law Commission Report, *op.cit.*, para. 79, note 74.

The domestic jurisdiction of magistrates is now contained in the Domestic Proceedings and Magistrates' Courts Act 1978[18] which replaces the old non-cohabitation orders with powers to make orders for the protection of a party to a marriage or a child of the marriage.[19] These include a power to order one party to leave the matrimonial home or an order prohibiting one party from entering the matrimonial home.[20] These orders do not have the effect of orders of judicial separation and, although there does not appear to be any specific amendment of section 18 of the 1973 Act, it is thought that such orders would likewise be excluded from the operation of that section.

Commorientes

Husbands and wives are particularly likely to be killed in common calamities and thus *commorientes* problems arise not infrequently.[21] In cases of testamentary succession the position will be governed by the well-known presumption in section 184 of the Law of Property Act 1925[22] to the effect that the younger will be presumed to have survived the elder but this provision is expressly excluded in cases of intestacy concerning the entitlement of a surviving spouse. Instead the distribution proceeds in such cases on the basis that, whatever be the respective ages of the parties, the husband or wife had not survived the intestate. The reason for this is that, if section 184 were to be applied to cases where spouses died intestate in a common calamity, it would result, in the typical case where the husband is older than his wife, in all (or most) of his property passing to the wife and then (in the absence of issue) her estate would pass to her next-of-kin. This was thought not to be consistent with the presumed intention of the parties which would probably be in favour of the husband's next-of-kin taking his property and the wife's next-of-kin taking hers. Accordingly, the law was modified to this effect by the Intestates' Estates Act 1952,[23] which added the following provision as subsection (3) to section 46 of the 1925 Act:

> "Where the intestate and the intestate's husband or wife have died in circumstances rendering it uncertain which of them survived the other and the intestate's husband or wife is by virtue of section one hundred and eighty four of the Law of Property Act

[18] The Act came into force November 1, 1979.
[19] ss.16–18.
[20] s.16(3).
[21] See *e.g. Re Howard* [1944] P. 39.
[22] The provision has been fully considered by the House of Lords in *Hickman* v. *Peacey* [1945] A.C. 304, to which reference should be made.
[23] s.1(4), a change was thought to be particularly necessary in 1952 in view of the greatly increased benefits provided by that Act for a surviving spouse. It was not thought to be appropriate that the estate should be directed to one side of the family by legal fiction. However like much of the amendments introduced in 1952, the provision is poorly drafted.

1925 deemed to have survived the intestate, this section shall, nevertheless, have effect as respects the intestate as if the husband or wife had not survived the intestate."

Thus, in the example given above where both spouses have died intestate, the husband's estate will pass as if he were a widower to his family and the wife's estate to her family. It must be noted that this result will apply where it is "uncertain which of them survived the other" and thus will not apply where the order of deaths is certain, however short an interval has elapsed between them. Thus, if a husband and wife are involved in a car crash and the husband is killed instantly but the wife dies later that same day in hospital, neither section 184 nor section 46(3) can have any operation. Further, it will be noticed that the section will only apply where, if section 184 applied, the other spouse would be deemed to have survived the intestate spouse *i.e.* where the elder spouse dies intestate. Section 46(3) will then apply whether or not the other spouse dies intestate. Suppose that a husband and his younger wife die in a *commorientes* situation and that the husband dies intestate but the wife leaves a valid will giving all her property to the husband. In such a case section 184 will apply to the wife so that her bequest to her husband will lapse and her family will take on her intestacy and section 46(3) will apply to the husband so that his family will take on his intestacy. However, if the ages are reversed so that the intestate husband is younger than his testate wife, section 46(3) will not apply. In such a case section 184 will apply to the wife's estate and it will go to her husband's estate and both her and his estate will then go to his family on his intestacy, again by virtue of section 184. This is because section 46(3) only applies where the intestate's spouse is deemed by section 184 to survive the intestate which is not so in the last example.

It seems that the section would be equally applicable to cases of partial intestacy since "intestate" is defined to include a person who leaves a will but dies intestate as to some beneficial interest in his real or personal estate.[24] Further, section 49(1) provides that "... this Part of this Act shall have effect as respects the part of his property not so disposed of..." and section 46(3) is in "this Part." It seems that section 46(3) would only apply to the intestate part of the property in cases of partial intestacy, whilst section 184 would apply to the testate part. This is because section 46(3) states "... this section shall, nevertheless, have effect as respects the intestate as if..." and "this section" refers to section 46 which only governs the distribution on intestacy. Thus, if a husband older than his wife bequeaths a legacy of £10,000 to his wife but dies with his wife in a *commorientes* situation intestate as to the rest of his estate, it seems that section 184 will

[24] 1925 Act, s.55(i)(vi); (1953) 16 M.L.R. 208, 209.

govern the wife's entitlement to the legacy but section 46(3) will exclude her from the intestate part of the estate.[25]

It can be emphasised that the section only applies to husbands and wives and has no application to other classes of relatives, for example, brothers or sisters, to whom section 184 applies in the usual way.[26] If, for example, two spinster sisters both die intestate in a common calamity, the property of the elder will pass to the younger and both estates will pass to the younger's next-of-kin. This is satisfactory in most cases since spinster sisters will usually have the same next-of-kin but suppose that the younger sister has an illegitimate child. Likewise, where a widowed mother dies in a common calamity with her married only child, the child's spouse will take the mother's estate.

Comment

A provision on the lines of section 46(3) would appear to be desirable to ensure that the law of intestacy accords with the presumed wishes of the parties. As presently drafted it applies only to the intestate part of an estate and consideration could be given to rendering the section applicable to cases where the younger spouse dies intestate and the older dies testate and to govern also the testate succession in partial intestacies. It might also be desirable to extend the section to cover parties other than a husband and wife. However, it is suggested that the main difficulty with the section centres on the fact that it will only apply in a true *commorientes* situation and yet the same solution seems equally desirable in cases where one spouse survives the other by a very short period. It would seem desirable for the legislation to be redrawn with reference to the spouse surviving the intestate for a specified period on the lines of the South Australian legislation "where an intestate and his spouse die within twenty-eight days of each other, this Part applies as if the spouse had not survived the intestate."[27]

[25] It will be appreciated that s.46(3) only affects the intestate entitlement and does not, for example, affect the survivorship to joint property which will be governed by s.184. This is because s.184 refers to "... all purposes affecting the title to property."

[26] *Re Grosvenor* [1944] Ch. 138, the Court of Appeal decision in *Hickman* v. *Peacey, supra*; *In the Estate of Dixon* [1969] 2 N.S.W.R. 223.

[27] Administration and Probate Act, 1919–1925, s.72(*e*); see also Queensland, Succession Act 1981, s.35(2), 30 days. In New Zealand (Simultaneous Deaths Act 1958) and Western Australia (Property Law Act 1969–1973) the test is where "... two or more persons have died at the same time or in circumstances which give rise to a reasonable doubt as to which of them survived the other or others"; see Hardingham, *op.cit.* p. 489. The American Uniform Probate Code has a provision, 2–104, to the effect that in order to qualify as an heir a person must survive the decedent for 120 hours.

Where the marriage has been dissolved or annulled

Divorce

A spouse whose marriage has been dissolved by decree absolute of divorce has no entitlement on intestacy to his or her former spouse's estate,[28] although it is of course clear that under the present English law a former wife, or a former husband[29] who has not remarried, can apply for a discretionary award of financial provision out of the intestate's estate under the Inheritance (Provision for Family and Dependants) Act 1975. In certain cases a decree nisi can be rescinded or a decree absolute might itself be void,[30] in which case, presumably, the marriage would be regarded as subsisting and the surviving spouse would be entitled on intestacy.

A decree nisi does not, however, generally change the status of marriage and so the spouse of an intestate who dies between the decree nisi and the decree absolute will be entitled. This was the case in *Re Seaford (decd.)*[31] where it was held that a spouse could succeed to the intestate estate of the other. The husband had died before the lodgment of the notice of application to make a decree nisi absolute with the consequence that the substratum of the divorce suit had been destroyed, the lodgment of the notice was a nullity and no decree absolute could be made. Accordingly, the wife was entitled to letters of administration of his estate.[32]

Voidable marriages

A voidable marriage is in all respects a valid marriage until a decree of nullity is pronounced. Thus, if either party dies before a decree is granted, a voidable marriage must be treated as valid for all purposes and for all time.[33] Therefore, if no decree has been obtained before the death intestate of one of the parties to such a marriage, the other party is entitled as a surviving husband or wife. This point was established

[28] In *The Estate of Wallas* [1905] P. 326; Bromley, *Family Law*, 6th ed., p. 232.

[29] s.1(1)(*b*); "former wife" or "former husband" originally defined in s.25(1) of the 1975 Act has been redefined by s.25(2) of the Matrimonial and Family Proceedings Act 1984; see *post* p. 359.

[30] Bromley, *op. cit.*, p. 227; p. 194.

[31] [1968] P. 53, reversing Cairns J., [1967] P. 325. See also *Re Allan, Allan* v. *Midland Bank Executor and Trustee Co.* [1954] Ch. 295; *Re William's Settlement* [1929] 2 Ch. 361; *Re Slaughter, Trustee Corporation Ltd.* v. *Slaughter* [1945] 1 Ch. 355, cases where a divorced wife was not entitled under wills and settlements.

[32] An alternative approach to the effect of a decree nisi on intestate succession, would be to provide that once such a decree has been obtained the property should devolve as if the surviving spouse had predeceased the deceased, analogously to judicially separated spouses, see *ante* p. 162. See the Victorian Marriage Act 1958 s.159(3), Hardingham, *op. cit.* pp. 390, 391. It might be thought that this would be more in accord with the parties' presumed intentions and the safety net of an application under the Inheritance (Provision for Family and Dependants) Act 1975 would presumably be applicable.

[33] *per* Bromley, *Family Law*, 6th ed. p. 73. See also *De Reneville* v. *De Reneville* [1948] P. 100, Lord Greene M.R. at p. 111.

in the modern law by *Re Roberts* (*decd.*),[34] where the surviving party to a voidable marriage applied for and obtained letters of administration to the estate of the other party to the marriage on the footing of an intestacy. This application was resisted by the defendant, who was the beneficiary under an earlier will, on the grounds that at the time when the deceased went through the ceremony of marriage he was suffering from senile dementia and other mental illness so as not to have the necessary capacity to marry. On this basis it was submitted that the marriage was voidable and as such was ineffective to revoke the earlier will. There were two statutory provisions to be considered both originally enacted in the Nullity of Marriage Act 1971[35] and now consolidated in the Matrimonial Causes Act 1973.[36]

Sections 1 and 2 of the 1971 Act set out the grounds on which marriages were void and voidable respectively and in the new classification the effect of lack of consent on the grounds of duress mistake or unsoundness of mind was deliberately changed from making a marriage void to making a marriage voidable.[37] Secondly, it was enacted in 1971 that thenceforth a decree of nullity granted on the ground that a marriage was voidable should operate to annul the marriage only as respects any time after the decree had been made absolute and that notwithstanding the decree the marriage should be regarded as if it had existed up to that time.[38] Applying these provisions it was held that a marriage which was voidable always revoked an earlier will of a party to the marriage, whether or not the marriage was subsequently annulled. Accordingly (since the marriage in question had not been annulled), the plaintiff was entitled to letters of administration on the basis of an intestacy and no doubt took most of the estate as the surviving spouse.

Whether or not the marriage has been annulled by decree *inter vivos*, it will be effective to revoke an earlier will under section 18 of the Wills Act 1837 because it is not necessary for the application of that provision that the marriage subsists at the death, merely that it has been a valid marriage at some time after the will has been made.[39] The decree, if granted, does not have retrospective effect.[40] However, if a decree of nullity has been obtained *inter vivos*, that will certainly affect the intestate entitlement of the "former spouse" since such a decree operates to annul the marriage as respects any time after the

[34] [1978] 1 W.L.R. 653.

[35] ss.2 and 5, with effect from July 31, 1971.

[36] ss.12(*c*) and 16.

[37] Now 1973 Act, s.12(*c*).

[38] s.5, now the 1973 Act, s.16. It will be noticed that both of these provisions represented changes in the law effected by the 1971 Act. The *Re Roberts* situation could not have arisen with reference to the pre-1971 position.

[39] A new provision has been substituted for the original s.18 of the 1837 Act, by the Administration of Justice Act 1982 s.18 but this does not affect the general rule.

[40] 1973 Act s.16, *supra*.

decree has been made.[41] Thus, if the marriage has been annulled, the other party to the marriage, by analogy with a divorced spouse, will have no claim as a spouse on intestacy. There remains, however, the possibility of an application under the Inheritance (Provision for Family and Dependants) Act 1975 as a former spouse (provided that the party has not remarried[42]) since that category is defined to include for the purposes of that Act a person whose marriage with the deceased was during the deceased's lifetime annulled by a decree of nullity.[43]

Void marriage

A void marriage is no marriage at all and the parties never acquire the status of husband or wife.[44] It is void *ab initio* and there is theoretically no necessity for a decree of nullity, which is merely declaratory,[45] but such a decree will undoubtedly clarify the position on the death of one of the parties.[46] A party to a void marriage, whether formally annulled or not, strictly has no claim to the spouse's entitlement on the intestacy of the partner[47] but there remains the possibility of an application under the Inheritance (Provision for Family and Dependants) Act 1975 leading to the making of a discretionary award. If the marriage has been declared null by a decree during the lifetime of the parties, the survivor can claim as a "former wife" or "former husband."[48] Further, where the marriage has not been annulled during the lifetime of the parties, the innocent party to a void marriage can have *locus standi* as a "husband" or "wife."[49] This is a desirable safeguard where, for example, the deceased partner had suppressed a previous marriage and had

[41] *Ibid.*

[42] 1975 Act, s.1(1)(*b*).

[43] 1975 Act, s.25(1); see Matrimonial and Family Proceedings Act 1984, s.25(2); *post* p. 359.

[44] See Bromley, *Family Law*, 6th ed., pp. 71, 74; *De Reneville* v. *De Reneville*, [1948] P. 100, see Lord Greene M.R. at p. 111.

[45] See *Re Roberts* (*decd.*) [1978] 1 W.L.R. 653 at p. 655.

[46] *Ibid.* The grounds on which marriages are void are set out in the Matrimonial Causes Act 1973 s.11.

[47] *Re Roberts* (*decd.*), *supra*, see Buckley L.J., at p. 660, and Goff L.J. at pp. 662, 663.

[48] See *post*, Chap. 18. It can be noted that for the purposes of the 1975 Act a "former wife" or "former husband" means a person whose marriage with the deceased was during the deceased's lifetime dissolved or annulled by a decree of divorce or of nullity of marriage granted under the law of any part of the British Isles, or which is entitled to be recognised as valid by the law of England and Wales; 1975 Act, s.25(1) as substituted by Matrimonial and Family Proceedings Act 1984, s.25(2).

[49] See *post*, Chap. 18. For the purposes of the 1975 Act any reference to a wife or husband shall be treated as including a reference to a person who in good faith entered into a void marriage with the deceased unless either (a) the marriage of the deceased and that person was dissolved or annulled during the lifetime of the deceased and the dissolution or annullment is recognised by the law of England and Wales, or (b) that person has during the lifetime of the deceased entered into a later marriage, s.25(4). See also s.25(5) referring to "remarriage."

bigamously married the other partner who thought that he or she was contracting a valid marriage.[50]

Parties to polygamous marriages

The entitlement of the surviving party or parties to a polygamous marriage on the death intestate of the other, is considered in Chapter 16.

Spouse entitled in two capacities

Australian case

The unusual situation of a spouse being entitled in two capacities arose in the Australian case of *Re Morrison*,[51] where the widow was also the intestate's cousin. There were a number of other cousins who were entitled as next-of-kin. It was held that the widow, in addition to taking her share as such, was entitled to share in the balance of the estate as one of the next-of-kin. The judge saw no reason why a person who stood in two distinct relationships to the intestate should not be entitled to the share appropriate to each of those relationships. This precise problem could not arise under the current English law since, if a widow survives and the only other relatives are cousins, the widow will take the whole estate as the surviving spouse.[52] In fact it is difficult to see how any double entitlement of a spouse could arise under English law since a person cannot marry his or her niece or nephew[53] and so could not also be entitled in that capacity.

PERSONS ENTITLED AS ISSUE

Meaning of issue

Introduction

The Administration of Estates Act 1925 refers in the table of distribution in section 46 to the intestate leaving "issue" or "no issue" and the entitlement is expressed to be "on the statutory trusts for the issue of the intestate." These trusts are set out in section 47(1)(i) and the primary entitlement is "... in equal shares if more than one, for all or any of the children or child of the intestate...," with a substitutional entitlement "... for all or any of the issue... of any child of the intestate who predeceases the intestate.... "[54] It is necessary in this section to consider who is so entitled as "issue" or "a child," with particular reference to the problems posed by illegiti-

[50] The surviving partner might also be able to apply as a "dependant" under s.1(1)(*e*).
[51] *Trustees Executors and Agency Co. Ltd.* v. *Comport* [1945] A.L.R. 138.
[52] s.46(1).
[53] Marriage Act 1949, Sched. 1, as amended by the Marriage (Enabling) Act 1960, and the Children Act 1975. It is possible for cousins to be entitled twice over, see *post*.
[54] See also s.47(1)(iii) "... of a child of the intestate.... "

mate, legitimated and adopted children, and to consider also the entitlement of children of void, voidable and polygamous marriages.

It can be noted initially that "issue" bears its usual meaning of descendants of all degrees and is not confined to children,[55] whereas "child" or "children" in its ordinary meaning refers to the first generation of legitimate descendants of the parent by any marriage.[56] The requirement in section 46 is that the deceased should leave issue and section 47(1)(i) states that the child or children should be "living at the death of the intestate."[57] If the child predeceases the intestate, then, if his issue are to take his share, it is essential that the issue are living at the death of the intestate. Where a parent and a child die in a common calamity, the *commorientes* provisions in section 184 Law of Property Act 1925 will be applicable to determine the order of deaths so that the younger will be presumed to survive the elder.[58]

It can be emphasised that issue always take on the "statutory trusts"[59] under which only children have a primary entitlement; grandchildren and great-grandchildren take only by representation or substitution *per stirpes*. This is so even if all the first generation children are dead so that the "issue" is composed exclusively of a class of grandchildren. It will be appreciated that taking *per stirpes* in this way rather than *per capita* can lead to striking and apparently anomalous differences in the size of the shares to be taken by individuals.[60]

En ventre sa mère

References to a child or issue living at the death of any person include a child or issue *en ventre sa mère* at the death.[61] Such children will obviously be born within the usual one-year period of administration.

Step-children

It will be appreciated that unadopted step-children, *i.e.* the children of the other party to the marriage by a third party, have no entitlement

[55] See *Williams on Wills*, 5th ed., p. 589.

[56] *Ibid.*, p. 585.

[57] Subject to the entitlement of children *en ventre sa mère*, at the date of the death, s.55(2), see *infra*.

[58] Provided, of course, that the condition precedent to the operation of that section is satisfied.

[59] As defined in s.47.

[60] Thus if the three children, A, B and C, of the intestate are all dead and A leaves one child P, B two, Q and R, and C three, S, T, U, then P takes a one-third share, Q and R one-sixth shares, and S, T and U one-ninth shares.

[61] 1925 Act s.55(2), this provision is necessary because a child *en ventre sa mère* is not normally regarded as satisfying a requirement of "living at" or "surviving" a particular time, *Villar* v. *Gilbey* [1907] A.C. 139; *Elliott* v. *Joicey* [1935] A.C. 209; but see the new s.33 of Wills Act 1837 added by Administration of Justice Act 1982 expressly including such children. See generally, *Williams on Wills* 5th ed. pp. 582, 583.

on intestacy.[62] They may, however, be able to apply under the Inheritance (Provision for Family and Dependants) Act 1975 as "a child of the family" for financial provision out of the estate.[63]

Illegitimate children

Introduction: pre-1969 position

The common law attitude was that any reference to a "child" or "children" or "issue" meant legitimate persons only,[64] *i.e.* a child whose parents were married to each other at the time of conception or at the time of birth or both.[65] Accordingly, the prima facie rule at common law before the enactment of the Family Law Reform Act 1969 was that illegitimate children had no entitlement on the death intestate of their parent and likewise the parent had no entitlement on the death intestate of the child.[66] However, even before 1969 the strict application of this rule had been modified by statute. The provision in section 9 of the Legitimacy Act 1926[67] applied where the mother of an illegitimate child[68] died intestate[69] and did not leave any legitimate surviving issue, in which case the illegitimate child (or if he was dead his issue) was entitled to take under his mother's intestacy the interest to which he would have been entitled if he had been born legitimate.[70] Similarly, where the illegitimate child died intestate, the mother had rights of entitlement as if the child had been born legitimate and she had been the only surviving parent.[71] It will be noticed that the

[62] Such children are not kin; see *Re Leach* (*decd.*) [1985] 2 All E.R. 754, at p. 759.

[63] s.1(1)(*d*); see *Re Callaghan* (*decd.*) [1984] 3 All E.R. 790; *Re Leach (decd.) supra*; see *post* p. 364. In 1976 it was indicated (in answer to a Parliamentary question) that the Treasury Solicitor's practice was not to claim *bona vacantia* where it appeared to him that step-children would have a valid claim under the 1975 Act. There remains also the possibility of an *ex gratia* payment out of *bona vacantia* for such children, see *post* p. 277.

[64] See *Williams on Wills*, 5th ed., p. 570. See in *Re Makein* (*decd.*) [1955] 1 Ch. 194; *Wilkinson* v. *Adam* (1813), Ives. & Bea. 422; *Hill* v. *Crook* (1873) L.R. 6 H.L. 265; *Guardians of Woolwich Union* v. *Guardians of Fulham* [1906] 2 K.B. 240. But would also presumably include a child conceived before the marriage of its parents and born after the death of its father.

[65] Bromley, *Family Law*, 6th ed., pp. 255 *et seq.*

[66] See Harman J. in *Re Makein* (*decd.*) [1955] 1 Ch. 194 at p. 200, 201, "In fact it is admitted that the law of intestacy makes no provision, for a natural child cannot by the law of England succeed on intestacy to any part of the estate of his father, though he may under the Legitimacy Act 1926 (s.9) succeed to his mother's property if she have no lawful issue."

[67] Which came into force on January 1, 1927.

[68] Not being a legitimated person, *ibid.*, see *post* p. 178.

[69] As respects all or any of her real or personal property, *ibid.*

[70] The section did not apply to or affect any express dispositions or entailed property, s.9(3).

[71] s.9(2). Subject of course to the prior rights on intestacy of any widow or widower of the illegitimate person.

provisions only applied to a mother and her child, and then only in the absence of legitimate issue,[72] and as such was clearly unsatisfactory. Section 9 of the 1926 Act was repealed by section 14(7) of the Family law Reform Act 1969 in respect of deaths after January 1, 1970 and the wider provisions of that Act now govern the situation.

Death intestate after 1970

The reforms embodied in the Family Law Reform Act 1969 were based on the recommendations of the Report of the Committee on the Law of Succession in relation to Illegitimate Persons[73] (the "Russell Committee"). The Committee recommended that for the purpose of intestate succession there should be no distinction between a woman's legitimate and illegitimate children[74] and that a similar right of succession should apply to a man's illegitimate children.[75] However, the Committee did not think it appropriate that an illegitimate child should participate in any estate other than that of the person responsible for that birth: "... it would not be right to impose a system of intestate succession which could, for example, lead to participation of a daughter's bastard in the intestacy of that daughter's parent when such participation might be directly opposed to the wishes of the latter, who, indeed, might know nothing of the bastard."[76] This comment clearly bases the proposals on the presumed intention of the intestate which, it is submitted, is the correct approach but the assumption made as to the presumed wishes is at least questionable. Further and conversely, it was not thought appropriate that any person other than a surviving spouse, issue, or parent of an illegitimate child should be able to succeed to the illegitimate child's estate.[77] These recommendations are reflected in section 14 of the 1969 Act which provides that an illegitimate child can inherit on the death intestate of his or her parent and that a parent can inherit on the death intestate of his of her illegitimate child.[78] Part IV of the 1925 Act is amended accordingly.

[72] The provisions were apparently based on the presumed wishes of the deceased but were criticised on this basis by the Russell Committee, Report of the Committee on the Law of Succession in Relation to Illegitimate Persons 1966, Cmnd. 3051, para. 31.

[73] 1966 Cmnd. 3051, see Stone, (1967) 30 M.L.R. 552.

[74] para. 31.

[75] para. 46, "... in cases in which paternity is established or not disputed." But subject to the "rule of convenience," s.14(4) *post*, so far as father's rights to succeed on the intestacy of his illegitimate child. See the "note of dissent" by Munro-Lucas-Tooth, *ibid.*

[76] para. 32.

[77] *Ibid.*

[78] s.14(3). The full provision is set out in Appendix A. For academic comment on the Act see Samuels, 34 Conv. 247 and the articles noted in n. 1 of that article. Note that

Some points can be noted on the provision. First, the 1969 Act does not affect any rights under the intestacy of a person dying before January 1, 1970.[79] Secondly, the provisions do not apply to or affect the right of any person to take any entailed interest in real or personal property.[80] Thirdly, references in section 50(1) of the 1925 Act[81] to Part IV of the Act in a document, will or codicil taking effect after January 1, 1970 include references to section 14 of the 1969 Act.[82] Fourthly, an "illegitimate child" does not include a legitimate or adopted child.[83] Fifthly, for the purposes of succession by a parent to the intestate estate of an illegitimate child, the child shall be presumed not to have been survived by his father unless the contrary is shown.[84] Sixthly, the Act does not differentiate between adulterous, incestuous and other illegitimate children.[85]

It will be seen that the legislation does not distinguish between mothers and fathers[86] and that the illegitimate child takes whether or not there are legitimate issue and on the basis of equality. However, it must be emphasised that the Act is limited to succession between illegitimate children and their parents and does not entitle an illegitimate child to share on the intestacy of his or her grandparents

the effect of the legislation is not exclusively beneficial since the entitlement of illegitimate children on the intestacy of their parent can prejudice the position of the "common law" husband or wife, by excluding the Crown's entitlement to *bona vacantia* and thus precluding any possibility of an *ex gratia* payment to the spouse. Consider the position where a man and a woman live together as husband and wife and have illegitimate children. On the death intestate of the man the children will have rights of inheritance under the 1969 Act to his estate; the woman has none. Previously, in the absence of other relatives, the estate would pass on *bona vacantia* to the Duchy or the Crown who could recognise by *ex gratia* payments the moral claims of the woman. Now she will have to rely on her right of application as a dependant, under the Inheritance (Provision for Family and Dependants) Act 1975.

[79] s.14(9).

[80] s.14(5).

[81] Which relates to the construction of documents.

[82] s.14(6).

[83] s.14(8), repealed by Children Act 1975, see *post* for position of legitimated and adopted children.

[84] s.14(4). This is a rule of convenience to resolve a problem that might arise on the intestacy of an illegitimate person who leaves no issue to take. In such a case the mother and the father, if both survive, would be entitled (subject to the rights of the illegitimate's surviving spouse) to share equally in the estate, or if one be dead the other would be entitled to the whole. But since in many cases the identity of the father would be unknown it is desirable to exclude him by presumption in such cases. See Russell Committee, *op. cit.* para. 47 see Samuels, 34 Conv. 253.

[85] Russell Committee, *op. cit.* para. 56. Nor was it thought to be practical to attempt any distinction between children with whom there has been at some stage a true familial relationship and those who have at an early age been, so to speak, jettisoned by the mother, *ibid.* para. 31.

[86] Except in respect of s.14(4) noted above. If the child was rich then the father would have an interest in publicising his parentage.

or brothers and sisters or uncles and aunts.[87] This is an important limitation and the consequences merit fuller illustration and emphasis.

Grandchildren

Suppose that a widow dies intestate after 1970 and has had three children: A, an illegitimate child who survives her; B, an illegitimate child who predeceased her leaving an illegitimate child D and a legitimate child E; and C, a legitimate child who predeceased her leaving an illegitimate child F and a legitimate child G. The estate will be divided into three shares.[88] A will take one[89]; B's share will pass to E, since the illegitimate child D is not entitled to share in the intestacy of his grandparent; and G will take C's share likewise to the exclusion of F.[90] If B or C were survived only by illegitimate children, it would seem that the shares would fail, and that A would be absolutely entitled to the whole estate.[91] Conversely, if an illegitimate person survives his parents and dies unmarried and without issue, his grandparents will not be entitled to take on intestacy.[92]

Personal representatives

The entitlement of illegitimate children could place personal representatives in a difficult position in view of the problems of proving paternity or simply discovering the existence of illegitimate children. Accordingly, it is provided by way of protection that trustees or personal representatives may convey or distribute the estate to the persons entitled thereto without having ascertained that there is any person entitled as an illegitimate child or their issue or as a father of an illegitimate child.[93] It will be noticed that this provision confers no

[87] See Ryder 24 C.L.P. 162. It is interesting to note that under some Commonwealth legislation illegitimate children are not subject to such limitations in the law of intestate succession, see Hardingham, Neave and Ford, *op. cit.* pp. 394, 395, discussing the legislation in Victoria, New South Wales, South Australia, Queensland, Tasmania, Northern Territory, New Zealand. The Australian Capital Territory legislation restricts succession by, and to, a parent and the illegitimate child, see Hardingham Neave and Ford, *op. cit.* pp. 397, 398.

[88] Under the 1925 Act s.47(1)(i).

[89] The 1969 Act s.14(1).

[90] This is because the inclusion of illegitimate issue or children is restricted by s.14(3) to "the issue of the intestate," or "the child or children of the intestate" and a grandchild is not, of course, such a person. See Russell Committee, *op. cit.* para. 33 ". . . where a bastard dies in his mother's lifetime and would, had he survived her, have been beneficially interested in her estate on intestacy, only his *legitimate* issue her surviving should stand in his shoes, as is the case at present."

[91] This does not seem very satisfactory and it is doubtful if it accords with the presumed wishes of the intestate. There is accordingly a case for suggesting a reform of s.14(3) to include illegitimate issue of a legitimate or illegitimate child of the deceased who has predeceased the intestate, *i.e.* that illegitimate grandchildren should be able to take by representation.

[92] And nor in fact will anyone else, and the estate will pass as *bona vacantia*. See *post.*

[93] 1969 Act, s.17.

protection so far as the entitlement of the mother is concerned. In addition personal representatives are not to be liable to any such person of whose claim they have not had notice at the time of the distribution but that this is not to prejudice the right of any such person to follow the property, or any property representing it, into the hands of any person, other than a purchaser, who may have received it.[94]

The question of proving the paternity of an illegitimate child will inevitably raise difficulties for the personal representatives. The Russell Committee thought that affiliation orders could not be regarded as sufficiently reliable to be taken as conclusive proof for the purpose of succession.[95] It was thought that the determination of paternity should be left to the decision of the court based on the evidence of the cases, with proof required beyond the balance of probabilities, save only for the presumption enacted as section 14(4) of the 1969 Act that a father of an illegitimate person should be presumed not to have survived the child unless the contrary was proved. This attitude might well result in many cases in the practical exclusion of the illegitimate child from sharing in its natural father's intestate estate.[96] There remains, however, the possibility of a claim under the Inheritance (Provision for Family and Dependants) Act 1975, either as a "child of the family"[97] or as a "dependant."[98]

Illegitimacy: proposals for reform

The legal position of non-marital children has recently been fully considered by the Law Commission,[99] including the rights of inheritance of illegitimate persons. The Commission noted[1] the present law, including the limited rights of inheritance conferred by the Family Law Reform Act 1969, and stated the argument of

[94] *Ibid.*, as to tracing property see Pettit, *Equity and the Law of Trusts*, 5th ed., pp. 446 *et seq.*

[95] Cmnd. 3051, para. 39. It is interesting to note that many Commonwealth and foreign jurisdictions have formulated principles based on voluntary recognition whether formal or informal but there are no such provisions in English law. See, for example, the Northern Territory of Australia's Administration and Probate Ordinance 1969, s.71(5); "For the purposes of this section (*entitlement of illegitimate child on intestacy of parent*) a person shall not be taken to be the father of an illegitimate child unless he has acknowledged, in writing, that he is the father of the child or has been adjudged by a court to be the father of the child, and in the case where the child died before that person, the person so acknowledged the child, or has been so adjudged, before the death of the child." See the Note of Dissent by Munro-Lucas-Tooth, *ibid.*, and Stone, 30 M.L.R. 557–559.

[96] The use of blood tests to resolve paternity provided by ss.20–25 of the 1969 Act, are obviously inapplicable in succession cases; see Bromley, *Family Law* 6th ed., pp. 262–265.

[97] 1975 Act, s.1(1)(*d*), see *post* Chap. 18.

[98] *Ibid.* s.1(1)(*e*).

[99] See Working Paper No. 74 and Report No. 118, Fam. Law: Illegitimacy (1982).

[1] See Report, the whole of Part VIII, Inheritance, particularly paras. 8.7 to 8.16.

principle against extending the rights of the non-marital child to inherit on intestacy as follows.

> "... it is right that the non-marital child should be able to inherit on the intestacy of either of his parents, who have moral and may have legal responsibilities for him, and who can be presumed to have wished to benefit him. However, this does not apply to remoter relations, since the deceased may not know of the illegitimate beneficiary, let alone wish to benefit him. It could even be said that a relation of this kind, such as a grandparent, might choose to die intestate on the assumption that his or her estate would go to the grandchildren of marital birth and that it would be wrong in such circumstances partially to frustrate the grandparent's positive intentions by allowing other grandchildren to share."

The Law Commission were not persuaded by these arguments.[2] First, it was thought that the Family Law Reform Act 1969 had decided the principle but that the incomplete rights of succession provided by that Act were illogical. Secondly, an extension of the rights to inherit on intestacy would render the position more consistent with testamentary succession. Thirdly, the present position is justified on the basis of the presumed wishes of the grandparent to exclude illegitimate grandchildren; this is dismissed as speculation. Fourthly, the present English law is inconsistent with the European Convention on Human Rights and the European Convention on the Legal Status of Children Born out of Wedlock to which the United Kingdom is a signatory.[3] Accordingly, the Law Commission concluded that there was no sufficient argument of principle to justify retention of the existing rules discriminating against illegitimate persons in relation to intestate succession.[4] The Commission recommended change and included a clause in their draft Bill to entitle an illegitimate child to the same rights on intestacy as those of a legitimate child.[5] It is understood that legislation is to be introduced to implement this recommendation.

[2] See paras. 8.9 to 8.12.

[3] "A child born out of wedlock shall have the same right of succession in the estate of its father and its mother and of a member of its father's or mother's family, as if it had been born in wedlock."

[4] para. 8.13.

[5] Clause 24 of the proposed Family Law Reform Bill provided:

"24.—(1) In section 14 of the Family Law Reform Act 1969 (which enables an illegitimate child to succeed on the intestacy of parents and parents to succeed on the intestacy of an illegitimate child) for subsection (1) to (5) there shall be substituted the following subsections—

"(1) Where any person dies intestate in respect of all or any of his real or personal property, an illegitimate person, and any person related to an illegitimate person, shall be entitled to take any interest therein as if the illegitimate person had been born legitimate.

Legitimated and adopted children

Legitimation

Where the parents of an illegitimate child marry one another the effect is to render that child legitimate from the date of the marriage.[6]

The initial legislative provision was contained in the Legitimacy Act 1926 and provided for legitimation by marriage provided that neither parent was married to a third person at the time of the birth.[7] The latter limitation was removed by the Legitimacy Act 1959, and both Acts were repealed and new provisions enacted by the Children Act 1975. The Legitimacy Act 1976 consolidated the previous legislation and now contains the relevant provisions. Accordingly the entitlement of legitimated children has to be considered with reference to deaths before and after January 1, 1927,[8] after October 29, 1959 and after January 1, 1976.[9]

The general rule expressed in the 1975 and 1976 Acts is that a legitimated person, and any other person, shall be entitled to take any interest as if the legitimated person had been born legitimate.[10] Thus a legitimated person will share in the intestacy of his or her parents, or in the intestacy of his or her brother or sister, and vice versa.[11] It will be appreciated that since the coming into force of the Family Law

(2) For the purposes of subsection (1) of this section, an illegitimate person shall be presumed not to have been survived by his father or by any person related to him through his father, unless the contrary is shown.'

(2) The amendment by this section of section 14 of the Family Law Reform Act 1969 does not affect any rights under the intestacy of a person dying before the coming into force of this section; and section 14 of that Act, as it has effect immediately before the coming into force of this section, shall continue to have effect, in relation to a person dying, or in relation to an instrument inter vivos made, after the coming into force of that section and before the coming into force of this section.
(3) In section 17 of the Family law Reform Act 1969 (which provides protection for trustees and personal representatives) in paragraph (a) after the words "the father of" there shall be inserted the words 'or on any person related through the father to.' "

[6] Legitimacy Act 1926 s.1(1).

[7] *Ibid.*, s.1(2).

[8] See *Re Mitchell* (*decd.*) [1954] Ch. 525.

[9] The Children Act 1975 repealed the earlier legislation and enacted a new code to be found in Sched. 1. The 1976 Act consolidated the earlier legislation and the law is set out in Sched. 1 to the 1976 Act, with effect from August 22, 1976.

[10] s.5(3). The Act extends the rights of legitimated persons to succeed under dispositions taking effect before the legitimation; see Cretney, 126 New L.J. 8.

[11] Subject to the prior entitlement of a spouse, or issue. For the purposes of the Act provisions of the law of intestate succession applicable to the estate of a deceased person shall be treated as if contained in an instrument executed by him (while of full capacity) immediately before his death, s.5(2). Note that the rule in s.5(4) to the effect that a disposition which depends on the date of birth of a child shall be construed as if a legitimate child had been born on the date of legitimation, does not operate to modify contingencies relating to age. Thus a legitimated person will still obtain a vested interest under the statutory trusts in s.47(1)(i) at the age of 18 years; see s.5(5).

Reform Act 1969 an illegitimate child and his or her parents have mutual rights of inheritance on intestacy in any event. However, it will be recalled that this Act confers no intestate entitlement to or by other relatives of an illegitimate person[12] and it is in these cases that legitimation will be of most significance. Thus, if a legitimate child has predeceased his parents leaving legitimate, legitimated and illegitimate children surviving, the former two classes will share in the intestacy of their grandparent but not the latter. The position will be similar where nephews and nieces take a brother's or sister's share by representation.

Section 5(4) of the 1976 Act provides that two or more illegitimate children who are legitimated on the same date are to be regarded as born on that date in the order of their actual birth.[13] This provision also applies to intestacy[14] but, apart from the *commorientes* provision in section 184 Law of Property Act 1925,[15] can have no relevance to intestacy because in no circumstance is an older member of a class preferred to a younger.

The final provision to note is that, if an illegitimate child dies and subsequently his parents marry so that the deceased would, if living at the time of the marriage, have become a legitimate person, he is regarded as such for the purpose of succession by or to his spouse, children and remoter issue.[16] In fact it will make no difference to succession by or to a person's spouse or children whether he is regarded as legitimate or illegitimate.[17] However, it will make a difference to succession to his grandfather's or brother's estate, where illegitimate children are not entitled.[18]

Adoption

There have been successive statutory provisions governing the property rights of adopted children commencing with the Adoption of Children Act 1949,[19] the Adoption Acts 1950[20] and 1958,[21] the Children Act 1975,[22] and the Adoption Act 1976.[23] The latter Act has

[12] See *ante* p. 173.
[13] s.5(4)(*b*).
[14] By virtue of s.5(2).
[15] By which the younger person is deemed to have survived the elder where the order of deaths is uncertain. If this is so, then the entitlement would depend on the application of two legal fictions!
[16] s.5(6).
[17] See *supra* p. 173.
[18] *Ibid.*
[19] Which came into force on January 1, 1950.
[20] Which came into force on October 1, 1950 and repealed the 1949 Act.
[21] Which came into force on April 1, 1959, and repealed the 1950 Act.
[22] Which came into force on January 1, 1976 and repealed the 1958 Act.
[23] Which will replace the provisions in the Schedule to the 1975 Act. In order to identify the relevant sections of each of these Acts see the destination table in the 1976 Act.

not yet been brought fully into force but in effect simply re-enacts in this connection the provisions in the Children Act 1975, which came into force on January 1, 1976. The basic provision in the 1976 Act is to the effect that an adopted child shall be treated in law, where the adopters are a married couple, as if he had been born as a child of the married couple or, if there is a single adopter, as if he had been born to the adopter in wedlock[24] and is not to be regarded as if he were the child of any other person.[25] This wording ensures that an adopted child will take as issue on the death intestate of his adoptive parents[26] and the adopted children of a child,[27] who predeceases the intestate, will share in their grandparent's estate.[28] Likewise an adopted child will share in appropriate cases as a brother or sister of the whole[29] or half blood[30] and the adopted issue of a brother or sister can take their parent's share by representation. Conversely, on the death intestate of an adopted child, the relatives will share as if the child had been natural born legitimate offspring.

Equally, however, the exclusionary effect of the words "and is not to be regarded as if he were the child of any other person"[31] must be noted. This will have the effect of excluding the child not only on the intestacy of the natural parents and grandparents, but from the intestacy of natural collateral relatives as well.[32]

Similarly to the rules applicable to legitimated persons noted above, the date of adoption is regarded as the date of birth for some purposes[33] but this is not to affect any reference to the age of a child.[34] These rules apply to intestate succession by virtue of the provision in section 46(4) Adoption Act 1976 "... provisions of the law of intestate succession applicable to the estate of a deceased person shall be treated as if contained in an instrument executed by him (while of full capacity) immediately before his death." However, it has been

[24] s.39(1).
[25] s.39(2).
[26] Thus a child adopted by his grandparents on the death of his parents will rank as a legitimate child and not *per stirpes* as a grandchild, which could have important consequences where the child was illegitimate or had been advanced by his grandparents.
[27] Whether legitimate, illegitimate, legitimated or adopted.
[28] Contrast illegitimate children, *ante*.
[29] Where both parents adopt the child.
[30] Where only one parent adopts the child.
[31] See *supra*, s.39(2).
[32] It is interesting to note that South Australian legislation preserves, in some cases, an adopted child's rights of intestate succession upon the death intestate of any collateral or lineal next of kin of his deceased parents notwithstanding a subsequent adoption, Adoption of Children Act 1966–1976, s.30(3), see Hardingham, Neave and Ford *op. cit.* pp. 399; 400.
[33] s.42(2), but for the reasons discussed above this will, in fact, have little relevance in intestate succession.
[34] *Ibid.*

pointed out[35] that these provisions can have no practical effect in cases of intestacies since under the statutory trusts only persons "living at the death of the intestate" can qualify and thus a person adopted after the death will be excluded since he will be regarded as having been born on the date of the adoption.[36]

Protection of personal representatives

It will sometimes be difficult for personal representatives to be aware of the existence of adopted or legitimated children and so there are provisions for their protection. They are relieved of any duty to enquire whether any person has been adopted or legitimated in so far as that fact could affect the entitlement to the property.[37] There is no liability to such a person if the personal representatives have no notice before distribution,[38] but this is not to prejudice the right of any person to follow the property, or any property representing it, into the hands of another person, other than a purchaser, who has received it.[39]

Marriages which have been dissolved or annulled

Children of divorced parents

A child born during the subsistence of the marriage to parents who subsequently divorce is legitimate and entitled to share in his parent's intestacy as such. It would seem that, even if his parents divorce before his birth, he will be regarded as their legitimate offspring if he was conceived during the marriage.[40]

Children of a voidable marriage

Historically a decree of nullity on the grounds that a marriage was voidable had retrospective effect and thus rendered the children illegitimate. The position is now governed by section 16 of the Matrimonial Causes Act 1973 which provides that the decree shall operate to annul the marriage only as respects any time after the decree has been made absolute and the marriage is to be regarded,

[35] Cretney, 126, New L.J. 7, notwithstanding that in general terms the Act extends the right of succession of adopted persons to dispositions taking effect before the adoption, *ibid.*
[36] s.47(1)(i).
[37] Legitimacy Act 1976, s.7(1); Adoption Act 1976, s.45(1).
[38] *Ibid.* s.7(2); *ibid.* s.45(2).
[39] *Ibid.* s.7(3); *ibid.* s.45(3).
[40] *Knowles* v. *Knowles* [1962] P. 161, see Bromley, *Family Law*, 6th ed. p. 256.

notwithstanding the decree, as if it had existed up to that time.[41] Thus children born between the date of the marriage and the decree are to be regarded as legitimate. Further, a voidable marriage can operate to legitimate previously illegitimate children of the parties to the marriage.[42]

Children of a void marriage

The status of children of a void marriage is now governed by section 1 of the Legitimacy Act 1976 to the effect that such a child is to be treated as the legitimate child of his parents if at the time of the act of intercourse resulting in the birth (or at the time of the celebration of the marriage if later) both or either of the parties reasonably believed that the marriage was valid.[43] This provision is limited to cases where the father of the child was domiciled in England and Wales at the time of the birth or, if he died before the birth, was so domiciled immediately before his death.[44] In cases to which this provision is not applicable, the children of a void marriage will be regarded as illegitimate and their entitlement will be governed accordingly.

Issue of polygamous marriage

The entitlement of issue of a polygamous marriage to succeed on the intestacy of their parent is considered *post* in Chapter 16.

OTHER RELATIVES ENTITLED

Methods of ascertaining next-of-kin

Next-of-kin

Modern legal systems basically adopt one of two methods of ascertaining the next-of-kin entitled on intestacy. The Statute of Distribution 1670 identified the order of entitlement by classifying

[41] Re-enacting the Nullity of Marriage Act 1971, s.5, which applied to decrees on or after July 31, 1971. In respect of decrees before that date the position was governed by s.4(1) of the Law Reform (Miscellaneous Provisions) Act 1949: "where a decree of nullity is granted in respect of a voidable marriage, any child who would have been the legitimate child of the parties to the marriage if it had been dissolved, instead of being annulled on the date of the decree, shall be deemed to be their legitimate child notwithstanding the annulment." That section repealed s.7(2) of the Matrimonial Causes Act 1937 which applied to earlier cases. See generally on the effect of voidable marriages in the law of succession, *Re Roberts* (*decd.*) [1978] 1 W.L.R. 653.

[42] Legitimacy Act 1976, s.2.

[43] Re-enacting the provisions in the Legitimacy Act 1959, s.2, which did not affect any rights under the intestacy of a person dying before the Act, *i.e.* October 29, 1959; s.2(4).

[44] s.1(2). For discussion of the difficulties of construction posed by this section, see Bromley, *Family Law* 6th ed. p. 267.

relatives according to their degree of relationship to the deceased.[45] Under this system the degree of relationship corresponds to the number of steps that the relative stands away from the intestate so that a parent is a relative of the first degree, a brother a relative of the second degree and so on.

However, although this approach has a superficial logic and simplicity, few jurisdictions feel it appropriate to apply it in its pure form, without significant modification. These modifications, influenced by policy, rapidly destroy both the logic and the simplicity of the system. For example, under the Statute of Distribution 1670 it was provided that a surviving father took to the exclusion of a mother, who was thus only entitled if there was no surviving father and who then shared equally with the surviving brothers and sisters if any.[46] In addition children of a deceased brother or sister were entitled to stand

[45] Sometimes referred to as the civil law system. A typical formula for ascertaining the next of kin according to this method can be found in The Republic of Eire's Succession Act 1965, s.71(2) as follows:

> "Degrees of blood relationship of a direct lineal ancestor shall be computed by counting upwards from the intestate to that ancestor, and degrees of blood relationship of any other relative shall be ascertained by counting upwards from the intestate to the nearest ancestor common to the intestate and that relative, and then downward from that ancestor to the relative, but where a direct lineal ancestor and any other relative are so ascertained to be within the same degree of blood relationship to the intestate, the other relative shall be preferred to the exclusion of the direct lineal ancestor."

See also the Scottish system of intestate succession, Succession (Scotland) Act 1964, s.2; Walker, *Principles of Scottish Private Law*, 2nd ed., pp. 1920, 1921. See also the following Australian legislation: Victoria, Administration and Probate Act 1958, s.52; Western Australia, Administration Act 1903–1976, s.14; and Tasmania, Administration and Probate Act 1935, s.44, see Hardingham, Neave and Ford, *Wills and Intestacy*. Degrees of relationship can be classified as follows:

Relatives of the First Degree:	Father Mother
Relatives of the Second Degree:	Grandparents Brothers Sisters
Relatives of the Third Degree:	Great Grand Parents Uncles Aunts Nephews Nieces
Relatives of the Fourth Degree:	Grand aunts Grand uncles First cousins Grand nephews Grand nieces
Relatives of the Fifth Degree:	Parents first cousins First cousins once removed
Relatives of the Sixth Degree:	Second cousins First cousins twice removed

[46] See *ante* p. 36.

in the place of their parent and take their parent's share.[47] Thus it could be that a mother (a relative of the first degree) would share the estate with brothers and sisters (relatives of the second degree) and with children of deceased brothers and sisters (relatives of the third degree).[48] Similar modifications are to be found in the Commonwealth statutes which retain the old system.[49] It will be seen, therefore, that considerations of policy overrule the strict logic of the approach and result in a distribution which is complex and arbitrary,[50] prompting the framers of the 1925 code to seek an entirely fresh approach.

1925 Act

The first step was to ascertain the usual distribution of estates on death as expressed in wills. From this study it was possible to identify the range of relatives that it was usually thought appropriate to benefit and the order of priority amongst such relatives. The legislation could then provide for the entitlement of such relatives having regard to the prior entitlement of the spouse and issue. The results of the study indicated that a fairly narrow range of relatives should be entitled on intestacy and section 46 of the Administration of Estates Act 1925 identifies these relatives descriptively and exclusively as the next-of-kin and places them in an order of entitlement. This approach has no regard to degrees of relationship so that, for example, brothers and sisters and their issue are preferred to grandparents, and, whereas grand uncles and aunts (*i.e.* the brothers and sisters of the deceased's grandparents) are excluded, first cousins (*i.e.* the children of the deceased's parent's brothers and sisters) are included, although both are relatives of the fourth degree.[51]

It is submitted that this method of ascertaining next-of-kin is to be preferred. The exclusive list of relatives identified by their descriptive name is simpler and clearer and more readily understood by the layman. Indeed it can be said that the civil law method is incomprehensible to the layman which is a serious objection for two reasons. First, it is important that people should be able readily to understand the distribution of intestate estates in order that they can decide whether it is desirable to override that distribution by making

[47] But only if there were also surviving brothers or sisters; if there were none then the nephews and nieces were entitled in their own right as relatives of the third degree, and would be excluded by a mother.

[48] Likewise it was thought that brothers and sisters should take ahead of grandparents.

[49] See, for example, the State of Victoria's Administration and Probate Act 1958, s.52.

[50] A further objection to the civil law method is that under the formula the range of next-of-kin is potentially very wide, and can include (in the absence of closer relatives) *e.g.* second cousins, great grandparents and grand uncles and aunts. It is arguably not appropriate that such remote relatives should have any claim on an intestate's estates.

[51] Indeed it is theoretically possible for a first cousin twice removed, who stands six steps away from the deceased in relationship, to succeed on intestacy.

a will.[52] Secondly, since laymen will in many cases be concerned with the administration of deceased's estates, it is important that the order of entitlement and method of distribution should be clear and comprehensible.[53]

The Administration of Estates Act 1925 confines the persons who can take in the case of intestacy to a comparatively narrow class of relatives, namely those who are within the degrees of grandparents or descendants of grandparents.[54] The next-of-kin entitled are exclusively named within this class and no other persons have any entitlement under the 1925 Act[55]; in the absence of any such relatives,[56] the property will pass as *bona vacantia* to the Crown or the Duchy, as the case might be.[57]

Persons entitled as relatives

Parent

"Parent" means the natural father or mother of the deceased, whether the child was legitimate or illegitimate.[58] Adoptive parents will be entitled[59] but a step-parent[60] is not entitled and nor, of course, is a parent-in-law. The natural parent of an adopted child is excluded by virtue of the provision in the Adoption Act 1976 that an adopted child is to be treated in law, where the adopters are a married couple, as if he had been born as a child of the marriage, and in any other case, as if he had been born to the adopter in wedlock,[61] and an adopted child is to be treated in law as if he were not the child of any person other than the adopters or adoptee.[62] The parent of a legitimated child will take, of course, on the intestacy of that child.[63]

[52] This point is admittedly somewhat theoretical since many people fail to make wills no doubt out of ignorance, lethargy or reluctance to contemplate death!

[53] The identification of the class of next-of-kin entitled is clear (although illegitimacy and in-law relationships could cause problems) but the entitlement, *e.g.* under the statutory trusts, could present difficulties to the layman.

[54] *Per* Clausen J. in *Re Bridgen, Chayter* v. *Edwin* [1938] 1 Ch. 205 at p. 209.

[55] There remains the possibility of an application under the Inheritance (Provision for Family and Dependants) Act 1975, see *post*, or the possibility of an *ex gratia* payment by the Crown out of *bona vacantia*.

[56] Including their issue where these can take by representation.

[57] See s.46(1)(vii), and *post* p. 275.

[58] Family Law Reform Act 1969 s.14(2), see *ante*, p. 173. But note the presumption in s.14(4) that an illegitimate child is presumed to have survived his father.

[59] Adoption Act 1976, s.39, see *ante* p. 179.

[60] *i.e.* the husband or wife of the real parent but who is not the parent of the deceased.

[61] Adoption Act 1976 s.39(1).

[62] Adoption Act 1976 s.39(2).

[63] Legitimacy Act 1976 s.5(3); the parent will take as if the legitimated person had been born legitimate. The mother, at least, would take even if the child were illegitimate but legitimation renders the succession subject to the Legitimacy Act 1976 and not the Family Law Reform Act 1969 and thus the presumption that the father had predeceased the child in s.14(4) of the latter Act will have no place.

Brother or sister

In appropriate circumstances brothers and sisters of the whole or the half blood are entitled to share on intestacy "on the statutory trusts," which will let in their issue (*i.e.* the intestate's nephews and nieces) to take by substitution.[64] Brothers and sisters of the whole blood comprehend persons who have both natural parents in common with the deceased and brothers and sisters of the half blood, persons who have one natural parent in common with the deceased. Brothers or sisters "in law" (*i.e.* the spouse of a natural brother or sister or the deceased's spouse's brothers or sisters) or step-brothers or sisters (*i.e.* the children of a person who is not the natural parent of the deceased but who is the spouse of the natural parent of the deceased) are not included. The only exception to the exclusion of all but natural brothers and sisters relates to adopted brothers and sisters. By virtue of the provision in section 39 of the Adoption Act 1976[65] a person who has been formally adopted by the parent(s) of the deceased (whether blood related or not) stands on all fours with natural children of the parent and can thus inherit as a brother or sister on intestacy. Likewise such a person would rank as "issue" of a deceased brother or sister and would thus be able to take by substitution.[66] By virtue of the same legislation the natural brother or sister of an adopted person will have no claims since the adopted person is deemed not to be the child of any person but the adopters.[67]

An illegitimate person has no right to inherit on the intestacy of his illegitimate brothers or sisters of the whole or the half blood.[68] Nor can such a person inherit on the death intestate of his legitimate brother or sister of the half blood.[69] Nor has a legitimately born person any right to inherit on the intestacy of his or her illegitimate brother or sister of the half blood.[70] In the former case in the absence of a spouse or issue no one has any entitlement to the illegitimate's intestate estate which accordingly passes to the Duchy or the Crown as *bona vacantia.*[71] Where, however, an illegitimate person has been legitimated by the marriage of his or her parents, he or she will, of course, be able to take

[64] See s.46(1), discussed, *post.*
[65] *Ante*, p. 179.
[66] Under s.47(1)(i), (3), (4).
[67] Adoption Act 1976 s.39(2).
[68] Ryder 24 C.L.P. 162.
[69] If the brother or sister is legitimate the illegitimate person can only be related in the half blood since otherwise the marriage would have legitimated him. If there are surviving legitimate brothers or sisters, they will be related in the whole blood and exclude the illegitimate in any event under s.46.
[70] Ryder, *op. cit.*
[71] The Russell Committee 1966, Cmnd. 3051, noted that in such cases "it is the practice to recognise moral claims of the survivor," by making *ex gratia* payments to the natural brothers or sisters. If this is so, it is difficult to see why the position is not formalised, since the exclusion of natural brothers and sisters in these circumstances will be contrary to the presumed wishes of the intestate in many cases.

any interest as if he or she had been born legitimate.[72] Thus a legitimated person can take on the intestacy of a legitimate brother or sister and a legitimate person can take on the intestacy of a legitimated brother or sister.

Uncles and aunts

Very similar rules apply to persons qualified to take as uncles or aunts or as issue thereof. Only persons so related by blood (whether of the whole or the half blood) are entitled, thus excluding relationships by affinity (*i.e.* the spouse of a natural uncle or aunt, or the natural uncles and aunts of the deceased spouse).[73] The same exceptions in favour of adopted and legitimated persons apply as above by virtue of the Adoption Act 1976[74] and the Legitimacy Act 1976.[75]

Nephews, nieces, cousins

Issue of deceased brothers and sisters or uncles and aunts, as the case might be, are entitled to take under the statutory trusts their deceased parent's share. Issue of unlimited degree are entitled under these trusts but, of course, the existence of a child of a closer generation will exclude all members of subsequent generations within the same *stirpes*. Thus a nephew excludes a great nephew of the same *stirpes* and a first cousin excludes a first cousin once removed.[76] It is noticeable that nephews, nieces and first cousins are never entitled under the intestacy rules in their own right *per capita*, but can only take under the statutory trusts by representation *per stirpes*. This is so even if all the members of the primary class are dead, *i.e.* brothers and sisters, or uncles and aunts, and the substituted class of issue are solely entitled.[77] It is possible for children to be first cousins twice over, *i.e.* where the intestate's father's sister had married the intestate's mother's brother, and there is Commonwealth authority to the effect that in this situation the children do not take a double share.[78]

[72] Legitimacy Act 1976 s.5(3).

[73] As to illegitimate relationships see the provisions in the Family Law Reform Act 1969, s.14, discussed above.

[74] s.39(1), (2).

[75] s.5(3).

[76] It can be suggested that it could be desirable to limit the entitlement of issue taking by substitution to the first generation only.

[77] In such cases the individual entitlement of each member of the class of nephews or nieces, etc. is likely to vary from family to family. Thus if the deceased's brother had three children and his sister had only one, and assuming that both brother and sister are dead, the former children will take one-sixth shares, whilst the latter will take a one-half share. This inequality of shares to be taken by relatives of the same relationship to the deceased seems undesirable. It can be suggested that in such cases, where the substituted class are in effect primarily entitled, the entitlement should be *per capita* in equal shares.

[78] *In the Estate of Cullen, (decd.)*, (1976) 14 S.A.S.R. 456; distinguishing *Re Morrison, Trustees Executors and Agency Co. Ltd.* v. *Comport*, [1945] V.L.R. 123 where a widow stood in two distinct relationships, *i.e.* as the widow and as one of the next-of-kin, and was held entitled to take a share appropriate to each of those relationships.

References to next-of-kin

References to Statutes of Distribution

Testators and settlors sometimes identify the beneficiaries entitled under wills or trusts by describing them as the "next-of-kin according to the statutes of distribution" or as "the next-of-kin on intestacy,"[79] The construction of such gifts is provided for by section 50 of the 1925 Act and depends upon whether the instrument or will takes effect before or after January 1, 1926. In the former case section 50(2) provides:

> "Trusts declared in an instrument *inter vivos* made, or in a will coming into operation, before the commencement of this Act by reference to the Statutes of Distribution, shall, unless the contrary thereby appears, be construed as referring to the enactments (other than the Intestates' Estates Act, 1890) relating to the distribution of effects of intestates which were in force immediately before the commencement of this Act."

Such cases will obviously be met less frequently in the modern law but the relevant construction is illustrated by cases such as *Re Sutcliffe*,[80] *Re Sutton*[81] and *Re Hooper's Settlement*[82] which also provides some discussion of the expression of a contrary intention within the section.

It was pointed out in *Re Sutton*[83] that section 50 refers not to the Statute of Distribution but to the Statutes of Distribution and "... this is not a statutory short title, although it is a well recognised phrase in common use at the date of the testator's will and at the passing of the Administration of Estates Act for compendious reference to a number of statutes regulating the devolution and distribution of property on an intestacy." The Intestates' Estates Act 1890 was not regarded as falling within the expression.[84]

In the case of post-1926 wills or trusts the position is governed by section 50(1)

> "(1) References to any Statutes of Distribution in an instrument *inter vivos* made, or in a will coming into operation after the commencement of this Act, shall be construed as references to

[79] See the analogous form of wording in *Re Mitchell* (*decd.*) [1954] 1 Ch. 525, which did not involve a reference within s.50; see *ante*, p. 7. Dispositions within s.50 and analogous "as an intestacy" clauses, are cases of testate and not intestate succession; see *ante* p. 6.

[80] [1929] 1 Ch. 123.

[81] [1934] 1 Ch. 209; *Re Jackson* (1944) 113 L.J. Ch. 78 (will in 1901).

[82] [1943] 1 Ch. 116. See also the difficult decision of *Re Gilligan* [1950] P. 32 on the construction of "next-of-kin" under the Statute of Distribution in (the old) s.18 of the Wills Act 1837.

[83] *Supra, per* Luxmoore J. at p. 216.

[84] *Re Morgan* [1920] 1 Ch. 196.

this Part of this Act; and references in such an instrument or will to statutory next-of-kin shall be construed, unless the context otherwise requires, as referring to the persons who would take beneficially on an intestacy under the foregoing provisions of this Part of this Act."

It is clear that section 50(1) covers two situations. First, a reference to any Statutes of Distribution, in which case the requirement that such a gift should be construed as referring to the persons identified in Part IV of the Act[85] is mandatory. Secondly, a reference to "statutory next-of-kin," in which case the construction in favour of Part IV of the Act can be displaced where "the context otherwise requires."[86] It would seem that such a context will only be found where "... the will (or other instrument) read as a whole, clearly indicates that the testator, when referring to 'statutory next-of-kin,' means a different class of persons from those entitled on intestacy under the Administration of Estates Act, 1925."[87]

It will be appreciated that the persons entitled as "next-of-kin" do not comprehend the whole class of persons identified as possibly entitled under the Administration of Estates Act 1925 but only those persons who in the circumstances would actually be entitled under the intestacy.[88]

Where there is an express reference to the statutes, the class take as tenants in common in the shares in which they would have taken on an intestacy.[89] This is because, where a testator gives a direction for a class of persons to take according to the Statute of Distribution, that is to be regarded not merely as a direction to point out or discover the persons who are to take but as affecting the interests so to be taken.[90]

Presumption of death

Common law presumption

Difficulties can arise where the person prima facie entitled as next-of-kin on intestacy has disappeared and there is no knowledge of

[85] Including a widow see, *obiter* in *Re Gilligan* [1950] P. 32 at p. 37; *ratio* in *Re Krawitz Will Trusts* [1959] 1 W.L.R. 1192.

[86] See Russell 68 L.Q.R. 455, commenting on Whitehall, 67 L.Q.R. 351.

[87] *Ibid.* at p. 456.

[88] *Re Bridgen* [1938] 1 Ch. 205 at p. 210, leaving open the question whether minors would take subject to the contingencies expressed in the statutory trusts.

[89] *Per* Lord Evershed M.R. in *In Re Gansloser's Will Trusts* [1952] Ch. 30 at p. 42, citing Lord Romilly M.R. in *Eagles* v. *Le Breton* (1873) L.R. 15 E.q. 148. But where there is no express reference to the statutes but the gift is construed as next-of-kin, then there is nothing to displace the ordinary rule that under a gift to a class without words of severance all the members of the class take as joint tenants. *Ibid.* See *Re Kilvert* [1957] 1 Ch. 388.

[90] *Bullock* v. *Downes* (1860) 9 H.L. Cas. 1 at p. 16; see *Re Kilvert, supra*; *Re Nightingale* [1909] 1 Ch. 385.

whether he or she is alive or dead. In such cases the common law presumption of death might apply to facilitate the distribution of the estate. This presumption is most often invoked in matrimonial cases to determine the marital status of a person or the validity of a second marriage[91] but it would seem to be equally applicable to establish the death of a potential beneficiary on intestacy. The leading modern case, where the circumstances in which the presumption will arise were stated, is *Chard* v. *Chard*.[92] First, there must have been a continuous absence for at least seven years during which there is no acceptable affirmative evidence that the person was alive; secondly, that there are persons who would be likely to have heard of him or her over that period; thirdly, that those persons have not heard of him; and fourthly, that all due enquiries have been made appropriate to the circumstances. If all these requirements are met, the person in question will be presumed to have died at some time during that period. These rules are strictly applied and all must be satisfied if the presumption is to arise.[93]

However, an important limitation to the presumption, particularly when applied to succession cases, must be noted. Although the court might be able to conclude that a person is dead, there is no presumption as to the time when that death took place. The rule was established by *Re Phene's Trusts*[94]: if a person has not been heard of for seven years, there is a presumption of law that he is dead but at what time within that period he died is not a matter of presumption but of evidence and the onus of proving that the death took place at any particular time within the seven years lies upon the person who claims a right to the establishment of which that fact is essential.[95] This principle was applied in *Re Rhodes*[96] where the court had no doubt that the presumption of death should be applied but the difficulty centred on ascertaining who were his next-of-kin at his death and, since different classes were entitled at different times, of ascertaining the date when he in fact died.[97] In the absence of evidence as to when he died, the court was forced to the conclusion that neither

[91] See Bromley, *Family Law*, 6th ed. pp. 65, 66; *Cross on Evidence*, 5th ed. pp. 140–145; Stone, 44 M.L.R. 516. See also statutory references to the seven year-period, Marital Causes Act 1973, s.19(3); Offences against the Person Act 1861, s.57.

[92] [1956] P. 259 at p. 272, concerned with the validity of a second marriage.

[93] See Cross, *op. cit.*, pp. 141, 142; *Re Watkins* [1953] 1 W.L.R. 1323; *Prudential Assurance Co.* v. *Edmunds* (1877) 2 App.Cas. 487; *Bradshaw* v. *Bradshaw* [1956] P. 274; see also Commonwealth authorities considered by Hardingham, Neave and Ford, *op. cit.* pp. 490–494.

[94] (1869) L.R. 5 Ch.App., 139, a succession case.

[95] There is no presumption of law in favour of the continuance of life, *ibid.* and see *Re Aldersey* [1905] 2 Ch. 181, presumed not to have survived beyond date last heard of.

[96] (1887) 36. Ch.D. 586.

[97] It was found that the intestate had died by 1880, and there were two sets of claimants, his next-of-kin as at 1873, and his next-of-kin as at 1880.

class of next-of-kin had made out a claim to the fund and the case was sent back for further inquiry.[98]

There is no presumption that a person presumed dead died without issue or unmarried and proof of these matters must be established by evidence.[99] It would seem that this burden can easily be discharged by slight evidence.[1]

Benjamin Order

Another helpful device in the case of uncertain deaths is the so-called Benjamin Order[2] whereby personal representatives can be given leave of the court to distribute the estate on the basis that a particular person did not survive the deceased.

[98] The judge suggested that the competing claimants should come to some arrangement for the distribution of the fund, *supra*, at p. 592. The decision in *In Re Westbrook's Trusts* noted in [1873] W.N. 167, indicating the end of the period as the date of death was not followed.

[99] See Cross, *op. cit.* p. 145, and cases there cited.

[1] *Ibid.*

[2] *Re Benjamin* [1902] 1 Ch. 723; *Re Green's Will Trusts, Fitzgerald-Hart* v. *Att.-Gen.* [1985] 3 All E.R. 455; see Parry and Clark, *The Law of Succession*, 8th ed. p. 349.

CHAPTER 11

THE ENTITLEMENT OF A SPOUSE

INTEREST IN THE RESIDUARY ESTATE

Introduction

The person qualified to take as a husband or wife on intestacy has been considered in the previous chapter and it is now necessary to consider the extent of the entitlement. The pre-1925 rules and the entitlement in respect of deaths between January 1, 1926[1] and January 1, 1953[2] have been considered so that this and the succeeding chapters will consider the distribution of the estate under the Administration of Estates 1925 Act, as amended by the Intestates' Estates Act 1952.[3]

Two initial points on the spouse's entitlement can be noted. First, the legislation refers to the intestate "leaving a husband and or wife"[4] so that the spouse must survive the deceased.[5] There is no entitlement of the estate of a deceased spouse. Secondly, there is no distinction between the entitlement of a husband or a wife on intestacy[6] and, although the legislation refers throughout to "a husband or wife," the expression "the spouse" will be used for convenience in this discussion.[7]

In order to ascertain the surviving spouse's entitlement on the death intestate of the other spouse it is necessary to distinguish three situations.

The spouse's entitlement

Spouse takes whole estate absolutely

The spouse will take the whole estate absolutely in three situations:

[1] The date when the Administration of Estates Act 1925 came into force.

[2] The date when the Intestates' Estates Act 1952 came into force.

[3] And as amended by the subsequent statutory instruments affecting the fixed net sum, and the capitalisation of the life interest see *post.* In the case of deaths after January 1, 1967 as amended by the Family Provision Act 1966.

[4] s.46(1)(i).

[5] The effect of s.46(3), *commorientes*, has been considered above.

[6] And for all purposes of distribution or division under s.46, a husband and wife are to be treated as two persons, s.46(2). Contrast the pre-1925 position.

[7] The 1952 Act refers to "the spouse" in the headings to s.2, right of surviving spouse to have life interest redeemed, and in the Second Schedule, rights of surviving spouse as respects the matrimonial home, but in both cases the legislation refers to the husband or wife.

(i) where the estate does not exceed £40,000 in value[8];
(ii) where the deceased left no issue, and the estate does not exceed £85,000[9];
(iii) where the deceased left no issue, no parent, or brother or sister of the whole blood, or issue of a brother or sister of the whole blood.[10]

Spouse and issue

If the intestate leaves a spouse and issue (whether or not there are other relatives), then the spouse takes[11]:

(i) the personal chattels absolutely,[12] and
(ii) in the case of deaths on or after March 1, 1981, a fixed net sum of £40,000,[13] with interest thereon from the date of the death at the rate of 6 per cent. per annum,[14] and
(iii) a life interest in one-half of the residuary estate[15] with remainder on the statutory trusts for the issue.[16]

Spouse and no issue but specified relatives

If the intestate leaves a spouse and

(a) no issue but
(b) one or more of the following relatives, a parent, a brother, or sister of the whole blood, or issue of a brother or sister of the whole blood.

then the spouse takes[17]:

(i) the personal chattels absolutely,[18] and
(ii) in the case of deaths on or after March 1, 1981, a fixed net sum

[8] In the case of deaths after March 1, 1981; in the case of deaths before that date, the amount was £25,000; in the case of deaths before March 15, 1977, the amount was £15,000; in the case of deaths before July 1, 1972 the amount was £8,750; in the case of deaths before January 1, 1967 the amount was £5,000 and in the case of deaths before January 1, 1953, the amount was £1,000; see *post.*
[9] In the case of deaths after March 1, 1981, in the case of earlier deaths with reference to the dates noted above, the amount was £55,000; £40,000; £30,000; £20,000; and £1,000.
[10] s.46(1)(i)(*l*).
[11] s.46(1)(2).
[12] Discussed *post* p. 196.
[13] S.I. 1981 No. 255; in the case of deaths before March 1, 1981, the amount of the fixed net sum was £25,000; in the case of deaths before March 15, 1977, the amount was £15,000; in the case of deaths before July 1, 1972, the amount was £8,750; in the case of deaths before January 1, 1967, the amount was £5,000; and in the case of deaths before January 1, 1953, the amount was £1,000.
[14] With effect from October 1, 1983; previously the rate was 7 per cent. with effect from September 15, 1977; 4 per cent. with effect from January 1, 1953; and 5 per cent. with effect from January 1, 1926.
[15] Discussed *post* p. 211.
[16] The other half is held on the statutory trusts for the issue of the intestate.
[17] s.46(1)(i)(3).
[18] Discussed *post* p. 196.

of £85,000,[19] with interest thereon from the date of the death at the rate of 6 per cent. per annum,[20] and

(iii) an absolute interest[21] in one-half of the residuary estate.[22]

Other persons entitled

The meaning of "personal chattels," the entitlement to the fixed net sum and the effect of the life interest are fully discussed in the next sections. Some preliminary points relating to the possibility of other persons also being entitled and thus affecting the entitlement of the spouse will be noted here.

The phrases "leaving no issue" and "leaving issue"[23] mean "leaving no issue who attain an absolutely vested interest,"[24] or who do obtain such an interest, respectively.[25] Issue obtain a vested interest under the statutory trusts when they attain the age of eighteen or marry under that age.[26] The immediate entitlement of the spouse will, however, be determined at death and, if there are minor children then alive, the spouse will be entitled initially as if there were issue.[27] If all of those children subsequently fail to attain a vested interest the entitlement of the spouse will have to be reassessed as if there were no issue. Thus (in the absence of the other specified relatives) the spouse's life interest will become absolute or, if he or she has exercised the right to capitalise the life interest,[28] the spouse will become entitled to the rest of the estate. If it becomes apparent that there are "no issue" but there are one or more of the specified relatives, then the spouse will be entitled as if that had been the position at death. Where there is a spouse and no issue or parent but there are brothers and sisters of the whole blood, then similar provisions apply.[29] The possibility of such an enlargement of the spouse's interest will not assist the spouse when considering whether to invoke the right of

[19] S.I. 1981 No. 255; in the case of deaths before March 1, 1981, the amount of the fixed net sum was £55,000; in the case of deaths before March 15, 1977, the amount was £40,000; in the case of deaths before July 1, 1972, the amount was £30,000; in the case of deaths before January 1, 1967, the amount was £20,000; and in the case of deaths before January 1, 1953, the amount was £1,000.

[20] With effect from October 1, 1983; previously the rate was 7 per cent. with effect from September 15, 1977; 4 per cent. with effect from January 1, 1953; and 5 per cent. with effect from January 1, 1926.

[21] Expressed to be held "in trust absolutely."

[22] The other half goes to the parent(s) or to the brother(s) and/or sister(s).

[23] In s.46(1); as to the meaning of "issue," see previous Chapter.

[24] s.47(2)(*b*).

[25] s.47(2)(*c*).

[26] s.47(1)(i) as amended, in the case of deaths after January 1, 1970, by the Family Law Reform Act 1969, s.3(2).

[27] Thus s.47(2)(*c*) see above, can strictly have no effect where minor children are alive at the death, and the legislation could have been better drafted.

[28] s.47A, see *post*.

[29] This clarifying section was added by the 1952 Act, s.1(3)(*c*). The subsection refers only to the situation in s.46(1)(*i*), *i.e.* where the intestate leaves a husband or wife, and thus is confined to brothers or sisters of the *whole* blood.

appropriation of the matrimonial home under the Second Schedule to the 1952 Act.[30] This right is exercisable "in or towards satisfaction of any absolute interest of the surviving husband or wife in the real and personal estate of the intestate," but must be exercised within twelve months[31] of the death. Thus the extent of the absolute interests must be ascertained for this purpose within this period and a subsequent enlargement, which may only become apparent many years later, will not assist.

The reference in section 47(4) to leaving or not leaving a member of the class of brothers or sisters or issue of brothers and sisters is construed as a reference to the intestate leaving or not leaving a member of that class who attains an absolutely vested interest. Thus on the subsequent total failure of this class (and assuming there is no parent surviving) the spouse will become entitled to the whole residuary estate absolutely.

Spouse's absolute interest

Entitlement

It has been seen that one of the principal objects of the Intestates' Estates Act 1952 was to increase the spouse's absolute entitlement and this objective has certainly been achieved in the modern law.[32] In cases, which can be regarded as the majority of intestate estates, where the estate does not exceed £40,000[33] or £85,000[34] in value (as the case might be) the spouse will be absolutely entitled to the whole estate.[35] Although the "fixed net sum" is expressed to be "charged" on the residuary estate, it is in effect an absolute entitlement.

Secondly, only issue, parents or brothers or sisters of the whole blood or their issue can prevent a spouse from taking an absolute interest in the whole residuary estate whatever the value.[36] In cases where the relatives mentioned above survive, the spouse will take an absolute interest in one-half of the residuary estate.[37]

Thirdly, the spouse is entitled to the personal chattels absolutely.[38]

Fourthly, where by reason of surviving issue the spouse is entitled to a life interest in the estate,[39] this can be capitalised at the election of

[30] See *post*.
[31] Para. 3(1), subject to extension in exceptional circumstances, s.3(3).
[32] See *ante*.
[33] Where there are issue, see *ante*. and *post*.
[34] Where there are no issue but specified relatives, see *ante*, and *post*.
[35] Particularly so because the matrimonial home will commonly be owned as joint tenants or in common with the deceased spouse; see *post* p. 216.
[36] s.46(1)(i). Where these relatives survive as minors there is the possibility of the enlargement of the spouse's interest should they fail to attain their majority see *ante*.
[37] s.46(1)(i).
[38] s.46(1)(i).
[39] s.46(1)(i).

the wife under section 47A. If this is done, the spouse will take the capital sum as an absolute interest.[40]

The spouse's absolute entitlement in the estate will in practice be satisfied by an appropriation under section 41 of the Administration of Estates Act 1925[41] or, more specifically, by exercising the right to require appropriation of the matrimonial home under Schedule 2 to the 1952 Act.[42]

Personal chattels

Definition

Section 46(1) of the 1925 Act provides that "the surviving husband or wife shall take the personal chattels absolutely." The Act defines "personal chattels" for this purpose in section 55(1)(x)[43] as follows:

> " 'Personal chattels' mean carriages, horses and stable furniture and effects (not used for business purposes), motor cars and accessories (not used for business purposes), garden effects, domestic animals, plate, plated articles, linen, china, glass, books, pictures, prints, furniture, jewellery, articles of household or personal use or ornament, musical and scientific instruments and apparatus, wines, liquors, and consumable stores, but do not include any chattels used at the death of the intestate for business purposes nor money or securities for money."

It has been pointed out judicially that the definition is a curious collocation of terms,[44] an *omnium gaterum*,[45] and that the enumeration of specific articles is neither happy nor clear.[46] The initial reference to "carriages, horses, stable furniture . . . " clearly dates the provision and in many respects the definition is inappropriate to cover modern chattels, such as items of sporting or recreational use. In the absence of a more modern formulation the judges have adopted a liberal construction so that Burgess V.-C. in *Re Crispin's Will Trusts*[47] observed that in all the reported cases a somewhat extended meaning had been given to the literal wording of the section.[48]

It will be noticed that the definition is essentially a list of specific

[40] See *post* p. 212.
[41] See *ante* p. 125.
[42] See *post* p. 228.
[43] Originally enacted as s.154(1)(iv), Law of Property Act 1922 (hereinafter also referred to as the "L.P.A. 1922") and amended by the Law of Property Amendment Act 1924 (hereinafter also referred to as the "L.P.A.A. 1924"), Sched. 7, para. 14.
[44] *Per* Stamp J, in *Re Reynolds' Will Trusts, Dove* v. *Reynolds* [1966] 1 W.L.R. 19 at p. 22.
[45] *Per* Vaisey J. in *Re Chaplin (decd.), Royal Bank of Scotland* v. *Chaplin* [1950] 1 Ch. 507 at p. 509.
[46] *Ibid.*
[47] [1975] 1 Ch. 245 at p. 248, reversed on appeal.
[48] This approach applies particularly to the construction of the phrase "articles of personal use," see *post*.

items but includes the non-specific phrase "articles of household or personal use or ornament." So far as the specific items are concerned, the suggestion that a restrictive meaning must be placed on the plain words of the provision by reason of one word's juxtaposition to other words in the provision has been rejected. Thus Danckwerts J. in *Re Hutchinson (decd.)*[49] refused to restrict "horses" to those used for domestic purposes (in view of the juxtaposition with "carriages" and "stable furniture") so as to exclude race horses kept purely for recreation. The question is simply whether the article comes within the ordinary meaning of the word used,[50] for example, jewellery as in *Re Whitby*,[51] horses as in *Re Hutchinson*[52] and clocks (furniture) as in *Re Crispin's Will Trusts*."[53] Reference has been made to the *Shorter Oxford Dictionary* to ascertain the meaning of the words and the ordinary meaning will be adhered to[54] so that, for example, the stamp collection in *Re Reynold's Will Trusts*[55] could not be regarded as a "book."

Other items which have been held to fall within the specific enumeration include: a cow or a pig or other domestic animal kept purely for the owner's own use[56]; garden implements[57]; cut but unmounted diamonds[58]; books, maps and antique silver,[59] and a collection of paintings and books.[60] Although "money" is expressly excluded, it would seem that a collection of coins or notes, where the items are rare or antique, would be viewed differently.[61]

Articles of personal use

Where an article is not specifically identified in the definition, it can be included as an "article of personal use" and this phrase has been generously construed by the courts.[62] Thus the stamp collection in *Re*

[49] [1955] 1 Ch. 255, not following *Re Hall* [1912] W.N. 175, or *Re White* [1916] 1 Ch. 172 where references in wills to carriages were held not to include a motor car.

[50] *Per* Russell L.J. in *Re Crispin's Will Trusts* [1975] 1 Ch. 245 at p. 251.

[51] [1944] Ch. 210. "Jewellery" would cover jewels collectively and gems sold by jewellers just as it covers jewels made up into articles of adornment such as a brooch.

[52] *Supra.*

[53] *Supra.*

[54] *Re Whitby* [1944] Ch. 210 at p. 213.

[55] *Supra*, but it was included as a personal chattel. The collection consisted of a number of stamp albums together with a number of boxes containing loose stamps and also other philatelic equipment. As to the meaning of "books" see *Re Tomline's Will Trusts* [1931] 1 Ch. 521.

[56] *Re Ogilby, Ogilby* v. *Wentworth-Stanley* [1942] 1 Ch. 288, dicta at p. 289, but not, of course, if kept for business purposes.

[57] *Ibid.*

[58] *Re Whitby, supra*, as jewellery.

[59] *Re Crispins Will Trusts, supra*, not affected by the appeal.

[60] *Per* Stamp J. *obiter* in *Re Reynold's Will Trusts*, [1966] 1 W.L.R. 19 at p. 23 "Pictures" would include old masters of inestimable value, counsel in *Re Crispin*, [1975] 1 Ch. 245.

[61] See *Re Collins' Settlement Trusts* [1971] 1 W.L.R. 37, where a coin collection was included in a bequest of personal effects.

[62] *Re Reynold's Will Trusts* [1966] W.L.R. 19, *per* Stamp J. at p. 22.

Reynolds Will Trusts,[63] although not a "book," "... was in truth an article of personal use within the meaning of that expression." Likewise in *Re Crispin's Will Trusts*[64] a watch could not be regarded as "furniture" but fell within the general phrase as an article of personal use. In *Re Chaplin (decd.)*[65] the question arose whether a motor yacht could be regarded as being within the general phrase and Vaisey J. held that it was. A motor car, although now specifically mentioned, has also previously been included in a specific bequest expressed generally.[66] The testator in *Re Collin's Settlement Trusts*[67] bequeathed "such articles of furniture and personal effects as she shall select...." The phrase "personal effects" was regarded as analogous to the phrase "personal chattels" and was held to include a stamp collection, a coin collection and a motor car. There would seem to be little doubt that "wearing apparel" would be included as articles of personal use.[68]

The liberal interpretation given to the phrase "articles of personal use" will greatly assist in solving some of the problems presented by the out of date wording of the provision. Thus, if a motor yacht used for recreational purposes is included, there seems little doubt that other recreational equipment, such as sailing boats, wind-surfers, caravans, tents and sports equipment of all kinds, would be included. The more modern items of twentieth century adult leisure activities, such as video cassette recorders, electronic computers and calculators, could also no doubt be included in the phrase and might also be deemed to fall within "musical and scientific instruments and apparatus."

Relevant and irrelevant considerations

In most cases, perhaps, the value of the items included in the definition will not be great, or form a large percentage of the value of the estate, but it seems clear that these questions are irrelevant. Thus in *Re Crispin's Will Trusts*[69] the first instance judge was influenced by the fact that the value of the collection of clocks and watches in question in the case was some £54,000 out of a total estate of £83,000.

[63] *Supra.*
[64] [1975] 1 Ch. 245, *per* Russell L.J. at p. 252.
[65] *Royal Bank of Scotland* v. *Chaplin* [1950] Ch. 507.
[66] *Re White* [1916] 1 Ch. 172, the bequest was of "furniture and all other articles of personal, domestic or household use."
[67] [1971] 1 W.L.R. 37.
[68] There is an express inclusion of "wearing apparel" in the Statutory Will Form 2, definition of "Personal chattels" which in other respects is virtually identical to the definition in s.55(1)(x), see *post* p. 203.
[69] *Arkwright* v. *Thurley* [1975] 1 Ch. 245, it should be pointed out that Burgess V.-C.'s consideration of the value was in the context of the testator's intention.

The Court of Appeal thought that this was a wholly irrelevant consideration.[70]

Collections of articles present other questions: is the method and purpose of acquisition, for example, whether purchased as an investment or built up gradually as a hobby, relevant? Does it make any difference if the articles were on the one hand kept by the deceased and frequently "cherished by eye and hand"[71] or, on the other, if they were stored in a bank vault for safe keeping? To answer these questions it seems that a distinction should be drawn between articles which fall within the enumeration of specific articles, where it would appear that these factors would not be significant, and articles that can only be included as "articles of personal use," where these considerations assume more importance. Thus in *Re Crispin's Will Trusts*[72] the court was concerned with the question whether the clocks were "furniture" within the definition and Russell L.J. stated:

> "So far as the clocks are concerned, in our opinion a clock, whether long case or bracket, is an article of furniture in the ordinary sense of the word, and it matters not whether it is keeping good or bad time or no time at all, whether it is standing in the room in the testator's house which is in everyday use or stored in a locked room therein, or stored at a repository, or on loan to a museum. The fact that it is one of a collection of clocks bought by the testator or inherited by the testor from another seems to us nothing to the point."

However, when considering in the same case whether the watches could be regarded as articles of personal use, the court thought[73]:

> "A watch is in its nature an article of personal use, and in the present case we regard the cherishing by eye and hand of the collection as well as the wearing of selected items from time to time as bringing them within the definition of articles of personal use."

Further, the judge expressly stated that, when considering whether an article is within the general phrase, an examination of the circumstances of the particular article may be required in addition to its physical character.[74] The fact that an item is one of a collection, which could be said to be a hobby of the testator or intestate, will

[70] *Per* Russell L.J. [1975] 1 Ch. 245 at p. 250. See also *Re Collins' Settlement Trusts* [1971 1 W.L.R. 37 where the stamp collection was valued at some £6,000 and Brightman J. rejected the argument that the testator could not have intended so valuable an asset to fall within the bequest of personal effects.

[71] See Russell L.J. in *Re Crispins' Will Trusts, supra*, at p. 252.

[72] *Ibid.* at p. 251.

[73] *Ibid.* at p. 251.

[74] *Ibid.*

incline the court towards regarding it as an article of personal use.[75] Stamp J. in *Re Reynolds' Will Trusts*[76] thought that the method of acquisition was relevant and he thought that a collection wholly bought from a dealer could hardly be said to be an article of personal use. Although the soundness of this proposition was doubted in *Re Crispin's Will Trusts*,[77] that was in the context of a consideration of specifically enumerated articles rather than articles of personal use. Clearly, if an item falls squarely within "furniture" or "plate" or "pictures," it might well be that the method of acquisition is irrelevant. However, when trying to bring an unspecified item like a stamp or coin collection within the phrase "an article of personal use," the method of acquisition seems more pertinent[78] but, even in such cases, it could be said that the manner of use and enjoyment by the deceased is more important than the method of acquisition.[79] The purpose of acquisition is another factor relevant to the general phrase. A collection purchased solely as an investment and kept in a bank or other secure place and rarely "cherished by eye or hand" could hardly be regarded as an article of personal use[80] but, if the items were within the specific enumeration, the purpose of acquisition is less important; Stamp J. comments in *Re Reynolds' Will Trusts*,[81] "A man could collect paintings or books which were an investment but nevertheless within the definition contained in section 55(1)(x)."

Business purposes

The definition specifically excludes "any chattels used at the death of the intestate for business purposes."[82] Since these concluding words

[75] *Ibid.* see also Stamp J. in *Re Reynolds' Will Trusts, supra* [1966] 1 W.L.R. 19 p. 22, where the way in which the testator had built up his stamp collection as his principal hobby was an important factor. Likewise in *Re Collins' Settlement Trusts* [1971] 1 W.L.R. 37 at p. 39, where the fact that the testator had assembled his stamp collection personally over a period of many years as a hobby, was regarded as significant.

[76] *Supra.*

[77] *Supra.*

[78] See note 5 *supra.*

[79] See R.E.M. (1966) 82 L.Q.R. 18, at p. 20. As this note points out as originally enacted the definition of "personal chattels" in L.P.A. 1922, s.154(1)(iv) included the words "... do not include any chattels acquired for business purposes." The L.P.A.A. 1924 changed these words to the present "... do not include any chattels used at the death of the intestate for business purposes." This lends some support for the view that the use at death is the correct criteria rather than the circumstances of acquisition. See also Ryder (1975) 39 Conv. 72. "... if A acquires a collection formed by someone else and keeps it in his flat, he may make 'personal use' of it by looking after it, making additions to it, or indeed merely examining and enjoying it from time to time, and if he does any of these things, the things comprised in it surely become articles of personal use."

[80] Contrast *Re Collins' Settlement Trusts, supra*, where the collection was kept in a large wooden cabinet in the deceased's house. Likewise in *Re Reynolds' Wills Trusts* the collection was kept at the deceased's house.

[81] *Supra*, at p. 23.

[82] s.55(1)(x); see R.E.M. (1966) 82 L.Q.R. 18.

apparently govern the whole provision, it seems tautologous for the section to include also in two places the qualification "not used for business purposes."[83] However, the difference in wording might be significant. The general qualification relates to the time of the death but the specific qualifications do not so refer. Consider the position of a chattel, which for many years was used for business purposes but which, by reason of the retirement of the user from his employment, was used at the time of the death exclusively for personal purposes. The general phrase would not exclude such a chattel so that, for instance, a typewriter so used could be included but the specific phrases could be construed as excluding the article so that a car would not pass. This seems to be an odd conclusion and it is suggested was not intended. It would seem preferable that the relevant use in all cases should be that at the date of death.[84]

A further difference which is likely to arise, particularly with reference to cars, is where the chattel is used partly for business purposes and partly for personal private use. The section refers simply to "business purposes," without any qualification such as "solely" or "substantially," and thus such chattels are in danger of exclusion.[85] A car used partly for business purposes would seem to fall within the excluding words. In this respect the New Zealand legislation[86] seems preferable since it refers to "any chattel used exclusively or principally at the death of the intestate for business purposes." The exclusion of such chattels in English law is a serious limitation on the spouse's entitlement and it is suggested that some modification on the New Zealand lines is desirable.

The English decisions on the exclusion of chattels used for business purposes can now be considered. An illustrative case is *Re Ogilby*[87] where the deceased owned a home farm with a substantial acreage and live and dead stock valued at between £1,400 and £1,500 including a herd of pedigree cattle and thirty-five head of sheep. It was argued that the herd of pedigree cattle was a personal chattel within the definition because the intestate carried on the breeding of cattle not as a business, because she consistently made a loss, but as a hobby. This contention was rejected on the basis that there was a farming business being carried on and all the live and dead stock were being used for the purpose of that business. Some relevance was attached to the fact that during the intestate's lifetime she had claimed on a business basis for the enterprise in respect of rates and taxes. In contrast in *Re Hutchinson (decd.)*[88] the deceased owned a stud farm, which was run

[83] Qualifying "stable furniture and effects" and "motor cars and accessories."
[84] See *Miller* v. *Miller* [1950] N.Z.L.R. 945 which refers to this difficulty but was concerned with the analogous but differently worded, New Zealand legislation.
[85] See Bicknell, 116 New L.J. 1287, 1288.
[86] See *post.*
[87] *Ogilby* v. *Wentworth-Stanley* [1942] 1 Ch. 288.
[88] *Holt* v. *Hutchinson* [1955] 1 Ch. 255.

as a business, but he also had twelve racehorses in training at a separate establishment. The judge decided that the racehorses were kept purely for the purpose of recreation and thus passed as personal chattels to the widow.

Motor cars

One of the most valuable and important chattels likely to be found in many estates will be a motor car. "Motor cars and accessories" are expressly included in the definition as specific items and thus in straightforward cases will pass to the surviving spouse. Clearly, the reference to the plural will include all cars owned by the deceased at the death (unless used for business purposes) and there seems no reason why vintage or veteran cars, even if bought as an investment, should not be included.[89] "Accessories" provide more difficulty. Obviously, accessories attached to the car, such as radios or special wheel trims, would pass and so, presumably, would articles used to maintain or service the car such as tools, jacks, battery chargers and the other miscellaneous paraphernalia found in twentieth-century suburban garages. But would the phrase include a trailer for towing a boat or carrying camping equipment? And what about a caravan or horse-box or trailer tent? In fact these items could clearly be included under the general phrase "articles of personal use" and so perhaps the discussion is academic. Indeed, cars have been included in the general phrase in *Re White*,[90] and in *Re Collins*[91] a car was held to be included in a bequest of "personal effects." The general phrase also seems to include motor bicycles, motor caravans, lorries, jeeps and all other forms of mechanical conveyance, provided they were used personally and not for business.

The section is at pains to exclude cars "used for business purposes" and the construction of this phrase has been considered above. The exclusion obviously has particular relevance to cars since it is probable that the majority of cars owned by people in employment are to some extent used for business purposes. Clearly, company-owned cars are excluded but there is in fact no express requirement in the section that the deceased should actually *own* the car or any other chattel, although this is usually assumed. An immediate problem, again of particular relevance to cars, concerns the article that is subject to an hire-purchase agreement, *i.e.* an agreement whereby the ownership of the goods rests with the hirer, the possessor having an option to purchase when the last instalment of the purchase money has been paid. Do such articles pass to the widow? It has been

[89] There seems no requirement that the vehicle should actually go, or be in use etc. Would a mere shell, *i.e.* a car without an engine be included?

[90] [1916] 1 Ch. 172.

[91] [1971] 1 W.L.R. 37. See also the New Zealand case of *Miller* v. *Miller*, [1950] N.Z.L.R. 945 on an analogous, but in some respects wider, provision.

suggested that they would not.[92] The framers of the New Zealand definition of "personal chattels"[93] felt that it was necessary to include such chattels expressly, thus giving some indirect support to the view that the basic definition does not include them.

A further point arises from the New Zealand legislation. It has been decided under that legislation that the spouse is entitled to the car in its condition at the death. Thus in *Wilson* v. *Commissioner for Stamp Duties*[94] it was held that, following the fatal accident of a husband in his car, his widow was entitled only to the value of the damaged car and not to the full insurance value paid to the estate.[95]

Partial intestacy

Where the deceased dies partially intestate, the requirement that a spouse must account for benefits received under the will[96] does not apply to "personal chattels specifically bequeathed."

Wills

A virtually identical definition of "personal chattels" is included in Form 2 of the Statutory Will Forms 1925, which is sometimes expressly included in wills.[97] Likewise, testators sometimes expressly incorporate the definition in their wills by a bequest of "all my personal chattels as defined by the Administration of Estates Act

[92] Bicknell, 116 New L.J. 1289, 1288.

[93] s.2 consolidating Administration Act 1969 which follows the English legislation up to the phrase "... consumable stores ... " and then provides: "... which immediately before his death were owned by him or in which immediately before his death he had an interest as grantor under an instrument by way of security, or as purchaser under a hire purchase agreement within the meaning of the Hire-Purchase Act 1971 or under an agreement that would have been such a hire purchase agreement if the purchaser were not engaged in the trade or business of selling goods of the same nature or description as the goods referred to in the agreement; but does not include any chattels used exclusively or principally at the death of the intestate for business purposes or money or securities for money."

See also the definition of "household chattels" in s.56(14) of the Republic of Eire's Succession Act 1965, and the definition of "furniture and plenishings" in s.8(6) of The Succession (Scotland) Act 1964. Both of these provisions seem to have been influenced by the 1925 Act and cannot be regarded as improvements thereon. See also the definition of "household chattels" in New South Wales, Probate and Administration Act 1898, s.61A(2) which is more restrictive; and the Australian Capital Territory, Administration and Probate Ordinance, 1929, s.44(1); and the Northern Territory Administration and Probate Ordinance 1969, s.61(1), which both refer to "exclusively for business purposes," see Hardingham, Neave and Ford, *op. cit.* pp. 439–442.

[94] [1948] N.Z.L.R. 1208.

[95] This was justified on the grounds that the car though damaged survived the intestate's death, and it was the car, not the insurance value to which the spouse was entitled. This might strictly be so but it could perhaps be argued without undue strain, that the insurance money represented the car, so as to pass the full value.

[96] s.49(1)(*aa*) of the 1925 Act; see *post* p. 288.

[97] Made pursuant to L.P.A. 1925, s.179. The form includes "wearing apparel"; has the word "also" before "musical," and states that the definition "shall not" include any chattels used at the death for business purposes.

1925" and, indeed, some of the leading decisions on the phrase are such cases.[98] It would seem that the definition is given, in the absence of any indication of a contrary intention, the same construction in such wills cases as it is given in the case of intestacy.[99]

The fixed net sum

The entitlement

The spouse's entitlement to a "fixed net sum" or, as it is sometimes called, "the statutory legacy"[1] is an important feature of the modern scheme of intestate succession. The seminal legislation was the 1890 Intestates' Estates Act which provided that, where there were no surviving issue and the estate was valued at less than £500, a widow was to be entitled to the whole estate[2] and that, where the estate exceeded that sum, the widow was to have a charge upon the whole estate for £500.[3] This idea was incorporated into the 1925 legislation which initially provided that, where the intestate was survived by a husband or wife, "the residuary estate of the intestate (other than the personal chattels) should stand charged with the payment of a net sum of one thousand pounds, free of death duties and costs, to the surviving husband or wife with interest thereon from the date of death at the rate of five pounds per cent. per annum until paid or appropriated."[4] It will be noticed that both widows and widowers were entitled to this sum and that the amount was constant whatever other relatives also survived.

By the middle of the century this provision in favour of a surviving spouse was looking decidedly ungenerous and the Morton Committee[5] recommended a substantial increase. This was enacted by the Intestates' Estates Act 1952 which, in the context of a general revision of the spouses entitlement on intestacy, provided for a sum of £5,000 where there were also issue surviving, and of £20,000 where there were no issue but certain other specified close relatives.[6] These sums applied in the case of deaths intestate on or after January 1, 1953. These figures in turn became out of date and in inflationary times it

[98] As in *Re Whitby's* [1944] 1 Ch. 210; *Re Chaplin (decd.)* [1950] 1 Ch. 507; *Re Crispin's Will Trusts* [1975] 1 Ch. 245; *Re Reynold's Will Trusts* [1966] 1 W.L.R. 19, see also *Re Collins' Will Trusts, Donne* v. *Hewetson* [1971] 1 W.L.R. 37, where the bequest was "articles of furniture and personal effects."

[99] Russell L.J. in *Re Crispin's Will Trusts, supra*, pp. 250, 251. See *Williams on Wills*, (1980) 5th ed. pp. 531, 532.

[1] See, for example, Goff J. in *Re Bowen-Buscarlet's Trusts, Northam* v. *Bowen-Buscarlet* [1972] 1 Ch. 463 at p. 468.

[2] s.1.

[3] s.2. See discussed *ante*, p. 37. The sum was charged on both realty and personalty thus providing the first true assimilation of the two in the law of intestate succession but was confined to the widow, a widower already having greater rights.

[4] s.46(1)(i).

[5] Committee on the Law of Intestate Succession, 1951, Cmd. 8310.

[6] s.1(2).

was thought to be unwieldy to require formal legislation every time an increase was needed and so the Family Provision Act 1966 introduced a more flexible method of provision. Section 1 of that Act provided that, in the case of intestacies occurring on or after January 1, 1967, the surviving spouse should be entitled not to a specified sum but to a "fixed net sum," and the 1925 Act was amended accordingly.[7] The amount of this fixed net sum was initially fixed by the Act at £8,750, where the intestate left issue, and £30,000 where the intestate left the specified class of close relatives but no issue.[8] It was further provided that the amount of these net sums could be increased from time to time by order of the Lord Chancellor.[9] This power has been invoked on subsequent occasions so that, in the case of deaths on or after July 1, 1972, the entitlement was to £15,000 (if there were issue) and £40,000 (if there were no issue but specified relatives)[10]; in the case of deaths on or after March 15, 1977, the entitlement was to £25,000 and £55,000 respectively.[11] The current entitlement in the case of deaths on or after March 1, 1981 is to £40,000 and £85,000 respectively.[12]

The amount of the statutory legacy has thus been progressively raised in line with inflation and more particularly it is suggested in line with the value of dwelling-houses.[13] A spouse has a statutory right[14] to require the appropriation of the matrimonial home in satisfaction of any absolute interest that he or she might have in the residuary estate and in most cases in practice this means in satisfaction of the statutory legacy. It is thus important that the entitlement should bear some relation to the value of the matrimonial home, particularly in view of the fact that it has only recently been established[15] that, if the house is worth more than the spouse's absolute interest in the estate, he or she can pay the balance out of other funds.[16] Although the Lord Chancellor seems vigilant in

[7] s.1(2)(*a*), also amending any reference to the sums in s.46(4) and s.48(2)(*a*), s.1(2)(*b*). The Act came into force on January 1, 1967 by virtue of S.I. 1966 No. 1453.

[8] s.1(1).

[9] *Ibid.* and s.1(1), (3), (4).

[10] Family Provision (Intestate Succession) Order 1972 (S.I. 1972 No. 916).

[11] *Ibid.* 1977 (S.I. 1977 No. 415).

[12] *Ibid.* Order 1981 (S.I. 1981 No. 255).

[13] Thus in 1971 the office of population, censuses and surveys, social security division, carried out a survey on matrimonial property which indicated that only 12 per cent. of the couples who owned their matrimonial home estimated its value at more than £8,000, see Todd and Jones, *Matrimonial Property*, 1972. At that time the amount of the lower fixed net sum was £8,750; shortly afterwards it was raised to a minimum of £15,000.

[14] Intestates' Estates Act 1952, Sched. 2, see *post*.

[15] See *Re Phelps* (*decd.*), *Wells* v. *Phelps* [1978] 1 W.L.R. 1501, fully discussed *post*.

[16] If the house is owned by the spouses as tenants in common in shares that will of course halve the effective value of the house for the purposes of appropriation. It should be noted however that the legislation provides no direct link between the statutory legacy and the matrimonial home, which can cause difficulties. See *post*, p. 338.

increasing the fixed net sum, it is tempting to suggest, in times of rapid inflation, that some form of index linking of the amount payable would be desirable. Such a scheme, however, would inevitably create complexity and uncertainty in the law and perhaps the fixed sums are preferable.

Where a spouse receives testamentary benefits in a partial intestacy there is a duty to account for the value of such benefits in diminution of the entitlement to the fixed net sum. This is fully discussed *post*.

Interest

Under the 1925 Act as originally enacted the statutory legacy bore interest at 5 per cent. per annum from the date of the death and this interest was charged on the capital and not on the income of the residue.[17] Following the recommendation of the Morton Committee[18] the 1952 Act reduced the rate of interest payable to 4 per cent. per annum.[19] and added a new sub-section (4) to section 46 declaring that this interest should be primarily payable out of income.[20] With the greater fluctuations of interest rates applicable in modern times it was thought that the rate payable on the statutory legacy should be capable of being varied by statutory instrument and this was provided by section 28 of the Administration of Justice Act 1977. Accordingly the 1925 Act was amended to read simply "at such rate as the Lord Chancellor may specify by order."[21] An order was then laid before Parliament stating "for the purposes of Section 46(1)(i) of the Administration of Estates Act 1925 as it applies both in respect of persons dying before 1953 and in respect of persons dying after 1952, the specified rate of interest shall be 7 per cent. per annum."[22] A subsequent order, with effect from October 1, 1983, reduces the rate of interest to 6 per cent. per annum.[23] It will be noticed that these variations in the rate of interest payable apply not to the dates of the death but to periods related to specific dates. Thus, where the complexity of the administration causes delay in paying the statutory legacy, the rates of interest payable will vary; for example, if the intestate dies in October 1982 and the statutory legacy was paid in April 1984, the rate of interest payable from October 1982 to October

[17] s.46(1), *Re Saunders, Public Trustee* v. *Saunders* [1929] 1 Ch. 674.
[18] Committee on the Law of Intestate Succession 1951, Cmd. 8310.
[19] s.1(2), in the case of deaths after January 1, 1953.
[20] Which means that the interest is no longer a permissible deduction in calculating the value of the net estate.
[21] s.28(1) which came into force on September 15, 1977, S.I. 1977 No. 1490 adding also a new subsection (1A) to s.46 referring to such orders. The 1977 Act also introduced a new method of quantifying the spouse's life interest on redemption, see *post*.
[22] With effect from September 15, 1977 (1977 S.I. No. 1491).
[23] Intestate Succession (Interest and Capitalisation) Ord. 1983 (No. 1374).

1983 would be 7 per cent. and from October 1983 to April 1984 would be 6 per cent.

Valuation of estate

The valuation of the estate relative to the amount of the fixed net sum to which the spouse is entitled can be important since, if the spouse is entitled to the whole estate, only one administrator is required and the administration of the estate is greatly simplified. If the estate exceeds £40,000 in value and there are also surviving children, then a life interest will arise and possibly minority interests, in which case two or more personal representatives are required and the estate will be subject to trusts.[24] It would seem that for this purpose the estate should be valued at the time of distribution, although it is the practice in straightforward cases to accept the probate valuation.

Nature of the interest

The 1925 Act charges the sum on the residuary estate but it is in practice an absolute gift and is paid to the spouse as such.[25] Thus the right of a surviving spouse to require the appropriation of the matrimonial home "... in or towards satisfaction of any absolute interest of the surviving husband or wife in the real and personal estate of the intestate"[26] is, as noted above, most frequently exercised with reference to the statutory legacy. The personal representatives may raise the amount of the fixed net sum or any interest thereon on the security of the whole or any part of the residuary estate (other than personal chattels) so far as the estate is sufficient for that purpose and in so far as the sum has not been satisfied by an appropriation.[27] In a case where the estate included property in England and overseas it was held that s.46 can only impose a charge for the statutory legacy on the proceeds of the English property.[28]

[24] Where this situation arises because of an increase in the value of the estate during the administration period, an additional administrator may need to be appointed. Thus where an estate was originally valued at £38,000 the surviving spouse will be solely entitled, but if that estate increases in value during the administration to £45,000 then surviving issue will become entitled. As to permissible deductions for the purpose of arriving at this valuation see Tristram and Coate's *Probate Practice* (1983) 26th Ed. p. 203.

[25] It is not a registerable charge under the Land Charges Act 1972.

[26] Intestates' Estates Act 1952, Sched. 2, para. (1).

[27] s.48(2), as amended, of the 1925 Act. As to appropriation and the statutory legacy see post.

[28] *Re Collens (decd.) Royal Bank of Canada (London) Ltd.* v. *Krogh* [1986] All E.R. 611, s.46 cannot impose a charge on assets not devolving under English law since such charge is part of the English law of succession, *per* Browne-Wilkinson V.-C. at p. 616. See further discussed *post*, p. 311.

Contingent partial intestacies: payment of the statutory legacy

It is clear from the cases of *Re McKee*[29] and *Re Bowen-Buscarlet's Will Trusts*,[30] that section 46 of the 1925 Act is applicable to so-called contingent partial intestacies, *i.e.* situations where the intestacy only becomes apparent subsequent to the death by reason of the subsequent failure of remainder interests. In such cases a difficulty arises where the widow is entitled to the subsisting life interest,[31] regarding the manner of payment of the statutory legacy. When the intestacy becomes apparent, the reversionary interest will become subject to the distribution on intestacy and the widows entitlement to the statutory legacy will be the primary entitlement.[32] Thus the question arises whether the statutory legacy is payable immediately, so that the reversionary estate will stand charged with the immediate payment of the legacy, or whether the legacy is payable only when the property became undisposed of, *i.e.* at the termination of the widow's life interest, in which case, of course, it would be payable not to the widow but to her personal representatives. This point is not clearly resolved by any of the statutory provisions[33] and has caused judicial difficulties and disagreement. In *Re McKee*[34] however, the Court of Appeal were unanimous; Lawrence L.J. stated the conclusion as follows[35]:

> "Under the effective provisions of the will the only duty of the trustees during the life of the widow is to preserve the capital of the residuary estate intact and pay the income arising therefrom to the widow during her life. On her death but not until then, it will be the duty of the trustee to distribute the corpus of the residuary estate. Being undisposed of, the trustee will then have to distribute the estate in accordance with the provisions of section 46 of the Act of 1925. In *Cooper* v. *Cooper*,[36] Lord Cairns expressed the opinion that the Statute of Distributions ought to be looked at as in substance nothing more than a will made by the

[29] [1931] 2 Ch. 145, see Lawrence L.J. at p. 161, confirming Maugham J. at first instance, *supra*, at pp. 151, 152. In *Re McKee* it will be recalled an intestacy became evident at a time subsequent to the testator's death by reason of the total failure of the class of brothers and sisters who were to take in remainder after the widow's life interest. Although the property which would fall in at the death of the life tenant was not within the phrase "the residuary estate of an intestate" it was notwithstanding thought to be subject to the provisions of s.46 of Part IV of the Act.

[30] [1972] Ch. 463; see also *Re Thornber* [1937] 1 Ch. 29 at p. 35.

[31] As in *Re McKee*, supra.

[32] See *ante.*

[33] It would appear that the legislation failed to foresee these situations therefore not making any provision. If this was an understandable omission in 1925 it was not in 1952 since the decision in *Re McKee* in 1931 ([1931] 2 Ch. 145) had highlighted the problem. The only reference in the 1952 Act to these cases is the obscurely worded, and probably superfluous, provision in s.49(4), which was added to the 1925 Act by the 1952 Act, consequential to the new s.47A; see *post.*

[34] *Supra,* where in fact the precise point in issue was not really argued.

[35] [1931] 2 Ch. 145 at p. 161; see also Romer L.J. at p. 167.

[36] (1874) L.R. 7 H.L. 53 at p. 66.

> Legislature for the intestate. Applying that principle to the present case, the provisions of section 46 of the Act of 1925, so far as applicable in the circumstances, should be read into the will of the testator after the determination of the life interest of the widow, as if they had been inserted in place of the trust for his surviving brothers and sisters."

Accordingly the widow was not entitled to any immediate payment in respect of the property subsequently shown to be undisposed of but on her death her personal representatives would be entitled to receive the statutory legacy[37] out of that property with interest thereon at 5 per cent.[38] from the testator's death.

A different view was adopted in *Re Bowen-Buscarlet's Will Trusts*[39] where the point arose because the deceased had effectively disposed of his residuary estate to his widow for her life but failed to provide for the remainder. The deceased left issue which meant that the widow's entitlement was to the personal chattels (which were not in issue and presumably bequeathed to the wife under the will), a life interest in half of the residuary estate, which was consumed by her testamentary life interest under the will, and to a statutory legacy, subject to the duty to account. On the authority of *Re McKee* it would have seemed that the widow would not have been entitled to an immediate charge in respect of this legacy but that her personal representatives would have been entitled on her death. Goff J., however, distinguished *Re McKee* and came to a different conclusion. He decided that the joint effect of the will and the statute was to give the widow a life interest and that, subject thereto, the residuary estate stood charged with an immediate payment to her of the statutory legacy, there being no warrant for making it a charge in favour of her personal representatives.[40]

An important point to bear in mind in relation to the cases is that *Re McKee* was decided before the Intestates' Estates Act 1952, and *Re Bowen-Buscarlet* after. This is significant because that Act added a

[37] At that time, the amount of the statutory legacy was £1,000, and there was no requirement for the widow to account in the partial intestacy for testamentary benefits.

[38] As the rate then was.

[39] *Northam* v. *Bowen-Buscarlet* [1972] 1 Ch. 463; following *Re Douglas Will Trusts* [1959] 1 W.L.R. 744, where the court decided that the legacy was payable at the date of the testator's death.

[40] In *Re Bowen-Buscarlet*, it was thought that the correct question to pose in these cases was simply whether the widow was entitled to payment of the statutory legacy out of the residuary estate as a whole, analogously to the position where a testator gives a life interest in residue to a beneficiary and subject thereto gives a deferred pecuniary legacy to which the same beneficiary is, or becomes, entitled, in which case that beneficiary can call for immediate payment of the legacy, since it is deferred only to his own interest, see counsels argument, [1972] 1 Ch. 463 at p. 465.

requirement that the widow should account for testamentary benefits against her entitlement to the fixed net sum. Goff J. commented[41]:

> "It is also interesting to observe that Maugham J., in *Re McKee*[42] felt himself fortified by the fact that, whereas under the law as it stood then, certain persons had to bring into account interests which they took under the will, a widow was not so accountable. That has now been changed by section 49(1)(*aa*) of the Administration of Estates Act 1925 (an amendment made by the Intestates' Estates Act 1952). If, of course, the decision in *Re McKee* were authority, settling the law and binding upon me, I do not think I could regard that provision as amending the law by a sidewind, but it is, I think, a consideration which one is entitled to have in mind when the point comes to be argued that the provision which Maugham J. thought helped him to his conclusion is not, now, open. There is moreover an indication in support of the conclusion I have reached in that the new section directs the widow to bring into account an actuarial valuation of her life interest. If Parliament regarded the law as being such that the widow had no beneficial interest and there was merely a charge in favour of her estate, one would have thought that the direction would have been to bring in the actual value of the life interest as ascertained on the date of her death and the legislature would not have speculated where there could be certainty."

In so far as the two cases are in conflict, *Re Bowen-Buscarlet*[43] would appear to be the better authority in the modern law.[44] The case seems more consistent with fundamental principles in that the statutory charge introduced by section 46 would seem to be an immediate charge in the widow's favour and not in favour of her personal representatives. If that charge is postponed to her own life interest then it seems difficult to avoid the conclusion that the widow can say "That life interest is mine and the charge is mine, and I merge the two and claim immediate payment."[45] Further the duty to account under section 49(1)(*aa*) only operates sensibly in such cases if the widow has an immediate entitlement to the statutory legacy, rather than an entitlement for her estate. In many cases the point will be of academic rather than practical importance in the modern law in view of the requirement of section 49(1)(*aa*)[46] that the widow should account for beneficial interests acquired under the will against the entitlement to the fixed net sum. The life interest under the will is such an interest

[41] *Ibid.* at p. 469.
[42] *Supra.*
[43] [1972] 1 Ch. 463.
[44] See for example, Parry and Clark, *The Law of Succession* (1983) 8th Ed. pp. 94, 95. The decision in *Re Bowen-Buscarlet, supra* was followed in *Re Wade* [1980] Qd. 70.
[45] *Per* Goff J. in *Re Bowen-Buscarlet, supra*, at p. 469.
[46] Introduced by Intestates' Estates Act 1952, see *post.*

and will be valued on an actuarial basis at the date of the deceased's death and, if that exceeds the amount of the fixed net sum, the widow will have no entitlement to a statutory legacy in any event.

The requirement to account

The Intestates' Estates Act 1952 introduced the requirement that a spouse should account for testamentary benefits against the entitlement to the statutory legacy. This provision[47] is discussed *post* in Chapter 15 on Partial Intestacy.

Spouse's life interest

Situation in which arises

It has been seen[48] that under the Intestates' Estates Act 1952[49] the only situation in which a life interest can arise is where the deceased leaves a spouse and issue.[50] The spouse will then take a life interest in one-half of the residuary estate with remainder to the issue on the statutory trusts.[51] In all other cases the spouse will take either the whole or one-half of the estate absolutely. This change is to be welcomed both as a considerable simplification of the law and as a greatly increased and more valuable provision for the spouse. Thus the capital will be available for unfettered investment or to purchase an annuity or for fiscally advantageous dispositions in favour of children.[52] The administration of estates will be simplified by the once for all distribution without the necessity for continuing trusts to administer the life interests.

However, even where there are surviving issue, so that a life interest arises initially, that can be turned into an absolute entitlement. If the spouse and the surviving issue are all of full age, then these persons, as they are solely entitled, can join together and divide the estate in accordance with the rule in *Saunders* v. *Vautier*.[53] Similarly, the spouse and issue could join together to make tax effective variations or disclaimers within two years of the death pursuant to section 142 of the Inheritance Tax Act 1984 (inheritance tax) and section 49 of the Capital Gains Tax Act 1979 (capital gains tax).[54] Alternatively, the spouse can exercise the rights conferred on her by section 47A of the

[47] The amended Administration of Estates Act 1925, s.49(1)(*aa*).
[48] See *ante*, Chap. 2 s.46(1) of the 1925 Act as originally enacted.
[49] Applicable to deaths on or after January 1, 1953.
[50] Following the recommendations of the report of the Committee on the Law of Intestate succession, Cmd. 8310.
[51] In addition to the personal chattels, and the statutory legacy, of course.
[52] A life interest would constitute an interest in possession and be liable to the charging provisions of capital transfer tax; see Inheritance Tax Act 1984, ss.49–57. A capital entitlement can be diminished by taking advantage of the yearly exception for transfers *inter vivos*, see Inheritance Tax Act 1984, s.19.
[53] (1941) Cr. & Ph. 240.
[54] See full discussion, *ante* p. 119.

1925 Act[55] to require the personal representative to capitalise the life interest. This process must now be considered.

Redemption of life interest

The 1925 Act as originally enacted conferred a power on personal representatives to redeem the spouse's life interest with the consent of the spouse. This provision was repealed in 1952 and replaced (for deaths after January 1, 1953) by the more far-reaching provisions of section 47A of the 1925 Act, Subsection (1) provides as follows:

> "Where a surviving husband or wife is entitled to a life interest in part of the residuary estate, and so elects, the personal representatives shall purchase or redeem the life interest by paying the capital value thereof to the tenant for life, or the persons deriving title under the tenant for life, and the costs of the transaction; and thereupon the residuary estate of the intestate may be dealt with and distributed free from the life interest."

It will be seen that the section confers a right, not merely a power, and that the natural effect of redemption will be to free the residuary estate from the life interest but reduce it by the amount of the capital sum paid.[56] The right has to be invoked by the spouse notifying the personal representatives in writing and such a notification is not revocable except with the consent of the personal representatives.[57] This election must be made within twelve months of the date when representation to the estate was first taken out.[58] The court is empowered to extend the period in circumstances where the time limit would operate unfairly.[59]

It is most unlikely at the present day that the spouse would be a

[55] Added by the 1952 Act. One advantage of so doing is to convert the entitlement to an absolute interest which will then be available for an appropriation of the matrimonial home under the 2nd Sched. to the 1952 Act, see *post.*

[56] s.47A(6). Where there are two or more personal representatives all must be notified, *ibid.* If the tenant for life is the sole personal representative then notice must be given to the Senior Registrar of the Family Division, s.47A(7), as amended by the Supreme Court Act 1981, Sched. 5.

[57] s.47A(6). There might well be advantages to other beneficiaries in the spouse's life interest being redeemed and thus freeing the assets and this would no doubt be borne in mind by the personal representative.

[58] s.47A(5). However a grant limited to settled land or to trust property is to be left out of account and likewise a grant limited to real estate or to personal estate when a grant limited to the remainder of the estate has been made or is made at the same time. s.47A(9).

[59] s.47A(5). These circumstances are identified as being, in consequence of the representation first taken out being probate of a will subsequently revoked on the ground that the will was invalid; or in consequence of a question whether a person had an interest in the estate, or as to the nature of an interest in the estate, not having been determined at the time when representation was first taken out; or in consequence of some other circumstances affecting the administration or distribution of the estate.

minor at the death of the intestate,[60] but to meet this possibility it is provided that an election by a minor spouse shall be as valid and binding as if the spouse were of full age.[61] However, the personal representatives will not be able to pay the capital sum directly to a minor and so they are instructed to deal with it in the same manner as any other part of the residuary estate to which the minor is entitled.[62]

In cases of total intestacy an election under the section can only be made if at the time of the election the whole of the relevant part of the residuary estate consists of property in possession.[63] The reason for this rule is that it is generally undesirable to realise reversionary interests until they fall into possession.[64] Where the estate consists of property partly in possession and partly in reversion then the life interest can be regarded as two separate life interests in the respective parts of the property so that an election can be confined to the part in possession.[65] In cases of partial intestacy, where the will created a life interest in property in possession and the remaining interest forms part of the residuary estate, an election is not possible with respect to that property since, until the life interest determines, the property is not in possession.[66] Where in such a case the testamentary life interest is in favour of the spouse, it might be advantageous to disclaim the testamentary life interest.

The personal representatives can raise the capital sum required for the purpose of redemption of the life interest of the spouse, or any part thereof, on the security of the whole or any part of the residuary estate of the intestate—other than the personal chattels.[67] Alternatively, the capital sum or any part may be satisfied by an appropriation under the statutory power.[68]

It can be noted that there are no adverse inheritance tax consequences on the exercise of this election by the spouse since, for the purposes of the charging provisions of that tax, the spouse is treated as if he or she had been initially entitled to the capital sum.[69]

Capitalisation

The capital value payable to the spouse on redemption of the life

[60] By virtue of the reduction in the age of majority to 18 by the Family Law Reform Act 1969.

[61] s.47A(8).

[62] *Ibid.* Thus the usual trusts until majority will apply with provision for maintenance and advancement.

[63] s.47A(3).

[64] See Graham, (1952) 16 Conv. 402, 410.

[65] s.47A(3), see Graham, *op. cit.*

[66] s.49(4), amending s.47A(3) in such cases, the provision is, to say the least, poorly drafted, but its import seems clear.

[67] s.48(2)(*b*), and the costs of the transaction.

[68] s.41, see *post.*

[69] Finance Act 1975, s.47(3); there is no question of a chargeable transfer of value of the capital. See now Inheritance Tax Act 1984, s.145.

interest was previously calculated in accordance with rules laid down in subsection (2) of section 47A.[70] These rules still apply in respect of deaths between January 1, 1953 and September 15, 1977 but have since been superseded and will not be discussed in detail here. In respect of deaths occurring after September 15, 1977 entirely new rules have been provided for calculating the capital value of a life interest in the residuary estate.[71] The value is calculated with reference to the tables set out in the Schedule to the Order, and reproduced in Appendix 2.[72] The first step is to ascertain, by reference to the index compiled by the *Financial Times*, the Institute of Actuaries and the Faculty of Actuaries, the average gross redemption yield on medium coupon fifteen-year Government stocks at the date on which the election was exercised or, if the index was not compiled on that date, by reference to the index on the last date before that date on which it was compiled.[73] The second step is to find the column which corresponds to that yield in whichever of the tables set out in the Schedule is applicable to the age and sex of the surviving spouse.[74] The capital value is then the product of the part of the residuary estate (whether or not yielding income) in respect of which the election was exercised and the multiplier shown in the appropriate column opposite the age which the surviving spouse had attained at the date on which election was exercised.[75] There follow some examples illustrating these rules.

> Assume that a 50-year-old widow was elected to capitalise her life interest in one-half of a residuary estate which is worth £50,000. Assume also that the average gross redemption yield on medium coupon fifteen year Government stocks is 15 per cent. Then the multiplier ascertained by reference to the tables is 0.855 and the capital value of the life interest is £50,000×0.855, *i.e.* £42,750.
> If the case concerned a 70-year-old widower and the relevant rate of interest was 10 per cent., the multiplier would be 0.452 and the value thus £22,600.
> If the case concerned is a 30-year-old wife, and the relevant rate of interest was 12 per cent., the multiplier would be 0.906 and the value thus £45,030.

[70] See *Halsbury's Laws*, Vol. 17, para. 1385. Now repealed by the Administration of Justice Act 1977, s.28(2).

[71] The change was effected by the Administrative Justice Act 1977, s.28(3) adding new subsections (3A) and (3B) to s.47A, which enabled the rules to be provided by statutory instrument. The relevant instrument is the Intestate Succession (Interest and Capitalisation) Ord. 1977 (S.I. 1977 No. 1491). Where the spouse and issue are all of full age and sui juris they can agree under the rule in *Saunders* v. *Vautier* (1841) Cr. & Ph. 240 as to the capital share to be taken by the spouse.

[72] Art. 3; see *post* p. 494.

[73] Art. 3(2).

[74] *Ibid.*

[75] Art. 3(3).

The matrimonial home

The succession to the matrimonial home on intestacy is considered in the next Chapter.

CHAPTER 12

THE MATRIMONIAL HOME

INTRODUCTION

The matrimonial home will have a unique and pre-eminent importance on the death of one party to a marriage. The increase in the ownership by married couples of the house in which they live has been one of the most important trends in modern property law and, where the deceased owned the house solely, or as a tenant in common with the surviving spouse, the matrimonial home will, in the majority of modern estates, be the most important asset of the estate.[1] Further, the matrimonial home will have a singular importance to the surviving spouse who will be most anxious to ensure continued occupation and succession to the house. It is therefore surprising that the code of intestate succession does not provide any direct rights of inheritance to the matrimonial home in favour of the surviving spouse and in this respect the prevalent code betrays its origins in the 1925 reforms.[2] Instead the succession to the house by the surviving spouse is achieved by indirect methods, either by virtue of the *jus accrescendi* where the house is in joint names or by the right of appropriation where a proprietary interest in the house forms part of the deceased spouse's residuary estate. An initial step in determining the succession will be to ascertain, by judicial declaration if necessary, the exact proprietary interests of the spouses in the house.

FREEHOLD PROPERTY

Proprietary rights in the matrimonial home

Legal estate in both spouses

In the simplest case the house on acquisition will have been expressly conveyed or transferred to the spouses jointly, or upon trust for themselves as joint tenants beneficially.[3] In such cases, provided

[1] Thus in 1972 when the Office of Population Censuses and Surveys carried out a survey of matrimonial property, only 5 per cent. of the couples surveyed estimated the value of their assets, excluding the matrimonial home and current bank account, as more than £10,000. See Todd and Jones, *Matrimonial Property*, 1972. As to the devolution of assets, see *ante*, Chap. 6.

[2] The Morton Committee, 1951 Cmd. 8310, considered the inheritance to the matrimonial home but did not recommend that the surviving spouse should be given any automatic or direct rights of inheritance thereto; see *ante* p. 45.

[3] The express declaration of the beneficial interest is conclusive in the absence of fraud or mistake, *Pettitt* v. *Pettitt* [1970] A.C. 777; *Goodman* v. *Gallant* [1986] 1 All E.R. 311.

there has been no *inter vivos* severance,[4] the *jus accrescendi* will apply on death to the advantage of the surviving spouse[5] and technically the house will form no part of the estate of the deceased spouse or feature in the succession at all.[6] Where a house has been simply conveyed to the parties without words of severance or other express reference to the beneficial interest, then, in the absence of a contrary intention or contributions in unequal shares, the house will be presumed to have been acquired by the parties as joint tenants.[7] A tenancy in common will arise where the house is expressly conveyed or transferred to the parties in shares[8] or where the property was acquired by the unequal contributions of the parties to the purchase.[9] Where the matrimonial home is beneficially owned by the spouses in shares, the share of the deceased spouse will form part of his or her residuary estate and will be subject (in the absence of express testamentary disposition) to the rules of intestacy.[10]

Legal estate in the name of one spouse

Where the legal title to the house is vested in one spouse alone, the position is very much more complex.[11] It is possible for the court to conclude that the house was owned both legally and beneficially by the legal title holder to the exclusion of the other spouse. In such cases, where the title holder is the first to die, the surviving spouse will have

[4] As to which see L.P.A. 1925, s.36(2); *Re Draper's Conveyance* [1969] 1 Ch. 486; *Burgess* v. *Rawnsley* [1975] Ch. 429; *Nielson-Jones* v. *Fedden* [1975] Ch. 222; *Harris* v. *Goddard* [1983] 1 W.L.R. 203; *Barton* v. *Morris* [1985] 2 All E.R. 1032. And also provided there has been no subsequent variation by written agreement.

[5] Where, as will usually be the case, the spouses are the co-owners, this will ensure that the property passes on death to the appropriate successor. But where the other joint tenant is not the surviving spouse then the rule will put the property beyond the reach of the surviving spouse since it will not form part of the residuary estate of the intestate within s.46, of the 1925 Act, and will not therefore be subject to the statutory scheme of intestate succession. This problem has been recognised by the Inheritance (Provision for Family and Dependants) Act 1975 s.9(1), which provides that joint property can by order of the court under that Act be deemed to be part of the deceased's estate. It can thus be made subject to a discretionary order under that Act in favour of the spouse in an appropriate case; see *post*.

[6] The interest of the deceased in joint property is regarded as an interest ceasing on death, and thus does not devolve on the personal representatives, s.1(1) A.E.A. 1925. In such cases it will be noticed that on intestacy the surviving spouse will in effect "inherit" the house, and in addition will be entitled to the full statutory legacy which could be regarded as an over provision since few intestate estates will exceed £40,000 in value excluding the value of the matrimonial home.

[7] *Cowcher* v. *Cowcher* [1972] 1 W.L.R. 425.

[8] Usually "in equal shares" but any quantum of interest can be specified.

[9] *Cowcher* v. *Cowcher supra*, in such cases the rules of equity will determine the beneficial interests although the legal estate will of course be held as joint tenants upon the statutory trusts; see *Gissing* v. *Gissing* [1970] 2 All E.R. 780 and cases concerning cohabitants such as, *Burns* v. *Burns* [1984] 1 All E.R. 244 and *Grant* v. *Edwards* [1986] 2 All E.R. 426.

[10] A.E.A. 1925, s.1(1) and s.33.

[11] For a full discussion reference should be made for example, to Cretney, *Family Law* (4th ed.) Chap. 21.

to rely on the indirect rights embodied in the entitlement to the statutory legacy, and the right of appropriation conferred by the 1952 Intestates' Estates Act,[12] to ensure the succession to the house.

However, in many cases where the legal title is in the name of one party alone, the other spouse will be able to point to the parties' intentions, perhaps evidenced by contributions, either direct or indirect, to the acquisition of the house and in some cases the courts have recognised the equitable proprietary interests of the non-owning spouse by the application of resulting and constructive trusts.[13] The principles which underlie such an approach are to be found in a developing area of law of recognised complexity and uncertainty which it is beyond the scope of this work to discuss in detail. The full discussion must be sought in specialist works.[14] The leading authorities of *Gissing* v. *Gissing*,[15] *Pettitt* v. *Pettitt*[16] and *Cowcher* v. *Cowcher*,[17] amongst others, are well known. Additionally, there have been a number of cases, in which Lord Denning M.R. has been prominent, where a beneficial interest has been conferred on the non-owning spouse by the use of a constructive trust without reference to the parties' intentions.[18] It is difficult to predict how this approach will develop, particularly since the Court of Appeal decision in *Burns* v. *Burns*[19] (a case concerning cohabitants) seems to indicate a return to orthodoxy. Indeed, this area of law is in need of statutory clarification and it is perhaps to be regretted that the Law Commission's proposals[20] for a statutory scheme of co-ownership of the matrimonial home were not adopted in some form. In the absence of such

[12] See the 2nd Sched., fully discussed *post.* This right is rendered effective by two factors. First, the amounts of the fixed net sum to which the spouse is entitled on intestacy have been progressively raised to ensure that the spouse has an absolute entitlement in the estate equivalent to the value of the matrimonial home, see *ante.* p. 204. Secondly, the house and the contents (in the form of personal chattels) are protected from disposal during the administration except for want of other assets, 1925 Act s.33(1), personal chattels; para. 4(1), 2nd Sched. to the 1952 Act, the house.

[13] Such an interest could be joint but is very much more likely to be in common, *i.e.* the statement of distinct shares. *Cowcher* v. *Cowcher* [1972] 1 W.L.R. 425. The surviving spouse will then be entitled to his or her own share as of right and the deceased spouse's share will form part of his estate.

[14] For example in Cretney, *Family Law*, 4th ed. Chapter 21, who also discusses relevant statutory provisions such as the Married Women's Property Act 1964 and s.37 of the Matrimonial Proceedings and Property Act 1970.

[15] [1971] A.C. 886.

[16] [1970] A.C. 777.

[17] [1972] 1 W.L.R. 425.

[18] See *Heseltine* v. *Heseltine* [1971] 1 W.L.R. 342; *Hazell* v. *Hazell* [1972] 1 W.L.R. 301 and *Hall* v. *Hall* (1981) 3 Fam.L.R. 379. See also the similar wide ranging use of constructive trusts in cases such as *Hussey* v. *Palmer* [1972] 1 W.L.R. 1286; *Bannister* v. *Bannister* [1948] 2 All E.R. 133; and *Binions* v. *Evans* [1972] Ch. 359. Some of the most striking developments have concerned the entitlement of cohabitants in the quasi-matrimonial home, as to which see, briefly, *post.*

[19] [1984] Ch. 317 *i.e.* a return to the stricter approach embodied in *Pettitt* v. *Pettitt supra,* and *Gissing* v. *Gissing, supra.* But see *Grant* v. *Edwards* [1986] 2 All E.R. 426.

[20] Third Report on Family Property; the Matrimonial Home (Co-Ownership and Occupation Rights) and Household Goods (Law Comm. No. 86).

certainty, in cases of dispute the resolution of the extent of the spouses' beneficial ownership of the matrimonial home on death can necessitate an application for judicial declaration.

Other points

It should be noted that where all the parties entitled to the succession are of full age and *sui juris*,[21] usually the spouse and children, they can join together and agree the succession to the matrimonial home perhaps in the form of a tax effective variation within the capital taxes Acts.[22] Further, where the total value of the estate including the full value of the matrimonial home does not exceed £40,000 (where there are also issue) or £85,000 (where there are no issue but specified relatives), then the surviving spouse will be absolutely entitled to the whole estate without the necessity to ascertain the beneficial shares in the house. Finally, the succession to the matrimonial home can be ensured or varied by an order made under the Inheritance (Provision for Family and Dependants) Act 1975.[23]

Possession and control over the house

It will usually be regarded as essential that during the course of the administration the surviving spouse should not be put out of possession of the matrimonial home. Where the surviving spouse is a co-owner of the house, no problem will arise since he or she will be entitled to possession of the house by virtue of ownership. Where the house was owned by the deceased spouse alone, although the surviving spouse might be absolutely entitled to the whole of the intestate spouse's estate including the matrimonial home, he or she has no recognisable rights in the property during the course of the administration.[24] Until the house is formally transferred by assent to the spouse, he or she has no legal or equitable proprietary interest in the unadministered assets of the intestate estate, but strictly has merely a chose in action to ensure due administration of the deceased's estate.[25]

However, the possession of the house can be ensured by section 43 of the Administration of Estates Act 1925, which applies to both

[21] *Saunders* v. *Vautier* (1841) 4 Beav. 115.

[22] See *post* p. 119; Inheritance Tax Act 1984, s.142(2); Capital Gains Tax Act 1979, s.49.

[23] See *post* Chap. 18.

[24] The statutory restriction on disposal of the house in solvent estates, in para. 4 of the Second Schedule to the 1952 Act,[3] see *post*, can obviously serve to protect the surviving spouse's possession and control over the house.

[25] See the discussion above, p. 93 and *Commissioner of Stamp Duties (Queensland)* v. *Livingstone* [1965] A.C. 694; *Dr. Barnardo's Homes National Incorporated Association* v. *Commissioner for Special Purposes of the Income Tax Acts* [1921] 2 A.C. 1; *Eastbourne Mutual Building Society* v. *Hastings Corporation* [1965] 1 W.L.R. 861; *Lall* v. *Lall* [1965] 1 W.L.R. 1249; and *Re K. (decd.)* [1985] 2 All E.R. 833.

testate and intestate estates.[26] Although the section is headed "Obligations of personal representative as to giving possession of land . . . ," it is in fact expressed permissively: "A personal representative before giving an assent or making a conveyance in favour of any person entitled, may permit that person to take possession of the land. . . . " The section has not been specifically amended with reference to the right to require appropriation introduced by the 1952 Act[27] but would seem undoubtedly to apply in such cases. Such possession, if granted, does not prejudice the right of the personal representative to take or resume possession or his power to convey the land as if he were in possession thereof, should the need arise.[28] The power is subject to the interest of any lessee, tenant or occupier in possession or in actual occupation of the land[29] but this will not arise in the usual matrimonial home situation where the spouses occupy the house exclusively as a matrimonial home.[30]

Beneficial interest in a quasi-matrimonial home

Cohabitant

The courts have been increasingly concerned in recent years with the determination of the beneficial interests of unmarried couples in the house in which they live together as husband and wife. Where the house has been expressly conveyed or transferred to the couple in joint names or in shares that will usually determine the matter. However, in many of these cases the legal title will be in the name of one partner alone and the other will claim a share of the beneficial interest.[31] The determination of this claim can have obvious effects on the entitlement of the relatives (perhaps of an estranged spouse) where the property owning partner dies intestate. It is not possible in this work to explore fully the complexities of this area of law but the range of possible solutions and approach can be illustrated by contrasting

[26] And whether the death occurred before or after the commencement of the Act, s.43(3).

[27] See *post* p. 228. The Second Schedule contains no right or power to take or retain possession until the appropriation is made, but does provide that the house should not be disposed of in course of administration without the written consent of the spouse, para. 4(1), see *post* p. 237.

[28] Subject, of course, to para. 4(1) *supra.*

[29] s.43(1), as in *Williams* v. *Holland* [1965] 1 W.L.R. 739, personal representative entitled to possession as against anyone entitled on intestacy.

[30] "Rights of Occupation" under the Matrimonial Homes Act 1983 cease on death, s.2(4).

[31] It will be appreciated that an unmarried cohabitant has no entitlement on intestacy and thus a claim to a beneficial share of the house will often be a significant way of effecting an "inheritance" to the assets on the death of the other partner intestate. There remains also, of course, the possibility of an application under the Inheritance (Provision for Family and Dependants) Act 1975, see *post* Chap. 18.

two of the leading cases. In *Eves* v. *Eves*[32] a man and woman, both married to other people, began to cohabit intending to marry when they were free to do so. A house was acquired for their joint habitation and was conveyed into the sole name of the man on the alleged grounds that the woman was too young to participate in the conveyance. Although the woman made no direct financial contribution to the purchase of the house, she did a great deal of work to the house and significantly improved it. When the relationship broke up some five years later, the question of the extent of the beneficial interests in the house arose. The Court of Appeal decided that the woman was entitled to a quarter share in the equity of the house, Lord Denning M.R. referring to the conduct of the parties at the time of the acquisition of the house and to the fact that it would be inequitable to deny her a share. In contrast, in *Burns* v. *Burns*[33] a differently constituted Court of Appeal denied any interest to a woman who had cohabited with the legal owner of the house for seventeen years. The court stated that, where property had been purchased in the man's sole name without the woman making any direct contribution to the purchase price or without the parties making an agreement or declaration regarding the beneficial interest in the property, there was a prima facie inference that the man was the sole legal and beneficial owner. This closer regard to strict property rights, in accordance with the principles enunciated in *Gissing* v. *Gissing* and *Pettitt* v. *Pettitt*, probably represents the likely course of the law in this area.

Leasehold Property

Introduction

If the deceased spouse was the tenant of the house under a fixed term or periodic tenancy which has not expired, then on death the lease will vest in the personal representatives in the usual way.[34] The death of the tenant does not automatically terminate the lease but might in accordance with the terms of the lease occasion a notice to quit.[35] It is possible in the case of a periodic tenancy that if a surviving spouse stays in possession and pays rent to the landlord, he or she will

[32] [1975] 1 W.L.R. 1338; see also *Cooke* v. *Head* [1972] 1 W.L.R. 518; *Bernard* v. *Joseph* [1982] Ch. 391; *Re Evers' Trust* [1980] 1 W.L.R. 1327; *Gordon* v. *Douce* [1983] 1 W.L.R. 563; *Grant* v. *Edwards* [1986] 2 All E.R. 426.

[33] [1984] Ch. 317; see also *Richards* v. *Dove* [1974] 1 All E.R. 888. Lord Denning M.R. in cases such as *Eves* had shown a willingness to use constructive trusts to ensure a share for the non-title-owning party. The Court of Appeal in *Burns* insisted that an entitlement could only be shown by proof of a resulting trust.

[34] Administration of Estates Act 1925 (hereinafter also referred to as the "A.E.A. 1925"), s.1(1), "real estate" is, for the purposes of this section, defined to include leasehold interests, s.3(1)(i) *ibid.* *Doe* d. *Hull* v. *Wood* (1845) 14 M. & W. 682. Such a devolution does not amount to a breach of a covenant against assignment, sub-letting or parting with the possession of the property subject to the lease without the consent of the landlord, *Seers* v. *Hind* (1791) 1 Ves. 294; *Parry* v. *Harbert* (1539) 1 Dyer 45b.

[35] *Rees* v. *Perrot* (1830) 4 C. & P. 230. Such a notice should be served on the executor, or administrator, of if none on the President of the Probate Division, A.E.A. 1925 s.9.

become the tenant in his or her own right but for this to happen it is essential that the landlord should accept the rent from him or her in the capacity of a tenant.[36] The spouse will not become the tenant if the landlord thinks he or she is paying the rent as the agent of the deceased, or as his or her legal personal representative or as a beneficiary under the will.[37]

It will, however, be appreciated that these points noted under the general law will apply in comparatively few tenancies. The majority of matrimonial homes that are subject to a tenancy will be either local authority lettings (council houses) or protected or statutory tenancies under the Rent Acts. These tenancies are discussed more fully in the next sections but it should be emphasised at the outset that it is most unlikely in either case that an effective notice to quit will, or can be, served on the death of the tenant spouse who leaves the surviving spouse living in the house.[38]

Private sector tenancies

Rent Acts

The Rent Act 1977[39] provides a scheme of statutory succession to statutory tenancies which will override both the contractual entitlement and the testate or intestate provisions. The main features of this succession can be noted briefly.

Spouse. The Housing Act 1980[40] has amended the First Schedule to the Rent Act 1977 in respect of a death of the original tenant on or after November 28, 1980. The Schedule[41] originally conferred a prior right of succession to the statutory tenancy where "... the original tenant was a man who died leaving a widow who was residing with him at his death. . . . "[42] The provision was thus confined to the widow, and then only if she was residing with the deceased tenant, and this remains the position in respect of deaths before November 28, 1980. It will be noticed that a widower was not included in this provision and had to claim under the third paragraph as a "member of the

[36] *Ticknor* v. *Buzzacott* [1965] 1 Ch. 426.

[37] *Ibid per* Plowman J. at p. 435.

[38] See generally Hill and Redman, *Landlord and Tenant*, 16th ed.; Woodfall, *Landlord and Tenant*, vol. 1, p. 808.

[39] s.2(1)(*b*) and Sched. 1, re-enacting earlier legislation to similar effect. Amended by the Housing Act 1980 s.76 which is in turn now replaced by Housing Act 1985. The succession arose initially out of the definition of tenant in the Increase of Rent and Mortgage Interest (Restrictions) Act 1920 s.12(1)(*g*) which included the widow of a tenant or a member of the tenant's family who was residing with him at the time of his death. The succession was put on a more formal basis by the Rent Act 1965, s.13 and re-enacted in the Rent Act 1968, Sched. I.

[40] s.76. See now 1985 Housing Act.

[41] Which is a re-enactment of earlier legislation, namely Rent Act 1968, Sched. I, paras. 1–9, which in turn had re-enacted earlier provisions.

[42] Rent Act 1977, Sched. 1, para. 2.

original tenants' family," in which case he might have to compete for the tenancy with other members of the family.[43] These differential requirements could be regarded as anomalous and the restrictions have now been removed, in respect of deaths after November 28, 1980, by section 76 of the Housing Act 1980, which substitutes the following paragraph for the original paragraph 2 in the Schedule to the 1977 Act: "The surviving spouse (if any) of the original tenant if residing in the dwelling house immediately before the death of the original tenant, shall after the death be the statutory tenant if and so long as he or she occupies the dwelling house as his or her residence."[44] Thus the provision now applies equally to a surviving widower who was not the original tenant and merely requires the surviving spouse to have been residing in the house at the death and not *with* the tenant. The Rent Acts permitted two statutory successions and the original requirement was likewise that the first successor should be a man who died leaving a widow who was residing with him at his death.[45] This has now been similarly amended to refer to "... The surviving spouse (if any) of the first successor, if residing in the dwelling-house immediately before the death of the first successor, shall after the death be the statutory tenant if and so long as he or she occupies the dwelling house as his or her residence."

A "widow" under the original formulation or a "surviving spouse" under the amendment does not include a mistress,[46] or a divorced wife but it appears that a widow does not lose her right to remain in possession by remarriage.[47]

Member of the tenants' family. If there is no spouse[48] but a member of the original tenant's family was residing with him or her at the time of and for the period of six months immediately before his or her death, then that person becomes the statutory tenant if and so long as he or she occupies the dwelling-house as his or her residence.[49] It has been noted that, under the Schedule to the Rent Act 1977 as originally enacted, a widower was entitled, if at all, under this paragraph[50] but this will no longer apply in respects of deaths after November 28, 1980 where by reason of the Housing Act amendment noted above a surviving spouse will now have a prior claim under the earlier paragraph.

[43] As in *Williams* v. *Williams* [1970] 1 W.L.R. 1530, husband and son.
[44] s.76(1).
[45] Rent Act 1977, Sched. 1, para. 6.
[46] As to succession to statutory tenancies by unrelated co-habitants see *post* p. 225.
[47] *Apsley* v. *Barr* [1928] N.I. 183.
[48] As amended by the Housing Act 1980 s.76, in respect of deaths after November 28, 1980, originally if there was no widow.
[49] Para. 3.
[50] See *e.g.* *Williams* v. *Williams* [1970] 1 W.L.R. 1530, a case which also illustrates that in some situations there may be two claimants as members of the tenant's family, and that the court will have to weigh the relative claims of each and decide between them.

So far as persons other than the widower are concerned, the prerequisites to establishing a claim to succession are threefold. First, the person should be a member of the original tenant's family; secondly, he or she should have been residing with the original tenant at the time of and for the period of six months immediately before his death; and, thirdly, he or she should have been occupying the dwelling-house as his or her residence. It is beyond the scope of this work to consider these requirements in detail, for which reference should be made to specialist works on the Rent Acts,[51] but one or two points can be noted shortly. The meaning of the phrase "member of the original tenant's family" has been considered in several recent decisions, notably by the House of Lords in *Carega Properties S.A.* v. *Sharratt.*[52] Viscount Dilhorne[53] stated that the meaning of the phrase is a question of law and that it is for the judge to construe the statute and to state his conclusion as to the meaning to be given to the word "family" in the context in which it appears, giving it, unless the context otherwise requires, its ordinary natural meaning. The word is not synonymous with "household." In the same case Lord Diplock[54] accepted the following formulation by Russell L.J. in *Ross* v. *Collins*[55]:

> "Granted that 'family' is not limited to cases of a strict legal familial nexus, I cannot agree that it extends to a case such as this.[56] It still requires, it seems to me, at least a broadly recognised *de facto* familial nexus. This may be capable of being found and recognised as such by the ordinary man where the link would be strictly familial had there been a marriage, or where the link is through adoption of a minor *de jure* or *de facto*, or where the link is 'step-' or where the link is 'in-law' or by marriage. But two strangers cannot, it seems to me, ever establish artificially for the purposes of this section a familial nexus by acting as brothers or as sisters, even if they call each other such and consider their relationship to be tantamount to that. Nor, in my view, can an adult man and woman who establish a platonic relationship establish a familial nexus by acting as a devoted brother and sister or father and daughter would act, even if they address each

[51] See, for example, Pettit, *Private Sector Tenancies*, 2nd ed. (1981) pp. 92–98.

[52] *sub. nom. Joram Developments Ltd.* v. *Sharratt* [1979] 1 W.L.R. 928, affirming the decision of the Court of Appeal [1979] 1 W.L.R. 3. See also *Helby* v. *Rafferty* [1979 1 W.L.R. 13]; *Dyson Holdings Ltd.* v. *Fox* [1975] 3 All E.R. 1030; *Ross* v. *Collins* [1964] 1 W.L.R. 425; *Hawes* v. *Evenden* [1953 1 W.L.R. 1169; *Gammans* v. *Ekins* [1950] 2 K.B. 328; *Brock* v. *Wollams* [1949] 2 K.B. 388.

[53] *Supra*, at p. 932.

[54] *Supra*, at p. 931.

[55] [1964] 1 W.L.R. 425 at p. 432.

[56] A case where a spinster who had no relationship by blood or marriage with the statutory tenant (who was some 40 years older) had looked after him devotedly for a substantial time before his death, the relationship being described as being something intermediate between a daughter and a sister, or on the other side, something between a father and an elder brother.

other as such and even if they refer to each other as such and regard their association as tantamount to such. Nor, in my view, would they indeed by recognised as familial links by the ordinary man."

Applying these principles in *Carega Properties S.A.* v. *Sharratt*[57] the House concluded that a man, who had lived with the tenant for twenty years before her death on a platonic basis as equivalent to aunt and nephew, was not entitled to succeed to the tenancy as a member of her family on her death.[58]

Thus it would seem that a real rather than a *de facto* relationship is necessary, which can be established by blood or marriage including situations where the link is "step-" or "in-law."[59] One exception to this appears from *Brock* v. *Wollams*[60] where there had been a *de facto* adoption of a child at the age of five and a long continuance of the child and parent *de facto* relationship and this was held to be sufficient. It has also been accepted that two persons living together as man and wife can provide the necessary element of relationship and this increasingly important situation will be considered in the next section.[61]

"*Common law husbands and wives.*" In recent years the courts have had to consider the entitlement to succession by an unrelated cohabitant of the tenant where the relationship is that of common law man and wife and this situation needs to be noted briefly. An examination of the cases reveals an apparent change in judicial attitude, from the somewhat uncompromising refusal to recognise the entitlement of such a person in *Gammans* v. *Ekins*[62] in 1950 to the acceptance of a common law wife in *Dyson Holdings Ltd.* v. *Fox*[63] in 1975.

The point has been considered by the Court of Appeal in *Watson* v.

[57] *Supra.*

[58] The court has rejected, in *Gammans* v. *Ekins, supra,* the notion that "... two old cronies of the same sex innocently sharing a flat," could establish the required relationship.

[59] See Lawton L.J. in *Joram Developments Ltd.* v. *Sharratt* [1979] 1 W.L.R. 3 at p. 9. In *Jones* v. *Whitehill* [1950] 2 K.B. 204 the niece of the tenant's wife succeeded.

[60] [1949] 2 K.B. 388.

[61] See Brown L.J. in *Joram Developments Ltd.* v. *Sharratt, supra*; at p. 12, who refers to these two situations as the only *de facto* relationships that would suffice for the purpose of the Act.

[62] [1950] 2 K.B. 328.

[63] [1975] 3 All E.R. 1030. See also *Hawes* v. *Evenden* [1953] 1 W.L.R. 1169. It was likewise accepted by the Court of Appeal in *Helby* v. *Rafferty* in [1979] 1 W.L.R. 13, that it was possible for a relationship between an unmarried man and an unmarried woman living together over a very long period to constitute a family relationship for the purpose of succession under the Rent Acts, although on the facts of that case, the Court did not consider that the situation was proved since the woman was anxious to retain her independence and had not adopted the character of a wife. The duration, permanence and stability of the relationship are important factors, likewise the presence of children and the adoption of the name of the man by the woman.

Lucas[64] where a married man, with one child of the marriage, was separated from his wife and had lived with another woman (who was the tenant in question) for some twenty years as man and wife. The circuit judge had declared that the man was not entitled to succeed to the tenancy on the death of the woman and on appeal Oliver L.J. agreed with that conclusion.[65] The majority in the Court of Appeal, however, thought that, notwithstanding the fact that the man had throughout remained married to his wife and that the co-habitees had continued to use their own names, the man was entitled to a declaration that he was a member of the tenant's family for the purposes of the Schedule.

Residing with. It has been noted that the original wording in the Rent Act 1977 referred to both the widow and the member of the tenant's family "residing with" the tenant.[66] This will no longer apply, in the case of deaths after 1980, to the spouse because the substituted wording refers simply to the spouse "residing in" the house.[67] It is hoped that this will be a more straightforward provision than the concept of "residing with." The latter phrase is applicable in respect of deaths before November 28, 1980 and with reference to all successions by a person as a member of the tenant's family. The detailed construction of this phrase is beyond the scope of this book but has been considered in several judicial decisions[68] and by specialist commentaries[69] to which reference should be made.

Two occasions. The statutory tenancy can devolve on two occasions and two only. The person entitled to the first transmission, whether a spouse or a member of the tenant's family, is termed "the first successor."[70] On that person's death the tenancy can devolve a second time either to his or her spouse or to a member of his or her family subject to the same requirements as apply to the first transmission.[71] There can be no further succession on the death of the second

[64] [1980] 1 W.L.R. 1493.

[65] The Lord Justice thought that *Dyson Holdings Ltd.* v. *Fox*, supra, rested on its own facts and stood at the very limit of any ordinarily accepted or acceptable definition of a family relationship, and thought the case to be distinguishable. The majority, however, regarded themselves as bound by that decision and applied it. It might be that *Dyson Holdings* is vulnerable to review by the House of Lords, which was not undertaken in *Carega Properties S.A.* v. *Sharratt*, because the House was not there concerned with the position of a "common law husband or wife," see Lord Diplock [1979] 1 W.L.R. 928 at p. 930.

[66] Which was the re-enactment of earlier legislation.

[67] See Housing Act 1980, s.76.

[68] See *e.g. Edmunds* v. *Jones* [1957] 1 W.L.R. 1181n; *Collier* v. *Stoneman* [1957] 1 W.L.R. 1108; *Foreman* v. *Beagley* [1969] 1 W.L.R. 1387; and *Morgan* v. *Murch* [1970] 1 W.L.R. 778.

[69] Pettit, *Private Sector Tenancies*, 2nd ed. (1982) p. 96.

[70] Rent Act 1977, Sched. 1, para. 4.

[71] *Ibid.* paras. 5, 6, and 7.

successor.[72] This second transmission is subject to some exceptions to which reference can be made in specialist texts.[73]

Statutory succession: public sector tenancies

Secure tenancies

The 1980 Housing Act[74] introduced a new category of secure tenancies and contained new provisions providing security of tenure for such tenants and introducing a system of statutory succession, analogous to that applicable to private sector tenancies and the Rent Act 1977.[75] The relevant provisions are now included in sections 87–90 of the Housing Act 1985. Secure tenancies include primarily and most importantly local authority tenancies and other forms of public and quasi-public tenancy where, for example, the landlord is the Commissioner for the New Towns or a development corporation or housing corporation.[76] The condition precedent to the succession is that the person to succeed should be an individual occupying the dwelling-house as his only or principal home at the time of the tenant's death.[77] Only the tenant's spouse or another member of the tenant's family who has resided with the tenant throughout the period of twelve months ending with the tenant's death can qualify.[78] The spouse is preferred to another member of the family and, in the case of dispute between the latter, the successor can be selected by the landlord.[79]

It can be noticed that, in contrast to the Rent Act provision, only one transmission is allowed since a tenant who was a successor is excluded and such a person is defined in section 31(1) (1985 Act, s.88) to include a person who had the tenancy vested in him by virtue of section 30 (1985 Act, s.87).[80] Likewise excluded is a person who was a joint tenant and has become the sole tenant[81] and, in certain circumstances, a tenant who is the successor to a previous periodic tenancy.[82] However, a tenant who has succeeded to a previous tenancy under the first schedule to the Rent Act 1977, is not regarded as a successor for the purposes of succession to a secure tenancy under the Housing Acts. In other respects the legislation is similar to the Rent Act provision.[83]

[72] *Ibid.*
[73] Paras. 9, 10, and 11. See Pettit, *op. cit.* pp. 97, 98.
[74] ss.28–50, succession on the death of the tenant was governed by the provisions in s.30. See now ss.87–90 of the Housing Act 1985.
[75] 1st Sched., see *ante* p. 222.
[76] Housing Act 1980, s.28, now ss.79–86 of the Housing Act 1985.
[77] s.30(2), (1985 Act, s.87).
[78] *Ibid.*
[79] s.30(3), (1985 Act, s.89).
[80] s.31(1)(*a*), (1985 Act, s.88).
[81] s.31(1)(*b*), (1985 Act, s.88).
[82] s.31(2), (1985 Act, s.88).
[83] See *ante*, p. 222.

Agricultural premises

Protected occupiers by succession

Reference should be made to The Rent (Agriculture) Act 1976 sections 3 and 4 which provides for the succession by a spouse to be "a protected occupier of the dwelling-house" on the death of the spouse.[84] There are provisions analogous to those of the Rent Act relating to succession by members of the original occupier's family where there is no spouse.[85] The Housing Act 1980 amends this legislation by changing the requirement that the spouse or member of the family should be "residing with" the occupier at the death to a requirement of "residing in the dwelling-house immediately before his death."[86] The details of this legislation can be found in specialist texts.[87]

APPROPRIATION OF THE MATRIMONIAL HOME UNDER THE 1952 ACT

Introduction

Personal representatives have wide powers of appropriation which can be used to enable a beneficiary to receive particular assets of the deceased, *in specie*, notwithstanding an express or statutory trust for sale. There is a limited power of appropriation under the common law[88] and clearly a will can include an express power to enlarge the statutory powers.[89] The latter can be relevant in cases of partial intestacy but does not need to be further discussed here. The main powers of appropriation which are relevant to cases of intestacy are the general statutory power in section 41 of the 1925 Act and the extensive rights conferred on a surviving spouse to require appropriation of the matrimonial home conferred by the Second Schedule to the Intestates' Estates Act 1952. The general power conferred by section 41 has been considered above,[90] but its inter-relation with the rights conferred by the Schedule are apparent since the rights under the Schedule are expressed to be "... in exercise of the power conferred

[84] s.3(2).
[85] s.3(3).
[86] s.76. The 1976 Act already conferred equal rights of succession on widowers and widows, so no change was needed in 1980 in this respect.
[87] See Scammell and Densham, *Law of Agricultural Holdings*, 6th ed. (1978). Note that the succession to agricultural tenancies provided by the Agriculture (Miscellaneous Provisions) Act 1976, ss.18–24 was abolished, subject to exceptions, by the Agricultural Holdings Act 1984. See now Agricultural Holdings Act 1986, Pt. IV.
[88] See *Williams on Wills*, 5th ed. (1980), pp. 179–186.
[89] *Ibid.* An express power could, for example, dispense with the consents required by the 1925 Act, s.41.
[90] See *ante* p. 125.

by section forty-one of the principal Act. . . . "[91] Thus Templeman L.J. in *Re Phelps (decd.)*[92]:

> "The effect of paragraph 5(2) is that for the purposes of Schedule 2 a transaction which in essence is partly appropriation and partly sale becomes an appropriation, and Schedule 2 must be read as if section 41 of the 1925 Act included this new hybrid power of appropriation. When a widow, pursuant to paragraph (1) of Schedule 2, requires the personal representatives to appropriate, in exercise of the power conferred by section 41, she is requiring them to exercise that power as enlarged by paragraph 5(2)."

The Schedule has the effect of widening the statutory power in section 41, principally by converting the power into a right.[93] This is not, however, to be taken as conferring any equitable interest in the matrimonial home before appropriation so as, for instance, to give the spouse *locus standi* to defend an action for possession by the registered proprietor.[94] Nor is the spouse to be regarded as being in a position analogous to a beneficiary who has an option to purchase an asset at the death of the testator.[95]

The basic provision

Paragraph 1(i) of the Schedule provides that (subject to the provisions of the Schedule)

> ". . . where the residuary estate of the intestate comprises an interest in a dwelling-house in which the surviving husband or wife was resident at the time of the intestate's death, the surviving husband or wife may require the personal representative, in exercise of the power conferred by section forty-one of the

[91] Para. 1(1); see also paras. 1(3), 3(2), 5(2), 6(2) and 7(2).

[92] [1980] Ch. 275 at pp. 278–279; see also Bridge L.J. *ibid*, at p. 280 ". . . the extended power of appropriation is to be 'included' in the power of appropriation under s.41 of the Administration of Estates Act 1925 . . . ," and Buckley L.J. *ibid* at p. 281. *Robinson* v. *Collins* [1975] 1 W.L.R. 309, at p. 314 per Pennycuick V.-C., ". . . Schedule 2 of the 1952 Act imports the provision for appropriation contained in s.41 of the 1925 Act. . . . " The power in s.41 will remain important in those cases where the Schedule is inapplicable *e.g.* to short leases, or in cases where the 12 month time limit under the Schedule has expired.

[93] See Buckley L.J. in *Re Phelps (decd.)* [1980] Ch. 275; Pennycuick V.-C. in *Robinson* v. *Collins* [1975] 1 W.L.R. 309. Further it is expressly provided in para. 1(3) that the right is not restricted by the requirements in s.41(5) that the personal representatives should have regard to the rights of any person, who may come into existence after the date of the appropriation, or, who cannot be found or ascertained at the time of appropriation.

[94] *Lall* v. *Lall* [1965] 1 W.L.R. 1249. The surviving spouses' rights are no greater than those of a residuary legatee of a testate estate, as to which see *Commissioner of Stamp Duties* v. *Livingston* [1965] A.C. 694.

[95] *Per* Pennycuick V.-C. in *Robinson* v. *Collins* [1975] 1 W.L.R. 309 at p. 314, rejecting an argument based on *Talbot* v. *Talbot* [1968] A.C. 1 and thus a contention that the asset should be valued at death.

principal Act (and with due regard to the requirements of that section as to valuation) to appropriate the said interest in the dwelling house in or towards satisfaction of any absolute interest of the surviving husband or wife in the real and personal estate of the intestate."

Each of the elements of this provision must be considered in turn and the first phrase to consider is "the residuary estate of the intestate." It is provided by the Schedule that it should ". . . be construed as one with Part IV of the principal Act" (para. 7(2)) and therefore the definition of the phrase in section 33 of the 1925 Act will govern the provision. This has been considered above and reference can be made to that discussion.[96]

Clearly the Schedule will apply in cases of total intestacy and (in contrast to section 41) cannot apply in cases of wholly testate succession. However, the reference in paragraph 1(1) is to "the residuary estate of the intestate" and "an intestate" is defined by the Act to include a person who leaves a will but dies intestate as to some beneficiary interest in his real or personal estate.[97] Accordingly the Schedule would seem to be applicable in cases of partial intestacy but the definition of "the residuary estate of the intestate" in section 33 refers strictly to the *undisposed* of property[98] and so it is submitted that the rights conferred by the Schedule can be invoked only when the dwelling-house is undisposed of and thus forms part of the intestate estate.[99] However, the alternative view is arguable, namely that, since "intestate" is defined to include a person who dies partially intestate, the Schedule is applicable if a dwelling-house forms part of the residuary estate whether that is undisposed of or subject to testamentary provision.[1]

A further difficulty centres on the question whether the appropriation can be made only in satisfaction of the spouse's *intestate* interests or whether it can be made, in cases of partial intestacy, partly in satisfaction of intestate and partly in satisfaction of testate interests, or indeed wholly in satisfaction of testate interests. Paragraph 1(i), as set out above, refers to the appropriation being made ". . . in or towards satisfaction of any absolute interest of the surviving husband

[96] See *ante* p. 78.

[97] s.55(1)(vi). It can be noted that the Schedule has to be construed as one with Pt. IV of the principal Act and the definition section is in Pt. V of the Act. However Pt. V is clearly supplemental (and described as such) to Pt. IV and would seem to be applicable in the absence of any contrary intention in the Schedule.

[98] See s.33(2), (4), and discussion above.

[99] See also s.5(1) ". . . purchasing out of the estate of the intestate an interest in a dwelling-house."

[1] s.41 of the principal Act which is in effect incorporated into the Schedule prevents an appropriation being made, "so as to affect prejudicially any specific devise or bequest," and clearly this would prevent any appropriation of a house that had been specifically devised, but leaves open the point where the house is part of the residuary estate.

or wife in the real personal estate of the intestate,"[2] and is thus not expressly limited to the intestate part of that estate. It is therefore arguable that the rights under the Schedule could, in cases of partial intestacy, be invoked in satisfaction of testamentary absolute interests or in satisfaction of intestate and partly of testate benefits. This conclusion is supported by the definition of "intestate" noted above.

However, it is submitted that a narrow view should be taken of the Schedule and that the rights should be regarded as applicable only when the dwelling-house is undisposed of and that the appropriation should be only in satisfaction of intestate benefits. This is because the failure of any interest, however small, in a testamentary scheme will give rise to a partial intestacy and a broader view of the Schedule would confer rights of appropriation in such cases, which it is submitted was not intended by the framers of the 1952 Act.[3]

An interest in a dwelling-house

It has been seen that the intestate must have had "an interest" in a dwelling-house and this requirement must now be considered. So far as the "interest" is concerned, clearly an absolute or concurrent interest in a freehold estate will suffice, but it would seem that an interest solely as a mortgagee would not. The Schedule applies to leasehold property provided that the lease has not less than two years to run from the date of death.[4] Tenancies which the landlord can, by notice given after the death, determine within the two years are also excluded.[5] It would seem also that Rent Act statutory tenancies are excluded since such tenancies do not pass on the death of the tenant to the personal representatives but are subject to their own scheme of statutory succession.[6] However, short leases are included if the surviving spouse would in consequence of an appropriation become entitled under the Leasehold Reform Act 1967 to acquire the freehold or an extended leasehold.[7] The general power in section 41 can be used to appropriate short leases.[8]

Dwelling-house

It will be noticed that paragraph 1 of the Schedule refers to the

[2] See also para. 5(2), and para. 1(4) which although clearly including a specific kind of intestate benefit does not expressly so limit the phrase.

[3] The plain fact is that the Schedule, like other parts of the 1952 Act, is poorly drafted and raises but does not solve these problems.

[4] Para. 1(2)(*a*).

[5] Para.1(2)(*b*). A mere licence to occupy as in *Somma* v. *Hazelhurst*, [1978] 1 W.L.R. 1014, would not seem to suffice. But see *Street* v. *Mountford* [1985] 2 All E.R. 289.

[6] As to which, see *post*.

[7] s.7(8)(*a*)(9), or if the deceased spouse was entitled to acquire the freehold or an extended lease under the Act, and had given notice of his or her desire to do so, and the benefit of that notice was appropriated with the tenancy, *ibid* s.7(8)(*b*).

[8] See *ante* p. 125.

interest being "in a dwelling house,"[9] whereas section 5 of the 1952 Act (which incorporates the Schedule) refers to "the matrimonial home" and so does the heading and the marginal note to the schedule. It would have been preferable if the legislation had avoided this difference of terminology and if a single phrase had been fully defined by the Schedule. The main guidance offered is the requirement that the dwelling-house must be one "... in which the surviving husband or wife was resident at the time of the intestate's death."[10] In straightforward cases, where the spouses live together in a single house, this will cause no problem and the dwelling-house will be the matrimonial home. However, it will be noticed that there is no requirement that the spouses should actually be living together in the house. The only requirements are that the surviving spouse was resident in a house at the date of the death and that the house is part of the residuary estate of the other. Accordingly, if the spouses are living apart, a house owned by the husband, in which the wife lived, would be within the Schedule on the death intestate of the husband.[11] Further problems arise where the parties have two houses and live alternately in each.[12] The Schedule refers to the house "in which the surviving husband or wife was resident" at the time of the intestate's death but it is not thought that this would be interpreted too strictly. The concept of residence is wider than mere occupation[13] and according to the ordinary and accepted meaning of the term it would seem perfectly possible to be "resident" in more than one house at the time of the intestate's death. In such cases it would seem that the surviving spouse would have to make a choice since the Schedule, by continually referring to "the dwelling-house," would not seem to enable the spouse to require more than one house to be appropriated towards his or her share.

The expression "dwelling-house" in the Schedule expressly includes a garden or portion of ground attached to and usually occupied with the dwelling-house or otherwise required for the amenity or convenience of the dwelling-house.[14] Also, where part of a building was at the date of the death of the intestate occupied as a separate dwelling, that dwelling is treated as a dwelling-house for the purpose of the Schedule.[15] Problems still remain, however. For example, is a "mobile home" or a house-boat a dwelling-house?[16]

In certain circumstances, because of the physical circumstances

[9] Para. 1(1), and throughout the Schedule.
[10] Para. 1(1).
[11] *Ibid.*
[12] *e.g.* a flat in London and a country house, or a holiday home.
[13] See *e.g.* the tax case of *Levene* v. *I.R.C.* [1928] A.C. 25.
[14] Para. 7(1).
[15] Para. 1(5).
[16] They are expressly included, in some circumstances, in the law of burglary, see Theft Act 1968, s.9(3).

regarding the dwelling-house, the rights conferred by the Schedule cannot be exercised without an order of the court,[17] for which either the personal representatives or the surviving husband or wife may apply.[18] The order will only be granted if the court is satisfied that the exercise of the right is not likely to diminish the value of other assets of the estate or to make them more difficult to dispose of.[19] The circumstances where such an order are necessary are[20]:

1. where the dwelling-house forms part of a building and an interest in the whole of the building is comprised in the residuary estate;
2. where the dwelling-house is held with agricultural land and an interest in the agricultural land is comprised in the residuary estate;
3. where the whole or a part of the dwelling-house was at the time of the intestate's death used as a hotel or lodging house;
4. where a part of the dwelling-house was at the time of the intestate's death used for purposes other than domestic purposes.

If the court declines to make the order, it may authorise the personal representatives to dispose of the interest in the dwelling-house within the twelve-month period.[21]

Surviving husband or wife

The right of appropriation under the Schedule is conferred only on a "husband or wife"[22] and again, in so far as the Schedule must be construed as one with Part IV of the principal Act,[23] the same meaning must apply. Reference can be made to the discussion above as to the problems of entitlement of "common law husbands and wives," divorced or judicially separated spouses and parties to void, voidable and polygamous marriages.[24]

Where the surviving husband or wife is a person of unsound mind, or a defective, then the committee or receiver, or the court if necessary, can make the relevant election.[25] In the unlikely event of the spouse being a minor, he or she can nonetheless make the election on his or her own behalf or consent to the personal representatives selling within the twelve months.[26]

[17] Para. 2.
[18] Para. 4(2).
[19] Para. 2.
[20] Para. 2.
[21] Para. 4(2).
[22] Para. 1(1), and throughout the Schedule.
[23] Para. 7(2).
[24] See *ante*, Chap. 10.
[25] Para. 6(1).
[26] Para. 6(2); the provisions of s.41 as to obtaining the consent of the minor's parent or guardian or of the court, on behalf of the minor do not apply, *ibid.*

In or towards satisfaction

The Schedule provides for an appropriation of "the said interest in the dwelling house in or towards satisfaction of any absolute interest" of the surviving spouse in the estate.[27] Clearly this will allow an appropriation in cases where the value of the interest is equal to or exceeds the value of the dwelling-house but the Schedule goes beyond this and includes also the right to pay equality money where the house exceeds the interest in value.[28] This is an important extension of the powers available under section 41.[29] Paragraph 5(2) expressly provides that an appropriation of the dwelling-house can be made partly in satisfaction of an interest in the residuary estate of the intestate and partly in return for a payment of money by the surviving spouse to the personal representatives. The construction and effect of this provision was the subject of the decision in *Re Phelps decd.*,[30] where the husband died intestate leaving a widow. At the death they were both living in the house which was their matrimonial home. The house formed part of the deceased's residuary estate but its value was greater than that of the widow's absolute interest in the estate.[31] The widow wanted to have the house appropriated to her under the Schedule and she was willing to pay equality money to make up for the difference in value. At first instance, Foster J.[32] decided that the right conferred by paragraph 1 of the Schedule was only to require appropriation "in or towards satisfaction" of any absolute interest and that this wording did not confer any right where the asset exceeded in value the interest. In forming this conclusion the judge was influenced by the power conferred by section 41 which is limited to appropriating assets of equal or lesser value than the interest.[33] However, this decision ignores the wording in paragraph 5(2) and in view of this provision the Court of Appeal reversed the decision.[34] Templeman L.J. explained the position[35]:

> "Where the dwelling-house and the widow's interests are equal in value the personal representatives are required to appropriate in satisfaction of the widow's interest; where the dwelling-house is worth less than the widow's interest, they are required to appropriate towards satisfaction of the widow's interest; and where the dwelling-house is worth more than the widow's interest they are required to appropriate, in the words of para. 5(2) 'partly

[27] Para. 1(1).
[28] Para. 5(2).
[29] See above.
[30] [1978] 1 W.L.R. 1501, reversed on appeal, [1980] Ch. 275.
[31] The widow was entitled to the current fixed net sum of £8,750 whereas the house was worth £12,000.
[32] *Supra.*
[33] *Supra.* p. 125.
[34] *Supra,* see Templeman L.J., [1980] Ch. 275 at p. 279.
[35] *Ibid.* at p. 279.

in satisfaction' of the interest 'and partly in return for a payment of money.' "

The conclusion of the court was thus expressed by Bridge L.J. as follows[36]:

> "It must follow, I think, that the only sensible purpose which can be ascribed to paragraph 5(2) is to extend by implication the ambit of paragraph 1(1) to enable the surviving spouse to require appropriation of the matrimonial home partly in satisfaction of his or her interest in the deceased spouse's estate and partly in return for a payment of money."

Absolute interest

The appropriation can only be made in or towards satisfaction of "... any absolute interest of the surviving husband or wife in the real and personal estate of the intestate."[37] The spouse's absolute interests under an intestacy are[38]:

> where there are no issue or other specified relatives, in the whole estate;
> where there are issue or other specified relatives, in the fixed net sum (which will surely be the primary interest for this purpose);
> where there are no issue but specified relatives, in one-half of the estate;
> where there are issue, the capital value of the life interest in one-half of the estate, if the spouse has elected to have the interest redeemed under section 47A.[39]

It has been suggested above that the fixed net sum has been increased progressively in recent years in line with the rise in house values. In *Re Phelps (decd.)*, it will be recalled, the then current fixed net sum was only £8,750 against the value of the house of (say) £12,000.[40] The estate, however, had a gross value of £356,000 and the spouse was entitled to a life interest in one-half[41] but she had made an ineffectual attempt to notify the personal representatives of her election to have her life interest capitalised.[42] This led to the problem

[36] *Ibid.* at p. 280.
[37] Para. 1(1).
[38] s.46(1), see *ante* p. 192. The personal chattels are also taken absolutely but these can be ignored in most cases, as being of little value, but see *Re Crispin's Will Trusts* [1975] Ch. 245.
[39] This is expressly included under the Schedule see para. 1(4).
[40] The Probate value was £11,000; it was subsequently valued at £15,000 which the spouse refused to accept. The figure of £12,000 is used as an example by the Court of Appeal [1979] 3 All E.R. 373.
[41] See the decision at first instance [1978] 3 All E.R. 395.
[42] The notice was sent before letters of administration were obtained and not to the personal representatives; see the requirements in s.47A(6). A subsequent attempt to rectify the situation was out of time, see s.47A(5).

of the shortfall in value which has been discussed above. Both the right under the Schedule[43] and the right under section 47A[44] must be exercised by due notice within twelve months of the grant and care is obviously needed to ensure that both of these notices are correctly sent.

Valuation

When considering an appropriation, the valuation of the interest in the estate, on the one hand, and the asset to be appropriated, on the other, will be of crucial importance. In cases of total intestacy there will be little problem in valuing the spouse's absolute interests in the residuary estate since in most cases the statutory legacy will be the relevant interest. Where the deceased leaves a spouse but no issue, the valuation of the spouse's absolute entitlement to one-half of the estate should also present little difficulty[45] and likewise the capital value of the spouse's life interest, where there is issue, which the spouse has elected to have redeemed.[46]

The valuation of the dwelling-house is subject to a statutory provision. First, it is provided that the surviving husband or wife may require the personal representative to have the deceased's interest in the dwelling house valued in accordance with section 41 of the principal Act and to inform him or her of the result of that valuation before he or she decides whether to exercise the rights conferred by the Schedule.[47] Secondly, for the purposes of such appropriation, section 41 provides that the personal representative may ascertain and fix the value of the asset and shall for that purpose employ a duly qualified valuer in any case where that may be necessary.[48] It is settled that under section 41 the relevant value of the appropriated asset is the value at the date of appropriation and not at the death[49] and it was decided in *Robinson* v. *Collins*,[50] that the same rule applies to the valuation of the dwelling house under the Schedule. In that case the question was crucial since the house had virtually doubled in value between the death and the appropriation and Pennycuick V.-C. could see no reason for departing from the general rule applicable to appropriation under section 41.[51]

> "If Parliament had intended that the appropriation should take effect retrospectively as at the date of death, one would have

[43] *i.e.* as to appropriation of the dwelling house, para. 3(1), see *post* p. 237.
[44] *i.e.* as to redemption of the life interest, s.47A(5).
[45] Under s.46(1), see *ante*. p. 193.
[46] As to the method of capitalisation see *ante* p. 212.
[47] Para. 3(2).
[48] s.41(3).
[49] *Robinson* v. *Collins* [1975] 1 W.L.R. 309; *Re Charteris* [1917] 2 Ch. 379, see *ante* p. 125.
[50] *Supra.*
[51] *Supra*, at p. 125.

expected this result to be achieved by plain words. The words actually used are quite inapt to achieve such a result. No injustice is involved in this conclusion. There is no reason that I can see why the widow rather than the other next of kin should benefit from rising house prices, or indeed, in the contrary case, less familiar in the circumstances of today, suffer from a fall in house prices."

This rule is clearly to the spouse's disadvantage in times of inflation and it behoves a spouse to make a decision as soon as possible, giving rise to the criticism that the spouse might be forced into a hasty decision or be prejudiced by the tardiness of the personal representative in making the appropriation.

Restrictions on disposition

During the twelve-month period the personal representatives cannot without the written consent of the surviving spouse sell or otherwise dispose of the interest in the dwelling-house except in the course of administration owing to want of other assets.[52] The court can, however, authorise the personal representatives to sell the interest within the period.[53] If the court has ordered an extension of the period under the provisions noted above, the above two provisions apply to the extended period.[54] However, these provisions relating to restrictions on disposition of the interest do not apply where the surviving spouse is the sole personal representative.[55] In such cases the spouse has effective control over the property.

Notwithstanding these restrictions, if the house is sold then the purchaser is protected and the surviving spouse has no rights under the Schedule against the purchaser.[56] When the twelve-month time limit has expired the personal representatives may forthwith sell and the sale will be unimpeachable.

Procedure

The right must be invoked by notifying the personal representative in writing[57] within twelve months[58] from the first taking out of representation with respect to the intestate's estate.[59]

For the purposes of this notification, where there are two or more

[52] Para. 4(1).
[53] Para. 4(2).
[54] Para. 4(3).
[55] Para. 4(4).
[56] Para. 4(5).
[57] Para. 3(1)(*c*).
[58] Para. 3(1)(*a*).
[59] For this purpose a grant limited to settled land or to trust property, is to be left out of account and likewise a grant limited to real estate or to personal estate unless a grant limited to the remainder of the estate has previously been made or is made at the same time, para. 3(3) incorporating s.47A(9) of the principal Act.

personal representatives of whom one is the surviving husband or wife, all except the spouse will be notified.[60] If the surviving spouse is the sole personal representative, doubts have been expressed as to whether the Schedule can be invoked at all[61] but it seems that it can and an additional personal representative should be appointed.[62] Where there are such additional personal representatives, the rule which precludes a trustee from purchasing trust property is expressly excluded so as not to prevent the surviving husband or wife from purchasing out of the estate of the intestate an interest in the dwelling-house.[63] Once the notification in writing has been made, it is not revocable except with the consent of the personal representatives.[64] The right is not exercisable after the death of the surviving husband or wife.[65]

An extension of the twelve-month period can be applied for on the grounds that the twelve-month period will operate unfairly for any of the following reasons[66]: first, in consequence of the representation first taken out being probate of a will subsequently revoked on the ground that the will was invalid[67]; secondly, in consequence of a question whether a person had an interest in the estate, or as to the nature of an interest in the estate not having been determined at the time when representation was first taken out[68]; thirdly, in consequence of some other circumstances affecting the administration or distribution of the estate, which satisfy the court that the limitation to the twelve-month period would operate unfairly.[69]

Comment

It is submitted that the absence of a simple and direct right of inheritance to the matrimonial home is to be regretted. The present system appears to be based on, and works most effectively where, the home is owned by the husband who dies first. However, the legislation fails to recognise the increasing trend towards the joint ownership of the matrimonial home. In such cases the spouse will "inherit" the home under the *jus accrescendi* and in addition will still be entitled to the full value of the fixed net sum. It can be suggested that this is a

[60] Para. 3(1)(*c*).

[61] See Graham (1952) 16 Conv. 402, 417. Perhaps s.41 could be invoked by a spouse who is sole personal representative.

[62] Para. 3(1)(*c*).

[63] Para. 5(1).

[64] Para. 3(2). It is difficult to see the reason for this rule or how the consent could be refused in normal cases.

[65] Para. 3(1)(*b*).

[66] Para. 3(3) incorporating s.47A(5) of the 1925 Act. It can be noted that there is no time limit in s.41 so that although that power will be limited to the period of administration, it could be exercised more than twelve months from the death.

[67] *Ibid.*

[68] *Ibid.*

[69] *Ibid.*

double provision for the spouse to the exclusion, in most cases, of any inheritance by the children. It is suggested that there should be, at least, more correlation between the ownership and destination of the matrimonial home and the entitlement to the fixed net sum.[70] A direct system of inheritance to the home could enable the spouse's other entitlements to be considered afresh, particularly with reference to the children's claims.

[70] If the Law Commission's suggested presumption of joint ownership had been adopted, see Report No. 86 referred to above, p. 218 then it is submitted the amount of the fixed net sum would also have needed reconsideration.

CHAPTER 13

THE ENTITLEMENT OF ISSUE

The categories of person who are entitled to take as issue have been described in Chapter 10 and it is now necessary to consider the extent of the entitlement of such children or other issue.

THE ENTITLEMENT

Introduction

Leaving issue

The Administration of Estates Act 1925 requires that the intestate should "leave issue"[1] and so, obviously, children, grandchildren or more remote issue must survive the intestate, except that "references to a child or issue living at the death of any person include a child or issue en ventre sa mere at the death."[2] Further, the presumption that the younger survives the elder in a *commorientes* situation, which is embodied in section 184 of the Law of Property Act 1925, will apply to children or issue on intestacy so that children will always be presumed to have survived their parents.[3]

The entitlement of issue on intestacy is expressed in section 46(1) to be "on the statutory trusts" and such trusts are defined in section 47 which is considered more fully in the following sections. Under these trusts issue attain a vested interest at eighteen years of age[4] or on marriage under that age and, strictly speaking, "leaving issue" or "leaving a child or other issue" is construed as "leaving issue who attain an absolutely vested interest."[5] Where all the children survive and they are all of full age, they will be absolutely entitled and the distribution of the estate can proceed on that basis. However, where there are minor children (or minor grandchildren of deceased children) the possibility that they will not attain a vested interest does not affect the initial distribution. The share attributable to issue will be set aside on the statutory trusts and the estate will be distributed initially as if there were issue. Should all of those issue fail to attain a vested interest, there will then be "no issue"[6] and the part of the estate

[1] s.46(1).
[2] s.55(2).
[3] The exclusion of s.184, by s.46(3) of the Administration of Estates Act 1925 in cases of intestacy is confined to husbands and wives.
[4] s.47(1), as amended in respect of deaths on or after January 1, 1970, by s.3(2) of the Family Law Reform Act 1969.
[5] s.47(1)(*c*) and likewise conversely "leaving no issue," s.47(1)(*b*).
[6] s.47(2)(*b*).

held on the statutory trusts will have to be redistributed on that basis. Thus section 47(2) provides:

> "If the trusts in favour of the issue of the intestate fail by reason of no child or other issue attaining an absolutely vested interest—
> (*a*) the residuary estate of the intestate and the income thereof and all statutory accumulations, if any, of the income thereof, or so much thereof as may not have been paid or applied under any power affecting the same, shall go, devolve and be held under the provisions of this Part of this Act as if the intestate had died without leaving issue living at the death of the intestate. . . . "[7]

The entitlement of issue

Spouse and issue

(a) Where the estate does not exceed the amount of the fixed net sum, currently £40,000,[8] the issue have no entitlement.
(b) Where the estate exceeds the amount of the fixed net sum currently £40,000, then subject to the spouse's entitlement to
  (i) the personal chattels absolutely;
  (ii) the fixed net sum, currently £40,000;
  (iii) a life interest in one-half of the residuary estate;

the issue are entitled to:

(a) an interest in remainder under the statutory trusts in one-half of the residuary estate and,
(b) an immediate interest under the statutory trusts[9] in the other half of the residuary estate.[10]

The necessity for a grant to be made to a trust corporation or to two or more individuals where under the intestacy any beneficiary is a minor or where a life interest arises, can be noted.[11]

[7] Thus the entitlement of the surviving spouse might subsequently become enlarged. When it becomes apparent subsequent to the death that the trusts in favour of issue have wholly failed, then the entitlement is ascertained with reference to the intestates death, not to the position at the date of failure. Thus the personal representatives of a parent who survived the intestate but died before the failure of the trusts for issue, will be entitled rather than say a surviving brother or sister; see *Re McKee* [1931] Ch. 145; *Re Bowen-Buscarlet* [1972] 1 Ch. 463; *Re Williams* (*decd.*) [1937] N.Z.L.R. 870, *Re Sawyer's Will* (1931) 26 Tas.L.R. 161.

[8] S.I. 1981 No. 255; in the case of deaths before March 1, 1981, the amount of the fixed net sum was £25,000; in the case of deaths before March 15, 1977, the amount was £15,000; in the case of deaths before July 1, 1972, the amount was £8,750 in the case of the deaths before January 1, 1967, the amount was £5,000; and in the case of deaths before January 1, 1953, the amount was £1,000. As to when the estate is valued for this purpose, see *ante* p. 207.

[9] s.46(1)(i).

[10] See *post*.

[11] Supreme Court Act 1981, s.114.

Issue and no spouse

If the intestate leaves issue but no husband or wife, the residuary estate of the intestate is held on the statutory trusts for such issue.[12]

It will be noticed that the entitlement of "issue" on intestacy is constant and does not vary with the number or the degree of relationship of such issue. Thus a single child will have the same entitlement as a class of 10 children or, where all the children have predeceased the intestate, as a single grandchild. This is in contrast to the position in some Australian states. In Queensland, for example,[13] if there is a spouse and one child, the child is entitled to one-half but, if there are two or more children, the children are entitled to two-thirds.

The statutory trusts

Section 47

The entitlement of issue on intestacy is not expressed as an immediate absolute interest but the whole or one-half, as the case may be, of the residuary estate is held "on the statutory trusts for the issue of the intestate."[14] These trusts are simple trusts and would appear to supersede the statutory trust for sale imposed on death by section 33(1).[15] This is because, once the residuary estate has been ascertained, the trust for sale can be regarded as *functus officio* and displaced by the imperative trusts of section 46 and section 47.

The statutory trusts are defined in section 47(1)(i) as follows:

> "In trust in equal shares if more than one, for all or any, the children or child of the intestate,[16] living at the death of the intestate, who attain the age of eighteen years[17] or marry under that age, and for all or any of the issue living at the death of the intestate who attain the age of eighteen years or marry under that age, of any child of the intestate who predeceases the intestate, such issue to take through all degrees, according to their stocks, in equal shares if more than one, the share which their

[12] s.46(1)(ii).

[13] Succession Act, 1981 2nd Sched., Pt. I, item 2. See likewise in Western Australia, Administration Act, 1903–1976, section 14(3), Item 3; Australian Capital Territory, Administration and Probate Ordinance, 1929, Part I, item 2, *ibid.* Northern Territory; see Hardingham Neave and Ford, Wills and Intestacy pp. 341 *et seq.*

[14] s.46(1), s.47(1)(2)(3). These provisions are not affected by the Intestates' Estates Act 1952 but were amended in respect of deaths on or after January 1, 1970 by the Family Law Reform Act 1969 by the substitution of the age of "eighteen years" for the previous "twenty-one years" and by the inclusion of illegitimate children: s.14.

[15] See *ante*, Chap. 6.

[16] The reference to child or children has effect as if it included a reference to any illegitimate child or children of the intestate, Family Law Reform Act 1969, s.14(3)(*b*).

[17] The age of 18 years was substituted for 21 years in respect of the estate of an intestate dying after January 1, 1970, s.3(2).

parent would have taken if living at the death of the intestate, and so that no issue shall take whose parent is living at the death of the intestate and so capable of taking."

It can be seen that the effect of this provision is to create a stirpital distribution whereby the children of the intestate will take primary shares and the children of deceased children, *i.e.* grandchildren of the intestate, will take their parent's share by representation.

Stirpital distribution

Children

The first task is to ascertain the position of the intestate's children. All children[18] who are living at the death of the intestate (including a child *en ventre sa mère* at the death[19]) will be entitled to a share. Additionally, a share will have to be allocated to each of the children who have predeceased the intestate leaving issue surviving, the issue of such a child being entitled to the share which their parent would have taken had he or she survived.[20] Children who have predeceased the intestate without leaving issue surviving will be ignored, as will the children of children, *i.e.* grandchildren, who survive the intestate.[21] Having thus ascertained the number of shares into which the "issues entitlement" in the residuary estate must be divided, the entitlement can be considered. Each of the children so qualified to a share, who has either attained the age of eighteen years[22] or has married under that age,[23] will be immediately and absolutely entitled to his or her share. The shares of children who have not attained a vested interest will be held for them on the statutory trust contingently on their attaining the age of eighteen years or marrying under that age. Should such a child fail to attain a vested interest, his or her notional share will accrue to the other shares to be held absolutely or contingently on trust for the other children or issue as the case may be. If all the children (or issue taking deceased children's shares) fail to attain a vested interest, the estate will be distributed as if the intestate had left no issue.[24]

[18] Including, legitimate, illegitimate, adopted and legitimated children, see *ante* Chap. 10.

[19] s.55(2). The *commorientes* presumption in s.184 of the Law of Property Act 1925 (hereinafter also referred to as the "L.P.A. 1925"), will apply so that children will be presumed to have survived their parent.

[20] s.47(1)(i).

[21] s.47(1)(i) "... so that no issue shall take whose parent is living at the death of the intestate and so capable of taking."

[22] Family Law Reform Act, s.3(2). A person attains a particular age at the commencement of the relevant anniversary of the date of his birth, *ibid.* s.9.

[23] The requirement is not to be married at the death, but to have been married so that a divorced or widowed child will be entitled.

[24] s.47(2)(*b*). The position where a child has been guilty of the criminal homicide of the intestate, and where a child disclaims his intestate benefit, is considered *post*, in Chap. 17.

Vesting of the interest

The children[25] will become entitled to an absolute interest when they attain the age of eighteen years, in the case of deaths on or after January 1 1970[26], or marry under that age. In view of the reduction in the age of majority it is now less likely that a child's interest will vest by reason of marriage under age but, where it does so, it presents a problem for the personal representatives since an infant cannot give a good receipt for capital[27] so as to provide an adequate discharge for the personal representatives. In such cases they can appoint trustees to hold the interest.[28]

The rules relating to the vesting of interests create an apparent gap in the statutory trusts which can be noted. Suppose that there is a child living at the death of the intestate who has an illegitimate child and then dies unmarried and under the age of eighteen. In such a case the child fails to attain a vested interest and so his or her interest in the intestate estate fails but his illegitimate child cannot take his or her share for two reasons. First, the parent did not predecease the intestate and thus the substitutional provisions do not apply and, secondly, there is no direct right of inheritance of an illegitimate grandchild.[29] Presumably in such cases the share attributed to the infant child goes to increase the shares of the other children, if there were any, or goes on failure of issue if there were not. It will be appreciated that this problem will only arise where the child has an illegitimate child since, if the child marries, the child's share will vest and can pass on the death of the child after the intestate according to the will or intestacy of the child.

Grandchild and remoter issue: per stirpes

Under the statutory trusts the child or children of the intestate have the primary entitlement and are entitled in their own right; more remote issue have a secondary entitlement and take by representation and not in their own right. Thus grandchildren and remoter issue are

[25] Likewise also the vesting of the shares taken by issue.

[26] Family Law Reform Act 1969, s.3(2).

[27] It is provided that when an infant marries such infant shall be entitled to give valid receipts for the income of the infant's share or interest, s.47(1)(ii); but a married infant still cannot give a good receipt for capital.

[28] s.42(1) which provides that where an infant is absolutely entitled on the intestacy of a person, the personal representatives may appoint a trust corporation of two or more individuals not exceeding four (whether or not including the personal representatives or one or more of the personal representatives) to be the trustee or trustees of such share for the infant. On such an appointment the personal representatives are discharged from all further liability in respect of such share, which may be retained in its existing condition or state of investment or may be converted into money and such money may be invested in any authorised investment. It will be noticed that this provision has a very limited operation and does not confer a general power on personal representatives to appoint trustees. See *ante* p. 124.

[29] See *ante*, Chap. 10.

not entitled *per se* but are merely entitled to the share to which their deceased parent or grandparent would have been entitled if he or she had survived the intestate.[30] This creates a *per stirpes* distribution, *i.e.* a scheme of entitlement by virtue of descent through the stalks or branches of the family. There are four fundamental rules which govern such a distribution. First, the nearest generation of issue will always take to the exclusion of more remote issue within the same branch or sub-branch, thus surviving children always exclude their own children, *i.e.* grandchildren, and grandchildren likewise exclude their own children, *i.e.* great grandchildren. Secondly, children of the same parent will always share equally, thus the intestate's children share equally and the children of a deceased child, *i.e.* grandchildren, will share equally. Thirdly, each branch of the family will take equal shares but there may be inequality of entitlement of individuals of the same degree of relationship to the intestate from one branch to another.[31] Fourthly, issue are entitled to any degree within each branch of the family subject to the rules above, so that it is possible for a more remote descendant to take along with, and possibly a greater share than, less remote descendants.[32]

Comment

It is suggested that the present *per stirpes* division in section 47(1)(i) is not satisfactory and is in need of modification. The most pointed anomaly occurs when there are no surviving children and the entitlement is between surviving grandchildren, *i.e.* the children of the intestate's deceased children. The present provision will usually result in inequality of shares to be taken by each grandchild and the possibility of a greatgrandchild not only taking along with grandchildren but taking a larger share than some of them.[33] Other modern intestacy codes have avoided such a result by a provision requiring a simple *per capita* distribution amongst grandchildren in such cases.[34]

[30] Thus grandchildren have no possible entitlement if their parent survives the intestate even if the child only does so by the effect of the *commorientes* presumption in s.184, L.P.A. 1925. It can be suggested that a provision making the child's interest conditional on him surviving the intestate by, say, 14 days, with a provision in favour of the child's issue if he does not, would be preferable.

[31] For example: suppose the intestate had four children A,B,C,D; A predeceases leaving no issue; B predeceases leaving one child P; C predeceases leaving two children Q and R; and D survives and has a child S. There are three qualifying branches of the family and the shares will be: P, one third; Q and R one sixth each; and D, one third. S will take nothing. If P had predeceased leaving a child T, T would take P's one-third share. The inequality of shares taken by grandchildren and the possibility of a more remote relative taking a greater share than a less remote relative (T over Q and R) are apparent.

[32] See the example in n. 31 above.

[33] See the example above.

[34] See *e.g.* the South Australian provision, Administration and Probate Act, 1919–1975, s.72(i): "... (d) if the intestate is survived by grandchildren and by no other issue

Another anomaly is that, although the reference in section 46(1) on entitlement is to issue, section 47(1)(i) clearly demands that the *per stirpes* division, *i.e.* the quantification of the number of branches or stirpes of the family, should be at the level of children whether there are any or not. Thus in the example above, where all the children predecease leaving issue, the shares of the grandchildren are quantified with reference to the number of children. It would seem to be preferable for the rule to be that the number of quantifying stirpes or branches of the family is determined at the nearest generation of which there were surviving members, *i.e.* grandchildren in the example above.[35] Such a provision appears in the American Uniform Probate Code.[36] That code also contains an alternative provision modifying the strict *per stirpes* division where the class entitled includes both children and grandchildren. It is provided that, where there are surviving members of the nearest generation (children), they take a full *per stirpes* share but, where there are also surviving children (grandchildren) of deceased members of that generation (children), then the shares of the deceased members of that generation (children) are treated as one mass and the failed shares are divided equally between the surviving members of the next generation (grandchildren) *per capita.* It will be noticed that this will ensure that, where grandchildren are entitled, they take equal shares.[37]

(apart from issue of those grandchildren) those grandchildren are entitled to the whole or that part (as the case may be) of the intestate estate in equal shares."

Similarly in Victoria, Administration and Probate Act 1958 S.52(i)(8)(vi) "where brothers' and sisters' children are entitled and all the brothers or sisters of the intestate have died before him or her such children shall not take as representatives and all such children shall take in equal shares."

An example will illustrate the problem. Assume that the testator had four children, A, B, C, D who all predeceased him. A has one child P, B has two children Q and R and C has three children, S, T, and U, who survive the deceased. D's child V predeceases the deceased leaving a child W. In this case none of the children are entitled, yet the division is still *per stirpes.* Thus P takes a quarter share, Q and R take an eighth share each, S, T and U take a twelfth share each and W takes a quarter share, although he is a more remote relative than P, Q, R, S, T or U. If the law were amended on the lines of the Australian provision noted above, then all the grandchildren would take equal shares to the exclusion of W.

[35] This possible construction of a *per stirpes* statutory provision was discussed but rejected in the American decisions in *Maud* v. *Catherwood* (1945) 67 Cal.App.2d. 636; and in *Lombardi* v. *Blois* (1964) 230 Cal.App.2d. 191. It is submitted that s.47(1)(i) cannot also be so construed.

[36] s.2–106 provides: "If representation is called for by this Code, the estate is divided into as many shares as there are surviving heirs in the nearest degree of kinship and deceased persons in the same degree who left issue who survive the decedent, each surviving heir in the nearest degree receiving one share and the share of each deceased person in the same degree being divided among his issue in the same manner."

[37] "Modified s.2–106"; also involving changes to s.2–103(1); (3) and (4) by replacing the wording on representation with the words "to be distributed *per capita* at each generation as defined in s.2–106."

Issue taking by representation

Many of the points noted above with reference to the children's entitlement apply also to issue taking by representation. Thus the issue will attain a vested interest at eighteen or marriage[38] and "leaving issue" means leaving issue who attain such a vested interest.[39] The shares of issue who fail to attain such an interest will accrue in the first place to the shares of their brothers or sisters or, if they are the only member of the class, to the shares of the other children of the intestate.

Maintenance and advancement

Where the estate is held on the statutory trusts for infant children or issue the statutory powers of maintenance in section 31 and of advancement in section 32 of the Trustee Act 1925 apply[40] in the ordinary way. The personal representatives may at their sole discretion pay or apply to the minor's parent or guardian such sums as may be reasonable for the maintenance, education or benefit of the minor.[41] In exercising this discretion they will have regard to the age of the minor and his requirements and generally to the circumstances of the case and in particular to what other income, if any, is applicable for this purpose.[42] Any income not so used will be accumulated.[43]

Likewise the power in section 32 will enable not more than one-half of the minor's presumptive share to be applied for the advancement or benefit of the minor.[44] However, where a spouse has a life interest in the fund, the consent of the spouse is required[45] and, when the minor becomes absolutely and indefeasibly entitled to his share, any such advancements must be brought into account.[46]

Use of chattels

It is expressly provided[47] that the personal representatives may permit any infant contingently interested to have the use and

[38] See *ante*.
[39] s.47(2)(*c*).
[40] s.47(1)(iii).
[41] Trustee Act 1925, s.31(1). See more fully discussed in Pettit, *Equity and The Law of Trusts*, th ed., pp. 392–403.
[42] *Ibid.*
[43] s.31(2).
[44] s.32(1)(*a*); see Pettit, *op. cit*, pp. 400–403.
[45] s.32(1)(*c*) the consenting spouse must be of full age and consent in writing.
[46] s.32(1)(*b*).
[47] s.47(1)(iv).

enjoyment of any personal chattels in such manner and subject to such conditions (if any) as the personal representatives may consider reasonable, without liability for any consequential loss.

LIABILITY TO ACCOUNT FOR ADVANCEMENTS

Equitable principles and the Statute of Distributions

Equitable courts have traditionally assumed an intention by a father or person in *loco parentis* to benefit children equally, an idea which found expression in the maxim, "Equity leans against double portions."[48] This assumption gave rise to the equitable doctrines of satisfaction and performance[49] and underlies the requirement to account under express hotchpot clauses in wills.[50] It is accordingly not surprising to find analogous provisions in the law of intestate succession which were included in the Statute of Distribution 1670 as follows[51]:

> "... in case any child, other than the heir at law, who shall have any estate by settlement from the said intestate, or shall be advanced by the said intestate in his lifetime by portion not equal to the share which will be due to the other children by such distribution as aforesaid; then so much of the surplusage of the estate of such intestate, to be distributed to such child or children as shall have any land by settlement from the intestate, or were advanced in the lifetime of the intestate as shall make the estate of all the said children to be equal as near as can be estimated. But the heir at law, notwithstanding any land that he shall have by descent or otherwise from the intestate, is to have an equal part in the distribution with the rest of the children, without any consideration of the value of the land which he has by descent, or otherwise from the intestate."

The Statute of Distribution was repealed in 1925[52] and the requirement to account was replaced by the present provision in section 47(1)(iii) of the Administration of Estates Act 1925. It is thus not necessary to consider the Statute in detail but one or two points can be noted as providing some analogy and contrast with the modern provision. The 1670 statute only required advancements by portion to children to be brought into account, although issue taking a child's

[48] This maxim can be regarded as an application of two other maxims, "Equality is Equity" and "Equity implies an intention to fulfil an obligation" See Keeton, *Introduction to Equity*, 6th ed., pp. 114–117; 200–215.

[49] See Keeton, *op cit.* and *Snell's Principles of Equity*, 28th ed. pp. 505 *et seq.*

[50] See *Williams on Wills*, 5th ed., pp. 734 *et seq.*

[51] s.3, see more fully discussed in Williams, Mortimer and Sunnucks 16th ed. (1982), pp. 883–886.

[52] Administration of Estates Act 1925 (hereinafter also referred to as "the A.E.A. 1925"), s.54 and Sched. 2.

share by representation had to account for any advancements made to that child.[53] This remains the same under the new legislation.

The position is similar in respect of the rule under the statute that the liability to account was only exercisable for the benefit of other children and not for the benefit of other persons entitled on the intestacy, such as a spouse.[54] However, it was repeatedly held that the liability to account under the statute did not apply in cases of partial intestacy,[55] although after 1925 there is a further provision imposing a duty to account for testamentary benefits.[56] It is clear that the 1925 legislation applies equally to gifts made by a father or a mother[57] but the 1670 statute was confined to gifts by a father or by a person in *loco parentis.*[58] Finally, the liability to account under the statute arose when a child was "advanced... by portion" whereas the 1925 legislation refers to money or property which has been transferred to a child "... by way of advancement or on the marriage of a child.... [59] The earlier legislation thus had more analogy with the equitable presumptions against double portions.

Accounting for inter vivos advancements

Section 47(1)(iii)

Following the repeal of the Statute of 1670 the reformers of the law in 1925 had to decide whether to include a similar accounting requirement in the new scheme of intestate succession. They were persuaded that such a provision was necessary and, seeing that the 1670 provision had produced some anomalies, thought no doubt that they would improve the position.[60] Accordingly, section 47(1)(iii) requires advancements to children to be brought into account on intestacy but the inclusion of this provision has been a matter of regret. Danckwerts J. commented in *Re Morton*[61]:

> "For some reason, which is difficult to fathom, but presumably with an idea of producing fairness, the draftsmen of the Administration of Estates Act 1925 introduced hotchpot provisions into the Sections of the Act dealing with intestacy. It

[53] *Re Scott* [1903] 1 Ch. 1, a case on double portions; *Weyland* v. *Weyland* (1742) 2 Atk. 632.
[54] *Kircudbright* v. *Kircudbright* (1802) 8 Ves.Jun. 51 at p. 64.
[55] *Re Roby* [1908] 1 Ch. 71, and cases cited therein, see Harman J. in *Re Young* [1951] 1 Ch. 185 at p. 188.
[56] s.49 of the 1925 Act.
[57] See, for example, *Hardy* v. *Shaw* [1976] 1 Ch. 82.
[58] *Holt* v. *Frederick* (1726) 2 P.Wms. 356.
[59] See more fully discussed *post.*
[60] *Per* Harman J. in *Re Young* [1951] 1 Ch. 185 at p. 188.
[61] [1956] 1 Ch. 644 at p. 647; see also Harman J. *op cit.*

> seems to me that they made a great mistake in so doing, and that it would have been far better to have left the whole thing out."[62]

Be that as it may, English law has retained a requirement to account on intestacy and the statutory provision must be considered in some detail. Section 47(1)(iii) of the Administration of Estates Act 1925 commences with the introductory words "where under this Part of this Act the residuary estate of an intestate, or any part thereof, is directed to be held on the statutory trusts for the issue of the intestate, the same shall be held upon the following trusts, namely. . . . " The requirement to account is one of the terms of those trusts. Subsection (iii) is in the following terms:

> "Where the property held on the statutory trusts for issue is divisible into shares, then any money or property which, by way of advancement or on the marriage of a child of the intestate, has been paid to such child (including any life or less interest and including property covenanted to be paid or settled) shall, subject to any contrary intention expressed or appearing from the circumstances of the case, be taken as being so paid or settled in or towards satisfaction of the share of such child or the share which such child would have taken if living at the death of the intestate, and shall be brought into account, at a valuation (the value to be reckoned as at the death of the intestate), in accordance with the requirements of the personal representatives."

The basic effect of the section

The basic purpose and effect of section 47(1)(iii) are clear, namely to ensure equality of total shares, *i.e.* of both *inter vivos* and intestate benefits, taken by each child or by each stirpes of the family in cases where a child has predeceased the intestate leaving issue. This remains its sole justification and in simple cases the provision achieves its objectives. An example will illustrate how the section operates. Suppose that an intestate leaves three children, A, B and C, who are entitled under the statutory trusts to a fund of £10,000. Suppose that child A has received *inter vivos* an advance of £2,000. The £2,000 is accounted for by notionally adding it to the distributable estate on intestacy making a notional total of £12,000. This represents the total sum to be divided equally between the children in shares of £4,000 each. The £2,000 brought in for accounting purpose

[62] It is noticeable that some of the Australian states have followed his advice and have abandoned all hotchpot requirements on intestacy, namely, New South Wales, Queensland, Western Australia and New Zealand. See Hardingham, Neave and Ford *Wills and Intestacy*. See also Lee, *Manual of Queensland Succession Law*, 1975 pp. 167, 168. These omissions have been prompted by the feeling that hotchpot provisions are outdated and are more trouble than they are worth.

is taken out of A's share, leaving a distribution of the £10,000, as to £2,000 to A, £4,000 to B, and £4,000 to C and resulting in equality of total shares of £4,000 for each child.

A question of construction

Subsection 47(1)(iii) refers to money or property paid to, or settled for, a child "by way of advancement." This is a crucial phrase which must be considered carefully. The first question to arise is whether the phrase has the same meaning as the words "advanced . . . by portion" in the Statute of Distribution. If it does, decisions on the old statute can be referred to for assistance in construing the new. However, there are two points which can be made to support a negative answer to this question. First, as Jenkins L.J. observed in *Re Hayward* (*decd.*),[63] the provision in section 47(1)(iii) of the 1925 Act departs radically from the language of the Statute of Distribution, containing as it does no reference at all to portions, save in so far as a reference to portions is to be imported by implication from the use of the word "advancement." Secondly, although the Administration of Estates Act 1925 is a consolidating Act, it consolidates the Law of Property Act 1922 and the Law of Property (Amendment) Act 1924 and can be regarded as a reforming Act so far as the Statute of Distribution is concerned.[64] Nevertheless it is clear that the weight of judicial authority is in favour of regarding cases on the Statute as relevant to the construction of the new subsection.[65] The clearest judicial comment to this effect is that of Jenkins L.J. in *Re Hayward*[66] who, having indicated the differences in wording noted above, concluded that decisions upon the old Act are generally speaking applicable to the new. Accordingly, the judge derived most assistance from Jessel M.R.'s judgment in *Taylor* v. *Taylor*[67] in 1835 and referred also to the decisions in *Re Lacon*[68] in 1891 and *Re Scott*[69] in 1903. Indeed at one point in his judgment Jenkins L.J. referred[70] to Jessel M.R.'s decision in *Taylor* v. *Taylor*[71] as ". . . indicating . . . the kinds of payment which should be regarded as advancements by portion for the purposes of this provision."[72] However, the judge had recognised earlier that the position under the Statute was not exactly synonymous with that under the Act since the former included any provision made for a

63 [1957] 1 Ch. 528 at p. 535.
64 See Farrand, (1961) 25 Conv. 468 at p. 472.
65 See Farrand, *supra*, at p. 472, who also concluded that "advancements" in intestacy has the same meaning as in the equitable presumption against double portions, which although supported to some extent by Jenkins L.J. in *Re Hayward*, *supra* can be regarded as being more doubtful.
66 *Supra*, at p. 535.
67 (1875) L.R.20 Eq. 155.
68 [1891] 2 Ch. 482, a case on double portions.
69 [1903] 1 Ch. 1, likewise.
70 [1957] 1 Ch. 528 at p. 541.
71 *Supra*.
72 *i.e.* s.47(1)(iii).

child by way of settlement but under the Act "... it is not every settlement the benefits taken under which must be brought into account, but the settlement must be either by way of advancement or on the marriage of the child concerned."[73]

In the most recent decision on the provision, *Hardy* v. *Shaw*,[74] the judge likewise relied on pre-1925 cases, deriving most assistance from *Taylor* v. *Taylor*.[75] With these preliminary points in mind it is now possible to consider the meaning of an advancement for the purposes of section 47(1)(iii).

The meaning of "advancement"

Definition

There is no statutory definition of an advancement for the purposes of section 47(1)(iii)[76] and reference must be made to the case law. The nearest definition of what is an advancement is to be found in the judgments[77] of Jessel M.R. in *Taylor* v. *Taylor*.[78] In the first of the two judgments delivered by him in the case, Jessel M.R. said[79]:

> "I have always understood that an advancement by way of portion is something given by the parent to establish the child for life, or to make what is called a provision for him—not a mere casual payment of this kind. You may make the provision by way of marriage portion on the marriage of the child. You may make it on putting him into a profession or business in a variety of ways: you may pay for a commission, you may buy him the goodwill of a business and give him stock-in-trade; all these things I understand to be portions or provisions. Again, if in the absence of evidence you find a father giving a large sum to a child in one payment, there is a presumption that that is intended to start him in life or make a provision for him; but if a small sum is so given you may require evidence to show the purpose. But I do not think that these words 'by portion' are to be disregarded, nor is the word 'advancement' to be disregarded. It is not every payment made to a child which is to be regarded as an advancement, or advancement by way of portion. In every case to which I have been referred there has either been a settlement itself, or the purpose for which the payment was made has been shewn to be that which everyone would recognise as being for establishing the child or making a provision for the child."

[73] *Supra*, at pp. 537, 538.
[74] [1976] 1 Ch. 82.
[75] *Supra*.
[76] Contrast the Republic of Eire's Succession Act 1965, s.63(6) which defines an "advancement" for the purposes of an analogous accounting provision.
[77] *Per* Jenkins L.J. in *Re Hayward* (decd.), [1957] 1 Ch. 528 at p. 537.
[78] (1875) L.R.20 Eq. at pp. 155, 157, 158.
[79] *Supra* at p. 157.

In the second judgment the Master of the Rolls said[80]:

> "nothing could be more productive of misery in families than if he were to hold that every member of the family must account strictly for every sum received from a parent. According to his view, nothing was an advancement unless it were given on marriage, or to establish the child in life. Prima facie, an advancement must be made in early life; but any sum given by way of making a permanent provision for the child would come within the term establishing for life."

These principles were applied to the facts of the case and it was decided that the following were advancements by portion for the purposes of the Statute: payment of the admission fee to one of the Inns of Court in the case of a child intended for the Bar; the price of a commission and outfit of a child entering the army; the price of plant and machinery and other payments for the purpose of starting a child in business. However, the following were held not to be advancements by portion: payment of a fee to a special pleader in the case of a child intended for the Bar; the price of outfit and passage money to an officer in the army and his wife on going out to India with his regiment; payment of debts incurred by an officer in the army; assisting a clergyman in paying his house-keeping and other expenses.

Points from the older decisions can be noted shortly. In *Re Lacon*[81] the transfer of two shares in a family business was shown not to be a gift by way of portion but as remuneration for the recipient's services as manager. In *Re Scott*[82] it was emphasised that "the time, circumstances and manner of the gift" must be looked at. The circumstances in that case rebutted the prima facie inference that a gift of £5,000 by a father to his son was a portion.

Important factors

It has been seen from Jessel M.R.'s judgment that a presumption of advancement can arise where a large sum is given by a parent to a child in one payment. Thus the size of the gift both absolutely and relatively can be an important factor. In *Re Hayward (decd.)*[83] the intestate had made *inter vivos* nominations of £315 National Savings Certificates and £191 in the Post Office Savings Bank in favour of his son. The nominations operated as dispositions in favour of the son

[80] *Supra* at p. 158.
[81] [1891] 2 Ch. 482, a case on the equitable presumption against double portions.
[82] [1903] 1 Ch. 1, a case on double portions. The father was wealthy, left a £250,000 estate and some of the money given was used to pay off debts.
[83] [1957] 1 Ch. 528; see generally (1953) 73 L.Q.R.21, where it is pointed out that "A revocable nomination taking effect at an uncertain time (namely, that of a father's death) would normally be an unusual way for setting a son up for life, unless, indeed, the father's business was providing a career for the son which would probably come to an end with the father's death, so that the son had to be started afresh, as it were."

taking effect on the father's death but revocable meanwhile.[84] The question arose whether these sums should be brought into account as advancements within section 47(1)(iii). There were only two relevant considerations apparent from the facts. First, the age of the son which was 43 at the time of the nomination and 46 at the time of the death.[85] This factor was prima facie against the view that there was an advancement. Secondly, there was the size of the gifts both absolutely and relative to the size of the estate. The nominations totalled some £500 and the total estate was worth some £1,800, giving a proportion between a quarter and a fifth. Jenkins L.J. thought that the size of the fund was the primary consideration rather than the proportion.[86]

> "I think, in order to raise a prima facie case for accounting it must be shown that the fund in question was sufficiently substantial in itself to be in the nature of a permanent provision, without pressing too far the question of proportion."

As the judge pointed out, an intestate who only had £50 in the world, £25 in cash and £25 in National Savings Certificates, could otherwise properly be held to be making a permanent provision for one of his sons by giving him a nomination in respect of the certificates because they represented no less than half of his estate. Accordingly, the Court of Appeal concluded that the nominations were not advancements and did not need to be brought into account under section 47(1)(iii).[87] One further point appears from the case: the two nominations were made on separate occasions, (albeit within a month of each other) and it is clear that the court will not add up several small amounts to a more significant total.

The decision in *Re Hayward* was applied in the more recent case of *Hardy* v. *Shaw*[88] where the size of the gift was also an important factor. The case concerned the shares in a family business, which were originally wholly owned by the father and his three children, who all worked in the business. One of the children, a daughter, married a

[84] There is no evidence of the son's means or needs at the time, or of the purpose for which the nominations were made.

[85] In view of Jessel M.R.'s observations in *Taylor* v. *Taylor* (1875) L.R.20 Eq. 155, 158 that prima facie an advancement must be made early in life. Sellers L.J. commented in *Re Hayward*, at p. 543, that if the son had been 20 years younger, it might have been sufficient.

[86] At p. 542.

[87] Confirming Upjohn J's decision to the same effect, [1956] 1 W.L.R. 1490. All the judges thought that the size of the gift, £500, made the case borderline. In *Re Scott* [1901] 1 Ch. 1, a case on double portions, £5,000 was regarded as a large sum, against an estate of £200,000–£250,000. But in *Re Livesey* [1953] 1 W.L.R. 1115, a case on double portions, farms and a mortgage of £30,000 although of considerable value, were held not to amount to an advancement. Jenkins L.J. in *Re Hayward*, *supra*, at p. 541, dismissed this authority as having turned on the language of the particular document and of being of no assistance to the case before him.

[88] [1976] 1 Ch. 82.

man of whom the father disapproved and then ceased to work in the business, whereupon the father declared that she was to have no further shares in the business. The father left all of his estate, including his shares, to the mother by will and after his death the mother decided to give these shares to the two sons who were carrying on the business. Respecting the husband's wishes, the mother gave no shares to the daughter who had married. The mother then died intestate and the daughter, excluded from the *inter vivos* gift, claimed that her brothers should bring the value of the donated shares into account under section 47(1)(iii) against the shares to which they were entitled in the mother's estate. The first point to decide was whether the *inter vivos* transfers of shares were in the nature of advancements within the section. The court held that they were, as being a permanent provision for them. This conclusion was fortified by the facts that, viewed in the abstract, the value of the shares was substantial and, looked at relatively to the mother's whole estate, they were still substantial.[89] The court thought that this was a crucial consideration in the light of *Re Hayward*.[90] Goff J. commented[91]:

> "If 'advancement' had to be construed narrowly as a gift establishing a young person for life, or in the case of an older person, as meeting some particular need, for example expansion of his business or money required to buy out the share of a deceased or outgoing partner, then this transfer would not, in my judgment be an advancement. But it is clear, I think, from the passages [*cited above*] from the two judgments of Jessel M.R.,[92] and what Jenkins L.J. said in *Re Hayward*[93] that it is wider than any such narrow construction and includes everything which may fairly be described as a permanent provision."

The earlier cases had emphasised that prima facie an advancement was a gift made early in life and it has been seen that in *Re Hayward*[94] this was regarded as an important consideration.[95] However, less importance was attached to this factor in *Hardy* v. *Shaw* where the transfer of shares was regarded as an advancement even though the donees were at the time of the gift mature in age and already established in business. In the last case the fact that the gifts were

[89] *Supra, per* Goff J. at p. 89.
[90] *Supra.*
[91] At p. 88.
[92] In *Taylor* v. *Taylor* (1875) L.R.20 Eq. 155.
[93] [1957] Ch. 528.
[94] *Supra.*
[95] The donee was aged 43, and Seller L.J. commented that the position might well have been different if the donee had been 20 years younger. See also *National Trustees, Executors & Agency Co.* v. *Ward* [1896] 2.A.L.R. 119; *Re Lamshed* [1970] S.A.S.R. 224.

intended to be in the nature of a permanent provision for the donees was regarded as more important.[96]

It was further argued in *Hardy* v. *Shaw* that, even if the transfers were advancements, the liability to account had, on the facts, been excluded by a contrary intention, *i.e.* an intention to prefer the sons at the expense of the daughter. This was rejected in the decision and this aspect of the case, and the proof of a contrary intention within section 47(1)(iii), is more fully discussed later.

Marriage

Section 47(1)(iii) refers to gifts "by way of advancement or on the marriage of a child of the intestate" and it would seem that these are alternative requirements. If this is so, there will be no necessity to show that a gift made on marriage is in the nature of an advancement. However, the two were linked historically since it was assumed that a substantial gift or settlement made on the marriage of a child was intended to establish that child for life. It would seem desirable to limit the duty to account in the modern law to substantial gifts on marriage to avoid any requirement that a child should account for a modest wedding present from his parents.

Other requirements of the section

Children

Section 47(1)(iii) only applies "Where the property held on the statutory trusts for issue is divisible into shares." This limits the application of the provision to cases where there is more than one branch or *stirpes* of the family entitled to a share as issue.[97] Thus an only child (in the absence of issue entitled to take a deceased's child's share by representation) need never account. Advances to a child are accountable only for the benefit of other members of the class of issue,[98] and need not be accounted for the benefit of a spouse.[99]

The subsection is also clearly confined to gifts to children[1] of the intestate, and the equitable principles relating to persons standing "*in loco parentis*" have no application.[2] This latter point will effectively exclude any question of accounting for gifts to, for example, nephews or grandchildren or children of the family. Adopted, legitimated and

[96] There was no evidence of intention in *Re Hayward, supra.*

[97] *Re Ashton* [1934] 78 S.J.803, only daughter need not account.

[98] *Re Heather* [1906] 2 Ch. 230, child need not account for the benefit of a stranger. See also *Re Vaux* [1938] Ch. 581 the decision on this point was not affected by the subsequent Court of Appeal decision at [1939] Ch. 465; and *Meinertzagen* v. *Walters* (1872) 7 Ch.App. 670 at p. 674.

[99] Who is the only relative who can take with issue on intestacy.

[1] "... a child of the intestate ...," "... to such child ...," "... of such child, ...," s.47(1)(iii).

[2] See Farrand, (1961) 25 Conv. 468 at p. 473.

illegitimate children will be included in accordance with the relevant legislation relating to them.[3] A further point is that the section refers to gifts to the child "by the intestate" and there is nothing in section 47(1)(iii) or in section 55(1)(vi) (where "intestate" is defined) to confine the provision to gifts by fathers. Thus, in contrast to the previous position, a gift by way of advancement by a mother to her child would be accountable.[4]

Since only gifts to children are accountable there is no requirement for grandchildren or other issue to account for advancements made directly to them. However, grandchildren or other issue who take a deceased child's share by representation must account for any advances made *inter vivos* to their parent or ancestor, *i.e.* to the child whose share they take.[5] Thus the subsection provides "... be taken as being so paid or settled in or towards satisfaction of the share of such child or the share which such child would have taken if living at the death of the intestate." This rule can be illustrated by an example. Suppose that an intestate had two children, A and B, and had made an advancement of £5,000 to A who had predeceased the intestate leaving two children, C and D. Suppose also that the intestate had advanced £10,000 to C. If the total estate to be distributed on the statutory trusts is £10,000, the division will be as follows:

Estate	£10,000
Add advance to A	5,000
	£15,000

	C and D	B
	£7,500	£7,500
Take out advance to A	£5,000	
	£2,500	£7,500

C does not have to account for his £10,000 advance.

However, the same rule will also apply where all the children have predeceased the intestate, leaving a class of grandchildren entitled as issue. Thus, suppose that in the above example B had also predeceased the intestate leaving a child, E. The distribution would be that C and D would share £2,500 (accounting for the advance to A but ignoring the advance to C) and E would take £7,500 (B's share). In this

[3] See *ante*, Chap. 10.
[4] See *Hardy* v. *Shaw* [1976] 1 Ch. 82, which was just such a case.
[5] *Re Scott* [1903] Ch. 1; *Re Binns, Public Trustee* v. *Ingle* [1929] 1 Ch. 677.

situation the rules look less satisfactory. It has been suggested above that, where no children survive but only grandchildren, a *per capita* distribution should be adopted instead of the present distribution *per stirpes*. It is probably preferable to abandon the requirements to account for advances but, if it is to be retained, it would seem that a fairer rule, coupled with the *per capita* distribution, would be for grandchildren to account for their own advances and not for those made to their parents.

The gift

The section refers generally to "money or property" and the latter word is widely defined in the Act to include "a thing in action and any interest in real or personal property."[6] The residuary estate will, by virtue of the statutory trust for sale,[7] be regarded as personalty but there is no room for the rule applicable to the equitable presumptions that only like property will be deemed in satisfaction of like. Real property will have to be brought into account, if the other requirements are satisfied, against the child's interest in the intestate personal estate.[8]

The duty to account relates to money or property "paid to such child by the intestate or settled by the intestate for the benefit of such child."[9] A life or less interest is included, as is property covenanted to be paid or settled.[10] The section applies in cases of total intestacy (partial intestacies being governed by section 49(1)(*a*) which extends section 47(1)(iii)[11]) and thus contemplates *inter vivos* gifts rather than testamentary gifts. However, the provision will also apply to two forms of gift which take effect on death but are not testamentary, namely nominations and *donationes mortis causa*. It was argued in *Re Hayward* (*decd.*)[12] that a nomination[13] was in its nature akin to a will and thus converted a total intestacy to a partial intestacy. This was rejected by the Court of Appeal who pointed out that a nomination operates as a disposition in favour of the nominee taking effect on the death of the nominator and revocable by the nominator at any time in

[6] 1925 Act, s.55(1)(xvii). Although the section refers primarily to money or property as a physical or tangible thing, it also expressly includes interests in property, see Danckwerts J. in *Re Morton* [1956] 1 Ch. 644 at p. 647.

[7] 1925 Act, s.33.

[8] See Farrand, *op. cit.*, p. 470.

[9] s.47(1)(iii). Although it could be argued that "money" is qualified by the word "paid" and "property" by the word "settled," this seems unduly technical and restrictive. The intention is surely to include both outright gifts of money or property and settlements of both money or property, see Ryder 26 C.L.P. 209; some of the Australian formulations are better worded, see Hardingham, Neave and Ford, *op. cit.*, Chap. 29.

[10] *Ibid.*

[11] See *post*, Chap. 15.

[12] [1957] 1 Ch. 528.

[13] In this case National Savings Certificates and money in the Post Office Savings Bank (now the National Savings Bank) were nominated. See *ante*, Chap. 3.

his lifetime and thus is analogous to a revocable *inter vivos* settlement.[14]

Donationes mortis causa have been considered in an earlier chapter,[15] and, although they are regarded as a singular form of gift, being amphibolous in nature,[16] it is submitted that they would be regarded as *inter vivos* rather than testamentary gifts for the purpose of section 47(1)(iii). Accordingly, a donee might have to account for a *donatio* in an appropriate case.

Paid or settled

The section refers to money or property which "... has been paid to such child by the intestate or settled by the intestate for the benefit of such child...."[17] This will include property settled by the parent on such trusts that the child takes a primary life interest but no more.[18] Difficulties arise, however, where under a pre-existing settlement the parent has a life interest in a fund with remainder to the children and the parent assigns or surrenders his interest in the fund to the children or where the parent has a power of appointment over settled funds and appoints the fund in favour of his children. The problem in such cases is that the property is not the property of the intestate, although the child is undoubtedly benefitted by the act of the parent, and the question arises whether the child would have to account for such benefit on the subsequent death intestate of the parent. This was considered by Clauson J. in *Re Reeve*[19] where it was decided that the children need not account. In that case funds had been settled on a husband and wife for life with remainder to such of the husband's children as he should appoint. The husband, having survived his wife, appointed part of the fund in favour of his son, part in favour of his daughters and surrendered his life interest in the respective parts in their favour. It was decided that the appointments were not within the provisions of section 47(1)(iii) because the transfers of funds were not payments by the intestate: they were payments by the trustees by virtue of the exercise of a power of appointment which had to be read into the original settlement.[20] The funds were not funds which would, had the appointments not been made, have been part of the intestate's estate.[21] The surrenders of the life interest made no difference since the children were in any event entitled to the remainder interest in default of appointment under the settlement and so there was nothing

[14] *Per* Jenkins L.J. at pp. 533, 538.
[15] See *ante* p. 56; see also *Williams on Wills*, 5th ed., p. 8.
[16] *Per* Buckley J. in *Re Beaumont* [1901] 1 Ch. 889 at p. 892.
[17] s.47(1)(iii).
[18] *Re Grover's Will Trusts, National Provincial Bank Ltd.* v. *Clarke* [1971] 1 Ch. 168 *per* Pennycuick J. at p. 174.
[19] [1935] 1 Ch. 110.
[20] *Per* Clauson J. at p. 117.
[21] *Ibid.* at p. 119.

which could be said to have been paid to them by the intestate. Even if it could be argued that the life interest which the father surrendered was "money or property which by way of advancement . . . has been paid to such child," it would not assist because the property which is paid or settled has to be brought into account at a valuation to be reckoned at the time of the death of the intestate and it is obvious that in the case of a life interest previously surrendered the value of the interest at the death is nil. There would therefore be nothing to bring into account.[22]

Re Reeve[23] thus puts on section 47(1)(iii) a restrictive interpretation which could be regarded as inconsistent with the spirit of the provision, although perhaps dictated by the specific wording of the subsection. The exclusion of such property from the effect of section 47(1)(iii) has been pointed out by Professor Farrand[24] to be inconsistent with authorities on the analogous equitable presumptions but can be justified in so far as the fundamental basis of accounting provisions is to ensure equality of total shares in the *parent's* property. On this basis appointments under special powers would be excluded but appointments under general powers would be included.

Some final points can be noted shortly. Although the subsection seems most apt to cover direct transfers of money or property by a parent to a child, it would presumably also include indirect transfers, such as where a parent buys a house and directs the vendor to convey it into the name of a child.[25] Secondly, the forgiveness of an *inter vivos* debt owed by the child to the parent could be regarded as an advancement. In *Re Lamshed*[26] a father made a substantial loan to his daughter and her husband and provided that, if he should predecease the date of repayment (which he did), the loan was to be regarded as a gift. It was held that the sum involved was an advancement and accountable. Thirdly, it has been held in another Australian case that the mere prospect of benefit under a power of appointment is not an interest that needs to be accounted.[27]

[22] *Ibid.* at p. 117. However the father had also paid over a sum of money to the trustees of the son's marriage settlement pursuant to a covenant in the settlement that he would so do. This was held to be accountable within s.47(1)(iii), notwithstanding that the property was transferred to the son's trustees rather than directly to the son.

[23] *Supra.*

[24] 25 Conv. 468, at p. 474.

[25] In such a case the presumption of advancement would rebut the inference of a resulting trust, see Pettit, *Equity and the Law of Trusts*, (1984) 5th ed., 121.

[26] [1970] S.A.S.R. 224.

[27] *Re Cooper* [1964–65] N.S.W.R. 1067, capital left to a wife for life with a power to appoint the remainder among the children of the deceased's first marriage. The wife was still living at the death of the intestate husband and it was held that the children's interest under the settlement was speculative and need not be accounted for *vis-à-vis* the children of the second marriage.

Mandatory

The section provides that the advancements should be brought into account "in accordance with the requirements of the personal representatives." This renders the section mandatory and it cannot be argued that the personal representatives have a discretion whether to require the advances to be brought into account or not.[28]

Contrary intention

Section 47(1)(iii) provides that the duty to account is "subject to any contrary intention expressed or appearing from the circumstances of the case."[29] If an intention is expressed at the time of the advance or, it would seem, subsequently in terms that the gift is made without duty to account, there will be no problem. More difficult will be the proof of such an intention as a matter of inference from the circumstances of the case.[30] There are two stages to consider. First, the circumstances of the case may indicate that the *inter vivos* gift was not by way of advancement, in which case there will be no duty to account. Secondly, the provision may be prima facie in the nature of an advancement but the duty to account be negatived by a contrary intention. In *Re Hayward*[31] in 1957 the court decided that there was no advancement and thus no duty to account. In *Hardy* v. *Shaw*[32] it was decided that there had prima facie been an advancement and the question whether the duty to account was negated by a contrary intention had to be considered. The facts of the case have been set out above but can be noted again briefly. The case concerned a gift of shares in a family business. The business was originally wholly owned by the father and his three children, who all worked in the business. One of the daughters then married a man of whom her father disapproved and she ceased to work in the business. The father stated that she was to have no further shares in the business. When the father died he left all his shares to his widow, who transferred them *inter vivos* to the two children who were still involved with the business to the exclusion of the married daughter. The mother died intestate and the excluded daughter claimed that the benefited children should account under section 47(1)(iii) for the shares transferred to them *inter vivos*. It was held that the transfer of the shares *inter vivos* was an advancement within section 47(1)(iii), and this aspect of the decision

[28] *Hardy* v. *Shaw* [1976] 1 Ch. 82 at p. 87; see also Farrand, (1961) 25 Conv. 468 at p. 479. Although, of course, the donor can exclude the requirement to account by a contrary intention relating to the advancement.

[29] A provision which did not appear in the Statute of Distribution 1670.

[30] The presumptions against double portions could be rebutted by circumstances showing that equality was not the intention of the father, see Bowen L.J. in *Re Lacon* [1891] 2 Ch. 482 at p. 498.

[31] [1957] 1 Ch. 526.

[32] [1976] 1 Ch. 82.

has been discussed above.[33] It was then alleged that the duty to account had been negatived by a contrary intention appearing from the circumstances of the case but Goff J. rejected this submission for the following reasons. First, the onus of proving such a contrary intention rests on the benefited children since, subject to this qualification concerning contrary intention, the Act is mandatory.[34] Secondly, the test to be applied to the circumstances is subjective and not objective: do the circumstances require an inference that the donor's intention was that the gift should not be brought into hotchpot?[35] Thirdly, the question to be asked is whether the facts as a whole indicate an intention on the part of the donor, not simply to anticipate the provision which the donees would receive on their death, but an intention and desire to prefer them to the excluded child not only in point of time but in point of the amount and nature of that provision.[36] Applying these guidelines, the judge concluded that the benefited children had not discharged the onus of proof to establish a contrary intention and that they should account.[37]

Valuation

Valuation of the advance

The section expressly states that the value of the advance is to be reckoned at the death of the intestate,[38] which has obvious implications for wasting or appreciating assets. It seems that only the value of the original advance has to be considered and not property into which it has been changed or invested. Thus, if the donee had been given shares which had doubled in value between the date of the gift and the death, the increased value would have to be accounted for whereas, if the child had received a sum of money which he had invested in the shares, only the original sum would be accountable. Obvious problems arise where the property has been disposed of by the child during the deceased's lifetime. Suppose that a child had been given a house *inter vivos* as an advancement and had subsequently sold the house and invested the proceeds in a new house and that the value of the new house at the death is double the value of the original house at the date of the gift and 50 per cent. more than the value of the original

[33] *Ante* p. 254.
[34] *Ante*, at p. 87.
[35] *Ante*, at p. 89.
[36] *Ante*, at p. 89, applying *Re Lacon* [1891] 2 Ch. 482 at p. 496 with modifications to fit the case of an intestacy as distinct from double portions or ademption.
[37] The facts seemed to indicate that the mother intended to prefer the benefited children so far as the ownership of the business was concerned but this did not necessarily mean that she intended preferment of these children with respect to all the assets of her estate, see Goff J., *supra* at pp. 89, 90.
[38] s.47(1)(iii). The rule applicable to the equitable presumptions is that the advance is valued at the date of the advance. This avoids the difficulties noted in this section and seems preferable, see Farrand, *op. cit.* pp. 477, 478.

house at the date of disposal. The problem is easily posed but the Act provides no clear answer. What is needed are further provisions, analogous perhaps to those in section 10(3) and (4) of the Inheritance (Provision for Family and Dependants) Act 1975, which indicate that, for the purposes of that section in the case of a gift of money, the amount of the original gift is relevant; in the case of an asset retained, the value at the death; and in the case of an asset disposed of, the value at the date of disposal.[39]

Apart from outright transfers the section also comprehends "any life or less interest" and these likewise must be valued at the date of the death and not at the date of the gift, which has obvious advantages for the child.[40] Since section 47(1)(iii) confines the duty to account to children, the problems of valuation associated with section 49(1)(*a*)[41] where the deceased has settled property on a child for life with remainder to his issue do not arise. In such a case it seems clear that only the actuarial valuation of the child's life interest need be brought into account. As Danckwerts J. commented in *Re Morton* (*decd.*)[42]:

> "It seems to me, reading section 47 with such application as I can give it, that the life interests or less interests which are brought in at a valuation, must be brought in at a valuation appropriate to the nature of the interest—and that seems to me to require that the life interest should be valued according to the relevant actuarial considerations; and they cannot be brought in as if they were equivalent to an absolute interest in the capital. To value the interest as being equivalent to a gift of capital in a case where a person takes no more than a life interest seems to me contrary to fairness, commonsense and everything else."

It is submitted that this is the correct approach to section 47(1)(iii), although section 49(1)(*a*) introduces other considerations.[43]

Section 47(1)(iii) contains no provisions relating to the method of

[39] See Chap. 8.

[40] See *Re Reeve* [1935] 1 Ch. 110, discussed above which concerned a surrender of the intestate's life interest to the child, valued at nil; contrast *Re Morton*, [1956] 1 Ch. 644 where property was settled on a child for life, actuarially valued at the intestate's death.

[41] See discussed *post* with reference to *Re Young's Will Trusts* [1951] Ch. 185; *Re Morton, supra* and *Re Grover's Will Trusts* [1971] 1 Ch. 169.

[42] *Supra* at p. 649. The judge was primarily concerned with the construction of s.49(1)(*a*) in the case.

[43] There is, however, some support for the alternative approach, namely that where the fund is settled for the benefit of a child and his issue, the whole capital value of the fund must be brought in. Thus Pennycuick J. in *Re Grover's Will Trusts, supra*, at p. 174 commented that s.47(1)(iii) includes property settled for the benefit of the child, and "That, of course, includes property settled on such trusts that the child takes a primary life interest but no more." This does not necessarily mean that the capital of the fund is accountable in such a case, but it could be so interpreted, see Ryder, 26 C.L.P. 208 at p. 209. See also *Weyland* v. *Weyland* (1742) 2 Atk. 632 at p. 635 and *Re Lampshed* [1970] S.A.S.R. 224 at pp. 232, 233.

arriving at the valuation.[44] Presumably principles and powers similar to those contained in section 41 of the Act relating to the valuation of assets for the purposes of appropriation[45] would be applicable.[46]

Valuation of the estate

Section 47(1)(iii) contains no guidance as to the time when the estate, against which the advance will be brought into account, should be valued. It is usually stated that there are basically two alternative dates which could be adopted: either the estate could be valued at the date of the death or at the date of distribution. The same problem has arisen in relation to the equitable presumptions against double portions and on the construction of hotchpot clauses in wills resulting in two lines of cases, one of which favours the date of death as relevant,[47] the other the date of distribution.[48] There is, however, a difficulty in this simple dichotomy so far as the statutory trusts for issue on intestacy are concerned. Does the date of distribution relate to the time when the residuary estate of the intestate is ascertained and the property becomes subject to the statutory trusts and is divisible into notional shares or does it refer to the time when the estate will actually be distributed to the children? In cases where all the children, or issue, have immediate vested interests, these dates will correspond but where the children, or the issue taking a child's share, are minors the former date will occur towards the end of the administration period but the latter will be postponed perhaps for many years until the children or issue attain vested interests. It is submitted that under section 47(1)(iii) the date of distribution must be taken to refer to the former date and that there can be no justification for postponing the valuation of the estate until the time when the property is actually distributed. This is because the subsection demands that the advancement be taken as being in or towards satisfaction of the share of *the child* and there is an earlier reference to the estate being divisible into shares. This process will take place when the estate is initially put upon the statutory trusts so that minor children or issue will have contingent interests in notional shares, rather than interests in the undivided estate. Therefore, so far as intestacy is concerned, it is submitted that the date of distribution

[44] The section simply requires that the advances should be brought into account in accordance with the requirements of the personal representatives. This phrase seems to govern the whole clause, and not merely the valuation.

[45] See discussed *ante* p. 125.

[46] See also Trustee Act 1925, s.22(3).

[47] *Re Hargreaves* [1903] 88 L.T. 100; *Re Gilbert* [1908] W.N. 63; *Re Mansel* [1930] 1 Ch. 352; *Re Gunter* [1939] Ch. 985 and *Re Oram* [1940] Ch. 1001.

[48] *Re Ponser* [1908] 1 Ch. 828; *Re Craven* [1914] 1 Ch. 358; *Re Forster-Brown* [1914] 2 Ch. 584; *Re Cooke* [1916] 1 Ch. 480; *Re Tod* [1916] 1 Ch. 567; *Re Wills* [1939] Ch. 705; and *Re Hillas-Drake* [1944] Ch. 235; see Farrand, *op. cit.* p. 482.

must refer to the time when the estate initially becomes subject to the statutory trusts.

That, however, still leaves open the debate as to whether the estate should be valued at the date of distribution so defined or at the date of the intestate's death. There is no direct authority on the point so far as a hotchpot intestacy is concerned and it is submitted that the cases referred to above are of little assistance since they are concerned, in the main, with the construction of particular clauses in wills and do not consider the statutory provisions. The question was fully explored by Farrand in 1961[49] and his conclusion was as follows[50]:

> "It is submitted that it is only possible to conclude that Parliament's intention coincided with that attributed by the Court of Appeal to the testator in *Re Hargreves*,[51] namely that the property held on the statutory trusts for issue is also to be valued as at the death of the intestate for the purposes of hotchpot on intestacy.[52] Thus the values of both estate and advance will be artificially frozen at the same date, which is a convenient date in practice since the estate at least will then have been valued for estate duty[53] purposes."

In so far as this opinion precludes any suggestion of valuation at the date when the interests actually vest, *i.e.* when the children attain the age of eighteen years or marry, which may be many years after the death, it is clearly acceptable. It is suggested, however, that it would have been better expressed with reference to the date of distribution as defined above, *i.e.* at the end of the first phase of the administration when the net estate is ascertained. The reasons can be noted shortly as follows. Section 46(1) of the 1925 Act states that the residuary estate of an intestate shall be distributed in the manner or be held on the trusts mentioned in the section. This is amplified by section 47(1) which states that, where the residuary estate of an intestate is directed to be held on the statutory trusts for the issue, the same shall be held upon the trusts stated in that subsection, which includes sub-clause (iii) relating to advancements. Clearly, therefore, the statutory trusts relate to "the residuary estate of an intestate." This phrase is defined in section 33(4) to refer to the net estate which is available for distribution after the payment of debts, expenses, legacies (if any), etc. Accordingly, the requirement to account in section 47(1)(iii) is against the net residuary estate as so defined, *i.e.* the estate at the time of distribution when it becomes divisible into the beneficial shares.[54]

[49] 25 Conv. 468.
[50] See p. 484.
[51] *Supra.*
[52] See Farrand's note 18 at p. 485.
[53] As applicable in 1961.
[54] It is suggested that valuation of the estate at this time will ensure equality of total shares, see Simonds J. in *Hillas* v. *Drake* [1944] Ch. 235.

Gross or net value

The gift *inter vivos* might have become liable to inheritance tax as a result of the death occurring within seven years after the date of the gift[55] tax and, the tax being payable by the donee, there seems little doubt that it is the net value of the advance which has to be accounted for under section 47(1)(iii), and not the gross amount.[56] The same must apply to the estate on the arguments advanced above relating to the residuary estate, since section 33(4) clearly defines the phrase as relating to the net estate.[57]

In or towards satisfaction

The advance is brought into account "in or towards satisfaction" of the share to be taken by the child or by the issue of a deceased child. If the advance is less in value than the value of the share of the estate held on the statutory trusts, the child's share will be reduced accordingly. If the advance exceeds in value the share of the estate, the child will not receive any part of the estate. There can be no question in such a case of the child having to pay any money into the estate to achieve equality. Thus, if an intestate leaves two children, A and B, the value of the estate held on the statutory trusts is £10,000 and A has to account for an *inter vivos* advance of £12,000, B will take the whole estate of £10,000, and A will retain his whole advance of £12,000.

The duty to account in a partial intestacy

The requirements of section 49(1)(*a*) of the Administration of Estates Act 1925 relating to the duty to account for testamentary benefits against the entitlement to undisposed property in a partial intestacy is fully discussed in Chapter 15.

[55] Inheritance Tax Act 1984, s.7(1) as amended.

[56] As to interest on the advance see *Re Lambert* [1897] 2 Ch. 169; *Re Whiteford, Pugh's* v. *Whiteford* [1903] Ch. 889; *Re Davy* [1908] 1 Ch. 61; *Re Poyser* [1908] 1 Ch. 828; and Farrand, *op. cit.* p. 486.

[57] See Farrand, (1961) 25 Conv. 468 at p. 487. *Re Tollemache* [1930] W.N. 138 on estate duty to the contrary.

CHAPTER 14

THE ENTITLEMENT OF OTHER RELATIVES AND OF THE CROWN

ENTITLEMENT OF OTHER RELATIVES

Introduction

This chapter will consider the entitlement on intestacy of relatives other than the spouse and issue. The entitlement of such relatives has progressively been diminished in modern times to the advantage, largely, of the spouse. This reduction has been both in the range of relatives entitled in any event and in the proportion of the estate to which they are entitled. Before 1925 it was possible, in the absence of a spouse, issue and other next-of-kin, for a great grandparent and his or her issue to inherit personal estate on intestacy.[1] Such relatives were excluded in 1925 when a more restricted class of next-of-kin was defined but, under the scheme of entitlement originally enacted in 1925, relatives other than a spouse and issue could still be entitled to a significant share of the estate.[2] This was further restricted by the 1952 Intestates' Estates Act which, although leaving unchanged the range of relatives possibly entitled on intestacy, diminished severely the extent of that entitlement where there was also a spouse surviving. Thus only a parent, a brother or sister of the whole blood or issue thereof can prevent the absolute entitlement of the spouse where there is no surviving issue. The entitlement of these relatives has been further restricted by the substantial increases in the spouse's statutory legacy which have been provided for in recent years. In effect the estate will have to exceed some £100,000 in value for the relatives to have any significant entitlement where there is a surviving spouse.[3] Thus in most cases it is only where there is no surviving spouse and no issue that the other relatives will have any significant entitlement on intestacy.

Parents: the entitlement

The parents have no entitlement if there is surviving issue and only a residual entitlement if there is a survivng spouse.

[1] See Chap. 2 on the pre-1926 rules relating to the entitlement to personalty.
[2] See Chap. 2 on the entitlement on intestacy between 1926 and 1953. This chapter will consider the post-1953 law.
[3] See Chap. 11 on the entitlement of a spouse on intestacy.

Spouse and parent(s). If the intestate leaves no issue but a surviving spouse and a parent or parents, then the residuary estate, after the spouse's prior entitlement to the personal chattels and the fixed net sum of £85,000,[4] will be divided into two:

> as to one half, in trust for the surviving husband or wife absolutely and as to the other half, where the intestate leaves one parent or both parents,[5] in trust for the parent absolutely or, as the case may be, for the two parents in equal shares absolutely.[6]

Parents and no spouse. If the intestate leaves no surviving spouse and no issue but both parents, then the residuary estate is held in trust for the father and mother in equal shares absolutely.[7]

Parent and no spouse. If the intestate leaves no surviving spouse and no issue but a parent, then the residuary estate is held in trust for the surviving father or mother absolutely.[8]

Although in each case the entitlement is expressed to be "in trust" for the parent(s), it is in fact an absolute entitlement.[9]

A parent of an illegitimate child is entitled to succeed on the intestacy of that child by virtue of section 14(2) of the Family Reform Act 1969.[10] However an illegitimate child is presumed not to have been survived by his father unless the contrary is shown.[11]

Brothers and sisters: the entitlement

Brothers and sisters of the whole blood

If the intestate leaves no issue and no parent but a surviving spouse, then the residuary estate, after the spouse's prior entitlement to the personal chattels and the fixed sum of £85,000,[12] will be divided into two:

[4] In the case of deaths on or after March 1, 1981, S.I. 1981 No. 255; in the case of deaths before March 1, 1981, the amount of the fixed net sum was £55,000; in the case of deaths before March 15, 1977, the amount was £40,000; in the case of deaths before July 1, 1972, the amount was £30,000; in the case of deaths before January 1, 1967, the amount was £20,000; and in the case of deaths before January 1, 1953, the amount was £1,000.

[5] Whether or not brothers or sisters of the intestate or their issue also survive.

[6] s.46(1)(i)(3). Note that by virtue of s.46(2) a husband and wife, for all purposes of distribution or division, are to be treated as two persons. This will prevent any possibility of a tenancy by entireties in respect to the parent's entitlement.

[7] s.46(1)(iii).

[8] s.46(1)(iv).

[9] In the unlikely event that the parent is not of full age, the provisions of A.E.A. 1925, s.42(1) will apply, namely that the personal representatives will appoint two trustees, or a trust corporation to hold the property and will obtain a good discharge from the trustees.

[10] See *ante*, Chap. 10.

[11] Family Law Reform Act 1969, s.14(4).

[12] In the case of deaths on or after March 1, 1981; for deaths before that date see note 4, *supra*.

> as to one half, in trust for the surviving husband or wife, absolutely and, as to the other half, on the statutory trusts for the brothers and sisters of the whole blood of the intestate.[13]

If the intestate leaves no spouse, no issue and no parent, the residuary estate will be held:

> on the statutory trusts for the brothers and sisters of the whole blood of the intestate.[14]

Brothers and sisters of the half blood

If the intestate leaves no spouse, no issue, no parent and no brother or sister of the whole blood or issue thereof, then the residuary estate will be held:

> on the statutory trusts for the brothers and sisters of the half blood of the intestate.[15]

A brother or sister of the whole blood is a person who has both the same father and the same mother as the intestate. A brother or sister of the half blood is a person who has one parent only in common with the deceased. It will be noticed that the latter are not equally entitled on intestacy with the former. Only brothers and sisters of the whole blood can take along with a surviving spouse and brothers and sisters of the half blood will be wholly excluded by a spouse.[16] In addition the collaterals of the half blood do not take alongside the collaterals of the whole blood but will be excluded by a surviving brother or sister of the whole blood or any issue thereof. This position stems from the reforms in 1952 when the dichotomy was adopted as a matter of deliberate policy by the framers of the Intestates' Estates Act 1952.[17] It can be challenged on the grounds that it does not accord with the presumed intention of the intestate and that it is likely to produce disharmony within families. Consider the situation where a child of a previous marriage has been brought up on an equal basis with the children of a subsequent marriage, perhaps in ignorance of the true situation. It seems difficult to justify the exclusion of the first child on

[13] s.46(1)(i)(3), in this case s.47(4) applies, see *post*.
[14] s.46(1)(v).
[15] *Ibid.*
[16] This change was effected by the Intestates' Estates Act 1952, as a matter of deliberate policy.
[17] Based on the recommendations of the Morton Committee 1951, Cmd. 8310. The change seems to be based more on a desire to limit the occasions on which a spouse will take less than an absolute interest in the whole estate, rather than on a conscious discrimination against collaterals of the half-blood.

the subsequent intestacy of his half brothers.[18] The situation could, of course, easily be remedied by the legal adoption of the first child by the parties to the marriage but this step is not taken in many such cases.

It must also be noted that the child of the half-blood would be unlikely to have any right of recourse under the Inheritance (Provision for Family and Dependants) Act 1975 against the brother's or sister's estate.[19]

The statutory trusts

Applicability

The Act provides that brothers or sisters of the intestate should take on the statutory trusts. These trusts are defined in section 47(1) which, although primarily designed to govern the entitlement of issue, are expressly made applicable to brothers and sisters by section 47(3). The estate is held on trusts corresponding to the statutory trusts for the issue of the intestate as if such trusts were repeated with the substitution of references to the brothers and sisters for references to the children or child of the intestate.[20] However, the provision in section 47(1)(iii) relating to the duty to account[21] is expressly excluded from such trusts, so that there can be no question of brothers or sisters or their issue having to bring *inter vivos* gifts into hotchpot.[22]

The provision in section 47(1)(ii) relating to maintenance and advancement and in section 47(1)(iv) relating to the use of chattels

[18] It is interesting to note that many modern intestacy schemes in other English-speaking countries make no distinction between the entitlement of collaterals of the whole blood and collaterals of the half blood. See Republic of Eire, Succession Act 1965, s.72; Northern Ireland, Administration of Estates Act 1955, s.14, and all but New South Wales of the Australian and New Zealand schemes, see Hardingham, Neave and Ford, Wills and Intestacy, p. 352. There was no distinction between collaterals of the whole blood and collaterals of the half blood under the Statute of Distribution 1670. In view of the discord and unhappiness that the distinction could cause in families, it is submitted that the dichotomy should also be abandoned in England particularly since the increasing number of divorces and remarriages make the situation less exceptional than in earlier days.

[19] Applications by a "child of the family" under s.1(1)(*d*) relate to the estate of the parent, not to a brother or sister. Thus the only possibility is a claim under s.1(1)(*e*), which is unlikely to have any basis in the sort of situation under discussion. See *post*, Chap. 18.

[20] s.47(3).

[21] See fully discussed *ante* in Chap. 13.

[22] The subsection would in any event be inapplicable to brothers and sisters and their issue, in so far as the duty to account relates only to gifts by way of advancement, since this could not apply to a gift to a brother or sister. But see also the alternative "or on the marriage" which might otherwise apply. However it is interesting to note that in some Australian states, persons other than issue must account for *inter vivos* gifts under modified hotchpot provisions—see the legislation in South Australia, Administration and Probate Act 1919–1975, s.72k; Australian Capital Territory, Administration and Probate Ordinance, 1929, s.49B(3), (4), and Northern Territory, Administration and Probate Ordinance, 1969, s.68(3), (4). See Hardingham, Neave and Ford *op. cit.*, p. 404.

apply to the trusts for brothers and sisters as they apply to those for issue.[23]

Many of the points noted above with reference to the statutory trusts for issue and embodied in section 47(1)(i) apply equally here. First, the brothers and sisters (or their issue when they take their parent's share) will attain a vested interest at eighteen years[24] or on marriage.[25] Secondly, references in section 46(1)(i) to an intestate leaving or not leaving a member of the class of brothers and sisters of the whole blood or issue of such persons are construed as references to the intestate leaving or not leaving a member of that class who attains an absolutely vested interest.[26]

The shares of minor members of the class who fail to attain a vested interest will accrue to the other members of the class or to the other members of the branch of the family entitled if it is a substitutional share.[27]

Thirdly, although the entitlement of brothers and sisters (and grandparents, and uncles and aunts) is introduced by the words "for the following persons living at the death of the intestate," these words are not intended to exclude issue who take under the statutory trusts their deceased parent's share by representation.[28]

Fourthly, the effect of the statutory trusts is to create a *per stirpes* distribution. Although the issue of brothers and sisters of the whole blood are referred to in section 46(1), there is no direct entitlement conferred on such persons. The nephews and nieces, being children of both whole and half blood brothers and sisters, take if at all by substitution, *i.e.* they are entitled only where their parent has predeceased the intestate and then take the share their parent would have taken if he or she had survived the intestate. Thus, if an intestate leaves one surviving brother and there are two surviving children of a deceased brother, the brother takes one half share and the two children take the other share between them. Issue of any degree of a

[23] See *ante* p. 247.

[24] In the case of deaths on or after January 1, 1970, Family Law Reform Act 1969, s.3(2).

[25] s.47(1)(i).

[26] s.47(4). There is thus the possibility of the subsequent enlargement of the surviving spouse's interest if all the brothers and sisters of the whole blood, or their issue, fail to attain a vested interest. The subsection is limited to brothers and sisters of the whole blood, since brothers and sisters of the half blood are not included in s.46(1)(i)(3) and cannot take with a spouse. Where there is no spouse then the entitlement of both the whole blood and the half blood is governed by the clause in s.46(1)(v) which contains the wording "... but if no person takes an absolutely vested interest under such trusts, then ...." Thus it is clear that brothers and sisters (or their issue when they take their parents share by substitution) will only be entitled if at least one member of the class attains a vested interest, and there is no necessity for a further express provision to that effect.

[27] s.47(1)(i).

[28] See *Galloway* v. *Galloway* [1949] N.Z.L.R. 24. It is interesting to note that the parents are dealt with separately and are not included with the other relatives under this general phrase.

deceased brother or sister can take, subject to the rule that the nearer generation of issue will always exclude the more remote within the same *stirpes*.[29]

Finally, it can be re-emphasised, with reference to the issue of deceased brothers and sisters, that only legitimate, legitimated or adopted children are included. Illegitimate children are not included since the reforms embodied in section 14 of the Family Law Reform Act 1969 relate only to the entitlement of illegitimate children to succeed on their *parent's* intestacy.[30]

Section 47(5)

A new subsection (5) to section 47 was added by the Intestates' Estates Act 1952 but was shown to produce an anomaly, and to be superfluous in any event and was repealed by the Family Provision Act 1966.[31] It will shortly be noted here. The subsection provided that, if trusts in favour of any class of relatives of the intestate (other than issue) failed by reason of no member of that class attaining an absolute vested interest, the residuary estate should be held as if the intestate had died without leaving any member of that class, or issue of any member of that class, living at the death of the intestate. The subsection was defective as drafted since it failed to include "or issue of any member of that class" in the opening premise but did include such a reference in the resulting hypothesis. The result was that, if no member of the class, *e.g.* brothers and sisters, or uncles and aunts, attained a vested interest, even if there were issue of that class surviving and capable of taking under the trusts, the class and their issue were wholly excluded in favour of the next class entitled. In *Re Lockwood*,[32] this absurd and capricious result was avoided by construing the class in the opening part of the section as not being

[29] This can lead to anomalies similar to those which have been illustrated above in Chap. 13 relating to issue. Thus relatives of the same degree can take unequal shares and a more remote relative can take a greater share than the closer relatives. This result would not have been possible under the Statute of Distribution 1670 which embodied two rules which were unwisely discarded in 1925. First, under the Statute it was provided that there could be no representation among collaterals after brothers' and sisters' children (s.4). The more remote issue, took if at all, in their own right as next-of-kin. Secondly, under the statute if all the brothers and sisters predeceased the intestate then their children did not take by representation but took *per capita* in their own right (s.4); see *Re Sutton* [1934] Ch. 217. It can be suggested that these rules are more in accordance with the intestate's presumed intention than the present provisions are. See also the current intestacy legislation in the Australian States of Victoria, Administration and Probate Act 1958, s.52(1)(*f*)(iii); Queensland, Succession Act, 1981, s.37(2); see Hardingham, Neave and Ford, *op. cit.*, pp. 347, 361. See also the Canadian cases of *Re Minor* [1945] 3 D.L.R. 474; *Re Drain* [1948] 2 D.L.R. 617; *Re Beaulieu* [1951] 4 D.L.R. 687; contrast *Re McIver* [1941] 57 B.C.R. 401.

[30] See *ante* p. 173; s.15 of the 1969 Act does not apply to intestacies.

[31] s.9, Sched. 2.

[32] *Atherton* v. *Brooke* [1958] Ch. 231; see Lodge (1956) 20 Conv. 399.

confined to the primary class of aunts and uncles in view of the "reference to issue" later in the section.[33]

In fact the subsection is unnecessary since the logical operation of the other provisions in section 46 and section 47 is to produce the desired result in any event.

Grandparents

The entitlement

If there is no surviving spouse, no issue, no parent, no brother or sister of the whole or half blood or issue thereof, the residuary estate will be held:

> in trust for the grandparents of the intestate, and if more than one survive the intestate, in equal shares.[34]

Uncles and aunts

The entitlement

If there is no surviving spouse, no issue, no parent, no brother or sister of the whole or half blood or issue thereof and no grandparent, the residuary estate will be held[35]:

> on the statutory trusts for the uncles and aunts of the intestate (being brothers and sisters of the whole blood of a parent of the intestate) but if no person takes an absolutely vested interest under such trusts; then: on the statutory trusts for the uncles and aunts of the intestate (being brothers and sisters of the half blood of a parent of the intestate).[36]

Most of the points already noted with reference to the statutory trusts applicable to the brothers' and sisters' share will also apply to the uncles and aunts. Thus the class will take vested interests at the age of eighteen years[37] or on marriage[38] and at least one member of the class must take an absolutely vested interest or the estate will pass to the relatives of the half blood (in the case of a class of the whole blood) or to the Crown as *bona vacantia* (in the case of a class of the half blood).[39] The distribution is *per stirpes* and issue of whatever degree can take their parent's share. The points noted above relating to the anomalies that this strict *per stirpes* distribution can produce, *i.e.* the

[33] Strictly "... but if no person takes an absolutely vested interest under such trusts...," s.46(1)(v).
[34] s.46(1)(v); see also s.46(2).
[35] s.46(1)(v).
[36] *Ibid.* See above for the meaning of the whole and the half blood. p. 269.
[37] In the case of deaths on or after January 1, 1970, Family Law Reform Act 1969, s.3(2).
[38] s.47(1)(i).
[39] s.46(1)(v).

inequality of shares taken by relatives equally related and the possible preference of a more remote relative over a nearer relative, apply also here. The same suggestions can be made for reform to bring the law more into line with the deceased's presumed intention.[40]

Another possible anomaly is in fact produced by the *per stirpes* distribution among uncles and aunts, namely the possibility of a person taking a double share. This can arise by virtue of a double entitlement as a cousin where the person's mother is a true aunt of the deceased and his father is a true uncle of the deceased. Suppose that the deceased's father's brother or sister marries the deceased's mother's sister or brother and that both parties of the marriage die leaving issue. It will be seen that the issue are first cousins of the deceased twice over and, since they take through distinct *stirpes* of the family, are presumably entitled to two shares. This is a factor of the *per stirpes* distribution and would be avoided if the issue of the primary class took *per capita* as suggested above.[41]

Other relatives

No entitlement

In the absence of a spouse, issue, parent, brother or sister of the whole or the half blood or issue thereof, or grandparent, or uncle or aunt of the whole or the half blood or issue thereof, the property will pass on intestacy to the Crown as *bona vacantia*.[42] Other relatives such as second cousins, greatgrandparents, grand uncles and aunts have no entitlement on intestacy. It will thus be noticed that the class of next-of-kin is somewhat restrictively defined in the modern law of intestate succession. It is submitted that this is correct as being consistent with the deceased presumed intention.[43] Further, any possible hardship or unfairness that might be occasioned to a remote relative can be

[40] *i.e.* representation should be limited to children of uncles and aunts, and where there are such children but all the uncles and aunts have predeceased the intestate, those children should share *per capita* and not *per stirpes.*

[41] As in South Australia, for example; see the case of *In the Estate of Cullen (decd.)* [1976] 14 S.A.S.R. 456 where a bachelor died intestate, leaving as next-of-kin 10 sets of first cousins who survived him. The intestate's father's sister had married the intestate's mother's brother, and three of the children of this marriage survived the intestate. It was held that these three children did not take a double share by virtue of being related as cousins on both sides of the family, but took equally *per capita* with the other first cousins of the intestate. The construction applicable in this case was that provided by the Statute of Distributions, under which it is clear that cousins took *per capita* and not by representation. See also *Re Morrison*; *Trustees, Executors and Agency Co. Loe.* v. *Comport* [1945] V.L.R. 123, where a woman was held to be entitled to two shares, one as the widow and another as a cousin. In *Cullen* the judge distinguished the case since in *Cullen* the claimants were only first cousins, twice over, so to speak, *i.e.* a claim as only one class of relative.

[42] s.46(1)(vi), see fully discussed in the next Chapter.

[43] If the deceased wishes to benefit more remote relatives he can make a will, as in, for example, *Re Barlow's Will Trusts* [1979] 1 W.L.R. 278 where there was an express devise to a great niece.

alleviated either by the exercise of the Crown's power to make *ex gratia* payments out of *bona vacantia*[44] or by an application under the Inheritance (Provision for Family and Dependants) Act 1975.

CROWN'S ENTITLEMENT TO BONA VACANTIA

Bona vacantia

The right of the Crown to succeed to the whole of the personal estate of a person dying intestate without next of kin as *bona vacantia* has been traced back to very early times.[45] In *Dyke* v. *Walford*,[46] which contains a useful historical review of the right, *Lord Kingsdown*[47] stated:

> "The origin of this right shows that, if it existed at all, it must have existed from the foundation of the Monarchy; it is the right of the Crown to "*bona vacantia*,' to property which has no other owner, . . . we consider it, therefore, to be perfectly clear that, at the date of the Charter [granted by Edward II, 1377] on which the Duchy claim is founded, the right in question was vested in the Crown, as one of its 'jura regalia' . . . ."

However, the right to *bona vacantia* existed only in relation to personal property; on a failure of heirs to real property the Crown was entitled to the property by way of escheat.[48] It is rare now for circumstances to arise which are governed by the pre-1925 law[49] and so it is not necessary for this discussion to consider the historical position further. The 1925 Act gives statutory formulation to the right to *bona vacantia*. Section 46(1) provides for the order of entitlement of relatives on intestacy and concludes in paragraph (vi):

> "In default of any person taking an absolute interest under the foregoing provisions, the residuary estate of the intestate shall belong to the Crown or to the Duchy of Lancaster or to the Duke of Cornwall for the time being, as the case may be, as *bona vacantia*, and in lieu of any right to escheat . . . ."

The first point to make with reference to the modern statutory

44 s.46(1)(vi), see *post*.
45 See *Re Sir Thomas Spencer Wells, Swinburne-Hanham* v. *Howard* [1933] 1 Ch. 29, at p. 49.
46 (1846) 5 Moore P.C. 434.
47 As he subsequently became, at p. 495. See also *Middleton* v. *Spicer* (1783) 1 Bro.C.C. 201 at p. 202, "The King is the owner of everything which has no other owner."
48 See Ing, *Bona Vacantia*, 1971, p. 38. This text contains a full consideration of *bona vacantia* in more detail than is possible here, and reference can be usefully made to it.
49 See the situations in which the pre-1925 law remains applicable in cases of intestacy, discussed *ante* pp. 27–35. See also the discussion *post* of the position where a foreign domicile is involved, where the Crown's rights could be said to be based on the common law, rather than the statutory rules. On the pre-1926 position see *Re Jones* [1925] 1 Ch. 340, trusts in will failed, no next-of-kin. Crown took only because indication in will that executor not to take beneficially.

entitlement is that it applies to both real and personal property including legal estates in freeholds. This change in the law is brought about by the combination of section 1 of the 1925 Act, which ensures the devolution of real estate to the personal representative, and section 33, which constitutes both real and personal property as part of "the residuary estate of the intestate" to which section 46 applies.[50]

Nature of the right

Historically the Crown's right to *bona vacantia* was a common law right based on the Royal prerogative and it would seem that the entitlement to ownerless property was one of the Crown's *jura regalia.*[51] An alternative view, and one which finds increasing acceptance in statutory codes, is that the Crown does not take *jus regalia* but takes as *ultimus haeres.*[52] The point, as will be seen, is not entirely academic where issues of private international law are involved. It is quite clear in view of the provisions of section 46(vi) that the Crown's primary right to *bona vacantia* on intestacy is now statutory rather than arising at common law. This does not, however, resolve the problem indicated above since the Act is silent as to the fundamental basis of this entitlement. There is some post-1925 authority on the point. Thus Wynn Parry J. in *Re Mitchell (decd.)*[53] thought that in the 1925 Act the words "as *bona vacantia*" were merely descriptive and in keeping with the statutory scheme, so that the Crown took directly under the statutory provision in section 46(1)(vi) and not by any prerogative right under which but for the statute it would otherwise have taken.[54] The decision in that case was that the Crown was entitled under a clause in a will which incorporated the intestacy provisions in the 1925 Act and this lends some support for the view that the Crown takes as *ultimus haeres.* Further indications to the same effect are the reference in the side note to the section, "Succession to real and personal estate on intestacy" and the inclusion of the Crown in much the same way as the other relatives. If this is so, the Crown might well be able to claim

[50] See the definition of "real estate" in s.55(1)(xix) leaseholds are included and also the equity of redemption in mortgaged premises. See *Re Sir Thomas Spencer Wells, supra.*

[51] *Per* Lord Kingsdown in *Dyke* v. *Walford* (1846) 5 moo.P.C. 434 at p. 495. See *Re Wells, Swinburne-Hanham* v. *Howard* [1933] 1 Ch. 29.

[52] *Per* Lord Mansfield in *Megit* v. *Johnson* (1780) 2 Dougl. (K.B.) 542. See Cohn, 17 M.L.R. 381, who indicates that most modern European codes provide for the Crown to take as *ultimus haeres,* as under Scottish law, see Walker, *Principles of Scottish Private Law,* 2nd ed., 1225, and the Republic of Eire's law, Succession Act 1965, s.73(1).

[53] *Hatton* v. *Jones* [1954] Ch. 525 at p. 529. *In the Estate of Hanley* [1941] 3 All E.R. 301 apparently to the contrary has now been reversed by the Non-Contentious Probate Rules 1954 (hereinafter also referred to as the "N.-C.P.R. 1954"), S.I. No. 796, r. 19, relating to the Crown's entitlement to a grant. See also the Australian case of *Re Bonner* [1963] Qd.R. 488.

[54] As to the situation where a foreign domicile is involved, see the discussions *post.*

under a testamentary gift to "statutory next-of-kin," in the absence of other relatives.[55]

When right arises

The Crown's right to *bona vacantia* arises whenever there is ownerless property within the realm and is not confined to cases of intestacy without next-of-kin.[56] However, cases of intestacy (or partial intestacy) are the most common instances of the operation of the doctrine. The most obvious case is where the intestate dies without being survived by any of the relatives specified in section 46 of the 1925 Act.

A claim to *bona vacantia* will arise also where there are surviving relatives but they are prevented for some reason from taking under the intestacy. One of the most frequent examples which arose on deaths between 1926 and 1970 was where the deceased was survived only by illegitimate children or where an illegitimate person died unmarried not survived by his or her mother.[57] The illegitimacy in such cases would disentitle the next-of-kin to succession.[58] However, this problem will be met less frequently in the case of deaths on or after January 1, 1970 since the effect of the Family Law Reform Act 1969[59] is to remove some of the disabilities previously attaching to illegitimacy in the law of succession.[60]

A surviving, but judicially separated, spouse has no right to succession[61] and, if he or she is the only relative, the Crown might be entitled. Likewise if the only relative otherwise entitled "feloniously" has killed the deceased[62] or disclaims the interest of intestacy.[63]

Ex gratia payments

Where the Crown or the Duchy is entitled to *bona vacantia* on intestacy, there is statutory recognition of the power to make *ex gratia*

[55] Ing, *op. cit.* pp. 46, 47 but not it is suggested under a gift simply to "next-of-kin" which suggest an actual blood relationship.

[56] See Ing, *Bona Vacantia*; other situations are *bona vacantia* arising on the dissolution of companies, or failure of trusts or incorporate associations ceasing to exist.

[57] See *ante* p. 172; See Ing, *op. cit.* It was the practice of the Crown to recognise the moral claims of illegitimate children, by making *ex gratia* payments, where appropriate, see *post.*

[58] See *Re Mitchell* [1954] 1 Ch. 525.

[59] s.14, see fully discussed *ante* p. 173.

[60] However the limitations of that legislation will be apparent and the Crown will be entitled to the estate of an illegitimate person who dies unmarried with no issue and no surviving parent.

[61] See *ante* p. 162; Matrimonial Causes Act 1973, s.18(2).

[62] See *post* p. 323; Ing *op. cit.* Chap. 17, and *Callaway* v. *Treasury Solicitor* [1956] Ch. 559; the Crown does not take the forfeited interests as *bona vacantia* if there are other relatives entitled.

[63] See *post* p. 339; Ing, *op. cit.* p. 207, and *Re Scott (decd.) Widdows* v. *Friends of the Clergy Corporation* [1975] 2 All E.R. 1033, the Crown does not take disclaimed benefits, if there are other relatives entitled.

payments to persons morally, but not legally, entitled to benefit from the estate. Section 46(1)(vi) of the 1925 Act provides:

> "The Crown or the said Duchy or the said Duke may (without prejudice to the powers reserved by section nine of the Civil List Act 1910[64] or any other powers), out of the whole or any part of the property devolving on them respectively, provide, in accordance with the existing practice, for dependants, whether kindred or not, of the intestate, and other persons for whom the intestate might reasonably have been expected to make provision."

The making of such grants is, of course, wholly discretionary and the section does not confer even a right of application as under the Inheritance (Provision for Family and Dependants) Act 1975. There are no formal procedures or rules regarding an application for an *ex gratia* payment but information and guidance on the making of a claim is supplied by the Treasury Solicitor on behalf of the Crown or the respective solicitors for the Duchies of Lancaster or Cornwall.[64] It has been indicated[65] that the Duchy is guided by the wishes of the deceased where these are apparent. Thus, where there is a will which fails by reason of defective execution or for other technical reasons, the beneficiaries of such a will will be regarded as having strong claims. Before the changes introduced by the Family Law Reform Act 1969 provision was often made in favour of illegitimate children or their parents.[66] Although such cases will no longer arise, provision can be made in favour of other relatives of an illegitimate person.[67] "Common law husbands and wives" will also have strong claims, as will unrelated or distantly related companions who have cared for the deceased at some sacrifice to themselves.[68] Such persons might also have the alternative of an application under the Inheritance (Provision for Family and Dependants) Act 1975 but must under that jurisdiction establish a dependency on the deceased within section 1(i)(*e*), section 1(3), and section 3(4).[69] The claim to an *ex gratia* payment might be more easily established. On the other hand the Inheritance (Provision for Family and Dependants) Act 1975 claim can be pursued notwithstanding the entitlement of other relatives on

[64] In 1982 it has been reported that the total amount of such *ex gratia* payments was £1,350,000; see *Daily Telegraph*, September 1, 1983.

[65] By the Chancellor of the Duchy of Lancaster in response to a parliamentary question; see Ing, *Bona Vacantia* (1971), Chap. 10.

[66] By virtue of the Family Law Reform Act 1969, s.14, illegitimate children can now succeed on the intestacy of their parent and vice versa.

[67] *i.e.* relatives other than a parent (and a spouse and issue of course) who have no rights of inheritance to the estate of an illegitimate child, and vice versa.

[68] See *ante* p. 162.

[69] Likewise a judicially separated spouse, or the issue of a person disqualified by the rule of public policy from inheriting, see *ante* p. 162 and *post* p. 339.

intestacy whereas the Crown's entitlement, and thus the payments, can only arise on failure of relatives.[70]

Grant of administration

If a person dies intestate and without next-of-kin, then, in the absence of a person with a prior title, the Treasury Solicitor or the solicitor to the Duchy will apply for a grant of administration on behalf of the Crown or the Duchy.[71] It is interesting to note that in answer to a parliamentary question the Minister of State to the Treasury indicated that during the twelve months up to September 30, 1976 the Treasury Solicitor had administered on behalf of the Crown some 2,905 estates having a total value of approximately £2,267,000.[72] Although the vast majority of such estates are of small value, *i.e.* under £5,000, there have been estates of over £500,000 with the largest estate being worth £650,000.[73]

Conflict of laws

The entitlement of the Crown to property situate in the United Kingdom of a person who dies with a foreign domicile has been the subject of contrasting decisions. These cases are discussed *post* in Chapter 16 entitled "Conflict of Laws."

[70] *Re Wilkinson (decd.), Neales* v. *Newell* [1978] Fam. 22; *Re Beaumont (decd.), Martin* v. *Midland Bank Trust Co. Ltd.* [1980] Ch. 444; *Jelley* v. *Iliffe* [1981] 2 W.L.R. 801, fully discussed *post*.

[71] See, *op. cit.* pp. 63–80; for the practice see Williams, Mortimer and Sinnucks, *op. cit.* p. 874; p. 267.

[72] More recent figures indicate, for 1982, 2,700 estates totalling £3,150,000.

[73] Similarly there is a newspaper reference to an estate of £380,000 left by a recluse widow who died intestate with no known relatives.

Chapter 15

PARTIAL INTESTACY

Application of the Scheme of Distribution

Section 49 of the Administration of Estates Act 1925 states

> "Where any person dies leaving a will effectively disposing of part of his property, this Part of this Act shall have effect as respects the part of his property not so disposed of subject to the provisions contained in the will and subject to the following modifications."

It is accordingly clear that the basic scheme of entitlement set out in section 46 of the Act and discussed in the preceding chapters applies to the undisposed of property where a person dies partially intestate. Three matters need to be considered further: first, the definition of a partial intestacy; secondly, the effect of the testamentary provisions; and, thirdly, the statutory modifications which relate mainly to the requirement to account for testamentary benefits.

Meaning of a partial intestacy

Definition

A partial intestacy is not defined by the statute and the dichotomy between a total and a partial intestacy is not expressly stated. There is the statutory reference in section 49(1) set out above and section 55(1)(vi) defines "an intestate" as including a person who leaves a will but who dies intestate as to some beneficial interest in this real or personal estate. Beyond those provisions reference must be made to case law for further definition. It can be said that a partial intestacy refers to the situation where the testator has made some effective testamentary dispositions but has failed to dispose effectively of some part of his assets or of some beneficial interest in his estate.[1] The reasons for this failure can be diverse and the cases suggest an initial distinction between "immediate partial intestacies" and "contingent partial intestacies."[2] The dichotomy between these two situations is relevant to the applicability of the statutory trust for sale in section 33 of the 1925 Act.[3] It is clear, however, that all cases of partial intestacy

[1] Romer L.J. in *Re Thornber* [1937] 1 Ch. 29 at p. 35.
[2] See Maugham J. in *Re McKee* [1931] 2 Ch. 145 at p. 148.
[3] See *ante* where it is concluded, on the authority of *Re McKee*, *supra*, that the statutory trust for sale applies to immediate partial intestacies but not to contingent partial intestacies.

are subject to the distributive provisions of the 1925 Act since, on the authority of both *Re McKee*[4] and *Re Bowen-Buscarlet's Will Trusts,*[5] section 49, and thus section 46, of the 1925 Act applies to both categories of partial intestacy.[6]

Most partial intestacies will be immediately apparent at the date of the death in the sense that it will be evident to the executors, after an examination of the will and the circumstances of the property and the family, that some property, or some interest in property, is undisposed of. This can arise in several ways. First, to take the simplest case, it might be that the testator's will fails to comprehend the whole of the disposable property in the testamentary dispositions, for example, where there is no residuary clause or where the residuary clause is limited to either realty or to personalty but does not cover both.[7] Similarly, where the testator revokes a gift of residue by codicil and fails to make any alternative provision.[8] Such instances can be regarded as cases of defective drafting and are obviously more likely to be met in home-made wills than in professionally drafted wills. Secondly, the will might purport effectively to comprehend all the property but one or more of the testamentary gifts might fail by operation of law. Thus a gift of residue might fail because the beneficiary has witnessed the will[9] or predeceased the testator[10] or be void for perpetuity, uncertainty, public policy, etc. An interesting illustration arose in *Re Sinclair (decd.)*[11] where it was held that a residuary gift to a wife, who was subsequently divorced, failed by virtue of section 18A of the Wills Act 1837 with the result that the property was undisposed of and passed on an intestacy. Thirdly, the *lacuna* may arise because a beneficiary under the will has disclaimed his or her testamentary benefits.[12] In some cases this may result in the property remaining subject to the testamentary provisions[13] but a disclaimer of a gift of residue will result in a partial intestacy.[14]

[4] [1931] 2 Ch. 145; see also Romer L.J. in *Re Thornber, supra.*

[5] [1972] 1 Ch. 463.

[6] Although the cases disclose a difference in approach as to the manner and effect of the applications of these sections, see *post* p. 283.

[7] See *Re Plowman* [1943] Ch. 269, where the testator failed to dispose of surplus income during the lifetime of an annuitant; see also *Re Tong* [1931] 1 Ch. 202, and *Re Martin* [1955] Ch. 698.

[8] As in *Re Midgley* [1955] Ch. 576.

[9] Wills Act 1837, s.15, as in *Ross* v. *Caunters* [1980] Ch. 297, for example.

[10] When the gift will lapse, as in *Re Berrey's Will Trusts* [1959] 1 W.L.R. 30; *Re Worthington* [1933] Ch. 771; *Re Beaumont's Will Trust* [1950] Ch. 462.

[11] [1984] 3 All E.R. 362 notwithstanding that there was a gift over in the event of the wife predeceasing the testator; affirmed by C.A. [1985] 1 All E.R. 1066. Contrast *Re Cherrington (decd.)* [1984] 1 W.L.R. 772. s.18A was added to the Wills Act 1837 by s.18(2) of the Administration of Justice Act 1982 and declares that a gift to a spouse who is subsequently divorced, lapses.

[12] As in *Re Sullivan* [1930] 1 Ch. 84; s.49(1) applied.

[13] Specific bequests which are disclaimed will fall into residue. A disclaimer of a life interest will accelerate a gift in remainder.

[14] See *Re Sullivan* [1930] 1 Ch. 84, discussed *post.*

Failure to dispose of an interest in property

In addition to cases where the testator has failed to dispose of property there can be cases where the testator has failed to dispose of an interest in property.[15] Such cases must be divided into two categories. First, there are those cases where an interest in property forms part of the assets of the estate, *e.g.* where the testator has a reversionary interest under his father's will and the will fails to dispose effectively of the interest, either because it is overlooked[16] or because the relevant testamentary dispositions fail.[17] Such cases will be subject to the statutory scheme.[18] The second category is where the *lacuna* arises because of a failure by the will to dispose effectively of the totality of the beneficial interest in property. The most obvious example of this is where the testator creates a life interest in property by will and fails to provide effectively for the remainder interest, either because the will makes no provision for it or because the disposition of the remainder fails for some reason.[19] These categories can be further divided into those cases where the failure to dispose of the whole interest is immediately apparent at the death[20] and cases where the failure becomes apparent only at a time subsequent to the death. *Re McKee*[21] provides the best illustration of the latter type. A testator gave his residuary estate to his wife for life and after her death to divide the same between such of his brothers and sisters who survived the widow. At the testator's death the widow and brothers and sisters were living but subsequently, during the lifetime of the widow, all the brothers and sisters died. This was categorised as "a contingent partial intestacy" since at the death the whole interest in the property may or may not have been effectively disposed of depending on subsequent contingencies and events such as whether any of the brothers or sisters survived the widow.[22] Similarly, where there is a direction to accumulate residue for a permitted period, at the expiration of which the fund is to be distributed between a class satisfying certain conditions or contingencies, and members of the

[15] See s.55(1)(vi).

[16] See *Re Gillett's Will Trusts* [1950] Ch. 102, surplus income undisposed of.

[17] See *Re Vander Byl, Fladgate* v. *Fore* [1931] 1 Ch. 216, ineffective exercise of a general power of appointment.

[18] s.55(1)(vi); making s.33, 46 and 49 applicable. See also s.55(1)(xvii). "Property" includes "any interest in real or personal property" see *Re Tong* [1931] 1 Ch. 202, *per* Romer L.J. at p. 213.

[19] See *Re Bowen-Buscarlet's Will Trusts* [1972] 1 Ch. 463.

[20] As in *Re Bowen-Buscarlet's Will Trusts, supra*, and *Re Thornber* [1937] 1 Ch. 29 direction to accumulate surplus income of residue and at the end of the period to hold in trust for the testator's children; testator dies without issue.

[21] *Supra.*

[22] See also *Re Young's Will Trusts* [1951] 1 Ch. 185; *Re Morton* [1956] 1 Ch. 644, and *Re Grover's Will Trust* [1971] Ch. 168, in each case the distribution on intestacy fell to be decided many years after the testator's death. On the recognition of the differing approach necessary in cases where there is no intestacy apparent at the death of the testator, see Harman J. in *Re Midgley (decd.)* [1955] 1 Ch. 576 at p. 584.

class are living at the death but fail to satisfy the conditions at the end of the accumulation period.

The New Zealand case of *Re Williams*[23] provides a similar example and the position was explained as follows[24]:

> "Because the persons whom the testator selected to have the ultimate residue after the death of his wife were those of his brothers and sisters who should be living at the death of his wife, and because all his brothers and sisters have died, and because his wife is still alive, it becomes clear that, although he made a will, it is, in the events that have actually happened, a will that does not completely dispose of his property. It is a will which, in the circumstances that have arisen, fails to indicate where the ultimate residue is to go after the death of his wife. There is therefore an intestacy. But it is an intestacy of the kind that is called partial. It relates to only part of the estate. What it relates to is merely a residuary capital interest after the death of the wife and the termination of her life interest. Further this partial intestacy is of the kind which is called contingent; that is to say, it was not clear at the date of the death of the testator whether or not there was any intestacy. Had any brother or sister survived the wife, there would have been no intestacy. It is now clear, however, that there is a partial intestacy, in that the testator has not completely disposed of his property by will."

Personal representatives of intestate beneficiaries

It is clear from the cases of *Re McKee*[25] and *Re Bowen-Buscarlet*[26] that, in the case of intestacies which arise or become apparent at a time subsequent to the death,[27] the persons entitled as the intestate beneficiaries are ascertained at the date of the death and not at the date when the intestacy arises or becomes apparent; where those persons have survived the intestate but predeceased the later date, then their personal representatives will be entitled. The point was clearly expressed in the New Zealand case referred to in the previous section[28]:

> "I have a clear opinion that although at the date of the testator's death it was impossible to say whether he had died testate or

[23] [1937] N.Z.L.R. 872.

[24] *Per* Callan J. at pp. 873, 874 see also *Pead* v. *Pead* [1912] 15 C.L.R. 510; *Re Sawyer's Will* [1931] 26 Tas.L.R. 161.

[25] [1931] Ch. 145.

[26] [1972] 1 Ch. 463.

[27] *i.e.* in the typical *Re McKee* situation where there is an effective life interest but the remainder fails.

[28] *Re Williams (decd.)* [1937] N.Z.L.R. 872 at p. 874 per Callan J., it is appreciated that the case was concerned with the relevant New Zealand legislation but in this respect it is thought that the English rule is the same.

> partially intestate now that it is clear that he did in fact die partially intestate, the persons to take under these rules of law must be settled by considering, as the appropriate point of time, the date of the testator's death and not any later date; not, for example, the date on which it first became clear that he was a person who had died partially intestate."[29]

It can be noted that the person(s) so identified will be entitled to the property then in the possession of the deceased and to property which falls into the estate after the intestate's death. Thus, where mines and minerals came into the intestate's estate after his death and after the death of his widow who survived him, her estate was nonetheless entitled to share in the mines and minerals.[30]

The application of the statutory trust for sale

The statutory trust for sale imposed by section 33 of the Administration of Estates Act 1925 is generally applicable to partial intestacies. However, it has been shown above[31] in a discussion of the decision in *Re McKee*[32] that the statutory trust is inappropriate to cases of contingent partial intestacies.

THE WILL

Testamentary provisions

The law of intestacy is applicable to govern the distribution of the estate which is not governed by an effective testamentary provision. Thus intestate succession is always subject to and subservient to the provisions of any will. A glance at the 1925 Act reveals that both section 33 (which imposes the trust for sale in subsection (7)) and section 49(1) (which provides for the distribution in cases of partial

[29] The personal representatives of the widow and the brothers and sisters (who had all survived the deceased but predeceased the intestacy) were entitled. This meant that the issue of these brothers and sisters were not automatically entitled by representation to their parent's share; whereas the issue of brothers and sisters, who predeceased the intestate, were. See also *Re Sawyer's Will* [1931] 26 Tas.L.R. 161; *Pead* v. *Pead* [1912] 15 C.L.R. 510. It will be noticed that the legislation throughout identifies the date of the death as the relevant time. "on the death of a person intestate" (s.33(11); "...of every person dying after..." (s.45(1); "...intestate leaves"; s.46(1) and "intestate" is defined as including "... a person who leaves a will but dies intestate as to...," and s.49(1) likewise, "where any person dies...." There is no reference to a person being "found to be intestate" or to "where an intestacy arises."

[30] *Re Jardine* [1956] 3 D.L.R. (2d) 262; *Bullock* v. *Downes* (1860) 9 H.L.C. 1; *Gundry* v. *Pinniger* (1851) 14 Beav. 94. The rule in the case of wills providing that on failure of a gift it shall go to the next-of-kin is that the succession is determined at the date of the testator's death rather than at the date of the failure of the gift or the date of distribution. The provisions of the intestacy legislation contain nothing to the contrary and indeed tend to emphasise that succession is determined as at the date of the intestate's death, *per* Johnson J.A. in *Re Jardine*, *supra*, on Canadian legislation. It is thought that the position in England is the same.

[31] See Chap. 5.

[32] [1931] 2 Ch. 145.

intestacy) state that the application of those sections in cases of partial intestacy is "subject to the provisions contained in the will." Thus, where there is a will, it is dominant and can affect both the entitlement and the manner of distribution of the undisposed of property. It has been said that the approach to adopt in cases of partial intestacy is to regard the provisions of intestate succession as a will made by the legislature to be read into the testator's will.[33] On this basis sections 33, 46, 47 and 48 ought to be applied only so far as that can be done consistently with the terms of the will[34] so that, for example, section 33 will not govern the manner in which funeral expenses or legacies are to be paid if there is express provision covering this question in the will.[35] An emphatic example would be one of those rare cases where the testator has foreseen the possibility of the failure of his testamentary provisions and has included an express clause to govern the entitlement. "In the event of any of my property being undisposed of by this my will and the provisions of section 49 taking effect, I direct that any such property shall be dealt with . . . " in a particular way.[36]

The testamentary provisions must, however, be operative and effective since no regard will be had to modifications of the statutory rules by provisions which have become inoperative by disclaimer or lapse.[37] This principle can be illustrated by the decision in *Re Sullivan*[38] concerning the disposition of certain royalties where the question arose whether the money should be regarded as capital or income.[39] There was a provision in the will to the effect that the royalties should be regarded as capital but this was with reference to certain trusts which failed, giving rise to an intestacy.[40] It was held that the widow should take the royalties as income, disregarding the testator's direction which was regarded as inoperative.[41]

The decision in *Re Sullivan* was applied in *Re Thornber*[42] where there was a direction to accumulate surplus income for the ultimate benefit of children. The testator died without issue and it was held

[33] *Per* Lawrence L.J. in *Re McKee, Public Trustee* v. *McKee* [1931] 2 Ch. 145 at p. 155, citing Lord Cairns in *Cooper* v. *Cooper* (1874) L.R. 7 H.L. 53, at p. 66 " . . . To make a will for the intestate in those respects in which he failed himself so to do."
[34] *Per* Maugham J. in *Re McKee, supra*, at p. 148.
[35] *Ibid.* at p. 151; see *Re Taylor's Estate and Will Trusts* [1969] 2 Ch. 245.
[36] See Romer L.J. in *Re Thornber* [1937] 1 Ch. 29 at pp. 36, 37.
[37] *Per* Maugham J. in *Re Sullivan* [1930] 1 Ch. 84 at p. 87.
[38] *Supra.*
[39] Royalties are wasting property to which the rule in *Howe* v. *Lord Dartmouth* (1802) 7 Ves. 137 applies, but s.33(5) excludes that rule, see *ante*, p. 84.
[40] The trusts were in favour of the wife and issue; the wife disclaimed and there was no issue.
[41] The testator's direction was intended to diminish the wife's interest for the benefit of children, but in fact there were no children. The wife in effect had exchanged a life interest in limited property under the will, for a statutory life interest in more valuable property.
[42] *Crabtree* v. *Thornber* [1937] 1 Ch. 29.

that there was no effective disposal by the will of the residuary estate and that the direction to accumulate was not applicable on intestacy. The dispositions in the will had entirely failed and so there was no provision contained in the will to which the property, which in fact was not effectively disposed of by the will, was subject.

The correct approach in such cases was stated as follows by Romer L.J. in *Re Thornber*[43]:

> "... when you have ascertained what interest has been undisposed of by the testator you then look at the will to see whether as regards that interest he has given any directions and, if he has, those directions must be attended to."

Thus, if the testator had foreseen the possibility of partial intestacy and had included express directions as to the distribution of that property, *e.g.* exclusion of illegitimate children or a *per capita* distribution to issue, that would govern the matter. However, a specific direction relating to the property, which fails, cannot apply for that direction will fail with the gift.

Greater difficulties surround a general direction in the will, *i.e.* one not specifically referred to any particular disposition but included as a general clause in the will. It will be a matter of construction whether administrative clauses relating to, for example, investment, apportionment or hotchpot will govern also the property distributable on intestacy. In the case of general clauses relating to entitlement, *e.g.* the exclusion of particular persons from classes or the preference in terms of double shares of named individuals, the answer seems again to be simply in the construction of the particular will.

Leaning against intestacy

The overriding importance of the will, if any, can be further illustrated by reference to the many judicial statements to the effect that, where possible, the court will lean against a finding of intestacy. Since most of the cases concern the construction of particular clauses in wills, the principle is perhaps more accurately stated as a presumption against a partial intestacy.[44] An early case where the point was expressed is *Booth* v. *Booth*[45] where the Master of the Rolls commented:

> "Every intendment is to be made against holding a man to die intestate who sits down to dispose of the residue of his property."

[43] *Supra*, at p. 36. The provisions relating to the accumulation were not provisions relating to any interest of which the testator had failed to dispose, *ibid.*

[44] As such the principle is really an aspect of the construction of wills and more fully discussed in texts such as *Williams on Wills* (1980) 5th ed., pp. 439–440.

[45] (1799) 4 Ves. 399 at p. 407. See also *Re Redfern* (1877) 6 Ch.D. 133 at p. 136; *Kirby-Smith* v. *Parnell* [1903] 1 Ch. 483 at p. 489, *Lightfoot* v. *Maybery* [1914] A.C. 782 at p. 802; *Re Hooper* [1936] 1 Ch. 442 at p. 446; *Re Bampfield* [1944] 4 D.L.R. 593.

The justification is obvious. If a testator has executed a will in solemn form, the courts should assume that he did not intend to make it a solemn farce.[46] The principle is perhaps better regarded as a rule of construction rather than as a legal presumption and it has been described as a "golden rule of construction."[47] As such, a full discussion of the principle is better left to specialist texts[48] relating to the construction of wills but one or two brief judicial references can usefully be included here. Buckley J. has explained the principle as follows[49]:

> "First, I ought to read the whole of the will and from it ascertain the testator's intention. Secondly, in ascertaining the intention, I ought to a certain extent—we all know what the expression means—to lean against an intestacy, and not to presume that the testator meant to die intestate if, on a fair construction, there is reason for saying the contrary."

However, the limits to the principle have been pointed out by Romer L.J. in *Re Edwards*[50]:

> "It is said that the court leans against an intestacy. I do not know whether that expression at the present day means anything more than this, that in cases of ambiguity you may, at any rate in certain wills, gather an intention that the testator did not intend to die intestate but it cannot be that, merely with a view to avoiding intestacy, you are to do otherwise than construe plain words according to their plain meaning. A testator may well intend to die intestate. When he makes a will he intends to die testate only so far as he has expressed himself in his will."[51]

The same cautious approach is apparent in the more recent decision in *Re Wragg (decd.)*[52] where the Court of Appeal decided, as a matter of construction in favour of an intestacy. Lord Evershed commented[53]:

> "I feel, if I may say so, some sympathy for the learned judge's view, since when a will has been (as this obviously was)

[46] *Per* Lord Esher M.R. in *Re Harrison* (1885) 30 Ch.D. 390 at p. 393; applied in *Re Messenger's Estate* [1937] 1 All E.R. 355; and in *Re Turner* [1949] 2 All E.R. 935 at p. 936.
[47] *Ibid.*
[48] Such as *Williams on Wills, op. cit.*
[49] *Kirby-Smith* v. *Parnall* [1903] 1 Ch. 483 at p. 489; see also Parker J. in *Re Hobson, Barwick* v. *Holt* [1912] 1 Ch. 626 at p. 636.
[50] [1906] 1 Ch. 570 at p. 574. But see Parker J. in *Re Hobson* [1912] 1 Ch. 626 at p. 634; and Lord Greene M.R. in *Re Abbott* [1944] 2 All E.R. 457 at p. 459.
[51] Thus the intention to die intestate can have no place where the testator has attempted to dispose of the whole of the residue. See also Romer L.J. and Lord Evershed M.R. in *Re Wragg (decd.)* [1959] 1 W.L.R. 922 at pp. 929, 930.
[52] [1959] 1 W.L.R. 922.
[53] At p. 929.

> professionally prepared there is a natural inclination against a result that means that the draftsman left a lacuna in his draft. Still, as Romer L.J. has pointed out, the court should not, I think, on that ground alone, lean too heavily against a construction that produces an intestacy; and certainly cannot in order to avoid that result, misconstrue the language of the instrument. I may perhaps also add, that in these matters naturally the Court of Appeal may have to take a rather stricter view than a judge of the first instance."

A further point to make is that the notion that a will is intended to comprehend all the deceased's property might be less persuasive with reference to property acquired after the date of the execution of the will and which thus could not have been within the contemplation of the testator at that time.[54]

THE STATUTORY MODIFICATIONS

Section 49(1) of the 1925 Act, which has been set out above, expressly renders the distribution of intestacy subject to three modifications. First, paragraph (*aa*), which was added by the Intestates' Estates Act 1952,[55] requires a spouse to account for testamentary benefits against the fixed net sum. Secondly, paragraph (*b*) states that: "the personal representative shall, subject to his rights and powers for the purposes of administration, be a trustee for the persons entitled under this part of this Act in respect of the part of the estate not expressly disposed of unless it appears by the will that the personal representative is intended to take such part beneficially." This provision speaks for itself, and indeed hardly needs to be expressly stated.

The third modification included in section 49(1) in paragraph (*a*) relates to the requirements of issue to account for testamentary benefits and must be discussed more fully.

Duty of spouse to account in a partial intestacy

Husband or wife

There never has been any duty on spouses to account for *inter vivos* benefits on intestacy, whether total or partial. The considerations relating to advancements which underlie section 47(1)(iii) have no relevance to the spouse.[56] Likewise, under the legislation originally

[54] *Re Methuen and Blore's Contract* (1881) 16 Ch.D. 696 at p. 699.

[55] s.3(2), with effect from January 1, 1953.

[56] Since the spouse takes singly and not as a member of a class there can be no considerations of "equality of shares." It has been said that the object of the section is to produce "fair results", *per* Megarry V.-C. in *Re Osoba (decd.)* [1978] 2 All E.R. 1099 at p. 1102.

enacted in 1925 the spouse had no duty to account for testamentary benefits in a partial intestacy but such a requirement was introduced by the Intestates' Estates Act 1952. This change was thought to be necessary because of the greatly increased provision for the spouse by way of the statutory legacy and it will be noticed that the duty to account is only against the entitlement to the fixed net sum. Section 3(2) of the Intestates' Estates Act 1952 accordingly added a new subsection (*aa*) to section 49(1) which applies in the case of deaths on or after January 1, 1953:

> "where the deceased leaves a husband or wife who acquires any beneficial interests under the will of the deceased (other than personal chattels specifically bequeathed) the references in this Part of this Act to the fixed net sum payable to a surviving husband or wife, and to interest on that sum, shall be taken as references to the said sum diminished by the value at the date of death of the said beneficial interests, and to interest on that sum as so diminished, and, accordingly, where the said value exceeds the said sum, this part of this Act shall have effect as if references to the said sum, and interest thereon, were omitted."

Various points need to be considered under this provision and it is convenient to take them in the order in which they arise in the section. The spouse accounts for "any beneficial interests under the will" and this obviously embraces any form of bequest or devise or share of residue. It does not cover, for example, *inter vivos* gifts, nominations, *donationes mortis causa* or property acquired by virtue of *jus accrescendi* applicable to joint property. It will include, however, life and other forms of limited interest as well as absolute or outright gifts.[57]

The references in section 49(1)(*aa*) to "beneficial interests" and to "property" are wide enough to include a beneficial interest in property abroad as well as property in England. Thus in *Re Osoba (decd.)*[58] the testator who was domiciled in Nigeria made a specific bequest of the rents of leasehold property in Nigeria to his wife and disposed of his residuary estate, which included a house in London, to his wife on trust. In fact the court adopted a construction which avoided a partial intestacy arising but the court commented *obiter* that, if the residuary estate had been undisposed of, the duty to account in the partial intestacy would have included the testamentary benefits in the Nigerian houses.

Finally, by virtue of section 46(3)[59] the personal representative can employ a duly qualified valuer in any case where that is necessary to

[57] See *Re Bowen-Buscarlet* [1972] 1 Ch. 463. Likewise in s.49(1)(*a*).
[58] *Osoba* v. *Osoba* [1978] 1 W.L.R. 791, reversed in part at [1979] 1 W.L.R. 247.
[59] Added by the 1952 Act and specifically limited to s.49(1)(*aa*).

value the spouse's beneficial interest under the will or, presumably, to value the property undisposed of.

"Other than personal chattels"

The spouse does not have to account for the value of the personal chattels if these are specifically bequeathed to her. This provision would cover the case where the will makes such a specific bequest[60] but would not seem to cover a case where the spouse is entitled to the personal chattels as part of the residue. Presumably, if some items which would fall within the definition of personal chattels in section 55(1)(x) are specifically bequeathed to the spouse, and others elsewhere, the spouse would not have to account. The position is less clear but, it is suggested, similar if the spouse acquires the chattels under a bequest of "the contents of my house" or "such of my personal effects as she might choose."

In many cases the personal chattels will be of little value and would in any event be extremely difficult to value, which is perhaps the explanation for the exception, but this is not necessarily so. For example, the collection of clocks in *Re Crispin's Will Trusts*[61] was of considerable value and in such a case the exclusion of a duty to account is of importance to the spouse.

Fixed net sum

The duty to account is only against the fixed net sum and does not affect any other entitlement of the spouse on intestacy.[62] It is, therefore, only where an entitlement to the fixed net sum arises, *i.e.* where there is a spouse and also one or more of the following, namely issue, parent, brother or sister of the whole blood or issue thereof, that the spouse will have to account.[63] If there are none of these specified relatives, the spouse will be absolutely entitled to the whole intestate estate.

An example will illustrate how section 49(1)(*aa*) will affect the entitlement. Suppose that an estate includes £125,000 to be distributed on a partial intestacy and that the spouse has received testamentary benefits valued at £100,000. Suppose also that the persons entitled to share in the partial intestacy are the spouse and a brother. The prima facie entitlement under section 46 is that the spouse takes a statutory legacy of £85,000 and one-half of the residue absolutely, and the other half goes to the brother. Thus, if there were no duty to account, the spouse would take a total of £205,000 (£100,000+£85,000+£20,000) and the brother would receive

[60] Bequest to spouse of "all my personal chattels as defined in s.55(1)(xi) of the A.E.A. 1925," as in *Re Crispin's Will Trusts, supra.*

[61] [1975] Ch. 245, see discussed *ante.*

[62] s.49(1)(*aa*).

[63] s.46(1).

£20,000. The effect of section 49(1)(*aa*) is that the testamentary benefits will eliminate the spouse's entitlement to the statutory legacy[64] but not affect the other entitlements. Thus the spouse will receive one-half of the intestate estate (£62,500) and the brother the other half. In this case the spouse will have received a total of £162,500 (£100,000+£62,500) and the brother £62,500.

If the testamentary benefits had been £50,000 but the facts were otherwise the same, the figures would be as follows. If there were no duty to account, the spouse would receive £155,000 (£50,000+ £85,000+£20,000) and the brother would receive £20,000. Applying section 49(1)(*aa*), the spouse would receive £50,000+£35,000 (*i.e.* £85,000 less £50,000)+£45,000 (*i.e.* half the residue), a total of £130,000. The brother would receive £45,000. It will thus be seen that the effect of requiring the spouse to account is to reduce the entitlement to the statutory legacy (to the advantage of the other relatives entitled) but not to affect the spouse's other entitlements on intestacy.

If instead of a brother in the above example there had been a surviving child, the figures would be as follows. The spouse would receive £50,000 (testamentary benefits), no statutory legacy (£50,000 exceeds £40,000) and the residuary estate would be held as to one-half, *i.e.* £62,500, in trust for the spouse for life with remainder to the issue and as to the other half on statutory trusts for the issue. If section 49(1)(*aa*) had not been enacted, the spouse would take £50,000 plus £40,000, and the residuary estate would have been reduced to £85,000.

Disclaimer

In some circumstances there can be fiscal advantages in disclaiming testate or intestate benefits and this is considered in a subsequent chapter.[65] Because the testamentary benefits will operate to diminish the statutory legacy, it is possible to envisage situations where it would be advantageous for a spouse to disclaim a benefit under a will and rely on her intestate entitlement. One such case is where the residuary estate is bequeathed to a spouse for life with no effective disposition of the remainder interest. Suppose that the residuary estate is worth £100,000, that a 50-year-old widow is given a life interest therein and that the only surviving relative is a brother. As the will stands there is an immediately apparent partial intestacy,

[64] ". . . where the said value exceeds the said sum, this Part of this Act shall have effect as if references to the said sum and interest thereon were omitted": s.49(1)(*aa*).

[65] See Chap. 7 on the fiscal consequences, and Chap. 17 on disclaimer generally; see also *Re Scott* [1975] 2 All E.R. 1033; *Re Harker's Will Trusts*, [1969] 1 W.L.R. 1124; *Re Kebty-Fletcher's Will Trusts* [1967] 3 All E.R. 1076; *Re Davies* [1957] 3 All E.R. 52; *Re Taylor* [1957] 1 W.L.R. 1043, and discussion *post*, as to the effect of a disclaimer on intestate distribution.

analogous to the situation in *Re Bowen-Buscarlet's Will Trusts,*[66] and on the authority of that case the estate will stand charged with the immediate payment of the statutory legacy. However, the value of the life interest will have to be brought into account so that in effect the spouse will get little other than the testamentary life interest.[67] On the other hand, if she disclaims the life interest, the whole £100,000 becomes immediately distributable on intestacy (assuming there is no effective disposition of the remainder) and the spouse becomes entitled absolutely to £85,000 (assuming no other testamentary benefits) plus one-half of the remainder.[68] This is clearly advantageous to the spouse.

If instead of a brother in the above example there had been a surviving child, different considerations come into play. Although the amount of the statutory legacy is smaller, the spouse will be entitled in addition to a life interest in one-half of the residuary estate and on intestacy the spouse has the statutory right in section 47A to demand capitalisation of that life interest.[69] There is no corresponding right to capitalise a testamentary life interest and therefore it can be advantageous for a spouse to disclaim a testamentary life interest (assuming that there is no gift in remainder) and in effect exchange it for an intestacy life interest which can be converted into an absolute interest.[70] One obvious advantage of taking an absolute interest on intestacy is that the spouse can then take advantage of the right to demand appropriation of the matrimonial home in satisfaction of that absolute entitlement.[71]

The duty of issue to account in a partial intestacy

Introduction

The Statute of Distribution 1670 did not apply to partial intestacies[72] and so there was no duty to account for *inter vivos* or testamentary benefits. This was no doubt regarded as anomalous in

[66] [1972] Ch. 463, discussed *ante* p. 281.

[67] If the life interest is valued at £80,000 then she will get the rest of the statutory legacy, *i.e.* £5,000 plus one-half of the remainder, *i.e.* £7,500. A total of £12,500 absolutely plus a life interest valued at £80,000.

[68] *i.e.* £7,500, giving a total of £92,500, all absolutely.

[69] 1925 Act, s.47A as amended by 1952 Act; see *ante* p. 212.

[70] Thus on the figures above the spouse would as the will stands be entitled only to life interests under the will and the intestacy; the statutory legacy will be eliminated by the value of the testamentary life interest. If she disclaims then she will be entitled to the statutory legacy of £40,000 absolutely, plus a life interest in one-half of the residue, *i.e.* £30,000, which can be converted to a sum of £24,000 (using a multiplier of 0.800). A total of £64,000 absolutely.

[71] See *post*—There is a power, but not a right, to appropriate in cases of testate succession, 1925 Act, s.41.

[72] See *e.g.* Harman J. in *Re Young, Young* v. *Young* [1951] 1 Ch. 185 at p. 188. The distribution was however followed by analogy to govern undisposed of property in a partial intestacy.

1925 and the legislation introduced a limited duty to account under section 49(1)(*a*). It is debatable whether this was either necessary or desirable,[73] and it is interesting to note that many Commonwealth countries have abandoned the idea.[74] However, the basic justification for the duty to account remains valid, namely that it fulfils the intestate's presumed intention that his children should share in his estate equally. It is this notion which underlies the hotchpot provisions in section 49(1)(*a*) since the unforeseen effects of rules of law invalidating testamentary dispositions can result in great inequality between a class of children. Consider the simple case where the residue is bequeathed equally between named children and the spouse of one child witnesses the will.[75] That share will fail and, in the absence of other provisions, will fall to be divided equally between the children, but the other children will also take their testamentary shares in full. The hotchpot provisions in section 49(1)(*a*) are intended to remedy such cases of inequality by requiring the other children to bring their testamentary shares into account. Thus in the circumstances described above the failed share will wholly accrue to the excluded child and equality between the children will be achieved.

The presumed intention to benefit children equally was never applied to other classes of relative so that there never has been any statutory requirement for brothers or sisters or nephews or nieces to account.

Section 47(1)(iii) on partial intestacy

There seems to be no doubt that section 47(1)(iii) applies to impose a duty to account for *inter vivos* advances to a *child* where the child (or his issue) are entitled under a partial intestacy. This requirement will, in appropriate cases, be additional and not alternative to the duty to account for testamentary benefits under section 49(1)(*a*). The reasons for this are twofold. First, section 47(1)(iii) refers throughout to "the

[73] See Danckwerts J. in *Re Morton* [1956] 1 Ch. 644 at p. 647. See also Harman J. in *Re Young, Young* v. *Young*, *supra*.

[74] Reference can be made to Australian and New Zealand legislation which illustrates the whole range of possible approaches. (See generally Hardingham, Neave and Ford, *Wills and Intestacy*, Chap. 29). New South Wales and Western Australia (Wills Probate and Administration Act 1898 (N.S.W.) and Administration Act 1903–1976, (W.A.)), retain the old pre-1925 rules that previously applied in England, and thus require no accounting at all in a partial intestacy. In Queensland (Succession Act, 1981, s.38) and New Zealand (Administration Act 1969, s.79(2)), only the spouse need account against the statutory legacy. Victoria (Administration and Probate Act 1958, s.53(a)) and Tasmania (Administration and Probate Act 1935, ss.44(4) and 47(a)), follow the English 1925 legislation. In the Australian Capital Territory (Administration and Probate Ordinance, 1929, s.49D) and in the Northern Territory (Administration and Probate Ordinance, 1969, s.70), the spouse, children, brothers and sisters and uncles and aunts are obliged to account, and in South Australia (Administration and Probate Act 1919–1975, s.72K(1)(b)), any intestate successor must account for the value of a benefit received by him under the intestate's will.

[75] And thereby, of course, preclude that child from taking his share under the will, Wills Act 1837, s.15.

intestate" and by section 55(1)(vi) the word includes a person who leaves a will but dies intestate as to some beneficial interest in his real or personal estate. Secondly, section 49(1) expressly states that "... this Part of this Act [*which includes section 47(1)(iii)*] shall have effect as respects the part of his property not so disposed of subject to the provisions contained in the will and subject to the following modifications:–" There is nothing in the succeeding provisions inconsistent with the application of section 47(1)(iii).[76]

The first point to ascertain on a partial intestacy is whether there have been any *inter vivos* dispositions to a child which have to be accounted for against the share of that child. This involves identical considerations as in cases of total intestacies save only the possibility of a contrary intention being expressed in the will.[77] Without wishing to repeat the earlier discussion four points can be emphasised on the application of section 47(1)(iii) to cases of partial intestacy. First, only advances to *children* need to be regarded[78]; secondly, issue taking by representation must account for advances to their parent (or ancestor) in respect of the share which they take[79]; thirdly, the duty to account is only required for the benefit of the other children or issue and not for the benefit of *e.g.* a spouse.[80] Finally, whereas under section 49(1)(*a*) the duty to account is for "any beneficial interests acquired by any issue of the deceased under the will," section 47(1)(iii) is limited to advancements.

Accounting for testamentary benefits

Section 49(1)(*a*) was intended to ensure that any benefits taken by issue under the will should be brought into account against their entitlement under a partial intestacy. The section is, however, very poorly drafted and its precise scope and effect are far from clear.[81] The section provides:

> "The requirements of section 47 of this Act as to bringing property into account shall apply to any beneficial interests acquired by any issue of the deceased under the will of the deceased, but not to beneficial interests so acquired by any other persons."

Danckwerts J. has commented in *Re Morton*[82]:

[76] The wording of s.49(1)(*a*) essentially expresses an additional, and not an alternative requirement.

[77] There seems to be nothing in s.47(1)(iii) which requires the contrary intention to be expressed *inter vivos*, although by the nature of the provision it will usually be so if it appears at all.

[78] Whereas *issue* must account for testamentary benefits under s.49(1)(*a*).

[79] Ditto under s.49(1)(*a*).

[80] Ditto under s.49(1)(*a*).

[81] See Ryder, (1973) 26 C.L.P. 208 for a compelling analysis of the section and the cases decided thereon.

[82] [1956] Ch. 644 at p. 647.

"I think section 49(1)(*a*) is as bad a piece of draftsmanship as one could conceive, in many respects. It says 'the requirements.' What requirements? I am told the requirements are to be found in section 47(1)(iii). There one finds certain provisions which are not by themselves particularly apt for application to something else."[83]

The reason for this is that section 47(1)(iii) is a straightforward provision under which, against the stirpital share of any child, there is to be brought into account any money paid by way of advancement or on the marriage of the child or settled for the benefit of the child. Only advancements to children are included although, if by reason of the death of such a child his issue are entitled under the statutory trust to that share, the issue must account for advancements to the child but need not account for advancements to them.

Section 49(1)(*a*) is in express terms an annex to section 47(1)(iii) and seeks to apply that section to cases of partial intestacy.[84] Thus it might be thought that the duty to account would be the same save only for a reference to beneficial interests acquired under the will instead of *inter vivos* gifts by way of advancement. However, as Pennycuick J. commented in *Re Grover*,[85] it is impossible so to read section 49(1)(*a*) without a hopeless contortion of language since section 49(1)(*a*) demands that *issue* should account for testamentary benefits and not simply children.[86] Therein lies the major difficulty with the section

[83] What are to be regarded as "the requirements" of that subsection? Is it simply the basic requirement to account or are all the subsidiary rules in s.47(1)(iii) also incorporated? These latter include the following phrases: "by way of advancement or on the marriage of the child"; "subject to any contrary intention expressed or appearing from the circumstances in the case"; "in or towards satisfaction"; "the value to be reckoned as at the death of the intestate . . . " etc. There is no guidance in the section but at first sight only the basic process of accounting, and not these rules, would seem to be included. This is because the sections are clearly incompatible in major respects—"child" in s.47(1)(iii), "issue" in s.49(1)(*a*), and the restriction in s.47(1)(iii) to "by way of advancement or on the marriage of the child" would clearly seem to be inappropriate to testamentary benefits. Further the phrase "the requirements of the personal representatives" is used in s.47(1)(iii) in a general rather than a particular sense, and perhaps "the requirements" in s.49(1)(*a*) should be considered likewise. There is also the point that s.49(1) states that the section is "subject to the provisions contained in the will" and so the "contrary intention" point in s.47(1)(iii) is not needed. However, on the other hand s.49(1)(*a*) contains no provisions relating to valuation and, at first sight, it would seem to be convenient to incorporate the rule in s.47(1)(iii) to cover this point.

[84] *Per* Pennycuick J. in *Re Grover's Will Trusts* [1971] Ch. 168 at p. 173.

[85] *Supra*, at p. 173.

[86] It is submitted that the legislature probably did not intend any fundamental inconsistency and that the sections could, with more sympathetic interpretation have been reconciled. Under s.47(1)(iii) only advancements to children have to be brought into account but the duty to so account is not confined to children but extends also to issue taking by representation; they do not account for their own benefits, they account for their parent's benefit. It is submitted that it is possible that the legislation intended a similar result in cases of partial intestacy, namely, children account for

since it has been decided that "issue" in section 49(1)(*a*) means children or remoter issue and that issue must account not only for any *inter vivos* advancements received by their parent or ancestor (being a child of the deceased) but also for any benefits which they have received under the will, although they need not account for any *inter vivos* benefits that they have received. This can lead to obvious anomalies depending on whether a grandchild is benefited under the will or *inter vivos*. Suppose, for example, that a sum of £12,000 is distributable on a partial intestacy amongst two children, A and B, and D the surviving child of a deceased child, C. Suppose also that A, C and D have been advanced £3,000 each *inter vivos* and that D has been bequeathed a legacy of £3,000. The benefits given to A and C *inter vivos* must be brought into account and so must the testamentary benefit given to D but not the gift to D *inter vivos*. This results in a distribution of £4,000 to A, £7,000 to B and £1,000 to D.

Closer analysis of section 49(1)(*a*) reveals other problems which arise where one member of the class of children has predeceased the intestate leaving issue surviving him who take their parent's share. Suppose that other children also survive and that one of the grandchildren taking by representation has benefited under the will. Prima facie the undisposed of property is divided into shares according to the number of branches of the family. The benefited grandchild must account "in accordance with the requirements of section 47" and, when that section is referred to, it is seen that it provides that the accounting is against "the share of that child," *i.e.* not the share of the grandchild but the share of the *child*. Therefore, on a strict interpretation the benefited grandchild will bring his benefit into account not against his own share but against his parent's share, which will reduce the entitlement of the whole class of grandchildren equally to the advantage of the benefited grandchild and to the prejudice of the others. Presumably, a section based on the desire to achieve equality cannot have been intended to have this result and so the wording of the section must be modified to the effect that the

their own testamentary benefits and issue taking by representation account for their parent's testamentary benefits. Issue in fact will only take if their parents have predeceased the intestate, but (old) s.33 of the Wills Act 1837, will frequently save such gifts from lapse, thus making the point viable. On this interpretation issue would not account for their own testamentary benefits. However, it is quite clear from the cases, *Re Young* [1951] Ch. 185, 190; *Re Morton* [1956] Ch. 644, 648; *Re Grover's Will Trusts* [1971] Ch. 168, see Ryder, (1973) 26 C.L.P. 208 at p. 210, that this construction is not possible.

grandchild accounts against his own share and not against his parent's share.

Successive interests

The problem relating to the construction of section 49(1)(*a*) which has most exercised the courts is raised by successive interests to a child and his issue.[87] The point is simply put: suppose a testator provides that a fund shall be enjoyed by a child for life with remainder to his issue and leaves other property undisposed of. The child, having survived, is entitled to share in the partial intestacy and having been benefited under the will must account. But does he account merely for what *he* has received, *i.e.* for an actuarial valuation of the life interest? Or, since "issue" must account under section 49(1)(*a*), does he account for his own and his issue's interest, *i.e.* the whole capital value of the fund? It is submitted that, if one has regard merely to the intent of the sections, it would be clear that the former solution is correct. The child is benefited under the will and the child accounts for that benefit against the share to which he would otherwise be entitled under the intestacy. Pennycuick J. thought likewise in *Re Grover's Will Trusts.*[88]

> "A possible construction . . . which I confess appeals to me, was that it must be treated on some *reddendo singula singulis* principle with the consequence that any descendant of the testator who acquires a beneficial interest under his will brings that interest, and nothing more, into account against his share under the partial intestacy. So, for instance, a child of the testator would bring into account any beneficial interest acquired by that child under the will, but nothing more, and similarly a grandchild of the testator would bring into account any beneficial interest taken by that grandchild. It is accepted, I think, on all hands that that is so as regards a grandchild."[89]

However, Pennycuick J. was forced in *Re Grover*,[90] to an alternative construction by previous decisions. These dictated that in such cases the child accounts not only for his own interest but *per stirpes* for the collective interests taken by himself and his issue. In a sentence, any member of a family belonging to a certain branch must bring in everything that has been taken or acquired under the will by that

[87] See the cases referred to in n. 86.

[88] [1971] Ch. 168 at p. 174.

[89] The concluding reference to a grandchild is obscure, does it mean that the *per capita* construction would apply where the testamentary benefit is to a grandchild for life, remainder to his issue?—or simply that the grandchild only accounts for his own benefit when the limitation is to a child for life remainder to his issue?; see Ryder (1973) 26 C.L.P. 208 at pp. 215, 216.

[90] *Supra.*

branch.[91] The decisions which adopt this construction must now be considered.

The first of the cases is *Re Young, Young* v. *Young*,[92] where a testator directed his trustee to hold his residuary estate, after the death of his widow, as to five-sevenths in trust for his children in equal shares. As to one of the remaining sevenths he directed that it was to be held at the discretion of the trustees to pay or apply the income or capital for the maintenance and support of one of his children, X, or any child or children of his during his life, and after his death to distribute any unapplied surplus between X's children. The testator died intestate as respects the remaining one seventh share. The question arose as to what share X's personal representatives (X now being dead) had to bring into account against his entitlement on the partial intestacy. The choice lay between saying that, since X was now dead, he in fact took nothing personally for which he should account, or that X and his children owned the total interest in the one-seventh share and must account for its capital value. The latter view was preferred, Harman J. stating[93]:

> "It seems to me that in the words 'any beneficial interests acquired by any issue of the deceased,' 'issue' must mean children or remoter issue. So it seems to me that what is to be brought into account is the beneficial interest which the issue acquired. Who are the issue in question? The father and children, the two generations between them, are the issue, and it seems to me, therefore, that anything that the father and children together acquired under the will is a beneficial interest acquired by the issue."[94]

The next case to consider is *Re Morton*[95] where the same point arose with reference to the entitlement to an undisposed of share of residue. One-half of the residuary estate was held in trust for a daughter for life with remainder to her children in equal shares and the other half for a

[91] *Per* Harman J. in *Re Young* [1951] Ch. 185 at p. 189. Note that in so far as the case was decided before the enactment of the 1952 Intestates Estates Act, the failure of that Act to modify the construction could be regarded as being tacit legislative approval for the interpretation.

[92] *Supra.* The power to distribute the income, in the event of some income not being applied during the father's lifetime, to other members of the family, was disregarded since it never arose.

[93] *Supra*, at p. 190.

[94] Harman J. was no doubt influenced by the wording of s.49(1)(*a*) "any beneficial interests acquired by any issue of the deceased"; this is in contrast with the wording in s.47(1)(iii) which refers to "any life or less interest," thus it was natural to bring into account the capital of the fund, "not *quoad* capital in the same sense as a fund settled for the benefit of a child is brought in under section 47, but *quoad* the sum of the beneficial interests in the fund," *per* Pennycuick J. in *Re Grover's Will Trusts* see *post.* Ryder doubts whether *Re Young* is in fact correctly decided, (1973) 26 C.L.P. 208, 220–222.

[95] [1956] Ch. 644.

son for life with a remainder which failed for remoteness and thus fell to be distributed on a partial intestacy. Did the child have to account for the capital value of one-half of the residuary estate or merely for an actuarial valuation of the life interest? It was held that the child should account for the value of the interest actually taken and not the capital value of the settled share. It would appear from the facts that a life interest was the only interest taken by that branch of the family because the remainder interest was void for perpetuity. On that basis the decision is unremarkable and indeed consistent with *Re Young.*[96] Pennycuick J. reconciled the cases as follows in *Re Grover's Will Trusts.*[97]

> "At first sight there appears to be a cleavage of view between Harman J. and Danckwerts J. as to the effect of section 49. If, indeed, there were such a cleavage my duty, I apprehend, would be to put on section 49 such construction as I thought right. But on further analysis, and particularly having regard to the explanation given to me by counsel for the trustee in bankruptcy of the son, of the facts in the two cases, I think that the cleavage is probably more apparent than real. In each case the learned judge held, or Danckwerts J. apparently took it for granted, that the interest to be brought into account by a child of the testator included not only the interest taken by the child himself but the interest taken by any issue of such child. The difference between the two cases is that in *Re Young*[98] the interests of the child and the child's children, disregarding an interest under the protective trust which Harman J. was prepared to disregard, together amounted to the entire interest in the fund. Therefore it was simple and natural to bring the capital of the fund into account not *quoad* capital in the same sense as a fund settled for the benefit of the child is brought in under section 47, but *quoad* the sum of the beneficial interests in the fund.
>
> In *Re Morton*[98] there were other beneficial interests in the fund; so that method could not be adopted and what had to be done was to value severally the beneficial interests. It does not appear from the judgment but I imagine that in the case of the daughter, Edith Harriet Hutton, who had a child who attained 21 years, the capital value of her share would have been brought in as representing their combined beneficial interests. Once it is accepted that in each of those cases the learned judge applied the same basic principle, *i.e.* that the child must bring in his beneficial interest and also the beneficial interest of any of his

[96] *Supra.*
[97] *Supra* at p. 178. Danckwerts J. in *Re Morton, supra,* referred to *Re Young, supra,* in a way which did not indicate that he was dissenting from that decision.
[98] *Supra.*

issue, then I must clearly follow those decisions and apply the same principle in the present case."

However, it can also be appreciated why the cases are often regarded as indicating different approaches. On the one hand, in *Re Young*[99] Harman J. clearly contrasted two approaches to the section and preferred the view that:

"Any member of the family belonging to a certain branch must bring in everything that has been taken or acquired under the will by that branch."

In contrast, Danckwerts J. in *Re Morton*[1] stated the rule in terms which seem more consistent with the alternative view canvassed by Harman J.

"It seems to me, reading section 47 with such application as I can give to it, that the life interests or less interests which are brought in at a valuation, must be brought in at a valuation appropriate to the nature of the interest—and that seems to me to require that the life interest should be valued according to the relevant actuarial considerations; and they cannot be brought in as if they were equivalent to an absolute interest in the capital. To value the interest as being equivalent to a gift of capital in a case where a person takes no more than a life interest seems to me contrary to fairness, common sense and everything else. Accordingly, I so hold."

However, as indicated above the decisions were reconciled in the most recent case where the point was considered, namely *Re Grover's Will Trusts*.[2] The facts were that one moiety of the residuary estate of a testator was settled for the benefit of a son who subsequently died so that it fell to be dealt with on the footing of a partial intestacy. The other moiety was settled for the benefit of the testator's daughter on protective trusts during her life and after her death for all her children who should attain the age of 21 years or previously marry. Apart from the widow's entitlement, who had in fact predeceased the son, the next-of-kin were the deceased son and the daughter and the question arose as to what interests the daughter had to bring into account against her entitlement to the son's moiety. Pennycuick J. held that the daughter must account for the whole of the second moiety, following the approach adopted by *Re Young*[3] and *Re Morton*[4]:

[99] *Supra*, at p. 189, although usually regarded as a statement of principle by Harman J., the quote was in fact made in the context of stating a view or argument on the matter.
[1] *Supra*, at p. 649.
[2] *Supra*.
[3] *Supra*.
[4] *Supra*.

> "Once it is accepted that the daughter and her children have to bring into account interests which together amount to the entire capital of one moiety of the residuary estate, that really is the end of the matter."[5]

However, the judge felt forced to this conclusion by the two previous authorities and, as indicated at the beginning of this section, would have preferred the alternative construction if the matter had been free from authority.[6]

Comment

It has already been submitted that the law is unsatisfactory in the present state of the authorities: the *per capita* construction in cases of successive interests seems preferable to the *per stirpes*. The real problem centres on Harman J.'s dictum "Any member of the family belonging to a certain branch must bring in everything that has been taken or acquired under the will by that branch."[7] This must be limited to the context in which it was stated, *i.e.* to cases where there are successive interests to one branch of a family. Without this restriction it would have absurd consequences. Consider the case where a child receives a share of residue under the will and a further share is undisposed of and passes on intestacy. Suppose also that all the grandchildren, including the two children of the child referred to above, have been given legacies of £5,000 each. The child must clearly account for his share of residue but cannot possibly be intended to account for his children's legacies.[8]

A further problem explored by Professor Ryder[9] is whether a person who takes under the statutory trusts on a partial intestacy must bring into account an interest taken under the will by his parent or ancestor who predeceased the testator. Again it is suggested that the legislation never intended such a result, which is certainly not productive of fairness between the class of grandchildren since (under the old law) the parent's share probably passes to the spouse and not to the issue.

Consider also the situation where the testator creates a testamen-

[5] *Per* Pennycuick J. in *Re Grover, supra*, at p. 178. The daughter in fact had a "protected" life interest but the possiblity of the discretionary trusts coming into effect was ignored by the judge, since no forfeiture had in fact occurred.

[6] See *ante* p. 297.

[7] In *Re Young's Will Trusts* [1951] Ch. 185 at p. 189. Described as "extremely wide" by Pennycuick J. in *Re Grover's Will Trusts* [1971] Ch. 168 at p. 176; see Ryder (1973) 26 C.L.P. 208 at p. 219.

[8] See Ryder *op. cit.* at p. 216.

[9] *Op. cit.* at p. 218. The example is, a testator makes a specific gift to his son A but dies intestate as to the residuary estate. A predeceases the testator leaving a son B who survives the testator. Other children of the testator are living at his death. The gift to A is saved from lapse by (the old) s.33 of the Wills Act 1837, and falls into A's estate. Must B bring the value of this gift into account? Under the new s.33 (as substituted by s.19 of the Administration of Justice Act 1982) the gift would take effect as a gift to the issue and thus might well have to be accounted.

tary trust in favour of his grandchildren at 18, if more than one in equal shares, and at the death there is one infant grandchild but the possibility of more being born. For what, and when, does the grandchild account against a share to which he is also entitled under the partial intestacy? Suppose that the fund is put upon discretionary trusts for the class of grandchildren and immediately after the death the trustee appoints the whole capital to one grandchild. Must he account for nothing, or for the whole fund?

Beneficial interest

Section 49(1)(*a*) applies to "any beneficial interests acquired . . . under the will." This will include absolute and life interests[10] and also a beneficial interest acquired by virtue of the exercise by the will of a general power of appointment (including the statutory power to dispose of entailed interests) but not of a special power of appointment.[11]

Valuation

It has been seen on the authority of *Re Young*[12] and *Re Morton*[13] that, if the child and his issue enjoy the totality of the interests in a settled fund, the capital value of the fund will be brought in but, if they enjoy only limited interests, those interests will be valued on an actuarial basis. The question remains as to when those interests should be valued. Section 47(1)(iii) states clearly that the interest ". . . shall be brought into account at a valuation (the value to be reckoned as at the death of the intestate)" and, in so far as section 49(1)(*a*) incorporates this subsection, it can clearly be argued that the same rule applies to the testamentary benefits. However, as Pennycuick J. commented in *Re Grover*,[14] all sorts of difficulties arise in taking the date of death for the valuation when there is a partial intestacy and the various interests on intestacy do not fall into possession until long after the death of the testator. Such will be the case with so-called contingent partial intestacies[15] and in such cases it may be necessary ". . . in applying section 49, to depart from the words in brackets in section 47."[16] Whichever rule is taken will cause practical problems but fewer perhaps when the date of death is adopted, which will at least avoid problems of changes of investment.

Further, although it is often not easy to value property retrospectively, there will at least be the probate valuation to provide a basis.

[10] *Re Young, Young* v. *Young* [1951] 1 Ch. 185; *Re Morton (decd.) Morton* v. *Morton* [1956] 1 Ch. 644.
[11] s.49(2).
[12] [1951] Ch. 185.
[13] [1956] Ch. 644, as applied in *Re Grover's Will Trusts* [1971] Ch. 168.
[14] *Ibid.* at p. 178.
[15] See *ibid.*
[16] *Per* Pennycuick J. *supra.*

Judges will no doubt hope to avoid such problems, as Pennycuick J. was able to do in *Re Grover*, since in that case, whatever date was taken, he had to compare like with like, *i.e.* the failure of one moiety of residue to be distributed between two children, one of whom took the other moiety.

Finally, it can be noted that, although there are no rules relating to valuation in section 49(1)(*a*), the 1952 Act added subsection (3) to section 49 to the following effect: "For the purpose of paragraph (*aa*) in the foregoing provisions of this section the personal representative shall employ a duly qualified valuer in any case where such employment may be necessary." This provision is, of course, limited to accounting by a spouse but it is strange that, if it was thought necessary in that context, an analogous provision was not thought necessary where issue account.

Subject to the provisions contained in the will

Section 49(1)(*aa*) is expressed mandatorily, "... shall be taken...," "... shall have effect...," but must presumably be qualified by the introductory wording of section 49(1) which states that the application of the Act is "... subject to the provisions contained in the will and subject to the following modifications."[17] Since few testators will foresee and provide expressly for the possibility of a partial intestacy, there is unlikely to be any provision of the will exempting the issue from the duty to account. It is possible that testamentary provisions might have that effect by implication where, for instance, there is an intention appearing from the will to benefit children unequally, such as where the sons are to receive twice the shares of the daughters or son A is given a substantial legacy and son B a nominal legacy.[18]

[17] Although s.49(1)(*a*) itself is mandatory.

[18] Another problem is whether an *inter vivos* statement within s.47(1)(iii) would suffice to exclude the requirement to account under s.49(1)(*a*), or whether *only* the provisions of the will are relevant. This depends upon whether the contrary intention point is regarded as "a requirement of s.47" and thus incorporated into s.49(1)(*a*).

Part Four

MATTERS AFFECTING ENTITLEMENT

CHAPTER 16

CONFLICT OF LAWS

INTRODUCTION

Issues of private international law can arise in the law of intestate succession where the deceased had, or may have had, a foreign domicile or where he or she owned foreign assets. In such cases there may be a conflict or a choice of law available varying with the jurisdiction adopted. There are established rules to determine the fundamental questions, namely according to what law should the intestate beneficiaries be identified and in what proportions should the estate be distributed amongst them. They will be considered shortly in this Chapter.[1] The Crown's entitlement to *bona vacantia* where the deceased had a foreign domicile can conveniently also be discussed under this heading. Other private international law questions relating to succession on intestacy concern the entitlement of the spouse and issue where the marriage is polygamous and these too will be considered.

THE CHOICE OF LAW

Movables and immovables

The rules of private international law which determine the choice of law governing the entitlement on intestacy depend on the distinction between movable and immovable property,[2] the former being governed by the law of the domicile and the latter being subject to the *lex situs*.[3] The distinction is crucial but a detailed examination is beyond the scope of this work. A brief discussion referring to one or two relevant cases on intestate succession can, however, be included.

Movables are literally things which can be moved[4] and so would include most property classified for other purposes in English law as personal property. Conversely, immovables would include real property. The concept of movability is not entirely satisfactory, however, since it applies literally only to tangible property and intangible property, such as choses in action which are classified as

[1] Full discussions are available in the specialist texts: Dicey and Morris. *The Conflict of Laws*, 10th ed., (1980) Chap. 23; Cheshire and North, *Private International Law*, 10th ed. (1979). See also A. E. Gotlieb, 26 I.C.L.Q. 734 at pp. 774; 786–798.

[2] See the specialist texts referred to above.

[3] See *post*.

[4] Thus in *Re Hoyles* [1911] 1 Ch. 179, Cozens-Hardy M.R. at p. 183 "Immovable property includes all rights over things which cannot be moved, whatever be the nature of such rights or interests."

movables, would not be covered.[5] Nor must it be thought that the dichotomy corresponds exactly to the distinction familiar in other areas of English law between personalty and realty. Leasehold interests in land in England, for example, are regarded as immovables and so are interests under unexecuted trusts for sale. This last point was the subject of some controversy, so far as intestate succession was concerned, until resolved by Russell J. in *Re Berchtold*[6] to the effect that when a person domiciled in a foreign country dies intestate having an interest in the proceeds of sale of English freeholds which are subject to a trust for sale, but not yet sold, the interest is an immovable and the succession thereto is governed by the *lex situs.* That decision was distinguished in *Re Cutcliffe's Will Trust*[7] which concerned the classification of the proceeds of sale of real estate subject to the Settled Land Acts 1882–1887 where there was a specific statutory provision[8] to the effect that the investments in such cases should for all purposes of devolution be considered as land. The court considered in view of this provision that the stock devolved as an an immovable.

There is some inconsistency between these decisions. Both cases proceeded on the initial basic principle that the question whether particular property is a movable or an immovable is decided according to the *lex situs.*[9] On that basis, if the English doctrine of conversion operates to change realty to personalty, prima facie *Re Berchtold,* is wrongly decided. Russell J. avoided that conclusion as follows[10]:

> "Thus the interest of the taker is personal estate. But this equitable doctrine of conversion only arises and comes into play where the question for consideration arises as between real estate and personal estate. It has no relation to the question whether property is movable or immovable. The doctrine of conversion is that real estate is treated as personal estate, or personal estate is treated as real estate; not that immovables are turned into movables, or movables into immovables."

However, in *Re Cutcliffe's Will Trusts*[11] the provisions of a statute stating that capital money was to be considered as land was applied so that the stock, into which the money had been invested, devolved as

[5] See Dicey and Morris *op. cit.*, p. 524.

[6] [1923] 1 Ch. 192. See also *Re Burke* [1928] 1 D.L.R. 318, real property in Saskatchewan although subject to an agreement for sale was an immovable and distribution on the death intestate of the owner domiciled out of the jurisdiction was therefore governed by the law of Saskatchewan.

[7] [1940] 1 Ch. 565.

[8] 1882 Act, s.22(5), now S.L.A. 1925, s.75(5).

[9] See Russell J. in *In Re Berchtold, supra* at p. 199; Morton J. in *Re Cutcliffe's Will Trusts, supra,* at p. 571.

[10] *Supra* at p. 206.

[11] *Supra.*

an immovable even though Russell J.'s reasoning above could have been applied. The cases are distinguishable and *Re Berchtold*[12] can strictly be confined to the effect of the doctrine of conversion with the *Re Cutcliffe*[13] approach to be preferred on the general question.

Movables

General rule

It is settled law that intestate succession to movables is governed by the law of the deceased's last domicile. The rule was stated by Jenkins L.J. in *In the Estate of Maldonado (decd.)*[14]:

> "The general rule to be applied in a case such as this is summed up in the maxim *mobilia sequuntur personam* and is thus stated in *Dicey's Conflict of Laws*: Rule 177. The distribution of the distributable residue of the movables of the deceased is (in general) governed by the law of the deceased's domicile (*lex domicilii*) at the time of his death."[15]

A further statement of the general principle is that of Kekewich J. in *Re Barnett's Trusts*[16] as follows:

> "When you come to the distribution of the property of the deceased, then you must follow the law of the domicile of the deceased, whether it is according to some statute, or what we call the common law, whether it is among relations, because they claim in that character, or among persons entitled under a will: in whatever aspect it is looked at, the distribution must follow the law of the domicile."

Immovables

General rule

Intestate succession to immovables is governed by the *lex situs* or *lex loci* and not by the law of the domicile. Kay J. stated the rule quite

[12] *Supra*, compare *Re Midleton's Settlement* [1947] 1 Ch. 583.
[13] *Supra*.
[14] *State of Spain* v. *Treasury Solicitor* [1954] P. 223 at p. 245, the case concerned the Crown's entitlement to *bona vacantia* and is discussed *post*, p. 313. The rule has been established for over 200 years, see Barnard J. in *Maldonado, supra*, at p. 266; *Pipon* v. *Pipon* (1744) Amb. 25; *Duncan* v. *Lawson* (1889) 41 Ch.D. 394; *Freke* v. *Lord Carbery* (1873) L.R. 16 Eq. 461 at p. 466; *Balfour* v. *Scott* (1793) 6 Bro.C.C. 550; *Ewing* v. *Orr Ewing* (1885) 10 App.Cas. 502; *Re Ralston* [1906] V.L.R. 689 at p. 701. *Re Collens (decd.), Royal Bank of Canada (London) Ltd.* v. *Keogh* [1986] 1 All E.R. 611.
[15] Reference must be made to specialist texts for the rules governing domicile.
[16] [1902] 1 Ch. 847 at pp. 856, 857. However if the law of the domicile dictates that successions are governed by the national law of the deceased, this will govern the succession. Thus in *Re O'Keefe Poingdestre* v. *Sherman* [1940] 1 Ch. 124 a citizen of Eire died domiciled in Italy which by national law directed the distribution to be according to the law of the domicile of origin, *i.e.* Eire.

clearly in *Duncan* v. *Lawson*[17]:

> "But the *lex loci* governs the devolution of *inmobilia* in case of intestacy, just as it does of freehold property. There is no possibility of doubt that, if the Scotch heir and the English heir were different persons, the English heir and not the Scotch heir would take the undisposed of freeholds in England.... At this stage of the proceedings the *lex loci* must determine, independently of the testator's domicile, to whom such distribution must be made."

The basic reason for this rule has been stated to be "that immovable property, that is land or things appurtenant to land, forms part of the actual territory controlled by the law of the place, and by international comity and for manifest convenience is deemed to be, for the purposes of descent and inheritance, regulated by the *lex loci*."[18]

A modern application of the rule is provided by *Re Osoba (decd.)*[19] where a testator domiciled in Nigeria died leaving leasehold property in Nigeria and a freehold house in London. It was common ground that the English house devolved according to English law as being the *lex situs*.[20] Likewise in *Re Collens (decd.)*[21] it was common ground between counsel that the succession to the English immovable property on the intestacy of the deceased was regulated by the domestic English law of intestacy.

Double entitlement

Statutory Legacy

The dichotomy gives rise to an anomaly because there appears to be no provision requiring the spouse or children to account, against intestate benefits under one jurisdiction, for intestate benefits acquired under another jurisdiction. Thus the likelihood is that, where land is situated in a country other than the place of domicile, there is the possibility of a double entitlement. This was indeed the result in *Re Rea*[22] where a man died intestate domiciled in Ireland leaving real and personal property in Ireland and real estate in Victoria. It was decided that the widow was entitled to two statutory legacies, one provided by the Irish law and one provided by the Victorian statute, payable out of the proceeds of sale of the real property. As the judge commented[23]:

[17] (1889) 41 Ch.D. 394 at p. 397, (leaseholds in England of a person domiciled in Scotland devolved according to English law) referring to *Freke* v. *Lord Carbery* (1873) L.R. 16 Eq. 461 at p. 466 and *In the Goods of Gentili* (1875) I.R. 9 Eq. 541. See also *Balfour* v. *Scott* (1793) 6 Bro.C.C. 550.

[18] *Per* Lord Porter, Irish Master of the Rolls, in *Rea* v. *Rea* [1902] 1 I.R. 451 at p. 461, citing Lord Selborne in *Freke* v. *Lord Carbery* (1873) L.R. 16 Eq. 461.

[19] [1978] 1 W.L.R. 791.

[20] *Per* Megarry V.-C. at p. 793.

[21] *Royal Bank of Canada (London) Ltd.* v. *Krogh* (1986) 1 All E.R. 611 at pp. 613, 614.

[22] [1902] 1 I.R. 451, followed in *Queensland Trustees Limited* v. *Nightingale* [1904] 4 S.R.N.S.W. 751.

[23] At p. 465.

"It seems [clear] to me that she must have both, where both are secured as charges by independent Acts of different legislatures each having full jurisdiction over the respective subject matters."

As has been forcefully pointed out by Morris,[24] this is an absurd result but would seem to be dictated by a strict application of the present rules. A view which Browne-Wilkinson V.-C. shared, but he was reluctantly forced to a similar conclusion in *Re Collens (decd.)*.[25] The deceased died intestate domiciled in Trinidad and Tobago and his estate consisted of property in Trinidad and Tobago, Barbados and the United Kingdom. He was survived by a widow and children and the widows entitlement over the Trinidad and Tobago estate was satisfied by a deed of compromise under which she took $1M. She then claimed that she was entitled to the appropriate statutory legacy as a charge on the English immovable property by virtue of section 46 of the Administration of Estates Act 1925.[26] It was held that section 46 could only regulate succession to immovable property situated in England and could not operate to create a charge on assets the succession to which was regulated by a foreign law.[27] Accordingly the charge created by section 46 on the English immovable property was not satisfied out of the overseas estate, it thus remained unsatisfied, and was payable. The judge recognised that it was unjust that the widow took not only one third of the estate under Trinidad and Tobago law but in addition the further capital sum under English law, but it was not possible on the construction of the 1925 Act to find in favour of the children.[28]

Partial intestacy

However, a rather different approach has been indicated in an English decision concerning a partial intestacy. The point was raised by the facts in *Re Osoba (decd.)*[29] where a testator domiciled in Nigeria

[24] (1969) 85 L.Q.R. 339 at p. 349; see *Re Ralston* [1906] V.L.R. 689 where the *Re Rea* decision was considered. The *Re Rea* conclusion would be avoided by an assimilation of the rules applicable to movable and immovable property. Morris (*op. cit.* at pp. 363–370) discusses several other examples illustrating the absurd results which the different rules relating to the law of the domicile and the *lex situs*, can produce and it is difficult not to agree with Morris' forceful conclusion that the difference in approach should now be abandoned in favour of a common system based on the *lex domicilii*. This is particularly so now when the widow's statutory legacy on intestacy is so large; when *Re Rea* was decided in 1902 the widow was entitled under the 1890 Act to a legacy of only £500, and under the Victorian statute to a legacy of £1,000.

[25] *Supra*; applying *Re Rea, supra*.

[26] The deceased died in 1966 and thus the charge was for £5,000.

[27] *Supra*, at p. 616. Even though the judge was prepared to hold that the definition of "the residuary estate of the intestate" in s.33(4), as being the net proceeds of sale of real or personal estate, included assets which do not fall for purposes of succession to be regulated by English law; at p. 615.

[28] As the judge commented the truth of the matter is that the draftsman of the 1925 Act did not have the present circumstances in mind and thus made no adequate provision.

[29] *Osoba* v. *Osoba* [1978] 1 W.L.R. 791.

made a will bequeathing to his wife and daughter the rents from leasehold property in Nigeria[29a] and leaving the residue, which included a house in London, on the same trusts. The house in London was subject to English law and it was argued as a matter of construction that it was undisposed of and thus passed on an intestacy. It was further contended that under the hotchpot provisions in section 49 the testamentary benefits relating to the foreign trusts would have to be brought in to account in the intestacy. This would mean that the daughter would have to account to the advantage of the son who received no testamentary benefits. In fact the court decided in favour of a division of the residue into equal shares and thus avoided the intestacy. Megarry V.-C. did, however, comment *obiter* on the hotchpot point[30]:

> "As at present advised I can see no rational ground on which it could be said that under section 49 of the Administration of Estates Act 1925, as amended, only English property has to be brought into account. The wording of section 49(1)(*aa*) and (*a*) is in terms of 'beneficial interests' and 'property,' and these expressions seem to me to be perfectly capable of embracing beneficial interests in property abroad as well as at home. Any other rule would also obviously be capable of producing most unfair results. In my judgment the hotchpot provision must apply where ever the property in question may be."

Comment

The persistence of English law in insisting on the dichotomy between the law applicable to the intestate succession to movable and immovable property must be regarded as unfortunate. The distinction could be justified, perhaps, and caused less difficulties at a time when English law had distinct and separate systems of succession to real and personal property. In view of the fact that the debts were payable primarily out of the personal property, it seemed sensible that the *lex domicilii* should apply to movables and, since realty was not primarily liable for debts, little inconvenience was caused by applying the *lex situs.* However, now that English law has a unified system of succession the dichotomy appears illogical and inconvenient. Some of these difficulties have been illustrated by the cases above, but as Morris[30a] has cogently pointed out, the present rules produce anomalies even when simply applied to different jurisdictions within the United Kingdom. For example, it could be crucial whether a matrimonial home is situated in England or in Scotland. Suppose that

[29a] Despite an expression of purpose the gift was construed as absolute.
[30] At p. 796.
[30a] (1969) 85 L.Q.R. 339; Dicey and Morris, *op. cit.*, pp. 613, 614; a view forcefully endorsed by Browne-Wilkinson V.-C. in *Re Collens, Supra*, at p. 616..

a married person with a Scottish domicile dies and the couple live in a house in England. The surviving spouse will take the personalty (movables) under the Scottish intestacy laws and the house will be governed by the English law, including the right of appropriation under the Second Schedule to the 1952 Act.

THE CROWN'S ENTITLEMENT TO BONA VACANTIA

Deceased with foreign domicile

Where the deceased had a foreign domicile, the intestate succession to his movable estate will be governed by the law of that domicile.[31] However, when such a person dies without heirs a contest can arise between the entitlement of the English Crown to personal property situated in England and the claim of the foreign state to such property. The resolution of this contest would seem to depend on whether the foreign state of the domicile takes as *ultimus haeres*, in which case there would seem to be a true succession to be determined in favour of the foreign state by the ordinary principles of private international law, or whether the foreign state takes as *jus regale*, in which case it would not be regarded as a matter of succession to which the law of the domicile should apply. In such a case the English Crown will claim the property by paramount prerogative.

The historical view on the point was that the Crown or state prima facie took by virtue of a *jus regale* but the more modern statutory codes of intestate succession, including the provisions of section 46 of the Administration of Estates Act 1925, more usually provide for the Crown or state to take as *ultimus haeres*.[31a] The distinction was first recognised judicially in *Re Barnett's Trusts*[32] which illustrates the traditional, pre-1925, *jus regale* approach. In that case an Austrian was entitled to a fund in court in this country and died in Vienna an illegitimate without heirs. By Austrian law the succession in such a case was confiscated as heirless property by the state. It was held that the Austrian government was not entitled since the claim was not in the nature of a succession and that the English Crown's entitlement was paramount.[32a]

> "When there is no heir, some paramount authority steps in and claims it, not as against any one, but because there is no one to claim it at all."

And likewise[33]:

[31] See *ante* p. 309. The succession to immovables is in any event governed by the *lex situs*, see *ante* p. 309 and so no problem of entitlement arising out of the competing state claims can arise.
[31a] See Cohn (1954) 17 M.R.L. 381. See *post*, note 41.
[32] [1902] 1 Ch. 847.
[32a] *Per* Kekewich J., *supra*, at p. 859.
[33] *Ibid.* at pp. 857, 858.

"It is because there is no one who can claim through the deceased that the Crown steps in and takes the property. The Crown takes it because it is, as it is described in the cases, *bona vacantia*. It is property which no one claims—property at large—there is no succession. The Crown does not claim it by succession at all, but because there is no succession . . . "

" . . . [W]hat the [*Austrian*] code says is that it is confiscated as heirless property—that is, as property which we call in England *bona vacantia*. It is property to which there is no heir, because neither country admits the right of the passing traveller, and therefore the property must fall to the Crown as a matter of right in the exercise of its sovereign power."

The Crown was also held to be entitled in *In the Estate of Musurus (decd.)*[33a] where a Turkish woman domiciled in Turkey died in 1915 intestate and without heirs leaving certain personal property in England. Both the Turkish government and the English Crown claimed the property. Sir Boyd Merriman P.[34] regarded the claim of the Turkish Government as a "regalian claim" and as such it did not prevail against the corresponding claim of the English Crown.

A contrast to these two decisions is provided by the more recent decision in *In the Estate of Maldonado (decd.)*[35] which illustrates the modern approach to current intestacy codes. Jenkins L.J. recognised the distinction drawn in the earlier cases, stating first the traditional view[36]:

" . . . if, according to the law of the foreign state in which the deceased is domiciled, there is no one entitled to succeed to the movable property of the deceased owing, for example, to the bastardy of the deceased, or to the failure of kin near enough in degree to qualify for succession under the law of the domicile, and, by the law of the foreign state, the state itself is, in such circumstances entitled to appropriate the property of the deceased as ownerless property by virtue of some *jus regale* corresponding to our own law of *bona vacantia*, English law will not recognise the claim of the foreign state as part of the law of succession of the domicile, but will treat it merely as being the assertion by the foreign state of a prerogative right which has no extra-territorial validity and one which must yield to the corresponding prerogative right of the Crown."

By way of contrast the court recognised that[37]:

33a [1936] 2 All E.R. 1666.

34 At p. 1667.

35 *State of Spain* v. *Treasury Solicitor* [1954] P. 223.

36 At p. 246.

37 *Ibid.*

> "... The law of the relevant foreign state, however may be such as to constitute the state itself the successor to the deceased in the absence of any individual with a proper right of succession under that law, and the question then arises whether the claim of the foreign state should be recognised under the general rule as being the claim of a person entitled to succeed according to the law of the domicile, or whether it should be treated as falling within the exception, on the ground that the claim of the foreign state, as self-constituted successor, does not differ in substance, or in principle, from a claim by a foreign state by virtue of its paramount right to ownerless property within its dominion as *bona vacantia* or the equivalent."

These principles had to be applied to the facts of the case which were simply that the deceased, a Spanish subject domiciled and resident in Spain, died intestate, leaving no next-of-kin, with personal estate in England. The State of Spain claimed a grant of administration to the personal estate of the deceased in England as sole and universal heir to his estate by Spanish law. Barnard J.[38] found on the evidence that the State of Spain was by Spanish law constituted a true heir on intestacy, just as any individual heir. This finding was regarded by the Court of Appeal[39] as conclusive of the issue:

> "If by the law of Spain it is possible to limit or define the individuals who can claim to be successors, namely, individuals having some connection by blood or marriage with the deceased. I can see no reason why, in default of there being such an individual, the law of Spain should not nominate or constitute as heir any person or corporation, including the state itself."

The decision of the Court of Appeal was stated by Morris L.J. as follows[40]:

> "As it is established in this case, and has not been challenged in this court, that by Spanish law the State of Spain is the heir of the deceased and is as truly the heir as any individual heir would be, I can see no reason why the English courts should decline to recognise this particular heir. In my opinion, the substance of the matter is that by the law to which reference is made, property in England is not left ownerless but is to pass to an heir; that being the State of Spain."

This is the more likely conclusion in the modern law since most continental codes will provide for the state to take as *ultimus haeres* and it has been submitted above that this is the position of the Crown

[38] *Supra*, at p. 231.
[39] See Lord Evershed M.R. at p. 244, 245.
[40] At pp. 251, 252.

under the 1925 Act according to the decision in *Re Mitchell (decd.)*.[41] Quite apart, however, from its entitlement on intestacy under the statutory code for want of other next-of-kin, it is submitted that the Crown still enjoys its prerogative right to ownerless property in England.[42] Accordingly, the English Crown will still exercise its regalian rights to ownerless personal property where, having consulted the law of intestacy in the country of the domicile, that law in effect provides for no true succession to the property, but there is in effect simply a regalian claim by the foreign state.[43]

THE ENTITLEMENT WHERE THE MARRIAGE WAS POLYGAMOUS

The entitlement of the surviving party to a polygamous marriage

There are two questions to be considered in this section. First, is a party to a polygamous marriage[44] entitled to take on the death intestate of the other as the surviving husband or wife? Secondly, if a man dies leaving more than one such wife, are they all entitled to share in his intestacy and, if so, in what shares? It will be assumed for the purposes of this discussion that English law governs the succession.[45]

Entitlement

Historically the question would at first sight have been answered in the negative bearing in mind Lord Penzance's classic definition of marriage in *Hyde* v. *Hyde*[46]:

> "I conceive that marriage, as understood in Christendom, may . . . be defined as the voluntary union for life of one man and one woman to the exclusion of all others."

However, Lord Penzance himself expressly disclaimed any intention of deciding upon the rights of succession or legitimacy, with which he was not concerned in the case.[47] Further, there has been a change in attitude in recent years towards polygamous marriages and a greater readiness to recognise and accept their validity.[48] Thus the

[41] [1954] Ch. 525, see *supra*, *Re Hanley* [1941] 3 All E.R. 301, to the contrary cited but not referred to in the judgment. See also *In the Estate of Maldonado*, *supra*, Barnard J. citing *Re Hanley*, at p. 232. The latter case was also cited in *Re Mitchell*, but ignored. The Court of Appeal did not express a view on the nature of the Crown's right under the 1925 Act since the issue in question referred solely to the nature of the State of Spain's right.

[42] This must be so since the Crown's right to *bona vacantia* is not limited to cases of intestacy, see Ing, *Bona Vacantia*.

[43] See p. 61.

[44] See generally, Bromley, *Family Law*, 6th ed., (1981) p. 54.

[45] See the discussion *ante*. Intestate succession to movables is governed by the law of the domicile, whilst immovables are subject to the *lex situs*.

[46] (1866) L.R. 1 P. & D. 130 at p. 133.

[47] *Supra*, at p. 138, see Foster J. in *Re Sehota (decd.)* [1978] 3 All E.R. 385 at p. 389.

[48] See Lord Parker in *Mohamed* v. *Knott* [1968] 2 All E.R. 563, at p. 567.

Matrimonial Proceedings (Polygamous Marriages) Act 1972[49] enabled parties to a polygamous marriage to seek matrimonial relief in English courts, although of course that Act had no direct bearing on the entitlement on intestacy. There is in fact no direct authority[50] but it is submitted with some confidence that a party to a polygamous marriage would be entitled as a husband or wife on the intestacy of the other. This view is supported by dicta in the cases, and by writers on private international law.[51]

A useful judicial statement is that of Lord Greene M.R. in *Baindail* v. *Baindail*[52]:

> "If a Hindu domiciled in India died intestate in England leaving personal property in this country, the succession to the personal property would be governed by the law of his domicile; and in applying the law of his domicile effect would have to be given to the rights of any children of the Hindu marriage and of his Hindu widow, and for that purpose the courts of this country would be bound to recognise the validity of a Hindu marriage so far as it bears on title to personal property left by an intestate here."

This dictum was applied in *Coleman* v. *Shang*[53] by the Judicial Committee of the Privy Council who concluded that, in dealing with personal property in Ghana of an intestate domiciled and validly married in that country in accordance with its laws, the courts of Ghana in the application of the English Statute of Distribution 1670, which applied at that time to govern the distribution of an intestate's estate in Ghana, would be entitled to apply the words "wife" or "widow" to all persons regarded as lawful wives or widows according to the law of Ghana. This decision was based on general principles but reinforced by the application of the English Interpretation Act 1889 to the effect that the words in the singular, *i.e.* "wife," included the plural unless there was something in the subject or contract repugnant to such a construction. Accordingly, since the word "wife" is used in a similar context in both the 1670 Statute of Distribution and the 1925

[49] Now reenacted as s.47 of the Matrimonial Causes Act 1973.

[50] In *Bamgbose* v. *Daniel* [1955] A.C. 107 where the Privy Council was concerned with the entitlement of issue of a polygamous marriage, see *post*, the point was expressly left open. Although the deceased had apparently nine polygamous wives no claim was put forward in the case by any person as a widow of the deceased. Lord Keith, commented, p. 119 "Whatever difficulties may arise in the case of the mothers of the children, the claims of the children as lawful children of the deceased must, in their Lordships opinion, be considered independently."

[51] See Hartley, (1969) 32 M.L.R. 171; Morris, *The Conflict of Laws,* (3rd ed. 1984) pp. 130, 131; and Cheshire and North, *Private International Law*, 10th ed., (1979) p. 311.

[52] [1946] P. 122 at p. 127. See also the note on the *Sinha Peerage Case*, [1946] 1 All E.R. 348n, Lord Maugham L.C. at p. 349.

[53] [1961] A.C. 481. The court decided that the sole surviving child of a previous marriage and the wife of the intestate, were entitled to a joint grant of letters of administration.

Administration of Estates Act, it is thought that a similar construction would govern the modern statute. Further, the Interpretation Act 1978 also provides that, unless the contrary intention appears, "words in the singular include the plural."[54]

Additional support for this view can be found now in a first instance decision on the Inheritance (Provision for Family and Dependants) Act 1975, namely *Re Sehota (decd.)*.[55] In that case the plaintiff and the husband were married in India in 1937, the marriage being potentially polygamous under Indian law. In 1948 the husband married a second wife in India and later the husband and both wives acquired an English domicile of choice. In 1976 the husband died and left all his property to his second wife. The first wife then applied under the Inheritance (Provision for Family and Dependants) Act 1975 for reasonable provision to be made for her. The question arose whether by reason of her polygamous marriage she had *locus standi*. The court decided that she did. This conclusion was supported by two main considerations. First, on the fundamental issue, English law had recognised polygamous marriages other than for the purposes of enforcing matrimonial duties or obtaining relief for a breach of marital obligations.[56] Thus "... there are purposes for which a polygamous marriage will be recognised as a valid marriage in this country, and also that in some statutes the word 'wife' may be construed as covering a polygamous married wife."[57] Secondly, the 1972 Act had rendered the recognition of polygamous marriages more compelling. The inclusion of a polygamous wife in these circumstances was supported also by the decision in *Chaudhry* v. *Chaudhry*[58] where the judge had taken the view that the 1972 Act had abolished the rule in *Hyde* v. *Hyde*.[59] In that case it was held that a party to a potentially polygamous marriage was a "husband or wife" for the purposes of section 17 of the Married Woman's Property Act 1882. It is submitted that a party to a polygamous marriage[60] would by analogy be regarded as entitled as a spouse under section 46 of the 1925 Act.

The share

If the marriage is only potentially polygamous there will be no problem in determining the share of the spouse but obvious

[54] s.6(*c*).

[55] [1978] 1 W.L.R. 1506. Foster J. thought that the issue was a question for the law of succession and was uninfluenced by the rule in *Hyde* v. *Hyde, supra*, since Lord Penzance had excluded questions of succession from his comments in that case, and in any event the Polygamous Marriages Act 1972 had abolished the *Hyde* v. *Hyde* rule.

[56] *Chaudhry* v. *Chaudhry* [1976] Fam. 148 at p. 153.

[57] *Per* Salmon L.J. in *Din* v. *National Assistance Board* [1967] 2 Q.B. 213 at p. 220, with reference to the National Assistance Act 1948.

[58] [1976] Fam. 148.

[59] *Supra.*

[60] *A fortiori* if the marriage is only potentially polygamous.

difficulties arise where the marriage is actually polygamous, as Lord Tucker observed in *Coleman* v. *Shang*[61]:

> "Difficulties may no doubt arise in the application of [*the decision in Baindail* v. *Baindail*[62]] in cases where there are more than one widow, both in dealing with applications for the grant of letters of administration and in the distribution of the estate, but they can be dealt with as and when they arise."

Some indication of the solution in such cases can be found in decisions on the estates of deceased Chinese who died domiciled in Malaya leaving more than one widow. In such cases it has been held that the several widows together constitute the "wife" and share the wife's share between them, rather than each being entitled to a full share as a wife. Thus Viscount Finlay stated in *Cheang Thye Phin* v. *Tan Ah Loy*[63]:

> "With regard to Chinese settled in Penang the Supreme Court recognises and applies the Chinese law of marriage. It is not disputed that this law admits polygamy. By a local Ordinance the Statute of Distribution has been applied to Chinese successions, and the courts have treated all the widows of the deceased as entitled among them to the widows share under the statute."

It is submitted that this would be the position if a man died domiciled in England survived by two or more widows and the estate fell to be distributed according to the Administration of the Estates Act 1925. It must be admitted, however, that such an approach would require division of the "personal chattels" which would obviously cause problems.[64] Further problems would centre on the spouse's right under the Intestates' Estates Act 1952[65] to require the matrimonial home to be appropriated in or towards the spouse's absolute share on intestacy. There is as yet no indication of how such problems would be resolved. In any event it is clear from *Re Sehota*[66] that any unfairness to one of the wives could be remedied under the Inheritance (Provision for Family and Dependants) Act 1975.

[61] [1961] A.C. 481 at p. 495. See also Lord Keith in *Bamgbose* v. *Daniel* [1955] A.C. 107 at p. 120.

[62] [1946] P. 122.

[63] [1920] A.C. 369 at p. 372. See also *Choo Eng Choon, Choo Ang Chee* v. *Neo Chan Neo* (the six widows case) (1908) 12 Str. Settlements Rep. 120; *Khoo Hooi Leong* v. *Khoo Hean Kwee* [1926] A.C. 529; and *Khoo Hooi Leong* v. *Khoo Chong Yeok* [1930] A.C 346. See Hartley 32 M.L.R. 172, who thought that division was the best solution in such cases. See also *Dawodu* v. *Danmole* [1962] 1 W.L.R. 1053.

[64] In South Australia it is possible for both a lawful and a "putative" spouse to share on intestacy and in the case of dispute regarding the division of the personal chattels, the statute provides for a sale and division of proceeds, see *ante*, p. 162.

[65] 2nd Sched., see discussed *post*, p. 228.

[66] *Supra.*

Issue of polygamous marriages

It has been seen that illegitimate children are entitled to share on the death intestate of their parents after January 1, 1970. This has greatly simplified the entitlement of children of a polygamous marriage since, whether they are regarded as legitimate or illegitimate, they will be entitled as issue. However, since this rule only applies to children inheriting on their parents intestacy, and vice versa, the problem remains, to a smaller extent, in respect of the entitlement of grandchildren or brother or sisters or their issue, and the relevant authorities must shortly be considered.[67] This discussion is concerned only with the status of the child; the entitlement will be governed either by the *lex situs*[68] or by the *lex domicilii*[69] and has been discussed above.

Parties domiciled abroad

Legitimacy is decided, according to the ordinary rules of the conflict of laws, by the law of the domicile.[70] Thus, where the parties to the marriage are domiciled abroad and the polygamous marriage is recognised by that law, the issue will be entitled to be regarded as legitimate. The rule was expressed by Lord Maugham L.C.[71]:

> "On the other hand it cannot, I think be doubted now (notwithstanding some earlier *dicta* by eminent judges) that a Hindu marriage between persons domiciled in India is recognised by our court, that such issue can succeed to property in this country. . . . "

In that case Lord Maugham L.C. followed "the very clear and well expressed exposition" of the conclusion reached in *Re Goodman's Trust*[72]:

Cotton L.J. said in that case[73]:

> " . . . I am of opinion that if a child is legitimate by the law of the country where at the time of its birth its parents were domiciled, the law of England, except in the case of succession to real estate in England, recognizes and acts on the status thus declared by the law of the domicile."

[67] See generally Cheshire and North's, *Private International Law*, 10th ed. (1980) p. 310; Morris, *The Conflict of Laws*, 3rd ed., (1984) p. 184; Hartley, (1969) 32 M.L.R. 170.
[68] In the case of immovables.
[69] In the case of movables.
[70] Cheshire and North, *op. cit.* pp. 440 *et seq.*; Morris, *op. cit.* pp. 182 *et seq.*; the domicile decides the status of the child; but either the *lex situs*, in the case of immovables, or the *lex domicilii*, in the case of movables, will govern the entitlement to succession on intestacy, Cheshire and North, *op. cit.* p. 456.
[71] *The Sinha (Peerage) case* [1939], 171 L.J. 350, noted, [1946] 1 All E.R. 348. See Cheshire and North, *op. cit.*, p. 310 and Lord Penzance in *Hyde* v. *Hyde* (1866) L.R. 1 P. & D. 130 at p. 138.
[72] (1881) 17 Ch.D. 266.
[73] At p. 292.

And James L.J. said[74]:

> "It must be borne in mind that the Statute of Distributions is not a statute for Englishmen only, but for all persons, whether English or not, dying intestate and domiciled in England, and not for any Englishman dying domiciled abroad.... And, as the law applies universally to persons of all countries, races, and religions whatsoever, the proper law to be applied in determining kindred is the universal law, the international law, adopted by the comity of States. The child of a man would be his child so ascertained and so determined."

These propositions were applied by the Judicial Committee of the Privy Council in *Bamgbose* v. *Daniel*[75] where the deceased died domiciled in Nigeria and intestate. The court had to consider the claims of children of nine polygamous marriages contracted in Nigeria according to local customary law. The relevant enactment to determine the succession was the English Statute of Distribution 1670. The court decided that, subject to the children establishing their status of legitimacy under the law of their domicile, they came within the class of persons entitled to succeed under the 1670 statute. Lord Morton expressed the opinion that there was little doubt that under well-accepted principles no ground existed for excluding the children from taking their rights of succession if they were legitimate children of the deceased under the law of their domicile.[76] The decision expressly recognised that, if a child is legitimate by the law of the country where at the time of its birth its parents were domiciled, the English law of succession to personalty recognises that status and that this principle is applicable to children of polygamous unions.[77]

However, in the passage cited above Lord Maugham[78] expressly reserved the position of inheritance to real estate before the Law of Property Act 1925 and of the devolution of entailed interests as equitable interests before or since that date.[79] This is because it is difficult to reconcile the issue of polygamous wives with the common law concept of "heirship" and so the limitation might still apply in those exceptional cases where intestate succession depends on the pre-1925 law."[80]

[74] *Ibid.* at p. 300. The decision and the reasoning of the majority in that case has not been questioned in any subsequent case, *per* the Privy Council in *Bamgbose* v. *Daniel* [1955] A.C. 107.

[75] [1955] A.C. 107.

[76] Applying *Re Don's Estate* (1857) 4 Drew 194, 197; *Re Goodman's Trusts* (1882) 17 Ch.D. 266.

[77] *Supra*, at pp. 118, 119, applying *Re Goodman's Trusts, supra.*

[78] *The Sinha (Peerage) Case, supra*, at p. 349.

[79] Descent to the heir was abolished by s.45 of the 1925 Act, except as regards entailed interests, s.45(2); see *ante.*

[80] The pre-1925 rules were preserved for a few purposes, principally entails, by ss.45(2) and 51 of the 1925 Act. See Cheshire and North, *op. cit.* p. 311; Morris, *op cit.* p. 184.

Parties domiciled in England

Where the parties are domiciled in England, the position, as a distinguished commentator has noted, is more difficult.[81] It seems inevitable that the status of the children would depend on the validity of the marriage.[82] If the marriage is only potentially polygamous, the issue can be regarded as legitimate but, if the marriage is actually polygamous, the issue would strictly be regarded as illegitimate and succession on intestacy would depend on that status.[83]

[81] Hartley, (1969) 32 M.L.R. 171.

[82] As to the recognition of polygamous marriages see Cheshire and North, *op. cit.* pp. 295 *et seq.*; Morris, *op. cit.* p. 175.

[83] Hartley, *op. cit.* comments, "... the law cannot be said to be settled but it would clearly be undesirable if the status of legitimacy were denied to the children of immigrants in these circumstances. If, moreover ... a polygamous wife is entitled to share in the estate of her husband on intestacy, it would be anomalous if the claims of her children were rejected on the ground that they were illegitimate. In view of these considerations an English court might today uphold the children's legitimacy," but this was written before the Family Law Reform Act 1969 removed the anomaly.

CHAPTER 17

FAILURE OF BENEFIT

INTRODUCTION

The code of intestate succession is mandatory and admits of no statutory exceptions other than the *commorientes* provision applicable to a husband and wife.[1] However, it is quite clear that the person prima facie entitled to succeed may be excluded, in particular situations by, for example, the effect of the rule of public policy preventing a murderer taking any benefit from his victim's estate. The entitlement may also be altered by post-death variations or disclaimers and these and other rules affecting disinheritance will be considered in this chapter.

EXCLUSION BY RULE OF PUBLIC POLICY

Introduction

Killer of deceased

It is an established principle of public policy that a person who has been criminally responsible for the death of another cannot take by succession on the death. A clear statement of the rule is that of Vaisey J. in *Re Callaway*[2]:

> "Now this rule, based on public policy, is that no person is allowed to take any benefit arising out of a death brought about by the agency of that person acting feloniously, whether it be a case of murder or manslaughter."

This rule is referred to as the "forfeiture rule" in The Forfeiture Act 1982 which modifies the previous effect of the rule in important ways, by providing relief from the rule in some cases and by conferring *locus standi* on guilty persons affected by the rule to apply for financial provision out of the deceased's estate under the Inheritance (Provision for Family and Dependants) Act 1975. The Act[3] refers to the forfeiture rule as meaning the rule of public policy which in certain

[1] s.46(3), see *ante* p. 164.

[2] [1956] 1 Ch. 559 at p. 562. See also *Cleaver* v. *Mutual Reserve Fund Life Association* [1892] 1 Q.B. 147 at p. 155; *In the Estate of Crippen* [1911] P. 108 at p. 112; *In the Estate of Hall* [1914] P. 1 at p. 5; *Re Giles (decd.)* [1972] Ch. 544 at pp. 551, 552; *Re Royse (decd.)* [1984] 3 W.L.R. 784; *Re K. (decd.)* [1985] 1 All E.R. 403; [1985] 2 All E.R. 833, C.A. A useful discussion of the rule can be found in Ing, *Bona Vacantia*, 1971.

[3] See s.1(1).

circumstances precludes a person who has unlawfully killed another from acquiring a benefit in consequence of the killing.[4] The common law rule will be discussed initially and a consideration of the provisions of the 1982 Act will follow.

Basis of the rule

The rule is firmly based on public policy[5] and it has been said that it is something which is really part of the common law of the land and not dependent upon statute.[6] This strictly remains the position after the Forfeiture Act 1982 since that Act is not a statutory formulation of the rule but merely a recognition and alleviation of it.

The rule is often spoken of in terms of long standing[7] but in 1892 Fry L.J. in *Cleaver's case* was unable to find any authority directly asserting the principle.[8] This case is accordingly the earliest authority in which a clear and explicit statement of the rule appears. Fry L.J. expressed the rule in a frequently-cited passage as follows:

> "The principle of public policy invoked is in my opinion rightly asserted. It appears to me that no system of jurisprudence can with reason include amongst the rights which it enforces rights directly resulting to the person asserting them from the crime of that person."

The explanation for the rule can be found in the, sometimes emotional justification for the principle[9]:

> "The human mind revolts at the very idea that any other doctrine could be possible in our system of jurisprudence."

However, the more modern cases have emphasised that neither the deserving of punishment nor the carrying of a degree of moral culpability has ever been a necessary ingredient of the crime which will attract the application of the rule.[10] Any such enquiry has been

[4] Including persons who have unlawfully aided, abetted, counselled or procured the death of that other: s.1(2).

[5] See *e.g.* Lord Esher M.R. in *Cleaver* v. *Mutual Reserve Fund Life Association* [1892] 1 Q.B. 147 at p. 152; Vaisey J. in *Re Callaway* [1956] 1 Ch. 559 at p. 562; Farwell J. in *Re Pitts* [1931] 1 Ch. 546 at p. 550; *Re Royse (decd.)* [1984] 3 W.L.R. 784.

[6] *Per* Cozens-Hardy M.R. in *In the Estate of Hall* [1914] P. 1 at p. 5.

[7] See *e.g.* Pennycuick V.-C. in *Re Giles (decd.), supra.*

[8] *Supra.* Although the judge thought that the decision of the House of Lords in *Fauntleroy's case* (1830) 4 Bli.N.S. 194, proceeded on the basis of the principle and could be regarded as a particular illustration of it. See also Cozens-Hardy M.R. in *In the Estate of Hall, supra,* at p. 5. *Cleaver's* case is usually regarded as the seminal decision by, for example, Cozens-Hardy M.R. *supra,* and Pennycuick V.-C. in *Re Giles (decd.), supra,* at pp. 549, 550. The rule appears to have developed in response to the Forfeiture Act 1870, which abolished the rule that a felon's property was forfeit to the Crown.

[9] *Per* Sir Samuel Evans P. in *In the Estate of Crippen* [1911] P. 108 at p. 112.

[10] *Per* Pennycuick V.-C. in *Re Giles (decd.)* [1972] Ch. 544 at pp. 551, 552; see also *Re Dellow's Will Trust* [1964] 1 W.L.R. 451.

dismissed as "... very noxious—a sentimental speculation as to the motives and degree of moral fault of a person who has been justly convicted."[11] It is this uncompromising attitude, typified by the hard case of *Re Giles (decd.).*[12] discussed *post*, which led to the enactment of the relief provided by the Forfeiture Act 1982.[13]

Application to intestate succession

The rule is now stated in section 1(1) of the Forfeiture Act 1982 but previously had no statutory embodiment and was not recognised in the Administration of Estates Act 1925 as an exception to the prima facie scheme of entitlement. In view of the fact that on intestacy the succession is by force of express statutory provisions, it could be argued that the rule had no application in cases of intestacy. Joyce J. in *Re Houghton*[14] inclined to this view on the basis that a rule of public policy could not override the clear provisions of a statute. Dissent from this opinion was, however, expressed by Farwell J. in *In Re Pitts.*[15] He thought that the rule was applicable to cases of intestacy and that the provisions of section 46 of the 1925 Act, however pre-emptory, would be read and construed subject to the public policy rule.[16] The controversy was resolved by Clauson J. in *Re Sigsworth*[17] which established that the rule did apply to exclude a murderer from claiming the statutory benefits arising in the case of his victim's intestacy. The general words of the Act, which might include cases obnoxious to the principle, must be read and construed as being subject to it and so we have "... an extraordinary instance of Judge-made law invoking the doctrine of public policy in order to prevent what is felt in the particular case to be an outrage.... "[18] In 1971 Pennycuick V.-C. in *Re Giles (decd.)*[19] had no doubts:

"And the cases have established beyond question that a person so

[11] *Per* Hamilton L.J. in *In the Estate of Hall, supra*, at pp. 7, 8.
[12] *Supra.*
[13] See *post.*
[14] [1915] 2 Ch. 173, adopting American opinions, see also *Re Sangal* [1921] V.L.R. 355 at p. 359 where it was argued that the provisions of a statute cannot be said to bend before the doctrine of public policy; the court was not however so persuaded.
[15] [1931] 1 Ch. 546 at p. 550. See likewise in *Re Pollock* [1941] 1 Ch. 219 at p. 222.
[16] This opinion was strictly *obiter* since the point did not specifically arise in that case and Farwell J. expressly declined to decide it. See also the *obiter* comments in *Re Crippen* [1911] P. 1.
[17] [1935] 1 Ch. 89, citing Fry L.J. in *Cleaver* v. *Mutual Reserve Fund Life Association* [1892] 1 Q.B. 147 at p. 156. The application of the rule to cases of intestacy was regarded as established by Pennycuick V.-C. in *Re Giles* [1972] Ch. 544 at pp. 551, 552 and by the Court of Appeal in *Re Royse (decd.)* [1984] 3 W.L.R. 784. See also the Commonwealth authorities of *Nordstrom* v. *Baumann* (1962) 31 D.L.R. (2d) 255 at p. 263; *Re Medaini* [1927] 4 D.L.R. 1137; *Re Sangal* [1921] V.L.R. 355; *Re Cash* (1911) 30 N.Z.L.R. 577; *Re Tucker* (1920, 21 S.R. (N.S.W.) 175; *Re Plaister* (1934) 34 S.R. (N.S.W.) 547; *Re Pechar* [1969] N.Z.L.R. 574; and *Re Dreger* (1975) 69 D.L.R. (3d) 47.
[18] *Per* Harvey J. in *Re Tucker, supra*, at p. 181.
[19] [1972] Ch. 544 at pp. 551, 552 applied in *Re Royse (decd.)* [1984] 3 W.L.R. 784.

convicted of manslaughter is disqualified from taking a benefit under the will or intestacy of the person whom he has killed."

The Forfeiture Act 1982[20] clearly recognises the application of the rule to beneficial interests in property acquired under the law relating to intestacy.

The rule is based on policy and, it would seem, has little reference to the presumed intention of the intestate. Although in most cases the exclusion of the criminal would no doubt be consistent with the wishes of the deceased, this is not necessarily so and yet in such cases the rule would seem to apply. An obvious example would be the case of a mercy killing with the agreement of the deceased. There is no authority directly in point but it seems, consistent with the general statements of the rule, that the killer would be excluded in such cases. It has been emphasised that the motive for the killing is irrelevant[21] and in *Re Dellow's Will Trusts*,[22] where there was some evidence to suggest that it was a mercy killing, the judge applied the rule although he was at great pains to point out that it was not a crime to which deep stigma should attach.[23]

Statement of the rule

Murder

The rule applies where the successor has murdered the deceased,[24] whether or not there has been a conviction for the crime.[25] It can be noted immediately that the Forfeiture Act 1982 contains no provisions for relief for a person who stands convicted of murder.[26]

[20] s.2(4)(*a*)(i).

[21] *Re Cash* (1911) 30 N.Z.L.R. 577; *Re Plaister* (1934) 34 S.R. (N.S.W.) 547; Chadwick, 30 L.Q.R. 212; *cf.* Goodhart, 88 L.Q.R. 13. The acquisition of property was not the motive for the killing in either *Cleaver's* case, *supra*, or *Crippen's* case.

[22] *Supra*, a wife killed her husband who was very seriously ill and helpless and it appeared that the wife was deeply concerned for him particularly in the event of his surviving her. See also *Re Callaway, supra.*

[23] Consider also the situation where there is an interval between the attack and the death and some indication of forgiveness by the deceased for the attacker; see Chadwick, (1914) 30 L.Q.R. 212; Youdan (1973) 89 L.Q.R. 236 and Taschereau J. in the Canadian case of *Lundy* v. *Lundy* (1895) 24 S.C.R. 650 at p. 653. It is clear that the rule can apply even where there has been no conviction, *Re Dellow's Will Trusts* [1964] 1 W.L.R. 451.

[24] *Cleaver* v. *Mutual Reserve Fund Association* [1982] 1 Q.B. 147; *In the Estate of Crippen* [1911] P. 108. *Re Sigsworth* [1935] 1 Ch. 89; *Re Pollock* [1941] 1 Ch. 219; *Re Callaway* [1956] Ch. 559.

[25] But the rule does not apply where the verdict is "not guilty by reason of insanity" (or previously "guilty but insane") *In Re Pitts* [1931] 1 Ch. 546; *Re Pollock* [1941] 1 Ch. 219; see also *Re Pechar* [1969] N.Z.L.R. 574; *Re Plaister* (1934) 34 S.R. (N.S.W.) 547; *Bauman* v. *Nordstrom* (1961) 27 D.L.R. (2d) 634; *Re Jane Tucker* (1920) 21 S.R. (N.S.W.) 175. As to proof of the conviction see Civil Evidence Act 1968, s.11, overruling *Hollington* v. *Hewthorn* [1943] 1 K.B. 587; see also *In the Estate of Crippen* [1911] P. 108.

[26] s.5.

Manslaughter

A leading authority on the application of the rule in cases of manslaughter is *In the Estate of Hall*[27] where Hamilton L.J. commented as follows:

> "On the main question *Cleaver's case*[28] binds our judgment. All the members of the Court express their decision on this part of the case in terms as applicable to murder as to manslaughter. True that was a case of murder, but I do not think that, by using terms wide enough to cover manslaughter, the members of the Court supposed themselves to be speaking *obiter*, or were in fact doing so. The principle can only be expressed in that wide form. It is that a man shall not slay his benefactor and thereby take his bounty, and I cannot understand why a distinction should be drawn between the rule of public policy where the criminality consists in murder and the rule where the criminality consists in manslaughter."

In the modern case of *Re Giles (decd.)*[29] the rule was applied to disentitle a widow who was convicted of the manslaughter of her husband. She pleaded not guilty to the charge of murder but guilty to manslaughter by reason of diminished responsibility and that plea was accepted. An order was made under section 60 of the Mental Health Act 1959 that she be admitted to and detained in Broadmoor. It was contended on behalf of the widow, who was the sole beneficiary under her husband's will, that the verdict and sentence implied no moral blameworthiness on her part so that the rule of public policy did not apply. This was firmly rejected by Pennycuick V.-C., who stated that the rule applied to all cases of culpable homicide, murder or manslaughter and that the deserving of punishment and moral culpability were not necessary ingredients for the application of the rule.[30] It is suggested that a case such as *Re Giles* would now attract the relief provided by the Forfeiture Act 1982.[31] This decision was regarded as for all practical purposes indistinguishable by the Court of Appeal in *Re Royse*[32] where Ackner L.J. stated:

> "It has not been, nor could it have been, disputed that the appellant, having been convicted of the manslaughter of her husband by stabbing him, was disqualified from taking any

27 [1914] P. 1 at p. 7.
28 [1892] 1 Q.B. 147.
29 [1972] Ch. 544. See also *Re K. (decd.)* [1985] Ch. 85; [1985] 2 All E.R. 833, C.A.
30 Although the judge accepted that the principles of public policy on which the courts act, can change over the generations he declined the opportunity which the introduction of diminished responsibility by the Homicide Act 1957 afforded, of limiting the application of the rule, *ibid.* at p. 1146.
31 See *post.*
32 [1984] 3 W.L.R. 784 at p. 786. See further discussed *post*, following *Re Giles (decd.)*, *supra* and *Cleaver's* case, *supra.*

> benefit under his will, or on his intestacy if he had died intestate, even though the sentence passed on her was one of detention for hospital treatment under section 60 of the Mental Health Act 1959, and was therefore a sentence designed to be remedial in nature and not by way of punishment."

However, there are dicta in cases concerning entitlement under insurance policies[33] which suggest that the public policy rule will only apply in manslaughter cases where there is actual or threatened violence. Pennycuick V.-C., held in *Re Giles*[34] that the motor manslaughter cases were inapplicable to a case concerning succession on death but Vinelott J., in *Re K. (decd.),*[35] more recently has referred to them and been influenced by them. There are indications in *Re K.* that the judge did not regard the rule as applicable to all cases of manslaughter but only to cases involving violence. On the facts before him a wife had threatened her husband with a loaded shot gun which went off and killed him, and Vinelott J. had no doubt that the rule applied in such cases.[36]

Other crimes

The earlier statements of the rule were often expressed with reference to "felony"[37] and this term is apt to cover murder, manslaughter, infanticide[38] and child destruction.[39] Pennycuick V.-C., in *Re Giles (decd.),*[40] appeared to confine the rule to culpable homicides, murder or manslaughter. However, other formulations of the rule are wider and refer simply to "the crime."[41] The question accordingly arises whether other crimes involving death would attract the principle and in particular whether the rule would disentitle a person who had been responsible for the death of the intestate by reckless driving.[42] There appears to be no reported English decision on the point, which is surprising since the situation is not unlikely, but

[33] See *Gray* v. *Barr, Prudential Assurance Co. Ltd. (third party)* [1971] 2 Q.B. 544; *R.* v. *National Insurance Co., ex p. Connor, sub nom. R.* v. *Chief National Commissioner, ex p. Connor* [1982] Q.B. 758.
[34] *Supra.*
[35] [1985] Ch. 85; affirmed by Court of Appeal [1985] 2 All E.R. 833, C.A.
[36] The widow was charged with murder and pleaded guilty to manslaughter, of her husband. She was made subject to a probation order for two years and the judge clearly regarded it as a case to which no great moral condemnation applied. The Court of Appeal did not need to discuss the point in any detail but implicitly agreed with Vinelott J.; see Ackner L.J., *supra,* at p. 836.
[37] See *e.g., In the Estate of Hall* [1914] P. 1 at p. 6; in *Re Callaway* [1956] 1 Ch. 559 at p. 562. The abolition of the distinction between "felony" and misdemeanour, Criminal Law Act 1967, s.1, does not appear to have affected the rule.
[38] Infanticide Act 1938.
[39] Infant Life (Preservation) Act 1929.
[40] [1972] Ch. 544 at pp. 551, 552.
[41] *Cleaver* v. *Mutual Reserve Fund Life Association* [1892] 1 Q.B. 147 at p. 156; *In the Estate of Crippen* [1911] P. 108 at p. 112.
[42] Road Traffic Act 1972, s.1.

the majority of academic opinion[43] seems to favour the view that the rule is not applicable to such cases.[44] The Forfeiture Act 1982, however, refers to "unlawfully killed" (section 1(1)(2); section 2(1)) and to "an offence of which unlawful killing is an element" (section 2(3)), which would seem to admit the possibility that killing by reckless driving might be included. In any event, in cases where the offender had been convicted under section 1 of the Road Traffic Act 1972, relief under the 1982 Act would now be available.[45]

Letters of administration

The facts in *In the Estate of Crippen*[46] were that a man who had been convicted of the wilful murder of his wife had, after his conviction and before his own death by execution, made a will appointing a person his executrix and universal legatee. That person claimed as such executrix to administer the murdered wife's estate and as legatee to be entitled to the murdered wife's property. The Court of Probate thought that the facts clearly raised "special circumstances" within section 73 of the Law of Probate Act, 1857[47] and the executrix was passed over and letters of administration were granted to the deceased woman's sister:

> "It is clear that the law is that no person can obtain or enforce any rights resulting to him from his own crime; neither can his representative claiming under him, obtain or enforce any such rights."[48]

Persons claiming through the offender

It is clear that the rule of public policy applies not only to exclude the criminal but also to exclude any person claiming through or under him. This was established in the seminal decision of *Cleaver* v. *Mutual*

[43] See Earnshaw and Pace, (1974) 37 M.L.R. 481 at p. 495; Youdan (1973) 89 L.Q.R. 235 at p. 239; Goodhart, (1972) 88 L.Q.R. 13; Hardingham, Neave and Ford, *Wills and Intestacy* p. 227. But see Miller, (1970) 35 M.L.R. 426 at p. 427.

[44] An analogous question has been considered in the insurance cases, *e.g. Tinline* v. *White Cross Insurance Association Ltd.* [1921] 2 K.B. 327; *Beresford* v. *Royal Insurance Co. Ltd.* [1938] 2 K.B. 197; *Hardy* v. *Motor Insurer's Bureau* [1964] 2 Q.B. 745, but Pennycuick V.-C. in *Re Giles* [1972] Ch. 544 refused to consider them and thus it seems that little guidance can be derived from them on the application of the rule in cases of intestate succession. See also *Gray* v. *Barr* [1971] 2 Q.B. 554 (Insurance case); and *Cleaver's* case, *supra*, (trust under the Married Women's Property Act 1882) and *Re K. (decd.)* [1985] Ch. 85; [1985] 2 All E.R. 833.

[45] Consider also the crime of aiding and abetting another's suicide, Suicide Act 1961, s.2; see Ing, *op. cit.*, pp. 221, 222; In the Canadian case of *Whitelaw* v. *Wilson* [1934] 2 D.L.R. 554 a husband who had aided his wife's suicide was excluded from benefiting under her will and also under the resultant intestacy. There is no reported English authority. The Forfeiture Act 1982 includes (s.1(2)), persons who aid, abet, counsel or procure another to murder.

[46] [1911] P. 108.

[47] Subsequently, Judicature Act 1925, s.162, now Supreme Court Act 1981, s.116.

[48] *Per* Sir Samuel Evans, at p. 112, citing *Cleaver's* case [1892] 1 Q.B. 147.

Reserve Fund Life Association[49] where Lord Esher M.R. expressed the point as follows:

> "That the person who commits murder, or any person claiming through him or her, should be allowed to benefit by his or her criminal act, would no doubt be contrary to public policy."[50]

Thus, where a murderer dies after his victim, *e.g.* by suicide or execution, the testate or intestate successors of the murderer cannot claim any part of the property which, but for the application of the rule, would have passed by succession from the victim to the murderer. Consider also the case where a son attacks his father, the son dies and then the father dies. In such a case, if the father dies intestate and if the son leaves issue, the issue, *i.e.* grandchildren, would prima facie be entitled to take their father's share *per stirpes*[51] but they will be excluded by the rule since they claim through their father. Relief under the 1982 Act might now be available to them.

However, the rule will not apply where the innocent beneficiaries, although related to the murderer, have an alternative and independent right to succeed.[52] Thus in *Cleaver's* case the husband had effected life insurance on his life with his wife named as a beneficiary. The wife was convicted of murdering her husband and later assigned her right to the insurance money. The court applied the rule of public policy so as to exclude the wife's estate and her assigns, with the result that the moneys formed part of the insured father's estate. Lord Esher M.R. explained the decision[53]:

> "I think that, if the court were to deprive the children of the insured, who do not claim through their mother, of the insurance-money under such circumstances, on the ground of public policy, it would be a gross injustice. Anyone claiming through the wife is shut out by the rule of public policy; so that any assignee from her, or other person claiming through her cannot recover the money; but the rule of public policy does not apply as between executors representing the estate of the insured and the defendants and, therefore, their rights and liabilities must be governed by the contract."

[49] [1892] 1 Q.B. 147 at p. 152.

[50] See also Sir Samuel Evans P. in *In the Estate of Crippen* [1911] P. 108 at p. 112, who stressed that the criminal's representatives (the criminal having been executed) was also excluded as claiming under the criminal.

[51] s.46(1)(i).

[52] *Per* Fry L.J. in *Cleaver's* case [1892] 1 Q.B. 147 at p. 155.

[53] *Ibid.* at p. 155.

Similarly, in *Re Gore*,[54] grandparents were allowed to claim the estate of their murdered granddaughter by reason of their relationship to her and were not regarded as claiming through the estate of the father who had been excluded by the rule. The same principle would seem to apply where the death serves to increase the shares of other intestate successors. If a son kills his father and brother in the same incident, an innocent sister will take an increased share in both estates by virtue of the death of the one brother and the exclusion of the other. Her entitlement is independent of the crime.

A more difficult question is whether the rule applies to exclude the offender when the benefit to him is indirect although related to the crime. Consider the situation where a son, anticipating the imminent death of his father from natural causes, murders his sister in order to increase his inheritance on the father's death. Clearly, it could be argued in such a case that the son benefits from his crime but the benefit is indirect rather than direct. An analogous example might be that of a grandchild who murders his father in order that he might inherit under his grandfather's intestacy by taking the share to which his father would have been entitled if he had survived the intestate.[55] There is no explicit English authority on these points but it has been suggested that the rule would apply[56] and this seems to be consistent with the statement of the rule in the Forfeiture Act 1982 which refers to "acquiring a benefit in consequence of the killing."[57] If such cases are subject to the rule, it seems difficult to envisage relief being available under the Act.[58]

The effect of disentitlement

If the person primarily entitled to the testate or intestate estate, whether original or by reason of exclusion from testate succession, is excluded from the succession by the rule of public policy and no relief

[54] [1972] 23 D.L.R. (3d) 534. It will be noticed that grandparents have a direct right of inheritance on intestacy, whereas grandchildren only take *per stirpes*. Compare *Re Dreger* [1977] 69 D.L.R. (3d) 47 where the husband's (murderer) next-of-kin were excluded from taking any part of the wife's (victim) estate because they had no independent claim to her estate.

[55] 1925 Act, s.46(1)(i).

[56] Hardingham, Neave and Ford, *Wills and Intestacy*, p. 229.

[57] s.1(1).

[58] Consider also the situation where the murderer inherits property as the heir to the beneficiary of the victim's estate, *i.e.* the victim leaves his property to X and X leaves his property to the murderer. This point has not apparently arisen in an English case but can be well illustrated by a South African case *Ex p. Steenkamp and Steenkamp* [1952] 1 S.A. 744 where it was held that the murderer could benefit. A man murdered his parents-in-law and was sentenced to life imprisonment. His parents-in-law bequeathed their property to their grandchildren, the children of their daughter and the murderer. One of the grandchildren died shortly after the grandparents and the court held that the murderer could succeed on intestacy to the estate of that child which consisted mainly of the property which the child had inherited from his murdered grandparents. The benefit in this case stemmed directly from the relationship not the crime.

is thought to be appropriate, the question arises how the estate should be distributed. It is established that the rule excludes the criminal, his representatives and anyone claiming through or under him.[59] The alternative methods of dealing with the succession are either to regard the Crown as entitled to the excluded share as *bona vacantia* or to distribute the estate amongst the other next-of-kin as if the murderer had not survived the deceased.

These alternatives were canvassed by Clauson J. in *Re Sigsworth*[60] but the question was expressly left open by the judge in that case[61] and the point was for many years unresolved by direct authority. There was some indication from *Cleaver's* case[62] that in such cases the property should be distributed amonst the other beneficiaries and not be forfeit to the Crown. However, that was a case concerning the entitlement under a policy of insurance effected under the Married Women's Property Act 1882 and so the result largely depended on the terms of the contract and the effect of the resultant trusts.

The point directly arose for decision in *Re Callaway*[63] in 1956. A testatrix had appointed her daughter as sole executrix and constituted her the sole beneficiary. The daughter murdered her mother and then committed suicide. Her estate was clearly excluded from taking any share under the resulting intestacy. The only other next-of-kin was a son and the question arose whether he was solely entitled to the whole estate or whether he was only entitled to his half-share with the Crown taking the excluded daughter's share as *bona vacantia.* It was held that the son was entitled to the whole estate of his mother to the exclusion of the Crown. The judge did not consider the metaphorical expression "struck out"[64] as being particularly happy or helpful but found it difficult to suggest a more appropriate expression. On this basis the son had to be regarded as the only qualified member of the class of next-of-kin. The judge felt compelled to this conclusion, which he reached with reluctance, by the then state of the authorities, commenting that he thought it unfortunate that in none of the previous cases was the Crown represented to argue the case on behalf of *bona vacantia.* The judge thought that there was great force in the contention that the rule does no more than exclude the culprit and

[59] It is of course quite clear that if the criminal is prevented by the rule from taking any testate benefit, he will also be excluded from taking under the resultant intestacy, *Re Callaway* [1956] 1 Ch. 559; *Re Giles (decd.), supra.*

[60] [1935] 1 Ch. 89 at p. 93.

[61] Because the Attorney-General was not represented in the case to argue on behalf of the Crown.

[62] *Cleaver* v. *Mutual Reserve Fund Life Association* [1892] 1 Q.B. 147.

[63] [1956] 1 Ch. 559.

[64] Vaisey J. *supra*, at p. 563; see also Lopes L.J. in *Cleaver's* case, *supra*, at p. 161. A similar result had been arrived at earlier in the Australian case of *Re Jane Tucker* (1920) 21 S.R. (N.S.W.) 175; but see *Davis* v. *Worthington* [1978] W.A.R. 144, gift to P if he should survive the intestate by 14 days; P did so but murdered the testator, since no alternative provision, intestacy.

that, while it may accelerate subsequent existing interests, it cannot create any new interests, with the consequence that the forfeited interest is one to which nobody is entitled and therefore goes to the Crown as *bona vacantia.*[65] Indeed the judge went so far as to indicate, in case the case was to go to a higher court, that, in the absence of authority,[66] he would have so decided it.

This view in favour of *bona vacantia* had great attraction for, as Vaisey J. pointedly asked, "why should Mrs. Stone's crime endow the plaintiff even to the extent of half of Mrs. Callaway's estate? Seeing that her crime was against the Queen's peace, why should not the Crown, rather than the Plaintiff, get the benefit from it?"[67]

The same thought would seem to underly the *obiter* comment of Walton J. in *Re Scott (decd.), Widdows* v. *Friends of the Clergy Corporation,*[68], a case concerned with the consequence of a disclaimer:

> "After all, if a person is entitled to take because of some offence against the Queen's peace, it is by no means a surprising conclusion that the Queen should be entitled to take the interest which the person is thus debarred from taking."

However, the judge in that case was concerned with the effects of a disclaimer which, as an act of parties, is clearly distinguishable from exclusion by application of the rule of public policy. In fact, so far as it is relevant to this discussion, he decided that the effect of a disclaimer was similarly to benefit the other person entitled on intestacy to the exclusion of the Crown.[69]

Whatever view is taken of the merits of the decision in *Re Callaway*[70] it must be taken as establishing the point, at least in cases where there are other members of the same class entitled to take on intestacy such as where a sister is disentitled as the murderer but other brothers and sisters are capable of taking.[71]

A further problem, which was posed but not answered in *Re*

[65] *Ibid.*

[66] Mainly *Cleaver's* case, *supra*, but which was in fact clearly distinguishable, since the Crown was not represented. See also the cases noted in Ing, *op. cit.*, pp. 220–222, *Re Merrett's Settlement Trusts, The Times*, November 3, 1955; *Re Peacock* [1957] Ch. 310; *Re the Estate of Robertson* (1963) 107 S.J. 318; and *Re C. H. Forster* (unreported).

[67] *Supra*, at p. 563

[68] [1975] 1 W.L.R. 1260 at p. 1271, see fully discussed, *post.*

[69] *Ibid.*

[70] *Supra.*

[71] Ing queries whether the same rule would apply where there are no other members of the same class capable of inheriting but where there are more remote relatives living. It is at least arguable in such cases that the Crown could step in and take the property as *bona vacantia*, although Ing admits that the chances of success in such cases must be small in the present state of the authorities. Ing notes (at p. 224) that, "It is not the practice of the Treasury Solicitor to assert a claim to property as *bona vacantia* by reason of the rule of public policy where the deceased person, *i.e.* the victim of the crime, was survived by innocent kin within the degrees of relationship set out in section 46(1) of the 1925 Act."

Callaway,[72] arises where the criminal was entitled under his victim's will to a life interest with remainder to his own issue. Would there be an acceleration of the issue's interests, so as to exclude after born issue, or would there be no acceleration but an intestacy as to the income during the criminal's life? There is no authority on the effect of the rule of public policy in such cases.[73]

Joint tenancy

It will not infrequently be the case that the substantial asset in issue, where one spouse has been convicted of the unlawful killing of the other, will be the matrimonial home held in joint names. The case of *Re K. (decd.)*[74] specifically decides that the effect of the forfeiture rule in such cases is to sever the joint tenancy so that the convicted party keeps his or her share but that the other share forms part of deceased's estate.[75] The forfeiture rule will then operate to disentitle the convicted party from inheriting that share under the will or intestacy. However, this is a situation where relief might be available under The Forfeiture Act 1982. Such relief was granted in *Re K. (decd.)*[76] to enable the convicted widow to inherit the whole interest in the home.

The Forfeiture Act 1982

Relief

This Act, which came into force on October 13, 1982,[77] provides relief from forfeiture of inheritance for persons guilty of unlawful killing and refers to the entitlement of such persons to apply for financial provision out of the deceased's estate under the Inheritance (Provision for Family and Dependants) Act 1975.[78] The 1982 Act recognises in section 1 the common law rule based on public policy[79] and then provides in section 2(1) that, where a court determines that the forfeiture rule would preclude the offender from "acquiring any interest in property," the court can make an order modifying the

[72] *Supra.*
[73] See the cases on the analogous situation where there has been a release, *Re Kebty-Fletcher's Will Trusts* [1969] 1 Ch. 339 and *Re Harker's Will Trusts* [1969] 1 W.L.R. 1124.
[74] [1985] Ch. 85, Vinelott J. who specifically deals with the point. Affirmed on other grounds by the Court of Appeal [1985] 2 All E.R. 833. In that case the house was worth some £85,000 and the widow (who had been convicted of her husband's manslaughter) was prima facie entitled to the whole estate for life under the will.
[75] A similar result is achieved in other jurisdictions by holding that the survivor holds one-half of the accrued interest on constructive trust for the deceased's estate.
[76] *Supra.*
[77] s.7(2). The Act is poorly drafted and its deficiencies have been exposed in *Re Royse (decd.)* [1984] 3 W.L.R. 784 and *Re K. (decd.)* [1985] Ch. 85; [1985] 2 All E.R. 833 CA.
[78] The Act also contains provisions relating to the entitlement to social security benefits, s.4.
[79] See *ante*.

effect of that rule. Interests in property include all benefits by way of succession, including expressly those which the offender would have acquired under the law relating to intestacy.[80] It is then provided that an order under section 2 may modify the effect of the forfeiture rule in respect of any such interest in property subject to the rule.[81] This may be done in either or both of the following ways:[82] first, where there is more than one such interest, by excluding the application of the rule in respect of any (but not all) of those interests; secondly, in the case of any such interest in property, by excluding the application of the rule in respect of part of the property. At first sight it would seem that the effect of these provisions is to preclude the court from relieving the applicant from the consequences of the rule altogether. This ridiculous conclusion was avoided in *Re K. (decd.)*[83] by Vinelott J. who thought that section 2(5) was intended to enlarge the power conferred by subsection (1) of section 2 by making it clear that the court is not bound either to relieve against the operation of the forfeiture rule altogether or not to relieve against the operation of the rule at all. In that case a widow had been found guilty of the unlawful manslaughter of her husband and the criminal court, who clearly had some sympathy for her, had given her a non-custodial sentence. Under the will she was entitled to a life interest in the whole of the considerable estate. Vinelott J. exercised the jurisdiction under the Act to relieve her wholly from the effect of the forfeiture rule in respect of the whole of the property.[84] This decision was affirmed on appeal; Ackner L.J. emphasised that the discretion under section 2(2) was very wide and he could see no reason to interfere with the way the judge had exercised it.[85]

Subject to any such modification, the forfeiture rule has its usual effect.[86] The exercise of the powers is entirely discretionary and governed by the terms of section 2(2):

> "The court shall not make an order under this section modifying the effect of the forfeiture rule in any case unless it is satisfied

[80] s.2(4)(*a*)(i); also included are interests under the deceased's will; nominations; *donatio mortis causa*, and property in trust, see s.2(4)(*a*) and (*b*).

[81] s.2(5).

[82] s.2(5)(*a*)(*b*).

[83] [1985] Ch. 85; [1985] 2 All E.R. 833, C.A. In truth the legislation appears to be defective.

[84] Although there were other relatives capable of inheriting there was no one to whom the deceased was under any moral obligation. Even so it does seem a very generous provision indeed for the widow.

[85] [1985] 2 All E.R. 833.

[86] s.2(6). The order is not to affect any interest in property which in consequence of the rule, has been acquired before October 13 by a person other than the offender or a person claiming through him, s.2(7), as to which see *Re K. (decd.)*, *supra*. It was specifically decided in that case that the beneficiaries under an unadministered estate do not have such an interest which would preclude the operation of the Act; see Ackner L.J. *supra*, at pp. 836–839.

> that, having regard to the conduct of the offender and of the deceased and to such other circumstances as appear to the court to be material, the justice of the case requires the effect of the rule to be so modified in that case."

The decision in *Re K. (decd.)*, discussed above indicates that in appropriate cases the discretion will be exercised boldly.

The offender

The 1982 Act refers throughout to "unlawful killing" but contains in section 5 an important and imperative exclusion of any possibility of relief for a person who stands convicted of murder.[87] Thus the jurisdiction to grant relief will be applicable, so far as the offender is concerned, to cases of manslaughter and other cases of unlawful killing.

There seems little doubt that the legislation was prompted by unease over cases such as *Re Giles (decd.)*[88] where, it will be recalled, a wife was found guilty of the manslaughter of her husband on the grounds of diminished responsibility and, although made subject to a hospital order, was still regarded as subject to the rule. So-called mercy killings, where the conviction is manslaughter, are another obvious example. Indeed most cases of voluntary manslaughter, including, for example, cases of provocation, would have some grounds for attracting relief. Similarly, some cases of infanticide, child destruction, complicity in the suicide of another and causing death by reckless driving could no doubt be suitable cases for relief. *Re K. (decd.)*,[89] discussed above, provides a useful illustration of how the jurisdiction can be applied in a manslaughter case.

Forfeiture rule and family provision

Where the Forfeiture Act 1982 is not applicable

The relationship between the forfeiture rule and the jurisdiction under the Inheritance (Provision for Family and Dependants) Act 1975, where the Forfeiture Act 1982 is not applicable,[90] has been

[87] s.5. This does not exclude the possiblity of relief for innocent persons who claim through the murderer, see *post*.

[88] [1972] Ch. 544.

[89] [1985] Ch. 85; [1985] 2 All E.R. 833, C.A.

[90] The Act came into force on October 13, 1982. Proceedings for the relief provided by the Act must be commenced within three months of the conviction, s.2(3). The applicant in *Re Royse (decd.)* [1984] 3 All E.R. 339 was convicted in July 1979, nearly three years before the 1982 Act was passed and thus was precluded from applying for relief under that Act. It was argued that she could apply notwithstanding for financial provision under the 1975 Act. This was not accepted. The 1982 Act is not retrospective, see Ackner L.J. in *Re Royse*, *supra* at p. 343 save that it is provided that an application can be made notwithstandng that the unlawful killing occurred before the passing of the Act, s.7(4). This on its own did not assist the applicant in *Re Royse.*

considered by the Court of Appeal in *Re Royse (decd.)*[91] In that case Ackner L.J. was clear that, on an interpretation of sections 1 and 2 of the 1975 Act, there were no qualifying grounds on which to base an application under that Act in a case to which the forfeiture rule applied because the absence of reasonable financial provision for the person convicted could not be attributed either to the deceased person's will or to the intestacy laws where relevant. The absence of provision was solely the result of the rule of public policy.[92] The court rejected the argument that provision granted under the 1975 Act was not a benefit accruing to the convicted person directly from his crime but was merely a benefit accruing from the exercise of the court's discretion. Slade L.J. could not see that it made any difference that an award under the 1975 Act was at the court's discretion.[93] Accordingly, in *Re Royse*, the court reluctantly[94] dismissed an application for reasonable provision out of the deceased's estate[95] where the applicant had been convicted of the manslaughter of the deceased.

Forfeiture Act 1982

This Act came into force on October 13, 1982 and includes an express provision[96] to the effect that the forfeiture rule shall not be taken to preclude any person from making an application under the Inheritance (Provision for Family and Dependants) Act 1975 or for variation of periodical payments[97] or maintenance agreements[98] under the Matrimonial Causes Act 1973. At first sight this would seem to enable persons disentitled from inheritance by the operation of the rule of public policy to apply for financial provision out of the estate under the 1975 Act. In other words it would seem superficially that the forfeiture rule no longer applies to the 1975 Act. However, if *Re Royse*[99] is correctly decided, this does not seem to be the position. To quote Ackner L.J. in that case:[1]

> "Although section 3 removes the automatic time bar imposed by the forfeiture rule on proceedings under the 1975 Act, the terms of that Act still have to be complied with. As previously stated,

[91] [1984] 3 W.L.R. 784.
[92] At p. 787.
[93] At p. 789. The judge also thought that if the legislature had intended in any way to mitigate the rigours of the forfeiture rule it would have expressly said so.
[94] The circumstances were described as "a very sad case."
[95] It was argued unsuccessfully that although the time bar precluded on application for relief under the 1982 Act, there was no time bar to an application under the 1975 Act.
[96] s.3(1), (2)(*a*). "s.3 is not merely declaratory. In my judgment it did alter the law. Parliament recognised that the forfeiture did apply to the 1975 Act and accordingly s.3 made special provision for that and the other legislation referred to in the section," *per* Ackner L.J. in *Re Royse (decd.)* [1984] 3 W.L.R. 784 at p. 789.
[97] 1973 Act, s.31(6).
[98] 1973 Act, s.36(1).
[99] [1984] 3 W.L.R. 784.
[1] At p. 789.

since the terms of the will, or the law relating to intestacy if that had been applicable were such as to make reasonable financial provision, the grounds under the 1975 Act would not be established."

Slade L.J. said:

"... I still do not see how section 3 would enable the appellant to succeed in her present application. Even assuming that, procedurally, she is not precluded from making the application under the 1975 Act, it still would be necessary for her to satisfy the precondition set out in section 2(1) of the 1975 Act in order to persuade the court to exercise the discretionary jurisdiction under that Act in her favour. This for reasons which I have already given she could not in my opinion do."

The reasons referred to by Slade L.J. are that the essential precondition in section 2(1) of the 1975 Act is that it must be the effect of the will or the intestacy that fails to make reasonable provision for the applicant and, in cases to which the rule of public policy applies, it is not. The failure to receive adequate provision is a consequence of his or her own act, coupled with the forfeiture rule.[2] Thus it is difficult to see how a person in the position of the applicant in *Re Royse*[3] could succeed in a simple application under the 1975 Act even if brought after the 1982 Act was fully in force. The solution, of course, is to apply initially under the 1982 Act for a discretionary order modifying the effects of the forfeiture rule on the prima facie will or intestacy entitlement.[4] If the provision thereunder is then thought to be inadequate, an application can be made under the 1975 Act for greater provision.[5] In this way the applicant will be able to point to the will or intestacy provision as inadequate and will not simply be relying on disinheritance by the effect of the forfeiture rule.

It might have been preferable if section 3 had conferred a direct entitlement on a person convicted of the unlawful killing of the deceased to apply, and in appropriate cases to succeed, for reasonable financial provision out of the deceased estate.[6] Such a change would

[2] At p. 792.

[3] *Supra*, or in *Re Giles (decd.)* [1972] Ch. 544.

[4] Under s.2 see Vinelott J. in *Re K. (decd.)* [1985] Ch. 85 at p. 101; [1985] 2 All E.R. 833, C.A.

[5] Thus the 1975 Act jurisdiction becomes supplemental to the effective invocation of the 1982 Act jurisdiction, except presumably in those cases where the will or intestacy makes no provision for the applicant.

[6] A person convicted of the murder of the deceased can make no application under the 1982 Act, s.5.

have required explicit wording, including an express amendment of section 2 of the 1975 Act.[7]

In any event it would appear that the primary remedy for persons subject to disinheritance by the forfeiture rule would be an application for relief under the 1982 Act where a successful application would assist. The exercise of the discretion under the 1982 Act is likely to be similar to that under the 1975 Act and it is difficult to envisage cases where an unsuccessful applicant under one would be successful under the other. In entertaining a claim by a person who, apart from the interest forfeited, would have had a claim under the joint effect of the 1975 Act and section 3 of the 1982 Act, the court must be entitled to have regard to the principles and the considerations set out in the 1975 Act.[8]

Exclusion or Variation by Act of Parties

Disclaimer

The prima facie entitlement on intestacy can be affected by a post-death disclaimer or variation by the persons entitled. Such actions can have tax consequences which have been considered above. First there must be a consideration of disclaimers of intestate benefits.[9]

Disclaimer is a refusal to accept an interest[10]—as the old saying goes "... nobody can put an estate into another in spite of his teeth."[11] In *Townson* v. *Ticknell*, Abbott C.J. said[12]:

> "The law certainly is not so absurd as to force a man to take an estate against his will. Prima facie, every estate, whether given by will or otherwise, is supposed to be beneficial to the party to whom it is so given. Of that, however, he is the best judge, and if it turn out that the party to whom the gift is made does not

[7] Referring to a failure of provision by virtue of the operation of the forfeiture rule as an additional alternative to the failure of the will or intestacy to make adequate provision.

[8] *Per* Vinelott J. in *Re K. (decd.), supra.* Such a person cannot be in a worse position than one for whom no provision is made under the deceased's will or by virtue of his intestacy and who accordingly can only claim under the 1975 Act as applied by s.3 of the 1982 Act. *Ibid.* See also [1985] 2 All E.R. 833, C.A.

[9] For a general discussion of disclaimers see, Williams on Wills, 5th ed. (1980) Chap. 36, and Ing, *Bona Vacantia*, Chap. 19, but note now *Re Scott (decd.)* [1975] 1 W.L.R. 1260.

[10] *Per* Walton J. in *Re Scott (decd.)* [1975] 1 W.L.R. 1260.

[11] *Thompson* v. *Leach* (1690) 2 Vent. 198 at p. 206; *Townson* v. *Ticknell* (1819) 3 B. & Ald. 31 at pp. 36, 37; see Goodhart (1976) 40 Conv. 293.

[12] *Supra*, at pp. 36, 37. See also *Re Wimperis* [1914] 1 Ch. 502; *Re Stratton's Disclaimer* [1958] 1 Ch. 42.

> consider it beneficial, the law will certainly, by some mode or other, allow him to renounce or refuse the gift."

There is no doubt that a legatee or devisee can disclaim testate benefits but the question arises whether it is possible to disclaim an interest under an intestacy. It is submitted with some confidence that intestate benefits can be disclaimed.

First, it was assumed by the court in *Re Scott* (*decd.*) that an intestate benefit could be disclaimed and the case concentrated on the effects of such disclaimer on the beneficial entitlement.[13] It is true to say that this decision surprised many commentators since there had previously been a fairly widespread assumption that intestate benefits could not be disclaimed because they were provided by statutory provisions which are expressed imperatively.[14] Consequently, the *Re Scott* assumption was immediately challenged[15] on the basis that intestate benefits do not require acceptance but vest automatically on the death of the intestate by force of the statutory provisions; the beneficiary is not given a choice whether to accept or disclaim. It is submitted, however, that this view of intestate entitlement is not correct because the only automatic vesting at the moment of death is in the Probate judge.[16] The estate then vests in the administrators when appointed who hold it for the purposes of administration.[17] It is only when the residuary estate of the intestate[18] is ascertained at the end of the first phase of administration that any beneficial interests arise.[19] It is clear that until that time the intestate beneficiaries have no defined interest in any of the assets of the estate but only an inchoate right to ensure due administration.[20]

It can be concluded therefore that, since a beneficiary has no interest in the estate until the residue is ascertained, it cannot be said that the interest vests in him automatically. He would thus appear to be entitled, so long as the residue is unascertained, to take steps to prevent the vesting in him of an interest under the intestacy, that is to

[13] *Supra.* The possibility that intestate interests could not be disclaimed does not seem to have been argued in the case. See also *Re Taylor* [1957] 1 W.L.R. 1043.

[14] See Goodhart (1976) 40 Conv. 293; Oughton, (1977) 41 Conv. 260, who thought that the absence of any English cases on the point before 1975 was an illustration of the principle that the most obvious cases are not litigated. There is no statutory recognition of the possibility that the intestate benefits could be disclaimed. But see Ing, *Bona vacantia*, who, writing in 1971, seemed to assume that an intestate benefit could be disclaimed.

[15] *Ibid.*

[16] Administration of Estates Act 1925 (hereinafter also referred to as the "A.E.A. 1925"), s.9.

[17] 1925 Act, ss.32, 33.

[18] s.33(4) defines this phrase which is the subject of the beneficial interests set out in Pt. IV of the Act.

[19] See Pinkerton (1978) 42 Conv. 213.

[20] See *Eastbourne Mutual Building Society* v. *Hastings Corporation* [1965] 1 W.L.R. 861; *Lall* v. *Lall* [1965] 1 W.L.R. 1249; *Barnado's Homes* v. *Special Income Tax Commissioners* [1921] A.C. 1; *Re K. (decd.)* [1985] 2 All E.R. 833 and discussion, *ante* at p. 93.

disclaim.[21] Once a beneficiary does acquire an interest, whether legal or equitable, on the making of an assent, it would appear clear from first principles that he can no longer be rid of it by means of a disclaimer.[22]

This analysis is supported by the Inheritance Tax Act 1984 which confers in section 142 statutory recognition of the fact that intestate benefits can be disclaimed. The wording of the provision refers to "... or the benefit conferred by any of those dispositions is disclaimed ... " and "any" refers to " ... by will, under the law relating to intestacy or otherwise ... "[23]

Non tax effect of a disclaimer

Assuming that it is possible to disclaim, before acceptance, interests on intestacy, the effect of such a disclaimer must now be considered. It has been indicated already that there appeared to be no English decision on this point before *Re Scott (decd.)*[24] because, perhaps, it had always been assumed that disclaimer was not possible on intestacy. In that case there was a testamentary gift to a brother and sister for life with remainder contingently to the brother's children and, should that gift fail, an ultimate remainder to two named charities. At the testatrix's death both the brother and the sister were very elderly and the brother had no children. Within a year of the death the brother and sister executed deeds which disclaimed their interests in the residue under the will or on intestacy. It will be noticed on these facts that the initial disclaimer was of testate benefits, giving rise to a partial intestacy, but that these interests on intestacy were also disclaimed. The judge[25] assumed without question that the rights could be disclaimed and this assumption would seem to be equally applicable to cases of a total intestacy where the disclaimer is in respect of such interests initially. Various alternative solutions were

[21] Pinkerton, *op. cit.* p. 219. It is interesting to note that in New Zealand it is specifically provided that a successor may disclaim the whole of his interest on intestacy, by deed, within one year of the first grant of administration: Administration Act 1969, s.81. The fact that a statutory provision to this effect is thought necessary, could be taken as indicating that there was no such right at common law. A similar statutory provision putting the question beyond doubt, might be thought to be desirable in English law.

[22] Disclaimers once made can only be retracted if no-one has altered their position in reliance on the disclaimer, *Re Cranstoun* [1949] Ch. 523, see Parry and Clark, *The Law of Succession*, 8th ed. (1983) p. 342. However, a formal disclaimer under s.81 of the New Zealand legislation is irrevocable, s.81(4)(*a*); see Hardingham, Neave and Ford, *Wills and Intestacy*, p. 433.

[23] A restricted interpretation would confine the effects of the section to the *variation* of intestate benefits, but it is submitted, such a narrow reading is not justified. See also Capital Gains Tax Act 1979, s.49(6)–(10); see discussion *ante* p. 120.

[24] [1975] 1 W.L.R. 1260.

[25] Walton J., *supra*, see pp. 1268, 1269. It is, of course, possible to disclaim testamentary benefits, thus creating a partial intestacy and then to claim rights on intestacy. There might be advantages in so doing where the testamentary benefits have to be brought into account in a partial intestacy, under s.49(1) of the 1925 Act, see *ante*, p. 291.

canvassed in the case as to how the estate should be distributed in consequence of the disclaimers.

The first possible solution was to say that the interests of the charities were accelerated so that the income, pending the birth of any child of the brother, which was very unlikely, should be paid to the charities. This was rejected because the interests of the charities were contingent.[26] The judge was attracted by an alternative argument, namely that the income should be accumulated for a period of twenty-one years from the death of the testatrix or until the prior death of the survivor of the brother or sister and then be added to the capital. This approach could not be adopted because it was thought to be contrary to the testatrix's intention. It was decided that the property devolved, in the absence of any alternative, as on a partial intestacy but the question remained who was entitled to it. The Crown claimed the property as *bona vacantia* on the basis that it had by virtue of the disclaimer become ownerless. Walton J. rejected this argument; he thought that the property was not ownerless but part of the estate of the deceased.[27]

> "The effect of a disclaimer is not to throw the property on to the scrap heap, but to refuse to accept it in the first place, leaving the ownership with the people or the interest, or the estate, or whatever, from which it was derived in the first place."[28]

That being so, the contest was between the next-of-kin of the intestate. The judge had no doubt that, if some but not all of the members of a class prima facie entitled on intestacy disclaimed, the remaining members of the class would take the whole interest between them.[29] Thus, in the case before him, if the brother alone had disclaimed, the sister would have been entitled to the whole interest. Analogously, therefore, the judge concluded that, if all the members of the class who were prima facie entitled on intestacy disclaimed as on the facts before him, they should all be left out of account. There being no members of that class, the estate would then fall to be distributed amongst the next class of successors entitled under the statute. This was explained as follows[30]:

[26] Applying *Re Townsend's Estates* (1886) 34 Ch.D. 357, distinguishing *Jull* v. *Jacobs* (1876) 3 Ch.D. 703, and somewhat unconvincingly *Re Taylor* [1957] 1 W.L.R. 1043.

[27] *Supra.* at pp. 1271, 1272. This is consistent with the decisions on the application of the rule of public policy excluding a murderer from benefitting under his victim's will or intestacy, although the two situations are clearly distinguishable, see *Re Callaway* [1956] Ch. 559, and discussion, *supra.* It is interesting to note that Ing, *op. cit.* p. 212, writing in 1971, also thought that the effect of a disclaimer of an intestate benefit by one member of the class of beneficiaries entitled would be to increase the share of the other members of the class, referring to *Re Callaway, supra, Re Peacock* [1957] Ch. 310, and *Re Coleman and Jarrom* (1876) 4 Ch.D. 165.

[28] *Per* Walton J., *supra*, at pp. 1271, 1272.

[29] *Supra*, at pp. 1270–1272; see *Re Callaway, supra*, and Ing, *op. cit.* at p. 212.

[30] At pp. 1270–1272.

> "It seems to me that the absolutely inevitable result, where all the members of any one particular class have disclaimed, is to say, 'very well, for the purposes of the distribution of this estate, that class must simply be left out of consideration.' And in the present case, that means that when applying section 46(1)(v) of the 1925 Act to the estate of the deceased, one must leave out 'first,' because all the members of that class have disclaimed. 'Secondly,' and 'thirdly,' will go because there are no members of those classes anyway, and one will then land up on 'fourthly.' And it seems to me that is the sensible and logical and intelligible way of dealing with the matter."[31]

Re Scott[32] leaves some important questions unanswered. If a child disclaims his entitlement on the intestacy of his parent, does that have the effect of benefiting his issue or of benefiting the next class of persons entitled? Likewise, if a brother or sister disclaims, does that benefit his or her child? It will be appreciated that grandchildren and nephews and nieces have no entitlement in their own right on intestacy but merely take by representation the share which their parent would have taken if he or she had not pre-deceased the intestate.[33] If the parent survives but disclaims, it seems unnatural to say that he or she has pre-deceased the intestate so as to confer a share by representation on his or her issue. If that is so, the effect of a disclaimer would be to exclude both the parent and his issue to the advantage of the next class entitled under the intestacy. This seems the better view, although it could obviously be contended that, where a parent disclaims, his share is to pass "as if he or she had pre-deceased the intestate," in which case his or her issue would be entitled. The point is unresolved by authority. It is interesting to note that in New Zealand, where there are specific statutory provisions governing disclaimers on intestacy, the effect of the legislation is that the person disclaiming is deemed to have predeceased the intestate and his or her issue may take the disclaimed interest by representation.[34]

[31] It was argued in the case that the same result could have been achieved having regard to the words of the statute. The concluding words at the end of the first, second and fourth paras. in section 46(1)(v) are "if no person takes an absolutely vested interest under such trusts," and these words would seem to cover the case where the reason why a person does not take an absolutely vested interest is because the person has disclaimed his interest. But this was not adopted by Walton J. apparently on the grounds that it would not apply to para. (3) (grandparents) where the words are "if there is no member of this class." Accordingly a wider principle was required. Ing, *op. cit.*, p. 213 writing in 1971, thought that where there were no other members of the entitled class, the interest might possibly be ownerless and *bona vacantia*.

[32] *Supra.*

[33] s.47(1)(i), s.47(3).

[34] Administration Act 1969, s.81, see Hardingham, Neave and Ford, *Wills and Intestacy*, pp. 432, 433.

Another point which did not arise for decision in *Re Scott*,[35] but which is explored by Ing,[36] is the effect of disclaimer by a spouse of her intestate benefits. These include absolute interests such as the personal chattels, interests "charged" on the residuary estate and a life interest in the residue. Ing concludes so far as the latter two interests are concerned that, since they are clearly interests in the residuary estate, a disclaimer of them will simply swell the residuary estate to the benefit of the issue or next category of relative entitled. Ing suggests, however, that the personal chattels could be viewed differently in view of the provisions of section 46(1)(1) by which the personal chattels are expressly excluded from the residuary estate (the entitlement is to the residuary estate "other than the personal chattels") and that, where the spouse disclaims all his or her interest on intestacy the chattels might pass as *bona vacantia.*

The fiscal consequences of a variation or disclaimer made within two years of death[37] have been considered above.[38]

Assignment of interest

There is, of course, no reason why an intestate benefit once accepted cannot be assigned. The tax consequences of such an assignment when amounting to a variation within two years of death have been considered above.[39] It can be noted that, where a parent prima facie entitled on intestacy wishes to benefit his children in his place, this should be effected by express assignment within section 142(1) of the Inheritance Tax Act 1984, and not simply by disclaimer.[40]

Exclusion by Direction or Act of Deceased

Attempted exclusion by direction

Rule in Lett v. Randall

A consequence of the mandatory nature of the code of intestate succession is the rule that a person cannot, by *inter vivos* direction or by will, purport to exclude all of his next of kin from their statutory

[35] *Supra.*
[36] *Op. cit.*, pp. 214, 215.
[37] See Inheritance Tax Act 1984, s.142(1) and Capital Gains Tax Act 1979, s.49(6).
[38] *Ante*, p. 119.
[39] See *ante*.
[40] This is because the likely effect of disclaimer will be to benefit the next class entitled to take not the issue of the disclaiming party; see *ante*.

entitlement on intestacy. This is a long-established rule which was stated as follows by Stuart V.-C. in *Lett* v. *Randall*[41]:

> "It was asked during the argument in *Pickering* v. *Stamford*[42] whether, supposing the testator annexed a clause of exclusion from any further part of his estate to the legacy he gave to each of the next of kin, would that have excluded everyone to whom the Statute of Distribution gave the property in case of intestacy? The answer must be certainly not if the clause of exclusion extends to all the next-of-kin, for then there could be no one in whose favour the exclusion could operate, and therefore the attempt to exclude being made universal becomes nugatory and fails. It would be as nugatory as an universal exclusion of all mankind. But although by making the declaration of exclusion from any further share too extensive it becomes inoperative, nevertheless, where it has a limited operation, so as to give a benefit to other persons, it may unquestionably be valid. But the exclusion by declaration of one or some only of the next of kin, if it be valid, must enure to the benefit of the rest, and has the same effect as a gift by implication to them of the share of those who are excluded."

More recently Kay J. applied the rule in *Re Holmes*,[43] stating:

> "A testator cannot deprive those who are by law entitled to his estate by words of exclusion only. He can only do that by giving the estate to somebody else. The simple case is where the testator makes a will and says, 'I declare that my heir-at-law should take no part of my real estate.' That is a perfect *brutum fulmen*. The heir-at-law does not take under the will, but by the general law of succession, and the testator can only deprive him of it by making a will and giving the property to somebody else. The same rule applies, and has been held to apply again and again, in the case of

[41] (1855) 3 Sm. & G. 83 at p. 89, where a testator gave his widow an annuity by will and declared that the provision was intended to be taken in discharge of all claims which she may at any time have in the estate on his death. A portion of the estate was left undisposed of and it was held that the widow was excluded from participating in the property, of which the testator died intestate. In that case the fact that there was an intestacy apparent on the face of the will was regarded as an important circumstance enabling the court to distinguish other cases where all the property was actually disposed of by the will but became distributable through an unforeseen accident. An example of the latter sort of case is *Pickering* v. *Lord Stamford* (1791) 3 Ves. 332, where the widow was held entitled to the intestate benefit additional to the testamentary provision expressed to be in satisfaction of her claims; see also *Penny* v. *Milligan* [1907] 5 C.L.R. 349.

[42] *supra.*

[43] (1890) 62 L.T. 383, where the testator's will provided "... and hereby utterly and for ever excluding any and all relatives except my two dear nieces aforesaid ... from any and all advantages or benefit in this my last will and testament." The residue of the testator's estate in the case was undisposed of and the court held that it devolved upon the whole class of statutory next-of-kin without restriction to the two nieces. See also *Vachell* v. *Breton* (1706) Bro.P.C. 51 "10/– and no more."

> the next-of-kin. A testator cannot deprive his next-of-kin who take in succession to him by law except by making a will and disposing of the property to somebody else. If he does not do that, the next of kin have by law, the right of succession to his personal estate."

However, there are two qualifications to this rule which must be noted. First, it is possible that, as in *Re Holmes*,[44] the direction is so worded as to preclude the named next-of-kin from taking under the will of the testator but not from taking on his intestacy.[45]

Secondly and more importantly, a clause excluding some of the next of kin may be construed as a gift by implication to the others and clearly a testator can vary the statutory entitlement by disposing of the property to specified persons. The line between simple exclusion and a gift by implication to the others can be difficult to draw but an illustrative case is *Bund* v. *Green*.[46] A testator directed that L. S., G. S., and his brother and two sisters should not be entitled to take any share of his personal estate of which he might happen to die intestate but should be wholly excluded therefrom in the same manner as if they had all died in his lifetime. There was an intestacy as to residue and it was held that the next of kin, other than the five persons named who were excluded, were entitled. In a short judgment Hall V.-C. stated that it was a matter of construction and that the provision should be regarded by implication as a gift to the statutory next of kin other than the persons excluded. Clearly such a gift by implication can only apply where some, but not all, of the class of next-of-kin are excluded.

In the most recent decision on the point, *Re Wynn (decd.)*,[47] Warner J. has stated the principle in terms of a settled rule of construction:

> "In my view such a direction (*i.e. that one or some of the testator's next of kin shall take no share in his property*) will operate as such an implied gift unless there is something in the will to indicate a contrary intention."

That view was applied to a will which simply read "I Olga Wynn, revoke all previous wills today, 9th January 1981. I hereby wish that all I possess is not given to my husband Anthony Wynn." It was decided that the will was effective to dispose of the whole of her estate

[44] *supra*.
[45] *Per* Warner J. in *Re Wynn (decd.)* [1984] 1 W.L.R. 237 at p. 240; see also *Ramsay* v. *Shelmerdine* (1865) L.R. 1 Eq. 129; and *Sykes* v. *Sykes* (1868) L.R. 4 Eq. 200, affd. L.R. 3 Ch.App. 301.
[46] (1879) 12 Ch.D. 819; see also *Johnson* v. *Johnson* (1841) 4 Beav. 318 probably incorrectly decided, see Warner J., in *Re Wynn (decd.)*, *supra*, at p. 241. See also *Re Snider* (1974) 46 D.L.R. (3d) 161; *Bateman* v. *Bateman* [1941] 3 D.L.R. 762.
[47] *Supra* at p. 241.

in favour of the persons other than Mr. Wynn entitled thereto on intestacy.[48]

Gift over on intestacy

An analogous rule is that a gift over which is to take effect on the intestacy of the donee is void as repugnant to the ownership vested in the donee.[49] An example is provided by the case of *Re Dixon*[50] where the testator gave shares to his daughters absolutely and added a gift over in the case of any child dying "... without a will and childless." The entire gift over was held void for repugnancy. The principle was stated by Turner L.J. in *Holmes* v. *Godson*[51]:

> "... the law has said that, if a man dies intestate, the real estate shall go to the heir, and the personal estate to the next of kin, and any disposition which tends to contravene that disposition which the law would make is against the policy of the law and therefore void."[52]

However, these cases relate to conditions and it might be that the principle would have no application to a gift which took the form of a determinable fee.[53] It is clear that such a fee can be made determinable on bankruptcy[54] and thus perhaps on intestacy.

Widow contracting out: separation agreement

The question which arises under this heading is the effect of a separation agreement between husband and wife in terms excluding the widow from sharing in her husband's intestacy or under his will. There does not appear to be any modern English authority on the point but reference can be made to the Canadian decision of *Re Rist*[55] where Ford J.A. stated:

[48] Rejecting the persuasive arguments of counsel, first, that *Bund* v. *Green* should be distinguished because in that case the testator had expressly referred to intestacy and secondly, that the attempt to exclude Mr. Wynn failed because there was no indication on the will of a positive intention to benefit the other persons entitled on intestacy. It is probable that most commentators would have stated the rule previously as a matter of construction and have required such positive evidence of a gift to the others. *Re Wynn* however establishes the gift by implication automatically in the absence of a contrary intention.

[49] *Holmes* v. *Godson* (1856) 8 D.M. & G. 152; *Re Dixon* [1903] 2 Ch. 458; *Re Ashton* [1920] 2 Ch. 481.

[50] *Supra.*

[51] *Supra*, at p. 165.

[52] Applied in *Re Patterson* [1939] V.L.R. 66 where a direction that on a donee's intestacy leaving issue part of the property in a testamentary gift to the donee, should go to third parties, was held void in that it would have the effect of altering the devolution of property prescribed by law.

[53] For the distinction between determinable fees and conditions subsequent, see Megarry and Wade, *Law of Real Property* (5th ed.), pp. 69, 70.

[54] See Trustee Act 1925, s.33.

[55] [1939] 2 D.L.R. 644; see *Slatter* v. *Slatter* (1834) 1 Y & C.Ex. 28.

> "There is I think ample authority for the proposition of law that a wife may forfeit her rights upon her spouse's intestacy by express agreement made either prior or subsequent to the marriage and indeed that an express or implied agreement may exist between the spouses excluding the survivor from any claim to the other's property on intestacy. . . .[56]
>
> This principle is distinct from and not inconsistent with the rule that a testator cannot deprive those who are by law entitled to his estate on intestacy by words of exclusion only. . . ."[57]

In that case there was a comprehensive clause in a separation agreement excluding the wife from benefit under her husband's estate[58] and it was held by the Alberta Supreme Court that the wife may so waive the rights accorded to her by statute under the intestacy of her husband.[59]

Contracts to bequeath or devise property

It is possible to affect the intestate entitlement to property on death by a *bona fide* contract made for valuable consideration by the deceased *inter vivos*.[60] A contract not to revoke a will does not prevent the revocation of the will but, if the will is revoked *inter vivos* by act of the party[61] and not by marriage,[62] the promisee may have an action against the estate for breach of contract.[63] If the benefit contracted for is a legacy, then, if the deceased has failed to leave the legacy, the promisee can claim payment from his estate.[64] Where the contract is to devise or bequeath specific property and the deceased disposes of it elsewhere by will, or dies intestate, then the personal

[56] Citing *Druce* v. *Denison* (1801) 6 Ves. 385; and *Gurly* v. *Gurly* (1840) 2 Dr. & Wal. 463. See also *Henderson* v. *Northern Trusts Co.* [1953] 1 D.L.R. 109; *Re James* [1950] 2 W.W.R. 313; *Penny* v. *Milligan* [1907] 5 C.L.R. 349.

[57] Citing *Re Holmes, Holmes* v. *Holmes* (1890) 62 L.T. 383; *Johnson* v. *Johnson* (1841) 4 Beav. 318, see *ante*.

[58] The clause was as follows: ". . . The said Kate Rist doth hereby covenant and agree with the said Thomas Rist that in case the said Thomas Rist shall predecease the said Kate Rist, testate or intestate the said Kate Rist shall have no right claim or demand of any nature or kind under the Intestate Succession Act or any Act or Law whatsoever against the estate of the said Thomas Rist, and also the said Kate Rist covenants with the said Thomas Rist that she will not in case the said Thomas Rist shall predecease her testate make any application claim or demand under the provisions of the Widow's Relief Act or under any other Act or Law either here or hereafter in force whatsoever with the object of obtaining an allowance out of the estate of the said Thomas Rist."

[59] A former spouse can on divorce in effect contract out of her rights under the Inheritance (Provision for Family and Dependants) Act 1975, see s.15 and discussion *post*.

[60] See generally, *Schaefer* v. *Schuhmann* [1972] A.C. 572 at pp. 585–587.

[61] *Robinson* v. *Ommanney* (1882) 21 Ch.D. 780; (1883) 23 Ch.D. 285.

[62] *Re Marsland* [1939] Ch. 820.

[63] *Robinson* v. *Ommanney*, *supra*.

[64] *Hammersley* v. *De Biel* (1845) 12 Cl. & Fin. 45, as a creditor if the estate is insolvent, *Graham* v. *Wickham* (1863) 1 De G.J. & Sm. 474. A covenant to leave a share of residue is treated differently, *Jervis* v. *Wolferstan* (1874) L.R. 18 Eq. 18, 24.

representative can be ordered to convey it to the promisee as the person beneficially entitled to it.[65] Such an order would have the effect of putting the property beyond the reach of the person otherwise entitled on intestacy. As Nicholls C.J. commented in a Tasmanian case[66]

> "All I propose to add to what I have already said on this case, is that the respondent's rights do not arise under the will. They arise contractually and exist independently of the will. If the testator had made no will, or had made a will leaving everything to his widow and daughter, he would have made a breach of his contract with the respondent. She would then have sued for damages for the breach, and the measure of her damages would have been the value of the testator's estate."

Similar considerations would presumably apply where the promise was to die intestate and confer benefits in that way and the deceased had made a will in breach of the agreement.

Constructive trust

Secret trusts

It is possible that, by reason of an *inter vivos* arrangement, the intestate's property might become subject to a constructive trust in favour of persons other than the prima facie intestate successor. The first of these situations is where the property is subject to a secret trust.[67] Suppose that the owner of property communicates to the intestate successor *inter vivos* that on his death he wishes the successor to hold the property not beneficially but on trust for a named beneficiary. If the successor accepts this trust, in reliance on which the owner fails to make a will, then on death the court will enforce the trust in favour of the secret beneficiary.[68] There seems no doubt that the principle is not confined to wills but applies also where the owner of property has refrained from disposing of it by will relying on the promise of the intestate successor to dispose of it in favour of the agreed beneficiary.[69]

[65] *Schaefer* v. *Schuhmann, supra*; *Synge* v. *Synge* [1894] 1 Q.B. 470; *Re Edwards, Macadam* v. *Wright* [1958] Ch. 168.
[66] *Re Richardson's Estate* [1934] 29 Tas.L.R. 149 at p. 155.
[67] See generally Pettit, *Equity and the Law of Trusts*, 5th ed. (1984), p. 106. There is some academic disagreement as to whether such trusts are express, implied or constructive but this need not be explored here.
[68] See *Ottaway* v. *Norman* [1972] Ch. 698; *Re Snowden (decd.)* [1979] Ch. 528.
[69] *Strickland* v. *Aldridge* (1804) 9 Ves. 516; *Re Gardner* [1920] 2 Ch. 523; *McCormick* v. *Grogan* (1869) L.R. 4 H.L. 82 at pp. 97, 98. See *Snell's Equity*, 28th ed., p. 111. The doctrine applies equally where the owner has been induced to revoke a will and thus die intestate, *Tharp* v. *Tharp* [1916] 1 Ch. 142.

Mutual wills

An analogous situation where a constructive trust will affect the beneficial entitlement to property on intestacy is where there are mutual wills.[70] Suppose that a husband and wife agree to make wills in common form, usually in favour of the survivor for life with remainder to their children, and that they agree that the wills shall not be revoked. If the first party dies consistently with the agreement, equity will enforce the agreement against the survivor by means of a trust. The will might well be revoked but this will not affect the trust. Nourse J. expressed the rule in the recent case of *Re Cleaver (decd.)*[70] as follows:

> "The principle of all these cases[71] is that a court of equity will not permit a person to whom property is transferred by way of gift, but on the faith of an agreement or clear understanding that it is to be dealt with in a particular way for the benefit of a third person, to deal with that property inconsistently with that agreement or understanding. If he attempts to do so after having received the benefit of the gift equity will intervene by imposing a constructive trust on the property which is the subject matter of the agreement or understanding."

The judge went on to emphasise the necessity of finding a legally-binding obligation[72] and it is interesting to note that Nourse J. thought that such an obligation gave rise to a constructive, rather than an implied, trust.[73]

Although the leading authorities[74] on the principle are all concerned with cases where the survivor had made a new will in breach of the agreement, the principle undoubtedly applies where the survivor simply revokes the mutual will and dies intestate.[75]

Performance

There is nineteenth century authority to the effect that the equitable doctrine of performance can sometimes affect intestate entitlement.

[70] See *Re Cleaver (decd.)* [1981] 1 W.L.R. 939, where the existence of mutual wills was established.

[71] Notably, *Dufour* v. *Pereira* (1769) 1 Dick. 419; *Gray* v. *Perpetual Trustee Co. Ltd.* [1928] A.C. 391; *Re Oldham* [1925] Ch. 75; *Birmingham* v. *Renfrew* (1937) 57 C.L.R. 666; *Ottaway* v. *Norman* [1972] Ch. 698.

[72] Referring to *Lord Walpole* v. *Lord Orford* (1797) 3 Ves. 402.

[73] This point is a matter of some controversy amonst textbook writers on the Law of Trusts; see, for example, Pettit, *Equity and the Law of Trusts*, 5th ed. (1984) p. 113.

[74] *Dufour* v. *Pereira, supra*; *Re Oldham* [1925] Ch. 75; *Re Hagger* [1930] 2 Ch. 190; *Re Green (decd.)* [1951] 1 Ch. 148. See also *Stone* v. *Hoskins* [1905] P. 194; *Gray* v. *Perpetual Trustee Co. Ltd.* [1928] A.C. 391.

[75] See Burgess (1970) 34 Conv. 230 at pp. 244, 245, on the basis that the effect of the mutual wills agreement is to take the property out of the estate so that the intestacy rules cannot affect it.

The point is best illustrated by reference to *Garthshore* v. *Chalie*[76] where there was a covenant in a marriage settlement by the husband in the event of his death, leaving his wife, and children, within six months after his decease to convey, pay and assign one full and clear moiety of all such real and personal estate as he shall be seised and possessed of, or entitled to, at his decease. It was held that on the principle of part performance, the widow was not entitled in addition to the moiety under the covenant to one-third of the residue of the personal estate by the intestacy of her husband. However, in a subsequent case[77] Sir James Wigram V.-C. commented that "... The decisions upon this question appears to me to be purely arbitrary." Although recognising that Lord Elden in the above case had referred the case to a principle, the Vice Chancellor found it difficult to see why the right of the widow to her distributive share should be excluded by her right under another contract.[78] It is not clear how these principles would affect the imperative statutory entitlement under the 1925 code. It would seem that in *Re Ashton*[79] the court did not think that a covenant to pay a gross sum *inter vivos* or within two years of death was satisfied or performed by the covenantee becoming entitled under the intestacy of the covenantor to a greater sum.

Unmarried minor

Finally, some reference can be made to what has been described as "one of the most awkward provisions of the 1925 Act,"[80] namely section 51(3). This provision governs the devolution of real property on the death of an unmarried minor and provides for a rather special form of inheritance in such cases. The subsection is in the following terms:

> "Where an infant dies after the commencement of this Act without having been married, and independently of this section he would, at his death, have been equitably entitled under a settlement (including a will) to a vested estate in fee simple or absolute interest in freehold land, or in any property settled to devolve therewith or as freehold land, such infant shall be deemed to have had an entailed interest, and the settlement shall be construed accordingly."

The effect of this provision has been summarised by Farwell J.[81] as follows: "In other words the Legislature says to the infant, 'If you

[76] (1804) 10 Ves. 1. See also *Blandy* v. *Widmore* (1716) 1 P.Wms. 324; *Lee* v. *Cox and D'Aranda* (1746) 3 Atk. 419; and *Goldsmid* v. *Goldsmid* (1818) 1 Swan s.219.
[77] *Salisbury* v. *Salisbury* (1848) 6 Hare 524.
[78] At p. 529. Referring also to the differences which exist where the obligation is to pay an annuity rather than a gross sum.
[79] (1934) 78 S.J. 803.
[80] *Williams on Title* 4th ed. 256; see also (1930) 74 S.J. 382.
[81] *Re Taylor* [1931] 2 Ch. 242 at p. 246.

attain twenty-one or marry the estate is yours absolutely. Otherwise it is only an entail.' " It is somewhat strange, however, because a minor cannot in general make a will,[82] nor can he dispose of an entailed interest under section 176 of the Law of Property Act 1925 and thus he cannot bar the entail.[83] Further, since by definition the minor must die unmarried, there cannot be any issue capable of inheriting under the entail. It will be appreciated that the Family Law Reform Act 1969 expressly states that the section conferring rights of succession on illegitimate children "... does not apply to or affect the right of any person to take any entailed interest in real or personal property."[84] Thus the effect of section 51(3) is to confer an interest which must fail immediately on the death of the minor with the inevitable result that it reverts back to the settlor. The consequence of this, in the absence of a gift over, is that, if the land was originally devised by will, it will fall into the settlor's residue or, if it was itself a gift of residue, will pass as on the settlor's intestacy. Why this result is regarded as more appropriate than the property being distributed in the usual way on the *child's* intestacy is, as mentioned above, obscure to say the least. Clearly, however, it is necessary to differentiate section 51(3) property[85] from the rest of the minor estate on death intestate.

[82] Wills Act 1837, s.7, as amended by the Family Law Reform Act 1969, s.3(1)(*a*) substituting 18 for 21 years.

[83] Which only applies to persons of full age, and which is thought to prevail over the exceptional privilege enabling infants to make a will if in actual military service etc.

[84] s.14(5).

[85] It would seem that leaseholds would not be included, nor property subject to a trust for sale. There is only one fully reported decision on s.51(3). *Re Taylor* [1931] 2 Ch. 242, a case with exceptional facts which could not in fact arise now but which can be shortly noted. Before 1926 an infant inherited land as eldest son on the death of his father intestate, subject to his mother's right of dower. The effect of the coming into force of the 1925 legislation was that he was treated as deriving his title under a settlement: Settled Land Act 1925, s.1(2)(ii)(*d*). The son then died an infant unmarried. It was held that the succession was governed by s.51(3), since that provision covered a notional settlement on intestacy (*i.e.* a settlement by virtue of the effect of the Settled Land Act 1925), with the result that the son was deemed to have an entail which ceased on his death and the property reverted to the settlor, his father. It was held further that the person entitled thereto was not the eldest son who was the heir, which would of course result in a circular succession, but the next heir, the father's younger son. The descent to the eldest son as heir was fully satisfied once and for all and on his death under 21 and unmarried the property went to the younger son as the next heir of the last purchaser, the intestate father, under the old rules of inheritance since it was a pre-1926 intestacy.

CHAPTER 18

FAMILY PROVISION

INTRODUCTION

The statutory code of intestacy provides for a fixed and certain distribution of the estate based on the presumed intention of the average intestate. As such it will provide a fair and reasonable distribution in most cases but inevitably will appear to operate unfairly in particular circumstances. The solution provided by English law to this problem is to supplement the fixed rules of intestacy by conferring jurisdiction on the court to make discretionary awards out of the estate in favour of specified classes of applicants.[1] In this way the undoubted merit of having a fixed and certain, and therefore simple and inexpensive to operate, system of intestate succession is not prejudiced but the entitlement can be varied by order of the court where necessary. It is submitted that this approach is to be preferred to the alternatives. A code of intestate succession alone could operate arbitrarily and unfairly in some cases; a discretionary system of intestate entitlement would render all estates uncertain and complex; and a system of fixed or prior rights of inheritance[2] would tend to be as arbitrary and sometimes as unfair as a fixed code of intestate succession. An alternative intermediate course is to empower the surviving spouse, and possibly the children, to set aside the will in favour of fixed rights of inheritance where the will makes inadequate provision for them. This system, which is common in the United States, depends on application by the spouse and is thus termed the "elective share" approach; it has not been adopted in England.[3]

THE JURISDICTION

In view of the necessity of having some system of supplementary

[1] The seminal legislation on family provision was the New Zealand, Testator's Family Maintenance Act 1906. All the Australian States and Territories subsequently followed that example. See Hardingham, Neave and Ford, *Wills and Intestacy* (1983) on the Commonwealth jurisdiction.

[2] Many jurisdictions do of course have a system of fixed or prior rights of inheritance which in effect limit testamentary power to the advantage of spouses and children. A case can obviously be made for such a system in preference to a system of application for discretionary awards, in cases of testate succession, but the arguments have minimal cogency in cases of intestate succession. See Law Commission Working Paper No. 42, p. 215; 52 Law Commission Report No. 52, p. 10; Guest, (1957) 73 L.Q.R. 74.

[3] See Tyler's *Family Provision*, 2nd ed. (1984), R. D. Oughton, for a full discussion of the policy, history, and substantive law relating to family provision.

jurisdiction in cases of intestacy, it is surprising that, although the Inheritance (Family Provision) Act 1938 introduced such a system in cases of testate succession, it was not until 1952 that it was made equally applicable to cases of partial or total intestacy.[4] The 1938 Act as originally enacted provided:

> "...and leaving a will then, if the court on application by etc.... is of opinion that the will does not make reasonable provision for the maintenance of that dependant...."

The jurisdiction was thus limited to a consideration of the provision made by will and no application could be made in cases of total intestacy. In cases of partial intestacy it would seem that the intestate benefits would have been disregarded.

This was amended in 1952 to read:

> "...that the disposition of the deceased's estate effected by his will, or the law relating to intestacy, or the combination of his will and that law, is not such as to make reasonable provision...."

The greatly increased entitlement of the surviving spouse on intestacy introduced by the 1952 Act could cause hardship to a divorced spouse, particularly where a long-standing "innocent" wife divorced her husband late in life, the latter remarrying and the new spouse inheriting on his intestacy. In 1958 legislation was introduced enabling former spouses to apply for financial provision out of the estate of the deceased and this jurisdiction was consolidated, as a parallel system of family provision, in section 26 of the Matrimonial Causes Act 1965. The Inheritance (Provision for Family and Dependants) 1975 Act assimilated this jurisdiction into the main body of the law of family provision.

Despite these successive amendments the 1938 Act was fundamentally restricted to a jurisdiction to provide maintenance for a limited class of applicants with no anti-avoidance provisions. The reforms in other areas of family law promoted by the Law Commission in the 1960s highlighted the deficiencies of the system, in particular the fact that a divorced spouse could be better off than a widowed spouse.[5] A thorough review of the position was conducted and various alterna-

[4] Intestates' Estates Act 1952, s.7 and Sched. 4, with effect from January 1, 1953. The change was made in response to a recommendation by the Morton Committee, 1951 Cmd. 8310. The reason was that the greatly increased provision for a spouse could work to the disadvantage of the children, particularly where they were the offspring of a previous marriage. The 1952 Act also increased the size of the awards that could be made in favour of a spouse, although it was not until the Family Provision Act 1966, that all restrictions on the amount of the award (although still limited to maintenance) were removed; see Tyler, *op. cit.*, pp. 20–22.

[5] This was because the Matrimonial Causes Act 1965 had conferred wide powers on the court to make financial and property provision for a divorced spouse, whilst a disinherited widow was restricted by the 1938 Act to an application for maintenance.

tive systems considered,[6] culminating in the Inheritance (Provision for Family and Dependants) Act 1975. This Act provided a new code of family provision based on the familiar supplementary system of discretionary provision but extended the classes of persons who could apply; it enabled spouses to apply for reasonable provision not limited to maintenance and contained anti-avoidance provisions. The jurisdiction emphatically embraces intestate and partially intestate estates with section 1(1) providing that the specified classes of applicants can

> "... apply to the Court for an order under section 2 of this Act on the ground that the disposition of the deceased's estate effected by his will or the law relating to intestacy, or the combination of his will and that law, is not such as to make reasonable financial provision for the applicant."[7]

Under the 1938 Act (as extended by the 1952 Act) it was expressly stated that the court "... shall not be bound to assume that the law relating to intestacy makes reasonable provision in all cases."[8] There is no such express provision in the 1975 Act but the assumption is implicit and there is a judicial comment to the effect that the problem must be exactly the same whether one is dealing with a will or an intestacy or a combination of both.[9] There are a number of reported cases concerning applications against an intestate estate. In *Kourkgy* v. *Lusher*,[10] which concerned an application by a mistress against a wife's entitlement on intestacy, Wood J. concluded:

> "Taking into account all the circumstances and all the relevant matters in section 3(1), (4) and (6), I am not satisfied that "the disposition of the deceased's estate by the law relating to intestacy is such as not to make reasonable financial provision for the plaintiff' or to put it differently, the plaintiff has failed to satisfy me that it was unreasonable in all the circumstances that she received no financial provision from the net estate of the deceased."

The claim in *Re Coventry (decd.)*[11] by an adult son against the wife's intestate entitlement also failed. More successful applicants against

[6] See the Law Commission's Working Paper No. 42 on Family Property Law; and Report No. 61, Second Report on Family Property: Family Provision on Death.

[7] It is beyond the scope of this book to discuss in detail the jurisdiction relating to family provision contained in the 1975 Act. However the Act is clearly relevant to some cases of intestacy and as reference has been made in earlier chapters to the jurisdiction, a brief consideration of the basic provisions will be included here with particular reference to the relevance of those provisions to cases of intestacy. For a full discussion see Tyler's *Family Provision*, 2nd ed., R. D. Oughton *op. cit.*

[8] s.1(8) added to the 1938 Act by the 1952 Act.

[9] *Per* Goff L.J. in *Re Coventry* [1980] Ch. 461 at pp. 471, 472.

[10] [1983] 4 F.L.R. 65, at p. 82, this case and those noted below are discussed more fully in this chapter.

[11] [1980] Ch. 461.

intestate estates are, however, illustrated by *Re Leach (decd.),*[12] (step-daughter against deceased's brothers and sister), *Re Kirby (decd.)*[13] (male cohabitant against son and daughter), *Harrington* v. *Gill*[14] (female cohabitant against daughter) and *Re Callaghan (decd.)*[15] (step-son against deceased's sisters).[15]

CLASSES OF APPLICANTS

Spouse

An application for financial provision out of the deceased's estate can be made only by persons who survive the deceased[16] and who fall within one of the specified classes in section 1. The first such category is "the wife or husband of the deceased."[17] An application can be made where the will or the law relating to intestacy, or the combination of the will and that law, is not such as to make "reasonable financial provision" for that person.[18] In the case of surviving spouses,[19] "reasonable financial provision" means "... such financial provision as it would be reasonable in all the circumstances of the case for a husband or wife to receive, whether or not that provision is required for his or her maintenance."[20] In the vast majority of cases of total intestacy the intestate entitlement of the spouse will satisfy this definition and no application for further provision will be supportable. However, it is possible to imagine cases where an application might succeed, as, for example, where the estate is very substantial and includes a business in which the spouse has been actively engaged during the marriage. In such a case the £40,000 statutory legacy and the life interest in one-half of the estate, assuming that there are also children surviving, might be regarded as inadequate.[21] It is perhaps unlikely in such cases that the deceased would have failed to make a will but the will might be invalid.

The jurisdiction of the court under the 1975 Act is not limited to the making of periodical payments or of lump sums[22] but includes also power to order the transfer or the settlement of specific property,[23] the acquisition and transfer of specific property[24] or the variation of ante- or post-nuptial settlements.[25] These powers might be relevant in cases

[12] [1985] 3 W.L.R. 413 C.A.
[13] [1982] 3 F.L.R. 249.
[14] [1983] 4 F.L.R. 265.
[15] [1984] 3 W.L.R. 1076.
[16] s.1(1).
[17] s.1(1)(*a*).
[18] s.1(1).
[19] Except for judicially separated spouses, s.1(2)(*a*).
[20] s.1(2)(*a*).
[21] See *e.g., Re Besterman (decd.)* [1984] Ch. 458, *post.*
[22] s.2(1)(*a*), and s.2(1)(*b*); see *Re Besterman (decd.), supra.*
[23] s.2(1)(*c*), s.2(1)(*d*).
[24] s.2(1)(*e*).
[25] s.2(1)(*f*).

of total intestacy where there is a surviving spouse. Further, the surviving spouse's entitlement on intestacy is limited to "the residuary estate of the intestate"[26] and this will not include property owned by the deceased as a joint tenant, or property disposed of *inter vivos* or subject to an effective contract to bequeath or devise by will, or property subject to a nomination or a *donatio mortis causa*.[27] The 1975 Act contains provisions to include, or to bring in by order of the court, each of these categories of property in the net estate which can be made subject to an order.[28] Thus, although on a total intestacy the spouse might be entitled to the whole estate, this entitlement may be illusory if the deceased has transferred his property *inter vivos* into the joint names of himself and another person or has voluntarily disposed of the property in favour of another shortly before his death. In such cases an application by a surviving spouse to invoke the wider powers under the 1975 Act might well be appropriate. The relevance of the 1975 Act jurisdiction in cases of partial intestacy will be apparent.

In addition the court is directed in cases of application by a spouse to have particular regard to the age of the applicant and the duration of the marriage, to the contribution made by the applicant to the welfare of the family of the deceased and to the provision which the applicant might reasonably have expected to receive if on the day on which the deceased died the marriage, instead of being terminated by death, had been terminated by a decree of divorce.[29] The judicial approach to the determination of an award with reference to these factors is well illustrated by the Court of Appeal decision in *Re Besterman (decd.)*[30] where a millionaire had by his will made inadequate provision for his widow and a large lump sum was awarded.[31]

Definition of wife or husband

A further aspect of the family provision jurisdiction relating to spouses is that the definition of "the wife or husband of the deceased" for the purposes of the 1975 Act is wider than the definition of such persons for the purposes of intestate succession. The position of divorced spouses is considered in the next section but it will be recalled that, by virtue of section 18(2) of the Matrimonial Causes Act

[26] Administrative Estates Act 1925 (hereinafter also referred to as the "A.E.A. 1925"), s.46(1); s.33(4).

[27] A.E.A. 1925, s.1(1).

[28] Net estate is widely defined by s.25(1). Property nominated and *donationes mortis causa* are included by s.8. Joint property can be treated as part of the net estate by s.9. s.10 contains powers to bring in certain *inter vivos* dispositions, and s.11 relates to contracts to make wills. See *post* p. 373.

[29] s.3(2).

[30] [1984] Ch. 458, see also *Re Bunning (decd.)* [1984] Ch. 480 where *Re Besterman* was applied and a widow was in effect given one-half of the spouses' joint assets.

[31] The case also illustrates the sort of circumstances where the absolute entitlement of a widow on intestacy might be regarded as inadequate.

1973, a judicially separated spouse is disentitled on intestacy.[32] Such a person can apply under the 1975 Act as a husband or wife save that the extended meaning of "reasonable financial provision" noted above[33] with reference to a spouse does not apply "... where the marriage with the deceased was the subject of a decree of judicial separation and at the date of death the decree was in force and the separation was continuing."[34]

It has also been noted above that a party to a void marriage has no entitlement on the intestacy of the other[35] but for the purposes of the 1975 Act[36]:

> "any reference to a wife or husband shall be treated as including a reference to a person who in good faith entered into a void marriage with the deceased unless either:
> (*a*) the marriage of the deceased and that person was dissolved or annulled during the lifetime of the deceased and the dissolution or annulment is recognised by the law of England and Wales, or
> (*b*) that person has during the lifetime of the deceased entered into a later marriage."

There may be some doubt whether a party to a polygamous marriage is entitled under the law of intestacy, but there is no doubt, on the authority of *Re Sehota (decd.)*,[37] that such a person can apply under the 1975 Act.

Further, the rule of public policy will (subject to the relief now available under the Forfeiture Act 1982) exclude from intestate benefit a person who has been criminally responsible for the death of the deceased.[38] Such a person can, however, apply for provision out of the estate under the 1975 Act by virtue of section 3 of the Forfeiture Act 1982.[39]

The right to claim under the 1975 Act against a deceased's spouse's

[32] See *ante*, p. 162.
[33] *Ante*, p. 356.
[34] s.1(2)(*a*).
[35] *Ante*. p. 169 where the marriage is voidable, but has not been annulled, the spouse would be entitled both under intestacy and the Act by virtue of s.16 of the Matrimonial Causes Act 1973, see *ante* p. 167.
[36] s.25(4).
[37] [1978] 1 W.L.R. 1506 (husband had left all his property to his second wife).
[38] See *ante*, p. 323.
[39] This Act came into force on October 13, 1982 and will govern applications made under the 1975 Act after that date. There was previously some doubt as to whether a person disentitled from testamentary or intestate inheritance by the rule of public policy could apply for discretionary relief under the 1975 Act. The Court of Appeal decided in *Re Royse (decd.)* [1984] 3 W.L.R. 784 that there could be no such application where the forfeiture rule applied. In that case the 1982 Act relief was not available to the applicant because the proceedings were commenced before that Act came into force, and in any event the applicant was out of time to apply for relief under that Act. See more fully discussed *ante*.

estate is personal to the surviving spouse and therefore ceases to exist on the death of the applicant.[40]

Former spouse

The second category of applicant identified by the 1975 Act is "a former wife or former husband of the deceased who has not remarried." This category was defined by the Act originally as meaning a person whose marriage with the deceased was during the deceased's lifetime dissolved or annulled by a decree of divorce or a nullity of marriage made under the Matrimonial Causes Act 1973,[41] The Matrimonial and Family Proceedings Act 1984 redefined the category as follows[42]:

> " 'former wife' or 'former husband' means a person whose marriage with the deceased was during the lifetime of the deceased either—
> (*a*) dissolved or annulled by a decree of divorce or a decree of nullity of marriage granted under the law of any part of the British Islands, or
> (*b*) dissolved or annulled in any country or territory outside the British Islands by a divorce or annulment which is entitled to be recognised as valid by the law of England and Wales; . . . "

The reference to "remarriage" includes a marriage which is by law void or voidable as to a person who has entered into such a marriage, and a marriage is treated for the purposes of the Act as a remarriage notwithstanding that the previous marriage of that party was void or voidable.[43]

An important point to note is that "reasonable financial provision" in the case of a former wife or husband, in contrast to the definition of that phrase in the case of a surviving wife or husband, means ". . . such financial provision as it would be reasonable in all the circumstances of the case for the applicant to receive for his or her maintenance."[44]

The word "maintenance" is not equivalent to providing for the wellbeing or benefit of the applicant[45] but is limited to payments which, directly or indirectly, enable the applicant in the future to discharge the cost of his daily living at whatever standard is

[40] *Whyte* v. *Ticehurst* [1986] 2 All E.R. 158.

[41] This meant that a person whose marriage was dissolved under other jurisdiction had to apply, if at all, under para. (*e*).

[42] 1984 Act, s.25(2).

[43] s.25(5).

[44] s.1(2)(*b*), see *Re Crawford (decd.)* [1983] 3 F.L.R. 273, it should not be assumed that "reasonable financial provision" under the 1975 Act was the same as an order for periodical payments during life under the Matrimonial Causes Act 1973 (hereinafter also referred to as the "M.C.A. 1973").

[45] Browne-Wilkinson J., in *Re Dennis (decd.)* [1981] 2 All E.R. 140 at p. 145, disapproving *Re Christie (decd.)* [1979] Ch. 168, applying *Re Coventry* [1980] Ch. 461.

appropriate to him or her.[46] This restricted view of the meaning of "maintenance" will obviously limit the scope of applications by former spouses and indeed by children and dependants who are likewise restricted to "maintenance."[47] However, in the case of applications by former spouses there is a further difficulty, namely the financial arrangements made by the court at the time of the divorce. In view of the wide powers available to the court under the Matrimonial Causes Act 1973[48] it is likely that the maintenance and property rights of the parties will already have been the subject of final resolution so that, as the Court of Appeal pointed out in *Re Fullard (decd.)*,[49] there will be few cases where an application by a former spouse for provision under the 1975 Act will succeed. Indeed the matter can be put beyond doubt by an order under section 15(1). This section, as originally enacted, provided that the court had power on the grant of a decree of divorce, nullity or judicial separation "... if the parties to the marriage agree ..." to order that one party should on the death of the other party be entitled to apply for an order under the Act. The Matrimonial and Family Proceedings Act 1984 substitutes the wording "... if it considers it just to do so may, on the application of either party to the marriage, order that the other party to the marriage shall not on the death of the applicant be entitled to apply for an order under section 2 of the [*1975*] Act."[50]

In other cases the fact that the applicant had been divorced from the deceased and the terms of the financial arrangements made by them on divorce are relevant matters for the court to have regard to under section 3(1)(*g*) of the 1975 Act.[51] Where the parties have settled their financial affairs on divorce with legal advice, it was stated in *Re Fullard*[52] that there had to be exceptional developments or conditions present at the date of death to show that reasonable maintenance within section 1(2)(*b*) had not been made for the former spouse by the agreed settlement. Examples of such exceptional circumstances provided by the Court of Appeal are where a long period of time has elapsed since the dissolution of the marriage in which there has been a continuing obligation by the deceased to make periodical payments to the former spouse and where the deceased is found to have a

[46] *Ibid.*, the application was by a son in the case, see *post.*

[47] At p. 145; see also *Jelley* v. *Illife* [1981] 2 All E.R. 29 at p. 34.

[48] See M.C.A. 1973, ss.23, 24.

[49] [1981] 3 W.L.R. 743, the parties were married in 1939 and divorced in 1977 when arrangements regarding the sharing of their assets (mainly the matrimonial home) were made. After the divorce the deceased lived with a woman to whom he left the whole of his estate. An application for financial provision by the former wife was unsuccessful.

[50] See also s.25(3) of the 1984 Act adding a new s.15A to the 1975 imposing further restrictions on applications under the Act where the court so orders pursuant to s.17 of the 1984 Act which relates to overseas divorces.

[51] *Re Fullard (decd.) supra*, at pp. 745, 746.

[52] *Supra.*

reasonable amount of capital in his estate or where the death unlocks a substantial capital sum from which the deceased, had he made a will immediately before his death, ought, within the criteria of the 1975 Act, to have made some provision for the surviving spouse.[53] However, it was thought doubtful whether the mere accretion of wealth after the dissolution of the marriage would of itself justify an application by a former spouse under the Act.

Thus it will be seen that the chances of a successful application by a former spouse under the 1975 Act in cases of intestacy are slim. Nevertheless the fact remains that the intestacy rules make absolutely no provision for a former spouse and it is possible to imagine deserving cases. Consider the case of the longstanding wife who was divorced, perhaps against her wishes,[54] late in life and where the deceased, who had remarried shortly before his death, left a considerable estate. In such a case the former spouse would surely have some chance of obtaining an award under the Act.

Administration of Justice Act 1982

The effect of dissolution or annulment of marriage on wills is governed, in the case of deaths on or after January 1, 1983,[55] by section 18A of the Wills Act 1837, added by section 18(2) of the Administration of Justice Act 1982. The section provides that, where after a testator has made a will, a decree of a court dissolves or annuls his marriage or declares it void, the will shall take effect as if any appointment of the former spouse as executor and trustee were omitted and "any devise or bequest to the former spouse shall lapse." In many cases this will result in a partial intestacy.[56] It is expressly provided that this provision "... is without prejudice to any right of the former spouse to apply for financial provision under the Inheritance (Provision for Family and Dependants) Act 1975."[57]

Children

There are two categories to consider here. Paragraph (*c*) of section 1(1) refers to "a child of the deceased" which includes an illegitimate child and a child *en ventre sa mère* at the death of the deceased.[58] Although not included expressly the phrase would undoubtedly also include by virtue of the relevant statutory enactments an adopted and

[53] *Supra*, at pp. 748, 749.
[54] By using the five-year separation ground, M.C.A. 1973, s.1(2)(*e*).
[55] s.73(6); s.76(11) A.J.A. 1982.
[56] Where the spouse is given a share in the residue where the spouse only has a life interest then s.18A(3) prevents the property becoming undisposed of and provides for an acceleration of the remainder interest.
[57] This seems to be a desirable safeguard and provides a remedy in cases of hardship. Note that if the testator remarries that will revoke the will and s.18A will no longer be applicable. See generally *Re Sinclair (decd.)* [1985] Ch. 446.
[58] s.25(1).

a legitimated child.[59] To this extent the definition of child corresponds with the meaning on intestacy; indeed the latter is obviously wider by including "issue."[60] The limited criteria for determining "reasonable financial provision" noted above with reference to former spouses also applies here. Thus it is not sufficient to show that the deceased could have been expected to make some provision for the child, there must have been a positive maintenance obligation. Minor or disabled or otherwise dependent children, will be able to satisfy this requirement more readily than will self-sufficient adult children. This can be illustrated by reference to the decision in *Re Coventry (decd.)*[61] which concerned an unsuccessful application by an adult son for provision out of his father's intestate estate. The deceased had married some fifty years before his death and the parties had purchased a house in which the wife was entitled to a third share. The wife had left the husband in 1957 and the adult son had then returned to live with his father in his house. The father died intestate and his widow was entitled to the whole of his estate which consisted solely of the house. The son, aged forty six, applied for financial provision out of the estate. The Court of Appeal,[62] in rejecting the application, stressed that the relevant question was not whether it might have been reasonable for the deceased to assist his son but whether in all the circumstances, looked at objectively, it was unreasonable that the effective provision governing the estate did not do so. The case indicates that "... an adult male in employment, and so capable of earning his own living ... " is unlikely to succeed in an application under the Act unless there is some special circumstance making the failure to make some financial provision unreasonable.[63] The mere fact that a son finds himself in necessitous circumstances is not by itself sufficient to establish a claim.

The same attitude is apparent in the more recent decision in *Re Dennis (decd.)*[64] where a claim by a 38-year-old able-bodied son received little sympathy. Browne-Wilkinson J. stated that a son is in the same position as all other able-bodied applicants and that a person who is physically capable of earning his own living faces a difficult task in getting provision made for him.[65] The judge emphasised that claims by persons other than spouses are limited to maintenance and

[59] See *ante* p. 178. Adoption Act 1976 and Legitimacy Act 1976.

[60] A.E.A. 1925, s.46(1).

[61] [1980] Ch. 461 contrast *Re Christie* [1979] Ch. 168 now regarded as discredited; and *Re Leach* [1985] 2 All E.R. 754, C.A.

[62] At p. 488 *per* Goff L.J.

[63] *Supra.* See Buckley L.J. at p. 495. The earlier decision of *Re Christie, Christie* v. *Keeble* [1979] Ch. 168 where an application by a son succeeded, was not followed and can be regarded as being of doubtful authority. See also *Re Dennis (decd.)* [1981] 2 All E.R. 140.

[64] [1981] 2 All E.R. 140, the application in fact was for permission to bring proceedings out of time under s.4 of the Act. The summons was dismissed.

[65] *Supra*, at p. 145.

that the applicant must show that the will fails to make provision for his maintenance.[66] He continued[67]:

> "But in my judgment the word 'maintenance' denotes only payments which, directly or indirectly, enable the applicant in the future to discharge the cost of his daily living at whatever standard of living is appropriate to him. The provision that is to be made is to meet recurring expenses, being expenses of living of an income nature. This does not mean that the provision need be by way of income payments. The provision can be by way of a lump sum, for example, to buy a house in which the applicant can be housed, thereby relieving him *pro tanto* of income expenditure. Nor am I suggesting that there may not be cases in which payment of existing debts may not be appropriate as a maintenance payment; for example, to pay the debts of an applicant in order to enable him to continue on a profit-making business or profession may well be for his maintenance."

However, notwithstanding this somewhat restrictive view, it is possible to imagine cases where an application by a child against the intestate estate of his parent might succeed. Thus a spouse might be entitled to the major part of an estate when already financially well off leaving a minor, disabled or otherwise necessitous child inadequately provided for. Likewise, the court might prefer to ensure the adequate maintenance of a middle-aged spinster daughter who had devoted her whole life caring for her parents and who found herself sharing an estate, largely consisting of the matrimonial home, with other brothers and sisters who were financially more secure and who had made little or no contribution to the care of their parents.

A useful illustrative case where the prima facie intestate entitlement of children was varied is provided by the Northern Irish case of *Campbell* v. *Campbell*.[68] A widow died intestate owning a farm and was survived by ten children and two children of a deceased son. One of the children had lived all his life on the farm and since his father's death had managed the farm with his mother. A grandson had also worked full time on the farm in return for his maintenance. It was held that both of them were entitled to apply under the Family Provision legislation as the law of intestacy did not make reasonable financial provision for them.[69]

[66] Following *Re Coventry (decd.), supra.*

[67] At pp. 145, 146.

[68] See [1983] C.L. 2648. The jurisdiction in Northern Ireland is to be found in the Inheritance (Provision for Family and Dependants) (Northern Ireland) Order 1979 (S.I. 1979 No. 924) which is in almost identical terms to the 1975 Act.

[69] The son was held to be entitled to occupy the dwellinghouse on the farm rent free for life, and to a twelve sixty-sixth share of the net estate. The grandson was entitled to a three sixty-sixth share of the net estate.

Child of the family

An additional category is defined in paragraph (*d*) which refers to "any person (not being a child of the deceased) who, in the case of any marriage to which the deceased was at any time a party, was treated by the deceased as a child of the family in relation to that marriage." Such a person will have no status under the intestacy rules but can apply under the Act for financial provision in the limited sense; thus the jurisdiction could be invoked on intestacy to ensure that step-children[70] share equally on intestacy with the other children. There are two useful cases on the paragraph. In *Re Leach*[71] a claim was successfully made by a step-daughter for one-half share of her step-mother's intestate estate (which otherwise passed to brothers and sisters). The court accepted that the phrase "child of the family in relation to that marriage" embraced a mature woman,[72] rejecting an argument that the court could not have regard to events after the marriage. A crucial factor in winning the award was that the bungalow which formed a large part of the estate of the deceased was financed mainly by the applicant's father. There was nothing to suggest that the deceased intended to die intestate but there was cogent evidence that the deceased intended the applicant to have half the value of the bungalow.[73] The Court of Appeal applied the earlier case of *Re Callaghan (decd.)*[74] where a successful claim was made by an adult child against his step-father's intestate estate. The judge thought that there was nothing in section 1(1)(*d*) of the 1975 Act to prevent an adult being a person who was "treated by the deceased as a child of the family" since eligibility depended on there being a relationship of parent and child and not on the age of the applicant. The application for provision was successful because the deceased had assumed considerable obligations and responsibilities for the child (and there were none such in relation to the deceased's sisters who were his next-of-kin under intestacy) and, further, much of the deceased's assets derived from the child's mother.[75]

Other dependants

The major extension to the class of potential applicants for financial

[70] *i.e.* the child of one but not the other party to the marriage. The category could also include a child who is not a child of either party to the marriage.

[71] [1984] F.L.R. 590; affirmed [1985] 2 All E.R. 754, C.A.

[72] She was aged 32 at the date of the marriage of her father and the deceased; aged 46 at the time of her father's death, and aged 55 at the time of her step-mother's death.

[73] See the very full analyses of the facts and the applicable law by Slade L.J. *Re Callaghan, post,* was applied but only very brief reference was made to *Re Coventry (decd.)* [1980] Ch. 461. The two step-children cases exhibit a more generous approach than is apparent in the earlier Court of Appeal case of *Re Coventry.*

[74] [1984] 3 W.L.R. 1076.

[75] Notwithstanding that the applicant was aged 47 and had a joint income with his wife of £11,750 a year. The estate was valued at £31,000 and the applicant was awarded a lump sum of £15,000.

provision which was introduced by the 1975 Act is contained in paragraph (*e*):

> "any person (not being a person included in the foregoing paragraphs of this subsection) who immediately before the death of the deceased was being maintained, either wholly or partly, by the deceased."

For the purposes of this paragraph:

> "... a person shall be treated as being maintained by the deceased, either wholly or partly, as the case may be, if the deceased, otherwise than for full valuable consideration, was making a substantial contribution in money or moneys worth towards the reasonable needs of that person."[76]

In respect of applications by such persons the court is directed to have regard to the extent to which and the basis upon which the deceased assumed responsibility for the maintenance of the applicant and to the length of time for which the deceased had discharged that responsibility.[77]

Clearly this paragraph can have direct relevance in cases of intestacy to ensure that some financial provision[78] is made for non-relatives who are not included in the statutory scheme. An obvious example is that of the unmarried co-habitee, the "common law husband or wife."[79] It is also apt to prefer a dependent relative, perhaps a sister or a niece who has cared for the deceased, to other relatives of the same class or to relatives who have a prior entitlement on intestacy. However, such a person must strictly satisfy the statutory qualifications noted above. The judicial attitude to such claims has been illustrated by three reported decisions: *Re Wilkinson (decd.)*,[80] *Re Beaumont (decd.)*[81] and *Jelley* v. *Iliffe*.[82] All three cases concern testate succession but the construction placed upon the relevant sections seem equally applicable to cases of intestate succession.[83] The factual situations were briefly as follows.

[76] s.1(3).
[77] s.3(4).
[78] In the limited sense, s.1(2)(*b*).
[79] See Purchas J. in *Re Kirby (decd.)* [1982] F.L.R. 249 at p. 251; "In this case the responsibility assumed by either or both of the parties to the long association cannot for practical purposes be distinguished from those accepted by a married couple towards each other. The only distinction is that in a marriage the obligations to support are formal whereas those in this association were informal but none the less effective for that."
[80] *Neale* v. *Newell* [1977] 3 W.L.R. 514.
[81] *Martin* v. *Midland Bank Trust Co. Ltd.* [1980] Ch. 444.
[82] [1981] 2 W.L.R. 801; see other cases on para. (*e*); *Harrington* v. *Gill* [1983] 4 F.L.R. 265; *Re Kirby (decd.)* [1982] 2 F.L.R. 249; *Kourkgy* v. *Lusher* [1983] 4 F.L.R. 65; *Re Cairnes (decd.)* [1983] 4 F.L.R. 225; *Malone* v. *Harrison* [1979] 1 W.L.R. 1353; *Re C. (decd.)* [1979] 123 S.J. 35.
[83] It could be argued that it would be easier for the applicant to challenge the entitlement under intestacy than it would be to challenge a will but the cases provide little if any support for that view.

In *Re Wilkinson*[84] the applicant was an elderly woman who had lived with, and cared for, her invalid sister during the last seven years of her life. In addition to providing care and companionship for her sister the applicant had assisted with light housework and cooking. She was bequeathed under her sister's will £5,000 and such furniture and household articles as she might choose, with the residue of the (presumably) considerable estate left elsewhere. *Re Beaumont (decd.)*[85] concerned an application by a "common law husband." The parties had lived together for thirty-six years as man and wife. The woman owned the bungalow in which they lived and there was some indication that the parties had never completely pooled their financial resources in the manner one would expect with a married couple. The woman died leaving an estate of £17,000 (mainly the bungalow) which was bequeathed entirely to her sisters.

In *Jelley* v. *Iliffe*[86] the applicant was a widower who had lived with the deceased in her house. The parties had pooled their financial resources and the applicant had provided some furniture for the house, had looked after the garden, had done household jobs and had provided the deceased with companionship. By her will the deceased had left all her property, including the house which was valued at £16,000 and the main asset, to her children and had made no provision for the applicant.

The cases establish the following propositions relevant to an application by a dependant for provision out of the deceased's estate.

1. The applicant must establish that he or she was "being maintained" by the deceased. This requirement is exhaustively defined in section 1(3) so that the state of affairs must fall within that definition: *Re Beaumont (decd.)*; *Jelley* v. *Iliffe*.[87]
2. The applicant must establish that he or she was "being maintained" "immediately before the death of the deceased" and what is important for this purpose is not the *de facto* situation existing at the moment of death but the general arrangements for maintenance which had existed during the deceased's lifetime; *ibid.*
3. The applicant must establish that the deceased had "assumed responsibility for the maintenance of the applicant," section 3(4)). This means "had undertaken to provide maintenance": *ibid.*
4. The bare fact that the applicant was being maintained by the deceased under an arrangement subsisting at the deceased's death is sufficient to, and generally does, raise a presumption

[84] *Supra.* The application was successful.
[85] *Supra.* The application was struck out.
[86] *Supra.* The application was allowed to proceed for trial.
[87] *Supra*; see also *Kourkgy* v. *Lusher* (1982) 12 Fam.Law. 86.

that the deceased had assumed responsibility for the applicant's maintenance. It is not necessary to prove that the deceased had intended to provide for the applicant after death. The approach is thus objective not subjective: *Jelley* v. *Iliffe*,[88] not following *Re Beaumont (decd.)*[89] on this point.

5. The exclusion of claims where the contribution towards the applicant's needs had been provided in return for full valuable consideration, section 1(3), is not restricted to contributions supplied under a contract, but extends to any contribution provided for full consideration: *Re Wilkinson (decd.)*[90]; *Re Beaumont (decd.)*[91]; *Jelley* v. *Iliffe*.[92]
6. In determining whether the claim was excluded by reason of consideration the court will take a broad, commonsense view of the relationship between the parties and will strike a balance between the benefits received by the applicant from the deceased and those provided by the applicant to the deceased: *Jelley* v. *Iliffe*.[93]

Applying these principles the court decided that the applicant in *Re Wilkinson*[94] had not provided full and valuable recompense for the benefits received and that her claim should succeed. The application in *Re Beaumont*[95] was struck out since the applicant had not established that the deceased had assumed responsibility for his

[88] *Supra.*

[89] *Supra.*

[90] *Supra.* The exclusion of applicants who have provided full valuable consideration for the benefits received was intended, no doubt, to exclude paid servants who will have to earn their salary or keep and to exclude residents in an old people's home who pay for their keep. But the provision, not being confined to contractual situations, has a much wider impact.

[91] *Supra.*

[92] *Supra*; see also *Re C.* [1979] 123 S.J. 35; *Malone* v. *Harrison* [1979] 1 W.L.R. 1353.

[93] *Supra.* The difficulty here is that the value of nursing assistance, or even domestic help, is considerable, whereas the value of accommodation and food etc. may not be great. Thus a person who devotedly nurses and cares for an elderly invalid over many years may find that the value of those services provided would outweigh the value of the benefits received in terms of accommodation etc. In such a case that person is in danger of being excluded from an application under the Act. This difficulty has been judicially recognised. In *Jelley* v. *Iliffe*, *supra*, at p. 811, 812, Griffiths L.J. said that the court must use common sense; "It cannot be an exact exercise of evaluating services in pounds and pence. By way of example, if a man was living with a woman as his wife and providing the house and all the money for their living expenses she would clearly be dependent on him, and it would not be right to deprive her of her claim by arguing that she was in fact performing services that a housekeeper would perform and it would cost more to employ a housekeeper than was spent on her and indeed perhaps more than the deceased had available to spend on her."

[94] *Supra.* There seemed to be no doubt that the deceased had made a substantial contribution in money or money's worth towards the applicant's reasonable needs but the applicant had to show that this had been otherwise than for full valuable consideration.

[95] The court thought that the facts indicated a situation where two people with independent means had chosen to pool their individual resources to enable them to live together without either undertaking any responsibility for maintaining the other.

maintenance but was allowed to stand in *Jelley* v. *Iliffe*[96] where the Court of Appeal took a rather different view as to the proof of this assumption of responsibility. The latter approach is clearly to be preferred since a requirement that the deceased should have intended to maintain the applicant after his death, or some wholly subjective indication of an assumption of responsibility, would be unduly restrictive of the legislation. The problem remains, however, of the exclusion of applicants who have provided full valuable consideration since this seems to favour the least meritorious applicants, *i.e.* the ones who have done little if anything in recompense for the benefits received, at the expense of the more deserving, *i.e.* those who have tried to contribute as much as possible in return for the benefits received.[97]

Subsequent authorities

Three subsequent cases concerning applications by dependants against intestate estates can be noted. In *Re Kirby (decd.)*[98] the plaintiff and the deceased had formed an association which lasted 35 years, living as man and wife but never marrying. The deceased woman died intestate leaving an estate of some £7,000 and the plaintiff applied for reasonable provision. The daughter who, together with a son, was equally entitled to the estate, failed in an attempt to have the application struck out as disclosing no reasonable cause of action. Similarly, in *Harrington* v. *Gill*[99] a female cohabitant succeeded in an action against an intestate estate which otherwise passed to a daughter. The net estate was worth £22,000 including the house in which they had cohabited. The trial judge had ordered that a lump sum of £5,000 to provide capital and a lump sum of £5,000 to provide income should be paid to the applicant. The Court of Appeal decided that a reasonable man in this deceased's circumstances would have wanted the plaintiff to remain in the house for her lifetime and varied the judge's order by adding a provision that the house be settled on the plaintiff for life. A mistress failed in *Kourkgy* v. *Lusher*[1] to win an award against a wife and indeed the claim was not strong. The court found that for a number of years before his death the deceased had been reluctant to commit himself financially on other

[96] The benefit of rent-free accommodation was a significant contribution to the reasonable needs of any person, and in the case of an old-age pensioner amounted to a substantial contribution. The provision of that benefit for eight years amounted to an assumption of responsibility for the applicant's maintenance.

[97] In view of this fact it might have been preferable if the legislation had omitted the reference to full valuable consideration and had simply allowed this factor to be taken into account in exercising its discretion. The court could thus exclude paid servants and persons who pay for their keep in a home, but include deserving applicants who had in fact provided considerable services in return for the benefits received.

[98] [1982] 3 F.L.R. 249.

[99] [1983] 4 F.L.R. 265.

[1] [1982] 3 F.L.R. 249.

than a cash basis to the relationship and there were indications that he had wished to divest himself of financial responsibility of a capital and lasting nature. A month before his (sudden) death, the deceased had not resumed cohabitation and had abandoned responsibility for the woman's maintenance. Accordingly, the court concluded that the applicant was not being maintained, either wholly or partly, by the deceased immediately before his death.

The Order of the Court

The question for decision

The proper approach to the resolution of the issues raised by an application under the Act was considered fully by the Court of Appeal in *Re Coventry*.[2] This concerned an application by a son so that the reasonable financial provision in question was restricted to maintenance and the Court's comments should be limited to such cases. A somewhat different approach might well be appropriate in the case of an application by a surviving spouse where a more generous criterion of provision is applicable.[3] The first point, made strongly by the Court of Appeal, was that the question to be resolved is *not*, "how should the available assets be fairly divided?"[4] The correct approach is to consider the matter in two stages. First, has the will or the rules of intestacy or the combination of both failed to make reasonable financial provision for the applicant? This is a question of fact but it is a value judgment, or a qualitative decision, and should be assessed objectively.[5] If this question is answered in favour of the applicant, the court should go on to consider the extent to which it should exercise its powers under the Act by making some sort of order for financial provision for the applicant out of the estate. This is a question of discretion.[6] The two questions are closely interrelated and were described by Goff L.J. as "a composite problem."[7]

A number of useful points emerge from the decision regarding these issues. First, the mere fact that the applicant is in necessitous

[2] [1980] Ch. 461. The first case on the 1975 Act to be considered by the Court of Appeal. The approach was approved and applied by the Court of Appeal in *Re Fullard (decd.)* [1981] 3 W.L.R. 743.

[3] See *ante*, p. 356 and s.1(2)(*a*), and (*b*).

[4] See Goff L.J., *supra*, at p. 486, 487.

[5] *Ibid.* ss.1(1), 2(1). The question whether the correct criterion was objective or subjective, was the subject of some dispute under the 1938 Act, until resolved in favour of the former, see *Re Goodwin* [1969] 1 Ch. 283. The court has regard to the facts existing at the date of the hearing, not at the date of the death, s.3(5). It can be emphasised that it is the will or the rules of intestacy that must fail to make reasonable provision, so that there will (apart from the enabling provisions of the 1982 Forfeiture Act where applicable) be no basis for a claim where the will makes adequate provision for a spouse who is precluded by the rule of public policy from taking any benefit; *Re Royse (decd.)* [1984] 3 W.L.R. 784.

[6] *Ibid.*

[7] *Ibid.*

circumstances, or even that he is near to the subsistence level, is not of itself sufficient to justify an award.[8] Goff L.J. stated[9]:

> "The question is not whether it might have been reasonable for the deceased to assist his son, the applicant, but whether in all the circumstances, looked at objectively, it is unreasonable that the effective provisions governing the estate did not do so."

Secondly, a moral obligation towards the applicant is not a prerequisite of a successful application[10] and in this respect there is no difference between will cases and cases of intestacy. Goff L.J. commented as follows in *Re Coventry*,[11] which was a case of intestacy:

> "... it was submitted that the question of moral obligation had only been raised in will cases, and that there was a difference between will cases where the testator had stated his wishes, and intestacies where he had not. As I see it, that is not an entirely correct dichotomy in any event, because a deceased person may have deliberately chosen to be intestate, and the provision provided by the legislative to cover the case where there is no will, or an incomplete will, may be as much the wishes of the deceased as those which he has expressed in a will. In my judgment, the problem must be exactly the same whether one is dealing with a will or an intestacy, or with a combination of both. The question is whether the operative dispositions make, or fail to make, reasonable provision in all the circumstances. Indeed I think any view expressed by a deceased person that he wishes a particular person to benefit will generally be of little significance, because the question is not subjective but objective."

Thirdly, it is inevitable that any award made in favour of the applicant will be at the expense of the testamentary or intestacy beneficiaries and the competing claims of each will have to be considered. In this connection, since intestate benefits can be regarded as something of a "windfall,"[12] they are perhaps more vulnerable than testate benefits.[13]

[8] At p. 488.
[9] *Ibid.*
[10] *Ibid.* A moral obligation can be relevant on the facts of a particular case to the issue of the reasonableness of the deceased's provision, or lack of it for the applicant. See also Ormrod L.J. in *Re Fullard (decd.), supra*, at p. 747.
[11] *Supra*, at p. 488.
[12] See Oliver J. in *Re Coventry, supra*, cited by Goff L.J. at p. 489.
[13] However in *Re Coventry* the spouse was the intestate beneficiary and she could show some colour of entitlement by virtue of cohabitation for 30 years. See also *Sivyer* v. *Sivyer* [1967] 1 W.L.R. 1482, a total intestacy case under the 1938 Act, where the deceased was intestate and at the time of his death there were only two persons having a call on his bounty namely, the applicant who was the daughter of his second wife, and the defendant who was his third wife. The daughter was aged 13 and in the

In determining the merits of an application, and in resolving the composite problem identified above, the court is directed to have regard to a number of matters set out in section 3 of the Act which include the relative fiancial resources and needs of the applicant and the persons otherwise entitled to the estate and the size and nature of the estate.[14]

The orders

The range of possible orders which the court can make by way of implementing an award under the Act has been mentioned already. The full list is contained in section 2 of the Act to which reference should be made.[15] In cases where the court is concerned to provide maintenance, *i.e.* where the applicant is a former spouse, a child or a dependant, an order for periodical payments will usually be appropriate[16] or, in the case of a small estate, a lump sum by way of maintenance.[17] However, in many such applications under the Act the crucial asset in question will be the house in which the parties were living before the death and which is also likely to be the only significant asset of the estate. Where the house is devised to a third party, or goes by the effect of the intestacy rules to a third party, the fundamental point of the application might well be to secure continued occupation of the house.[18] In such cases the power of the court to settle the property for the benefit of the applicant would seem appropriate.[19]

care of the local authority; the widow had some means. Under the intestacy provisions the widow inherited the whole of the small estate but the daughter was awarded a lump sum of £2,500. The court took note of the fact that most of the deceased's estate was derived from the daughter's mother.

[14] Para. (*g*) includes "any other matter, including the conduct of the applicant or any other person, which in the circumstances of the case the court may consider relevant." These factors are, of course, exactly the considerations which the fixed rules of intestacy cannot have regard to. Additional factors relating to spouses are contained in s.3(2); to children in s.3(3); and to dependants in s.3(4). Statements made by the deceased can be admitted as evidence, s.21.

[15] And to the consequential and supplemental powers in ss.2(2), 2(3) and 2(4).

[16] s.2(1)(*a*).

[17] s.2(1)(*b*).

[18] See *Re Wilkinson (decd.)* [1977] 3 W.L.R. 514; *Re Beaumont (decd.)* [1980] Ch. 444; *Jelley* v. *Iliffe* [1981] 2 W.L.R. 801, all cases of applications by dependants who had been living in the house before the death, which was devised elsewhere. In *Re Coventry* [1980] Ch. 461 the house passed to a separated spouse by virtue of the intestacy rules, and the applicant was a son who lived in the house. Consider also the obvious case where a spinster daughter has remained in the home and cared for her parents until their death, but where the house prima facie passes equally to her and her less deserving brothers and sisters.

[19] Thus providing "maintenance" (but hopefully avoiding settled land!); a transfer of the house would seem to be an over provision in such cases.

Where, however, the applicant is the surviving spouse and the house is devised elsewhere, the power simply to transfer the house will be significant.[20] In cases of intestacy the house will, in effect, pass in any event to the spouse but an award under the Act might assist, where the value of the house exceeds the value of the absolute interest taken by the spouse on intestacy, in providing the necessary equality money to enable an appropriation to be made.[21]

It will be appreciated that any award made under the Act will be to the prejudice of the testamentary or intestacy beneficiaries so that the incidence of the award will have to be considered. The Act contains power in section 2(4) for the court to make any consequential or supplemental orders that it thinks necessary or expedient and thus it can direct where the burden is to fall. In such cases the court should try to ensure that the order operates fairly as between one beneficiary of the estate and another.[22] In cases of partial intestacy it might be that the court would regard it as proper to fulfil the deceased's testamentary wishes as far as possible and to throw the burden of the award on the intestate part of the estate.[23]

There is provision for the making of interim orders.[24] In addition the court has supplementary powers to vary or discharge the original order or to suspend any provision of it temporarily and to revive the operation of any provision so suspended.[25]

It will be appreciated that such an agreed compromise could also constitute a variation for the purposes of section 142(1), of the Inheritance Tax Act 1984, again without prejudice to the inheritance tax position.[26]

Where such an order or compromise or variation is in favour of the surviving spouse, it will be covered by the usual spouse exemption. Conversely, additional inheritance tax might be payable where the order or variation is in favour of some person other than a spouse.[27]

NET ESTATE

Definition

Orders under the 1975 Act are made out of the "net estate" of the

[20] See s.2(1)(*c*).

[21] s.2(1)(*c*); or even to purchase and settle, or transfer, a house for the benefit of the spouse. For an illustration of the exercise of the discretion in favour of a spouse see *Re Besterman (decd.)* [1984] Ch. 458, where a substantial lump sum was awarded to a wife.

[22] See *ante*, Chap. 12.

[23] s.2(4).

[24] See s.5.

[25] See s.6 and *Fricker* v. *P. R. of Fricker* [1982] 3 F.L.R. 228.

[26] See *ante*. Note that in such cases an election must be made in writing to the Board. Similarly the compromise might fall within s.49(*b*) of the Capital Gains Tax Act 1979.

[27] See texts on capital tax, such as Foster's *Capital Taxes Encyclopaedia*, Part D.

deceased, as defined by that Act, whereas the entitlement under intestate succession is in "the residuary estate of the intestate."[28] The contrast between these provisions has already been mentioned above and the point was made that the 1975 Act can comprehend very much wider categories of property than does the 1925 Act.[29] The concept of the "net estate" is crucial to the effective working of the 1975 Act, and to the prevention of avoidance of the jurisdiction, and the definition will be considered briefly. "Net estate" is defined as including[30]:

"(*a*) all property of which the deceased had power to dispose by his will (otherwise than by virtue of a special power of appointment) less the amount of his funeral, testamentary and administration expenses, debts and liabilities, including any capital transfer tax payable out of his estate on his death;

(*b*) any property in respect of which the deceased held a general power of appointment (not being a power exercisable by will) which has not been exercised;

(*c*) any sum of money or other property which is treated for the purposes of this Act as part of the net estate of the deceased by virtue of section 8(1) or (2) of this Act; . . . "

Section 8(1) includes any sum of money which has been nominated in favour of any person and section 8(2) includes any sum of money or other property which has been received by any person as a *donatio mortis causa.*

"(*d*) any property which is treated for the purposes of this Act as part of the net estate of the deceased by virtue of an order made under section 9 of the Act."

Section 9 relates to property to which the deceased was beneficially entitled immediately before his death as a joint tenant.[31] The court can order that the deceased's severable share should be treated as part of his net estate.

"(*e*) any sum of money or other property which is by reason of a disposition or contract made by the deceased, ordered under section 10 or 11 of this Act to be provided for the purpose of the making of financial provision under this Act."

Section 10 enables the court to order a donee of property to bring into the estate "such sum of money or other property as may be specified in the order," section 10(2). The conditions precedent to such an order are, first, that the deceased had made a disposition in favour of the donee " . . . less than six years before the date of the

[28] s.25(1) of the 1975 Act; s.33(4) of the 1925 Act.
[29] See s.33(4) of the 1925 Act, *ante* p. 78.
[30] s.25(1).
[31] See *Kourkgy* v. *Lusher* [1983] 4 F.L.R. 65, where the deceased's half share in a matrimonial home was not brought into the estate.

death of the deceased" and "... with the intention of defeating an application for financial provision under this Act"[32]; secondly, that the donee did not provide full valuable consideration for the disposition[33]; thirdly, that the making of such an order would facilitate the making of an award for financial provision under the Act.[34] Clearly this jurisdiction could be invoked in cases where the deceased had deliberately disposed of his property shortly before death with the aim of defeating the intestate entitlement of his spouse or family on death. A particularly important illustration would be where the deceased had purported to transfer the matrimonial home to a third party to the great prejudice of the wife. If the disposition was made less than six years before the deceased's death, the court might order the donee, whether or not at the date of the order he holds any interest in the property disposed of to him or for his benefit by the deceased, to provide, for the purpose of making financial provision under the Act, such sums of money or other property as may be specified in the order.[35] Thus, if the house has been retained by the donee, the court might order its return and then transfer it to, or settle it on, the wife. If the house had been disposed of to a third party, the court would order the donee to provide a sum of money not exceeding the value of the house at the date of its disposal.[36]

A further method of possible avoidance is covered by section 11 which was enacted to deal with the problem highlighted by the decision in *Schaefer* v. *Schuhmann.*[37] In that case a testator had told his housekeeper that he was devising his house to her in his will providing that she was still employed in that capacity at the time of his death. Thereafter he paid her no more wages and the housekeeper acquiesced in the arrangement in the expectation of inheriting the house. It was held that this constituted a contract to devise the house by will and that the housekeeper was to be regarded as a creditor rather than a beneficiary of the estate. Accordingly the house did not form part of the deceased's net estate and was not property available to meet an order for family provision in favour of the deceased's daughter. This decision seemed to point the way to easy avoidance of the family provision legislation if a testator was so minded[38] since, instead of devising the house to a third party beneficially, the testator would devise it pursuant to some purported *inter vivos* contract. Section 11 of the 1975 Act is designed to prevent such avoidance by

[32] s.10(2)(*a*).
[33] s.10(2)(*b*).
[34] s.10(2)(*c*).
[35] s.10(2).
[36] s.10(4).
[37] [1972] A.C. 572.
[38] See Lord Simon's dissenting speech.

empowering the court, if certain conditions are fulfilled,[39] to order that the property should be available to meet a family provision order.

Procedure

Application must be made within six months of the date when representation with respect to the estate is first taken out.[40] The court has a discretion[41] in exceptional cases to extend the six months period. Proceedings are brought either in the High Court (Chancery or Family Division by originating summons[42]) which has unlimited jurisdiction, or in the County Court[43] where the value of the estate does not exceed the County Court limit.[44] For full details of the procedure reference should be made to the relevant court rules.[45]

[39] s.11(2), principally the contract must be voluntary and made with the intention of defeating an application for financial provision under the Act. The contract in *Schaefer* v. *Schuhmann*, *supra*, appeared to be bona fide and it is doubtful if it could have been upset under s.11 if then enacted.

[40] s.4; further defined by s.23 which excludes a grant limited to settled land or to trust property. The time limit runs from the date when an effective and valid grant is made. *Re Freeman (decd.)* [1984] 1 W.L.R. 1419.

[41] Guidance as to the exercise of this discretion has been provided in *Re Salmon (decd.)* [1981] Ch. 167; *Re Dennis (decd.)* [1981] 2 All E.R. 140; and *Escritt* v. *Escritt* [1982] F.L.R. 280.

[42] See R.S.C., Ord. 99.

[43] County Court Act 1984, s.25, previously s.52A of the County Court Act 1959. See County Court Rules 1981 (S.I. 1981 No. 1687), as amended.

[44] Originally £5,000, see s.22; subsequently raised to £15,000 and then to £30,000, with effect from December 1, 1981, see S.I. 1981 No. 1636.

[45] R.S.C., Ord. 99; C.C.C., 1981, Ord. 48.

APPENDICES

APPENDIX 1

STATUTES

ADMINISTRATION OF ESTATES ACT 1925

PART III

ADMINISTRATION OF ASSETS

Real and personal estate of deceased are assets for payment of debts

32.—(1) The real and personal estate, whether legal or equitable, of a deceased person, to the extent of his beneficial interest therein, and the real and personal estate of which a deceased person in pursuance of any general power (including the statutory power to dispose of entailed interests) disposes by his will, are assets for payment of his debts (whether by specialty or simple contract) and liabilities, and any disposition by will inconsistent with this enactment is void as against the creditors, and the court shall, if necessary, administer the property for the purpose of the payment of the debts and the liabilities.

This subsection takes effect without prejudice to the rights of incumbrancers.

(2) If any person to whom any such beneficial interest devolves or is given, or in whom any such interest vests, disposes thereof in good faith before an action is brought or process is sued out against him, he shall be personally liable for the value of the interest so disposed of by him, but that interest shall not be liable to be taken in execution in the action or under the process.

Trust for sale

33.—(1) On the death of a person intestate as to any real or personal estate, such estate shall be held by his personal representatives—

(*a*) as to the real estate upon trust to sell the same; and
(*b*) as to the personal estate upon trust to call in sell and convert into money such part thereof as may not consist of money,

with power to postpone such sale and conversion for such a period as the personal representative shall pay all such funeral, testamentary and proper, and so that any reversionary interest be not sold until it falls into possession, unless the personal representatives see special reason for sale, and so also that, unless required for purposes of administration owing to want of other assets, personal chattels be not sold except for special reason.

(2) Out of the net money to arise from the sale and conversion of such real and personal estate (after payment of costs), and out of the ready money of the deceased (so far as not disposed of by his will, if any), the personal representative shall pay all such funeral testamenary and administration expenses, debts and other liabilities as are properly payable thereout having regard to the rules of administration contained in this Part of this Act, and out of the residue of the said money the personal representative shall set aside a fund sufficient to provide for any pecuniary legacies bequeathed by the will (if any) of the deceased.

(3) During the minority of any beneficiary or the subsistence of any life interest and pending the distribution of the whole or any part of the estate of the deceased, the person representatives may invest the residue of the said money, or so much thereof as may not have been distributed, in any investments for the time being authorised by statute for the investment of trust money, with power, at the discretion of the personal representatives, to change such investments for others of a like nature.

(4) The residue of the said money and any investments for the time being representing the same, including (but without prejudice to the trust for sale) any part of the estate of the deceased which may be retained unsold and is not required for the administration purposes aforesaid, is in this Act referred to as "the residuary estate of the intestate."

(5) The income (including net rents and profits of real estate and chattels real after payment of rates, taxes, rent, costs of insurance, repairs and other outgoings properly attributable to income) of so much of the real and personal estate of the deceased as may not be disposed of by his will, if any, or may not be required for the administration purposes aforesaid, may, however such estate is invested, as from the death of the deceased, be treated and applied as income, and for that purpose any necessary apportionment may be made between tenant for life and remainderman.

(6) Nothing in this section affects the rights of any creditor of the deceased or the rights of the Crown in respect of death duties.

(7) Where the deceased leaves a will, this section has effect subject to the provisions contained in the will.

Administration of assets

34.—(1) Where the estate of a deceased person is insolvent, his real and personal estate shall be administered in accordance with the rules set out in Part I of the First Schedule to this Act.

(2) [*This subsection was repealed by the Administration of Estates Act* 1971 (*c.* 25), *s.*12 *and Sched.* 2, *Pt.* II.]

(3) Where the estate of a deceased person is solvent his real and personal estate shall, subject to rules of court and the provisions hereinafter contained as to charges on property of the deceased, and to the provisions, if any, contained in his will, be applicable towards the discharge of the funeral, testamentary and administration expenses, debts and liabilities payable thereout in the order mentioned in Part II of the First Schedule to this Act.

Charges on property of deceased to be paid primarily out of the property charged

35.—(1) Where a person dies possessed of, or entitled to, or, under a general power of appointment (including the statutory power to dispose of entailed interests) by his will disposes of, an interest in property, which at the time of his death is charged with the payment of money, whether by way of legal mortgage, equitable charge or otherwise (including a lien for unpaid purchase money), and the deceased has not by will deed or other document signified a contrary or other intention, the interest so charged shall, as between the different persons claiming through the deceased, be primarily liable for the payment of the charge; and every part of the said interest, according to its value, shall bear a proportionate part of the charge on the whole thereof.

(2) Such contrary or other intention shall not be deemed to be signified—

(*a*) by a general direction for the payment of debts or of all the debts of the testator out of his personal estate, or his residuary real and personal estate, or his residuary real estate; or
(*b*) by a charge of debts upon any such estate;

unless such intention is further signified by words expressly or by necessary implication referring to all or some part of the charge.

(3) Nothing in this section affects the right of a person entitled to the charge to obtain payment or satisfaction thereof either out of the other assets of the deceased or otherwise.

Effect of assent or conveyance by personal representative

36.—(1) A personal representative may assent to the vesting, in any person who (whether by devise, bequest, devolution, appropriation or otherwise) may be entitled thereto, either beneficially or as a trustee or personal representative, of any estate or interest in real estate to which the testator or intestate was entitled or over which he exercised a general power of appointment by his will, including the statutory power to dispose of entailed interests, and which devolved upon the personal representative.

(2) The assent shall operate to vest in that person the estate or interest to which the assent relates, and, unless a contrary intention appears, the assent shall relate back to the death of the deceased.

(3) The statutory covenants implied by a person being expressed to convey as personal representative, may be implied in an assent in like manner as in a conveyance by deed.

(4) An assent to the vesting of a legal estate shall be in writing, signed by the personal representative, and shall name the person in whose favour it is given and shall operate to vest in that person the legal estate to which it relates; and an assent not in writing or not in favour of a named person shall not be effectual to pass a legal estate.

(5) Any person in whose favour an assent or conveyance of a legal estate is made by a personal representative may require that notice of the assent or conveyance be written or endorsed on or permanently annexed to the probate or letters of administration, at the cost of the estate of the deceased, and that the probate or letters of administration be produced, at the like cost, to prove that the notice has been placed thereon or annexed thereto.

(6) A statement in writing by a personal representative that he has not given or made an assent or conveyance in respect of a legal estate, shall, in favour of a purchaser, but without prejudice to any previous disposition made in favour of another purchaser deriving title mediately or immediately under the personal representative, be sufficient evidence that an assent or conveyance has not been given or made in respect of the legal estate to which the statement relates, unless notice of a previous assent or conveyance affecting that estate has been placed on or annexed to the probate or administration.

A conveyance by a personal representative of a legal estate to a purchaser accepted on the faith of such a statement shall (without prejudice as aforesaid and unless notice of a previous assent or conveyance affecting that estate has been placed on or annexed to the probate or administration) operate to transfer or create the legal estate expressed to be conveyed in like manner as if no previous assent or conveyance had been made by the personal representative.

A personal representative making a false statement, in regard to any such matter, shall be liable in like manner as if the statement had been contained in a statutory declaration.

(7) An assent or conveyance by a personal representative in respect of a legal estate shall, in favour of a purchaser, unless notice of a previous assent or conveyance affecting that legal estate has been placed on or annexed to the probate or administration, be taken as sufficient evidence that the person in whose favour the assent or conveyance is given or made is the person entitled to have the legal estate conveyed to him, and upon the proper trusts, if any, but shall

not otherwise prejudicially affect the claim of any person rightfully entitled to the estate vested or conveyed or any charge thereon.

(8) A conveyance of a legal estate by a personal representative to a purchaser shall not be invalidated by reason only that the purchaser may have notice that all the debts, liabilities, funeral, and testamentary or administration expenses, duties, and legacies of the deceased have been discharged or provided for.

(9) An assent or conveyance given or made by a personal representative shall not, except in favour of a purchaser of a legal estate, prejudice the right of the personal representative or any other person to recover the estate or interest to which the assent or conveyance relates, or to be indemnified out of such estate or interest against any duties, debt, or liability to which such estate or interest would have been subject if there had not been any assent or conveyance.

(10) A personal representative may, as a condition of giving an assent or making a conveyance, require security for the discharge of any such duties, debt, or liability, but shall not be entitled to postpone the giving of an assent merely by reason of the subsistence of any such duties, debt or liability if reasonable arrangements have been made for discharging the same; and an assent may be given subject to any legal estate or charge by way of legal mortgage.

(11) This section shall not operate to impose any stamp duty in respect of an assent, and in this section "purchaser" means a purchaser for money or money's worth.

(12) This section applies to assents and conveyances made after the commencement of this Act, whether the testator or intestate died before or after such commencement.

Validity of conveyance not affected by revocation of representation

37.—(1) All conveyances of any interest in real or personal estate made to a purchaser either before or after the commencement of this Act by a person to whom probate or letters of administration have been granted are valid, notwithstanding any subsequent revocation or variation, either before or after the commencement of this Act, of the probate or administration.

(2) This section takes effect without prejudice to any order of the court made before the commencement of this Act, and applies whether the testator or intestate died before or after such commencement.

Right to follow property and powers of the court in relation thereto

38.—(1) An assent or conveyance by a personal representative to a person other than a purchaser does not prejudice the rights of any person to follow the property to which the assent or conveyance relates, or any property representing the same, into the hands of the person in whom it is vested by the assent or conveyance, or of any other person (not being a purchaser) who may have received the same or in whom it may be vested.

(2) Notwithstanding any such assent or conveyance the court may, on the application of any creditor or other person interested,—

(*a*) order a sale, exchange, mortgage, charge, lease, payment, transfer or other transaction to be carried out which the court considers requisite for the purpose of giving effect to the rights of the persons interested;
(*b*) declare that the person, not being a purchaser, in whom the property is vested is a trustee for those purposes;
(*c*) give directions respecting the preparation and execution of any conveyance or other instrument or as to any other matter required for giving effect to the order;
(*d*) make any vesting order, or appoint a person to convey in accordance with the provisions of the Trustee Act 1925.

(3) This section does not prejudice the rights of a purchaser or a person deriving title under him, but applies whether the testator or intestate died before or after the commencement of this Act.

Powers of management

39.—(1) In dealing with the real and personal estate of the deceased his personal representatives shall, for purposes of administration, or during a minority of any beneficiary or the subsistence of any life interest, or until the period of distribution arrives, have—

(i) the same powers and discretions, including power to raise money by mortgage or charge (whether or not by deposit of documents), as a personal representative had before the commencement of this Act, with respect to personal estate vested in him, and such power of raising money by mortgage may in the case of land be exercised by way of legal mortgage; and
(ii) all the powers, discretions and duties conferred or imposed by law on trustees holding land upon an effectual trust for sale (including power to overreach equitable interests and powers as if the same affected the proceeds of sale); and
(iii) all the powers conferred by statute on trustees for sale, and so that every contract entered into by a personal representative shall be binding on and be enforceable against and by the personal representative for the time being of the deceased, and may be carried into effect, or be varied or rescinded by him, and, in the case of a contract entered into by a predecessor, as if it had been entered into by himself.

(2) Nothing in this section shall affect the right of any person to require an assent or conveyance to be made.

(3) This section applies whether the testator or intestate died before or after the commencement of this Act.

Powers of personal representatives for raising money, &c.

40.—(1) For giving effect to beneficial interests the personal representative may limit or demise land for a term of years absolute, with or without impeachment for waste, to trustees on usual trusts for raising or securing any principal sum and the interest thereon for which the land, or any part thereof, is liable, and may limit or grant a rentcharge for giving effect to any annual or periodical sum for which the land or the income thereof or any part thereof is liable.

(2) This section applies whether the testator or intestate died before or after the commencement of this Act.

Powers of personal representative as to appropriation

41.[1]—(1) The personal representative may appropriate any part of the real or personal estate, including things in action, of the deceased in the actual condition or state of investment thereof at the time of appropriation in or towards satisfaction of any legacy bequeathed by the deceased, or of any other interest or share in his property, whether settled or not, as to the personal representative may seem just and reasonable, according to the respective rights of the persons interested in the property of the deceased:

Provided that—

(i) an appropriation shall not be made under this section so as to affect prejudicially any specific devise or bequest;

(ii) an appropriation of property, whether or not being an investment authorised by law or by the will, if any, of the deceased for the investment of money subject to the trust, shall not (save as hereinafter mentioned) be made under this section except with the following consents:—

(*a*) when made for the benefit of a person absolutely and beneficially entitled in possession, the consent of that person;

(*b*) when made in respect of any settled legacy share or interest, the consent of either the trustee thereof, if any (not being also the personal representative), or the person who may for the time being be entitled to the income:

If the person whose consent is so required as aforesaid is an infant or [is incapable, by reason of mental disorder

[1] This section is excluded in respect of requirements or consents made under Sched. 2, para. 6(2) to the Intestates' Estates Act 1952.

within the meaning of the Mental Health Act 1959 of managing and administering his property and affairs],[2] the consent shall be given on his behalf by his parents or parent, testamentary or other guardian, [. . .] or receiver, or if, in the case of an infant, there is no such parent or guardian, by the court on the application of his next friend;

(iii) no consent (save of such trustee as aforesaid) shall be required on behalf of a person who may come into existence after the time of appropriation, or who cannot be found or ascertained at that time;

(iv) if no [receiver is acting for a person suffering from mental disorder], then, if the appropriation is of an investment authorised by law or by the will, if any, of the deceased for the investment of money subject to the trust, no consent shall be required on behalf of the [said person];

(v) if, independently of the personal representative, there is no trustee of a settled legacy share or interest, and no person of full age and capacity entitled to the income thereof, no consent shall be required to an appropriation in respect of such legacy share or interest, provided that the appropriation is of an investment authorised as aforesaid.

(2) Any property duly appropriated under the powers conferred by this section shall thereafter be treated as an authorised investment, and may be retained or dealt with accordingly.

(3) For the purposes of such appropriation, the personal representative may ascertain and fix the value of the respective parts of the real and personal estate and the liabilities of the deceased as he may think fit, and shall for that purpose employ a duly qualified valuer in any case where such employment may be necessary; and may make any conveyance (including an assent) which may be requisite for giving effect to the appropriation.

(4) An appropriation made pursuant to this section shall bind all persons interested in the property of the deceased whose consent is not hereby made requisite.

(5)[3] The personal representative shall, in making the appropriation, have regard to the rights of any person who may thereafter come into existence, or who cannot be found or ascertained at the time of appropriation, and of any other person whose consent is not required by this section.

(6) This section does not prejudice any other power of appropriation conferred by law or by the will (if any) of the deceased, and takes effect with any extended powers conferred by the will (if any) of the

[2] Substituted by the Mental Health Act 1959 (7 & 8 Eliz. 2, c. 72), Sched. 7, Pt. I. See new Mental Health Act 1983.

[3] For the rights of the surviving spouse as respects the matrimonial home, see the Intestates' Estates Act 1952, Sched. 2, para. 1(3).

deceased, and where an appropriation is made under this section, in respect of a settled legacy, share or interest, the property appropriated shall remain subject to all trusts for sale and powers of leasing, disposition, and management or varying investments which would have been applicable thereto or to the legacy, share or interest in respect of which the appropriation is made, if no such appropriation had been made.

(7) If after any real estate has been appropriated in purported exercise of the powers conferred by this section, the person to whom it was conveyed disposes of it or any interest therein, then, in favour of a purchaser, the appropriation shall be deemed to have been made in accordance with the requirements of this section and after all requisite consents, if any, had been given.

(8) In this section, a settled legacy, share or interest includes any legacy, share or interest to which a person is not absolutely entitled in possession at the date of the appropriation, also an annuity, and "purchaser" means a purchaser for money or money's worth.

(9) This section applies whether the deceased died intestate or not, and whether before or after the commencement of this Act, and extends to property over which a testator exercises a general power of appointment, including the statutory power to dispose of entailed interests, and authorises the setting apart of a fund to answer an annuity by means of the income of that fund or otherwise.

Power to appoint trustees of infants' property

42.—(1) Where an infant is absolutely entitled under the will or on the intestacy of a person dying before or after the commencement of this Act (in this subsection called "the deceased") to a devise or legacy, or to the residue of the estate of the deceased, or any share therein, and such devise, legacy, residue or share is not under the will, if any, of the deceased, devised or bequeathed to trustees for the infant, the personal representatives of the deceased may appoint a trust corporation or two or more individuals not exceeding four (whether or not including the personal representatives or one or more of the personal representatives), to be the trustee or trustees of such devise, legacy, residue or share for the infant, and to be trustees of any land devised or any land being or forming part of such residue or share for the purposes of the Settled Land Act 1925 and of the statutory provisions relating to the management of land during a minority, and may execute or do any assurance or thing requisite for vesting such devise, legacy, residue or share in the trustee or trustees so appointed.

On such appointment the personal representatives, as such, shall be discharged from all further liability in respect of such devise, legacy, residue, or share, and the same may be retained in its existing condition or state of investment, or may be converted into money, and such money may be invested in any authorised investment.

(2) Where a personal representative has before the commencement of this Act retained or sold any such devise, legacy, residue or share, and invested the same or the proceeds thereof in any investments in which he was authorised to invest money subject to the trust, then, subject to any order of the court made before such commencement, he shall not be deemed to have incurred any liability on that account, or by reason of not having paid or transferred the money or property into court.

Obligations of personal representative as to giving possession of land and powers of the court

43.—(1) A personal representative, before giving an assent or making a conveyance in favour of any person entitled, may permit that person to take possession of the land, and such possession shall not prejudicially affect the right of the personal representative to take or resume possession nor his power to convey the land as if he were in possession thereof, but subject to the interest of any lessee, tenant or occupier in possession or in actual occupation of the land.

(2) Any person who as against the personal representative claims possession of real estate, or the appointment of a receiver thereof or a conveyance thereof, or an assent to the vesting thereof, or to be registered as proprietor thereof under the Land Registration Act 1925 may apply to the court for directions with reference thereto, and the court may make such vesting or other order as may be deemed proper, and the provisions of the Trustee Act 1925, relating to vesting orders and to the appointment of a person to convey, shall apply.

(3) This section applies whether the testator or intestate died before or after the commencement of this Act.

Power to postpone distribution

44. Subject to the foregoing provisions of this Act, a personal representative is not bound to distribute the estate of the deceased before the expiration of one year from the death.

PART IV

DISTRIBUTION OF RESIDUARY ESTATE

Abolition of descent to heir, curtesy, dower and escheat

45.—(1) With regard to the real estate and personal inheritance of every person dying after the commencement of this Act, there shall be abolished—

(*a*) All existing modes rules and canons of descent, and of devolution by special occupancy or otherwise, of real estate, or of a personal inheritance, whether operating by the general law or by the custom of gavelkind or borough english or by any other custom of any county, locality, or manor, or otherwise howsoever; and

(*b*) Tenancy by the curtesy and every other estate and interest of a husband in real estate as to which his wife dies intestate, whether arising under the general law or by custom or otherwise; and

(*c*) Dower and freebench and every other estate and interest of a wife in real estate as to which her husband dies intestate, whether arising under the general law or by custom or otherwise: Provided that where a right (if any) to freebench or other like right has attached before the commencement of this Act which cannot be barred by a testamentary or other disposition made by the husband, such right shall, unless released, remain in force as an equitable interest; and

(*d*) Escheat to the Crown or the Duchy of Lancaster or the Duke of Cornwall or to a mesne lord for want of heirs.

(2) Nothing in this section affects the descent or devolution of an entailed interest.

Succession to real and personal estate on intestacy

46.[4]—(1) The residuary estate of an intestate shall be distributed in the manner or be held on the trusts mentioned in this section, namely:—

(i) [If the intestate leaves a husband or wife, then in accordance with the following Table:

TABLE

If the intestate—	
(1) leaves— (*a*) no issue,[5] and (*b*) no parent,[6] or brother or sister of the whole blood, or issue of a brother or sister of the whole blood	the residuary estate shall be held in trust for the surviving husband or wife absolutely.

[4] The amendments to ss.46–49 have effect as respects a person dying intestate after January 1, 1953.

[5] In this Part of the Act, any reference to the issue of the intestate shall have effect as if it included a reference to any illegitimate child of his or to the issue of any such child: Family Law Reform Act 1969 (c. 46), s.14(3)(*a*).

[6] In this Part of the Act, any reference to the parent, parents, father or mother of the intestate shall have effect as if it were a reference to his natural parent, parents, mother or father: *ibid.* s.14(3)(*c*).

(2) leaves issue (whether or not persons mentioned in sub-paragraph (*b*) above also survive)

the surviving husband or wife shall take the personal chattels absolutely and, in addition, the residuary estate of the intestate (other than the personal chattels) shall stand charged with the payment of a [fixed net sum],[7] free of death duties and costs, to the surviving husband or wife with interest thereon from the date of the death of such rate as the Lord Chancellor may specify by order[8] until paid or appropriated, and, subject to providing for that sum and the interest thereon, the residuary estate (other than the personal chattels) shall be held—

(*a*) as one half upon trust for the surviving husband or wife during his or her life, and, subject to such life interest, on the statutory trusts for the issue of the intestate, and

(*b*) as to the other half, on the statutory trusts for the issue of the intestate.

(3) leaves one or more of the following, that is to say, a parent, a brother or sister of the whole blood, or issue of a brother or sister of the whole blood, but leaves no issue

the surviving husband or wife shall take the personal chattels absolutely and, in addition, the residuary estate of the intestate (other than the personal chattels) shall stand charged with the payment of a [fixed net sum],[9] free of death duties and costs, to the surviving husband or wife with interest thereon from the date of the death at such rate as the Lord Chancellor may specify by order,[10] until paid or appropriated, and, subject to providing for that sum and the interest thereon, the residuary estate (other than the personal chattels) shall be held—

[7] Substituted by the Family Provision Act 1966, s.1(2)(*a*). The sum is £40,000: Family Provision (Intestate Succession) Order 1981 (No. 255).

[8] Substituted by the Administration of Justice Act 1977 (c. 38), s.28(1). See the Intestate Succession (Interest and Capitalisation) Order 1983 (No. 1374) which provides that the specified rate of interest shall be 6 per cent. per annum.

[9] The sum is £85,000: Family Provision (Intestate Succession) Order 1981 (No. 255).

[10] See note 8, *supra*.

(*a*) as to one half in trust for the surviving husband or wife absolutely, and

(*b*) as to the other half—

(i) where the intestate leaves one parent or both parents (whether or not brothers or sisters of the intestate or their issue also survive) in trust for the parent absolutely or, as the case may be, for the two parents in equal shares absolutely

(ii) where the intestate leaves no parent, on the statutory trusts for the brothers and sisters of the whole blood of the intestate.][11]

[The fixed sums referred to in paragraphs (2) and (3) of this Table shall be of the amounts provided by or under section 1 of the Family Provision Act 1966.][12]

(ii) If the intestate leaves issue but no husband or wife, the residuary estate of the intestate shall be held on the statutory trusts for the issue of the intestate;

(iii) If the intestate leaves [no husband or wife and][13] no issue but both parents, then [...] the residuary estate of the intestate shall be held in trust for the father and mother in equal shares absolutely;

(iv) If the intestate leaves [no husband or wife][14] no issue but one parent, then [...] the residuary estate of the intestate shall be held in trust for the surviving father or mother absolutely;

(v) If the intestate leaves no [husband or wife and no issue and no][15] parent, then, [...] the residuary estate of the intestate shall be held in trust for the following persons living at the death of the intestate, and in the following order and manner, namely:—

First, on the statutory trusts for the brothers and sisters of the whole blood of the intestate; but if no person takes an absolutely vested interest under such trusts; then

Secondly, on the statutory trusts for the brothers and

[11] S.46(1)(i) was substituted by the Intestates' Estates Act 1952, s.1(2).
[12] Added by the Family Provision Act 1966, s.1(2)(*a*).
[13] Added by the Intestates' Estates Act 1952, s.1(3).
[14] See above, note 13.
[15] Substituted by *ibid.*

sisters of the half blood of the intestate; but if no person takes an absolutely vested interest under such trusts;

then

Thirdly, for the grandparents of the intestate and, if more than one survive the intestate, in equal shares; but if there is no member of this class; then

Fourthly, on the statutory trusts for the uncles and aunts of the intestate (being brothers or sisters of the whole blood of a parent of the intestate); but if no person takes an absolutely vested interest under such trusts; then

Fifthly, on the statutory trusts for the uncles and aunts of the intestate (being brothers or sisters of the half blood of a parent of the intestate); [. . .]

(vi) In default of any person taking an absolute interest under the foregoing provisions, the residuary estate of the intestate shall belong to the Crown or to the Duchy of Lancaster or to the Duke of Cornwall for the time being, as the case may be, as *bona vacantia*, and in lieu of any right to escheat.

The Crown or the said Duchy or the said Duke may (without prejudice to the powers reserved by section nine of the Civil List Act 1910, or any other powers), out of the whole or any part of the property devolving on them respectively, provide, in accordance with the existing practice, for dependants, whether kindred or not, of the intestate, and other persons for whom the intestate might reasonably have been expected to make provision.

[(1A) The power to make orders under subsection (1) above shall be exercisable by statutory instrument subject to annulment in pursuance of a resolution of either House of Parliament; and any such order may be varied or revoked by a subsequent order made under the power.][16]

(2) A husband and wife shall for all purposes of distribution or division under the foregoing provisions of this section be treated as two persons.

[(3) Where the intestate and the intestate's husband or wife have died in circumstances rendering it uncertain which of them survived the other and the intestate's husband or wife is by virtue of section one hundred and eight-four of the Law of Property Act 1925 deemed to have survived the intestate, this section shall, nevertheless, have effect as respects the intestate as if the husband or wife had not survived the intestate.

[16] Subsection added by Administration of Justice Act 1977 (c. 38), s.28(1).

(4) The interest payable on the [fixed net sum][17] payable to a surviving husband or wife shall be primarily payable out of income.][18]

Statutory trusts in favour of issue and other classes of relatives of intestate

47.—(1) Where under this Part of this Act the residuary estate of an intestate, or any part thereof, is directed to be held on the statutory trusts for the issue of the intestate,[19] the same shall be held upon the following trusts, namely:—

(i) In trust, in equal shares if more than one, for all or any the children or child of the intestate,[20] living at the death of the intestate, who attain the age of [eighteen years][21] or marry under that age, and for all or any of the issue living at the death of the intestate who attains the age [eighteen years] or marry under that age of any child of the intestate who pre-deceases the intestate, such issue to take through all degrees, according to their stocks, in equal shares if more than one, the share which their parent would have taken if living at the death of the intestate, and so that no issue shall take whose parent is living at the death of the intestate and so capable of taking;

(ii) The statutory power of advancement, and the statutory provisions which relate to maintenance and accumulation of surplus income, shall apply, but when an infant marries such infant shall be entitled to give valid receipts for the income of the infant's share or interest;

(iii) Where the property held on the statutory trusts for issue is divisible into shares, then any money or property which, by way of advancement or on the marriage of a child of the intestate, has been paid to such child by the intestate or settled by the intestate for the benefit of such child (including any life or less interest and including property covenanted to be paid or settled) shall, subject to any contrary intention expressed or appearing from the circumstances of the case, be taken as being so paid or settled in or towards satisfaction of the share of such child or the share which such child would have taken if living at the death of the intestate, and shall be brought into account, at a valuation (the value to be reckoned as at the

[17] Substituted by the Family Provision Act 1966, s.1(2)(*b*). The sum is £40,000 if the intestate leaves issue and £85,000 if the intestate leaves no issue: Family Provision (Intestate Succession) Order 1981 (No. 255).

[18] Added by the Intestates' Estates Act 1952, s.1(4).

[19] See *ante*, note 5.

[20] In this Part of the Act, any reference to the child or children of the intestate shall have effect as if it included a reference to any illegitimate child or children of his: Family Law Reform Act 1969 (c. 46), s.14(3)(*b*).

[21] These words were substituted, in respect of the estate of an intestate dying after January 1, 1970, for the words "twenty-one years" by *ibid.* s.3(2).

death of the intestate), in accordance with the requirements of the personal representatives;

(iv) The personal representatives may permit any infant contingently interested to have the use and enjoyment of any personal chattels in such manner and subject to such conditions (if any) as the personal representatives may consider reasonable, and without being liable to account for any consequential loss.

(2) If the trusts in favour of the issue of the intestate fail by reason of no child or other issue attaining an absolutely vested interest—

(*a*) the residuary estate of the intestate and the income thereof and all statutory accumulations, if any, of the income thereof, or so much thereof as may not have been paid or applied under any power affecting the same, shall go, devolve and be held under the provisions of this Part of this Act as if the intestate had died without leaving issue living at the death of the intestate;

(*b*) References in this Part of this Act to the intestate "leaving no issue" shall be construed as "leaving no issue who attain an absolutely vested interest;"

(*c*) References in this Part of this Act to the intestate "leaving issue" or "leaving a child or other issue" shall be construed as "leaving issue who attain an absolutely vested interest."

(3) Where under this Part of this Act the residuary estate of an intestate or any part thereof is directed to be held on the statutory trusts for any class of relatives of the intestate, other than issue of the intestate, the same shall be held on trusts corresponding to the statutory trusts for the issue of the intestate (other than the provision for bringing any money or property into account) as if such trusts (other than as aforesaid) were repeated with the substitution of references to the members or member of that class for references to the children or child of the intestate.

(4) References in paragraph (i) of subsection (1) of the last foregoing section to the intestate leaving, or not leaving, a member of the class consisting of brothers or sisters of the whole blood of the intestate and issue of brothers or sisters of the whole blood of the intestate shall be construed as references to the intestate leaving, or not leaving, a member of that class who attains an absolutely vested interest.

(5) [*Repealed by the Family Provision Act* 1966, *post, s.*9, *Sched.* 2.]

[**47A.**[22]—(1) Where a surviving husband or wife is entitled to a life interest in part of the residuary estate, and so elects, the personal representative shall purchase or redeem the life interest by paying the capital value thereof to the tenant for life, or the persons deriving title

[22] Added by the Intestates' Estates Act 1952, s.2(*b*).

under the tenant for life, and the costs of the transaction; and thereupon the residuary estate of the intestate may be dealt with and distributed free from the life interest.

(2) [*Repealed by the Administration of Justice Act* 1977 (*c.* 38), *s.*28(2).]

(3) An election under this section shall only be exercisable if at the time of the election the whole of the said part of the residuary estate consists of property in possession, but, for the purposes of this section, a life interest in property partly in possession and partly not in possession shall be treated as consisting of two separate life interests in those respective parts of the property.

[(3A) The capital value shall be reckoned in such manner as the Lord Chancellor may by order direct, and an order under this subsection may include transitional provisions.

(3B) The power to make orders under subsection (3A) above shall be exercisable by statutory instrument subject to annulment in pursuance of a resolution of either House of Parliament; and any such order may be varied or revoked by a subsequent order made under the power.][23]

(4) [*Repealed by the Administration of Justice Act* 1977 (*c.* 38), *s.*28(2).]

(5) An election under this section shall be exercisable only within the period of twelve months from the date on which representation with respect to the estate of the intestate is first taken out:

Provided that if the surviving husband or wife satisfies the court that the limitation to the said period of twelve months will operate unfairly—

(*a*) in consequence of the representation first taken out being probate of a will subsequently revoked on the ground that the will was invalid, or

(*b*) in consequence of a question whether a person had an interest in the estate, or as to the nature of an interest in the estate, not having been determined at the time when representation was first taken out, or

(*c*) in consequence of some other circumstances affecting the administration or distribution of the estate.

the court may extend the said period.

(6) An election under this section shall be exercisable, except where the tenant for life is the sole personal representative, by notifying the personal representative (or, where there are two or more personal representatives of whom one is the tenant for life, all of them except the tenant for life) in writing; and a notification in writing under this

[23] Subsections added by the Administration of Justice Act 1977 (c. 38), s.28(3). See the Intestate Succession (Interest and Capitalisation) Order 1983 (No. 1374).

subsection shall not be revocable except with the consent of the personal representative.

(7) Where the tenant for life is the sole personal representative an election under this section shall not be effective unless written notice thereof is given to the [[Senior Registrar][24] of the Family Division of the High Court][25] within the period within which it must be made; and provision may be made by probate rules for keeping a record of such notices and making that record available to the public.

In this subsection the expression "probate rules" means rules [of court made under section 127 of the Supreme Court Act 1981][26]

(8) An election under this section by a tenant for life who is an infant shall be as valid and binding as it would be if the tenant for life were of age; but the personal representative shall, instead of paying the capital value of the life interest to the tenant for life, deal with it in the same manner as with any other part of the residuary estate to which the tenant for life is absolutely entitled.

(9) In considering for the purposes of the foregoing provisions of this section the question when representation was first taken out, a grant limited to settled land or to trust property shall be left out of account and a grant limited to real estate or to personal estate shall be left out of account unless a grant limited to the remainder of the estate has previously been made or is made at the same time.]

Powers of personal representative in respect of interests of surviving spouse

48.—(1) [*Repealed by the Intestates' Estates Act* 1952 (15 & 16 *Geo.* 6 & 1 *Eliz.* 2, *c.* 64), *s.*2(*a*).]

(2) The personal representatives may raise—

(*a*) [the fixed net sum][27] or any part thereof and the interest thereon payable to the surviving husband or wife of the intestate on the security of the whole or any part of the residuary estate of the intestate (other than the personal chattels), so far as that estate may be sufficient for the purpose or the said sum and interest may not have been satisfied by an appropriation under the statutory power available in that behalf; and

(*b*) in like manner the capital sum, if any, required for the purchase or redemption of the life interest of the surviving husband or wife of the intestate, or any part thereof not satisfied by the application for that purpose of any part of the residuary estate of the intestate;

[24] These words were substituted by the Supreme Court Act 1981 (c. 48), Sched. 5.
[25] These words were substituted by the Administration of Justice Act 1970 (c. 31), s.1(6) and Sched. 2, para. 4.
[26] These words were substituted by the Supreme Court Act 1981 (c. 48), Sched. 5.
[27] Substituted by the Family Provision Act 1966, s.1(2)(*b*).

and in either case the amount, if any, properly required for the payment of the costs of the transaction.

Application to cases of partial intestacy

49.—(1) Where any person dies leaving a will effectively disposing of part of his property, this Part of this Act shall have effect as respects the part of his property not so disposed of subject to the provisions contained in the will and subject to the following modifications:—

[(*aa*) where the deceased leaves a husband or wife who acquires any beneficial interests under the will of the deceased (other than personal chattels specifically bequeathed) the references in this Part of this Act to the [fixed net sum][28] payable to a surviving husband or wife, and to interest on that sum, shall be taken as references to the said sum diminished by the value at the date of death of the said beneficial interests, and to interest on that sum as so diminished, and, accordingly, where the said value exceeds the said sum, this Part of this Act shall have effect as if references to the said sum, and interest thereon, were omitted.][29]

(*a*) The requirements [of section forty-seven of this Act] as to bringing property into account shall apply to any beneficial interests acquired by any issue of the deceased under the will of the deceased, but not to beneficial interests so acquired by any other persons:

(*b*) the personal representative shall, subject to his rights and powers for the purposes of administration, be a trustee for the persons entitled under this Part of this Act in respect of the part of the estate not expressly disposed of unless it appears by the will that the personal representative is intended to take such part beneficially.

[(2) References in the foregoing provisions of this section to beneficial interests acquired under a will shall be construed as including a reference to a beneficial interest acquired by virtue of the exercise by the will of a general power of appointment (including the statutory power to dispose of entailed interests), but not of a special power of appointment.

(3) For the purpose of paragraph (*aa*) in the foregoing provisions of this section the personal representative shall employ a duly qualified valuer in any case where such employment may be necessary.

(4) The references in subsection (3) of section forty-seven A of this Act to property are references to property comprised in the residuary estate and, accordingly, where a will of the deceased creates a life

[28] Substituted by the Family Provision Act 1966, s.1(2)(*b*).
[29] Added by the Intestates' Estates Act 1952, s.3(2).

interest in property in possession, and the remaining interest in that property forms part of the residuary estate, the said references are references to that remaining interest (which, until the life interest determines, is property not in possession).]

Construction of documents

50.—(1)[30] References to any Statutes of Distribution in an instrument *inter vivos* made or in a will coming into operation after the commencement of this Act, shall be construed as references to this Part of this Act; and references in such an instrument or will to statutory next of kin shall be construed, unless the context otherwise requires, as referring to the persons who would take beneficially on an intestacy under the foregoing provisions of this Part of this Act.

(2) Trusts declared in an instrument *inter vivos* made, or in a will coming into operation, before the commencement of this Act by reference to the Statutes of Distribution, shall, unless the contrary thereby appears, be construed as referring to the enactments (other than the Intestates' Estates Act 1890) relating to the distribution of effects of intestates which were in force immediately before the commencement of this Act.

Savings

51.—(1) Nothing in this Part of this Act affects the right of any person to take beneficially, by purchase, as heir either general or special.

(2) The foregoing provisions of this Part of this Act do not apply to any beneficial interest in real estate (not including chattels real) to which a lunatic or defective living and of full age at the commencement of this Act, and unable by reason of his incapacity, to make a will, who thereafter dies intestate in respect of such interest without having recovered his testamentary capacity, was entitled at his death, and any such beneficial interest (not being an interest ceasing on his death) shall, without prejudice to any will of the deceased, devolve in accordance with the general law in force before the commencement of this Act applicable to freehold land, and that law shall, notwithstanding any repeal, apply to the case.

For the purposes of this subsection, a lunatic or defective who dies intestate as respects any beneficial interest in real estate shall not be deemed to have recovered his testamentary capacity unless his [. . .] receiver has been discharged.

(3) Where an infant dies after the commencement of this Act

[30] Reference to this Part of this Act shall in relation to instruments made or instruments coming into operation after the commencement of the Intestates' Estates Act 1952 include references to Part I of that Act: *ibid.* s.6(2); and after the commencement of the Family Law Reform Act 1969 (c. 46) include references to Part IV of that Act: *ibid.* s.14(6).

without having been married, and independently of this subsection he would, at his death, have been equitably entitled under a settlement (including a will) to a vested estate in fee simple or absolute interest in freehold land, or in any property settled to devolve therewith or as freehold land, such infant shall be deemed to have had an entailed interest, and the settlement shall be construed accordingly.

(4) This Part of this Act does not affect the devolution of an entailed interest as an equitable interest.

Interpretation of Part IV

52. In this Part of this Act "real and personal estate" means every beneficial interest (including rights of entry and reverter) of the intestate in real and personal estate which (otherwise than in right of a power of appointment or of the testamentary power conferred by statute to dispose of entailed interests) he could, if of full age and capacity, have disposed of by his will.

PART V

SUPPLEMENTAL

General savings

53.—(1) Nothing in this Act shall derogate from the powers of the High Court which exist independently of this Act or alter the distribution of business between the several divisions of the High Court, or operate to transfer any jurisdiction from the High Court to any other court.

(2) Nothing in this Act shall affect any unrepealed enactment in a public general Act dispensing with probate or administration as respects personal estate not including chattels real.

(3) [*Repealed by Finance Act* 1975 (*c.* 7), *Sched.* 13.]

Application of Act

54. Save as otherwise expressly provided, this Act does not apply in any case where the death occurred before the commencement of this Act.

Definitions

55.—(1) In this Act, unless the context otherwise requires, the following expressions have the meanings hereby assigned to them respectively, that is to say:—

(i) "Administration" means, with reference to the real and personal estate of a deceased person, letters of administration, whether general or limited, or with the will annexed or otherwise:

(ii) "Administrator" means a person to whom administration is granted:

(iii) "Conveyance" includes a mortgage, charge by way of legal mortgage, lease, assent, vesting declaration, vesting instrument, disclaimer, release and every other assurance of property or of an interest therein by any instrument, except a will, and "convey" has a corresponding meaning, and "disposition" includes a "conveyance" also a devise bequest and an appointment of property contained in a will, and "dispose of" has a corresponding meaning:

(iv) "the Court" means the High Court, and also the county court, where that court has jurisdiction [. . .]

(v) "Income" includes rents and profits:

(vi) "Intestate" includes a person who leaves a will but dies intestate as to some beneficial interest in his real or personal estate:

(vii) "Legal estates" mean the estates charges and interests in or over land (subsisting or created at law) which are by statute authorised to subsist or to be created at law; and "equitable interests" mean all other interests and charges in or over land or in the proceeds of sale thereof:

(viii) "[person of unsound mind]"[31] includes a lunatic whether so found or not, and in relation to a [person of unsound mind][32] not so found; [*words repealed by the Mental Health Act* 1959 (7 *&* 8 *Eliz* 2, *c.* 72), *Sched.* 8, *Pt.* I] and "defective" includes every person affected by the provisions of section one hundred and sixteen of the Lunacy Act 1890 as extended by section sixty-four of the Mental Deficiency Act 1913 and for whose benefit a receiver has been appointed:

(ix) "Pecuniary legacy" includes an annuity, a general legacy, a demonstrative legacy so far as it is not discharged out of the designated property, and any other general direction by a testator for the payment of money, including all death duties free from which any devise, bequest, or payment is made to take effect:

(x) "Personal chattels" mean carriages, horses, stable furniture and effects (not used for business purposes), motor cars and accessories (not used for business purposes), garden effects, domestic animals, plate, plated articles, linen, china, glass, books, pictures, prints, furniture, jewellery, articles of household or personal use or ornament, musical and scientific instruments and apparatus, wines, liquors and consumable stores, but do not include any chattels used at the death of the intestate for business purposes nor money or securities for money.

[31] Substituted for "lunatic" by the Mental Treatment Act 1930, s.20(5).
[32] *Ibid.*

(xi) "Personal representative" means the executor, original or by representation, or administrator for the time being of a deceased person, and as regards any liability for the payment of death duties includes any person who takes possession of or intermeddles with the property of a deceased person without the authority of the personal representatives or the court, and "executor" includes a person deemed to be appointed executor as respects settled land:

(xii) "Possession" includes the receipt of rents and profits or the right to receive the same, if any:

(xiii) "Prescribed" means prescribed by rules of court [. . .]

(xiv) "Probate" means the probate of a will:

(xv) ["Probate judge" means the President of the Family Division of the High Court][33]

(xvi) [. . .][34]

(xvii) "Property" includes a thing in action and any interest in real or personal property:

(xviii) "Purchaser" means a lessee, mortagee or other person who in good faith acquires an interest in property for valuable consideration, also an intending purchaser and "valuable consideration" includes marriage, but does not include a nominal consideration in money:

(xix) "Real Estate" save as provided in Part IV of this Act means real estate, including chattels real, which by virtue of Part I of this Act devolves on the personal representative of a deceased person:

(xx) "Representation" means the probate of a will and administration, and the expression "taking out representation" refers to the obtaining of the probate of a will or of the grant of administration:

(xxi) "Rent" includes a rent service or a rent-charge, or other rent, toll, duty, or annual or periodical payment in money or money's worth, issuing out of or charged upon land, but does not include mortgage interest; and "rent charge" includes a fee farm rent:

(xxii) [. . .][35]

(xxiii) "Securities" include stocks, funds, or shares:

(xxiv) "Tenant for life," "statutory owner," "land," "settled land," "settlement," "trustees of the settlement," "term of years absolute," "death duties," and "legal mortgage" have the same meanings as in the Settled Land Act 1925 and "entailed interest" and "charge by way of legal mortgage" have the same meanings as in the Law of Property Act 1925:

[33] These words were substituted by the Administration of Justice Act 1970 (c. 31), s.1(6) and Sched. 2, para. 5.

[34] Words repealed by Supreme Court Act 1981 (c. 48), Sched. 7.

[35] Words repealed by Supreme Court Act 1981 (c. 48), Sched. 7.

(xxv) "Treasury solicitor" means the solicitor for the affairs of His Majesty's Treasury, and includes the solicitor for the affairs of the Duchy of Lancaster:

(xxvi) "Trust corporation" means the public trustee or a corporation either appointed by the court in any particular case to be a trustee or entitled by rules made under sub-section (3) of section four of the Public Trustee Act 1906 to act as custodian trustee:

(xxvii) "Trust for sale" in relation to land, means an immediate binding trust for sale, whether or not exercisable at the request or with the consent of any person, and with or without a power at discretion to postpone the sale; and "power to postpone a sale" means power to postpone in the exercise of a discretion:

(xxviii) "Will" includes codicil:

(2) References to a child or issue living at the death of any person include a child or issue *en ventre sa mere* at the death.

(3) References to the estate of a deceased person include property over which the deceased exercises a general power of appointment (including the statutory power to dispose of entailed interests) by his will.

Repeal

56. The Acts mentioned in the Second Schedule to this Act are hereby repealed to the extent specified in the third column of that Schedule, but as respects the Acts mentioned in Part I of that Schedule only so far as they apply to deaths occurring after the commencement of this Act.

Application to Crown

57.—(1) The provisions of this Act bind the Crown and the Duchy of Lancaster, and the Duke of Cornwall for the time being, as respects the estates of persons dying after the commencement of this Act, but not so as to affect the time within which proceedings for the recovery of real or personal estate vesting in or devolving on His Majesty in right of His Crown, or His Duchy of Lancaster, or on the Duke of Cornwall, may be instituted.

(2) Nothing in this Act in any manner affects or alters the descent or devolution of any property for the time being vested in His Majesty either in right of the Crown or of the Duchy of Lancaster or of any property for the time being belonging to the Duchy of Cornwall.

Short title, commencement and extent

58.—(1) This Act may be cited as the Administration of Estates Act 1925.

(2) [*Repealed by S.L.R. Act* 1950 (14 & 15 *Geo.* 6, *c.* 6).]

(3) This Act extends to England and Wales only.

TRUSTEE ACT 1925

PART II

GENERAL POWERS OF TRUSTEES AND PERSONAL REPRESENTATIVES

General Powers

Power of trustees for sale to sell by auction, &c.

12.—(1) Where a trust for sale or a power of sale of property is vested in a trustee, he may sell or concur with any other person in selling all or any part of the property, either subject to prior charges or not, and either together or in lots, by public auction or by private contract, subject to any such conditions respecting title or evidence of title or other matter as the trustee thinks fit, with power to vary any contract for sale, and to buy in at any auction, or to rescind any contract for sale and to re-sell, without being answerable for any loss.

(2) A trust or power to sell or dispose of land includes a trust or power to sell or dispose of part thereof, whether the division is horizontal, vertical, or made in any other way.

(3) This section does not enable an express power to sell settled land to be exercised where the power is not vested in the tenant for life or statutory owner.

Power to sell subject to depreciatory conditions

13.—(1) No sale made by a trustee shall be impeached by any beneficiary upon the ground that any of the conditions subject to which the sale was made may have been unnecessarily depreciatory, unless it also appears that the consideration for the sale was thereby rendered inadequate.

(2) No sale made by a trustee shall, after the execution of the conveyance, be impeached as against the purchaser upon the ground that any of the conditions subject to which the sale was made may have been unnecessarily depreciatory, unless it appears that the purchaser was acting in collusion with the trustee at the time when the contract for sale was made.

(3) No purchaser, upon any sale made by a trustee, shall be at liberty to make any objection against the title upon any of the grounds aforesaid.

(4) This section applies to sales made before or after the commencement of this Act.

Power of trustees to give receipts

14.—(1) The receipt in writing of a trustee for any money, securities, or other personal property or effects payable, transferable, or deliverable to him under any trust or power shall be a sufficient discharge to the person paying, transferring, or delivering the same and shall effectually exonerate him from seeing to the application of being answerable for any loss or misapplication thereof.

(2) This section does not, except where the trustee is a trust corporation, enable a sole trustee to give a valid receipt for—

(*a*) the proceeds of sale or other capital money arising under a [. . .][1] trust for sale of land;
(*b*) capital money arising under the Settled Land Act 1925.

(3) This section applies notwithstanding anything to the contrary in the instrument, if any, creating the trust.

Power to compound liabilities

15. A personal representative, or two or more trustees acting together, or, subject to the restrictions imposed in regard to receipts by a sole trustee not being a trust corporation, a sole acting trustee where by the instrument, if any, creating the trust, or by statute, a sole trustee is authorised to execute the trusts and powers reposed in him, may if and as he or they think fit—

(*a*) accept any property, real or personal, before the time at which it is made transferable or payable; or
(*b*) sever and apportion any blended trust funds or property; or
(*c*) pay or allow any debt or claim on any evidence that he or they think sufficient; or
(*d*) accept any composition or any security, real or personal, for any debt or for any property, real or personal, claimed; or
(*e*) allow any time of payment of any debt; or
(*f*) compromise, compound, abandon, submit to arbitration, or otherwise settle any debt, account, claim, or thing whatever relating to the testator's or intestate's estate or to the trust;

and for any of those purposes may enter into, give, execute, and do such agreements, instruments of composition or arrangement, releases, and other things as to him or them seem expedient, without being responsible for any loss occasioned by any act or thing so done by him or them in good faith.

Power to raise money by sale, mortgage, &c.

16.—(1) Where trustees are authorised by the instrument, if any, creating the trust or by law to pay or apply capital money subject to the trust for any purpose or in any manner, they shall have and shall

[1] These words were repealed retrospectively by the Law of Property (Amendment) Act 1926, Sched.

be deemed always to have had power to raise the money required by sale, conversion, calling in, or mortgage of all or any part of the trust property for the time being in possession.

(2) This section applies notwithstanding anything to the contrary contained in the instrument, if any, creating the trust, but does not apply to trustees of property held for charitable purposes, or to trustees of a settlement for the purposes of the Settled Land Act 1925, not being also the statutory owners.

Protection to purchasers and mortgagees dealing with trustees

17. No purchaser or mortgagee, paying or advancing money on a sale or mortgage purporting to be made under any trust or power vested in trustees, shall be concerned to see that such money is wanted, or that no more than is wanted is raised, or otherwise as to the application thereof.

Devolution of powers or trusts

18.—(1) Where a power or trust is given to or imposed on two or more trustees jointly, the same may be exercised or performed by the survivors or survivor of them for the time being.

(2) Until the appointment of new trustees, the personal representatives or representative for the time being of a sole trustee, or, where there were two or more trustees of the last surviving or continuing trustee, shall be capable of exercising or performing any power or trust which was given to, or capable of being exercised by, the sole or last surviving or continuing trustee, or other the trustees or trustee for the time being of the trust.

(3) This section takes effect subject to the restrictions imposed in regard to receipts by a sole trustee, not being a trust corporation.

(4) In this section "personal representative" does not include an executor who has renounced or has not proved.

Power to insure

19.—(1) A trustee may insure against loss or damage by fire any building or other insurable property to any amount, including the amount of any insurance already on foot, not exceeding three fourth parts of the full value of the building or property, and pay the premiums for such insurance out of the income thereof or out of the income of any other property subject to the same trusts without obtaining the consent of any person who may be entitled wholly or partly to such income.

(2) This section does not apply to any building or property which a trustee is bound forthwith to convey absolutely to any beneficiary upon being requested to do so.

Application of insurance money where policy kept up under any trust, power or obligation

20.—(1) Money receivable by trustees or any beneficiary under a policy of insurance against the loss or damage of any property subject to a trust or to a settlement within the meaning of the Settled Land Act 1925, whether by fire or otherwise, shall, where the policy has been kept up under any trust in that behalf or under any power statutory or otherwise, or in performance of any covenant or of any obligation statutory or otherwise, or by a tenant for life impeachable for waste, be capital money for the purposes of the trust or settlement, as the case may be.

(2) If any such money is receivable by any person, other than the trustees of the trust or settlement, that person shall use his best endeavours to recover and receive the money, and shall pay the net residue thereof, after discharging any costs of recovering and receiving it, to the trustees of the trust or settlement, or, if there are no trustees capable of giving a discharge therefor, into court.

(3) Any such money—

(*a*) if it was receivable in respect of settled land within the meaning of the Settled Land Act 1925, or any building or works thereon, shall be deemed to be capital money arising under that Act from the settled land, and shall be invested or applied by the trustees, or, if in court, under the direction of the court, accordingly;

(*b*) if it was receivable in respect of personal chattels settled as heirlooms within the meaning of the Settled Land Act 1925, shall be deemed to be capital money arising under that Act, and shall be applicable by the trustees, or, if in court, under the direction of the court, in like manner as provided by that Act with respect to money arising by a sale of chattels settled as heirlooms as aforesaid;

(*c*) if it was receivable in respect of property held upon trust for sale, shall be held upon the trusts and subject to the powers and provisions applicable to money arising by a sale under such trust;

(*d*) in any other case, shall be held upon trusts corresponding as nearly as may be with the trusts affecting the property in respect of which it was payable.

(4) Such money, or any part thereof, may also be applied by the trustees, or, if in court, under the direction of the court, in rebuilding, reinstating, replacing, or repairing the property lost or damaged, but any such application by the trustees shall be subject to the consent of any person whose consent is required by the instrument, if any, creating the trust to the investment of money subject to the trust, and, in the case of money which is deemed to be capital money arising

under the Settled Land Act 1925, be subject to the provisions of that Act with respect to the application of capital money by the trustees of the settlement.

(5) Nothing contained in this section prejudices or affects the right of any person to require any such money or any part thereof to be applied in rebuilding, reinstating, or repairing the property lost or damaged, or the rights of any mortgagee, lessor, or lessee, whether under any statute or otherwise.

(6) This section applies to policies effected either before or after the commencement of this Act, but only to money received after such commencement.

Deposit of documents for safe custody

21. Trustees may deposit any documents held by them relating to the trust, or to the trust property, with any banker or banking company or any other company whose business includes the undertaking of the safe custody of documents, and any sum payable in respect of such deposit shall be paid out of the income of the trust property.

Reversionary interests, valuations, and audit

22.—(1) Where trust property includes any share or interest in property not vested in the trustees, or the proceeds of the sale of any such property, or any other thing in action, the trustees on the same falling into possession, or becoming payable or transferable may—

(*a*) agree or ascertain the amount or value thereof or any part thereof in such manner as they may think fit;
(*b*) accept in or towards satisfaction thereof, at the market or current value, or upon any valuation or estimate of value which they may think fit, any authorised investments;
(*c*) allow any deductions for duties, costs, charges and expenses which they may think proper or reasonable;
(*d*) execute any release in respect of the premises so as effectually to discharge all accountable parties from all liability in respect of any matters coming within the scope of such release;

without being responsible in any such case for any loss occasioned by any act or thing so done by them in good faith.

(2) The trustees shall not be under any obligation and shall not be chargeable with any breach of trust by reason of any omission—

(*a*) to place any distringas notice or apply for any stop or other like order upon any securities or other property out of or on which such share or interest or other thing in acton as aforesaid is derived, payable or charged; or
(*b*) to take any proceedings on account of any act, default, or

neglect on the part of the persons in whom such securities or other property or any of them or any part thereof are for the time being, or had at any time been, vested;

unless and until required in writing so to do by some person, or the guardian of some person, beneficially interested under the trust, and unless also due provision is made to their satisfaction for payment of the costs of any proceedings required to be taken:

Provided that nothing in this subsection shall relieve the trustees of the obligation to get in and obtain payment or transfer of such share or interest or other thing in action on the same falling into possession.

(3) Trustees may, for the purpose of giving effect to the trust, or any of the provisions of the instrument, if any, creating the trust or of any statute, from time to time (by duly qualified agents) ascertain and fix the value of any trust property in such manner as they think proper, and any valuation so made in good faith shall be binding upon all persons interested under the trust.

(4) Trustees may, in their absolute discretion, from time to time, but not more than once in every three years unless the nature of the trust or any special dealings with the trust property make a more frequent exercise of the right reasonable, cause the accounts of the trust property to be examined or audited by an independent accountant, and shall, for that purpose, produce such vouchers and give such information to him as he may require; and the costs of such examination or audit, including the fee of the auditor, shall be paid out of the capital or income of the trust property, or partly in one way and partly in the other, as the trustees, in their absolute discretion, think fit, but in default of any direction by the trustees to the contrary in any special case, costs attributable to capital shall be borne by capital and those attributable to income by income.

Power to employ agents

23.—(1) Trustees or personal representatives may, instead of acting personally, employ and pay an agent, whether a solicitor, banker, stockbroker, or other person, to transact any business or do any act required to be transacted or done in the execution of the trust, or the administration of the testator's or intestate's estate, including the receipt and payment of money, and shall be entitled to be allowed and paid all charges and expenses so incurred, and shall not be responsible for the default of any such agent if employed in good faith.

(2) Trustees or personal representatives may appoint any person to act as their agent or attorney for the purpose of selling, converting, collecting, getting in, and executing and perfecting insurances of, or managing or cultivating, or otherwise administering any property, real or personal, moveable or immoveable, subject to the trust or forming part of the testator's or intestate's estate, in any place outside

the United Kingdom or executing or exercising any discretion or trust or power vested in them in relation to any such property, with such ancillary powers, and with and subject to such provisions and restrictions as they may think fit, including a power to appoint substitutes, and shall not, by reason only of their having made such appointment, be responsible for any loss arising thereby.

(3) Without prejudice to such general power of appointing agents as aforesaid—

(*a*) A trustee may appoint a solicitor to be his agent to receive and give a discharge for any money or valuable consideration or property receivable by the trustee under the trust, by permitting the solicitor to have the custody of, and to produce, a deed having in the body thereof or endorsed thereon a receipt for such money or valuable consideration or property, the deed being executed, or the endorsed receipt being signed, by the person entitled to give a receipt for that consideration;

(*b*) A trustee shall not be chargeable with breach of trust by reason only of his having made or concurred in making any such appointment; and the production of any such deed by the solicitor shall have the same statutory validity and effect as if the person appointing the solicitor had not been a trustee;

(*c*) A trustee may appoint a banker or solicitor to be his agent to receive and give a discharge for any money payable to the trustee under or by virtue of a policy of insurance, by permitting the banker or solicitor to have the custody of and to produce the policy of insurance with a receipt signed by the trustee, and a trustee shall not be chargeable with a breach of trust by reason only of his having made or concurred in making any such appointment:

Provided that nothing in this subsection shall exempt a trustee from any liability which he would have incurred if this Act and any enactment replaced by this Act had not been passed, in case he permits any such money, valuable consideration, or property to remain in the hands or under the control of the banker or solicitor for a period longer than is reasonably necessary to enable the banker or solicitor, as the case may be, to pay or transfer the same to the trustee.

This subsection applies whether the money or valuable consideration or property was or is received before or after the commencement of this Act.

Power to concur with others

24. Where an undivided share in the proceeds of sale of land directed to be sold, or in any other property, is subject to a trust, or forms part of the estate of a testator or intestate, the trustees or personal representatives may (without prejudice to the trust for sale affecting the entirety of the land and the powers of the trustees for sale in reference thereto) execute or exercise any trust or power vested in them in relation to such share in conjunction with the persons entitled to or having power in that behalf over the other share or shares, and notwithstanding that any one or more of the trustees or personal representatives may be entitled to or interested in any such other share, either in his or their own right or in a fiduciary capacity.

Power to delegate trusts during absence abroad

25.[2]—[(1) Notwithstanding any rule of law or equity to the contrary, a trustee may, by power of attorney, delegate for a period not exceeding twelve months the execution or exercise of all or any of the trusts, powers and discretions vested in him as trustee either alone or jointly with any other person or persons.

(2) The persons who may be donees of a power of attorney under this section include a trust corporation but not (unless a trust corporation) the only other co-trustee of the donor of the power.

(3) An instrument creating a power of attorney under this section shall be attested by at least one witness.

(4) Before or within seven days after giving a power of attorney under this section the donor shall give written notice thereof (specifying the date on which the power comes into operation and its duration, the donee of the power, the reason why the power is given and, where some only are delegated, the trusts, powers and discretions delegated) to—

(*a*) each person (other than himself) if any, who under any instrument creating the trust has power (whether alone or jointly) to appoint a new trustee; and

(*b*) each of the other trustees, if any;

but failure to comply with this subsection shall not, in favour of a person dealing with the donee of the powers, invalidate any act done or instrument executed by the donee.

(5) The donor of a power of attorney given under this section shall be liable for the acts or defaults of the donee in the same manner as if they were the acts or defaults of the donor.][3]

[(6)][4] For the purpose of executing or exercising the trusts or powers

[2] By the Powers of Attorney Act 1971 (*c.* 27), s.2, no instrument creating a power of attorney, and no copy of any such instrument shall be deposited or filed at the central office of the Supreme Court or at the Land Registry under this section, although any right to search for, inspect, copy, or obtain an office copy of, any such document deposited or filed before October 1, 1971, remains unaffected. Similarly, s.9 applies whenever the trusts, powers or discretions in question arose but does not invalidate anything done by virtue of this section. See also Enduring Powers of Attorney Act 1985.

[3] These subsections were substituted for the former subss. (1) to (8) by the Powers of Attorney Act 1971 (c. 27), s.9(1) and (2).

[4] The former subss. (9) and (10) now stand as subss. (6) and (7): *ibid.* s.9(1) and (3).

delegated to him, the donee may exercise any of the powers conferred on the donor as trustee by statute or by the instrument creating the trust, including power, for the purpose of the transfer of any inscribed stock, himself to delegate to an attorney power to transfer but not including the power of delegation conferred by this section.

[(7)][4] The fact that it appears from any power of attorney given under this section, or from any evidence required for the purposes of any such power of attorney or otherwise, that in dealing with any stock the donee of the power is acting in the execution of a trust shall not be deemed for any purpose to affect any person in whose books the stock is inscribed or registered with any notice of the trust.

[(8) This section applies to a personal representative, tenant for life and statutory owner as it applies to a trustee except that subsection (4) shall apply as if it required the notice there mentioned to be given—

(*a*) in the case of a personal representative, to each of the other personal representatives, if any, except any executor who has renounced probate;
(*b*) in the case of a tenant for life, to the trustees of the settlement and to each person, if any, who together with the person giving the notice constitutes the tenant for life;
(*c*) in the case of a statutory owner, to each of the persons, if any, who together with the person giving the notice constitute the statutory owner and, in the case of a statutory owner by virtue of section 23(1)(*a*) of the Settled Land Act 1925, to the trustees of the settlement.][5]

Indemnities

Protection against liability in respect of rents and covenants

26.—(1) Where a personal representative or trustee liable as such for—

(*a*) any rent, covenant, or agreement reserved by or contained in any lease; or
(*b*) any rent, covenant or agreement payable under or contained in any grant made in consideration of a rentcharge; or
(*c*) any indemnity given in respect of any rent, covenant or agreement referred to in either of the foregoing paragraphs;

satisfies all liabilities under the lease or grant [which may have accrued and been claimed][6] up to the date of the conveyance hereinafter mentioned, and, where necessary, sets apart a sufficient fund to answer any future claim that may be made in respect of any fixed and ascertained sum which the lessee or grantee agreed to lay out

[4] The former subss. (9) and (10) now stand as subss. (6) and (7): *ibid.* s.9(1) and (3).
[5] This subsection was substituted for the former subs. (11): *ibid.*
[6] These words are substituted by the Law of Property (Amendment) Act 1926, Sched.

on the property demised or granted, although the period for laying out the same may not have arrived, then and in any such case the personal representative or trustee may convey the property demised or granted to a purchaser, legatee, devisee, or other person entitled to call for a conveyance thereof and thereafter—

(i) he may distribute the residuary real and personal estate of the deceased testator or intestate, or, as the case may be, the trust estate (other than the fund, if any, set apart as aforesaid) to or amongst the persons entitled thereto, without appropriating any part, or any further part, as the case may be, of the estate of the deceased or of the trust estate to meet any future liability under the said lease or grant;

(ii) notwithstanding such distribution, he shall not be personally liable in respect of any subsequent claim under the said lease or grant.

(2) This section operates without prejudice to the right of the lessor or grantor, or the persons deriving title under the lessor or grantor, to follow the assets of the deceased or the trust property into the hands of the persons amongst whom the same may have been respectively distributed, and applies notwithstanding anything to the contrary in the will or other instrument, if any, creating the trust.

(3) In this section "lease" includes an underlease and an agreement for a lease or underlease and any instrument giving any such indemnity as aforesaid or varying the liabilities under the lease; "grant" applies to a grant whether the rent is created by limitation, grant, reservation, or otherwise, and includes an agreement for a grant and any instrument giving any such indemnity as aforesaid or varying the liabilities under the grant; "lessee" and "grantee" include persons respectively deriving title under them.

Protection by means of advertisements

27.—(1) With a view to the conveyance to or distribution among the persons entitled to any real or personal property, the trustees of a settlement or of a disposition on trust for sale or personal representatives, may give notice by advertisement in the Gazette, and [in a newspaper circulating in the district in which the land is situated][7-8] and such other like notices, including notices elsewhere than in England and Wales, as would, in any special case, have been directed by a court of competent jurisdiction in an action for administration, of their intention to make such conveyance or distribution as aforesaid, and requiring any person interested to send to the trustees or personal representatives within the time, not being less than two months, fixed in the notice or, where more than one notice is given, in

[7-8] These words are substituted by the Law of Property (Amendment) Act 1926, Sched.

the last of the notices, particulars of his claim in respect of the property of any part thereof to which the notice relates.

(2) At the expiration of the time fixed by the notice the trustees or personal representatives may convey or distribute the property or any part thereof to which the notice relates, to or among the persons entitled thereto, having regard only to the claims, whether formal or not, of which the trustees or personal representatives then had notice and shall not, as respects the property so conveyed or distributed, be liable to any person of whose claim the trustees or personal representatives have not had notice at the time of conveyance or distribution; but nothing in this section—

(*a*) prejudices the right of any person to follow the property, or any property representing the same, into the hands of any person, other than a purchaser, who may have received it; or

(*b*) frees the trustees or personal representatives from any obligation to make searches or obtain official certificates of search similar to those which an intending purchaser would be advised to make or obtain.

(3) This section applies notwithstanding anything to the contrary in the will or other instrument, if any, creating the trust.

Protection in regard to notice

28. A trustee or personal representative acting for the purposes of more than one trust or estate shall not, in the absence of fraud, be affected by notice of any instrument, matter, fact or thing in relation to any particular trust or estate if he has obtained notice thereof merely by reason of his acting or having acted for the purposes of another trust or estate.

Exoneration of trustees in respect of certain powers of attorney

29. [*This section was repealed by the Powers of Attorney Act* 1971 (*c.* 27), *s.*11(2), *and Sched.* 2.]

Implied indemnity of trustees

30.—(1) A trustee shall be chargeable only for money and securities actually received by him notwithstanding his signing any receipt for the sake of conformity, and shall be answerable and accountable only for his own acts, receipts, neglects, or defaults, and not for those of any other trustee, nor for any banker, broker, or other person with whom any trust money or securities may be deposited, nor for the insufficiency or deficiency of any securities, nor for any other loss, unless the same happens through his own wilful default.

(2) A trustee may reimburse himself to pay or discharge out of the trust premises all expenses incurred in or about the execution of the trusts or powers.

Power to apply income for maintenance and to accumulate surplus income during a minority

31.—(1) Where any property is held by trustees in trust for any person for any interest whatsoever, whether vested or contingent, then, subject to any prior interests or charges affecting that property—

(i) during the infancy of any such person, if his interest so long continues, the trustees may, at their sole discretion, pay to his parent or guardian, if any, or otherwise apply for or towards his maintenance, education, or benefit, the whole or such part, if any, of the income of that property as may, in all the circumstances, be reasonable, whether or not there is—
  (*a*) any other fund applicable to the same purpose; or
  (*b*) any person bound by law to provide for his maintenance or education; and

(ii) if such person on attaining the age of [eighteen years] has not a vested interest in such income, the trustees shall thenceforth pay the income of that property and of any accretion thereto under subsection (2) of this section to him, until he either attains a vested interest therein or dies, or until failure of his interest:

Provided that, in deciding whether the whole or any part of the income of the property is during a minority to be paid or applied for the purposes aforesaid, the trustees shall have regard to the age of the infant and his requirements and generally to the circumstances of the case, and in particular to what other income, if any, is applicable for the same purposes; and where trustees have notice that the income of more than one fund is applicable for those purposes, then, so far as practicable, unless the entire income of the funds is paid or applied as aforesaid or the court otherwise directs, a proportionate part only of the income of each fund shall be so paid or applied.

(2) During the infancy of any such person, if his interest so long continues, the trustees shall accumulate all the residue of that income in the way of compound interest by investing the same and the resulting income thereof from time to time in authorised investments, and shall hold those accumulations as follows:—

(i) If any such person—
  (*a*) attains the age of [eighteen years], or marries under that age, and his interest in such income during his infancy or until his marriage is a vested interest; or
  (*b*) on attaining the age of [eighteen years][9] or on marriage under that age becomes entitled to the property from

[9] These words were substituted by the Family Law Reform Act 1969 (c. 46), s.1(3) and Sched. 1, Pt. I.

which such income arose in fee simple, absolute or determinable, or absolutely, or for an entailed interest;

the trustees shall hold the accumulations in trust for such person absolutely, but without prejudice to any provision with respect thereto contained in any settlement by him made under any statutory powers during his infancy, and so that the receipt of such person after marriage, and though still an infant, shall be a good discharge; and

(ii) In any other case the trustees shall, notwithstanding that such person had a vested interest in such income, hold the accumulations as an accretion to the capital of the property from which such accumulations arose, and as one fund with such capital for all purposes, and so that, if such property is settled land, such accumulations shall be held upon the same trusts as if the same were capital money arising therefrom;

but the trustees may, at any time during the infancy of such person if his interest so long continues, apply those accumulations, or any part thereof, as if they were income arising in the then current year.

(3) This section applies in the case of a contingent interest only if the limitation or trust carries the intermediate income of the property, but it applies to a future or contingent legacy by the parent of, or a person standing in *loco parentis* to, the legatee, if and for such period as, under the general law, the legacy carries interest for the maintenance of the legatee, and in any such case as last aforesaid the rate of interest shall (if the income available is sufficient, and subject to any rules of court to the contrary) be five pounds per centum per annum.

(4) This section applies to a vested annuity in like manner as if the annuity were the income of property held by trustees in trust to pay the income thereof to the annuitant for the same period for which the annuity is payable, save that in any case accumulations made during the infancy of the annuitant shall be held in trust for the annuitant or his personal representatives absolutely.

(5) This section does not apply where the instrument, if any, under which the interest arises came into operation before the commencement of this Act.

Power of advancement

32.—(1) Trustees may at any time or times pay or apply any capital money subject to a trust, for the advancement or benefit, in such manner as they may, in their absolute discretion, think fit, of any person entitled to the capital of the trust property or of any share thereof, whether absolutely or contingently on his attaining any specified age or on the occurrence of any other event, or subject to a gift over on his death under any specified age or on the occurrence of any other event, and whether in possession or in remainder or reversion, and such payment or application may be made notwithstanding that the interest of such person is liable to be defeated by the exercise of a power of appointment or revocation, or to be diminished by the increase of the class to which he belongs:

Provided that—

(*a*) the money so paid or applied for the advancement or benefit of any person shall not exceed altogether in amount one-half of the presumptive or vested share or interest of that person in the trust property; and

(*b*) if that person is or becomes absolutely and indefeasibly entitled to a share in the trust property the money so paid or applied shall be brought into account as part of such share; and

(*c*) no such payment or application shall be made so as to prejudice any person entitled to any prior life or other interest, whether vested or contingent, in the money paid or applied unless such person is in existence and of full age and consents in writing to such payment or application.

(2) This section applies only where the trust property consists of money or securities or of property held upon trust for sale calling in and conversion, and such money or securities, or the proceeds of such sale calling in and conversion are not by statutue or in equity considered as land, or applicable as capital money for the purposes of the Settled Land Act 1925.

(3) This section does not apply to trusts constituted or created before the commencement of this Act.

Protective trusts

33.[10]—(1) Where any income, including an annuity or other periodical income payment, is directed to be held on protective trusts for the benefit of any person (in this section called "the principal beneficiary") for the period of his life or for any less period, then, during that period (in this section called the "trust period") the said income shall, without prejudice to any prior interest, be held on the following trusts, namely:—

(i) Upon trust for the principal beneficiary during the trust period or until he, whether before or after the termination of any prior

[10] By the Family Law Reform Act 1969, s.15(3), this section shall have effect, in relation to any disposition made after its coming into force, as if (a) the reference to children or more remote issue of the principal beneficiary included a reference to any illegitimate child of the principal beneficiary and to anyone who would rank as such issue if he, or some other person through whom he is descended from the principal beneficiary, had been born legitimate; and (b) the reference to the issue of the principal beneficiary included a reference to anyone who would rank as such issue if he, or some other person through whom he is descended from the principal beneficiary, had been born legitimate.

interest, does or attempts to do or suffers any act or thing, or until any event happens, other than an advance under any statutory or express power, whereby, if the said income were payable during the trust period to the principal beneficiary absolutely during that period, he would be deprived of the right to receive the same or any part thereof, in any of which cases, as well as on the termination of the trust period, whichever first happens, this trust of the said income shall fail or determine;

(ii) If the trust aforesaid fails or determines during the subsistence of the trust period, then, during the residue of that period, the said income shall be held upon trust for the application thereof for the maintenance or support, or otherwise for the benefit, of all or any one or more exclusively of the other or others of the following persons (that is to say)—

(*a*) the principal beneficiary and his or her wife or husband, if any, and his or her children or more remote issue, if any; or

(*b*) if there is no wife or husband or issue of the principal beneficiary in existence, the principal beneficiary and the persons who would, if he were actually dead, be entitled to the trust property or the income thereof or the annuity fund, if any, or arrears of the annuity, as the case may be:

as the trustees in their absolute discretion, without being liable to account for the exercise of such discretion, think fit.

(2) This section does not apply to trusts coming into operation before the commencement of this Act, and has effect subject to any variation of the implied trusts aforesaid contained in the instrument creating the trust.

(3) Nothing in this section operates to validate any trust which would, if contained in the instrument creating the trust, be liable to be set aside.

INTESTATES' ESTATES ACT 1952

An Act to amend the law of England and Wales about the property of persons dying intestate; and for purposes connected therewith.

[October 30, 1952.]

PART I

AMENDMENTS OF LAW OF INTESTATE SUCCESSION

1–4. [*These sections amend the Administration of Estates Act* 1925, *ss.*46–49, *ante, pp.* 387–396.]

Rights of surviving spouse as respects the matrimonial home

5. The Second Schedule to this Act shall have effect for enabling the surviving husband or wife or a person dying intestate after the commencement of this Act to acquire the matrimonial home.

PART III

GENERAL

Short title and commencement

9.—(1) This Act may be cited as the Intestates' Estates Act 1952.

(2) This Act shall come into operation on the first day of January, nineteen hundred and fifty-three.

SCHEDULES

FIRST SCHEDULE

[*This Schedule sets out ss.*46–49 *of the Administration of Estates Act* 1925, *ante, pp.* 387–396, *as amended by Part I of this Act.*]

SECOND SCHEDULE

RIGHTS OF SURVIVING SPOUSE AS RESPECTS THE MATRIMONIAL HOME

1.—(1) Subject to the provisions of this Schedule, where the residuary estate of the intestate comprises an interest in a dwelling-house in which the surviving husband or wife was resident at the time of the intestate's death, the surviving husband or wife may require the personal representative, in exercise of the power conferred by section forty-one of the principal Act (and with due regard to the requirements of that section as to valuation) to appropriate the said interest in the dwelling-house in or towards satisfaction of any absolute interest of the surviving husband or wife in the real and personal estate of the intestate.

(2) The right conferred by this paragraph shall not be exercisable where the interest is—

(*a*) a tenancy which at the date of the death of the intestate was a tenancy which would determine within the period of two years from that date; or

(*b*) a tenancy which the landlord by notice given after that date could determine within the remainder of that period.

(3) Nothing in subsection (5) of section forty-one of the principal Act (which requires the personal representative, in making an appropriation to any person under that section, to have regard to the rights of others) shall prevent the personal representative from giving effect to the right conferred by this paragraph.

(4) The reference in this paragraph to an absolute interest in the real and personal estate of the intestate includes a reference to the capital value of a life interest which the surviving husband or wife has under this Act elected to have redeemed.

(5) Where part of a building was, at the date of the death of the intestate, occupied as a separate dwelling, that dwelling shall for the purposes of this Schedule be treated as a dwelling-house.

2. Where—

(*a*) the dwelling-house forms part of a building and an interest in the whole of the building is comprised in the residuary estate; or

(*b*) the dwelling-house is held with agricultural land and an interest in the agricultural land is comprised in the residuary estate; or

(*c*) the whole or part of the dwelling-house was at the time of the intestate's death used as a hotel or lodging house; or

(*d*) a part of the dwelling-house was at the time of the intestate's death used for purposes other than domestic purposes,

the right conferred by paragraph 1 of this Schedule shall not be exercisable unless the court, on being satisfied that the exercise of that right is not likely to diminish the value of assets in the residuary estate (other than the said interest in the dwelling-house) or make them more difficult to dispose of, so orders.

3.—(1) The right conferred by paragraph 1 of this Schedule—

(*a*) shall not be exercisable after the expiration of twelve months from the first taking out of representation with respect to the intestate's estate;

(*b*) shall not be exercisable after the death of the surviving husband or wife;

(*c*) shall be exercisable, except where the surviving husband or wife is the sole personal representative (or, where there are two or more personal representatives of whom one is the surviving husband or wife, all of them except the surviving husband or wife) in writing.

(2) A notification in writing under paragraph (*c*) of the foregoing sub-paragraph shall not be revocable except with the consent of the personal representative; but the surviving husband or wife may require the personal representative to have the said interest in the dwelling-house valued in accordance with section forty-one of the principal Act and to inform him or her of the result of that valuation before he or she decides whether to exercise the right.

(3) Subsection (9) of the section forty-seven A added to the principal Act by section two of this Act shall apply for the purposes of the construction of the reference in this paragraph to the first taking out of representation, and the proviso to subsection (5) of that section shall apply for the purpose of enabling the surviving husband or wife to apply for an extension of the period of twelve months mentioned in this paragraph.

4.—(1) During the period of twelve months mentioned in paragraph 3 of this Schedule the personal representative shall not without the written consent of the surviving husband or wife sell or otherwise dispose of the said interest in the dwelling-house except in the course of administration owing to want of other assets.

(2) An application to the court under paragraph 2 of this Schedule may be made by the personal representative as well as by the surviving husband or wife, and if, on an application under that paragraph, the court does not order that the right conferred by paragraph 1 of this Schedule shall be exercisable by the surviving husband or wife, the court may authorise the personal representative to dispose of the said interest in the dwelling-house within the said period of twelve months.

(3) Where the court under sub-paragraph (3) of paragraph 3 of this Schedule extends the said period of twelve months, the court may direct that this paragraph shall apply in relation to the extended period as it applied in relation to the original period of twelve months.

(4) This paragraph shall not apply where the surviving husband or wife is the sole personal representative or one of two or more personal representatives.

(5) Nothing in this paragraph shall confer any right on the surviving husband or wife as against a purchaser from the personal representative.

5.—(1) Where the surviving husband or wife is one of two or more personal representatives, the rule that a trustee may not be a purchaser of trust property shall not prevent the surviving husband or wife from purchasing out of the estate of the intestate an interest in a dwelling-house in which the surviving husband or wife was resident at the time of the intestate's death.

(2) The power of appropriation under section forty-one of the principal Act shall include power to appropriate an interest in a dwelling-house in which the surviving husband or wife was resident at the time of the intestate's death partly in satisfaction of an interest of the surviving husband or wife in the real and personal estate of the intestate and partly in return for a payment of money by the surviving husband or wife to the personal representative.

6.—(1) Where the surviving husband or wife is a person of unsound mind or a defective, a requirement or consent under this Schedule may be made or given on his or her behalf by the committee or receiver, if any, or, where there is no committee or receiver, by the court.

(2) A requirement or consent made or given under this Schedule by a surviving husband or wife who is an infant shall be as valid and binding as it would be if he or she were of age; and, as respects an appropriation in pursuance of paragraph 1 of this Schedule, the provisions of section forty-one of the principal Act as to obtaining the consent of the infant's parent or guardian, or of the court on behalf of the infant, shall not apply.

7.—(1) Except where the context otherwise requires, references in this Schedule to a dwelling-house include references to any garden or portion of ground attached to and usually occupied with the dwelling-house or otherwise required for the amenity or convenience of the dwelling-house.

(2) This Schedule shall be construed as one with Part IV of the principal Act.

FAMILY LAW REFORM ACT 1969

PART II

PROPERTY RIGHTS OF ILLEGITIMATE CHILDREN

Right of illegitimate child to succeed on intestacy of parents, and of parents to succeed on intestacy of illegitimate child

14.—(1) Where either parent of an illegitimate child dies intestate as respects all or any of his or her real or personal property, the illegitimate child or, if he is dead, his issue, shall be entitled to take any interest therein to which he or such issue would have been entitled if he had been born legitimate.

(2) Where an illegitimate child dies intestate in respect of all or any of his real or personal property, each of his parents, if surviving, shall be entitled to take any interest therein to which that parent would have been entitled if the child had been born legitimate.

(3) In accordance with the foregoing provisions of this section, Part IV of the Administration of Estates Act 1925 (which deals with the distribution of the estate of an intestate) shall have effect as if—

(*a*) any reference to the issue of the intestate included a reference to any illegitimate child of his and to the issue of any such child;

(*b*) any reference to the child or children of the intestate included a reference to any illegitimate child or children of his; and

(*c*) in relation to an intestate who is an illegitimate child, any reference to the parent, parents, father or mother of the intestate were a reference to his natural parent, parents, father or mother.

(4) For the purposes of subsection (2) of this section and of the provisions amended by subsection (3)(*c*) thereof, an illegitimate child shall be presumed not to have been survived by his father unless the contrary is shown.

(5) This section does not apply to or affect the right of any person to take any entailed interest in real or personal property.

(6) The reference in section 50(1) of the said Act of 1925 (which relates to the construction of documents) to Part IV of that Act, or to the foregoing provisions of that Part, shall in relation to an instrument *inter vivos* made, or a will or codicil coming into operation, after the coming into force of this section (but not in relation to instruments *inter vivos* made or wills or codicils coming into operation earlier) be construed as including references to this section.

(7) Section 9 of the Legitimacy Act 1926 (under which an

illegitimate child and his issue are entitled to succeed on the intestacy of his mother if she leaves no legitimate issue, and the mother of an illegitimate child is entitled to succeed on his intestacy as if she were the only surviving parent) is hereby repealed.

(8) [*Repealed by Children Act* 1975 (*c.* 72), *Sched.* 4.]

(9) This section does not affect any rights under the intestacy of a person dying before the coming into force of this section.

Presumption that in dispositions of property references to children and other relatives include references to, and to persons related through, illegitimate children

15.—(1) In any disposition made after the coming into force of this section—

(*a*) any reference (whether express or implied) to the child or children of any person shall, unless the contrary intention appears, be construed as, or as including, a reference to any illegitimate child of that person; and

(*b*) any reference (whether express or implied) to a person or persons related in some other manner to any person shall, unless the contrary intention appears, be construed as, or as including, a reference to anyone who would be so related if he, or some other person through whom the relationship is deduced, had been born legitimate.

(2) The foregoing subsection applies only where the reference in question is to a person who is to benefit or to be capable of benefiting under the disposition or, for the purpose of designating such a person, to someone else to or through whom that person is related; but that subsection does not affect the construction of the word "heir" or "heirs" or of any expression which is used to create an entailed interest in real or personal property.

(3) In relation to any disposition made after the coming into force of this section, section 33 of the Trustee Act 1925 (which specifies the trusts implied by a direction that income is to be held on protective trusts for the benefit of any person) shall have effect as if—

(*a*) the reference to the children or more remote issue of the principal beneficiary included a reference to any illegitimate child of the principal beneficiary and to anyone who would rank as such issue if he, or some other person through whom he is descended from the principal beneficiary, had been born legitimate; and

(*b*) the reference to the issue of the principal beneficiary included a reference to anyone who would rank as such issue if he, or some other person through whom he is descended from the principal beneficiary, had been born legitimate.

(4) [*Repealed by Children Act* 1975 (*c.* 72), *Sched.* 4.]

(5) Where under any disposition any real or personal property or any interest in such property is limited (whether subject to any preceding limitation or charge or not) in such a way that it would, apart from this section, devolve (as nearly as the law permits) along with a dignity or title of honour, then, whether or not the disposition contains an express reference to the dignity or title of honour, and whether or not the property or some interest in the property may in some event become severed therefrom, nothing in this section shall operate to sever the property or any interest therein from the dignity or title, but the property or interest shall devolve in all respects as if this section had not been enacted.

(6) [*Repealed by Children Act* 1975 (*c.* 72), *Sched.* 4.]

(7) There is hereby abolished, as respects dispositions made after the coming into force of this section, any rule of law that a disposition in favour of illegitimate children not in being when the disposition takes effect is void as contrary to public policy.

(8) In this section "disposition" means a disposition, including an oral disposition, of real or personal property whether *inter vivos* or by will or codicil; and, notwithstanding any rule of law, a disposition made by will or codicil executed before the date on which this section comes into force shall not be treated for the purposes of this section as made on or after that date by reason only that the will or codicil is confirmed by a codicil executed on or after that date.

Meaning of "child" and "issue" in s.33 of Wills Act 1837

16.—(1) In relation to a testator who dies after the coming into force of this section, section 33 of the Wills Act 1837 (gift to children or other issue of testator not to lapse if they predecease him but themselves leave issue) shall have effect as if—

(*a*) the reference to a child or other issue of the testator (that is, the intended beneficiary) included a reference to any illegitimate child of the testator and to anyone who would rank as such issue if he, or some other person through whom he is descended from the testator, had been born legitimate; and

(*b*) the reference to the issue of the intended beneficiary included a reference to anyone who would rank as such issue if he, or some other person through whom he is descended from the intended beneficiary, had been born legitimate.

(2) In this section "illegitimate child" includes an illegitimate child who is a legitimated person within the meaning of the Legitimacy Act 1926 or a person recognised by virtue of that Act or at common law as having been legitimated.

Protection of trustees and personal representatives

17. Notwithstanding the foregoing provisions of this Part of this Act, trustees or personal representatives may convey or distribute any real or personal property to or among the persons entitled thereto without having ascertained that there is no person who is or may be entitled to any interest therein by virtue of—

(*a*) section 14 of this Act so far as it confers any interest on illegitimate children or their issue or on the father of an illegitimate child; or

(*b*) section 15 or 16 of this Act,

and shall not be liable to any such person of whose claim they have not had notice at the time of the conveyance or distribution; but nothing in this section shall prejudice the right of any such person to follow the property, or any property representing it, into the hands of any person, other than a purchaser, who may have received it.

18. [*Repealed by Inheritance (Provision for Family and Dependants) Act* 1975 (*c.* 63), *Sched.*]

Policies of assurance and property in industrial and provident societies

19.—(1) In section 11 of the Married Women's Property Act 1882 and section 2 of the Married Women's Policies of Assurance (Scotland) Act 1880 (policies of assurance effected for the benefit of children) the expression "children" shall include illegitimate children.

(2) In section 25(2) of the Industrial and Provident Societies Act 1965 (application of property in registered society where member was illegitimate and is not survived by certain specified relatives) for the words "and leaves no widow, widower or issue, and his mother does not survive him" there shall be substituted the words "and leaves no widow, widower or issue (including any illegitimate child of the member) and neither of his parents survives him."

(3) Subsection (1) of this section does not affect the operation of the said Acts of 1882 and 1880 in relation to a policy effected before the coming into force of that subsection; and subsection (2) of this section does not affect the operation of the said Act of 1965 in relation to a member of a registered society who dies before the coming into force of the said subsection (2).

INHERITANCE (PROVISION FOR FAMILY AND DEPENDANTS) ACT 1975

An Act to make fresh provision for empowering the court to make orders for the making out of the estate of a deceased person of provision for the spouse, former spouse, child, child of the family or dependant of that person; and for matters connected therewith.

1.—(1) Where after the commencement of this Act a person dies domiciled in England and Wales and is survived by any of the following persons:—

(*a*) the wife or husband of the deceased;
(*b*) a former wife or former husband of the deceased who has not remarried;
(*c*) a child of the deceased;
(*d*) any person (not being a child of the deceased) who, in the case of any marriage to which the deceased was at any time a party, was treated by the deceased as a child of the family in relation to that marriage;
(*e*) any person (not being a person included in the foregoing paragraphs of this subsection) who immediately before the death of the deceased was being maintained, either wholly or partly, by the deceased;

that person may apply to the court for an order under section 2 of this Act on the ground that the disposition of the deceased's estate effected by his will or the law relating to intestacy, or the combination of his will and that law, is not such as to make reasonable financial provision for the applicant.

(2) In this Act "reasonable financial provision"—

(*a*) in the case of an application made by virtue of subsection (1)(*a*) above by the husband or wife of the deceased (except where the marriage with the deceased was the subject of a decree of judicial separation and at the date of death the decree was in force and the separation was continuing), means such financial provision as it would be reasonable in all the circumstances of the case for a husband or wife to receive, whether or not that provision is required for his or her maintenance;
(*b*) in the case of any other application made by virtue of subsection (1) above, means such financial provision as it would be reasonable in all the circumstances of the case for the applicant to receive for his maintenance.

(3) For the purposes of subsection (1)(*e*) above, a person shall be treated as being maintained by the deceased, either wholly or partly, as the case may be, if the deceased, otherwise than for full valuable consideration, was making a substantial contribution in money or money's worth towards the reasonable needs of that person.

2.—(1) Subject to the provisions of this Act, where an application is made for an order under this section, the court may, if it is satisfied that the disposition of the deceased's estate effected by his will or the law relating to intestacy, or the combination of his will and that law, is not such as to make reasonable financial provision for the applicant, make any one or more of the following orders:—

(*a*) an order for the making to the applicant out of the net estate of the deceased of such periodical payments and for such term as may be specified in the order;
(*b*) an order for the payment to the applicant out of that estate of a lump sum of such amount as may be so specified;
(*c*) an order for the transfer to the applicant of such property comprised in that estate as may be so specified;
(*d*) an order for the settlement for the benefit of the applicant of such property comprised in that estate as may be so specified;
(*e*) an order for the acquisition out of property comprised in that estate of such property as may be so specified and for the transfer of the property so acquired to the applicant or for the settlement thereof for his benefit;
(*f*) an order varying any ante-nuptial or post-nuptial settlement (including such a settlement made by will) made on the parties to a marriage to which the deceased was one of the parties, the variation being for the benefit of the surviving party to that marriage, or any child of that marriage, or any person who was treated by the deceased as a child of the family in relation to that marriage.

(2) An order under subsection (1)(*a*) above providing for the making out of the net estate of the deceased of periodical payments may provide for—

(*a*) payments of such amount as may be specified in the order,
(*b*) payments equal to the whole of the income of the net estate or of such portion thereof as may be so specified,
(*c*) payments equal to the whole of the income of such part of the net estate as the court may direct to be set aside or appropriated for the making out of the income thereof of payments under this section,

or may provide for the amount of the payments or any of them to be determined in any other way the court thinks fit.

(3) Where an order under subsection (1)(*a*) above provides for the

making of payments of an amount specified in the order, the order may direct that such part of the net estate as may be so specified shall be set aside or appropriated for the making out of the income thereof of those payments; but no larger part of the net estate shall be so set aside or appropriated than is sufficient, at the date of the order, to produce by the income thereof the amount required for the making of those payments.

(4) An order under this section may contain such consequential and supplemental provisions as the court thinks necessary or expedient for the purpose of giving effect to the order or for the purpose of securing that the order operates fairly as between one beneficiary of the estate of the deceased and another and may, in particular, but without prejudice to the generality of this subsection—

(*a*) order any person who holds any property which forms part of the net estate of the deceased to make such payment or transfer such property as may be specified in the order;

(*b*) vary the disposition of the deceased's estate effected by the will or the law relating to intestacy, or by both the will and the law relating to intestacy, in such manner as the court thinks fair and reasonable having regard to the provisions of the order and all the circumstances of the case;

(*c*) confer on the trustees of any property which is the subject of an order under this section such powers as appear to the court to be necessary or expedient.

3.—(1) Where an application is made for an order under section 2 of this Act, the court shall, in determining whether the disposition of the deceased's estate effected by his will or the law relating to intestacy, or the combination of his will and that law, is such as to make reasonable financial provision for the applicant and, if the court considers that reasonable financial provision has not been made, in determining whether and in what manner it shall exercise its powers under that section, have regard to the following matters, that is to say—

(*a*) the financial resources and financial needs which the applicant has or is likely to have in the foreseeable future;

(*b*) the financial resources and financial needs which any other applicant for an order under section 2 of this Act has or is likely to have in the foreseeable future;

(*c*) the financial resources and financial needs which any beneficiary of the estate of the deceased has or is likely to have in the foreseeable future;

(*d*) any obligations and responsibilities which the deceased had towards any applicant for an order under the said section 2 or towards any beneficiary of the estate of the deceased;

(*e*) the size and nature of the net estate of the deceased;
(*f*) any physical or mental disability of any applicant for an order under the said section 2 or any beneficiary of the estate of the deceased;
(*g*) any other matter, including the conduct of the applicant or any other person, which in the circumstances of the case the court may consider relevant.

(2) Without prejudice to the generality of paragraph (*g*) of subsection (1) above, where an application for an order under section 2 of this Act is made by virtue of section 1(1)(*a*) or 1(1)(*b*) of this Act, the court shall, in addition to the matters specifically mentioned in paragraphs (*a*) to (*f*) of that subsection, have regard to—

(*a*) the age of the applicant and the duration of the marriage;
(*b*) the contribution made by the applicant to the welfare of the family of the deceased, including any contribution made by looking after the home or caring for the family;

and, in the case of an application by the wife or husband of the deceased, the court shall also, unless at the date of death a decree of judicial separation was in force and the separation was continuing, have regard to the provision which the applicant might reasonably have expected to receive if on the day on which the deceased died the marriage, instead of being terminated by death, had been terminated by a decree of divorce.

(3) Without prejudice to the generality of paragraph (*g*) of subsection (1) above, where an application for an order under section 2 of this Act is made by virtue of section 1(1)(*c*) or 1(1)(*d*) of this Act, the court shall, in addition to the matters specifically mentioned in paragraphs (*a*) to (*f*) of that subsection, have regard to the manner in which the applicant was being or in which he might expect to be educated or trained, and where the application is made by virtue of section 1(1)(*d*) the court shall also have regard—

(*a*) to whether the deceased had assumed any responsibility for the applicant's maintenance and, if so, to the extent to which and the basis upon which the deceased assumed that responsibility and to the length of time for which the deceased discharged that responsibility;
(*b*) to whether in assuming and discharging that responsibility the deceased did so knowing that the applicant was not his own child;
(*c*) to the liability of any other person to maintain the applicant.

(4) Without prejudice to the generality of paragraph (*g*) of subsection (1) above, where an application for an order under section 2 of this Act is made by virtue of section 1(1)(*e*) of this Act, the court

shall, in addition to the matters specifically mentioned in paragraphs (*a*) to (*f*) of that subsection, have regard to the extent to which and the basis upon which the deceased assumed responsibility for the maintenance of the applicant and to the length of time for which the deceased discharged that responsibility.

(5) In considering the matters to which the court is required to have regard under this section, the court shall take into account the facts as known to the court at the date of the hearing.

(6) In considering the financial resources of any person for the purposes of this section the court shall take into account his earning capacity and in considering the financial needs of any person for the purposes of this section the court shall take into account his financial obligations and responsibilities.

4. An application for an order under section 2 of this Act shall not, except with the permission of the court, be made after the end of the period of six months from the date on which representation with respect to the estate of the deceased is first taken out.

5.—(1) Where on an application for an order under section 2 of this Act it appears to the court—

(*a*) that the applicant is in immediate need of financial assistance, but it is not yet possible to determine what order (if any) should be made under that section; and

(*b*) that property forming part of the net estate of the deceased is or can be made available to meet the need of the applicant;

the court may order that, subject to such conditions or restrictions, if any, as the court may impose and to any further order of the court, there shall be paid to the applicant out of the net estate of the deceased such sum or sums and (if more than one) at such intervals as the court thinks reasonable; and the court may order that, subject to the provisions of this Act, such payments are to be made until such date as the court may specify, not being later than the date on which the court either makes an order under the said section 2 or decides not to exercise its powers under that section.

(2) Subsections (2), (3) and (4) of section 2 of this Act shall apply in relation to an order under this section as they apply in relation to an order under that section.

(3) In determining what order, if any, should be made under this section the court shall, so far as the urgency of the case admits, have regard to the same matters as those to which the court is required to have regard under section 3 of this Act.

(4) An order made under section 2 of this Act may provide that any sum paid to the applicant by virtue of this section shall be treated to such an extent and in such manner as may be provided by that order as having been paid on account of any payment provided for by that order.

6.—(1) Subject to the provisions of this Act, where the court has made an order under section 2(1)(*a*) of this Act (in this section referred to as "the original order") for the making of periodical payments to any person (in this section referred to as "the original recipient"), the court, on an application under this section, shall have power by order to vary or discharge the original order or to suspend any provision of it temporarily and to revive the operation of any provision so suspended.

(2) Without prejudice to the generality of subsection (1) above, an order made on an application for the variation of the original order may—

(*a*) provide for the making out of any relevant property of such periodical payments and for such term as may be specified in the order to any person who has applied, or would but for section 4 of this Act be entitled to apply, for an order under section 2 of this Act (whether or not, in the case of any application, an order was made in favour of the applicant);

(*b*) provide for the payment out of any relevant property of a lump sum of such amount as may be so specified to the original recipient or to any such person as is mentioned in paragraph (*a*) above;

(*c*) provide for the transfer of the relevant property, or such part thereof as may be so specified, to the original recipient or to any such person as is so mentioned.

(3) Where the original order provides that any periodical payments payable thereunder to the original recipient are to cease on the occurrence of an event specified in the order (other than the remarriage of a former wife or former husband) or on the expiration of a period so specified, then, if, before the end of the period of six months from the date of the occurrence of that event or of the expiration of that period, an application is made for an order under this section, the court shall have power to make any order which it would have had power to make if the application had been made before that date (whether in favour of the original recipient or any such person as is mentioned in subsection (2)(*a*) above and whether having effect from that date or from such later date as the court may specify).

(4) Any reference in this section to the original order shall include a reference to an order made under this section and any reference in this section to the original recipient shall include a reference to any person to whom periodical payments are required to be made by virtue of an order under this section.

(5) An application under this section may be made by any of the following persons, that is to say—

(*a*) any person who by virtue of section 1(1) of this Act has applied, or would but for section 4 of this Act be entitled to apply, for an order under section 2 of this Act,
(*b*) the personal representatives of the deceased,
(*c*) the trustees of any relevant property, and
(*d*) any beneficiary of the estate of the deceased.

(6) An order under this section may only affect—

(*a*) property the income of which is at the date of the order applicable wholly or in part for the making of periodical payments to any person who has applied for an order under this Act, or
(*b*) in the case of an application under subsection (3) above in respect of payments which have ceased to be payable on the occurrence of an event or the expiration of a period, property the income of which was so applicable immediately before the occurrence of that event or the expiration of that period, as the case may be,

and any such property as is mentioned in paragraph (*a*) or (*b*) above is in subsections (2) and (5) above referred to as "relevant property."

(7) In exercising the powers conferred by this section the court shall have regard to all the circumstances of the case, including any change in any of the matters to which the court was required to have regard when making the order to which the application relates.

(8) Where the court makes an order under this section, it may give such consequential directions as it thinks necessary or expedient having regard to the provisions of the order.

(9) No such order as is mentioned in sections 2(1)(*d*), (*e*) or (*f*), 9, 10 or 11 of this Act shall be made on an application under this section.

(10) For the avoidance of doubt it is hereby declared that, in relation to an order which provides for the making of periodical payments which are to cease on the occurrence of an event specified in the order (other than the remarriage of a former wife or former husband) or on the expiration of a period so specified, the power to vary an order includes power to provide for the making of periodical payments after the expiration of that period or the occurrence of that event.

7.—(1) An order under section 2(1)(*b*) or 6(2)(*b*) of this Act for the payment of a lump sum may provide for the payment of that sum by instalments of such amount as may be specified in the order.

(2) Where an order is made by virtue of subsection (1) above, the court shall have power, on an application made by the person to whom the lump sum is payable, by the personal representatives of the deceased or by the trustees of the property out of which the lump sum is payable, to vary that order by varying the number of instalments

payable, the amount of any instalment and the date on which any instalment becomes payable.

Property available for financial provision

8.—(1) Where a deceased person has in accordance with the provisions of any enactment nominated any person to receive any sum of money or other property on his death and that nomination is in force at the time of his death, that sum of money, after deducting therefrom any capital transfer tax payable in respect thereof, or that other property, to the extent of the value thereof at the date of the death of the deceased after deducting therefrom any capital transfer tax so payable, shall be treated for the purposes of this Act as part of the net estate of the deceased; but this subsection shall not render any person liable for having paid that sum or transferred that other property to the person named in the nomination in accordance with the directions given in the nomination.

(2) Where any sum of money or other property is received by any person as a *donatio mortis causa* made by a deceased person, that sum of money, after deducting therefrom any capital transfer tax payable thereon, or that other property, to the extent of the value thereof at the date of the death of the deceased after deducting therefrom any capital transfer tax so payable, shall be treated for the purposes of this Act as part of the net estate of the deceased; but this subsection shall not render any person liable for having paid that sum or transferred that other property in order to give effect to that *donatio mortis causa.*

(3) The amount of capital transfer tax to be deducted for the purposes of this section shall not exceed the amount of that tax which has been borne by the person nominated by the deceased or, as the case may be, the person who has received a sum of money or other property as a *donatio mortis causa.*

9.—(1) Where a deceased person was immediately before his death beneficially entitled to a joint tenancy of any property, then, if, before the end of the period of six months from the date on which representation with respect to the estate of the deceased was first taken out, an application is made for an order under section 2 of this Act, the court for the purpose of facilitating the making of financial provision for the applicant under this Act may order that the deceased's severable share of that property, at the value thereof immediately before his death, shall, to such extent as appears to the court to be just in all the circumstances of the case, be treated for the purposes of this Act as part of the net estate of the deceased.

(2) In determining the extent to which any severable share is to be treated as part of the net estate of the deceased by virtue of an order under subsection (1) above, the court shall have regard to any capital transfer tax payable in respect of that severable share.

(3) Where an order is made under subsection (1) above, the provisions of this section shall not render any person liable for anything done by him before the order was made.

(4) For the avoidance of doubt it is hereby declared that for the purposes of this section there may be a joint tenancy of a chose in action.

Powers of court in relation to transactions intended to defeat applications for financial provision

10.—(1) Where an application is made to the court for an order under section 2 of this Act, the applicant may, in the proceedings on that application, apply to the court for an order under subsection (2) below.

(2) Where on an application under subsection (1) above the court is satisfied—

(*a*) that, less than six years before the date of the death of the deceased, the deceased with the intention of defeating an application for financial provision under this Act made a disposition, and

(*b*) that full valuable consideration for that disposition was not given by the person to whom or for the benefit of whom the disposition was made (in this section referred to as "the donee") or by any other person, and

(*c*) that the exercise of the powers conferred by this section would facilitate the making of financial provision for the applicant under this Act,

then, subject to the provisions of this section and of sections 12 and 13 of this Act, the court may order the donee (whether or not at the date of the order he holds any interest in the property disposed of to him or for his benefit by the deceased) to provide, for the purpose of the making of that financial provision, such sum of money or other property as may be specified in the order.

(3) Where an order is made under subsection (2) above as respects any disposition made by the deceased which consisted of the payment of money to or for the benefit of the donee, the amount of any sum of money or the value of any property ordered to be provided under that subsection shall not exceed the amount of the payment made by the deceased after deducting therefrom any capital transfer tax borne by the donee in respect of that payment.

(4) Where an order is made under subsection (2) above as respects any disposition made by the deceased which consisted of the transfer of property (other than a sum of money) to or for the benefit of the donee, the amount of any sum of money or the value of any property ordered to be provided under that subsection shall not exceed the

value at the date of the death of the deceased of the property disposed of by him to or for the benefit of the donee (or if that property has been disposed of by the person to whom it was transferred by the deceased, the value at the date of that disposal thereof) after deducting therefrom any capital transfer tax borne by the donee in respect of the transfer of that property by the deceased.

(5) Where an application (in this subsection referred to as "the original application") is made for an order under subsection (2) above in relation to any disposition, then, if on an application under this subsection by the donee or by any applicant for an order under section 2 of this Act the court is satisfied—

(*a*) that, less than six years before the date of the death of the deceased, the deceased with the intention of defeating an application for financial provision under this Act made a disposition other than the disposition which is the subject of the original application, and

(*b*) that full valuable consideration for that other disposition was not given by the person to whom or for the benefit of whom that other disposition was made or by any other person,

the court may exercise in relation to the person to whom or for the benefit of whom that other disposition was made the powers which the court would have had under subsection (2) above if the original application had been made in respect of that other disposition and the court had been satisfied as to the matters set out in paragraphs (*a*), (*b*) and (*c*) of that subsection; and where any application is made under this subsection, any reference in this section (except in subsection (2)(*b*)) to the donee shall include a reference to the person to whom or for the benefit of whom that other disposition was made.

(6) In determining whether and in what manner to exercise its powers under this section, the court shall have regard to the circumstances in which any disposition was made and any valuable consideration which was given therefor, the relationship, if any, of the donee to the deceased, the conduct and financial resources of the donee and all the other circumstances of the case.

(7) In this section "disposition" does not include—

(*a*) any provision in a will, any such nomination as is mentioned in section 8(1) of this Act or any *donatio mortis causa*, or

(*b*) any appointment of property made, otherwise than by will, in the exercise of a special power of appointment,

but, subject to these exceptions, includes any payment of money (including the payment of a premium under a policy of assurance) and any conveyance, assurance, appointment or gift of property of any description, whether made by an instrument or otherwise.

(8) The provisions of this section do not apply to any disposition made before the commencement of this Act.

11.—(1) Where an application is made to a court for an order under section 2 of this Act, the applicant may, in the proceedings on that application, apply to the court for an order under this section.

(2) Where on an application under subsection (1) above the court is satisfied—

(*a*) that the deceased made a contract by which he agreed to leave by his will a sum of money or other property to any person or by which he agreed that a sum of money or other property would be paid or transferred to any person out of his estate, and

(*b*) that the deceased made that contract with the intention of defeating an application for financial provision under this Act, and

(*c*) that when the contract was made full valuable consideration for that contract was not given or promised by the person with whom or for the benefit of whom the contract was made (in this section referred to as "the donee") or by any other person, and

(*d*) that the exercise of the powers conferred by this section would facilitate the making of financial provision for the applicant under this Act,

then, subject to the provisions of this section and of sections 12 and 13 of this Act, the court may make any one or more of the following orders, that is to say—

(i) if any money has been paid or any other property has been transferred to or for the benefit of the donee in accordance with the contract, an order directing the donee to provide, for the purpose of the making of that financial provision, such sum of money or other property as may be specified in the order;

(ii) if the money or all the money has not been paid or the property or all the property has not been transferred in accordance with the contract, an order directing the personal representatives not to make any payment or transfer any property, or not to make any further payment or transfer any further property, as the case may be, in accordance therewith or directing the personal representatives only to make such payment or transfer such property as may be specified in the order.

(3) Notwithstanding anything in subsection (2) above, the court may exercise its powers thereunder in relation to any contract made by the deceased only to the extent that the court considers that the amount of any sum of money paid or to be paid or the value of any property transferred or to be transferred in accordance with the

contract exceeds the value of any valuable consideration given or to be given for that contract, and for this purpose the court shall have regard to the value of property at the date of the hearing.

(4) In determining whether and in what manner to exercise its powers under this section, the court shall have regard to the circumstances in which the contract was made, the relationship, if any, of the donee to the deceased, the conduct and financial resources of the donee and all the other circumstances of the case.

(5) Where an order has been made under subsection (2) above in relation to any contract, the rights of any person to enforce that contract or to recover damages or to obtain other relief for the breach thereof shall be subject to any adjustment made by the court under section 12(3) of this Act and shall survive to such extent only as is consistent with giving effect to the terms of that order.

(6) The provisions of this section do not apply to a contract made before the commencement of this Act.

12.—(1) Where the exercise of any of the powers conferred by section 10 or 11 of this Act is conditional on the court being satisfied that a disposition or contract was made by a deceased person with the intention of defeating an application for financial provision under this Act, that condition shall be fulfilled if the court is of the opinion that, on a balance of probabilities, the intention of the deceased (though not necessarily his sole intention) in making the disposition or contract was to prevent an order for financial provision being made under this Act or to reduce the amount of the provision which might otherwise be granted by an order thereunder.

(2) Where an application is made under section 11 of this Act with respect to any contract made by the deceased and no valuable consideration was given or promised by any person for that contract then, notwithstanding anything in subsection (1) above, it shall be presumed, unless the contrary is shown, that the deceased made that contract with the intention of defeating an application for financial provision under this Act.

(3) Where the court makes an order under section 10 or 11 of this Act it may give such consequential directions as it thinks fit (including directions requiring the making of any payment or the transfer of any property) for giving effect to the order or for securing a fair adjustment of the rights of the persons affected thereby.

(4) Any power conferred on the court by the said section 10 or 11 to order the donee, in relation to any disposition or contract, to provide any sum of money or other property shall be exercisable in like manner in relation to the personal representative of the donee, and—

(*a*) any reference in section 10(4) to the disposal of property by the donee shall include a reference to disposal by the personal representative of the donee, and (*b*) any reference in section 10(5) to an application by the donee under that subsection shall include a reference to an application by the personal representative of the donee;

but the court shall not have power under the said section 10 or 11 to make an order in respect of any property forming part of the estate of the donee which has been distributed by the personal representative; and the personal representative shall not be liable for having distributed any such property before he has notice of the making of an application under the said section 10 or 11 on the ground that he ought to have taken into account the possibility that such an application would be made.

13.—(1) Where an application is made for—

(*a*) an order under section 10 of this Act in respect of a disposition made by the deceased to any person as a trustee, or

(*b*) an order under section 11 of this Act in respect of any payment made or property transferred, in accordance with a contract made by the deceased, to any person as a trustee,

the powers of the court under the said section 10 or 11 to order that trustee to provide a sum of money or other property shall be subject to the following limitation (in addition, in a case of an application under section 10, to any provision regarding the deduction of capital transfer tax) namely, that the amount of any sum of money or the value of any property ordered to be provided—

(i) in the case of an application in respect of a disposition which consisted of the payment of money or an application in respect of the payment of money in accordance with a contract, shall not exceed the aggregate of so much of that money as is at the date of the order in the hands of the trustee and the value at that date of any property which represents that money or is derived therefrom and is at that date in the hands of the trustee;

(ii) in the case of an application in respect of a disposition which consisted of the transfer of property (other than a sum of money) or an application in respect of the transfer of property (other than a sum of money) in accordance with a contract, shall not exceed the aggregate of the value at the date of the order of so much of that property as is at that date in the hands of the trustee and the value at that date of any property which represents the first-mentioned property or is derived therefrom and is at that date in the hands of the trustee.

(2) Where any such application is made in respect of a disposition made to any person as a trustee or in respect of any payment made or property transferred in pursuance of a contract to any person as a

trustee, the trustee shall not be liable for having distributed any money or other property on the ground that he ought to have taken into account the possibility that such an application would be made.

(3) Where any such application is made in respect of a disposition made to any person as a trustee or in respect of any payment made or property transferred in accordance with a contract to any person as a trustee, any reference in the said section 10 or 11 to the donee shall be construed as including a reference to the trustee or trustees for the time being of the trust in question and any reference in subsection (1) or (2) above to a trustee shall be construed in the same way.

Special provisions relating to cases of divorce, separation etc.

14.—(1) Where, within twelve months from the date on which a decree of divorce or nullity of marriage has been made absolute or a decree of judicial separation has been granted, a party to the marriage dies and—

(*a*) an application for a financial provision order under section 23 of the Matrimonial Causes Act 1973 or a property adjustment order under section 24 of that Act has not been made by the other party to that marriage, or

(*b*) such an application has been made but the proceedings thereon have not been determined at the time of the death of the deceased,

then, if an application for an order under section 2 of this Act is made by that other party, the court shall, notwithstanding anything in section 1 or section 3 of this Act, have power, if it thinks it just to do so, to treat that party for the purposes of that application as if the decree of divorce or nullity of marriage had not been made absolute or the decree of judicial separation had not been granted, as the case may be.

(2) This section shall not apply in relation to a decree of judicial separation unless at the date of the death of the deceased the decree was in force and the separation was continuing.

15.—(1) On the grant of a decree of divorce, a decree of nullity of marriage or a decree of judicial separation or at any time thereafter the court, if it considers it just to do so, may, on the application of either party to the marriage, order that the other party to the marriage shall not on the death of the applicant be entitled to apply for an order under section 2 of this Act.

In this subsection "the court" means the High Court or, where a county court has jurisdiction by virtue of Part V of the Matrimonial and Family Proceedings Act 1984, a county court."[1]

[1] As substituted by s.8, Matrimonial and Family Proceedings Act 1984.

(3) Where an order made under subsection (1) above on the grant of a decree of divorce or nullity of marriage has come into force with respect to a party to a marriage, then, on the death of the other party to that marriage, the court shall not entertain any application for an order under section 2 of this Act made by the first-mentioned party.

(4) Where an order made under subsection (1) above on the grant of a decree of judicial separation has come into force with respect to any party to a marriage, then, if the other party to that marriage dies while the decree is in force and the separation is continuing, the court shall not entertain any application for an order under section 2 of this Act made by the first-mentioned party.

15A.[2]—(1) On making an order under section 17 of the Matrimonial and Family Proceedings Act 1984 (orders for financial provision and property adjustment following overseas divorces, etc.) the court, if it considers it just to do so, may, on the application of either party to the marriage, order that the other party to the marriage shall not on the death of the applicant be entitled to apply for an order under section 2 of this Act.

In this subsection 'the court' means the High Court or, where a county court has jurisdiction by virtue of Part V of the Matrimonial and Family Proceedings Act 1984, a county court.

(2) Where an order under subsection (1) above has been made with respect to a party to a marriage which has been dissolved or annulled, then, on the death of the other party to that marriage, the court shall not entertain an application under section 2 of this Act made by the first-mentioned party.

(3) Where an order under subsection (1) above has been made with respect to a party to a marriage the parties to which have been legally separated, then, if the other party to the marriage dies, while the legal separation is in force, the court shall not entertain an application under section 2 of this Act made by the first-mentioned party."

16.—(1) Where an application for an order under section 2 of this Act is made to the court by any person who was at the time of the death of the deceased entitled to payments from the deceased under a secured periodical payments order made under the Matrimonial Causes Act 1973, then, in the proceedings on that application, the court shall have power, if an application is made under this section by that person or by the personal representative of the deceased, to vary or discharge that periodical payments order or to revive the operation of any provision thereof which has been suspended under section 31 of that Act.

(2) In exercising the powers conferred by this section the court shall have regard to all the circumstances of the case, including any order which the court proposes to make under section 2 or section 5 of this

[2] Added by Matrimonial and Family Proceedings Act 1984, s.25(3).

Act and any change (whether resulting from the death of the deceased or otherwise) in any of the matters to which the court was required to have regard when making the secured periodical payments order.

(3) The powers exercisable by the court under this section in relation to an order shall be exercisable also in relation to any instrument executed in pursuance of the order.

17.—(1) Where an application for an order under section 2 of this Act is made to the court by any person who was at the time of the death of the deceased entitled to payments from the deceased under a maintenance agreement which provided for the continuation of payments under the agreement after the death of the deceased, then, in the proceedings on that application, the court shall have power, if an application is made under this section by that person or by the personal representative of the deceased, to vary or revoke that agreement.

(2) In exercising the powers conferred by this section the court shall have regard to all the circumstances of the case, including any order which the court proposes to make under section 2 or section 5 of this Act and any change (whether resulting from the death of the deceased or otherwise) in any of the circumstances in the light of which the agreement was made.

(3) If a maintenance agreement is varied by the court under this section the like consequences shall ensue as if the variation had been made immediately before the death of the deceased by agreement between the parties and for valuable consideration.

(4) In this section "maintenance agreement," in relation to a deceased person, means any agreement made, whether in writing or not and whether before or after the commencement of this Act, by the deceased with any person with whom he entered into a marriage, being an agreement which contained provisions governing the rights and liabilities towards one another when living separately of the parties to that marriage (whether or not the marriage has been dissolved or annulled) in respect of the making or securing of payments or the disposition or use of any property, including such rights and liabilities with respect to the maintenance or education of any child, whether or not a child of the deceased or a person who was treated by the deceased as a child of the family in relation to that marriage.

18.—(1) Where—

(*a*) a person against whom a secured periodical payments order was made under the Matrimonial Causes Act 1973 has died and an application is made under section 31(6) of that Act for the variation or discharge of that order or for the revival of the operation of any provision thereof which has been suspended, or (*b*) a party to a maintenance agreement within the meaning of section 34 of that Act has died, the agreement being one which provides for the continuation of payments thereunder after the death of one of the parties, and an application is made under section 36(1) of that Act for the alteration of the agreement under section 35 thereof,

the court shall have power to direct that the application made under the said section 31(6) or 36(1) shall be deemed to have been accompanied by an application for an order under section 2 of this Act.

(2) Where the court gives a direction under subsection (1) above it shall have power, in the proceedings on the application under the said section 31(6) or 36(1), to make any order which the court would have had power to make under the provisions of this Act if the application under the said section 31(6) or 36(1), as the case may be, had been made jointly with an application for an order under the said section 2; and the court shall have power to give such consequential directions as may be necessary for enabling the court to exercise any of the powers available to the court under this Act in the case of an application for an order under section 2.

(3) Where an order made under section 15(1) of this Act is in force with respect to a party to a marriage, the court shall not give a direction under subsection (1) above with respect to any application made under the said section 31(6) or 36(1) by that party on the death of the other party.

Miscellaneous and supplementary provisions

19.—(1) Where an order is made under section 2 of this Act then for all purposes, including the purposes of the enactments relating to capital transfer tax, the will or the law relating to intestacy, or both the will and the law relating to intestacy, as the case may be, shall have effect and be deemed to have had effect as from the deceased's death subject to the provisions of the order.

(2) Any order made under section 2 or 5 of this Act in favour of—

(*a*) an applicant who was the former husband or former wife of the deceased, or

(*b*) an applicant who was the husband or wife of the deceased in a case where the marriage with the deceased was the subject of a decree of judicial separation and at the date of death the decree was in force and the separation was continuing,

shall, in so far as it provides for the making of periodical payments, cease to have effect on the remarriage of the applicant, except in relation to any arrears due under the order on the date of the remarriage.

(3) A copy of every order made under this Act shall be sent to the principal registry of the Family Division for entry and filing, and a memorandum of the order shall be endorsed on, or permanently annexed to, the probate or letters of administration under which the estate is being administered.

20.—(1) The provisions of this Act shall not render the personal representative of a deceased person liable for having distributed any part of the estate of the deceased, after the end of the period of six months from the date on which representation with respect to the estate of the deceased is first taken out, on the ground that he ought to have taken into account the possibility—

(*a*) that the court might permit the making of an application for an order under section 2 of this Act after the end of that period, or

(*b*) that, where an order has been made under the said section 2, the court might exercise in relation thereto the powers conferred on it by section 6 of this Act,

but this subsection shall not prejudice any power to recover, by reason of the making of an order under this Act, any part of the estate so distributed.

(2) Where the personal representative of a deceased person pays any sum directed by an order under section 5 of this Act to be paid out of the deceased's net estate, he shall not be under any liability by reason of that estate not being sufficient to make the payment, unless at the time of making the payment he has reasonable cause to believe that the estate is not sufficient.

(3) Where a deceased person entered into a contract by which he agreed to leave by his will any sum of money or other property to any person or by which he agreed that a sum of money or other property would be paid or transferred to any person out of his estate, then, if the personal representative of the deceased has reason to believe that the deceased entered into the contract with the intention of defeating an application for financial provision under this Act, he may, notwithstanding anything in that contract, postpone the payment of that sum of money or the transfer of that property until the expiration of the period of six months from the date on which representation with respect to the estate of the deceased is first taken out or, if during that period an application is made for an order under section 2 of this Act, until the determination of the proceedings on that application.

21. In any proceedings under this Act a statement made by the deceased, whether orally or in a document or otherwise, shall be admissible under section 2 of the Civil Evidence Act 1968 as evidence of any fact stated therein in like manner as if the statement were a statement falling within section 2(1) of that Act; and any reference in that Act to a statement admissible, or given or proposed to be given, in evidence under section 2 thereof or to the admissibility or the giving in evidence of a statement by virtue of that section or to any statement falling within section 2(1) of that Act shall be construed accordingly.

22. [*Repealed by Administration of Justice Act* 1962, *s.*75(1), *Sched.* 9, *Pt.* 1. *The County Court Jurisdiction is now subject to County Courts Act* 1959, *s.*52A *added by* 1982 *Act, Part* II, *Sched.* 3.]

23. In considering for the purposes of this Act when representation with respect to the estate of a deceased person was first taken out, a grant limited to settled land or to trust property shall be left out of account, and a grant limited to real estate or to personal estate shall be left out of account unless a grant limited to the remainder of the estate has previously been made or is made at the same time.

24. Section 46(1)(vi) of the Administration of Estates Act 1925, in so far as it provides for the devolution of property on the Crown, the Duchy of Lancaster or the Duke of Cornwall as *bona vacantia*, shall have effect subject to the provisions of this Act.

25.—(1) In this Act—

"beneficiary," in relation to the estate of a deceased person, means—

(*a*) a person who under the will of the deceased or under the law relating to intestacy is beneficially interested in the estate or would be so interested if an order had not been made under this Act, and

(*b*) a person who has received any sum of money or other property which by virtue of section 8(1) or 8(2) of this Act is treated as part of the net estate of the deceased or would have received that sum or other property if an order had not been made under this Act;

"child" includes an illegitimate child and a child *en ventre sa mere* at the death of the deceased;

"the court" means unless the context otherwise requires[3] the High Court, or where a county court has jurisdiction by virtue of section 22 of this Act, a county court;

" 'former wife' or 'former husband' means a person whose marriage with the deceased was during the lifetime of the deceased either—

(*a*) dissolved or annulled by a decree of divorce or a decree of nullity of marriage granted under the law of any part of the British Islands, or

(*b*) dissolved or annulled in any country or territory outside the

[3] Added by Matrimonial and Family Proceedings Act 1984, s.8(2).

British Islands by a divorce or annulment which is entitled to be recognised as valid by the law of England and Wales;".[4]

"net estate," in relation to a deceased person, means:—

(*a*) all property of which the deceased had power to dispose by his will (otherwise than by virtue of a special power of appointment) less the amount of his funeral, testamentary and administration expenses, debts and liabilities, including any capital transfer tax payable out of his estate on his death;
(*b*) any property in respect of which the deceased held a general power of appointment (not being a power exercisable by will) which has not been exercised;
(*c*) any sum of money or other property which is treated for the purposes of this Act as part of the net estate of the deceased by virtue of section 8(1) or (2) of this Act;
(*d*) any property which is treated for the purposes of this Act as part of the net estate of the deceased by virtue of an order made under section 9 of the Act;
(*e*) any sum of money or other property which is, by reason of a disposition or contract made by the deceased, ordered under section 10 or 11 of this Act to be provided for the purpose of the making of financial provision under this Act;

"property" includes any chose in action;
"reasonable financial provision" has the meaning assigned to it by section 1 of this Act;
"valuable consideration" does not include marriage or a promise of marriage;
"will" includes codicil.

(2) For the purposes of paragraph (*a*) of the definition of "net estate" in subsection (1) above a person who is not of full age and capacity shall be treated as having power to dispose by will of all property of which he would have had power to dispose by will if he had been of full age and capacity.

(3) Any reference in this Act to provision out of the net estate of a deceased person includes a reference to provision extending to the whole of that estate.

(4) For the purposes of this Act any reference to a wife or husband shall be treated as including a reference to a person who in good faith entered into a void marriage with the deceased unless either—

(*a*) the marriage of the deceased and that person was dissolved or annulled during the lifetime of the deceased and the dissolution or annulment is recognised by the law of England and Wales, or

[4] Added by Matrimonial and Family Proceedings Act 1984, s.25(2).

(*b*) that person has during the lifetime of the deceased entered into a later marriage.

(5) Any reference in this Act to remarriage or to a person who has remarried includes a reference to a marriage which is by law void or voidable or to a person who has entered into such a marriage, as the case may be, and a marriage shall be treated for the purposes of this Act as a remarriage, in relation to any party thereto, notwithstanding that the previous marriage of that party was void or voidable.

(6) Any reference in this Act to an order or decree made under the Matrimonial Causes Act 1973 or under any section of that Act shall be construed as including a reference to an order or decree which is deemed to have been made under that Act or under that section thereof, as the case may be.

(7) Any reference in this Act to any enactment is a reference to that enactment as amended by or under any subsequent enactment.

26.—(1) Section 36 of the Matrimonial Causes Act 1973 (which provides for the alteration of maintenance agreements by the High Court or a county court after the death of one of the parties) shall have effect subject to the following amendments (being amendments consequential on this Act), that is to say—

(*a*) in subsection (3) for the words "section 7 of the Family Provision Act 1966" there shall be substituted the words "section 22 of the Inheritance (Provision for Family and Dependants) Act 1975," for the words from "the Inheritance (Family Provision) Act" to "net estate" there shall be substituted the words "that Act if the value of the property mentioned in that section" and for the words "section 26 of the Matrimonial Causes Act 1965 (application for maintenance out of deceased's estate by former spouse)" there shall be substituted the words "section 2 of that Act";

(*b*) in subsection (7) for the words from "section 7" to "subsection (5)" there shall be substituted the words "section 22 of the Inheritance (Provision for Family and Dependants) Act 1975 (which enables rules of court to provide for the transfer from a county court to the High Court or from the High Court to a county court of proceedings for an order under section 2 of that Act) and paragraphs (*a*) and (*b*) of subsection (4)" and for the words "any such proceedings as are referred to in subsection (1) of that section" there shall be substituted the words "proceedings for an order under section 2 of that Act."

(2) Subject to the provisions of this section, the enactments specified in the Schedule to this Act are hereby repealed to the extent specified in the third column of the Schedule; and in paragraph 5(2) of Schedule 2 to the Matrimonial Causes Act 1973 for the words "that

Act" there shall be substituted the words "the Matrimonial Causes Act 1965."

(3) The repeal of the said enactments shall not affect their operation in relation to any application made thereunder (whether before or after the commencement of this Act) with reference to the death of any person who died before the commencement of this Act.

(4) Without prejudice to the provisions of section 38 of the Interpretation Act 1889 (which relates to the effect of repeals) nothing in any repeal made by this Act shall affect any order made or direction given under any enactment repealed by this Act, and, subject to the provisions of this Act, every such order or direction (other than an order made under section 4A of the Inheritance Family Provision Act 1938 or section 28A of the Matrimonial Causes Act 1965) shall, if it is in force at the commencement of this Act or is made by virtue of subsection (3) above, continue in force as if it had been made under section 2(1)(*a*) of this Act, and for the purposes of section 6(7) of this Act the court in exercising its powers under that section in relation to an order continued in force by this subsection shall be required to have regard to any change in any of the circumstances to which the court would have been required to have regard when making that order if the order had been made with reference to the death of any person who died after the commencement of this Act.

27.—(1) This Act may be cited as the Inheritance (Provision for Family and Dependants) Act 1975.

(2) This Act does not extend to Scotland or Northern Ireland.

(3) This Act shall come into force on April 1, 1976.

5. Rights of legitimated persons and others to take interests in property

(1) Subject to any contrary indication, the rules of construction contained in this section apply to any instrument other than an existing instrument, so far as the instrument contains a disposition of property.

(2) For the purposes of this section, provisions of the law of intestate succession applicable to the estate of a deceased person shall be treated as if contained in an instrument executed by him (while of full capacity) immediately before his death.

(3) A legitimated person, and any other person, shall be entitled to take any interest as if the legitimated person had been born legitimate.

(4) A disposition which depends on the date of birth of a child or children of the parent or parents shall be construed as if—

(*a*) a legitimated child had been born on the date of legitimation,
(*b*) two or more legitimated children legitimated on the same date had been born on that date in the order of their actual births,

but this does not affect any reference to the age of a child.

(5) Examples of phrases in wills on which subsection (4) above can operate are—

1. Children of A "living at my death or born afterwards."
2. Children of A "living at my death or born afterwards before any one of such children for the time being in existence attains a vested interest, and who attain the age of 21 years."
3. As in example 1 or 2, but referring to grandchildren of A, instead of children of A.
4. A for life "until he has a child" and then to his child or children.

Note. Subsection (4) above will not affect the reference to the age of 21 years in example 2.

(6) If an illegitimate person or a person adopted by one of his natural parents dies, or has died before the commencement of this Act, and—

(*a*) after his death his parents marry or have married; and
(*b*) the deceased would, if living at the time of the marriage, have become a legitimated person,

this section shall apply for the construction of the instrument so far as it relates to the taking of interests by, or in succession to, his spouse, children and remoter issue as if he had been legitimated by virtue of the marriage.

(7) In this section "instrument" includes a private Act settling property, but not any other enactment.

6. Dispositions depending on date of birth

(1) Where a disposition depends on the date of birth of a child who was born illegitimate and who is legitimated (or, if deceased, is treated as legitimated), section 5(4) above does not affect entitlement under Part II of the Family Law Reform Act 1969 (illegitimate children).

(2) Where a disposition depends on the date of birth of an adopted child who is legitimated (or, if deceased, is treated as legitimated) section 5(4) above does not affect entitlement by virtue of paragraph 6(2) of Schedule 1 to the Children Act 1975.

(3) This section applies for example where—

(*a*) a testator dies in 1976 bequeathing a legacy to his eldest grandchild living at a specified time,
(*b*) his daughter has an illegitimate child in 1977 who is the first grandchild,
(*c*) his married son has a child in 1978,
(*d*) subsequently the illegitimate child is legitimated,

and in all those cases the daughter's child remains the eldest grandchild of the testator throughout.

7. Protection of trustees and personal representatives

(1) A trustee or personal representative is not under a duty, by virtue of the law relating to trusts or the administration of estates, to enquire, before conveying or distributing any property, whether any person is illegitimate or has been adopted by one of his natural parents, and could be legitimated (or if deceased be treated as legitimated), if that fact could affect entitlement to the property.

(2) A trustee or personal representative shall not be liable to any person by reason of a conveyance or distribution of the property made without regard to any such fact if he has not received notice of the fact before the conveyance or distribution.

(3) This section does not prejudice the right of a person to follow the property, or any property representing it, into the hands of another person, other than a purchaser, who has received it.

8. Personal rights and obligations

A legitimated person shall have the same rights, and shall be under the same obligations in respect of the maintenance and support of himself or of any other person as if he had been born legitimate, and, subject to the provisions of this Act, the provisions of any Act relating to claims for damages, compensation, allowance, benefit or otherwise by or in respect of a legitimate child shall apply in like manner in the case of a legitimated person.

ADOPTION ACT 1976

39. Status conferred by adoption

(1) An adopted child shall be treated in law—

(*a*) where the adopters are a married couple, as if he had been born as a child of the marriage (whether or not he was in fact born after the marriage was solemnized);

(*b*) in any other case, as if he had been born to the adopter in wedlock (but not as a child of any actual marriage of the adopter).

(2) An adopted child shall, subject to subsection (3), be treated in law as if he were not the child of any person other than the adopters or adopter.

(3) In the case of a child adopted by one of its natural parents as sole adoptive parent, subsection (2) has no effect as respects entitlement to property depending on relationship to that parent, or as respects anything else depending on that relationship.

(4) It is hereby declared that this section prevents an adopted child from being illegitimate.

(5) This section has effect—

(*a*) in the case of an adoption before January 1, 1976, from that date, and

(*b*) in the case of any other adoption, from the date of the adoption.

(6) Subject to the provisions of this Part, this section—

(*a*) applies for the construction of enactments or instruments passed or made before the adoption or later, and so applies subject to any contrary indication; and

(*b*) has effect as respects things done, or events occurring, after the adoption, or after December 31, 1975, whichever is the later.

the child shall be a citizen of the United Kingdom and Colonies as from the date of the adoption.

(2) In subsection (1) the reference to an adoption order includes a reference to an order authorising the adoption of a child in Scotland, Northern Ireland, the Isle of Man or in any of the Channel Islands.

(3) Where a Convention adoption order, or a specified order ceases to have effect, either on annulment or otherwise, the cesser shall not affect the status as a citizen of the United Kingdom and Colonies of any person who, by virtue of this section or section 19 of the Adoption Act 1958, became such a citizen in consequence of the order.

41. Adoptive relatives

(1) A relationship existing by virtue of section 39 may be referred to as an adoptive relationship, and—

(*a*) a male adopter may be referred to as the adoptive father;
(*b*) a female adopter may be referred to as the adoptive mother;
(*c*) any other relative of any degree under an adoptive relationship may be referred to as an adoptive relative of that degree,

but this section does not prevent the term "parent," or any other term not qualified by the word "adoptive" being treated as including an adoptive relative.

42. Rules of construction for instruments concerning property

(1) Subject to any contrary indication, the rules of construction contained in this section apply to any instrument, other than an existing instrument, so far as it contains a disposition of property.

(2) In applying section 39(1) to a disposition which depends on the date of birth of a child or children of the adoptive parent or parents, the disposition shall be construed as if—

(*a*) the adopted child had been born on the date of adoption,
(*b*) two or more children adopted on the same date had been born on that date in the order of their actual births,

but this does not affect any reference to the age of a child.

(3) Examples of phrases in wills on which subsection (2) can operate are—

1. Children of A "living at my death or born afterwards."

2. Children of A "living at my death or born afterwards before any one of such children for the time being in existence attains a vested interest and who attain the age of 21 years."

3. As in example 1 or 2, but referring to grandchildren of A instead of children of A.

4. A for life "until he has a child," and then to his child or children.

Note. Subsection (2) will not affect the reference to the age of 21 years in example 2.

(4) Section 39(2) does not prejudice any interest vested in possession in the adopted child before the adoption, or any interest expectant (whether immediately or not) upon an interest so vested.

(5) Where it is necessary to determine for the purposes of a disposition of property effected by an instrument whether a woman can have a child, it shall be presumed that once a woman has attained the age of 55 years she will not adopt a child after execution of the instrument, and, notwithstanding section 39, if she does so that child

shall not be treated as her child or as the child of her spouse (if any) for the purposes of the instrument.

(6) In this section, "instrument" includes a private Act settling property, but not any other enactment.

43. Dispositions depending on date of birth

(1) Where a disposition depends on the date of birth of a child who was born illegitimate and who is adopted by one of the natural parents as sole adoptive parent, section 42(2) does not affect entitlement under Part II of the Family Law Reform Act 1969 (illegitimate children).

(2) Subsection (1) applies for example where—

(*a*) a testator dies in 1976 bequeathing a legacy to his eldest grandchild living at a specified time,

(*b*) his daughter has an illegitimate child in 1977 who is the first grandchild,

(*c*) his married son has a child in 1978,

(*d*) subsequently the illegitimate child is adopted by the mother as sole adoptive parent,

and in all those cases the daughter's child remains the eldest grandchild of the testator throughout.

44. Property devolving with peerages etc.

(1) An adoption does not affect the descent of any peerage or dignity or title of honour.

(2) An adoption shall not affect the devolution of any property limited (expressly or not) to devolve (as nearly as the law permits) along with any peerage or dignity or title of honour.

(3) Subsection (2) applies only if and so far as a contrary intention is not expressed in the instrument, and shall have effect subject to the terms of the instrument.

45. Protection of trustees and personal representatives

(1) A trustee or personal representative is not under a duty, by virtue of the law relating to trusts or the administration of estates, to enquire, before conveying or distributing any property, whether any adoption has been effected or revoked if that fact could affect entitlement to the property.

(2) A trustee or personal representative shall not be liable to any person by reason of a conveyance or distribution of the property made without regard to any such fact if he has not received notice of the fact before the conveyance or distribution.

(3) This section does not prejudice the right of a person to follow the property, or any property representing it, into the hands of another person, other than a purchaser, who has received it.

46. Meaning of "disposition"

(1) In this Part, unless the context otherwise requires,—

"disposition" includes the conferring of a power of appointment and any other disposition of an interest in or right over property;

"power of appointment" includes any discretionary power to transfer a beneficial interest in property without the furnishing of valuable consideration.

(2) This Part applies to an oral disposition as if contained in an instrument made when the disposition was made.

(3) For the purposes of this Part, the death of the testator is the date at which a will or codicil is to be regarded as made.

(4) For the purposes of this Part, provisions of the law of intestate succession applicable to the estate of a deceased person shall be treated as if contained in an instrument executed by him (while of full capacity) immediately before his death.

(5) It is hereby declared that references in this Part to dispositions of property include references to a disposition by the creation of an entailed interest.

SUPREME COURT ACT 1981

PART V

PROBATE CAUSES AND MATTERS

105. Applications

Applications for grants of probate or administration and for the revocation of grants may be made to—

(a) the Principal Registry of the Family Division (in this Part referred to as "the Principal Registry"); or
(b) a district probate registry.

106. Grants by district probate registrars

(1) Any grant made by a district probate registrar shall be made in the name of the High Court under the seal used in the registry.

(2) No grant shall be made by a district probate registrar—

(a) in any case where there is contention, until the contention is disposed of; or
(b) in any case where it appears to him either—
  (i) that a grant ought not to be made without the directions of the High Court under subsection (4), or
  (ii) that a grant ought not to be made until any particular matter relating to the grant, or to an application for it, has been determined by the High Court otherwise than under that subsection.

(3) In any case where subsection (2)(b)(i) applies, the district probate registrar shall send a statement of the matter in question to the Principal Registry for the directions of the court.

(4) Where its directions are sought under subsection (3), the High Court may either direct the district probate registrar to proceed with the matter in accordance with such instructions as it may think necessary, or direct him to take no further action in relation to the matter.

107. No grant where conflicting applications

Subject to probate rules, no grant in respect of the estate, or part of the estate, of a deceased person shall be made out of the Principal Registry or any district probate registry on any application if, at any time before the making of a grant, it appears to the registrar concerned that some other application has been made in respect of that estate or, as the case may be, that part of it and has not been either refused or withdrawn.

108. Caveats

(1) A caveat against a grant of probate or administration may be entered in the Principal Registry or in any district probate registry.

(2) On a caveat being entered in a district probate registry, the district probate registrar shall immediately send a copy of it to the Principal Registry to be entered among the caveats in that Registry.

109. Refusal of grant where capital transfer tax unpaid

(1) Subject to subsections (2) and (3), no grant shall be made, and no grant made outside the United Kingdom shall be resealed, except on the production of an account prepared in pursuance of Part III of the Finance Act 1975 showing by means of such receipt or certification as may be prescribed by the Commissioners of Inland Revenue (in this and the following section referred to as "the Commissioners") either—

(a) that the capital transfer tax payable on the delivery of the account has been paid; or
(b) that no such tax is so payable.

(2) Arrangements may be made between the President of the Family Division and the Commissioners providing for the purposes of this section in such cases as may be specified in the arrangements that the receipt or certification of an account may be dispensed with or that some other document may be substituted for the account required by Part III of the Finance Act 1975.

(3) Nothing in subsection (1) applies in relation to a case where the delivery of the account required by that Part of that Act has for the time being been dispensed with by any regulations under section 94(1)(a) of the Finance Act 1980.

110. Documents to be delivered to Commissioners of Inland Revenue

Subject to any arrangements which may from time to time be made between the President of the Family Division and the Commissioners, the Principal Registry and every district probate registry shall, within such period after a grant as the President may direct, deliver to the Commissioners or their proper officer the following documents—

(a) in the case of a grant of probate or of administration with the will annexed, a copy of the will;
(b) in every case, such certificate or note of the grant as the Commissioners may require.

111. Records of grants

(1) There shall continue to be kept records of all grants which are made in the Principal Registry or in any district probate registry.

(2) Those records shall be in such form, and shall contain such particulars, as the President of the Family Division may direct.

112. Summons to executor to prove or renounce

The High Court may summon any person named as executor in a will to prove, or renounce probate of, the will, and to do such other things concerning the will as the court had power to order such a person to do immediately before the commencement of this Act.

113. Power of court to sever grant

(1) Subject to subsection (2), the High Court may grant probate or administration in respect of any part of the estate of a deceased person, limited in any way the court thinks fit.

(2) Where the estate of a deceased person is known to be insolvent, the grant of representation to it shall not be severed under subsection (1) except as regards a trust estate in which he had no beneficial interest.

114. Number of personal representatives

(1) Probate or administration shall not be granted by the High Court to more than four persons in respect of the same part of the estate of a deceased person.

(2) Where under a will or intestacy any beneficiary is a minor or a life interest arises, any grant of administration by the High Court shall be made either to a trust corporation (with or without an individual) or to not less than two individuals, unless it appears to the court to be expedient in all the circumstances to appoint an individual as sole administrator.

(3) For the purpose of determining whether a minority or life interest arises in any particular case, the court may act on such evidence as may be prescribed.

(4) If at any time during the minority of a beneficiary or the subsistence of a life interest under a will or intestacy there is only one personal representative (not being a trust corporation), the High Court may, on the application of any person interested or the guardian or receiver of any such person, and in accordance with probate rules, appoint one or more additional personal representatives to act while the minority or life interest subsists and until the estate is fully administered.

(5) An appointment of an additional personal representative under subsection (4) to act with an executor shall not have the effect of including him in any chain of representation.

115. Grants to trust corporations

(1) The High Court may—

(a) where a trust corporation is named in a will as executor, grant probate to the corporation either solely or jointly with any other person named in the will as executor, as the case may require; or

(b) grant administration to a trust corporation, either solely or jointly with another person;

and the corporation may act accordingly as executor or administrator, as the case may be.

(2) Probate or administration shall not be granted to any person as nominee of a trust corporation.

(3) Any officer authorised for the purpose by a trust corporation or its directors or governing body may, on behalf of the corporation, swear affidavits, give security and do any other act which the court may require with a view to the grant to the corporation of probate or administration; and the acts of an officer so authorised shall be binding on the corporation.

116. Power of court to pass over prior claims to grant

(1) If by reason of any special circumstances it appears to the High Court to be necessary or expedient to appoint as administrator some person other than the person who, but for this section, would in accordance with probate rules have been entitled to the grant, the court may in its discretion appoint as administrator such person as it thinks expedient.

(2) Any grant of administration under this section may be limited in any way the court thinks fit.

117. Administration pending suit

(1) Where any legal proceedings concerning the validity of the will of a deceased person, or for obtaining, recalling or revoking any grant, are pending, the High Court may grant administration of the estate of the deceased person in question to an administrator pending suit, who shall, subject to subsection (2), have all the rights, duties and powers of a general administrator.

(2) An administrator pending suit shall be subject to the immediate control of the court and act under its direction; and, except in such circumstances as may be prescribed, no distribution of the estate, or any part of the estate, of the deceased person in question shall be made by such an administrator without the leave of the court.

(3) The court may, out of the estate of the deceased, assign an administrator pending suit such reasonable remuneration as it thinks fit.

118. Effect of appointment of minor as executor

Where a testator by his will appoints a minor to be an executor, the appointment shall not operate to vest in the minor the estate, or any part of the estate, of the testator, or to constitute him a personal representative for any purpose, unless and until probate is granted to him in accordance with probate rules.

119. Administration with will annexed

(1) Administration with the will annexed shall be granted, subject to and in accordance with probate rules, in every class of case in which the High Court had power to make such a grant immediately before the commencement of this Act.

(2) Where administration with the will annexed is granted, the will of the deceased shall be performed and observed in the same manner as if probate of it had been granted to an executor.

120. Power to require administrators to produce sureties

(1) As a condition of granting administration to any person the High Court may, subject to the following provisions of this section and subject to and in accordance with probate rules, require one or more securities to guarantee that they will make good, within any limit imposed by the court on the total liability of the surety or sureties, any loss which any person interested in the administration of the estate of the deceased may suffer in consequence of a breach by the administrator of his duties as such.

(2) A guarantee given in pursuance of any such requirement shall enure for the benefit of every person interested in the administration of the estate of the deceased as if contained in a contract under seal made by the surety or sureties with every such person and, where there are two or more sureties, as if they had bound themselves jointly and severally.

(3) No action shall be brought on any such guarantee without the leave of the High Court.

(4) Stamp duty shall not be chargeable on any such guarantee.

(5) This section does not apply where administration is granted to the Treasury Solicitor, the Official Solicitor, the Public Trustee, the Solicitor for the affairs of the Duchy of Lancaster or the Duchy of Cornwall or the Crown Solicitor for Northern Ireland, or to the consular officer of a foreign state to which section 1 of the Consular Conventions Act 1949 applies, or in such other cases as may be prescribed.

121. Revocation of grants and cancellation of resealing at instance of court

(1) Where it appears to the High Court that a grant either ought not to have been made or contains an error, the court may call in the grant

and, if satisfied that it would be revoked at the instance of a party interested, may revoke it.

(2) A grant may be revoked under subsection (1) without being called in, if it cannot be called in.

(3) Where it appears to the High Court that a grant resealed under the Colonial Probates Acts 1892 and 1927 ought not to have been resealed, the court may call in the relevant document and, if satisfied that the resealing would be cancelled at the instance of a party interested, may cancel the resealing.

In this and the following subsection "the relevant document" means the original grant or, where some other document was sealed by the court under those Acts, that document.

(4) A resealing may be cancelled under subsection (3) without the relevant document being called in, if it cannot be called in.

122. Examination of person with knowledge of testamentary document

(1) Where it appears that there are reasonable grounds for believing that any person has knowledge of any document which is or purports to be a testamentary document, the High Court may, whether or not any legal proceedings are pending, order him to attend for the purpose of being examined in open court.

(2) The court may—

(a) require any person who is before it in compliance with an order under subsection (1) to answer any question relating to the document concerned; and
(b) if appropriate, order him to bring in the document in such manner as the court may direct.

(3) Any person who, having been required by the court to do so under this section, fails to attend for examination, answer any question or bring in any document shall be guilty of contempt of court.

123. Subpoena to bring in testamentary document

Where it appears that any person has in his possession, custody or power any document which is or purports to be a testamentary document, the High Court may, whether or not any legal proceedings are pending, issue a subpoena requiring him to bring in the document in such manner as the court may in the subpoena direct.

124. Place for deposit of original wills and other documents

All original wills and other documents which are under the control of the High Court in the Principal Registry or in any district probate registry shall be deposited and preserved in such places as the Lord Chancellor may direct; and any wills or other documents so deposited shall, subject to the control of the High Court and to probate rules, be open to inspection.

125. Copies of wills and grants

An office copy, or a sealed and certified copy, of any will or part of a will open to inspection under section 124 or of any grant may, on payment of the prescribed fee, be obtained—

(a) from the registry in which in accordance with section 124 the will or documents relating to the grant are preserved; or
(b) where in accordance with that section the will or such documents are preserved in some place other than a registry, from the Principal Registry; or
(c) subject to the approval of the Senior Registrar of the Family Division, from the Principal Registry in any case where the will was proved in or the grant was issued from a district probate registry.

126. Depositories for wills of living persons

(1) There shall be provided, under the control and direction of the High Court, safe and convenient depositories for the custody of the wills of living persons; and any person may deposit his will in such a depository on payment of the prescribed fee and subject to such conditions as may be prescribed by regulations made by the President of the Family Division with the concurrence of the Lord Chancellor.

(2) Any regulations made under this section shall be made by statutory instrument which shall be laid before Parliament after being made; and the Statutory Instruments Act 1946 shall apply to a statutory instrument containing regulations under this section in like manner as if they had been made by a Minister of the Crown.

127. Probate rules

(1) The President of the Family Division may, with the concurrence of the Lord Chancellor, make rules of court (in this Part referred to as "probate rules") for regulating and prescribing the practice and procedure of the High Court with respect to non-contentious or common form probate business.

(2) Without prejudice to the generality of subsection (1), probate rules may make provision for regulating the classes of persons entitled to grants of probate or administration in particular circumstances and the relative priorities of their claims thereto.

(3) Probate rules shall be made by statutory instrument subject to annulment in pursuance of a resolution of either House of Parliament; and the Statutory Instruments Act 1946 shall apply to a statutory instrument containing probate rules in like manner as if they had been made by a Minister of the Crown.

128. Interpretation of Part V and other probate provisions

In this Part, and in the other provisions of this Act relating to probate causes and matters, unless the context otherwise requires—

"administration" includes all letters of administration of the effects of deceased persons, whether with or without a will annexed, and whether granted for general, special or limited purposes;

"estate" means real and personal estate, and "real estate" includes—

(a) chattels real and land in possession, remainder or reversion and every interest in or over land to which the deceased person was entitled at the time of his death, and
(b) real estate held on trust or by way of mortgage or security, but not money to arise under a trust for sale of land, nor money secured or charged on land;

"grant" means a grant of probate or administration;

"non-contentious or common form probate business" means the business of obtaining probate and administration where there is no contention as to the right thereto, including—

(a) the passing of probates and administrations through the High Court in contentious cases where the context has been terminated,
(b) all business of a non-contentious nature in matters of testacy and intestacy not being proceedings in any action, and
(c) the business of lodging caveats against the grant of probate or administration;

"Principal Registry" means the Principal Registry of the Family Division;

"probate rules" means rules of court made under section 127;

"trust corporation" means the Public Trustee of a corporation either appointed by the court in any particular case to be a trustee or authorised by rules made under section 4(3) of the Public Trustee Act 1906 to act as a custodian trustee,

"will" includes a nuncupative will and any testamentary document of which probate may be granted.

FORFEITURE ACT 1982

An Act to provide for relief for persons guilty of unlawful killing from forfeiture of inheritance and other rights; to enable such persons to apply for financial provision out of the deceased's estate; to provide for the question whether pension and social security benefits have been forfeited to be determined by the Social Security Commissioners; and for connected purposes.

1.—(1) In this Act, the "forfeiture rule" means the rule of public policy which in certain circumstances precludes a person who has unlawfully killed another from acquiring a benefit in consequence of the killing.

(2) References in this Act to a person who has unlawfully killed another include a reference to a person who has unlawfully aided, abetted, counselled or procured the death of that other and references in this Act to unlawful killing shall be interpreted accordingly.

2.—(1) Where a court determines that the forfeiture rule has precluded a person (in this section referred to as "the offender") who has unlawfully killed another from acquiring any interest in property mentioned in subsection (4) below, the court may make an order under this section modifying the effect of that rule.

(2) The court shall not make an order under this section modifying the effect of the forfeiture rule in any case unless it is satisfied that, having regard to the conduct of the offender and of the deceased and to such other circumstances as appear to the court to be material, the justice of the case requires the effect of the rule to be so modified in that case.

(3) In any case where a person stands convicted of an offence of which unlawful killing is an element, the court shall not make an order under this section modifying the effect of the forfeiture rule in that case unless proceedings for the purpose are brought before the expiry of the period of three months beginning with his conviction.

(4) The interests in property referred to in subsection (1) above are—

(*a*) any beneficial interest in property which (apart from the forfeiture rule) the offender would have acquired—

(i) under the deceased's will (including as respects Scotland, any writing having testamentary effect) or the law relating to intestacy or by way of *ius relicti, ius relictae* or *legitim*;

(ii) on the nomination of the deceased in accordance with the provisions of any enactment;

(iii) as a *donatio mortis causa* made by the deceased; or

(iv) under a special destination (whether relating to heritable or moveable property); or

(*b*) any beneficial interest in property which (apart from the forfeiture rule) the offender would have acquired in consequence of the death of the deceased, being property which, before the death, was held on trust for any person.

(5) An order under this section may modify the effect of the forfeiture rule in respect of any interest in property to which the determination referred to in subsection (1) above relates and may do so in either or both of the following ways, that is—

a) where there is more than one such interest, by excluding the application of the rule in respect of any (but not all) of those interests; and

(*b*) in the case of any such interest in property, by excluding the application of the rule in respect of part of the property.

(6) On the making of an order under this section, the forfeiture rule shall have effect for all purposes (including purposes relating to anything done before the order is made) subject to the modifications made by the order.

(7) The court shall not make an order under this section modifying the effect of the forfeiture rule in respect of any interest in property which, in consequence of the rule, has been acquired before the coming into force of this section by a person other than the offender or a person claiming through him.

(8) In this section—

"property" includes any chose in action or incorporeal moveable property; and
"will" includes codicil.

3.—(1) The forfeiture rule shall not be taken to preclude any person from making any application under a provision mentioned in subsection (2) below or the making of any order on the application.

(2) The provisions referred to in subsection (1) above are—

(*a*) any provision of the Inheritance (Provision for Family and Dependants) Act 1975; and

(*b*) sections 31(6) (variation etc., of periodical payments orders) and 36(1) (variation of maintenance agreements) of the Matrimonial Causes Act 1973 and section 5(4) of the Divorce (Scotland) Act 1976 (variation etc., of periodical allowances).

4.—(1) Where a question arises as to whether, if a person were otherwise entitled to or eligible for any benefit or advantage under a relevant enactment, he would be precluded by virtue of the forfeiture rule from receiving the whole or part of the benefit or advantage, that question shall (notwithstanding anything in any relevant enactment) be determined by a Commissioner.

(2) Regulations under this section may make such provision as appears to the Secretary of State to be necessary or expedient for carrying this section into effect; and (without prejudice to the generality of that) the regulations may, in relation to the question mentioned in subsection (1) above or any determination under that subsection—

(*a*) apply any provision of any relevant enactment, with or without modifications, or exclude or contain provision corresponding to any such provision; and

(*b*) make provision for purposes corresponding to those for which provision may be made by regulations under section 115 of the Social Security Act 1975 (matters relating to adjudication).

(3) The power to make regulations under this section shall be exercisable by statutory instrument which shall be subject to annulment in pursuance of a resolution of either House of Parliament.

(4) Section 166(2) and (3) of the Social Security Act 1975 (provision about extent of power to make regulations) shall apply to the power to make regulations conferred by this section as it applies to the power to make regulations conferred by that Act, but as if for references to that Act there were substituted references to this section.

(5) In this section—

"Commissioner" has the same meaning as in the Social Security Act 1975; and

"relevant enactment" means any provision of the following and any instrument made by virtue of such a provision:

the Personal Injuries (Emergency Provisions) Act 1939,

the Pensions (Navy, Army, Air Force and Mercantile Marine) Act 1939,

the Polish Resettlement Act 1947,

the Family Income Supplements Act 1970,

the Social Security Act 1975,

Part II of the Social Security Pensions Act 1975,

the Child Benefit Act 1975,

Part I of the Supplementary Benefits Act 1976,

section 12 of the Social Security (Miscellaneous Provisions) Act 1977,

section 14 of the Social Security Act 1980,

and any other enactment relating to pensions or social security prescribed by regulations under this section.

5. Nothing in this Act or in any order made under section 2 or referred to in section 3(1) of this Act shall affect the application of the forfeiture rule in the case of a person who stands convicted of murder.

6. An Order in Council under paragraph 1(1)(*b*) of Schedule 1 to the Northern Ireland Act 1974 (legislation for Northern Ireland in the interim period) which contains a statement that it is made only for purposes corresponding to the purposes of this Act—

(*a*) shall not be subject to paragraph 1(4) and (5) of that Schedule (affirmative resolution of both Houses of Parliament); but
(*b*) shall be subject to annulment in pursuance of a resolution of either House.

7.—(1) This Act may be cited as the Forfeiture Act 1982.

(2) Section 4 of this Act shall come into force on such day as the Secretary of State may appoint by order made by statutory instrument; and sections 1 to 3 and 5 of this Act shall come into force on the expiry of the period of three months beginning with the day on which it is passed.

(3) This Act, except section 6, does not extend to Northern Ireland.

(4) Subject to section 2(7) of this Act, an order under section 2 of this Act or an order referred to in section 3(1) of this Act and made in respect of a person who has unlawfully killed another may be made whether the unlawful killing occurred before or after the coming into force of those sections.

ADMINISTRATION OF JUSTICE ACT 1985

50.—(1) Where an application relating to the estate of a deceased person is made to the High Court under this subsection by or on behalf of a personal representative of the deceased or a beneficiary of the estate, the court may in its discretion—

(*a*) appoint a person (in this section called a substituted personal representative) to act as personal representative of the deceased in place of the existing personal representative or representatives of the deceased or any of them; or

(*b*) if there are two or more existing personal representatives of the deceased, terminate the appointment of one or more, but not all, of those persons.

(2) Where the court appoints a person to act as a substituted personal representative of a deceased person, then—

(*a*) if that person is appointed to act with an executor or executors the appointment shall (except for the purpose of including him in any chain of representation) constitute him executor of the deceased as from the date of the appointment; and

(*b*) in any other case the appointment shall constitute that person administrator of the deceased's estate as from the date of the appointment.

(3) The court may authorise a person appointed as a substituted personal representative to charge remuneration for his services as such, on such terms (whether or not involving the submission of bills of charges for taxation by the court) as the court may think fit.

(4) Where an application relating to the estate of a deceased person is made to the court under subsection (1), the court may if it thinks fit, proceed as if the application were, or included, an application for the appointment under the Judicial Trustees Act 1896 of a judicial trustee in relation to that estate.

(5) In this section "beneficiary", in relation to the estate of a deceased person, means a person who under the will of the deceased or under the law relating to intestacy is beneficially interested in the estate.

(6) In section 1 of the Judicial Trustees Act 1896, after subsection (6) there shall be added—

"(7) Where an application relating to the estate of a deceased person is made to the court under this section, the court may, if it thinks fit, proceed as if the application were, or included, an application under section 50 of the Administration of Justice Act 1985 (power of High Court to appoint substitute for, or to remove, personal representative).".

APPENDIX 2

RULES AND ORDERS

NON-CONTENTIOUS PROBATE RULES 1954

Citation and commencement

1. These Rules may be cited as the Non-Contentious Probate Rules, 1954, and shall come into operation on the first day of October 1954.

Interpretation

2.—(1) The Interpretation Act 1889 shall apply to the interpretation of these Rules as it applies to the interpretation of an Act of Parliament.

(2) In these Rules, unless the context otherwise requires—

"The Act" means the Supreme Court Act 1981;

"Authorised officer" means any officer of a registry who is for the time being authorised by the President to administer any oath or to take any affidavit required for any purpose connected with his duties;

"The Crown" includes the Crown in right of the Duchy of Lancaster and the Duke of Cornwall for the time being;

"England" includes Wales;

"Gross value" in relation to any state means the value of the estate without deduction for debts, incumbrances, funeral expenses or estate duty;

"Oath" means the oath required by rule 6 to be sworn by every applicant for a grant;

"Personal applicant" means a person other than a trust corporation who seeks to obtain a grant without employing a solicitor, and "personal application" has a corresponding meaning;

"The President" means the President of the Family Division;

"The principal registry" means the principal registry of the Family Division;

"'Registrar' means a registrar of the principal registry and includes—

(i) in relation to an application for a grant made or proposed to be made at a district probate registry,

(ii) in rules 24, 42 and 60(2) in relation to a grant issued from a district probate registry and

(iii) in relation to rules 45, 46 and 47,

the registrar of that district probate registry."[1]
"Registry" means the principal registry or a district probate registry;
"The Senior Registrar" means the Senior Registrar of the Family Division or, in his absence, the senior of the registrars in attendance;
"Statutory guardian" means a surviving parent of an infant who is the guardian of the infant by virtue of section 3 of the Guardianship of Minors Act 1971;
"Testamentary guardian" means a person appointed by deed or will to be guardian of an infant under the power conferred by section 4 of the Guardianship of Minors Act 1971;
"The Treasury Solicitor" means the solicitor for the affairs of Her Majesty's Treasury and includes the solicitor for the affairs of the Duchy of Lancaster and the solicitor of the Duchy of Cornwall;
"Trust corporation" means a corporation within the meaning of section 128 of the Act as extended by section 3 of the Law of Property (Amendment) Act 1926;
"Will" includes a nuncupative will and any testamentary document or copy or reconstruction thereof.

(3) A form referred to by number means the form so numbered in the First Schedule; and such forms shall be used wherever applicable with such variations as a registrar may in any particular case direct or approve.

(4) Unless the context otherwise requires, any reference in these Rules to any rule or enactment shall be construed as a reference to that rule or enactment as amended, extended or applied by any other rule or enactment.

Application of other rules

2A. Subject to the provisions of these Rules and to any enactment, the Rules of the Supreme Court 1965 shall apply, with the necessary modifications, to non-contentious probate matters, save that nothing in Order 3 shall prevent time from running in the Long Vacation."[2]

Applications for grants through solicitors

3.—(1) A person applying for a grant through a solicitor may apply at any registry or sub-registry by post or otherwise.

(2) Every solicitor through whom an application for a grant is made shall give the address of his place of business within the jurisdiction.

Personal applications

4.—(1) A personal applicant may apply for a grant otherwise than by post at any registry or sub-registry or to any probate office

[1] Substituted by Non-Contentions (Amendment) Rules 1985, (S.I. 1985 No. 1232).
[2] Added by *ibid.*

established pursuant to any Order for the time being in force under section 104 of the Act.

(2) A personal applicant may not apply through an agent, whether paid or unpaid, and may not be attended by any person acting or appearing to act as his adviser.

(3) No personal application shall be received or proceeded with if—

(*a*) it becomes necessary to bring the matter before the Court on motion or by action;

(*b*) an application has already been made by a solicitor on behalf of the applicant and has not been withdrawn;

(*c*) the registrar otherwise directs.

(4) After a will has been deposited in a registry by a personal applicant, it may not be delivered to the applicant or to any other person unless in special circumstances the registrar so directs.

(5) A personal applicant shall produce a certificate of the death of the deceased or such other evidence of the death as the registrar may approve.

(6) A personal applicant shall supply all information necessary to enable the papers leading to the grant to be prepared in the registry, or may himself prepare such papers and lodge them unsworn.

(7) Unless the registrar otherwise directs, every oath, affidavit or guarantee required on a personal application (other than a guarantee given by a corporation in accordance with rule 38) shall be sworn or executed by all the deponents or sureties before an authorised officer.

(8) No legal advice shall be given to a personal applicant by any officer of a registry and every such officer shall be responsible only for embodying in proper form the applicant's instructions for the grant.

Duty of registrar on receiving application for grant

5.—(1) A registrar shall not allow any grant to issue until all inquiries which he may see fit to make have been answered to his satisfaction.

(2) The registrar may require proof of the identity of the deceased or of the applicant for the grant beyond that contained in the oath.

(3) Except with the leave of two registrars, no grant of probate or of administration with the will annexed shall issue within seven days of the death of the deceased and no grant of administration shall issue within fourteen days thereof.

(4) The registrar shall not require a guarantee under section 120 of the Act as a condition of granting administration to any person without giving that person or, where the application for the grant is made through a solicitor, the solicitor an opportunity of being heard with respect to the requirement.

Grants by district probate registrars

5A. (1) No grant shall be made by a district probate registrar

(*a*) in any case in which there is contention, until the contention is disposed of or

(*b*) in any case in which it appears to him that a grant ought not to be made without the directions of a judge or a registrar of the principal registry.

(2) In any case in which paragraph (1)(*b*) applies, the district probate registrar shall send a statement of the matter in question to the principal registry for directions.

(3) A registrar of the principal registry may either confirm that the matter be referred to a judge and give directions accordingly or may direct the district probate registrar to proceed with the matter in accordance with such instructions as are deemed necessary, which may include a direction to take no further action in relation to the matter.[3]

Oath in support of grant

6.—(1) Every application for a grant shall be supported by an oath in the form applicable to the circumstances of the case, which shall be contained in an affidavit sworn by the applicant, and by such other papers as the registrar may require.

(2) On an application for a grant of administration the oath shall state whether, and if so, in what manner, all persons having a prior right to a grant have been cleared off, and whether any minority or life interest arises under the will or intestacy.

(3) Where the deceased died on or after January 1, 1926, the oath shall state whether, to the best of the applicant's knowledge, information and belief, there was land vested in the deceased which was settled previously to his death and not by his will and which remained settled land notwithstanding his death.

(4) Unless otherwise directed by a registrar, the oath shall state where the deceased died domiciled.

Grant in additional name

7. Where it is necessary to describe the deceased in a grant by some name in addition to his true name, the applicant shall state in the oath the true name of the deceased and shall depose that some part of the estate, specifying it, was held in the other name, or as to any other reason that there may be for the inclusion of the other name in the grant.

Marking of wills

8. Every will in respect of which an application for a grant is made shall be marked by the signatures of the applicant and the person

[3] *Ibid.*

before whom the oath is sworn, and shall be exhibited to any affidavit which may be required under these Rules as to the validity, terms, condition or date of execution of the will:

Provided that where the registrar is satisfied that compliance with this rule might result in the loss of the will, he may allow a photographic copy thereof to be marked or exhibited in lieu of the original document.

Engrossments for purposes of record

9.—(1) Where the registrar considers that in any particular case a photographic copy of the original will would not be satisfactory for purposes of record, he may require an engrossment suitable for photographic reproduction to be lodged.

(2) Where a will contains alterations which are not admissible to proof, there shall be lodged an engrossment of the will in the form in which it is to be proved.

(3) Any engrossment lodged under this rule shall reproduce the punctuation, spacing and division into paragraphs of the will and, if it is one to which paragraph (2) of this rule applies, it shall be made bookwise on durable paper following continuously from page to page on both sides of the paper.

(4) Where any pencil writing appears on a will, there shall be lodged a copy of the will or of the pages or sheets containing the pencil writing, in which there shall be underlined in red ink those portions which appear in pencil in the original.

Evidence as to due execution of will

10.—(1) Where a will contains no attestation clause or the attestation clause is insufficient or where it appears to the registrar that there is some doubt about the due execution of the will, he shall, before admitting it to proof, require an affidavit as to due execution from one or more of the attesting witnesses or, if no attesting witness is conveniently available, from any other person who was present at the time the will was executed.

(2) If no affidavit can be obtained in accordance with the last foregoing paragraph, the registrar may, if he thinks fit having regard to the desirability of protecting the interests of any person who may be prejudiced by the will, accept evidence on affidavit from any person he may think fit to show that the signature on the will is in the handwriting of the deceased, or of any other matter which may raise a presumption in favour of the due execution of the will.

(3) If the registrar, after considering the evidence—

(*a*) is satisfied that the will was not duly executed, he shall refuse probate and shall mark the will accordingly;

(*b*) is doubtful whether the will was duly executed, he may refer the matter to the court on motion.

Execution of will of blind or illiterate testator

11. Before admitting to proof a will which appears to have been signed by a blind or illiterate testator or by another person by direction of the testator, or which for any other reason gives rise to doubt as to the testator having had knowledge of the contents of the will at the time of its execution, the registrar shall satisfy himself that the testator had such knowledge.

Evidence as to terms, condition and date of execution of will

12.—(1) Where there appears in a will any obliteration, interlineation, or other alteration which is not authenticated in the manner prescribed by section 21 of the Wills Act, 1837, or by the re-execution of the will or by the execution of a codicil, the registrar shall require evidence to show whether the alteration was present at the time the will was executed and shall give directions as to the form in which the will is to be proved:

Provided that this subparagraph shall not apply to any alteration which appears to the registrar to be of no practical importance.

(2) If from any mark on the will it appears to the registrar that some other document has been attached to the will, or if a will contains any reference to another document in such terms as to suggest that it ought to be incorporated in the will, the registrar may require the document to be produced and may call for such evidence in regard to the attaching or incorporation of the document as he may think fit.

(3) Where there is doubt as to the date on which a will was executed, the registrar may require such evidence as he thinks necessary to establish the date.

Attempted revocation of will

13. Any appearance of attempted revocation of a will by burning, tearing or otherwise, and every other circumstance leading to a presumption of revocation by the testator, shall be accounted for to the registrar's satisfaction.

Affidavit as to due execution, terms, etc., of will

14. A registrar may require an affidavit from any person he may think fit for the purpose of satisfying himself as to any of the matters referred to in rules 11, 12 and 13, and in any such affidavit sworn by an attesting witness or other person present at the time of the execution of a will the deponent shall depose to the manner in which the will was executed.

Wills not proved under section 9 of Wills Act, 1837

15. Nothing in rule 10, 11, 12 or 13 shall apply to any will which it is sought to establish otherwise than by reference to section 9 of the Wills Act, 1837, as explained by the Wills Act Amendment Act, 1852, but the terms and validity of any such will shall be established to the registrar's satisfaction.

Wills of persons on military service and seamen

16. If it appears to the registrar that there is prima facie evidence that a will is one to which section 11 of the Wills Act, 1837, as amended by any subsequent enactment applies, the will may be admitted to proof if the registrar is satisfied that it was signed by the testator or, if unsigned, that it is in the testator's handwriting.

Wills of naval personnel

17. Every application for a grant in respect of the estate of a person who has at any time served in the capacity to which the Navy and Marines (Wills) Act, 1865, applies shall be supported by a certificate of the Inspector of Seamen's Wills as to the existence of any will in his custody:

Provided that no such certificate shall be required where—

(*a*) the application relates to a will made after the deceased had ceased to serve in such capacity as aforesaid which revokes all previous wills made by him, or

(*b*) the deceased was at the date of his death in receipt of a pension in respect of his service.

Evidence of foreign law

18. Where evidence as to the law of any country or territory outside England is required on any application for a grant, the registrar may accept an affidavit from any person whom, having regard to the particulars of his knowledge or experience given in the affidavit, he regards as suitably qualified to give expert evidence of the law in question.

Order of priority for grant where deceased left a will

19. Where the deceased died on or after January 1, 1926, the person or persons entitled to a grant of probate or administration with the will annexed shall be determined in accordance with the following order of priority, namely:—

(i) The executor;

(ii) Any residuary legatee or devisee holding in trust for any other person;

(iii) Any residuary legatee or devisee for life;

(iv) The ultimate residuary legatee or devisee, including one entitled on the happening of any contingency, or, where the residue is not wholly disposed of by the will, any person entitled to share in the residue not so disposed of (including the Treasury Solicitor when claiming *bona vacantia* on behalf of the Crown), or, subject to paragraph (3) of rule 25, the personal representative of any such person:

Provided that: (*a*) unless a registrar otherwise directs a residuary legatee or devisee whose legacy or devise is vested in interest shall be preferred to one entitled on the happening of a contingency; and (*b*) where the residue is not in terms wholly disposed of, the registrar may, if he is satisfied that the testator has nevertheless disposed of the whole or substantially the whole of the estate as ascertained at the time of the application for the grant, allow a grant to be made (subject however to rule 37) to any legatee or devisee entitled to, or to a share in, the estate so disposed of, without regard to the persons entitled to share in any residue not disposed of by the will;

(v) Any specific legatee or devisee or any creditor or, subject to paragraph (3) of rule 25, the personal representative of any such person or, where the estate is not wholly disposed of by will, any person who, notwithstanding that the amount of the estate is such that he has no immediate beneficial interest therein, may have a beneficial interest in the event of an accretion thereto;

(vi) any specific legatee or devisee entitled on the happening of any contingency, or any person having no interest under the will of the deceased who would have been entitled to a grant if the deceased had died wholly intestate.

Grants to attesting witnesses, etc.

20. Where a gift to any person fails by reason of section 15 of the Wills Act, 1837, (which provides that gifts to attesting witnesses or their spouses shall be void), such person shall not have any right to a grant as a beneficiary named in the will, without prejudice to his right to a grant in any other capacity.

Order of priority for grant in case of intestacy

21.—(1) Where the deceased died on or after January 1, 1926, wholly intestate, the persons having a beneficial interest in the estate shall be entitled to a grant of administration in the following order of priority, namely:—

(i) The surviving spouse;

(ii) The children of the deceased, or the issue of any such child who has died during the lifetime of the deceased;

(iii) The father or mother of the deceased;
(iv) Brothers and sisters of the whole blood, or the issue of any deceased brother or sister of the whole blood who has died.

(2) If no person in any of the classes mentioned in sub-paragraphs (ii) to (iv) of the last foregoing paragraph survived the deceased, then, in the case of—

(*a*) a person who died before January 1, 1953, wholly intestate, or
(*b*) a person dying on or after January 1, 1953, wholly intestate without leaving a surviving spouse,

the persons hereinafter described shall, if they have a beneficial interest in the estate, be entitled to a grant in the following order of priority, namely:—

(i) Brothers and sisters of the half blood, or the issue of any deceased brother or sister of the half blood who has died;
(ii) Grandparents;
(iii) Uncles and aunts of the whole blood, or the issue of any deceased uncle or aunt of the whole blood who has died;
(iv) Uncles and aunts of the half blood, or the issue of any deceased uncle or aunt of the half blood who has died.

(3) In default of any person having a beneficial interest in the estate, the Treasury Solicitor shall be entitled to a grant if he claims *bona vacantia* on behalf of the Crown.

(4) If all persons entitled to a grant under the foregoing provisions of this rule have been cleared off, a grant may be made to a creditor of the deceased or to any person who, notwithstanding that he has no immediate beneficial interest in the estate, may have a beneficial interest in the event of an accretion thereto.

(5) Subject to paragraph (3) of rule 25, the personal representative of a person in any of the classes mentioned in paragraphs (1) and (2) of this rule or the personal representative of a creditor shall have the same right to a grant as the person whom he represents:

Provided that the persons mentioned in sub-paragraphs (ii) to (iv) of paragraph (1) and in paragraph (2) of this rule shall be preferred to the personal representative of a spouse who has died without taking a beneficial interest in the whole estate of the deceased as ascertained at the time of the application for the grant.

(6) In this rule references to children of the deceased include references to his illegitimate children, and "father or mother of the deceased" shall be construed accordingly.

Order for priority for grant in pre 1926 cases

21A. Where the deceased died before January 1, 1926, the person or persons entitled to a grant shall, subject to the provisions of any enactment, be determined in accordance with the principles and rules under which the court would have acted at the date of death.[4]

Right of assignee to a grant

22.—(1) Where all the persons entitled to the estate of the deceased (whether under a will or on intestacy) have assigned their whole interest in the estate to one or more persons, the assignee or assignees shall replace, in the order of priority for a grant of administration, the assignor or, if there are two or more assignors, the assignor with the highest priority.

(2) Where there are two or more assignees, administration may be granted with the consent of the others to any one or more (not exceeding four) of them.

(3) In any case where administration is applied for by an assignee, a copy of the instrument of assignment shall be lodged in the registry.

Joinder of administrator

23.—(1) An application to join with a person entitled to a grant of administration a person entitled in a lower degree shall, in default of renunciation by all persons entitled in priority to such last-mentioned person, be made to a registrar and shall be supported by an affidavit by the person entitled, the consent of the person proposed to be joined as personal representative and such other evidence as the registrar may require.

(2) An application to join with a person entitled to a grant of administration a person having no right thereto shall be made to a registrar and shall be supported by an affidavit by the person entitled, the consent of the person proposed to be joined as personal representative and such other evidence as the registrar may require:

Provided that there may without any such application be joined with a person entitled to administration—

(*a*) on the renunciation of all other persons entitled to join in the grant, any kin of the deceased having no beneficial interest in the estate, in the order of priority described in rule 21;

(*b*) unless a registrar otherwise directs, any person whom the guardian of an infant may nominate for the purpose under paragraph (4) of rule 31;

(*c*) a trust corporation.

Additional personal representatives

24.—(1) An application under section 114(4) of the Act to add a personal representative shall be made to a registrar and shall be supported by an affidavit by the applicant, the consent of the person

[4] *Ibid.*

proposed to be added as personal representative and such other evidence as the registrar may require.

(2) [*Revoked by Non-Contentious Probate (Amendment) Rules* 1967 (S.I. 1967 No. 748).]

(3) On any such application the registrar may direct that a note shall be made on the original grant of the addition of a further personal representative, or he may impound or revoke the grant or make such other order as the circumstances of the case may require.

Grants where two or more persons entitled in same degree

25.—(1) A grant may be made to any person entitled thereto without notice to other persons entitled in the same degree.

(2) A dispute between persons entitled to a grant in the same degree shall be brought by summons before a registrar.

(3) Unless a registrar otherwise directs, administration shall be granted to a living person in preference to the personal representative of a deceased person who would, if living, be entitled in the same degree and to a person not under disability in preference to an infant entitled in the same degree.

(4) The issue of a summons under this rule in a district probate registry shall be notified forthwith to the principal registry."[5]

(5) If the issue of a summons under this rule is known to a registrar, he shall not allow any grant to be sealed until such summons is finally disposed of.

Exceptions to rules as to priority

26.—(1) Nothing in rule 19, 21, 23 or 25 shall operate to prevent a grant being made to any person to whom a grant may or may require to be made under any enactment.

(2) The rules mentioned in the last foregoing paragraph shall not apply where the deceased died domiciled outside England, except in a case to which the proviso to rule 29 applies.

Grants to persons having spes successionis

27. When the beneficial interest in the whole estate of the deceased is vested absolutely in a person who has renounced his right to a grant and has consented to administration being granted to the person or persons who would be entitled to his estate if he himself had died intestate, administration may be granted to such person or one or more (not exceeding four) of such persons;

Provided that a surviving spouse shall not be regarded as a person in whom the estate has vested absolutely unless he would be entitled to the whole of the estate, whatever its value may be.

[5] *Ibid.*

Grants in respect of settled land

28.—(1) In this rule "settled land" means land vested in the deceased which was settled previously to his death and not by his will and which remained settled land notwithstanding his death.

(2) The special executors in regard to settled land constituted by section 22 of the Administration of Estates Act, 1925, shall have a prior right to a grant of probate limited to the settled land.

(3) The person or persons entitled to a grant of administration limited to settled land shall be determined in accordance with the following order of priority, namely:—

(i) The trustees of the settlement at the time of the application for the grant;
(ii) [*Revoked by Non-Contentious Probate (Amendment) Rules* 1967 (S.I. 1967 No. 748).]
(iii) The personal representative of the deceased.

(4) Where the persons entitled to a grant in respect of the free estate are also entitled to a grant of the same nature in respect of settled land, a grant expressly including the settled land may issue to them.

(5) Where there is settled land and a grant is made in respect of the free estate only, the grant shall expressly exclude the settled land.

Grants where deceased died domiciled outside England

29. Where the deceased died domiciled outside England, a registrar may order that a grant do issue—

(*a*) to the person entrusted with the administration of the estate by the court having jurisdiction at the place where the deceased died domiciled,
(*b*) to the person entitled to administer the estate by the law of the place where the deceased died domiciled,
(*c*) if there is no such person as is mentioned in paragraph (*a*) or (*b*) of this rule or if in the opinion of the registrar the circumstances so require, to such person as the registrar may direct,
(*d*) if a grant is required to be made to, or if the registrar in his discretion considers that a grant should be made to, not less than two administrators, to such person as the registrar may direct jointly with any such person as is mentioned in paragraph (*a*) or (*b*) of this rule or with any other person:

Provided that without any such order as aforesaid—

(*a*) probate of any will which is admissible to proof may be granted—
 (i) if the will is in the English or Welsh language, to the executor named therein;

(ii) if the will describes the duties of a named person in terms sufficient to constitute him executor according to the tenor of the will, to that person;

(*b*) where the whole of the estate in England consists of immovable property, a grant limited thereto may be made in accordance with the law which would have been applicable if the deceased had died domiciled in England.

Grants to attorneys

30.—(1) Where a person entitled to a grant resides outside England, administration may be granted to his lawfully constituted attorney for his use and benefit, limited until such person shall obtain a grant or in such other way as the registrar may direct:

Provided that where the person so entitled is an executor, administration shall not be granted to his attorney without notice to the other executors, if any, unless such notice is dispensed with by the registrar.

(2) Where a registrar is satisfied by affidavit that it is desirable for a grant to be made to the lawfully constituted attorney of a person entitled to a grant of administration and resident in England, he may direct that administration be granted to such attorney for the use and benefit of such person, limited until such person shall obtain a grant or in such other way as the registrar may direct.

Grants on behalf of infants

31.—(1) Where the person to whom a grant would otherwise be made is an infant, administration for his use and benefit until he attains the age of eighteen years shall unless otherwise directed and subject to paragraphs (3) and (5) of this Rule, be granted—

(*a*) to both parents of the infant jointly or to the statutory or testamentary guardian of the infant or to any guardian appointed by a court of competent jurisdiction, or

(*b*) if there is no such guardian able and willing to act and the infant has attained the age of sixteen years, to any next of kin nominated by the infant or, where the infant is a married woman, to any such next of kin or to her husband if nominated by her.

(2) Any person nominated under sub-paragraph (*b*) of the last foregoing paragraph may represent any other infant whose next of kin he is, being an infant below the age of sixteen years entitled in the same degree as the infant who made the nomination.

(3) Notwithstanding anything in this rule, administration for the use and benefit of the infant until he attains the age of eighteen years may be granted to any person assigned as guardian by order of a registrar in default of, or jointly with, or to the exclusion of, any such

person as is mentioned in paragraph (1) of this rule; and such an order may be made on application by the intended guardian, who shall file an affidavit in support of the application and, if required by the registrar, an affidavit of fitness sworn by a responsible person.

(4) Where a grant is required to be made to not less than two administrators and there is only one person competent and willing to take a grant under the foregoing provisions of this rule, administration may, unless a registrar otherwise directs, be granted to such person jointly with any other person nominated by him as a fit and proper person to take the grant.

(5) Where an infant who is sole executor has no interest in the residuary estate of the deceased, administration for the use and benefit of the infant until he attains the age of eighteen years shall, unless a registrar otherwise directs, be granted to the person entitled to the residuary estate.

(6) An infant's right to administration may be renounced only by a person assigned as guardian under paragraph (3) of this rule and authorised to renounce by a registrar.

Grants where infant co-executor

32.—(1) Where one of two or more executors is an infant, probate may be granted to the other executor or executors not under disability, with power reserved of making the like grant to the infant on his attaining the age of eighteen years, and administration for the use and benefit of the infant until he attains the age of eighteen years may be granted under rule 31 if and only if the executors who are not under disability renounce or, on being cited to accept or refuse a grant, fail to make an effective application therefor.

(2) An infant executor's right to probate on attaining the age of eighteen years may not be renounced by any person on his behalf.

Grants in case of mental or physical incapacity

33.—(1) Where a registrar is satisfied that a person entitled to a grant is by reason of mental or physical incapacity incapable of managing his affairs, administration for his use and benefit, limited during his incapacity or in such other way as the registrar may direct, may be granted—

(*a*) in the case of mental incapacity, to the person authorised by the Court of Protection to apply for the grant, or

(*b*) where there is no person so authorised, or in the case of physical incapacity—

(i) if the person incapable is entitled as executor and has no interest in the residuary estate of the deceased, to the person entitled to such estate;

(ii) if the person incapable is entitled otherwise than as

executor or is an executor having an interest in the residuary estate of the deceased, to the person who would be entitled to a grant in respect of his estate if he had died intestate;

or to such other person as a registrar may by order direct.

(2) Unless a registrar otherwise directs, no grant of administration shall be made under this rule unless all persons entitled in the same degree as the person incapable have been cleared off.

(3) In the case of mental incapacity, notice of intended application for a grant under this rule shall be given to the Court of Protection, except where the person incapable is an executor with no beneficial interest in the estate.

(4) In the case of physical incapacity, notice of intended application for a grant under this rule shall, unless a registrar otherwise directs, be given to the person alleged to be so incapable.

Grants to trust corporations and other corporate bodies

34.—(1) Where a trust corporation applies for a grant through one of its officers, such officer shall lodge a certified copy of the resolution authorising him to make the application and shall depose in the oath that the corporation is a trust corporation as defined by these rules and that it has power to accept a grant:

Provided that it shall not be necessary to lodge a certified copy of the resolution where the trust corporation

(*a*) has filed with the Senior Registrar a certified copy thereof identifying the authorised person or persons by the position held and it is deposed in the oath that the resolution is still in force or

(*b*) is a person holding an official position if the person through whom the application is made is included in a list filed with the Senior Registrar of persons authorised to make such applications.[6]

(2) Where a trust corporation applies for a grant of administration otherwise than as attorney for some person, there shall be lodged with the application the consents of all persons entitled to a grant and of all persons interested in the residuary estate of the deceased, unless the registrar directs that such consents be dispensed with on such terms, if any, as he may think fit.

(3) Where a corporation (not being a trust corporation) would, if an individual, be entitled to a grant, administration for its use and benefit, limited until further representation is granted, may be granted to its nominee or, if the corporation has its principal place of business outside England, its nominee or lawfully constituted attorney, and a copy of the resolution appointing the nominee or, as the case may be,

[6] *Ibid.*

the power of attorney, sealed by the corporation or otherwise authenticated to the registrar's satisfaction, shall be lodged with the application for the grant, and the oath shall state that the corporation is not a trust corporation.

Renunciation of probate and administration

35.—(1) Renunciation of probate by an executor shall not operate as renunciation of any right which he may have to a grant of administration in some other capacity unless he expressly renounces such right.

(2) Unless a registrar otherwise directs, no person who has renounced administration in one capacity may obtain a grant thereof in some other capacity.

(3) A renunciation of probate or administration may be retracted at any time on the order of a registrar:

Provided that only in exceptional circumstances may leave be given to an executor to retract a renunciation of probate after a grant has been made to some other person entitled in a lower degree.

(4) A direction or order under this rule may be made by either the registrar of a district probate registry where the renunciation is filed or a registrar of the principal registry.

Consent of administrator of enemy property

36. *Revoked by the Non-Contentious Probate (Amendment) Rules* 1974 (S.I. 1974 No. 597).

Notice to Crown of intended application for grant

37. In any case in which it appears that the Crown is or may be beneficially interested in the estate of a deceased person, notice of intended application for a grant shall be given by the applicant to the Treasury Solicitor, and the registrar may direct that no grant shall issue within a specified time after the notice has been given.

Guarantee

38.—(1) The registrar shall not require a guarantee under section 120 of the Act as a condition of granting administration except where it is proposed to grant it—

(*a*) by virtue of rule 19(v) or rule 21(4) to a creditor or the personal representative of a creditor or to a person who has no immediate beneficial interest in the estate of the deceased but may have such an interest in the event of an accretion to the estate;

(*b*) under rule 27 to a person or some of the persons who would, if the person beneficially entitled to the whole of the estate died intestate, be entitled to his estate;

(*c*) under rule 30 to the attorney of a person entitled to a grant;

(*d*) under rule 31 for the use and benefit of a minor;
(*e*) under rule 33 for the use and benefit of a person who is by reason of mental or physical incapacity incapable of managing his affairs;
(*f*) to an applicant who appears to the registrar to be resident elsewhere than in the United Kingdom;

or except where the registrar considers that there are special circumstances making it desirable to require a guarantee.

(2) Notwithstanding that it is proposed to grant administration as aforesaid, a guarantee shall not be required, except in special circumstances, on an application for administration where the applicant or one of the applicants is—

(*a*) a trust corporation;
(*b*) a solicitor holding a current practising certificate under the Solicitors Act 1974;
(*c*) a servant of the Crown acting in his official capacity;
(*d*) a nominee of a public department or of a local authority within the meaning of the Local Government Act 1972.

(3) Every guarantee entered into by a surety for the purposes of section 120 of the Act shall be in Form 1.

(4) Except where the surety is a corporation, the signature of the surety on every such guarantee shall be attested by an authorised officer, commissioner for oaths or other person authorised by law to administer an oath.

(5) Unless the registrar otherwise directs—

(*a*) if it is decided to require a guarantee, it shall be given by two sureties, except where the gross value of the estate does not exceed £5,000[7] or a corporation is a proposed surety, and in those cases one will suffice;
(*b*) no person shall be accepted as a surety unless he is resident in the United Kingdom;
(*c*) no officer of a registry or sub-registry shall become a surety;
(*d*) the limit of the liability of the surety or sureties under a guarantee given for the purposes of section 120 of the Act shall be the gross amount of the estate as sworn on the application for the grant;
(*e*) every surety, other than a corporation, shall justify.

(6) Where the proposed surety is a corporation there shall be filed an affidavit by the proper officer of the corporation to the effect that it has power to act as surety and has executed the guarantee in the manner prescribed by its constitution, and containing sufficient information as to the financial position of the corporation to satisfy

[7] Substituted by *ibid.*

the registrar that its assets are sufficient to satisfy all claims which may be made against it under any guarantee which it has given or is likely to give for the purposes of section 120 of the Act:

Provided that the Senior Registrar may, instead of requiring an affidavit in every case, except an affidavit made not less often than once in every year together with an undertaking by the corporation to notify the Senior Registrar forthwith in the event of any alteration in its constitution affecting its power to become surety under that section.

Particulars of estate to be filed, and sureties to justify, in certain cases

39. *Revoked by the Non-Contentious Probate (Amendment) Rules* 1971 (S.I. 1971 No. 1977).

Resealing of Scottish confirmations and Northern Irish grants, and transmission of English grants to Northern Ireland

40. *Revoked by the Non-Contentious Probate (Amendment) Rules* 1971 (S.I. 1971 No. 1977).

Resealing under Colonial Probates Acts, 1892 and 1927

41.—(1) An application under the Colonial Probates Acts, 1892 and 1927, for the resealing of probate or administration granted by the court of a country to which those Acts apply may[8] be made by the person to whom the grant was made or by any person authorised in writing to apply on his behalf.

(2) On any such application—

(*a*) an Inland Revenue affidavit or account shall be lodged as if the application were one for a grant in England;

(*b*) if a registrar so requires, the application shall be advertised in such manner as he may direct and shall be supported by an oath sworn by the person making the application.

(2A) On an application for the resealing of a grant of administration—

(*a*) the registrar shall not require sureties under section 11 of the Administration of Estates Act 1971 as a condition of resealing the grant except where it appears to him that the grant is made to a person or for a purpose mentioned in paragraphs (*a*) to (*f*) of rule 38(1) or except where he considers that there are special circumstances making it desirable to require sureties;

(*b*) rules 5(4) and 38(2), (4), (5) and (6) shall apply with any necessary modifications; and

(*c*) a guarantee entered into by a surety for the purposes of the said section 11 shall be in Form 2.

[8] Substituted by *ibid.*

(3) Except by leave of a registrar, no grant shall be resealed unless it was made to such a person as is mentioned in paragraph (*a*) or (*b*) of rule 29 or to a person to whom a grant could be made under the proviso to that rule.

(4) No limited or temporary grant shall be resealed except by leave of a registrar.

(5) Every grant lodged for resealing shall include a copy of any will to which the grant relates or shall be accompanied by a copy thereof certified as correct by or under the authority of the court by which the grant was made, and where the copy of the grant required to be deposited under subsection (1) of section 2 of the Colonial Probates Act, 1892, does not include a copy of the will, a copy thereof shall be deposited in the registry at the same time as the copy of the grant.

(6) The registrar shall send notice of the resealing to the court which made the grant.

(7) Where notice is received in the principal registry of the resealing of an English grant, notice of any amendment or revocation of the grant shall be sent to the court by which it was resealed.

Application for leave to sue on guarantee

41A. An application for leave under section 120(3) of the Act or under section 11(5) of the Administration of Estates Act 1971 to sue a surety on a guarantee given for the purposes of either of those sections shall, unless the registrar otherwise directs under rule 60, be made by summons to a registrar, and notice of the application shall in any event be served on the administrator, the surety and any co-surety.

Amendment and revocation of grant

42. If a registrar is satisfied that a grant should be amended or revoked he may make an order accordingly:

Provided that except in special circumstances no grant shall be amended or revoked under this rule except on the application or with the consent of the person to whom the grant was made.

Certificate of delivery of Inland Revenue affidavit

43. Where the deceased died before March 13, 1975, the certificate of delivery of an Inland Revenue affidavit required by section 30 of the Customs and Inland Revenue Act 1881, to be borne by every grant shall be in form 3.

Caveats

44.—(1) Any person who wishes to ensure that no grant is sealed without notice to himself may enter a caveat in any registry.

(2) Any person who wishes to enter a caveat (in this rule called "the caveator") may do so by completing form 4 in the appropriate book at the registry and obtaining an acknowledgement of entry from the

proper officer, or by sending through the post at his own risk a notice in form 4 to the registry in which he wishes the caveat to be entered.

(3) Where the caveat is entered by a solicitor on the caveator's behalf, the name of the caveator shall be stated in form 4.

(4) Except as otherwise provided by this rule, a caveat shall remain in force for the period of six months beginning with the date on which it is entered.

(4A) Where a caveator, within the last month of a period of six months described by paragraph (4) of this rule or of any additional period of six months prescribed by this paragraph, lodges at the Registry in which the caveat was entered a written application for its extension, the caveat shall (except as otherwise provided by paragraphs (8), (11) and (12) of this rule) remain in force for an additional period of six months.

(5) The Senior Registrar shall maintain an index of caveats entered in any registry and on receiving an application for a grant in the principal registry, or a notice of an application for a grant made in a district probate registry, he shall cause the index to be searched and shall notify the appropriate registrar in the event of a caveat having been entered against the sealing of a grant for which application has been made in a district probate registry.

(6) The registrar shall not allow any grant to be sealed if he has knowledge of an effective caveat in respect thereof:

Provided that no caveat shall operate to prevent the sealing of a grant on the day on which the caveat is entered.

(7) A caveat may be warned by the issue from the principal registry of a warning in form 5 at the instance of any person interested (in this rule called "the person warning") which shall state his interest and, if he claims under a will, the date of the will, and shall require the caveator to give particulars of any contrary interest which he may have in the estate of the deceased; and every warning or a copy thereof shall be served on the caveator.

(8) A caveator who has not entered an appearance to a warning may at any time withdraw his caveat by giving notice at the registry at which it was entered and the caveat shall thereupon cease to have effect and, if it has been warned, the caveator shall forthwith give notice of withdrawal of the caveat to the person warning.

(9) A caveator having an interest contrary to that of the person warning may, within eight days of service of the warning upon him inclusive of the day of such service, or at any time thereafter if no affidavit has been filed under paragraph (11) of this rule, enter an appearance in the principal registry by filing form 6 and making an entry in the appropriate book, and shall forthwith thereafter serve on the person warning a copy of form 6 sealed with the seal of the registry.

(10) A caveator having no interest contrary to that of the person

warning but wishing to show cause against the sealing of a grant to that person may, within eight days of service of the warning upon him inclusive of the day of such service, or at any time thereafter if no affidavit has been filed under paragraph (11) of this rule, issue and serve a summons for directions, which may include a direction for a caveat to cease to have effect[9] which shall be returnable before a registrar.

(11) If the time limited for appearance has expired and the caveator has not entered an appearance, the person warning may file in the principal registry an affidavit showing that the warning was duly served, and thereupon the caveat shall cease to have effect, provided that there is no pending summons issued under the last foregoing paragraph.[10]

(11A) Upon the commencement of a probate action the Senior Registrar[11] shall, in respect of each caveat then in force (other than a caveat entered by the plaintiff), give to the caveator notice of the commencement of the action and, upon the subsequent entry of a caveat at any time when the action is pending, shall likewise notify the caveator of the existence of the action.

(12) Unless a registrar of the principal registry by order made on summons otherwise directs—

(*a*) any caveat in force at the commencement of proceedings by way of citation or motion shall, unless withdrawn pursuant to paragraph (8) of this rule, remain in force until an application for a grant is made by the person shown to be entitled thereto by the decision of the court in such proceedings, and upon such application any caveat entered by a party who had notice of the proceedings shall cease to have effect;

(*b*) any caveat in respect of which an appearance to a warning has been entered shall remain in force until the commencement of a probate action;

(*c*) the commencement of a probate action shall, whether or not any caveat has been entered, operate to prevent the sealing of a grant (other than a grant under section 117 of the Act) until application for a grant is made by the person shown to be entitled thereto by the decision of the court in such action, and upon such application any caveat entered by a party who had notice of the action, or by a caveator who was given notice under paragraph (11A) of this rule, shall cease to have effect.

(13) Except with the leave of a registrar of the principal registry, no further caveat may be entered by or on behalf of any caveator whose

[9] Added by *ibid.*
[10] *Ibid.*
[11] Substituted by *ibid.*

caveat is either in force or has ceased to have effect under paragraph (11) or (12) of this rule.

(14) In this rule "grant" includes a grant made by any court outside England which is produced for resealing by the High Court.

Citations

45.—(1) Any citation may issue from the principal registry or a district probate registry and shall be settled by a registrar before being issued.[12]

(2) Every averment in a citation, and such other information as the registrar may require, shall be verified by an affidavit sworn by the person issuing the citation (in these Rules called "the citor") or, if there are two or more citors, by one of them:

Provided that the registrar may in special circumstances accept an affidavit sworn by the citor's solicitor.

(3) The citor shall enter a caveat before issuing a citation.

(4) Every citation shall be served personally on the person cited unless the registrar, on cause shown by affidavit, directs some other mode of service, which may include notice by advertisement.

(5) Every will referred to in a citation shall be lodged in a registry before the citation is issued, except where the will is not in the citor's possession and the registrar is satisfied that it is impracticable to require it to be lodged.

(6) A person who has been cited to appear may, within eight days of service of the citation upon him inclusive of the day of such service, or at any time thereafter if no application has been made by the citor under paragraph (5) of rule 46 or paragraph (2) of rule 47, enter an appearance in the registry from which the citation issued by filing form 6 and shall forthwith thereafter serve on the citor a copy of form 6 sealed with the seal of the registry.

Citation to accept or refuse or to take a grant

46.—(1) A citation to accept or refuse a grant may be issued at the instance of any person who would himself be entitled to a grant in the event of the person cited renouncing his right thereto.

(2) Where power to make a grant to an executor has been reserved, a citation calling on him to accept or refuse a grant may be issued at the instance of the executors who have proved the will or of the executors of the last survivor of deceased executors who have proved.

(3) A citation calling on an executor who has intermeddled in the estate of the deceased to show cause why he should not be ordered to take a grant may be issued at the instance of any person interested in the estate at any time after the expiration of six months from the death of the deceased:

[12] Added by *ibid.*

Provided that no citation to take a grant shall issue while proceedings as to the validity of the will are pending.

(4) A person cited who is willing to accept or take a grant may apply *ex parte* to a registrar for an order for a grant on filing an affidavit showing that he has entered an appearance and that he has not been served by the citor with notice of any application for a grant to himself.

(5) If the time limited for appearance has expired and the person cited has not entered an appearance, the citor may—

(*a*) in the case of a citation under paragraph (1) of this rule apply to a registrar for an order for a grant to himself;
(*b*) in the case of a citation under paragraph (2) of this rule, apply to a registrar for an order that a note be made on the grant that the executor in respect of whom power was reserved has been duly cited and has not appeared and that all his rights in respect of the executorship have wholly ceased;
(*c*) in the case of a citation under paragraph (3) of this rule, apply to a registrar by summons (which shall be served on the person cited) for an order requiring such person to take a grant within a specified time or for a grant to himself or to some other person specified in the summons.

(6) An application under the last foregoing paragraph shall be supported by an affidavit showing that the citation was duly served and that the person cited has not entered an appearance.

(7) If the person cited has entered an appearance but has not applied for a grant under paragraph (4) of this rule, or has failed to prosecute his application with reasonable diligence, the citor may—

(*a*) in the case of a citation under paragraph (1) of this rule, apply by summons to a registrar for an order for a grant to himself;
(*b*) in the case of a citation under paragraph (2) of this rule, apply by summons to a registrar for an order striking out the appearance and for the endorsement on the grant of such a note as is mentioned in sub-paragraph (*b*) of paragraph (5) of this rule;
(*c*) in the case of a citation under paragraph (8) of this rule, apply by summons to a registrar for an order requiring the person cited to take a grant within a specified time or for a grant to himself or to some other person specified in the summons;

and the summons shall be served on the person cited.

Citation to propound a will

47.—(1) A citation to propound a will shall be directed to the executors named in the will and to all persons interested thereunder, and may be issued at the instance of any citor having an interest contrary to that of the executors or such other persons.

(2) If the time limited for appearance has expired, the citor may—

(*a*) in the case where no person cited has entered an appearance, apply to a registrar for an order for a grant as if the will were invalid;

(*b*) in the case where no person who has entered an appearance proceeds with reasonable diligence to propound the will, apply to a registrar by summons (which shall be served on every person cited who has entered an appearance) for such an order as is mentioned in paragraph (*a*) above.

Address for service

48. All caveats, citations, warnings and appearances shall contain an address for service within the jurisdiction.

Application for order to bring in a will or to attend for examination

49.—(1) An application under section 122 of the Act for an order requiring a person to bring in a will or to attend for examination may, unless a probate action has been commenced, be made to a registrar by summons, which shall be served on every such person as aforesaid.

(2) An application under section 123 of the Act for the issue by a registrar of a subpoena to bring in a will shall be supported by an affidavit setting out the grounds of the application, and if any person served with the subpoena denies that the will is in his possession or control he may file an affidavit to that effect in the registry from which the subpoena issued.[13]

Limited grants under section 113 of Act

50. An application for an order for a grant under section 113 of the Act limited to part of an estate may be made to a registrar and shall be supported by an affidavit stating—

(*a*) whether the application is made in respect of the real estate only or any part thereof, or real estate together with personal estate, or in respect of a trust estate only;

(*b*) whether the estate of the deceased is known to be insolvent;

(*c*) that the persons entitled to a grant in respect of the whole estate in priority to the applicant have been cleared off.

[13] *Ibid.*

Grants of administration under discretionary powers of court, and grants ad colligenda bona

51. An application for an order for—

(*a*) a grant of administration under section 116 of the Act, or
(*b*) a grant of administration *ad colligenda bona,*

may be made to a registrar, and shall be supported by an affidavit setting out the grounds of the application.

Applications for leave to swear to death

52. An application for leave to swear to the death of a person in whose estate a grant is sought may be made to a registrar and shall be supported by an affidavit setting out the grounds of the application and containing particulars of any policies of insurance effected on the life of the presumed deceased.

Grants in respect of nuncupative wills and of copies of wills

53.—(1) An application for an order admitting to proof a nuncupative will, or a will contained in a copy, a completed draft, a reconstruction or other evidence of its contents where the original will is not available, may be made to a registrar:

Provided that where a will is not available owing to its being retained in the custody of a foreign court or official, a duly authenticated copy of the will may be admitted to proof without any such order as aforesaid.

(2) The application shall be supported by an affidavit setting out the grounds of the application and by such evidence on affidavit as the applicant can adduce as to—

(*a*) the due execution of the will,
(*b*) its existence after the death of the testator, and
(*c*) the accuracy of the copy or other evidence of the contents of the will,

together with any consents in writing to the application given by any persons not under disability who would be prejudiced by the grant.

Grants durante absentia

54. [*Revoked by the Non-Contentious Probate (Amendment) Rules* 1982 (S.I. 1982 No. 446).]

Application for order where case pending in district probate registry

55. [*Revoked by the Non-Contentious Probate (Amendment) Rules* 1967 (S.I. 1967 No. 748).]

Notice of election by surviving spouse to redeem life interest

56.—(1) Where a surviving spouse who is the sole personal representative of the deceased is entitled to a life interest in part of the residuary estate and elects under section 47A of the Administration of Estates Act, 1925, to have the life interest redeemed, he may give written notice of the election to the Senior Registrar in pursuance of subsection (7) of that section by filing a notice in form 7 in the principal registry or in the district probate registry from which the grant issued.

(2) Where the grant issued from a district probate registry, the notice shall be filed in duplicate.

(3) A notice filed under this rule shall be noted on the grant and the record and shall be open to inspection.

Information as to grants in district probate registries to be sent to principal registry

57.—(1) Notice of every application for a grant made in a district probate registry shall be sent by the registrar to the principal registry and shall be in the form of a document stating the full name of the deceased and the date of his death.

(2) No grant shall be made by a district probate registrar in any estate until he has received from the principal registry a certificate that no other application appears to have been made in respect of that estate.

(3) On receipt of the notice referred to in paragraph (1) above, the principal registry shall examine its records of current caveats, grants issued and applications for grants made elsewhere, and shall either give such a certificate or advise the district probate registrar of the reason why a certificate cannot be given.

(4) Each district probate registrar shall in respect of the district probate registry for which he is responsible send to the principal registry at intervals directed by the Senior Registrar a copy of every grant issued from, and will proved in, that district probate registry during that period.

(5) Each district probate registrar shall file and preserve all original wills proved in his registry.

(6) In this rule "district probate registry" includes a sub-registry and, in paragraph (1), a probate office and "grant" includes the resealing of a grant under the Colonial Probate Acts 1892 and 1927.[14]

Issue of copies of original wills and other documents

58.—(1) Where copies are required of original wills or other documents deposited under section 124 of the Act, such copies may be photographic copies sealed with the seal of the registry and issued as office copies and, where such office copies are available, copies

[14] *Ibid.*

certified under the hand of a registrar to be true copies shall be issued only if it is required that the seal of the Court be affixed thereto.

(2) Copies, not being photographic copies, of original wills or other documents deposited under the said section 124 shall be examined against the documents of which they purport to be copies only if so required by the person demanding the copy, and in such case the copy shall be certified under the hand of a registrar to be a true copy and may in addition be sealed with the seal of the Court.

Taxation of costs

59.—(1) Every bill of costs (other than a bill delivered by a solicitor to his client which falls to be taxed under the Solicitors Act 1974), shall be referred to a registrar of the principal registry for taxation and may be taxed by him or such other taxing officer as the President may appoint.

(2) The party applying for taxation shall file the bill and give to any other parties entitled to be heard on the taxation not less than three clear days' notice of the time appointed for taxation, and shall at the same time, if he had not already done so, supply them with a copy of the bill.

(3) If any party entitled to be heard on the taxation does not attend within a reasonable time after the time appointed, the taxing officer may proceed to tax the bill upon being satisfied that such party had due notice of the time appointed.

(4) The fees payable on taxation shall be paid by the party on whose application the bill is taxed and shall be allowed as part of the bill.

Power to require application to be made by summons or motion

60.—(1) A registrar may require any application to be made by summons to a registrar or a judge or to the court on motion.

(2) An application for an inventory and account shall be made by summons to a registrar.[15]

(3) A summons for hearing by a registrar shall be issued out of the registry in which it is to be heard.[16]

(4) A summons to be heard by a judge shall be issued out of the principal registry.

Transfer of applications to Principal Registry

60A. A district probate registrar to whom any application is made under these rules may order the transfer of the application to the principal registry.

[15] Substituted by *ibid.*
[16] Added by *ibid.*

Powers to make orders for costs

60B. On any application made to him by way of summons, the district probate registrar shall have full power to determine by whom and to what extent the costs are to be paid.[17]

Exercise of powers of judge during Long Vacation

61. All powers exercisable under these Rules by a judge in chambers may be exercised during the Long Vacation by a registrar of the principal registry.

Appeals from registrars

62.—(1) [*Revoked by Non-Contentious Probate (Amendment) Rules* 1967 (S.I. 1967 No. 748).]

(2) Any person aggrieved by a decision or requirement of a registrar may appeal by summons to a judge.

(3) If, in the case of an appeal under the last foregoing paragraph, any person besides the appellant appeared or was represented before the registrar from whose decision or requirement the appeal is brought, the summons shall be issued within seven days thereof for hearing on the first available day and shall be served on every such person as aforesaid.

Service of notice of motion and summons

63.—(1) A judge or registrar of the principal registry or where the application is to be made to a district probate registrar, that registrar[18] may direct that a notice of motion or summons for the service of which no other provision is made by these Rules shall be served on such person or persons as the judge or registrar may direct.

(2) Where by these Rules or by any direction given under the last foregoing paragraph a notice of motion or summons is required to be served on any person, it shall be served—

(*a*) in the case of a notice of motion, not less than five clear days before the day named in the notice for hearing the motion;

(*b*) in the case of a summons, not less than two clear days before the day appointed for the hearing, unless a judge or registrar at or before the hearing, dispenses with service on such terms, if any, as he may think fit.

Notices, etc.

64. Unless a registrar otherwise directs or these Rules otherwise provide, any notice or other document required to be given to or served on any person may be given or served by leaving it at, or by sending it by prepaid registered post or by recorded delivery to, that

[17] *Ibid.*
[18] *Ibid.*

person's address for service or, if he has no address for service, his last known address.

65, 66. [*Revoked by Non-Contentious Probate (Amendment) Rules* (S.I. 1985 No. 1232).]

Application to pending proceedings

67. Subject in any particular case to any direction given by a judge or registrar, these Rules shall apply to any proceeding which is pending on the date on which they come into operation as well as to any proceeding commenced on or after that date.

Revocation of previous Rules

68.—(1) The Rules, Orders and Instructions set out in the Second Schedule are hereby revoked.

(2) The following amendments shall be made in the Rules, Orders and Tables of Fees for the Court of Probate in respect of Contentious Business, dated July 30, 1862:—

(*a*) rules 7 to 12 shall be revoked;
(*b*) in rule 73 the words "and by motion upon affidavit when no suit is pending" shall be deleted.

ADMINISTRATION OF ESTATES

S.I. 1977 No. 1491

THE INTESTATE SUCCESSION (INTEREST AND CAPITALISATION) ORDER 1977

Made	- - - - - -	*4th September* 1977
Laid before Parliament -	-	*14th September* 1977
Coming into Operation -	-	*15th September* 1977

The Lord Chancellor, in exercise of the powers conferred on him by section 46(1)(i) of the Administration of Estates Act 1925, and by section 47A(3A) of that Act, hereby makes the following Order:—

Citation and Interpretation

1.—(1) This Order may be cited as the Intestate Succession (Interest and Capitalisation) Order 1977 and shall come into operation on September 15, 1977.

(2) The Interpretation Act 1889 shall apply to the interpretation of this Order as it applies to the interpretation of an Act of Parliament.

Interest on Statutory Legacy

2. For the purposes of section 46(1)(i) of the Administration of Estates Act 1925, as it applies both in respect of persons dying before 1953 and in respect of persons dying after 1952, the specified rate of interest shall be 7 per cent. per annum.
[Amended by 1983 order of same name, S.I. 1983 No. 1374, to 6 per cent]

Capitalisation of Life Interests

3.—(1) Where after the coming into operation of this Order an election is exercised in accordance with subsection (6) or (7) of section 47A of the Administration of Estates Act 1925, the capital value of the life interest of the surviving spouse shall be reckoned in accordance with the following provisions of this article.

(2) There shall be ascertained, by reference to the index compiled by the Financial Times, The Institute of Actuaries and the Faculty of Actuaries, the average gross redemption yield on medium coupon fifteen-year Government Stocks at the date on which the election was exercised or, if the index was not compiled on that date, by reference to the index on the last date before that date on which it was compiled; and the column which corresponds to that yield in

whichever of the Tables set out in the Schedule hereto is applicable to the sex of the surviving spouse shall be the appropriate column for the purposes of paragraph (3) of this article.

(3) The capital value for the purposes of paragraph (1) of this article is the product of the part of the residuary estate (whether or not yielding income) in respect of which the election was exercised and the multiplier shown in the appropriate column opposite the age which the surviving spouse had attained at the date on which the election was exercised.

Elwyn-Jones, C.

Dated September 4, 1977.

SCHEDULE

TABLE 1: **Multiplier to be applied to the part of the residuary estate in respect of which the election is exercised to obtain the capital value of the life interest of a surviving husband, when the average gross redemption yield on medium coupon fifteen-year Government Stocks is at the rate shown.**

AGE LAST BIRTHDAY OF HUSBAND	LESS THAN 8.50%	8.50% OR BETWEEN 8.50% AND 9.50%	9.50% OR BETWEEN 9.50% AND 10.50%	10.50% OR BETWEEN 10.50% AND 11.50%	11.50% OR BETWEEN 11.50% AND 12.50%	12.50% OR BETWEEN 12.50% AND 13.50%	13.50% OR BETWEEN 13.50% AND 14.50%	14.50% OR BETWEEN 14.50% AND 15.50%	15.50% OR MORE
16	0.882	0.897	0.908	0.917	0.923	0.927	0.931	0.934	0.936
17	0.879	0.895	0.906	0.915	0.921	0.926	0.930	0.933	0.935
18	0.876	0.892	0.904	0.913	0.920	0.925	0.929	0.932	0.934
19	0.873	0.890	0.902	0.911	0.918	0.923	0.928	0.931	0.933
20	0.870	0.887	0.900	0.909	0.917	0.922	0.926	0.930	0.933
21	0.866	0.884	0.897	0.907	0.915	0.921	0.925	0.929	0.932
22	0.863	0.881	0.895	0.905	0.913	0.919	0.924	0.928	0.931
23	0.859	0.878	0.892	0.903	0.911	0.918	0.923	0.927	0.930
24	0.855	0.875	8.890	0.901	0.909	0.916	0.921	0.925	0.929
25	0.852	0.872	0.887	0.898	0.907	0.914	0.920	0.924	0.928
26	0.847	0.868	0.884	0.896	0.905	0.912	0.918	0.923	0.926
27	0.843	0.864	0.880	0.893	0.903	0.910	0.916	0.921	0.925
28	0.838	0.860	0.877	0.890	0.900	0.908	0.914	0.919	0.923
29	0.834	0.856	0.873	0.887	0.897	0.905	0.912	0.917	0.922
30	0.828	0.851	0.869	0.883	0.894	0.903	0.910	0.915	0.920
31	0.823	0.847	0.865	0.879	0.891	0.900	0.907	0.913	0.918
32	0.818	0.842	0.861	0.876	0.887	0.897	0.904	0.911	0.916
33	0.812	0.837	0.856	0.871	0.884	0.893	0.901	0.908	0.913
34	0.806	0.831	0.851	0.867	0.880	0.890	0.898	0.905	0.911
35	0.799	0.825	0.846	0.862	0.875	0.886	0.895	0.902	0.908
36	0.792	0.819	0.840	0.857	0.871	0.882	0.891	0.899	0.905
37	0.785	0.813	0.834	0.852	0.866	0.878	0.887	0.895	0.902
38	0.778	0.806	0.828	0.846	0.861	0.873	0.883	0.891	0.898
39	0.771	0.799	0.822	0.840	0.856	0.868	0.879	0.887	0.894
40	0.763	0.792	0.815	0.834	0.850	0.863	0.874	0.883	0.890
41	0.755	0.784	0 808	0.828	0.844	0.857	0.869	0.878	0.886
42	0.746	0.776	0.801	0.821	0.838	0.852	0.863	0.873	0.881
43	0.737	0.768	0.793	0.814	0.831	0.845	0.857	0.868	0.876
44	0.728	0.759	0.785	0.806	0.824	0.839	0.851	0.862	0.871
45	0.719	0.750	0.776	0.798	0.816	0.832	0.845	0.856	0.866

TABLE 1: **Multiplier to be applied to the part of the residuary estate in respect of which the election is exercised to obtain the capital value of the life interest of a surviving husband, when the average gross redemption yield on medium coupon fifteen-year Government Stocks is at the rate shown.**

AGE LAST BIRTHDAY OF HUSBAND	LESS THAN 8.50%	8.50% OR BETWEEN 8.50% AND 9.50%	9.50% OR BETWEEN 9.50% AND 10.50%	10.50% OR BETWEEN 10.50% AND 11.50%	11.50% OR BETWEEN 11.50% AND 12.50%	12.50% OR BETWEEN 12.50% AND 13.50%	13.50% OR BETWEEN 13.50% AND 14.50%	14.50% OR BETWEEN 14.50% AND 15.50%	15.50% OR MORE
46	0.709	0.741	0.768	0.790	0.809	0.825	0.838	0.850	0.860
47	0.699	0.731	0.758	0.781	0.801	0.817	0.831	0.843	0.853
48	0.688	0.721	0.749	0.772	0.792	0.809	0.823	0.836	0.847
49	0.678	0.711	0.739	0.763	0.783	0.800	0.815	0.828	0.839
50	0.666	0.700	0.729	0.753	0.774	0.791	0.807	0.820	0.832
51	0.655	0.689	0.718	0.743	0.764	0.782	0.798	0.812	0.824
52	0.643	0.678	0.707	0.732	0.754	0.772	0.789	0.803	0.815
53	0.631	0.666	0.695	0.721	0.743	0.762	0.779	0.794	0.807
54	0.619	0.654	0.684	0.710	0.732	0.752	0.769	0.784	0.797
55	0.606	0.641	0.671	0.698	0.721	0.741	0.758	0.774	0.787
56	0.594	0.628	0.659	0.685	0.709	0.729	0.747	0.763	0.777
57	0.580	0.615	0.646	0.673	0.696	0.717	0.735	0.752	0.766
58	0.567	0.602	0.633	0.660	0.683	0.705	0.723	0.740	0.755
59	0.553	0.588	0.619	0.646	0.670	0.692	0.711	0.728	0.743
60	0.539	0.574	0.605	0.632	0.657	0.678	0.698	0.715	0.731
61	0.525	0.560	0.590	0.618	0.642	0.664	0.684	0.702	0.718
62	0.510	0.545	0.576	0.603	0.628	0.650	0.670	0.688	0.704
63	0.496	0.530	0.561	0.588	0.613	0.636	0.656	0.674	0.691
64	0.481	0.515	0.546	0.573	0.598	0.621	0.641	0.659	0.676
65	0.466	0.500	0.530	0.558	0.583	0.605	0.626	0.644	0.661
66	0.451	0.485	0.515	0.542	0.567	0.590	0.610	0.629	0.646
67	0.436	0.469	0.499	0.526	0.551	0.574	0.594	0.613	0.631
68	0.421	0.454	0.483	0.510	0.535	0.557	0.578	0.597	0.615
69	0.407	0.438	0.467	0.494	0.518	0.541	0.562	0.581	0.598
70	0.392	0.423	0.452	0.478	0.502	0.524	0.545	0.564	0.582
71	0.377	0.407	0.436	0.462	0.485	0.508	0.528	0.547	0.565
72	0.362	0.392	0.420	0.445	0.469	0.491	0.511	0.530	0.548
73	0.348	0.377	0.404	0.429	0.452	0.474	0.494	0.513	0.531
74	0.333	0.362	0.388	0.413	0.436	0.457	0.477	0.496	0.513
75	0.319	0.347	0.373	0.397	0.419	0.441	0.460	0.479	0.496

TABLE 1: **Multiplier to be applied to the part of the residuary estate in respect of which the election is exercised to obtain the capital value of the life interest of a surviving husband, when the average gross redemption yield on medium coupon fifteen-year Government Stocks is at the rate shown.**

AGE LAST BIRTHDAY OF HUSBAND	LESS THAN 8.50%	8.50% OR BETWEEN 8.50% AND 9.50%	9.50% OR BETWEEN 9.50% AND 10.50%	10.50% OR BETWEEN 10.50% AND 11.50%	11.50% OR BETWEEN 11.50% AND 12.50%	12.50% OR BETWEEN 12.50% AND 13.50%	13.50% OR BETWEEN 13.50% AND 14.50%	14.50% OR BETWEEN 14.50% AND 15.50%	15.50% OR MORE
76	0.305	0.332	0.357	0.381	0.403	0.424	0.443	0.461	0.479
77	0.292	0.318	0.342	0.365	0.387	0.407	0.426	0.444	0.461
78	0.278	0.304	0.328	0.350	0.371	0.391	0.410	0.427	0.444
79	0.265	0.290	0.313	0.335	0.355	0.375	0.393	0.410	0.427
80	0.253	0.277	0.299	0.320	0.340	0.359	0.377	0.394	0.410
81	0.241	0.264	0.285	0.306	0.325	0.343	0.361	0.377	0.393
82	0.229	0.251	0.272	0.292	0.310	0.328	0.345	0.361	0.377
83	0.218	0.239	0.259	0.278	0.296	0.313	0.330	0.346	0.361
84	0.207	0.227	0.246	0.265	0.282	0.299	0.315	0.331	0.345
85	0.196	0.216	0.234	0.252	0.269	0.285	0.301	0.316	0.330
86	0.186	0.205	0.223	0.240	0.256	0.272	0.287	0.302	0.315
87	0.177	0.195	0.212	0.228	0.244	0.259	0.274	0.288	0.301
88	0.168	0.185	0.201	0.217	0.232	0.247	0.261	0.275	0.288
89	0.159	0.176	0.191	0.207	0.221	0.235	0.249	0.262	0.275
90	0.151	0.167	0.182	0.197	0.211	0.224	0.237	0.250	0.262
91	0.144	0.159	0.173	0.187	0.201	0.214	0.227	0.239	0.251
92	0.137	0.151	0.165	0.179	0.192	0.205	0.217	0.229	0.240
93	0.130	0.144	0.158	0.171	0.183	0.196	0.208	0.219	0.230
94	0.124	0.138	0.151	0.163	0.175	0.187	0.199	0.210	0.221
95	0.119	0.132	0.144	0.156	0.168	0.179	0.190	0.201	0.212
96	0.113	0.126	0.138	0.149	0.161	0.172	0.182	0.193	0.203
97	0.108	0.120	0.132	0.143	0.154	0.164	0.175	0.185	0.195
98	0.103	0.115	0.126	0.137	0.147	0.157	0.167	0.177	0.187
99	0.098	0.109	0.119	0.130	0.140	0.150	0.159	0.169	0.178
100 and over	0.093	0.103	0.112	0.123	0.133	0.143	0.151	0.161	0.169

TABLE 2: **Multiplier to be applied to the part of the residuary estate in respect of which the election is exercised to obtain the capital value of the life interest of a surviving wife, when the average gross redemption yield on medium coupon fifteen-year Government Stocks is at the rate shown.**

AGE LAST BIRTHDAY OF WIFE	LESS THAN 8.50%	8.50% OR BETWEEN 8.50% AND 9.50%	9.50% OR BETWEEN 9.50% AND 10.50%	10.50% OR BETWEEN 10.50% AND 11.50%	11.50% OR BETWEEN 11.50% AND 12.50%	12.50% OR BETWEEN 12.50% AND 13.50%	13.50% OR BETWEEN 13.50% AND 14.50%	14.50% OR BETWEEN 14.50% AND 15.50%	15.50% OR MORE
16	0.892	0.905	0.915	0.922	0.927	0.930	0.933	0.936	0.937
17	0.889	0.903	0.913	0.920	0.925	0.929	0.933	0.935	0.937
18	0.887	0.901	0.911	0.919	0.924	0.929	0.932	0.934	0.936
19	0.884	0.899	0.910	0.917	0.923	0.928	0.931	0.934	0.936
20	0.882	0.897	0.908	0.916	0.922	0.927	0.930	0.933	0.935
21	0.879	0.895	0.906	0.915	0.921	0.926	0.929	0.932	0.934
22	0.877	0.893	0.904	0.913	0.920	0.925	0.928	0.931	0.934
23	0.874	0.890	0.902	0.911	0.918	0.923	0.927	0.931	0.933
24	0.871	0.888	0.900	0.910	0.917	0.922	0.926	0.930	0.932
25	0.868	0.885	0.898	0.908	0.915	0.921	0.925	0.929	0.932
26	0.864	0.882	0.896	0.906	0.914	0.920	0.924	0.928	0.931
27	0.861	0.879	0.893	0.904	0.912	0.918	0.923	0.927	0.930
28	0.857	0.876	0.891	0.901	0.910	0.916	0.921	0.925	0.929
29	0.853	0.873	0.888	0.899	0.908	0.915	0.920	0.924	0.928
30	0.849	0.869	0.885	0.896	0.906	0.913	0.918	0.923	0.926
31	0.845	0.866	0.882	0.894	0.903	0.911	0.916	0.921	0.925
32	0.840	0.862	0.878	0.891	0.901	0.908	0.914	0.919	0.923
33	0.836	0.858	0.875	0.888	0.898	0.906	0.912	0.918	0.922
34	0.831	0.853	0.871	0.884	0.895	0.903	0.910	0.916	0.920
35	0.826	0.849	0.867	0.881	0.892	0.901	0.908	0.913	0.918
36	0.820	0.844	0.863	0.877	0.889	0.898	0.905	0.911	0.916
37	0.815	0.839	0.858	0.873	0.885	0.895	0.902	0.909	0.914
38	0.809	0.834	0.853	0.869	0.881	0.891	0.899	0.906	0.911
39	0.803	0.828	0.848	0.864	0.877	0.888	0.896	0.903	0.909
40	0.796	0.822	0.843	0.860	0.873	0.884	0.893	0.900	0.906
41	0.790	0.816	0.838	0.855	0.869	0.880	0.889	0.897	0.903
42	0.783	0.810	0.832	0.850	0.864	0.876	0.885	0.893	0.900
43	0.775	0.803	0.826	0.844	0.859	0.871	0.881	0.889	0.896
44	0.768	0.796	0.820	0.838	0.854	0.866	0.877	0.885	0.893
45	0.760	0.789	0.813	0.832	0.848	0.861	0.872	0.881	0.889

TABLE 2: **Multiplier to be applied to the part of the residuary estate in respect of which the election is exercised to obtain the capital value of the life interest of a surviving wife, when the average gross redemption yield on medium coupon fifteen-year Government Stocks is at the rate shown.**

AGE LAST BIRTHDAY OF WIFE	LESS THAN 8.50%	8.50% OR BETWEEN 8.50% AND 9.50%	9.50% OR BETWEEN 9.50% AND 10.50%	10.50% OR BETWEEN 10.50% AND 11.50%	11.50% OR BETWEEN 11.50% AND 12.50%	12.50% OR BETWEEN 12.50% AND 13.50%	13.50% OR BETWEEN 13.50% AND 14.50%	14.50% OR BETWEEN 14.50% AND 15.50%	15.50% OR MORE
46	0.752	0.782	0.806	0.826	0.842	0.856	0.867	0.876	0.885
47	0.744	0.774	0.799	0.819	0.836	0.850	0.862	0.872	0.880
48	0.735	0.766	0.791	0.812	0.829	0.844	0.856	0.866	0.875
49	0.726	0.757	0.783	0.804	0.822	0.837	0.850	0.861	0.870
50	0.716	0.748	0.775	0.797	0.815	0.831	0.844	0.855	0.865
51	0.707	0.739	0.766	0.788	0.807	0.823	0.837	0.849	0.859
52	0.697	0.729	0.757	0.780	0.799	0.816	0.830	0.842	0.853
53	0.686	0.719	0.747	0.771	0.791	0.808	0.822	0.835	0.846
54	0.676	0.709	0.737	0.761	0.782	0.799	0.814	0.827	0.839
55	0.664	0.698	0.727	0.751	0.772	0.790	0.806	0.820	0.831
56	0.653	0.687	0.716	0.741	0.763	0.781	0.797	0.811	0.823
57	0.641	0.676	0.705	0.730	0.752	0.771	0.788	0.802	0.815
58	0.629	0.664	0.693	0.719	0.741	0.761	0.778	0.793	0.806
59	0.616	0.651	0.681	0.707	0.730	0.750	0.767	0.783	0.796
60	0.603	0.638	0.669	0.695	0.718	0.739	0.757	0.772	0.786
61	0.590	0.625	0.656	0.683	0.706	0.727	0.745	0.761	0.776
62	0.577	0.612	0.643	0.670	0.693	0.715	0.733	0.750	0.764
63	0.563	0.598	0.629	0.656	0.680	0.702	0.721	0.738	0.753
64	0.549	0.584	0.615	0.642	0.667	0.688	0.708	0.725	0.740
65	0.534	0.569	0.600	0.628	0.653	0.674	0.694	0.712	0.728
66	0.520	0.555	0.586	0.613	0.638	0.660	0.680	0.698	0.714
67	0.505	0.540	0.570	0.598	0.623	0.645	0.666	0.684	0.700
68	0.490	0.524	0.555	0.583	0.608	0.630	0.651	0.669	0.686
69	0.475	0.509	0.539	0.567	0.592	0.615	0.635	0.654	0.671
70	0.459	0.493	0.523	0.551	0.576	0.599	0.619	0.638	0.655
71	0.444	0.477	0.507	0.535	0.560	0.582	0.603	0.622	0.640
72	0.428	0.461	0.491	0.518	0.543	0.566	0.586	0.606	0.623
73	0.413	0.445	0.475	0.501	0.526	0.549	0.570	0.589	0.606
74	0.398	0.429	0.458	0.485	0.509	0.532	0.552	0.572	0.589
75	0.382	0.413	0.442	0.468	0.492	0.514	0.535	0.554	0.572

TABLE 2: **Multiplier to be applied to the part of the residuary estate in respect of which the election is exercised to obtain the capital value of the life interest of a surviving wife, when the average gross redemption yield on medium coupon fifteen-year Government Stocks is at the rate shown.**

AGE LAST BIRTHDAY OF WIFE	LESS THAN 8.50%	8.50% OR BETWEEN 8.50% AND 9.50%	9.50% OR BETWEEN 9.50% AND 10.50%	10.50% OR BETWEEN 10.50% AND 11.50%	11.50% OR BETWEEN 11.50% AND 12.50%	12.50% OR BETWEEN 12.50% AND 13.50%	13.50% OR BETWEEN 13.50% AND 14.50%	14.50% OR BETWEEN 14.50% AND 15.50%	15.50% OR MORE
76	0.367	0.397	0.425	0.451	0.475	0.497	0.517	0.536	0.554
77	0.352	0.381	0.408	0.434	0.457	0.479	0.499	0.518	0.536
78	0.337	0.365	0.392	0.417	0.440	0.461	0.482	0.500	0.518
79	0.322	0.350	0.376	0.400	0.423	0.444	0.464	0.482	0.500
80	0.307	0.334	0.360	0.383	0.406	0.426	0.446	0.464	0.482
81	0.293	0.319	0.344	0.367	0.389	0.409	0.428	0.446	0.463
82	0.279	0.304	0.328	0.351	0.372	0.392	0.410	0.428	0.445
83	0.265	0.290	0.313	0.335	0.355	0.375	0.393	0.410	0.427
84	0.252	0.276	0.298	0.319	0.339	0.358	0.376	0.393	0.409
85	0.239	0.262	0.284	0.304	0.323	0.342	0.359	0.376	0.392
86	0.227	0.249	0.269	0.289	0.308	0.326	0.343	0.359	0.374
87	0.215	0.236	0.256	0.275	0.293	0.310	0.327	0.342	0.357
88	0.204	0.224	0.243	0.261	0.279	0.295	0.311	0.327	0.341
89	0.193	0.212	0.230	0.248	0.265	0.281	0.296	0.311	0.325
90	0.182	0.201	0.218	0.235	0.251	0.267	0.282	0.296	0.310
91	0.173	0.190	0.207	0.223	0.239	0.254	0.268	0.282	0.296
92	0.164	0.180	0.197	0.212	0.227	0.242	0.256	0.269	0.282
93	0.155	0.171	0.187	0.202	0.216	0.230	0.243	0.256	0.269
94	0.147	0.162	0.177	0.192	0.205	0.219	0.232	0.244	0.256
95	0.139	0.154	0.168	0.182	0.195	0.208	0.221	0.233	0.244
96	0.132	0.146	0.159	0.173	0.185	0.198	0.210	0.222	0.233
97	0.125	0.138	0.151	0.164	0.176	0.188	0.199	0.211	0.222
98	0.118	0.130	0.143	0.155	0.167	0.178	0.189	0.200	0.210
99	0.110	0.122	0.134	0.146	0.157	0.168	0.178	0.189	0.199
100 AND OVER	0.102	0.114	0.125	0.137	0.147	0.158	0.167	0.178	0.188

INDEX